Critical Acclaim for
The Night Stalker

"Carlo has given us an astonishing portrait of a killer not seen since *In Cold Blood*."

—Denis Hamil, *NY Daily News*

"We've all read novelists and true crime writers who try to put you inside-the-mind-of-the-serial-killer, but I can't remember one that succeeded with the physical and psychological intimacy of this collaboration between the writer and the killer himself."

—John Strausbaush, *New York Press*

"An exceptionally well-told true crime tale."

—*Publishers Weekly*

"Phil Carlo paints a disturbing portrait of cold-blooded killer, Richard Ramirez. In the true crime tradition of *In Cold Blood* and *The Executioner's Song*, Carlo compellingly tells the ghastly story from numerous points of view, including those of Ramirez and two ingenious sheriff's detectives who finally cracked the case."

—*People Magazine*

". . . this book will provide true crime readers a chilling inside perspective of a serial killer."

—*Library Journal*

THE NIGHT

THE LIFE AND CRIMES

STALKER

OF RICHARD RAMIREZ

PHILIP CARLO

Pinnacle Books
Kensington Publishing Corp.

http://www.pinnaclebooks.com

PINNACLE BOOKS are published by

Kensington Publishing Corp.
850 Third Avenue
New York, NY 10022

First Pinnacle Printing: August, 1997

Printed in the United States of America
30 29 28 27 26 25

*Dedicated to all who have lost their lives
at the hands of serial murderers.*

ACKNOWLEDGMENTS

I wish to extend my gratitude to the following individuals, without whose kind support this book would not have been possible:

LASD Homicide detectives Sgt. Frank Salerno and Gil Carrillo, Capt. Ken Roe, Dr. Dale Griffis, Dr. Richard Ash, Jeffrey Hafer, Mary Meagher, Louis Carlo, Dante and Antonina Carlo, Doreen and Joseph Mannanice, Robert and Maxine Ganer, Beth McDermit, J. McNally, Ivelisse Reyes, Marcos Quinones at the NYPD Police Academy, Anthony Danza, Danny Aiello, Paul Herman, Brian Hamill, Tony Sirico, Chuck Zito, T. Conforte, Philip Monaco, Patrick Laudisina, Michael Kostrewa, and the Ramirez family; also, my agent, Frank Weimann. And, of course, my editor, Paul Dinas, and all the terrific people at Kensington Publishing, especially Karen Haas, Laura Shatzkin, and Diane Wright.

I also wish to thank Michaela Hamilton at Kensington Publishing for encouraging me to write the update for this tenth-anniversary edition of our book.

Those who are unhappy clutch at shadows, and to give themselves an enjoyment that truth refuses them, they artfully bring into being all sorts of illusions.

The Marquis de Sade
Crimes of Love

BOOK I

THE HUNTED

AND

THE HUNTERS

Swear on Satan you won't scream.

The Night Stalker

ONE

The downtown area around the Los Angeles Greyhound Bus Terminal is a very dangerous place after dark. Colorful legions of thieves, muggers, fences, crackheads, junkies, alcoholics, and ten-dollar whores prowl like hungry sharks around a bleeding man. Known as skid row, people here often sleep in the filthy, vermin-infested streets where they dropped the night before. If the great, grand City of Angels had an asshole, the downtown area around the terminal would undoubtedly be it.

It was from this place that he came, nameless and nocturnal, as silent and deadly as cyanide gas. He always wore black, with the brim of a black baseball cap pulled down low; even his socks and shoes were black. Thus attired, he moved about in shadows, blending and becoming one with them, rarely seen until it was too late.

At 8:30 on the evening of June 27, 1984, he copped two grams of cocaine from Roberto, a skinny Colombian who sold pure rock from the little park with the benches and the palm trees just in front of the terminal. It was a simple matter of saying, "Two grams" and shaking Roberto's hand, and all of a sudden the coke was in his hand. Roberto shook hands with dozens of people a day and was adept at passing the drug without being seen. It was like a magic trick.

Tonight, the man in black was driving a stolen dark-blue Toyota. However, no one paid particular attention to what he was driving; that was his business and, for the most part, people who moved through the underground empire of degradation and crime in downtown Los Angeles minded their own business. It was a very easy place to get lost in. There were transient hotels all over that rented rooms for eight to twelve dollars a night, no questions asked, no ID necessary. The Huntington, Cecil, Rosslyn, Ford, and Frontier were some of the places he'd go and binge on cocaine for several days straight, not eating or sleeping, answerable only to his addiction and the hot winds of his psychosis.

But tonight all his money had gone for the cocaine and he'd have to make do out in the open. He got into the car, drove a few blocks, and parked. He knew the mean, stinking, urine-stained streets and alleys as intimately as the palms of his large-knuckled hands. He had prearranged places where he'd go to get off without being disturbed. He got out of the car and walked to the back of an abandoned building just off Pico, anxious and in a hurry to get the drug into his system.

He removed two of the four glistening rocks from a neatly folded piece of aluminum foil and put them into a cut-down Pepsi can he carried in a little paper bag. He then spilled a tablespoon of bottled water into the can and quickly the coke melted and became one with the liquid. Moving his long, powerful fingers deftly, he took a syringe out of the bag and drew the cocaine-laden water into it. He then tied a piece of cord around the sinewy bicep of his left arm and waited for the basilic vein to swell.

It was a clear, hot summer night. He used light from a street lamp to see. Rats scurried about, not happy about his presence. When the vein stood out like a thick purple worm, he untied the cord and slowly slid in the needle, injecting the drug. The cocaine raced to his brain and limbs like a speeding train on its way to no good. He put the works and rocks back in the bag, stashed it, and hurried to the car—the drug heightening his senses, dilating his pupils.

Sweating, he began to cruise downtown, driving up and down its foul, sweltering streets—thinking about a hooker, a specific kind of sex. But he had to have money for that.

By trade he was a burglar, and he was good at his chosen profession. He knew how to get into any kind of home, even one with an alarm system, though he avoided alarms and dogs when possible. He drove in widening circles around the terminal. While he cruised, he listened to heavy metal music—Judas Priest, AC/DC, Black Sabbath, Billy Idol. He found the frantic beats and often violent lyrics stimulating. To him there were hidden, important messages in the music he related to and made his own. He thought that Idol's "Eyes without a Face"—about a murderer on a bus—very much reflected what he was about, for he often fantasized about killing people he saw on the bus as he was returning downtown after dropping off a hot car.

He returned to the alley a third time, shot up the rest of the cocaine, and resumed his cruising. He saw a few street hustlers who made him slow down and wave, but none who made him want to stop.

Money! To get what he wanted he had to have money.

As he drove and watched people walking on the sidewalks of Main, Broadway, and Spring, sitting in their cars waiting for red lights, he thought about violent sex and domination. The right time and place were essential for successful murder. He'd later reveal: *To be a good killer you have to plan things out carefully. You've got to be prepared in every way when the moment comes to strike; you cannot hesitate.*

Under the influence of cocaine, time goes by quickly; he was beginning to come down. The euphoric rushes he'd been traveling with were leaving him, replaced by an edgy, nervous anxiety, which could only be relieved with more cocaine.

He got on the 10 Freeway and drove for a few exits, got off at Alhambra, and looked for a situation he could exploit. He couldn't find one, returned to the freeway, and drove over to Glassel Park—a small community inhabited by low-income working people. Its population was 42,000. He drove without directions or map, his dark eyes searching the night, looking for a place where he could get in, get what he wanted, and get out.

He parked on Chapman Street, which ran parallel to the gentle, peaceful rolling hills of Forest Lawn Memorial Park. He sat in the car a few minutes and collected himself, put on dark-colored gardening gloves, and made sure no one was watching him.

When he was satisfied he was unobserved—he had a sixth sense about such things—he got out of the car and walked along the dark green cemetery wall, staying in shadows, taking long, silent steps.

Above, an ink-black sky was punctuated with glistening stars. Light from the stars and street lamps put a kind of luminous frosting on the tombstones, all neatly lined up and well cared for. Gauze-thin, silky clouds scudded across the night, momentarily blocking out the stars. In his mind he heard the howl of a wolf, imagined he was walking through thick fog.

He stopped in front of a two-story pink apartment building, not too well cared for, fifty feet wide, a hundred fifty feet deep. It was a barracks-like structure with an alley on the right that ran to the back of the building. The apartments were off this alley, five on the upper level, five on the lower, connected by rusting outdoor metal stairs.

He walked to the yard, studying the doors and windows with the experienced eye of a seasoned jeweler looking through a loupe. He quickly decided not to break into one of the rear apartments. If things went wrong back there, he could be trapped. He started back toward Chapman and stopped at apartment 2, the home of seventy-nine-year-old Jennie Vincow.

Jennie had thinning hair as white as salt, was 5'9", and weighed 190 pounds. She had two sons: Jack, who lived in apartment 9, upstairs, and Manny, who resided in Benson-hurst, Brooklyn.

Jennie had been living in Brooklyn with Manny until November 11, 1981. Manny had some "mental problems," Jack would later say, and he often fought with his mother. He had even struck her on several occasions. Jack thought it best if he brought his mother out to sunny California, where he could watch over her and get her what she needed. She had a very low electrolyte count and was always tired; just the act of walking was strenuous for her.

On this night her window was open, but there was a screen covering it. He made sure he wasn't being observed. A tall, bushy palm tree at the front of the building blocked any light from the street. He had no idea who lived in apartment 2, but it didn't matter. He'd make it his, neutralize whoever was inside and take what he wanted. He'd dominate; he'd control.

He was certain that Satan, archenemy of Christ, of all things good, was traveling with him, and that Satan would protect him so long as he stayed evil in his heart and showed no mercy.

The gloves made getting the screen off difficult, and he

had to remove one. He rarely took off his gloves, but tonight he was wired and jammed with the coming down of the cocaine, and his motor movements were off.

Carefully he pried the screen loose, silently put it down inside the apartment, and opened the window ever so slowly. He put his glove back on, grabbed the sill, and hoisted himself up and into the apartment in two easy movements, catlike, as silent as the turning of a page. Inside, he got down low and let his eyes adjust to the dark.

It was, he could quickly discern, a one-bedroom, and as soon as his eyes registered the poverty in which Jennie Vincow lived, he knew he'd come to the wrong place. It made him angry. Furious. Anger was a very difficult emotion for him to control.

Staying low, on the balls of his feet, he walked toward the bedroom and made out the form of Jennie Vincow, sleeping deeply under a brown-and-white plaid blanket, her breathing slow and labored. When he was sure she was alone, he took out a penlight and looked around the apartment. There was just about nothing worth stealing there, except, of course, Jennie Vincow's soul . . .

He spotted a suitcase at the foot of the bed and silently went for it, hoping there might be something in it he could sell—turn into currency, cocaine and sex. He opened it and found only wrinkled clothing. There was a dresser against the wall. Soundlessly he went through its drawers, but again he found nothing of value—no jewelry, no hidden cash. He stared at the sleeping form of Jennie Vincow, hate and anger welling up inside him, contorting his face into an animal-like snarl. He took out a razor-sharp six-inch hunting knife, approached the bed, and stood there, his heart now beating rapidly. He could feel hot blood pulsating at his temples and at the backs of his eyes.

Sexually excited by the prospect of what he was going to do, he raised the knife and plunged the full length of the blade into Jennie Vincow's chest. She woke up screaming; he kept stabbing. She tried to fight him off, but that was impossible: he slammed his hand over her mouth, raised her chin, and stabbed, then slashed her throat from ear to ear, cutting so deeply he nearly severed her head. Her body shook violently. She choked and gagged on her blood. The last image her dying eyes registered was of him—standing over her, killing her.

He pulled down the blanket and stabbed her deeply in the chest three more times, sexually charged by the plunging of the blade, propelled and spurred on by the certainty that he was one with Satan—one with evil.

Fascinated by what he'd just done—the blood, her gaping wounds, his omnipotent power—he excited himself for nearly an hour, drinking glass after glass of water, the small, hot, humid room filling with the fetid smell of blood, sweat and death.

Finished, he washed his hands in the bathroom sink and left the apartment as soundlessly as he'd come, taking a small, portable radio. Quickly, though not so fast that he'd draw attention to himself, he made his way back to the stolen car, got into it, and drove toward the corner.

It was now 5 A.M. and dawn was slowly filling a sad, tranquil sky. The horizon in the east was a deep indigo above big, puffy clouds that were stitched with the fiery threads of the rising sun. It was the time filmmakers call the "magic hour," when there is no glare in the air and color and dimension are sharper and more defined. People were on their way to early-morning jobs. Sparrows and finches chirped in trees that dotted the cemetery and lined the block.

He came to a stop sign on the corner of Weldon Avenue. He was going to run it, but something made him slow down; something held him back. As he started out again, an LAPD black-and-white came to a slow stop on the corner to his immediate right. His heart rolled over at the sight of the cruiser. The officer watched him pull away just half a block from where Vincow had been murdered. He had her blood all over his clothes and was in a stolen car with stolen property.

But Lucifer was with him, and he drove one way as the police cruiser took a left and moved in the opposite direction.

At 1:20 that afternoon, ten hours after the killer had left, Jack Vincow went to visit his mom. It was his custom to look in on her about that time every day. She liked Chicken McNuggets, and he'd gone and bought her some. He wanted to surprise her with them.

Jack was a pharmacist who had recently been laid off. The air conditioner in his car hadn't been working properly and he'd had it fixed that morning. Jennie liked to take rides in the cool car, and Jack thought today he'd take her for one after she'd had her McNuggets.

As soon as he got to the front door, he noticed the window screen was missing. Strange. He turned and looked for it but couldn't find it. He took out his keys to open the door. He expected it to be locked and didn't want to make his mom get up, but the door was open. That, too, registered as peculiar; his mother always kept the door locked. Chapman Street was not in a good area, and there were often break-ins and burglaries. As Jack entered his mother's apartment, he saw the screen sitting in the middle of the living room floor. There were blood smears on the walls, and the house had been ransacked.

"Mother . . . Mother, are you here? Mother?" he called into the ominous silence. There was no response. With trepidation he walked toward Jennie's bedroom, a feeling of dread welling up in him. The light in the bedroom was not good. Jennie was covered by a blanket. He grabbed it, lifted it, and saw the terrible destruction—the gaping, obscene wounds, the nearly detached head. He turned and ran from the apartment, yelling, "My mother's been murdered! Call the police!" He went straight to the managers of the building, a married couple named Laui and Rene Trinque, and banged on their door, calling out, "My mother's been murdered. Oh, God, please call the police!"

Rene hurried to the phone and dialed 911. Jack thought he'd better call, too. He ran up to his apartment, dialed 911, and repeated, "Someone's murdered my mother; please come quick!" He gave them the address and was told a car had already been dispatched.

He returned to the front of the building to wait for the authorities. It was now 1:40 P.M., hot and sticky. Up and down the block word spread quickly that there had been a murder, and a crowd was gathering. Jack walked back and forth, tears streaming down his face, sobbing, brokenhearted. He returned to his mother's apartment, opened the drapes, looked about for a few seconds, then went back outside.

The first police officer to get there was Lt. Buster Altizer.

He'd been the watch commander at the LAPD Northeast Station on North San Fernando Road when the call, a 187—a murder—had come in over the radio. The station was four blocks from Chapman, and Lt. Altizer was there in minutes. He parked out front and reluctantly got out of his air-conditioned car; it was a suffocating 96 degrees. Jack Vincow approached.

"Police?" he asked.

"That's right."

"I called; my mother's been murdered."

"Was it you who found the body, sir?"

"Yes . . . in her apartment, in the house. I'll show you."

Lt. Altizer followed Jack, dazed, round-shouldered, still crying, to the doorway of apartment 2. Jack did not want to go back in. He couldn't take seeing his mother like that again, he said.

"She's in the bedroom," he told Altizer, and pointed.

As soon as Altizer entered the apartment he could smell the murder; human death has a very distinct odor, one never forgotten once experienced. Slowly he made his way to the bedroom and saw the ransacking, the blood on the walls. He approached the bed, took in the destruction, the glassy stare in her eyes, and knew immediately this was a murder, a particularly sadistic, very brutal one. His job now was to contact LAPD Homicide and to seal the apartment. He went back outside and called for back-up and Homicide people. He then used yellow crime-scene tape he'd gotten out of the trunk of his car and cordoned off the alley and apartment. He asked Jack a few questions that Jack answered as best he could, but he was distraught, and talking coherently was difficult.

Seasoned homicide detectives Jesse Castillo and his partner, Mike Wynn, were the next to arrive. Altizer took them into the apartment. They saw the screen on the floor, the ransacking, and knew what it meant; they noted blood in the bathroom sink and surmised the killer had washed blood from his hands.

As they entered the bedroom, they took note of a dresser in the room with its drawers open and things strewn all over. They moved closer and studied Jennie Vincow's wounds. Homicide detectives all over the world are a hard lot; not much fazes them. But even for a homicide man, it is very unpleasant to see the murder of an elderly person.

Hard-jawed, cold-eyed, Castillo called for fingerprint people, photographers, criminalists, and someone from the coroner's office. Before the body could be disturbed in any way, it was legally mandated that a representative of the Los Angeles Coroner's Office be present. When John Hererra from the M.E.'s office arrived, the blanket covering Jennie's body was removed and bagged as evidence.

Now, for the first time, they all saw that Jennie had been stabbed repeatedly. There were wounds on her hands, indicating that she had tried to defend herself, to ward off the stabbing thrusts. On her back, neck, arms, and posterior, Hererra noted lividity (the coagulation of blood settling due to gravity). She had been wearing a blue nightgown and it was pushed up over her waist; he noted the crotch area of her girdle had been cut out and that there was a deep stab wound on her left inner thigh. Rigor mortis was present. Hererra used a scalpel and made an incision in Jennie Vincow's rib cage, then put a cooking-type thermometer into her liver. Its temperature when compared to the air temperature would give the approximate time of death. Her liver temperature was 94 degrees and the room temperature was 81 degrees, tentatively indicating she had been dead between eight and ten hours. Jennie was placed in a black body bag and taken to the county morgue for autopsy.

It was LAPD fingerprint expert Reynaldo Clara's job to find any latent prints the killer might have left. He arrived and dusted all over the house, tables, doorknobs, dresser drawers—anywhere there were smudges of blood—but he didn't find a single print. Clara and Castillo decided to ninhydrin the bathroom. Its surfaces were far too smooth for the powders to be effective in raising prints. Ninhydrate is a chemical that is sprayed on floors and walls. Its fumes attach to any prints, which can then be removed with lifting tape. But the chemical is very strong and toxic, and the process would not be done, it was further decided, until 9:30 A.M. the following morning.

Last, Clara focused his attention on the window, the probable source of entry. Wearing gloves, he took the screen into the bright California sunlight so he could see better. He dusted the screen with white fingerprint powder, finding four prints, three of them partially discernible, one smudged.

"Bingo!" he called out, and the other detectives and tech people came over. He showed them what he'd found—perhaps the clue that would solve the case. Clara lifted the prints with a special tape and glued the tape to a lifting card. He proceeded to dust the window itself and found two more prints, one usable, the other too smudged to be helpful, but he had found four reasonably good prints that could be used to identify the killer. It would take years for fingerprint experts to manually compare these partials with the millions of prints on file with LAPD. Before they could be of any use to them, a suspect would be needed to compare them to.

Dets. Castillo and Wynn questioned whoever they could find home at the Chapman apartment building, but no one had seen or heard anything. They searched the alley, a garbage dumpster out front, the street, the curbs, and the sidewalks for the knife, but couldn't find it. Detectives even climbed the cemetery wall and looked for it there—thinking the killer might have thrown it over the wall as he'd departed; they found nothing but some coins, dead flowers, used condoms, and empty beer bottles.

The following morning, LAPD fingerprint experts returned and sprayed the bathroom with ninhydrin. No additional prints were discovered.

At 11 A.M. an autopsy was done on Jennie Vincow by Dr. Joseph Cogan. He took particular note of the unusual wound to Jennie's neck: it was actually two deep stab wounds, one on either side of the windpipe, connected by a very deep slash. Her murderer, Dr. Cogan knew, had experience at killing and was good at it. Beyond that, however, he could offer little to further the investigation.

TWO

After murdering Jennie Vincow, the killer slipped deeper and deeper into intravenous cocaine addiction; the drug became his life, his main preoccupation. To get it he needed money, which he routinely secured by committing burglaries—frequently two and three a day.

Always wearing gloves, always wearing black, he'd silently slink in and out of people's homes, never leaving a clue, taking coin and stamp collections, televisions, VCRs, answering machines—anything he could carry, fence, and quickly turn into currency. Sleeping, eating, and washing didn't much matter to him, and he walked with a tawny, leathery smell about him, an odor witnesses would later describe to police and tell about in court.

He had no friends and was very untrusting of people—the consummate loner. Often he'd stay in his room from sundown to sunrise, shooting up cocaine, watching MTV, listening to heavy metal music, and fantasizing about extreme sexual violence: watching people suffer, squirm, and die.

For a true killer, a good murder is like a good meal: you want to make it last and get the most out of it.

Fused together by cocaine, his days melted into weeks, then months, and there was no new violence, but there were scores of break-ins and robberies. He felt certain that demons and Satan were protecting him and watching over him—and that he'd never get caught.

But he knew the cocaine made him make mistakes, made him paranoid; and in what he was doing, there was no room for mistakes. Faced with the sure reality of a death sentence, he swore off the drug. He smoked pot and drank once in a while, and that was it.

On March 17, 1985, he bought a .22-caliber revolver from a skinny, pockmarked Mexican who hung out at the terminal. A .22 slug at close range is lethal. It was, the killer knew, the preferred caliber of hitmen around the world.

The bullet enters the skull and zigzags about without exiting, causing havoc to the brain; it's almost always fatal.

He stole a car from a gas station while the owner went in to pay for gas. He immediately got on the Los Angeles freeway system with the sole intention of finding a victim, of killing a human being; that, he decided, was the greatest drug of all, the ultimate high.

This night he was wearing all black, with a dark blue AC/DC baseball cap. He had a Walkman on and listened to AC/DC's *Highway to Hell* album over and over, its hard-driving rhythms pumping him up with malicious intent.

Maria Hernandez was a petite, attractive brunette with large round eyes and clear olive skin. He spotted her on the freeway as she was driving her gold Camaro home from dinner at her boyfriend's in Monterey Park. As she left the freeway and made her way into the suburb of Rosemead—a lovely residential community of 46,000—he exited just behind her.

He followed her three blocks before she slowed and took a right into a new condominium community on Village Lane. He trailed her into the complex and watched her take a left and a right and pull into the last garage at the back of the condo she shared with her roommate, Dayle Okazaki, whose green Toyota wagon was already parked in the garage.

Earlier that evening Dayle, fourteen days away from her thirty-fifth birthday, had been visiting her mom and dad, watching television and talking. She was very pleased at her recent promotion to traffic supervisor with Los Angeles County. Dayle was one of three children from a close, supportive, loving family. She had attended Pasadena City College. An avid skier, she was also taking classes in cake decorating, flower arranging, computer programming, and self-defense. Dayle was a highly motivated woman who loved life and made the most of it. She had saved hard to buy the condominium she now shared with Maria.

As Maria pulled into the garage, the killer parked, got out of the car, and, robotlike, walked straight toward her, his steps and movements quick, his head low, as though he was looking at the ground. On both sides there were two-story tan stucco condos whose windows looked out into the alley. He carried nothing but the .22 he'd just bought—no ID, no change in his pockets, for coins could make noise. There was no sound but the silky rustling of thick palm trees.

When Maria stepped out of her car, she was holding her keys and a brown leather pocketbook. The entrance to the house was a door on the other side of the garage. She walked toward it, moving around the two cars. On the wall near the door was the button that opened and closed the garage. Maria pushed it and the door began to close.

At that moment, the killer bent down to enter the garage and walked straight toward Maria, while her back was still to him; as he bent, his AC/DC hat fell off. He raised the .22 and aimed it directly at her head.

Maria had to open two locks to get into the house. She opened one, heard a noise behind her, perhaps the falling hat, and turned. He was twenty feet away, walking toward her, pointing the gun with two hands right between her eyes. She could actually see down the barrel—

"No, God, please don't! No!" she screamed, automatically raising her hand.

He kept coming. When the gun was two feet from her face, the garage door finished closing and the light automatically went out, putting them in sudden darkness. At that instant he fired, but Maria had raised her right hand in defense and the bullet was miraculously deflected by the keys.

She went down, played dead.

He assumed he'd killed her, pushed her body aside and went up the ten stairs. He entered the house and found himself in a nicely appointed dining room just off a kitchen. There were small vases with flowers on the kitchen counters and the dining room table.

He spotted Dayle as she ducked behind a white-tiled kitchen counter, hoping he hadn't seen her. She was wearing a baggy Dodgers T-shirt and faded jeans. She had straight shoulder-length black hair, a heart-shaped face, and full, rounded lips; she was very pretty. He knew she'd come up again and he slowed his breathing, stayed still and quiet, and aimed his gun at blank space and waited.

In the garage, Maria stood, opened the garage door, and ran back down the alley and around to the front of the complex, confused and frightened, not knowing what to do.

After a few long seconds, Dayle's curiosity took over and she stood up slowly, shaking, trembling, to see if he had gone. She had no idea who he was or why he was there, but she'd heard the gunshot and had seen death in his black eyes as clearly as she'd seen anything in her life.

Just as she appeared at the top of the counter, he fired, shooting her squarely in the forehead, knocking her to the ground, a bullet hole the size of a dime immediately swelling, turning purple, spurting a finger of blood.

With muscles coiled, he turned and left by the front door. Maria saw his tall, gaunt figure in black hurrying down the walkway leading from the house. He spotted her and pointed the gun.

"Oh, please don't! Please don't kill me! Please don't shoot me again!" she pleaded, ducking behind an orange Volkswagen bug with a black top.

Thinking he'd already killed her, surprised to see her alive, he lowered his shaggy head and, still pointing the gun at her, hurried back to the stolen car, got in, and took off, letting Maria Hernandez live, creating the first witness.

As he drove away, he realized he'd lost his AC/DC cap when he'd bent to enter the garage.

Sexually charged by every aspect of the entire episode—the hunt, the stalk, the killing—he found his way onto the San Bernardino Freeway. As he drove, he repeatedly replayed in his mind what he'd just done—heard it, saw it, smelled it.

He looked to his right and spotted petite Veronica Yu as she exited the freeway at Monterey Park, a predominantly Asian community with a population of 65,000 and its own police department.

Yu, a thirty-year-old law student, was tired. She'd been visiting a close childhood friend, June Wang, and they had talked for many hours. She had gone to June's house in Arcadia at 10 A.M. that morning. It was St. Patrick's Day, and neither of the women had to work.

In Mandarin, Veronica's name was Tsai-Lian Yu. She had had lunch at June's house, and the two women, with June's one-and-a-half-year-old son, had gone out for dinner at the Edokyl Restaurant in Pasadena. Veronica, like June, had been born in Taiwan. Both women had immigrated to America seven years earlier and each spoke English with a strong accent. Veronica lived with her parents in Monterey Park. She was looking forward to a good night's sleep.

Quickly the killer turned the wheel of his car and for the second time that evening followed a woman picked solely at random as she drove home, having no idea that death stalked her.

When Veronica noticed the man in the Toyota and realized he was trailing her, she began looking for a police car. After another block, she pulled over to the curb and stopped her car to get a better look at him. He passed her up, thinking he'd find someone else, cursing her under his breath.

Now, though, she began to follow *him*. After going one block, he caught a red light on North Alhambra Avenue, a pleasant two-way street that leads directly to the 10 Freeway. He shut the lights, got out of the car, and approached her. The gun was tucked in his waistband, under a shiny black leather jacket.

He did not see Jorge Gallegos just down the street, sitting in his uncle's white Ford pickup with his girlfriend, Edith Alcaaz.

Veronica opened the window.

"Why you follow me?" she demanded, pointing an indignant finger at him.

"I'm not following. I thought I knew you," he said.

"No, you didn't. You follow me. Why? What you want?" She stared at him with disbelief, her almond-shaped eyes dark and angry above a delicate, lovely jawline.

"I wasn't. I thought I knew you," he repeated, seeing her death even before it happened.

"Liar," she said, her gaze defiantly meeting his. She began to back up. "I calling the police," she said, as she looked at the plate number of the stolen Toyota and remembered it.

"I'm telling you, I thought I knew you. I wasn't following you—"

"You follow me, I could tell. Why?"

He moved closer to the car, a plan of abduction, sadistic sex, and murder crystallizing in his mind. Suddenly, he reached out and grabbed Veronica by the shoulders and tried to pull her right out of the car window. She began to scream.

He couldn't get her out of the window; the driver's door was locked and he couldn't open it. He noticed the passenger door wasn't locked, vaulted over the car, and reached out to open the door. Quickly Veronica moved her right hand to try to lock the door, but not in time. He got into the car with her.

"What you want?" she pleaded of the man in black.

He said nothing, just pulled out the .22 and shot her in the side, under her right arm, seventeen inches from the top of her head. She opened the door to flee and he shot her again, in the lower back this time. She managed to get out of the car, lost a shoe, wobbled a few feet, and fell in the street, bleeding . . . dying.

"Help me! Help me, help!" she wailed.

"Bitch!" he said.

Laughing, he hurried to the Toyota, got in it, and drove to the freeway. He was certain that people had seen the car and knew it would be hot within minutes. He exited the freeway, got rid of the car, and took a bus back to downtown L.A., envisioning himself a soldier of Satan's, returning from battle with the infidels.

THREE

Maria Hernandez couldn't tell what kind of car he'd been driving, the color, or the license plate number. She was too upset to think straight.

After he'd left, she'd waited a few seconds, then ran back to the condominium. Her hand was bleeding and it hurt terribly, a burning, searing pain, but she ignored it. She was worried about Dayle.

Maria found her roommate lying facedown on the kitchen floor; there was a circle of thick blood around her head. She screamed Dayle's name, shook her shoulder, got no response. Crying hysterically, she ran upstairs, made sure no one was in the house, picked up the phone, and called the police.

Why, she kept asking herself, *did that madman in black try to kill her and shoot Dayle?* She called her boyfriend and told him what had happened. He said he'd be right over.

Los Angeles sheriff's deputies John Powell and Anthony Dallus were working the six-to-two shift that night. They received a call of a woman shot at 10:57 P.M., put on the siren and spinning red light, and hit the gas hard, arriving at the condominium in two minutes.

Officer Powell, a big, very serious man, knocked on the door. After a few moments, Maria opened it, holding a bloody towel to her right hand. She explained as best she could what had happened and took them up the seven steps that led to the second level. Officers Powell and Dallus saw an unmoving Dayle Okazaki lying on the kitchen floor. Powell bent down and felt for a pulse; there wasn't one.

The paramedics arrived and turned Dayle over. For the first time the sheriff's deputies and Maria saw the bullet hole in Dayle's forehead. The paramedics raised Dayle's shirt and tried to resuscitate her with electric shock, to no avail. She was pronounced dead at the scene. More sheriff's deputies arrived and they cordoned off the condo, the alley, and the garage with yellow crime-scene tape, then contacted Sheriff's Homicide. Maria was taken to the Beverly Hospital in Montebello.

Back in Monterey Park, Jorge Gallegos was the first person to reach Veronica Yu as she lay in the street. Her eyes were open and she was breathing, but she couldn't speak. He spoke English poorly, but still he asked her what happened—who that man was.

Edith's cousin, Joseph, came down from upstairs and told them he'd summoned the police. He had heard the screams for help and had gone to a veranda off his bedroom that faced Alhambra. He had seen the killer trying to pull Veronica out of the car and had immediately called the police. Other people came out of their homes and apartments and gathered around the dying woman.

The first officer to arrive was Ron Endo from the Monterey Police. As he pulled up, he saw Veronica in his headlights. He told everyone to move back and checked her pulse. It was weak, but she was still breathing. She was wearing brown slacks, a blue blouse, and a black jacket. One of her shoes was lying in the street. A silver chain and a round medallion were around her neck.

Both Jorge Gallegos and Joseph Duenas said they had seen what had occurred. Officer Gorajewski of the Monterey Police arrived and kept back a growing crowd.

As Officer Endo tried to get a statement from Veronica, she stopped breathing. Both he and Gorajewski administered CPR until a medical team arrived and took over. They decided to try and resuscitate her back at the Monterey Park Hospital and took her there, red lights spinning, siren screaming, shattering the otherwise tranquil Sunday night.

When Veronica arrived at the emergency unit of Garfield Hospital in Monterey Park, she was examined by Dr. Richard Tenn, who, after checking her vital signs, pronounced her dead.

Edith, Jorge, and Joseph Duenas were taken to the Monterey Park police station. There they gave statements to Det. Tony Romero.

Dep. Gil Carrillo of Los Angeles Sheriff's Homicide was home watching television that evening. It had been a lazy, relaxing Sunday, and Gil had spent the day with his family.

Gil was 6'4" and 280 pounds, with a thick head of shiny black hair and a surprisingly quick, ingratiating smile for a homicide cop. At thirty-four, Carrillo was the youngest detective in Sheriff's Homicide, which comprised five teams, each with twelve to sixteen detectives, including a lieutenant and usually five sergeants. They were responsible for solving all homicides in sixty-four of the ninety-six communities that made up the Los Angeles County complex. They worked on a rotating cycle, and Carrillo "caught" the Hernandez/Okazaki shootings.

Quickly Carrillo dressed, kissed his wife, Pearl, and said he'd see her when he got back. He never knew when he'd be able to return home and he had stopped giving her times. Gil and Pearl had three children: two girls, Rene and Tiffany, and a son, the youngest, Gil Jr., called J. R. Gil had grown up in Pico Rivera; he had six sisters to whom he was very close. He had fought in Vietnam at the height of the Tet Offensive. He received a Medal of Valor and a Bronze star. To date Gil had worked over 300 murder cases.

Carrillo lived ten minutes from Rosemead and arrived at the condo complex a little after midnight. Powell and Dallus briefed him on what had happened. He asked to talk to Maria and was told she'd been taken to the hospital. He first walked around back, duplicating the killer's footsteps. When he got to the open garage, the first thing he saw was the dark blue AC/DC baseball cap lying on the floor. He did not touch it. That would be done by the criminalists, who'd already been summoned.

He entered the garage and carefully walked to the east wall, where the entrance door was. He noted blood on the wall and Maria's keys and brown leather pocketbook on the floor. A washer, dryer, and hamper were against the north wall. He looked at everything carefully, his dark eyes filled with the dead serious, unwavering curiosity of a good homicide cop. He took a long, slow breath and went back to the front of the condo, walking with a heavy, lumbering step. It seemed the ground shook when Carrillo walked. He followed Officer Powell into the kitchen, noted the bullet hole in Dayle's forehead, and knew that death had probably been instantaneous, that the bullet was a small caliber and had done much damage to her brain. Carrillo's partner, Sgt. Jim Mercer, a heavyset man with a gruff personality, arrived, followed by people from the crime lab. It was their job to make sure any evidence found was properly categorized and preserved for court. They had photographers take pictures and fingerprint people, dust the garage door, the walls in the stairwell the killer used, the kitchen counter, and the front door. They found nothing but the prints of the two women.

At this point Carrillo was thinking the murder involved some kind of love triangle. It seemed the only explanation. Certainly robbery wasn't the motive, for nothing had been stolen—either from Maria or Dayle. The detectives spoke to all the neighbors they could find. No one had seen or heard anything. A .22 doesn't make much noise.

William Rainy, from the M.E.'s office, arrived, examined Dayle, officially pronounced her dead, and had her body removed for autopsy.

At 3 A.M. Carrillo was standing in the vestibule near the front door. All the lights in the house were on, and the tech people had brought in spotlights. A few neighbors still lingered at the taped barrier and talked about how dangerous the world had become, and what a nice woman Dayle Okazaki had been.

A small, reserved woman who'd obviously been crying timidly approached one of the deputies. She said she was Maria Hernandez's mother and that she wanted to go inside the house to get a few things for her daughter. The officer told her he would have to ask one of the homicide detectives if it was all right. He approached Carrillo and told him Maria's mom was there and what she wanted. Carrillo was deeply engaged in the investigation and asked the officer to tell Mrs. Hernandez he'd be out as soon as he could to talk with her. Carrillo's huge frame was silhouetted in the doorway. The deputy returned to Mrs. Hernandez and asked her to please wait. At that point she saw Carrillo for the first time and called out, "Gilbert . . . Gilbert, is that you?" Carrillo stopped what he was doing and walked toward Mrs. Hernandez, taking slow, curious steps, wondering who the hell was calling him Gilbert. He was known as Gil. He approached Mrs. Hernandez.

"Gilbert Carrillo, is that you?" she asked.

She looked familiar, but he couldn't place the face; he apologized and told her he didn't know who she was.

"Gilbert, I'm Pumpkin, your sister Rose's friend, remember? I'm Maria's mother."

"Oh, of course, I'm sorry," Carrillo said, and took Mrs. Hernandez to the side, away from the hurly-burly of the investigation. The Hernandezes had lived three doors away from Carrillo's parents' house in Pico Rivera, and they were good friends. Gil's mother was Maria's godmother.

Mrs. Hernandez told him what Maria had said about the attack and about Maria's injury: the middle joint of her index finger had been broken by the bullet and would have to be operated on. She also told Carrillo how the gun had gone off right in her daughter's face and how the keys had saved Maria's life. Carrillo had not seen Mrs. Hernandez or Maria for twenty-one years. He agreed that Maria was indeed lucky and asked if she had any idea who the assailant was.

"No. None. She never saw him before. He was just suddenly there—in the garage, walking right toward her."

"Please tell her I'll come by the hospital to see her later."

"I will. And please give your family my best."

Carrillo said he would. He went and retrieved what Mrs. Hernandez needed from the house, gave it to her, and returned to work.

He was eager to speak to Maria. He knew the Hernandezes were fine working people and Maria would tell him the truth. Getting people to tell the truth was Carrillo's specialty. He had a concerned, serious face, always talked gently, and was respectful. He was such a large, powerful man that people were caught off guard by his gentle demeanor. He often managed to get suspects to open up, to confess, with his concerned, sincere face and eyes.

Jim Mercer and Carrillo kicked ideas back and forth, talked over the love triangle aspect, and closed down the crime scene at 5 A.M. As Carrillo drove home that morning, a hot, fiery dawn was beginning to color the sky. He was tired and looked forward to a few hours of rest before he returned to work. Often he went about the business of catching murderers with very little sleep.

That afternoon Carrillo went to see Maria at the Beverly Hospital, finding her in a gleaming white hospital bed with a large bandage on her right hand and a very sad face. He hugged and kissed her hello and gave her his sincere condolences over the loss of her friend. Pulling a chair close to the bed, he parked his huge frame, crossed his legs, leaned forward, and asked Maria to tell him what the hell had happened.

A strong-willed woman of few words, she slowly and calmly recounted for him what she had seen. When asked who she thought the killer might be, she told him she honestly had no idea. She and Dayle had "no enemies, no estranged boyfriends, no weird phone calls, nothing like that."

"Why," he asked, "would this man just follow you into the garage and shoot you?"

Looking directly at him, her dark eyes unwavering, she told him it was an absolute mystery to her, and Carrillo believed her. He was an accurate judge of character, and he was sure Maria was telling the truth. He asked her if the AC/DC cap was hers or Dayle's. She said it wasn't. He asked her again to describe the man she'd seen in the garage.

"He was five ten, thin, with black hair and dark, real scary eyes. I was opening the door to the house when I heard a noise, like maybe his foot on the ground. I turned and there he was, walking straight toward me."

"Did he move quickly?"

"No, just walking normally, pointing the gun right at my face."

"Didn't say anything?"

"Not a sound."

He told her they had her pocketbook and keys and would return them as soon as possible. She thanked him. He said, "When you are up to it, I'd like you to take me through exactly what happened at your place, okay?"

"Of course . . . anything I can do to help."

"You're sure you never saw this guy before?"

"Never, I'm sure."

"You say you got a good look at him in the garage?"

"I saw his face clearly."

"I'd like you to work with a police artist and put a composite together as soon as possible—while the images are still fresh, all right?"

"Sure, send him over."

"You're up to it?"

"I'm up to it."

After talking a while longer, he stood, hugged her tightly, and left. She was, he knew, a very lucky young woman. If the key in her raised hand hadn't stopped the bullet, he'd probably be attending her funeral right now.

Relatively certain there was no "love triangle" at work here, Carrillo was more baffled than ever. *Why*, he kept asking himself, *would this guy in black shoot these two nice women?* He had two daughters of his own. He knew how Dayle's parents and her family were suffering. He knew, too, that if he found their daughter's killer, it would help ease their grief.

Early on in Carrillo's career, he had taken, at Cal State, an advanced criminal investigation course pertaining to sex crimes, taught by a retired FBI agent, Prof. Bob Morneau, who had helped put together the FBI's Behavioral Science Unit at Quantico, Virginia.

Professor Morneau taught Carrillo never to take the obvious for what it seemed when it came to killers; that to a serial murderer, just the act of killing was itself sexual. He told Carrillo, "If you go to a murder scene and the killer took a dump there, most guys would just say, hey look, the pig took a shit. But you, you must realize that by doing that, the killer is talking to you—telling you sex was a part of why he's killed and aim your investigation toward a sex offender. Remember: sex is whatever feels good."

Gil had learned well what Prof. Morneau had taught, and now he began wondering if *this* killer got off sexually by simply killing people.

As he was pondering that question, he heard about the Veronica Yu murder and called up Tony Romero at the Monterey Park stationhouse so they could exchange notes. Right off, Carrillo felt it was the same guy. Romero told him one of his witnesses, a Jorge Gallegos, had got a few numbers of the license plate, and they were trying to find the car. Carrillo asked Romero to keep him posted. The Monterey Park detective said he would.

Communication lags between the various law enforcement jurisdictions within Los Angeles County often made the already difficult job of hardworking investigators even more difficult.

The following morning, Dets. Carrillo and Mercer attended the autopsy of Dayle Okazaki at the Los Angeles Medical Examiner's Building. It was done in a very brightly lit white-walled room by Dr. Joseph Wegner, a seasoned, experienced pathologist whom Carrillo respected. The two detectives had to watch the entire procedure, which took seventy-two minutes. It was legally mandated that they, as the investigating officers, be present at the autopsy.

It began with the taking of weight and height. As Dr. Wegner worked, he dictated his findings into a tape recorder for his report, which would be typed up later that day. It was obvious the cause of death was the gunshot wound to the head. When Dr. Wegner opened up Dayle's skull, he could see massive damage to the brain. He found the .22 slug without much difficulty, cleaned it of brain matter, and turned it over to Carrillo, who noted the slug had become distorted from impacting with Dayle's skull. He put it in a small plastic bag and marked it number 85-7086, Dayle's autopsy number. Dr. Wegner then made a "Y" shape cut beginning above the pubic hair line. That done, Dayle Okazaki's chest cavity was pulled back and her organs were removed, examined, and weighed.

As Carrillo watched Dr. Wegner work with fast and knowing hands, his mind kept going back to what Maria had told him. He imagined how frightened Dayle must have been when she'd first seen her killer, having first heard a gunshot and then seen him pointing a gun at her. Carrillo was sure Dayle had seen her killer shoot her because she had been facing him.

She was, he thought, probably begging for mercy. He had no way of knowing that she had been hiding behind the kitchen counter when the bullet had struck her.

The killer had held the gun, Maria said, in a combat position, and he had also tried to shoot Maria in the head—a "kill shot." Maybe, Carrillo thought, the guy was a veteran, or someone who had been in law enforcement.

Deep in the pit of his stomach, he had a very bad feeling about the man who had put Dayle on the autopsy table. He believed the attack was totally random and that unless the man in black was stopped, he'd kill again, and soon.

After the autopsy, the two sheriff's detectives went back to the office. A copy of the drawing Maria had helped with was on Carrillo's desk. It was of a thin, gaunt face with dark, round, bulging eyes.

Carrillo often went to the sheriff's East L.A. office, where sheriff's detectives from different homicide teams would meet, using it as an informal annex to their office at the Justice Building.

At the East L.A. Station he ran into Rene Galindo, a deputy with the sheriff's office who did composites and took fingerprints. When Carrillo showed him the Hernandez drawing, his eyes swelled. He had done a composite drawing on a suspect who had tried to abduct a girl from Montebello. Rene thought they were similar. He got it, and when they compared Maria's drawing and Rene's composite, they were alike. Gil made a mental note to read the teletypes and see if he could find any more sex crimes by a guy in black.

That same morning Veronica Yu's autopsy was done by Dr. Susan Selser. Present at the autopsy were Monterey detective Tony Romero and his partner.

Initially, Romero believed Veronica's killer was probably a boyfriend, but after he'd spoken to Veronica's family and friends, he wasn't so sure this was a lover's quarrel gone bad. Robbery didn't seem to play into it, either: "Her pocketbook was sitting right there in the car, in plain view," reported the first officer on the scene.

Dr. Selser marked the bulletholes "1" and "2." She had no way of knowing the first slug was the one Veronica took in her side. Quickly she went about the business of taking Veronica's body apart to determine for the courts exactly how she had died. She noted the damage each of the bullets had done, their trajectories and angles. She removed the slugs and gave them to Det. Romero.

Later that day, Ballistics reported the rounds removed from Dayle Okazaki and Veronica Yu had "more than likely" been fired from the same gun, but the one extracted from Dayle had been too damaged for them to make an absolute ID. Gil Carrillo now sought the advice of Sgt. Frank Salerno.

"Frank was the absolute best we had, and I wanted to know what he thought," Carrillo recalled, "He had run the Hillside Strangler task force and he knew serial killers. You couldn't find a better homicide detective anywhere than Salerno."

FOUR

Frank Salerno was forty-six years old, 6'2" and 220 pounds, with intense light brown eyes that saw right through you and most everything else. He was a legend in Los Angeles law enforcement. His nickname was "the Bulldog," for when he got ahold of something, he didn't let go. He was an avid sportsman, a crack shot and gun aficionado who loved to hunt and fish; his greatest passion in life—aside from catching murderers—was duck hunting, which the walls in his house clearly attest to. They are covered with trophies.

To stay fit, Salerno went swimming every day in a twenty-by-thirty-five-foot pool in his backyard. His shoulders were wide, his arms thick with muscle, and he moved with the slow, sure confidence of a heavyweight prizefighter in his prime.

Salerno had built the pool with overtime money he'd earned while running the Hillside Strangler task force: he had worked on the case seven days a week for nearly four months, from October 31, 1977, to February 17, 1978, getting only a few hours' sleep per day.

The Hillside Strangler, as it turned out, was actually two cousins, Angelo Buono and Kenneth Bianchi, who'd impersonated policemen and abducted, tortured, sexually abused, and killed ten women whose nude bodies had been left—often in obscene positions—on hillsides scattered around Los Angeles communities. Several of the bodies were found in Glendale, which was where Angelo Buono had a car upholstery shop. It was Frank Salerno who'd found in the first victim's eyelid a tiny piece of thread that was matched with fabric used to upholster furniture—and so eventually tied Buono to the crimes.

Frank married his childhood sweetheart, Jayne, and they had three children—a girl, Terri, and two boys, Frank Jr. and Michael. Following in his famous dad's footsteps, Frank Jr. was a sheriff's deputy and hoped someday to be a homicide detective.

The son of Italian immigrants, Salerno never planned to become a detective. A good student and terrific athlete, he was accepted at Notre Dame University on a football scholarship after graduating from high school. His family was very proud. But he didn't feel comfortable at the prestigious institution, missed Jayne terribly, and decided to return to Los Angeles. He enrolled in Valley Junior College, and married.

When Jayne became pregnant, money problems forced Frank to quit school and join his family's upholstering business. But he found the work boring and repetitious. It was then he spotted a *Los Angeles Times* ad for a position in the sheriff's office promising good pay, a guaranteed pension, and challenging work. Frank applied and got the job and began his training.

Before any Los Angeles sheriff's deputy was allowed to work a beat, he had to put in at least a year as a guard at the L.A. County Jail. The experience the deputies received at the jail gave them insights into human nature and the criminal mentality which made them better cops.

After Salerno had done thirteen months at the jail it was time for him to be moved to a beat. He needed to fill out a form listing the three areas he'd like to work. For all three, he requested the East Los Angeles Station.

A sergeant called him on the side two days later and said: "Hey, Frank, you sure you want East L.A.? It's a rough section—"

"Yeah, that's what I want, I'm sure."

"They've got a real tough watch commander there."

"That's okay, thanks for asking."

Salerno's first partner was a black man named Willie Hill. Willie was 5'9", very muscular, keyed up, and fearless. Often in East L.A. there were bar fights and violent squabbles—involving pipes, bats, and broken bottles—which Frank and Willie Hill had to break up. Without hesitation, Willie would run into the fracas, sometimes involving ten people or more, and in no time he had everybody on the floor, meek and cooperative.

As a result of arrests he'd made, Salerno began to meet with the detectives frequently. They handled all the real crimes, and dealing with them made him want to be one so badly he could taste it.

The way to become a detective was to make a lot of quality felony arrests. Frank Salerno began to develop street informants and kept a black book with their names and the details and particulars of their knowledge. He always treated his contacts with respect and kept his word, and through a network of snitches he developed with his sincere eyes and ingratiating smile, he began to make many quality felony arrests—most of which held up in court. The detectives began noticing Frank Salerno.

In August of 1966, Salerno received his first taste of working as a station detective, and he enjoyed it immensely, telling Jayne he'd found his niche in life.

His shifts started at 5 P.M., then were changed to the twelve-to-eight graveyard shift. For the most part, he handled juvenile and gang-related incidents, though he always had his hands full: people committed all kinds of crimes all through the night.

The night hours eventually became a problem for Frank; by now he had three children he was seeing very little, which disturbed him deeply.

The only way he could get better hours and still work as a detective would be for him to pass the sergeant's test; he studied hard, took it in January, and passed, and his name was put on a list. He was told when an opening became available, he'd be assigned.

Bobby Penland, a friend of his from East L.A., said there was a position opening up in Narcotics and asked if he'd be interested in it. Salerno would have preferred to work Robbery-Homicide, but when he heard the hours were day shift and he'd be assigned to the East L.A. Station—and have weekends off—he couldn't say no.

Salerno soon began working as a narc out of East L.A. This was just before the cocaine-crack plague, and most of the busts he made were for heroin, marijuana, barbiturates, amphetamines—and all kinds of pills.

In September of 1967, Frank Salerno made sergeant and his dream of becoming a full-fledged detective finally came true. He was put in charge of a narcotics team consisting of eight men; their job was to do reconnaissance work—find out who was selling what where, and do undercover surveillance. It was exciting and challenging, and Frank enjoyed the work . . . but what he really wanted was to be a homicide detective—to work in the sheriff's much respected Homicide Bureau.

That year a new narcotics team was started up to deal with drug problems in Malibu and Topanga Canyon, and Frank was asked if he'd like to run it. He thought a change of scenery might be a good idea, and he and his men began to stake out Malibu and the Canyon, developing informants. Most of the busts they made were small-time dealers—one of whom was Charles Manson.

On weekends and most all his time off, Frank took his boys hunting and fishing. On Frank's vacation, he'd take off with his sons for the mountains. Jayne and Terri sometimes went, but mostly it was just the boys.

Early on Frank learned to never bring his work home. It was his sanctuary, his place for peace of mind, and what he saw on the job, in the streets, had no place in the Salerno home.

"When I'd get to the driveway and shut the car engine, I'd shut it all off inside. I didn't want what I do to ever enter my family life," he later related.

In 1971, Salerno was transferred to the Major Violations section of the sheriff's office. There they concentrated on making larger drug busts and did a lot of undercover, surveillance, and infiltration work. He found it exciting and challenging, and they were routinely making busts involving pounds and kilos of heroin and cocaine—the latter then just becoming the "in" drug. If it hadn't been for a new captain who Salerno could not get along with, he might have stayed in major violations for the rest of his career. But he transferred to Internal Affairs—the branch of the sheriff's office that polices the sheriff's deputies and detectives—and stayed there a year and a half.

However, he didn't particularly like the work and asked to be moved to Homicide. He wanted to go after killers—the criminals he perceived as the largest threat to society. Homicide was always looking for bright stars and clearly Salerno was a bright star; there was an opening—Sgt. Phil Brooks out of team 3 was being promoted—and Frank Salerno filled his spot.

Thirty-seven murders later, the day after Halloween of 1977, Salerno caught the murder of a woman named Judy Miller. Her nude body was found on a hill in La Crescenta, and she proved to be the second of the victims in the Hillside Strangler case. And so began one of the largest manhunts in California's history, spearheaded by Frank Salerno.

When Carrillo approached Frank about the Veronica Yu and Dayle Okazaki murders, and about the attempted abduction in Montebello, Frank listened carefully to what Carrillo had to say. He paid such intense attention to Carrillo, he made him feel like he was the only person in the room, though in truth there were fifty other hardworking detectives around them. He suggested Carrillo turn to crime reports, saying if Okazaki and Yu's killer was indeed a serial murderer and a rapist, there could very well be other crimes he'd committed but had not yet been tied to; he also suggested Carrillo look at recently released sex offenders.

"A man," Salerno said, "does not become a killer overnight."

Carrillo began to peruse police reports carefully, looking for a suspect who dressed in black, listened to heavy metal music, had a .22, was a sexual deviant, and enjoyed killing people.

As Carrillo continued to read, he tried to figure out why the man in black had let Maria Hernandez live—that, he reasoned, could very well be the key that cracked the case. Maria, in bad light, could easily have passed for an Asian. Maybe, he thought, the killer was a disgruntled, psychopathic Vietnam vet, who thought Maria was Asian and when he realized she wasn't Asian, the need to kill was somehow mitigated.

The more Carrillo thought it through, the more certain he

was a new kind of monster was roaming Los Angeles: an individual who was cunning, very deadly, and afflicted with an atavistic, perverse sexuality that drove him like a runaway train.

It stayed quiet until the end of March, when Carrillo read a teletype report of a man in black who had followed two young women and tried to get one of them into his car, a dark-colored BMW. The girls wrote down the plate number and it belonged to Paul Samuels. Carrillo ran the name to see if he had any priors and he didn't; Samuels, however, was a veteran, tall and thin, with black hair. Gil requested and got a surveillance of Samuels—headed by Sgt. Larry Brakebush.

On Friday, March 28, the L.A. sheriff's office surveillance team began trailing Paul Samuels around L.A. in his BMW, a fast car the detectives were hard pressed to keep up with. Carrillo was off that night, but he didn't want to miss the surveillance, so he drove his twenty-seven-foot Rickwood mobile home to the Hall of Justice. With two other detectives, Mike Bumcrot and Jimmy Mercer, he listened to the surveillance over the radio, and what they heard was the surveillance team losing Samuels.

Up until the time they lost him, Samuels was doing all kinds of strange things—backing up one-way streets, following girls who were obviously underage. To Gil, he was exhibiting clear signs of a sexual predator.

The following night the sheriff's office followed Samuels again. He went downtown and into some XXX sex shops. Now, more than ever, they were sure Samuels was the one. They tried to get a photo of him to show to Maria Hernandez, but Samuels moved too quickly and the glass of his BMW had tinted windows.

The surveillance team observed him talking with a few streetwalkers and finally managed to get a photograph of him. It was immediately shown to Maria Hernandez, and she tentatively identified Samuels.

The sheriff's office arrested Paul Samuels on Wednesday morning and went to his house, finding a large collection of pornography and a .38 revolver—not a .22. He was put in a lineup viewed by Maria Hernandez, Jorge Gallegos, Edith Alcaaz, Joseph Duenas, and three young people who had been abducted and sexually abused by a man in black. Samuels was not identified and was quickly released.

"He was a freak," Gil said later. "He just wasn't *our* freak."

Samuels was the only viable suspect they'd had.

Gil felt certain the killer would strike again, and soon; but he could do nothing more at this point than wait until he did strike—and hope he would make a mistake.

Neither Carrillo nor Salerno had any way of knowing then that the Okazaki/Yu murders were just the start of a crime spree unparalleled in the annals of crime history.

FIVE

Since he had murdered Dayle Okazaki and Veronica Yu, he'd been thinking long and hard about who he was and what he was about, and he decided to commit himself totally to domination. To murder. For him, the act of killing had become the ultimate high; for him, that's what life was now about.

He believed in his heart the more heinous and vicious his assaults, the more Satan would be pleased and thus afford him his fiery blessings.

He had plans to steal enough money to buy his own house somewhere quiet and set up a torture room in the basement where he could quench his thirst for sadistic sex and killing in complete privacy. He also had visions of filming his conquests and maybe even selling the films; he knew there was a market for such things.

Eight days after the Okazaki and Yu murders, he went out hunting again, getting on the San Gabriel River Freeway with another stolen Toyota. As always, he cruised with no particular direction in mind, the need to kill a human being burning inside him like a tropical fever. It was March 26.

He suddenly remembered a house in Whittier he'd robbed a year earlier—how wealthy the occupants had seemed—and he began to drive back there. Whittier was a wealthy upscale community with a population of 70,000, founded by Quakers in 1881, and known as a center for citrus, avocado, and walnut ranches. It was named after the Quaker poet John Greenleaf Whittier and had been Richard Nixon's hometown.

At 2 A.M. the killer shut the lights, turned off the engine and rolled to a silent silent stop in front of the home of Vincent and Maxine Zazzara on Strong Avenue. The night was somewhat overcast. A quarter moon shed very little light.

No cars were parked on the street except the stolen Toyota. Aside from the rustling of leaves and the sound of an occasional cricket, all was quiet. Slowly he got out of the car, his eyes moving about with the hungry intensity of a stalking jungle cat. He closed the door without a sound.

The Zazzara residence was a one-story brick structure on a half acre of land; there was a white ranch-style fence out front, and orange, lemon, and grapefruit trees grew on either side of the house. It had two large bay windows that faced Strong Avenue. Lights were on in the window to the left.

The killer, his heart beating as if he'd been running, sweat beading his forehead, walked to the lighted window and saw Vincent Zazzara sleeping on a plaid couch. A television was on. There was a round black glass table in front of the couch. On it was a plant with bright red flowers. Mr. Zazzara had apparently dozed off while watching television. Vincent Zazzara was a fun-loving gregarious man. He was a retired CPA, who now owned two pizza restaurants.

The killer continued on to the backyard, careful to avoid walking into anything. Midway there he looked into a second window and saw forty-four-year-old Maxine sound asleep in bed. The sight of a woman excited him sexually. He continued on and tried to get the screens off the windows, but couldn't. They were all closed and locked.

He walked further into the yard, turned, and scrutinized the back of the house carefully, spotting a smaller window at the southeast corner, higher up on the building than the others. He moved to it, but it was too high for him to get the screen off; he had no leverage. Again he walked into the yard, looking for something to stand on. Spotting an empty compound can, he placed it under the window, got on it, reached up, and removed the screen. He then pried the window open and pulled himself up and into a small room where the washing machine and dryer were kept. He reached down and untied and took off his shoes. In his stocking feet, he started toward an unsuspecting, soundly sleeping Vincent Zazzara, pulling the .22 revolver from his waistband. As he reached the front of the house, he raised the gun, and holding it in combat position, rushed into the den where Zazzara had fallen asleep. He aimed carefully and shot him in the left side of his head, just above the ear. Shocked and bleeding, Zazzara tried to stand and grab the intruder with the gun, but the small-caliber bullet zigzagged through his brain, cutting the carotid artery, and he lost motor movement. As his dying heart pumped, blood shot out of the wound in squirts and hit the wall three feet away.

At the sound of the gunshot, Maxine Zazzara woke with a start, wide-eyed, just as the killer rushed into the room, pointing the gun at her. She screamed. He slapped her, said, "Shut up, bitch! And don't look at me! Where's the money? Where's the jewelry?"

Maxine demanded that he leave.

He beat her, telling her not to look at him, forced her on her stomach and tied her hands together with a necktie he grabbed from a nearby closet. He gagged her, disabled the phones, then began frantically to ransack the bedroom—opening closets and drawers, looking for valuables—diamonds, gold, cash.

Maxine Zazzara knew there was a shotgun under the bed that her husband had bought the previous year after a burglary, saying if the burglar came back, he'd blow him to pieces.

She was a strong-willed woman, an attorney and not easily intimidated. She carried a .45 automatic in her purse for protection. She knew from her husband's labored breathing that he was dying, and she knew what was in store for her when the killer was finished looking for valuables. She wasn't about to let that happen. Her .45 was not within reach, but the shotgun under the bed was. She tried with every ounce of strength she had to untie the knots binding her hands. The killer was busy searching, putting whatever he wanted into a pillowcase, anxious to get to the woman, and so caught up in his hunt, he did not see Maxine free her hands, quickly roll off the bed, and reach for the heavy blue-black shotgun.

Maxine Zazzara was a religious woman. She did the accounting at the Trinity Baptist Church in Downey for free, and she sang in the church choir. She didn't, however, have the slightest compunction about what to do now. She drew out the shotgun, stood, and aimed it at the sweating man in black, who was throwing their possessions all over the place. His back was to her. He heard something, turned, and saw her pointing the big-bored shotgun at him.

He moved left and went for the gun in his pants.

She pulled the trigger; there was only a metallic click. The gun was empty. All the blood ran out of his face. Fury burst inside him. Maxine had not known Vincent had taken the shells out of the gun because their grandchildren had been visiting the house that weekend.

"Bitch! Motherfucker!" he said, raising the .22 and shooting her three times, the bullets knocking her down.

He beat her, kicked her, slapped her, furious she would defy him—try to kill *him*. He hurried to the kitchen, found a sharp, ten-inch-long carving knife, and returned to her, picked her up, put her on the bed, raised her purple nightshirt, and tried to cut her heart out. But he couldn't get through the rib cage and he left a gaping inverted cross sliced into her chest, over and below the left breast.

He decided on her eyes; that would be his way of having a piece of her soul. Quickly, yet carefully, he cut away her eyelids, removed both her eyes, and put them in a little jewelry box he had found, laughing as he did so.

Then he stabbed her in the stomach, throat, and pubic area.

He tried to have sex with her, but he was so shaken by her pointing the shotgun at him and pulling the trigger, he was unable to. He gathered what he could of value—a VCR, a video camera, jewelry, watches, and rings, and hastily put them in a pillowcase. He found Maxine's .45 and another shotgun, taking the shotgun but leaving the .45 on the bed next to Maxine.

There was a safe hidden in the house, but he didn't find it; he also missed an expensive coin collection in boxes in the living room near the family piano. There was a .22 target pistol in the boxes with the coins.

He left by the front door with Maxine Zazzara's blood all over his pants, hustled to the car, and got in it. He kept a shotgun between his legs, put the box with the eyes on the passenger seat, and drove to the corner, in a hurry to get to the freeway just two blocks away.

He was very angry at himself for letting Maxine Zazzara get the drop on him and vowed that would never happen again.

Suddenly, there was a police car behind him.

Earlier he had put a sticker on the rear bumper of the car that read, "America, love it or leave it," knowing most cops were patriotic and less likely to pull over a driver who so openly proclaimed his love of country. It usually worked. It did tonight, for he reached the freeway and got on it without being stopped.

First he went to his hotel room, washed the blood off, and changed his clothes. Then he proceeded to the home of his main fence. They'd met a year earlier at the bus terminal, and since then he'd been bringing him the fruits of his labor for hard cash, most times paid on the spot, no questions asked. The fence did not know his real name, nor did he know the fence's real name. That was the way it was on the street. The fence was always there and would receive him with a rigid smile and cold cash. He was a short, stocky man with a hard boxer's face. He hung out at MacArthur Park and in the downtown pool halls. The killer sold him the Zazzara jewelry and guns, pocketed the money, and drove around downtown L.A. looking for a prostitute, all sexually charged up by the violence.

He found a hooker on Sixth Street, just off Broadway. They agreed on a price for oral sex and she got into the car. He parked on a quiet street but couldn't get an erection. He asked to play with her feet—he was obsessed with feet. She let him, though reluctantly and without enthusiasm. He paid her and dropped her off where he'd found her.

He drove the car to Hollywood, abandoned it, took a bus back to downtown Los Angeles, and walked its mean streets until 6 A.M., when he returned to the rat-infested Cecil Hotel on Main, went to his room, looked at Maxine Zazzara's eyes, and laughed.

At 8:45 that evening, thirty-one-year-old Bruno Francisco Polo pulled into the Zazzara driveway. Both Maxine and Vincent Zazzara's cars were parked in the garage, and Polo noted that the light in the television room was on. It was his custom to drop off the receipts for the pizzeria in Whittier which he had managed for the last year. Before that, he had worked in Vincent's Downey store. He was close to the Zazzara family and had been at their Thanksgiving and Christmas dinners that year.

Polo opened the Whittier store at 11 A.M. and closed at 8 P.M. His usual route home took him right past the Zazzara

THE NIGHT STALKER / 53

residence. He had the money in a folded-up brown paper bag, the amount and date written on it in pencil. He noted the front door was half open and the screen door was unlocked, which was unusual. He rang the bell; no answer. He called out Vincent's name; still no answer. With some trepidation, he put the money in the front door mail slot and left.

The following morning, Polo returned to the Zazzara residence. He had a "bad feeling" about the door being opened the night before and Vincent not answering his knocking, ringing, and subsequent phone calls. When Polo saw the front door still ajar, in the same position, he got goose bumps. He rang the bell, knocked, and called Vincent's name, all to no avail. Something, he knew, was very wrong, and he walked back to his pickup. He didn't want to go into the house alone. He thought about calling Vincent's son, Peter, but he really didn't know if there was reason to yet. Instead, he quickly drove to the store in Downey, twenty minutes away, and told Al Persico about the Zazzara door being open and Vincent's not answering.

Persico told Polo he'd follow him back to the Zazzara residence. As they made their way there, Persico caught a red light and Polo arrived first, parked, got out of his pickup, and again walked to the front door and rang the bell. No response. Made bolder by the knowledge that Al would soon be there, he opened the screen door and slowly, hesitantly, entered the house and went left, toward the television room.

"Vincent . . . Vincent you here? Vincent?" he called out.

As he entered the den, he first saw Vincent's bare feet on the arm of the couch; they seemed a strange color, white and waxy. When he saw the dried blood around Vincent's ear, he thought Vincent had headphones on and that's why he'd not responded to his calls and knocks. He moved closer and suddenly realized it was blood he was looking at, and that Vincent was dead.

Bruno turned and ran, his face devoid of color. The world was suddenly upside down. He got in his car and began to drive away, went thirty feet, and realized there was nowhere for him to go. He was in shock. He backed up, got out of his pickup, and paced back and forth, in a panic. Al arrived and Bruno hurried to him and told him what he'd found. Al did not believe him; he said he must be mistaken—

"Look, go look, go see for yourself!" Bruno said.

Al entered the house, went straight to the den, and immediately knew Vincent was dead. He moved to the bedroom, took one look at Maxine, and hurried outside to join a distraught Bruno Polo. Bruno said he was calling Vincent's son, Peter. But he would not go back in the Zazzara house; he hurried across the street, found some neighbors home, and asked if he could please use the phone, as there had been a terrible, terrible tragedy. Bruno got Peter Zazzara on the line and told him briefly what had happened. Peter said he'd call the police and be right over.

First to arrive was fire captain Carl Allen with a firetruck and paramedics in a Medivac truck. It was never made clear why a firetruck had rolled, but there they were. Al outlined what he'd seen, and with two of his men, Capt. Allen entered the house, took one look at Vincent Zazzara, and immediately backed up and summoned the police.

The first policeman to arrive was Los Angeles sheriff's deputy Paul Archambault. He went inside, saw Vincent, saw what had been done to Maxine, and went straight back to his cruiser and called in the murders. He next sealed off the crime scene with yellow tape across the entire front of the Zazzara property. Neighbors began gathering. More deputies arrived. Peter Zazzara pulled up in his car. He had his fiancée and young daughter with him. Bruno and Dep. Archambault explained to him what they'd seen. Peter wanted to go into the house, but it was a crime scene now and no one would be allowed to enter but Sheriff's Homicide.

Homicide detectives Russ Uloth and J. D. Smith, assigned to team 4, caught the call and arrived at 12 P.M. Russ was in his late fifties, dapper, tall, and slender, with blond hair. Smith was 5'8", of medium build, with blond hair and a lot of freckles. They went inside with Dep. Archambault, took quick note of Vincent and Maxine's condition, the wounds, and the fact that the house had been ransacked. The two detectives went back outside and J. D. Smith summoned criminalists from the sheriff's department on his car phone. There was evidence everywhere that had to be gathered.

Together, the two detectives went around back and immediately saw the screen on the patio and the empty compound can with the killer's shoeprint clearly imprinted on it. Careful about where they walked, they moved closer and saw a dozen shoeprints in the flower bed, just under the window he'd entered through. Actually, there were two sets; one turned out to be Vincent Zazzara's and the other, they assumed correctly, was the killer's. They noted two pry marks on the window frame and the window itself. As they moved around the perimeter of the house, walking gingerly, their eyes looking about hungrily, they found more shoeprints on the east side, the place from which the killer had first seen Maxine.

Henry Laporte and John Garrision, from the sheriff's crime lab, arrived and took photographs of the bodies, the ransacking, the shoeprints, and the windows, at the direction of Det. Uloth. Criminalist Steve Renteria made plaster casts of both sets of shoeprints under the entrance window.

Sam Lorca from the medical office arrived and looked carefully at the wounds that had been inflicted on Vincent and Maxine and confirmed what Uloth and Smith had thought. Maxine's eyes had been taken. This gave Uloth and Smith a lot to think about. It was a rare occurrence, and they wondered what it meant. They found the cash bags Bruno had left, dated March 27, 28, and 29, in the mail drop with a lot of mail. They turned the bags over to a very distraught Peter Zazzara.

No one there that day linked the Zazzara murders to the killer's other assaults. There was no reason to. There was no commonality among them yet. The Vincow homicide had been handled by the LAPD and had happened over fifteen months earlier. Jennie Vincow had become just another murder statistic; the case was officially still open, but inactive.

Uloth and Smith stayed at the Zazzara residence until a little after 2 A.M. They interviewed friends and family members of the Zazzaras and had no idea who had committed the vicious double murder. They knew, though, the killer had a size 11 1/2 foot, wore Avia sneakers, and had taken a pair of brown human eyes.

They had learned that Vincent Zazzara had been in jail once, but had no association or business dealings with organized crime, which had briefly been suggested by Peter Zazzara, both to Russ Uloth and Paul Archambault.

The killer, the detectives knew, had searched the place frantically. There was a safe with a lot of cash in it, and maybe, they theorized, the killer had known about the safe. However, that would have made it an inside job. Persico, Bruno, and Zazzara's family all knew about the safe, and at that point, the detectives weren't ruling out anyone.

The missing eyes added a macabre twist to the crime. *Why,* they kept asking one another, *would the killer take the eyes? What the hell was that all about?*

Early the following morning, after very little sleep, Uloth and Smith attended the autopsies of the Zazzaras, which was done by Dr. Terence Allen. He first extracted the slug from Vincent's head; it, like the bullets removed from Dale Okazaki and Veronica Yu, was a .22. Dr. Allen said the gunshot was what had killed Vincent Zazzara.

He at first noted just two gunshot wounds to Maxine, but as the autopsy progressed, he discovered a third bullet lodged in her neck. She had died, he said, from the bullet wounds and had been cut afterward. Each of the slashes over her heart was four by four inches long. There were eight other stab wounds to her chest and two to the pubic area, as well as multiple stab-slash cuts to her throat.

Back in the Homicide squad room in the Hall of Justice Building on West Temple, Frank Salerno silently read Uloth's and Smith's memo. At the inception of all homicides, the detectives who catch the case fill out a simple form outlining the components and elements of the murder. It is theoretically a memo to the sheriff, but is supposed to be read by every officer there, so crime patterns can be discerned and solved quickly. Salerno went straight to Carrillo and told him there was a double murder in Whittier in which a .22 revolver had been used. Carrillo then spoke to Uloth and Smith and was filled in on the details, and the more he heard, the more he thought it was his man. When he learned Mrs. Zazzara's nightgown had been pulled up—"indicative of a sexual assault"—and that her eyes had been removed, he was even more convinced it was the man in black. Uloth and Smith, however, didn't share Carrillo's theory and told him so.

Carrillo turned to the bullets removed from the Zazzaras.

They were too damaged to be matched up with the ones recovered from Dayle Okazaki and Veronica Yu.

"Can't say it is, but can't say it isn't, either," Ballistics told Carrillo.

He went back to Salerno and told him how certain he was that one man had committed all three assaults. Salerno said it could very well be, but they'd have to wait and see—hope he made a mistake that would lead them to him. Salerno asked Carrillo if there was anything on the partial license plate gotten by Jorge Gallegos over in Monterey Park. Carrillo told him he'd called Monterey Park a couple of times and they'd said they were "on it."

"That could be," Salerno said, "the thing that breaks the case."

Neither man had any way of knowing the car the killer had been driving the night of the Okazaki/Yu killings had already been found and recovered by the Monterey Park police just two days after the assault. Monterey Park, however, did not connect it to the car used in the Yu killing. The vehicle had been towed to a garage the police used and was given back to its rightful owner.

It was never dusted for prints.

Uloth told Carrillo about a meeting detectives from Montebello, Monterey Park, and Pico Rivera were having about three abductions and sexual assaults. It was believed the same suspect had done the crimes because the descriptions matched and two of the victims had spoken about a bad odor coming from their assailant. The detectives had, Uloth said, matched up a shoeprint found in the Zazzaras' garden with a print discovered in wet cement near the attempted abduction of a girl from Los Angeles.

When Carrillo heard this, bells went off in his head. He went to the meeting with Uloth and Smith and listened as detectives from each jurisdiction told what they had: there were sodomy and handcuffs involved; both victims had been abandoned after the assault—one at a bus stop, the other at a park; the third had gotten away. As Carrillo listened to the descriptions matching up, he knew.

"It was like this heavy feeling I had in my gut. I was certain it was all the same guy. I just knew it," he'd later relate.

When each of the detectives finished, Carrillo stood and

told them what he had and what his theory was: "This is all one suspect."

No one there—eight detectives in all—agreed with Carrillo; they laughed at him. He was the youngest present and had been on team 3 for less than a year. He smiled and laughed along with his colleagues as they made fun of him, but he knew.

"I'm telling you, it's the same freak!" he said, laughing.

"That just doesn't fit," he was told. "No one suspect did all these crimes—"

"Bullshit. This dude did it all," Carrillo said.

And they laughed some more.

Back at the Sheriff's Homicide office, Carrillo went straight to Salerno and told him what he learned at the meeting and how he thought one man was responsible for everything, the abductions and sexual assaults, the Zazzara, Yu, and Okazaki murders, and the shooting of Maria Hernandez.

Salerno gave Carrillo a long, slow once-over, said, "It's possible," though his eyes said "It's unlikely," and they proceeded to see Capt. Bob Grimm. Grimm was a large man with thick black hair, a barrel chest, and dark circles under his eyes. He was an excellent judge of character, and he knew how to get the most out of the five homicide teams under his command, all of which worked out of the same long narrow office, filled with cluttered desks and ringing phones.

After hearing what Carrillo had to say, which Salerno said he agreed with, the captain suggested they form a small, informal task force to monitor and solve these murders, kidnappings, and sexual assaults. He put Salerno in charge. He was the perfect man for the job; he had learned much, Grimm knew, running the Hillside Strangler case.

Salerno picked J. D. Smith, Russ Uloth, Gil Carrillo, Jim Mercer, Bobby Ghan, and John Yarbrough, and they all began by reading crime teletypes from all over the huge expanse of Los Angeles County—looking for similarities in modus operandi (methods, dress, language, etc.).

At the end of March, Gil Carrillo met with Maria Hernandez at the condo in Rosemead. She still had a large bandage on her right hand. With time and therapy, the doctors said optimistically, the hand would be as good as new.

Gil and Maria entered the garage; slowly, she took him

through it all. He listened very carefully. She described and showed him how she'd got out of the car, walked to the door, opened its two locks, and pushed the button to close the garage. He timed how long it took for the garage to actually close after the button had been activated—it was eight seconds.

That meant, he theorized, the killer had to have been lying in wait for her or had come into the complex right behind her. Maria took him to the front of the house and showed him where she was standing when the killer walked out the front door.

"What exactly did you say?" he asked.

"When he saw me, he pointed the gun at me with two hands. I said something like, 'No, please don't shoot me again!' He put down the gun and ran to the car. I never saw it, but I heard it start up and pull away."

They went inside the house and Maria described exactly what she'd done. Gill had been hoping there was something he'd missed or overlooked, but as he thought about what Maria told him and showed him, he was even more baffled.

He asked her if anyone had been trailing her or Dayle. She said she was certain no one had been following her—she did not just go around the world wide-eyed and unseeing: she knew in today's society a woman had to be vigilant and was certain no one had been trailing her that night. She was positive Dayle would have told her about any strangers. Dayle had been taking self-defense courses and had been made more aware.

Carrillo drove her home, thanked her for her help, promised to do all he could, and started back to his cramped desk at the Hall of Justice. As he drove, he replayed the encounter in his mind.

Why, he kept wondering, did he let her live, after first being so intent upon killing her?

It didn't make sense.

SIX

Two weeks and four days after the murders of Vincent and Maxine Zazzara, on April 14, the killer woke up late in the day, casually walked out of the Cecil Hotel, turned left, had breakfast at Margarita's on Seventh, then went over to the Ye Hi pool parlor, also on Seventh. He still had money from the Zazzara score and he liked to shoot pool for cash. He liked to gamble. But he wasn't able to find a game this day and left the pool hall, smoking a joint as he walked to the Cameo Theater on Broadway, which showed porno movies twenty-four hours a day.

There, the killer sat in the musty, semen-laden dark and watched the huge genitals on the screen being pushed, prodded, probed, licked, and sucked.

Sometimes in porno films he'd see a woman with a pentagram on her body, and that would excite him. It was her, that kind of woman—a follower of Satan, of what was evil—that interested him and turned him on. She would be someone he could trust; she would be someone who'd understand his needs and not think he was strange, weird, or bizarre.

When he was a boy, he had read the story of Jack the Ripper, and it both fascinated him and had a profound effect on him: the fog, the Ripper being all in black, the cuts and eviscerations turned him on and led his thinking to the path of murder for sexual gratification and pleasure which would become his destiny.

It's like nothing else; you can't explain its intensity in words. To have that power over life—nothing is more sexually exciting; it's the ultimate, something very few people experience.

He particularly liked movies in which there was extreme violence—preferably of a sexual, occult nature. Films like *Nightmare on Elm Street, Friday the 13th, The Exorcist,* and *Dracula* were a great inspiration and turn-on to him. His favorite film was *The Texas Chainsaw Massacre.*

It was ahead of its time; it portrayed something that really exists in human nature, but no one will honestly admit.

His favorite book was Truman Capote's *In Cold Blood,* which depicts the shotgun murders of the Cutter family in Holcomb, Kansas, by two ex-con drifters by the names of Richard Hickirk and Perry Smith.

When he left the Cameo, he walked back to the pool hall and knocked a few balls around. As he played, listening to AC/DC's *Highway to Hell* album on earphones, he decided to take it all to the extreme, to go on a killing spree with stealth and careful planning that would make the whole world stop and take notice. He would be more famous than Jack the Ripper, more famous than any killer, ever.

Once there was a time when he had some remorse—had second thoughts about killing; but that was all a long time ago: *Psychopaths have no ethics, no scruples, and no conscience. Something inside is gone. They just aren't capable of those emotions. That's why killing is so easy for a real psychopath. Society has a lot of problems understanding that.*

He left the pool hall and stole a car he found in front of the Alexandria Hotel. He had the scanner with him he'd bought at a Radio Shack; it would enable him to listen in on police transmissions. He drove to the freeway and began to hunt, as he listened to loud heavy metal music.

AC/DC's "Night Prowler" was his favorite song: its lyrics spoke of an intruder sneaking into someone's room and into the womb. He felt that they'd written it for him, that Satan had inspired the group to do it as an anthem for him.

As he cruised different communities, blocks, avenues, streets—always near the freeway for a quick escape—he listened to police movement over the scanner. Again he got off the freeway at Monterey Park. Few cars were out. Most everyone was in a deep sleep; he had studied people's sleeping patterns and knew it was best to break into a home in the early-morning hours, between 2 and 4 A.M.

Veronica Yu had been killed in Monterey Park, and he knew the police there would be particularly vigilant, yet he still returned and cruised its quiet streets. There were no vehicles parked at the curbs; all were either in garages or in driveways.

He shut off the engine and lights, coasted to a noiseless stop on Trumbower Avenue, and sat still, listening carefully to the silence of the night. He reached down and tucked the top of his pants into his socks; he didn't want them getting caught on anything.

Just then Launie Dempster, who delivered the *Herald Examiner* in Monterey Park, drove by. During the day, Launie worked as a security guard at Rio Hondo College in Whittier. She was particularly vigilant, having received training from the security company she worked for—California Plant Protection. Launie saw him sitting there and thought he was "suspicious." As she looked at him, he stared right back at her. She reached the corner and turned, glad to be away from him. "He had very scary eyes," she'd later report.

Quietly, the killer opened and closed the car door and began walking south on Trumbower, staying in the shadows. He stopped in front of the home of sixty-six-year-old William Doi and his fifty-six-year-old invalid wife, Lillian.

Bill Doi had recently retired from his job as international sales manager at the Santa Fe Trail Trucking Company. Yesterday he had put a down payment on a brand new Ford van; he was planning to tour the country in it with his wife. Bill had had a heart attack in the spring of 1982, but his health had improved steadily, and he looked forward to the trip. Mrs. Doi had had a crippling stroke two years earlier; it was still very difficult for her to talk, and though she could not get about without the help of a wheelchair, she, too, was looking forward to the trip.

Bill had been born in Salinas, California. Because of his Japanese heritage, he was put in an Arizona relocation camp during World War II. When he was released from the camp, he joined the Army's 44th Regimental Combat Team and fought with distinction. After the service, he attended Northwestern University and worked as a shipping clerk to support his wife and young daughter, Linda. He worked his way up the corporate ladder to international sales manager. He was a member of the Eastside Optimists' Club; he was an extremely outgoing man with a great sense of humor. He played golf often and was a big Lakers fan. The Dois had one grandchild, whom Bill joyfully doted over and took to Japanese festivals, the beach, and carnivals.

In front of the Doi residence there was a lone lemon tree. The front door was in the center of the home, with picture windows to the left and a garage to the right. Above the garage there was a basketball hoop. Somewhere on the block a set of chimes made a shimmering, ethereal sound, which floated gently on the still, lemon-scented air. The sky was low and overcast; no moon or stars were visible. A slight rain began to fall. The killer liked the rain—fewer people were out, and it muffled the sound of gunshots nicely. He'd gotten rid of the .22 revolver, sold it to a fence for twenty bucks. He knew it was hot, and tonight he had a new weapon: a silver-plated .22 automatic.

He decided the Doi residence was the place and walked straight to the backyard, his steps quick and efficient, using the shadows.

It takes years to learn how to steal, to use the cover of night. It's not easy. You have to practice it. And you need someone who knows what they're doing to teach you. You've got to be aware of everything at once. And you always have to be careful about making noise. You've got to learn to move without noise.

In the backyard there was a pair of locked sliding glass doors. He saw alarm wires around the windows, but he found one that was open, covered only by a screen. He cut the screen, removed it carefully, reached in, and pushed the window up. He climbed into a rear bathroom, saying inside his head: *Satan, this, what I, your humble servant, am about to do, I do for you.*

He got down low and waited, making certain he hadn't been heard. Seconds later, he was up and moving through the house; there was a hall light on and it was easy to see. In the first bedroom he found an elderly Asian woman, Lillian Doi, sleeping soundly. He saw a wheelchair near her bed, which told him she was an invalid. As he moved to the bedroom of Bill Doi, he raised the gun and chambered it. The cold metallic click woke Bill instantly—he knew what it was, and he grabbed for the loaded 9-millimeter he kept in the nightstand. Bill was very security conscious; he had several handguns placed strategically around the house. As he grabbed his 9, the killer ran into the bedroom, saw Bill going for the gun, aimed, and holding the .22 in combat position, shot Bill just above the upper lip, right through the tongue.

Bill half fell from the bed, choking on the bullet lodged in the back of his throat. He tried to shoot Bill again, but the .22 jammed. Cursing, he returned to the hall, cleared the gun—leaving the shell on the floor—and went back to finish Bill. The bullet he had taken, tumbling after it had entered, had caused severe damage to his tongue, voicebox, and brain: he couldn't pick up the Walther and pull the trigger. He tried to beg for his life but could not articulate his words. Blood gushed from his mouth.

Lillian had awakened at the report of the .22. She heard Bill moaning, pleading incoherently with someone, but she couldn't move; she could only lie there wide-eyed, waves of fear washing over her, listening to the murder of the man she'd loved all her adult life.

Bill's pleas for mercy fell on deaf ears, for the killer returned to him. He used his gloved fists and beat Bill unconscious, kicking him viciously when he went down. He took Bill's Walther and hurried to Lillian's bedroom, walked to her bed, slapped her, and warned her not to scream.

"Shut up, or I'll kill you, bitch," he said. Even if she'd wanted to scream, she couldn't; since the stroke, verbal articulation had been difficult. He secured her hands with thumb cuffs, then proceeded to ransack the house, taking whatever jewelry and valuables he could find, throwing things all over. The jewelry he stole included Bill Doi's Omega Constellation watch, his Masonic ring, a jade ring, Lillian Doi's father's pocketwatch, and both their wedding bands.

Bill came to, moaning in pain as streams of blood ran from his nose and mouth. Immediately the killer ran back to him and knocked him unconscious again.

Excited by the shooting and the beating, the killer returned to Lillian's room and raped her, all the while demanding she not look at him. He was sexually charged up by the violence, the blood, his total domination—her absolute shock at what he was doing so dispassionately.

Finished, he kissed her, put what he was taking into two pillowcases, disabled one of the two phones in the house, and left without removing the thumb cuffs from Lillian's hands.

Again Bill came to. He realized the man in black had gone and he crawled, bleeding profusely, on his hands and knees, to his wife's room. He saw how the man had left her, with the cuffs, and his heart broke, for he knew what had happened. He had just enough strength left to get to the phone, pick it up, and say in a weak, barely discernible voice, "Help, please help me," before he passed out again.

Emergency operator Darlene Boese received the call. Before she could answer Bill, he'd blacked out. But she knew he was in serious trouble and dispatched fire department personnel, police, and an ambulance to Trumbower. The L.A. 911 system was "enhanced" and automatically displayed an address as soon as a call came in.

Bill regained consciousness. He called 911 a second time and repeatedly said, "Help me." Darlene Boese kept telling him that help was on its way. Crying, Lillian struggled to get up and forced the cuff off her right hand, leaving the thumb bleeding.

At 5:04 A.M., fire captain Norman Case and three firefighters pulled up in front of the Doi home. The sky was a low, deep gray, and a light rain still fell. Capt. Case got out of the firetruck, walked to the front door, and noted it was wide open. He rang the bell, calling out, "Fire department here! Fire department here to help!" Without getting a response, he walked into the house. His men waited outside. The red lights on the truck continued to spin.

Capt. Case saw a small woman wearing a blue nightgown babbling incoherently, the thumb cuffs hanging from her left hand. Lillian had summoned all the strength she could and managed to get up and move to the doorway, but she could go no further. She pointed to her right and Capt. Case saw Bill Doi for the first time. He was sitting in an easy chair near the phone, covered with blood, unconscious, his breathing labored and shallow. Case could see that Bill needed CPR and he hurried outside, told his men to bring in equipment, and ran back to Bill.

The killer had thrown things all over, and Case and his men had to clear the floor before they could even lay Bill down.

Monterey Park officer Michael Gorajewski arrived, knowing only that someone needed help. When he entered the house and saw Bill getting CPR, he thought it had probably been a heart attack. His eyes moved down the hall and he spotted Lillian, walked up to her, and noticed the left side of her face was swollen, that she had a black eye. Then he saw the thumb cuffs dangling from her left hand and realized this was no heart attack.

When he asked her what had happened, she could only mumble incoherently. Gorajewski searched the rest of the house; there could be, he knew, more victims—or a suspect still about. After his search, he returned to Lillian. Officer Arthur Brooks pulled up and Gorajewski outlined what they had and called it into Central. He went outside, retrieved yellow tape from his car trunk, and cordoned off the Doi residence.

Medivac 21 arrived and the medics took over, though the firemen continued to assist. Bill stopped breathing, but the Medivac personnel revived him with shock. He had to be taken to the hospital as soon as possible, and he was carefully secured to a stretcher and moved to an ambulance, which sped off for Garfield Hospital in Monterey Park. One of the firefighters stayed with the Medivac team. The others gathered their gear and returned it to the truck, planning to pick up their colleague, fireman Nordstrom, at the hospital.

Launie Dempster again drove past the Doi residence, returning from her paper route, and saw the police cars and ambulance and wondered if the guy she'd seen in the car had had anything to do with what had happened.

Gorajewski again tried to communicate with Lillian, to no avail. Later, when asked in court about her ability to talk, he said, "I was not getting any response back from her, other than mumbling, and I did not know if she was—what she was trying to tell me. She acknowledged I was speaking to her, but what she was trying to tell me, I do not know."

Officer Gorajewski pulled up a chair so she could sit down.

Officer Bill Reynolds arrived, was apprised of the situation, knelt down to be at eye level with Lillian, and calmly asked her what had happened.

Now, for the first time, in jumbled sentences, Lillian told the officers about a tall man in black with a gun and bad teeth. Officer Reynolds managed to get the cuffs off her other thumb. They put her in a squad car and drove her to the Monterey Park Hospital as the dawn of a new day began to stir the great metropolis of Los Angeles.

Bill Doi reached the hospital at 5:13 A.M. and was immediately taken to the emergency unit. Dr. Anthony Reid, who specialized in cardiology, was waiting for him. In the ambulance, all of Bill's vital signs had ceased. Dr. Reid examined him and found no blood pressure, no spontaneous respiration, no cardiac activity or oscillation of the heart on an electrocardiogram. Dr. Reid tried unsuccessfully to resuscitate Doi with electrical shock.

He pronounced Bill Doi officially dead at 5:29 A.M. He then took a good look at Bill's wounds, realized he'd been shot, and ordered X rays to determine where the bullet had lodged.

At 6:20 A.M., Monterey Park robbery-homicide detective Paul Torres arrived. He had caught the Doi case. He was greeted by Lt. James Burke, who filled him in on what they had. They didn't get many homicides in Monterey Park, and it was a rare thing for Monterey Park detectives to have to get out of bed to work a murder scene. Torres went back outside and began to look for clues. He found the Avia shoeprint in front of the Doi residence on a muddy island between the street and sidewalk. There was also a print of a combat boot. Torres called Officer Jiron over and asked to see the bottom of his boot. It matched the combat boot print. He told Jiron to cordon off the dirt island for the criminalists.

Det. Torres walked to the back of the house and noticed the Avia shoeprint under Lillian Doi's bedroom window and the master bath window. He continued to the yard and found more Avia prints on the rear patio and the screen lying on the ground. He saw the wide-open window and surmised that the killer had gone in there. Criminalists Joe Snyder and Linda Arthur arrived. Torres directed Snyder to the Avia shoeprints and asked him to plaster-cast them.

Gil Carrillo was called at home at 8:30 A.M. Monterey Park police had phoned the sheriff's office and asked specifically that Carrillo be sent over to the Doi crime scene. Carrillo never found out who'd exactly requested his presence, but he went straight from his home to Monterey Park, found Trumbower using his Thomas Guide, parked, and approached the front door of the Doi residence. Monterey Park detective Torres was surprised to see Gil and asked why he was there.

Carrillo explained that he'd gotten a call and had been asked to come.

"Well, we don't need your help. Thanks anyway," he was told.

Rather than get offended, Carrillo said he was wondering if perhaps this crime tied into a crime pattern he was investigating.

Det. Torres didn't like having Carrillo there; it was his case and in his jurisdiction, and Carrillo had no right to be there. From the front doorway Gil spotted an officer standing on the shell the killer had ejected in the hall.

Carrillo said, "I suggest you protect that evidence," pointing to the shell. His comment was not appreciated and he was thanked for coming but again told they didn't need his help. "Thanks anyway."

Nothing was said to Carrillo about the shoeprint or the thumb cuffs.

Angry, he returned to his car and drove to the sheriff's office. He knew why Det. Torres didn't want him there—no one wanted to be shown up—but still, he thought, they should have let him view the crime scene. And they'd been rude and disrespectful.

When he got back to the office, he told his team members how he'd been treated by Monterey Park. When asked by Salerno if he thought it was their man, Carrillo said he didn't know, that they wouldn't tell him anything. Salerno said he'd call Monterey Park and see what he could find out. He, too, was stonewalled.

Monterey Park, it seemed, didn't want the sheriff's office nosing around their investigations. If the case was solved, they would solve it.

Not knowing about the Avia shoeprints Torres had found, Carrillo went back to reading teletypes and looking for patterns.

SEVEN

Mabel Bell, eighty-three, and her invalid sister, Florence "Nettie" Lang, eighty-one, lived on North Alta Vista, on the outskirts of Monrovia. Getting to their house required driving up North Alta Vista, a lonely, twisting road that rose half a mile high.

Monrovia, twenty miles northeast of the city of Los Angeles, is a small town with big-city features and a population of 40,000. Named after William N. Monroe, a railroad construction engineer who laid out the town in 1886 after purchasing it for $30,000, Monrovia is situated below the majestic Sierra Madre Mountains in the beautiful San Gabriel Valley, between the cities of Duarte and Pasadena.

Mabel Bell's home stood by itself, isolated and distinct from any other. It is a plain beige frame-style affair with a garage on the right. Orange trees grow in the front yard. It, like the Zazzara residence, has a white picket fence out front.

Mabel Bell, or "Ma Bell," as she was known, was a strong, independent senior citizen who still drove around Monrovia on chores and enjoyed bridge games three times a week. She liked the seclusion of her house; crime was something she didn't much worry about. Most nights Ma Bell left her front door unlocked. She had moved to California from Oklahoma thirty-five years earlier, and folks there always left their doors unlocked. Every year Ma Bell contributed to the fund to keep the Statue of Liberty in good shape. She loved God, her country, her children, and her twelve grandchildren.

Ma Bell was widowed at an early age, and she had brought up two children without assistance. She had worked as a secretary for the Veron Tool Company for twenty-three years.

She now had twelve grandchildren and was the center of the family. She was white-haired and frail but moved like a woman fifteen years her junior. She had taken in her invalid sister, Nettie, two years earlier, rather than let her be institutionalized. The two sisters slept in different bedrooms. Ma Bell's was white, with ruffled Victorian curtains covering its two windows. Her bed had four dark wooden posts. At 11:40 P.M. on May 29, both sisters were sleeping soundly with the doors of the house unlocked.

On this night the killer was driving a gray Mercedes sedan he'd stolen from the parking lot of the Velvet Turtle Restaurant. He reached the bottom of North Alta Vista and started driving up it; he didn't look at a map or compass. He just went where his inner voice told him to go. North Alta Vista was not an easy street to find, but somehow that night he made his way up its winding, twisting curves, seeing nothing in the headlights but foliage, dusty cactus, tall palms, and cypress trees. The first residence he came to was Ma Bell's. He shut off the lights and engine and just sat there with the window open, listening and watching, taking in the night. It was absolutely quiet. He started the engine, put the lights back on, drove past Ma Bell's house, and didn't see another home for a half mile or so. He turned around and went back to the house; he wanted his car to be facing the direction he would flee when his work, his mission, was done.

He got out, careful not to slam the door, and walked to Ma Bell's front door. As always, he was wearing gloves and was not worried about fingerprints when he grabbed the doorknob, turned, and pushed. The door opened and he slowly walked into the modest home, hunching down low, all coiled aggression. He let his eyes get used to the dark, took out a flashlight, and found his way to the bedrooms. He could readily see that the occupants of the house were not too well off, that there was little of monetary value, and it made him angry.

He found Nettie Lang and quickly realized she was an elderly invalid. He then moved to Ma Bell's room and saw her asleep in bed. He searched the rest of the house and realized he'd come to the wrong place: there were no young women, and there was nothing much to steal.

He went to the kitchen for a knife he could use on the two old women, but he couldn't find one sharp enough, though he did find a red, wood-handled hammer. With it he returned to Nettie Lang's bedroom, walked up to her frail, sleeping form, and without hesitation, struck her in the head, sinking the hammer into her brain repeatedly. Then he used a piece of the electrical cord from a clock near the bed to bind her hands behind her back tightly. The clock dropped to the floor, stopped at 12:06 A.M. He proceeded to Ma Bell's room, not realizing he had stepped on the clock and left a bloody shoeprint.

Calling on Satan to watch what he was about to do, he raised the hammer and struck Ma Bell in the head. She woke up screaming, in a panic, thinking she was in the middle of a terrible nightmare.

"Shut up or I'll kill you! Where's the money? Where's the jewelry?" he demanded.

"I have no money! Get out of my house! Who are you?" Ma Bell managed to say, before he struck her again, sending brain matter about the room. He put on the lights, found duct tape, and used it to bind her ankles. He ripped the rest of the cord from Ma Bell's bedside clock, a four-by-five-inch white-faced General Electric, frayed the broken ends, plugged it back in, and used the exposed wire to shock a semiconscious Mabel Bell. He then took whatever of value he could find—some costume jewelry, watches, and a cassette player Ma Bell had gotten from her grandson, David Nipp, for her eighty-third birthday on April 6. It was the first one she had ever owned.

Sexually charged by the violence, the torture, he returned to Nettie Lang, ripped her nightgown off, and raped her.

Satan, he knew, would be pleased with this work, for it was cruel, brutal, and truly bestial.

It was time, he reasoned, to let the whole world know he walked with Satan, and he used Ma Bell's red lipstick to draw a pentagram (a five-pointed star in a circle) on the back of her left thigh and on the white wall over her head. A pentagram was the universally accepted symbol of Satan. He then drew a pentagram on Nettie Lang's bedroom wall. He ate a banana he found in the kitchen, drank a can of Mountain Dew and a Coke, urinated, and left, carrying a bloodstained pillowcase with the sisters' meager belongings in it over his shoulder like some Santa Claus from hell.

He jumped into the stolen Mercedes and drove back down the twisting turns of North Alta Vista, tires screeching, to the freeway and the foul-smelling obscurity of downtown Los Angeles.

The next evening, still driving the gray Mercedes, he went out hunting again, so sexually keyed up by the violence at Mabel Bell's home, he felt like he'd explode if he didn't have what he needed: to hurt, to control—to totally dominate a human being, then have sex.

Burbank was a large, well-off community with a population of 87,000, home of NBC and Disney. He cruised its sleepy streets and avenues close to the freeway. He had with him a set of regular cuffs, a .25 automatic, and the .22 auto.

Earlier, before he'd gotten on the freeway, he'd gone to the downtown Goodwill Mission, where there were boxes of books for the taking. He lined up a few boxes of these books on the back seat of the car so if he was shot at by police, the books would stop the slugs. He'd seen that in a movie. He parked on North Avon at 3:57 A.M., sat there a few minutes, and read the night, his senses heightened, keen, and sharp.

As Ma Bell and Nettie Lang still lay the way he'd left them—now twenty-six hours later—he got out of the car in Burbank and walked to a beige stucco house with a big bay window. Birds of paradise grew to the left of the window. There was a tall palm in the middle of the front yard which blocked out light from street lamps, shrouding the house in warm, still shadows. He decided this place was right and quickly walked to the backyard.

The windows were all closed and locked. So were the sliding glass doors. His eyes stopped on the puppy door at the bottom of the rear kitchen entrance. He got down on his knees, reached in and up through the little door, and quickly found the lock. With nimble, knowing fingers, he unlocked the door, stood up, and slowly entered the house, drawing the .22. Using a penlight to see, he moved straight to the bedroom of forty-two-year-old Carol Kyle, catwalked up to the bed, and saw a lone sleeping woman, yet his muscles stayed taut, his finger tight on the trigger. Until he knew the house was secured, "neutralized," he would not relax. To him, this was a military mission: he viewed himself as a commando fighting for the dark side of human nature.

He shined the light in her eyes, pushed her, and said, "Wake up, bitch! And don't scream, or I'll kill you. Don't make a fucking sound!" He put the gun to her head; she could feel its cold metal biting into her skin. "Understand?"

"I understand," she said.

"Who else is in the house?"

"Just my eleven-year-old son."

"Where is he?"

"In his room."

He pulled her out of bed and prodded her toward her son's bedroom. Inside she was panicking, but outside she stayed calm. Carol Kyle knew her and her son's lives depended on what she did, how she acted. She made up her mind to talk her way out of this. She was a registered nurse and knew how to stay calm in emergencies, knew how to deal with psychopaths.

When they reached the boy's room, she was about to open the door. However, Maxine Zazzara had gotten the drop on the killer, and he wouldn't trust or underestimate a woman again. He made her lie down and told her to stay on the floor or he'd kill her. Then he opened the door, put on the light, and charged into the room, hurling himself on the sleeping boy and putting the gun to his head.

"Don't fuckin' move. Don't look at me, and don't move!" the killer demanded.

To his astonishment, Carol Kyle came running into the room after him and jumped between him and her son, shielding the boy.

"Please don't hurt him. Take whatever you want, just don't hurt him, please!" she pleaded.

"Don't look at me," he said, and threw Carol on the bed, cuffing her and Mark together. He took them to a hall closet, put them in it, and closed the door, then quickly opened it to say, "You don't have any guns in here, do you?"

"No. I don't own any guns," Carol said. He didn't believe her and took them back to her room, laid them down, covered them with a sheet, and began ransacking the house frantically, cursing her, asking, "Where is it? Where is it?"

He made Carol and her son get up and put them back in

the closet. Again Carol heard him tearing her home apart. She held Mark with her free hand, reassured him, and told him to be brave. She remained calm and cool, lest Mark see her panic, which would only serve to fuel his anxiety. The killer came back, uncuffed Carol, cuffed both of Mark's hands behind his back, and left him in the closet.

He took Carol back to her bedroom, dragging her by the hair.

"Where's the jewelry?"

"I'll give you whatever I have, just please, don't hurt me or my children—"

"Children? How many you have?"

"My son . . . and a daughter—"

"Where is she?"

"She stayed at a friend's house."

"When's she comin' home?"

"Not until morning."

"Maybe I'll wait," he said, and laughed—a sickening hyena-like cackle, Carol thought. She did not find it funny; she knew what he'd do to her daughter. Carol felt sure and confident she could endure whatever he dished out, but the thought of her sixteen-year-old in this man's hands sent cold shivers up her spine.

"Where's the money and where's the jewelry?" he demanded. "And don't fuckin' look at me, bitch!"

Keeping her eyes down, though remembering the contours and lines of his high-cheekboned face, she said, "There is a jewelry box in my dresser," and led him to her dresser and put her hand in a top drawer.

He remembered Maxine Zazzara, the shotgun suddenly in her hands.

"Stop!" he demanded, "and raise your hand real slowly with the fingers spread, or I'll kill you."

She complied. She knew he'd kill her in a heartbeat. It was in his eyes as clear as blinking red lights.

"Don't do anything unless I fuckin' tell you, understand?" She nodded.

"If I give you something valuable, will you leave?" she asked.

"Yeah, sure, I'll leave," he told her, and laughed.

Carol wore a diamond teardrop on a thin gold chain around

her neck. It had been on her wedding ring, but she had had it made into a necklace two years after her husband had been killed. She took it off now and reluctantly gave it to him.

He pocketed it and led her over to the bed, tied her hands tightly behind her back with a pair of panty hose, covered her head with a pillow, and searched the bedroom, all the while playing over in his mind what he was going to do to her, constantly threatening her, cursing her, warning her not to look at him. He took whatever jewelry he could find, then went back to her.

"All right, where's the other diamonds? And where's the cash, bitch?" he demanded.

"I don't have any, I swear. I gave you the only valuable piece I have."

"Come on, don't give me that bullshit, this is a nice house and everything—"

"Listen, I'm poor. My husband left me the house; he died six years ago in a plane crash. Please don't hurt the boy. He's already been so hurt by his father's death—"

"Don't worry, you do what I say and you'll both be all right," the killer said. He viciously ripped off her nightgown, then her panties, pulled down his zipper, and forced her to orally copulate him. As he started to rape her, she told him she had her period, then that she had a disease. He told her to shut the fuck up or she was dead.

Carol did not resist him. She knew if she did in the slightest way he'd explode; he truly would kill her.

There was a terrible something brewing inside him; she could see it and feel it as tangibly as a summer lightning storm.

"The look in his eyes was absolutely demonic. Never had I seen eyes like his on a human being," she'd later tell police.

He turned her over and roughly sodomized her. Finished, he searched the place some more, making certain there were no hidden valuables anywhere, his movements quick, erratic. He was very nervous, and that worried Carol. He kept warning her not to look at him.

Hypersexual, unable to be satisfied, he sodomized her still again. She pleaded with him not to—told him it hurt, but her pain, her pleading, only served to turn him on more.

When he finished with Carol, he went into the kitchen for

something to drink. As always, when he was committing an assault, he was sweating heavily.

He returned from the kitchen and told Carol she wasn't bad, sexually, for her age. She thanked him, knowing that diplomacy was very necessary with him. She didn't want to do anything that would incite him—this bubbling volcano of a man with a gun and an atavistic need to hurt and draw blood.

Near dawn he was finally ready to leave. He asked her questions about how to get to the freeway. "He seemed confused about where he was," she would tell the police. "He thought he was in Glendale." She told him how to find the freeway, in a hurry to see him go.

"You must have had a very bad life to do this to me," she said.

"You're lucky I'm letting you live. I've killed a lot of people, you know." Again he let loose with his eerie laugh. "I'm going to bring your son in here—"

"Please don't let him see me naked like this. He's already been through so much."

He walked over to her, untied the stocking binding her right hand, and said, "Don't look at me, or I'll cut your eyes out." To her surprise, he gave her a second nightgown to cover herself with. He let Mark out of the closet, warning her and the boy not to look in his direction. He cuffed them both to the bed's headboard. The stocking was still tied to her left hand and she asked him to remove it. He found a pair of scissors and cut it off. He put the handcuff key on the mantel so her daughter, he said, could free her when she came home.

"You say anything about who I am and I'll have my friends come back here; say I had a mask on . . . I know where you live, remember," he told her.

"I won't," she said.

"Is this Glendale?" he asked.

"No, Burbank."

"Where's the freeway?" he asked again.

"Go to the corner and make a right."

"Oh, yeah," he said, and was gone. Carol heard a car start up out front. She thought it sounded like an old Oldsmobile she used to own. He had cut the phone line in the bedroom between the receiver and the base. Mark managed to reach the phone and punch in 911. The Los Angeles enhanced system of showing the address as soon as a call came in was enough to send assistance to the victims.

After the man had left Carol's house, he got back on the freeway and headed toward downtown L.A. It was still dark out. There was not much traffic; he did a steady seventy miles an hour and was soon far away from the pain, fear, and terror he'd just brought to North Avon.

And Mabel Bell and Nettie Lang had still not been discovered.

Officer Roger Cervenka stopped in front of Carol's house at 6:05 A.M. The sun was up now and he could see the house well. The call had been issued as a code 9—an "incomplete"—and Officer Cervenka didn't know what the problem was. However, he soon noticed Mark waving from the northeast bedroom window. As he got out of his patrol car, a second Burbank cruiser turned into the block and stopped, manned by Paul Barcus. The two officers found the front door locked. They walked to the back yard via the driveway, on the north side of the house, and noticed the back door was open about eight inches. They entered the residence, drawing their weapons. They found Carol and Mark as the killer'd left them. Briefly, she told them what happened. The two officers first made sure he'd left. When Cervenka's cuff key didn't fit, Carol mentioned the key on the mantel her assailant had said he'd put there. Officer Cervenka found the key and undid the cuffs. The law stipulated Carol be taken to the hospital for a rape examination. As they were leaving for the St. Joseph Medical Center in Burbank, Carol's daughter arrived. Mark was not hurt, and Carol decided it would be best if he didn't go to the hospital. Officer Barcus stayed at the house with the children to await the crime tech people.

Criminalist Bobby Cestaro from the Burbank Police arrived at 7:15 and dusted for fingerprints, though unsuccessfully. Officer Barcus gave him the handcuffs and key.

Though teletypes of the man-in-black's crimes had gone out, no one at the Burbank Police linked the rape of Carol Kyle to him, and no one contacted Sheriff's Homicide.

The day after the attack, an LAPD artist worked with Carol to create a composite of her attacker. When the artist finished, Carol wasn't satisfied. No matter how hard she tried, the artist couldn't capture the images she was giving him. The composite didn't resemble the Maria Hernandez composite.

Seventy-eight-year-old Carlos Valenzuela did gardening and handyman work in the Monrovia area. He'd known Mabel Bell for twenty-four years and took care of her yard and pool. He'd passed by the house on the morning of May 30, rung the bell, and knocked, without getting an answer. He came back the following morning and again rang the bell without getting an answer. He returned a third time on June 1, noticing two newspapers had not been picked up. He wondered if the sisters had gotten sick and entered the house, calling Mabel and Nettie's names out loud.

He found Nettie lying on her bed as the killer'd left her fifty-eight hours earlier, her eyes wide open, blood caked thick around her head. He saw her hands were tied behind her and noticed the pentagram on the wall. He ran from the house, making the sign of the cross, calling for Jesus to give him strength; some monster had attacked Nettie, tied her up, killed her. He quickly drove to Mabel Bell's neighbors and told them what he'd discovered, and they called 911.

As with the Zazzara and Doi assaults, the fire department arrived before the police, at 11:50 A.M. Medivac fireman Ken Struckus and his partner, Steve Ford, entered the house together. Ken found Mabel Bell first, immediately started giving her CPR, and cut the tape binding her ankles. He noticed throbbing brain matter protruding from the left side of her head, just above her ear. Mabel Bell was comatose. Fireman Ed Anderson assisted Ken. Steve found Nettie Lang. He was a professional and had treated all kinds of terrible wounds, but never anything like this: the bindings had caused Nettie's hands to swell obscenely, and they were blackened. There was so much swelling, the wire had cut into her skin, and the flesh on the backs of her hands had split like furrowed soil.

Steve tried to get some response from Nettie, but couldn't. She, too, was comatose and reacted only when an IV needle was inserted in her arm. Using their portable radio, they called for an ambulance. As the medics worked, Monrovia police officer James Old arrived, took one look at what happened, saw the pentagrams, the horrific injuries, and the ransacking, and called for detectives, before he cordoned off the house and grounds. Mabel and her sister were rushed to Arcadia Methodist Hospital and were examined there by Dr. Michael Agron. He could get no response from either woman. Their wounds were cleaned, and X rays were taken of their heads. Each had multiple fractures, with exposed brain matter visible to the naked eye. Dr. Agron noted that Nettie Lang had tears around her vagina, indicating she'd been sexually assaulted. He also noted the pentagram on the back of Mabel's left leg.

Homicide detective Mike Bumcrot and his new partner, Mike Robinson, out of team 4, Sheriff's Homicide, caught the Bell/Lang assault. There hadn't been a murder, but the attack was so severe and life-threatening that Monrovia officials decided to contact Sheriff's Homicide. (Monrovia did not have any homicide detectives.)

The two men got there at 3 P.M. They carefully directed criminalists Michelle LePiesto and Charles Vander Wende around the house and grounds. There were two half-eaten bananas and empty cans of Coke and Mountain Dew, which were collected for evidence. The wires the attacker tied the women with, the clock, and the urine in the toilet were also collected. Charles Vander Wende noted the footstep in blood on the clock, but did not identify the footwear.

As each of the people called to the crime scene did his job, a quiet resentment at what had been done in this house to two defenseless women became almost palpable. No one really knew what the pentagram meant, other than that the attacker had "some link to devil worship."

As no Avia shoe prints were outside, nor was a gun or knife used, this crime was not tied to the man-in-black. Detectives Bumcrot and Robinson went to the hospital to try to talk with Mabel and Nettie, but neither was coherent. As they entered Nettie's room, she began to moan and scream and turned away in abject fear at the sight of them.

When Carrillo heard about the asault from Mike Bumcrot,

he wasn't sure it had anything to do with his case. He drove out to the house and looked around, but didn't learn anything other than that the Bell residence was very secluded, unlike the Zazzara, Doi, and Okazaki residences. A pentagram had never been left behind before. Carrillo talked it over with Salerno, and he wasn't sure, either.

Usually, Salerno said, serial killers stick to the same type of victim. If their man had assaulted the two elderly women, he would be a new breed of killer: one whose victims could be anyone. His range, therefore, had absolutely no limit.

Dets. Bumcrot and Robinson learned that Mabel Bell never locked her door. She liked to see the good in people, and by locking her door, she was acknowledging something about human nature which she would rather not be aware of, one of her grandchildren told the detectives. Her children and grandchildren had implored her to lock the door, but she wouldn't listen.

"Monrovia," she'd said, "is a safe place. I'm not going to live like that—behind locked doors."

EIGHT

In early June, the killer again went hunting. As usual, he was in a Toyota he'd stolen with his pass key. He exited the freeway in Pico Rivera, looking for a house veiled by shadows. He cut the engine and lights and stopped in front of the home of John Rodriguez and his wife, Susan. Rodriguez was a Los Angeles sheriff's deputy who slept with his service revolver in the night table next to his bed. He had gone to sleep at 10 P.M. Susan had stayed up to watch the 11:30 news and now dozed on the couch in the living room.

The killer thought Rodriguez's house looked right, not realizing it was just a half-mile from the Zazzara murders, only three blocks from Gil Carrillo's mother's house. There was a lightbulb out in a fixture over the front door, the kind of thing he liked to exploit. He opened the car door without a sound, got out, and walked straight to the front door. It was locked. He tried the windows; they, too, were locked.

Sweating, with his heart pumping furiously, and sexually charged by the prospect of what he was about to do, he silently walked to the side of the house, where he found an unlocked dining room window. He removed the screen, but the window would not go up; dry paint had frozen it in place. He used a screwdriver, managed to separate the window from the window frame, and slowly began to push the window up. From inside the house he heard, "Honey, you open a window? John, that you . . . ?"

Rodriguez woke up at the sound of his wife's voice.

"What window?" he said, entering the living room.

"I just heard the window going up," Susan said from the couch.

"Well, it wasn't me, and that window's been sealed for two years—ever since I painted the house; you know that—"

"Well, I heard it go up."

"No way."

"John, I heard it go up," Susan insisted.

The killer's greatest asset, the element of surprise, had been lost, and he turned on his heels and hurried back to the car to flee to the freeway and continue his blood quest.

At 4 A.M., Carrillo received a call from an excited deputy in Pico Rivera.

"Gil," the deputy said, "we've got that shoeprint you're looking for out here."

"You sure?"

"Yes, sir."

"Where?"

"There was an attempted break-in at a deputy's house—"

"Are you shitting me?"

"No, sir. And the shoeprint is right under the window."

"You protect that with your life, understand? I'm on my way," Carrillo said. He hurried downstairs and sped over to Pico.

This was where Carrillo had grown up, where his family still lived. The man in black coming to Pico Rivera suddenly made this very personal. The killer, without knowing it, had invaded the sanctity of Gil Carrillo's very existence. He loved his mother and sisters dearly. Knowing the killer might have been hunting Pico Rivera tightened the muscles in his jaw and filled his stomach with an edgy, nervous anxiety.

When he arrived at the address, he was met by the deputy who'd called. He had cordoned off the house well, and when Carrillo pulled up, he was standing there at attention. It was still dark and the temperature was already in the mid 80s.

"This way, sir." The homicide detective followed, carrying his own flashlight, to the right side of the house. At a window midway to the yard, the deputy stopped and pointed.

He had, Carrillo noted with approval, put a box over the print.

"I thought it might rain, and I wanted to preserve the print," the deputy said.

"Good work—you did the right thing," Carrillo told him, as he carefully picked up the box and put his own flashlight on the print. It was the distinctive Avia shoe.

"The fucker's been here, all right!" he said. "That's it. That's his shoeprint! You did well."

"Thank you, sir. I listened to one of your classes on crime scenes."

"Well, you did it just right."

Gil called for tech people to dust the window for fingerprints and plaster-cast the shoeprint. He then went inside and interviewed John and Susan Rodriguez.

"God was looking over us," she said.

"I would've killed him for sure," John said.

As it turned out, the killer couldn't find a home to invade that night. He was angry and frustrated and continued to hunt, even after the sun had come up, something he usually didn't do. In Eagle Rock, he tried to abduct a girl, but she screamed, fought him off, ran, and got away. A neighbor in a ground-floor apartment heard her screams, saw what was happening, and dialed 911.

He took off and was racing back to the freeway—his sanctuary—when he went through a red light and was spotted by LAPD motorcycle officer John Stavros.

Officer Stavros turned on his siren and gave chase. As the man in black got on the freeway, he threw a gun and an ounce of pot out the car window, onto a secluded grassy knoll. Officer Stavros didn't see this.

Stavros quickly caught up to him and told him to pull over. He obeyed. The most Stavros had on him at that point was a stolen car, he figured.

Stavros asked him where he was going in such a hurry and demanded his license and registration. He sincerely told Stavros he didn't have his license or registration with him; that he'd forgotten his wallet at home.

Stavros made him get out of the car and put his hands on the front hood and searched him, finding nothing.

"Give me your name," Stavros said. "I'll call it in, and if everything's okay, I'll let you go with a ticket."

He gave him a phony name and a downtown address.

Stavros went back to his motorcycle to write up the ticket, and heard the call about an attempted abduction over the police radio. It gave a description of the stolen Toyota and a description of the suspect: "Mexican, black hair, driving a blue Toyota."

Officer Stavros did not realize the guy he'd pulled over was the suspect involved. However, the killer did, and as Stavros called in the plate number of the stolen Toyota, he made up his mind to run. He couldn't take any chances. If they linked him to what he'd done, he knew they'd kill him—one way or the other, for sure.

He wasn't ready to die.

Stavros walked back to him and said, "Hey . . . you're not that guy killing people in their homes, are you?"

"No way, man; when are you guys going to catch that motherfucker?"

"We'll get him."

"Hope so. I got a wife, you know."

"You sure you're not him?"

"Hey, man, it's not me, c'mon here."

Stavros returned to his motorcycle. The killer said a prayer to Satan, drew a pentagram on the hood of the car, and bolted like a jackrabbit. He had long, strong legs and had always been a fast runner. Stavros jumped on his cycle and tried to catch him, but he vaulted over a ten-foot fence, crossed a yard, an alley, and another yard, jumped on a bus, and got away.

Stavros went back to the car and searched it. He found a black leather wallet on the floor containing a hundred dollars in cash and an appointment card with a dentist, a Dr. Peter Leung, located in downtown Los Angeles; he also found a little black phonebook with six telephone numbers. Stavros learned the car was stolen and had it towed to a police lot, where it was left outside in the harsh summer sun. He didn't ask any tech people to dust it for prints, even though the driver was suspected of kidnapping—a major felony.

The man in black's prints were all over the car; he'd never had a chance to wipe them off. They were also on the hood next to the pentagram he had drawn.

* * *

That was the day of the annual picnic for the Sheriff Department's Homicide Bureau. All the teams were there with their wives and kids. They held it at Gull Park in Long Beach, a beautiful spot on a naval base right next to the ocean.

Carrillo was very excited about the shoeprint they'd found in Pico Rivera. It meant the killer was still active, and as long as he "worked," they'd get him.

After he'd finished his shift, he'd gone home, gotten a few hours of restless sleep, and then gone to the picnic with Pearl and the kids. Before they left, he called his sister, Rose, who lived with his mom, and told her to be careful.

"Make sure," he said, "to lock the door and windows. There's a real bad dude breaking into people's homes, and he just hit Pico."

Rose knew that for Gilbert to call and warn her, something serious must be happening, and she'd make sure to do as her brother'd said.

At the picnic Carrillo saw his lieutenant, Tony Toomey, and, all excited, he hurried over to him. "Tony, the fucker hit again last night! There was an attempted burglary at Deputy John Rodriguez's house in Pico. I went. It's the same print—that Avia shoeprint at Zazzara and the—"

"So what are you so excited about, Gil? It's not your case."

"Tony, it's all the same guy—he murdered that couple in Whittier—"

"Yeah, well, that's Uloth and Smith's case. Tell them about it and let them handle it."

"Tony, I'm telling you, it's all one guy. He did Okazaki, Yu, and the Zazzaras—and probably that Asian couple in Monterey Park, and maybe the two elderly sisters in Monrovia."

Lt. Tomey looked at Carrillo skeptically. He was one of the many detectives in Homicide who still didn't believe one man could be so varied in his crimes, and he had little enthusiasm for Carrillo's theories.

Later, Carrillo told Frank Salerno about the shoeprint at Rodriguez's house.

"So he's got a box over the print and he'll shoot someone before he'll let them near it. I picked up the box and there was that fucking print. He's still at it, Frank."

"His type doesn't stop until he's either dead or in jail."

"I told Toomey, and he's all, 'Well, what are you so excited about?' He still doesn't think it's the same guy."

Salerno said, "What we have to do is find out how many Avias were made and sold in Southern California. There could be two suspects wearing the same shoe."

"Don't think so—it's him. I'm sure. I feel it in my gut. I can sense the fucker out there. Frank, my mother lives in Pico, and so do four of my sisters."

"I know; you told me."

"There's never been a criminal like this guy—he's a first."

"Let's go talk to Grimm."

The two detectives approached Capt. Grimm and told him about the print in Pico. They agreed to have a strategy meeting Monday morning.

Monday morning things started happening.

Carrillo read the LAPD teletype report of the attempted abduction in Eagle Rock and the escape of the suspect—the driver of a stolen Toyota. He showed the report to Salerno, and the two of them took an informal ride over to the LAPD Northeast Station to speak to Officer Stavros. He had, they were told, taken the day off. Salerno asked to see what had been found in the car—but LAPD said no. They couldn't see anything until it was approved from above. The incident had happened in their jurisdiction, and the sheriff's office couldn't just come over asking to see their evidence; there was protocol—rules and regulations—to follow.

The two detectives protested, saying that it would take days to accomplish and any leads would be cold by then.

They were told it didn't matter.

Unless it was okayed from above, they couldn't see *anything*. Salerno suggested the car be fingerprinted. He was told it would be done.

Angry, frustrated, Salerno and Carrillo returned to the office and told Capt. Grimm what went down. Grimm was the kind of captain who went to the wall for his men. He picked up the phone and began making calls. Frank went to criminalist Jerry Burke and told him to find out everything there was to know about Avia Aerobic sneakers.

Later that morning Salerno, as the acting lieutenant for

team 3, had to put together the working schedule for the month. His partner, John Paillet, was in the hospital, having surgery, and Carrillo's partner, Jim Mercer, was on vacation. It seemed the perfect time for him and Carrillo to start working as a team, Salerno thought.

Partners in homicide investigations must be compatible. Detectives regularly spend more time with their partners than with their spouses. Salerno had wanted to work with Gil for a long while, and now the time had finally come.

He asked Carrillo if he'd like to be his *official* partner. Carrillo's eyes lit up, and a big smile creased his face. Of all the men in Homicide, of all the cops in the world, Frank Salerno was the one Gil Carrillo respected the most. He knew he could learn a lot from Salerno and knew the two of them as a team would "kick ass."

That night the two celebrated their union at Emi Lu's, at a small horseshoe-shaped bar in the Chinese restaurant Homicide frequented at the end of their shifts, when they were keyed up and unable to discuss what they'd seen or what they were feeling with their families.

The following day it was Carrillo and Salerno's turn for the next homicide. Patty Elaine Higgins of Arcadia, a twenty-eight-year-old schoolteacher, blond and attractive, had been found murdered by Don Bonelli, the foreman of a construction site next to the building where she lived. He had needed a phone at the job site and had asked Patty if he could run an extension off her line, for which he'd pay. Patty was an easygoing woman who liked to help whoever she could, and she said yes.

When she didn't show up for work or call, which was very unlike her, the Braddocks School called her. Don heard the insistent ringing and picked up the phone. A school official explained what had happened and asked him to please check on Patty. He said he'd be happy to and walked to the side door and knocked, getting no answer. He went around back and saw a broken windowpane in the back door, which was a foot ajar.

"Patty," he called. "Patty . . . you home?"

Silence.

He entered the house and saw it had been ransacked. He found Patty on the bathroom floor. Someone had beaten her brutally and nearly cut off her head. He turned, hurried to the phone outside, and punched in 911 with shaking fingers.

Carrillo lived closer to Arcadia and he arrived first, wearing a tie and jacket, even though the temperature was 102 degrees. The summer of 1985 would be the hottest summer in a hundred years.

The scene had been cordoned off by Arcadia policemen who'd initially responded to the call.

Carrillo was thinking, "It's him," and he looked for something to link this crime to him. As he was studying the soil under Patty's windows, looking for that Avia shoeprint, Salerno arrived, and they went inside.

Hunting was Salerno's passion in life, and now, as he studied the crime, his eyes changed—filled with the steady, deadly curiosity of the hunter. He got down on his knees and studied the wounds to Patty's neck carefully as Carrillo looked over his shoulder. The wound was a kind of stab-slash. Very lethal, quickly fatal.

There were bloody bruises on her outer knees, and her panties were rolled down in back. Salerno and Carrillo agreed she had been sodomized while she was on her hands and knees. They were both thinking it was their killer, but no gun had been used and there were no Avia shoeprints. The tech people arrived, and Salerno and Carrillo directed the fingerprinting and picture-taking—the collecting of the smallest pieces of evidence. They were not really sure if Patty was a victim of their killer or another.

Salerno would never forget how a little piece of fiber he'd found on the left eyelid of Judy Miller—Bianchi and Buono's second victim, led to evidence that became very damaging in court: Bianchi had blindfolded Judy with upholsterer's fabric, which tied the murder to Angelo Buono's shop on Colorado Street in Glendale.

Salerno found a metal pipe under Patty's bed from the construction site next door. "He probably used it to break the window to get in," he told Carrillo.

The crime scene had to be videotaped, and one of the tech people held a camera as Salerno walked through the crime—beginning at the front of the house and ending with a careful, minute inspection of Patty's body. The heat was choking and cloying, and both detectives took off their jackets.

With no apparent evidence tying the man in black to this crime, they discussed the possibility of one of the construction men being the murderer. Maybe, they reasoned, he'd seen her undressing through the window and decided to forcibly take what he saw. They wrote down all the workmen's names, which were checked for criminal histories. The sodomy and violence suggested the killer must have once been in prison. None of the workmen had an arrest record.

Carrillo noticed an ATM machine across the street from Patty's house and decided that checking who'd used a card the night before might provide a witness.

The bank's list included a pathologist they knew from the M.E.'s office. Gil phoned him and was shocked to learn Carrillo knew about a two-hundred-dollar withdrawal he'd made.

The detective said, "There was a very brutal murder in the house just across from the bank. Did you see anything un-usual—suspicious?"

"No, Gil. I'm sorry, I didn't."

And Carillo faced another dead end.

NINE

It was now July 2, and the heat was intense and oppressive, making even the simple act of walking very difficult. However, the heat did not dissuade the man in black from going back to work.

He had no idea, nor did he care, how many police were looking for him. He knew nothing of the ballistics tests, the shoeprints, or Carrillo's early certainty that there was a new kind of serial killer preying on the people of Los Angeles County.

Tonight, he returned to Arcadia, thinking the police wouldn't be expecting him back so soon. Arcadia was thirteen miles northeast of Los Angeles City. A beautiful residential community at the base of the scenic San Gabriel Mountains, with a population of 43,000, it is one of the nicest communities making up the ninety-six-city complex of Los Angeles County.

He parked a few blocks from the freeway, at Floral and Second, walked south two blocks to Haven, and he took a left, his eyes scrutinizing the homes he passed, looking for a vulnerability he could use.

The streets were abandoned because of the heat; the hum of air conditioners came from every home. As he walked, sweat poured from him, and he frequently had to wipe it from his face. He stopped at the home of seventy-five-year-old Mary Louise Cannon, a widow who lived alone. For long seconds he just stood there, making certain he wasn't being observed, making certain to stay in the shadows. The house was a beige ranch-style with a slanted brown shingled roof, and one car was parked in its driveway. All the lights were out. A well-trimmed cypress stood on the left. Brazenly, he walked straight to the right front window, took the screen off quickly, opened the window, and slipped inside as silently as a snake into still water.

Mary Louise Cannon had been born on a farm near Downey, attended business school, and married Darrel Cannon, an Arcadia horse trainer with his own business. She kept the books for the business, which was successful and enabled them to live well. Mary had had two bouts with cancer, but she had won both times. She was a very strong, independent woman, a fighter who loved her five grandchildren. She was excited about a planned trip to Australia with a senior citizens' group in a few weeks.

Yesterday, she'd gotten into an accident and her car had been damaged. She'd had to be driven home by a policeman.

After the killer's eyes adjusted to the dark, he moved toward the back of the house, hunching down low, all coiled aggression, using a penlight to see. He ascertained that Mary was alone and was angered by there being no young women in the house. He spotted a heavy milk-white vase-lamp on a dresser in her bedroom, picked it up with a gloved hand, and brought it down with all his might on Mary's head. She woke up screaming. He knocked her unconscious with his fist, choking and beating her even after she was unconscious. He then made his way to the kitchen and found a sharp, ten-inch-long butcher knife. Returning, he raised the knife, and without a second thought, plunged it into the left side of Mary's throat. He twisted and turned it and plunged it again and again and again in a killing frenzy. As he stole her life, he thought about Lucifer—how proud he must be of him.

He washed the blood off, then ransacked Mary's house, taking anything of value he could find. He left by the front door, walked back to the stolen Toyota, and drove straight to his fence.

Christine and Frank Starich had lived next door to Mary Cannon for twenty-five years. At 8 that morning, Frank came out of the house, soon followed by Christine, to work in their garden. It was already nearing 100 degrees, and they wanted to be finished before the sun had a chance to make it even hotter.

The Stariches watched over Mary. They were good friends as well as neighbors. Frank did little chores around her house. Christine was the first to notice the screen lying on Mary Cannon's lawn at about 8:20. She suggested that Frank put the screen back. Without a second thought, he walked over to the screen. It seemed odd that the latch which holds the screen in place had been bent forward. He got a hammer, screwdriver, and stepladder and went to the window. He had to hit the latch several times with the hammer to straighten it and Mary didn't stir, which he thought was peculiar. He put back his tools and resumed his gardening. Christine asked Frank if he'd seen Mary.

"No, not at all," he told her.

"That's odd. And look, her paper still hasn't been picked up, and the sprinkler'll be on any minute. Frank, she never lets her paper get wet . . . Something . . . something's wrong. Why don't you get the keys?"

For emergencies, Mary had given the Stariches a front door key. Frank opened the door and Christine entered, calling, "Mary? Mary, you here? Oh, Mary." Frank was right behind her. When she saw the ransacking, she stopped short.

"Something bad's happened here. Let's call the police," she said. They backed out of the house without seeing Mary. Christine called 911. A police car was dispatched, and Arcadia officer Ed Winter pulled up within a minute. Christine and Frank met him, told him about the screen and the ransacking, and Mary not answering their calls. The three of them returned to the house; Officer Winter opened the door and went in first, heading for Mary's bedroom on the left. He took one quick look at Mary, realized there'd been a brutal murder, and knew the scene had to be preserved for Homicide. He had to get the civilians out. He briefly described what he'd seen, making them leave, and called in a homicide.

Homicides in Arcadia are rare—one, at the most two, a year—so Sheriff's Homicide handles Arcadia's killings.

On the morning of July 2, Salerno and Carrillo drove to Mary's house in Frank's car. It was air-conditioned and a welcome respite from the temperature, but the ride was a short one and soon they were back in the wavering heat. Mary Cannon, they quickly realized, had been stabbed-slashed in the throat *exactly* as Patty Higgins had been.

"It's the same guy," Salerno said.

"The damage is identical," Carrillo agreed. "The fucker did them both!"

There had been no footprints at Patty's place, but there were here, in the nap of Mary's new rugs. They couldn't tell if it was the Avia, but they could readily see it was the same size and general shape. Salerno wanted to get it photographed and measured under the optimal conditions of the crime lab, and he told Lloyd Mahanay to cut the print out of the rug so it could be rushed to the lab, figuring the nap of the rug might rise and they'd lose the print entirely.

Using a roofer's knife, Lloyd cut the print from the rug and tacked it to some plywood. It was rushed to the lab.

The killer had left the knife covered with blood on the bed next to Mary. It was bagged for evidence. Lloyd Mahanay began taking pieces of the milk-white glass from Mary's face.

Now, truly for the first time, Salerno believed a full-blown serial killer—far more dangerous and malicious than Bianchi and Buono—was free in Los Angeles: "The knife wound tied Patty and Mary together, and the shoeprints tied in the Zazzara killings and abduction cases," Salerno later said. Despite a heavy, sickening feeling in his stomach, Salerno put aside any personal feelings he had and remained the consummate professional.

He noticed a small piece of bloody tissue on the floor and had criminalist Debbie Green bag it. Later that day, at the lab, they would see that the killer had stepped on this tissue with blood on his soles and had left a one-inch square print with the distinct waffle pattern of the Avia Aerobic shoe.

Here, too, Salerno made a video of the crime scene. Calmly, speaking clearly and without emotion, he took the camera through the entire crime, from the entrance to the victim, who'd been beaten and stabbed viciously.

Salerno's own mother was Mary Cannon's age, and as he worked, he kept thinking about how vulnerable she was.

At noon the temperature hit 106 degrees. It was the hottest day in a hundred years. When they were finished at Mary

Cannon's, they rode back to the Hall of Justice together. Salerno told Gil they were going to go to Grimm and get a proper task force started up to find the killer.

Salerno had already made up his mind that the task force would not become so large that investigators would end up working against one another, as had happened in the Hillside Strangler investigation, which at its height had 124 detectives on it. He would keep it lean, mean, and effective.

When they arrived at the sheriff's office, they learned that the shoeprint they'd found on Mary Cannon's rugs was the Avia; and the shoeprint on the clock at Ma Bell's house was now also positively linked to the Avia Aerobic shoe, size 11 1/2.

Salerno and Carrillo met with Capt. Bob Grimm, and Salerno ran down for him all the evidence they had linking the crimes. Grimm had a lot of respect for Frank. He gave him authority to use more men and run the investigation in any way he saw fit.

Salerno called a meeting of team 3 and described the linking elements.

"It's like a spiderweb, in that it's made up of many strands in a widening circle," he told them, and talked about the Avia shoeprints, the matching descriptions, the foul odor, the bad teeth, the thumb cuffs, the disabled phones, the ransacking, the similarities in wounds, the matching bullets, and the fact that the assailant wore cloth gloves all the time.

Now, for the first time, they were all hearing Frank Salerno saying what Carrillo had been saying all along, and now they believed it.

Salerno gave teams of detectives jobs to do: one team would read teletypes and spread the picture of the footprint and the composite; criminalist Jerry Burke would go to Portland, Oregon, to interview the designer of the Avia Aerobic shoe, Jerry Stubblefield. Another team would coordinate with different police jurisdictions for a smooth transfer of information. Carrillo was asked to follow up on the car Officer Stavros had pulled over.

TEN

The killer now knew that seasoned, hardened detectives, the best L.A. had, were looking for him, that cops on the beat and in cruisers all over the county knew about him, had seen the composite sketches of him—but still that didn't worry him unduly. He was confident that he was protected by Satan, and that as long as he followed the ways of Satan, showed no mercy, gave no quarter, he'd never get caught.

Tonight, he had altered his appearance: he'd slicked his hair back and now sported large, round, white-framed glasses. As he drove east in a stolen car on the 210, listening to AC/DC's *Highway to Hell* album, he drew strength and perverse sustenance from the hard, pumping rhythms and hidden meanings he believed lived between the lines.

He knew he was making history, that he'd be more famous than Jack the Ripper, who he believed had never been caught because he, too, walked with Satan.

He again reasoned the police would not expect him back in Arcadia, and so he went there, cruised it, then drove over to nearby Sierra Madre. The temperature had gone down and it was a cool 84 degrees; a quarter moon hung in the sky. He had a special affinity for the moon and felt it had a power he could use and draw on. It was, like him, of the night.

He remembered how fascinated he had been as a young boy by Barnabas Collins of *Dark Shadows*, the soap-opera series about a vampire, that was popular in the sixties.

The fog, the long, black cape, had a power, a threatening connotation that I wanted to make my own. Those things excite me. They always have. I was just born that way.

In Sierra Madre he drove north, toward the beautiful San

Gabriel Mountains, which were just visible in the light of the moon. He drove slowly, his eyes searching for an opportunity. The streets were very quiet in this wealthy, upscale community. He spotted deer feeding on flowers in people's front yards. He came to an intersection and saw the lights of a police cruiser to his left. He was listening to the scanner and heard that a citizen had phoned in a report of a prowler, who the police were now looking for. A second police cruiser pulled up behind him. His heart rose and lodged in his throat, but he stayed calm. He took a left, and the cruiser did, too. He had stolen the Toyota he was driving only a few hours earlier, and he hoped it hadn't been reported yet. The cruiser stayed with him a few blocks and turned off. As he listened to the police transmission, he realized they were actually looking for him—"the Valley Intruder," which was one of the names they were now calling him. Yet still he did not leave the area.

He continued toward the peaks of San Gabriel, parked on Arno Drive, at the base of the mountain, and studied the night like a scientist studies microbes under a microscope. Here, like all the places he picked, it was very quiet. The homes were expensive, with pools and gardens filled with colorful flowers. He opened and closed the car door without a sound and walked straight to an all-white ranch-style house with huge picture windows at the corner of Arno and Lelino. It was built on a raised piece of land half an acre in size. There were eighteen red-brick steps to the front door. Ivy and flowers grew on the soil incline that surrounded the house. He tried the back door. It was locked. He walked to the front of the house and tried that door; it was open. He took out the .22 automatic and slowly, cautiously, entered the home of Mr. and Mrs. Steve Bennett and their two children: Whitney, their sixteen-year-old daughter, and eighteen-year-old James.

Steve Bennett was an executive at Southern California Gas. The Bennetts had had another couple over for a Fourth of July get-together. At 9 P.M. they had gone out the front door to watch a fireworks display in the San Gabriel Valley. When it was over, they had all returned to the house but hadn't locked the front door. They customarily used the back door and when their company left that evening, they went out by the rear door, which Steve then locked. The Bennetts retired and were sleeping by 12:15 A.M. Whitney had gone to a party with friends in La Crescenta, then on to another one in La Canada. She had stayed out later than she should have and driven home faster than she should have.

Whitney had chestnut-brown hair, a cute upturned nose, and large, friendly blue eyes. She had arrived home a little before 1 A.M. and gone in through the rear door. Her dad had left her a check in the kitchen for a few things she needed. She wrote him a thank-you note, washed up, took off her jewelry, rings, and a watch, put them on her bedroom dresser, put on a nightgown, and went to bed.

Whitney's bedroom was to the right of the front door. The master bedroom was in the rear.

The killer stood still for thirty seconds, getting used to the dark, getting a feeling for the house. All was silent. He went right, and using a penlight to see, found Whitney's bedroom, entered it, and saw her sleeping soundly. He made his way to her dresser and pocketed the rings and watch. He knew whoever owned the house had money, and he wanted it. He knew, too, he had to neutralize the place before he could do anything to Whitney. He left her and walked to the Bennetts' bedroom. The door was slightly ajar. He used his light and saw they were sleeping soundly. Deciding not to use his gun, he went outside and retrieved the car's tire iron, planning to beat the Bennetts to death with it. As he was returning to the house, a police cruiser came down the block slowly. He ducked behind some foliage and watched the policemen drive by.

If he was ever caught, he had sworn to Satan, he'd go down fighting, rather than face prosecution, the disgrace, the hate, and finally what he knew would be the death sentence. For crimes like his, it could only be the death sentence, and that just wouldn't do; *he* would pick the time and place he was to die, and, he believed as long as he stayed true to his god, his lord, he'd have a place of honor and respect in the house of Satan, with plenty of slaves to do his bidding, to cower in abject fear of him.

He returned to Whitney's room. As he entered, he shone the penlight slowly over her lithe body. The sight of her so helpless, so much in his power, was very stimulating.

He walked to the bed, clamped his hand over her mouth,

and struck her with the tire iron, knocking her out, then struck her ten more times.

He decided he was going to use a knife; the knife would be quiet and he'd derive, he decided, more pleasure from a knife than from the tire iron.

Killing with a knife is very personal; you actually are holding it as it goes in, and when death comes, you can feel your victim dying through the knife. It's like sex.

He went to the kitchen in search of an appropriate blade.

He couldn't find a knife suitable for what he had in mind, and he went back to Whitney, still carrying the tire iron, which was now dripping with her blood. Excited by the violence, he was about to rape her, but, he reasoned, she could come to and start screaming, so he decided to kill her before he had his way with her. He looked for something he could strangle her with, studied a blue sash and a brown tie, and finally decided on the telephone wire.

Whitney was lying on the bed, on her stomach. He straddled her, wrapped the telephone cord around her neck, and pulled it close with all his strength, a terrific homicidal force; when he was in a killing mood, his strength was exceptional.

Suddenly, he saw sparks on the wire taking Whitney's life, and they caused him to hesitate. He saw a blue haze leaving her body—he figured it was her soul—and as he let go of the cord, Whitney sucked in desperately needed air. He'd never seen anything like that before, and it spooked him.

He exited by the bedroom window, hurrying back to the stolen car. Dawn was beginning to lighten the eastern sky. Birds were waking up, chirping merrily. He got in the car and pulled away, headed straight back toward the freeway, frustrated and angry—and in a foul mood.

It was, he decided, the power of Christ that had interceded and saved Whitney's life.

He wondered why it had happened—if it foretold of a weakening of his powers.

When he was two blocks from the freeway, the same police cruiser was suddenly behind him again. It followed him to the freeway entrance, but he was not pulled over, and he sped back to the safety of downtown Los Angeles, thirteen miles away.

He'd not managed to consummate the sexual assault on

Whitney and was all sexually keyed up—tight as a violin string—by the violence. He searched the downtown area for a prostitute, some way to relieve himself. He found one, a heavy Mexican with straight black hair and a very full chest, on Eighth Street. He had an intense foot fetish, and some of the prostitutes did not mind what he wanted to do with their feet, but this one laughed in his face when he told her he wanted to have sex with them. He threw her out of the car on Sixth Street, just off Main.

Angry, frustrated, he got rid of the car a few miles from the terminal, took a bus back to Main, and rented a room at the Hotel Lido.

But he couldn't sleep for a long while.

He just lay there, tossing, turning, smoking pot, planning new ways he could satisfy his hunger for sadism and murder.

He felt safe being close to the bus terminal all the time; if something went wrong, he could hop on a departing bus and be hundreds of miles from Los Angeles in no time. Buses were leaving at all hours, going in all directions.

At 5:45 that morning, Whitney woke up with a blinding, horribly painful headache, shocked to find herself backward in the bed, and doubly shocked by all the blood. She had no recollection of the attack at all. She began to scream and cry hysterically. She stumbled to the doorway of her bedroom and collapsed there, whimpering like an injured puppy, then screaming, "Daddy, Daddy, Daddy!"

Steve and his wife were awakened by Whitney's pleas. He jumped out of bed and ran toward her room. When he saw how badly she had been beaten, he nearly fell over. Both her eyes were swollen shut, and her head was distorted to twice its normal size; she was barely recognizable. He saw the bloody tire iron. He put a nightgown on her and summoned the police, his hands shaking. Mrs. Bennett tried to console Whitney. Steve kept asking her what happened, and Whitney kept saying she didn't know.

Earlier on the Fourth of July, there had been a murder at the Los Angeles Men's Central county jail. Team 3 was up, and Carrillo's old partner, Jim Mercer, and Bobby Morck got the call. Salerno and Carrillo were in the office, working the Valley Intruder case. Because there were a lot of witnesses to the jailhouse killing—fifty in all—Salerno said he and Gil would go to the jail with Mercer and Morck and help them interview some of the witnesses. They'd been working the Intruder killings every day and night, nonstop, and were bone tired, but their help was needed at the jail and they went without complaint. By the time they finished taking statements, it was 4 A.M. They made plans to meet at the office and drove home, truly exhausted, each wondering where the killer was, what he was doing, what he was thinking.

As Salerno was getting into bed, the phone rang. It was Gil.

"Well, we got another one, partner. In Sierra Madre. A teenage girl's been beaten and left for dead in her parents' home. It's him, Frank. I know it."

"I'll meet you there."

Salerno took a quick shower, shaved, put on a fresh shirt, tie, and jacket, and was out the door. Using his Thomas Guide, he found the Bennetts' home without difficulty. He was struck by the nice neighborhood and he admired how well all the homes were kept. People who lived here had money, and it showed. Crime in Sierra Madre was a rare thing. "You couldn't find a more idyllic community anywhere," Salerno would later say.

Carrillo had arrived first, and Frank found him interviewing Officer Gerald Skinner of the Sierra Madre Police. Steve and Anna Bennett had gone to the Arcadia Methodist Hospital with Whitney. Officer Skinner knew who Frank was and was slightly in awe. As Salerno and Carrillo walked the crime scene, looked for Avia prints, and studied Whitney's bedroom, Officer Skinner told them he had gotten there at 5:10 A.M., his partner had arrived at 5:12, and the paramedics, who had removed Whitney, had been there at 5:20. He described how he'd found Whitney, that she'd had no recollection of what had taken place. Carefully, the two homicide detectives scrutinized Whitney's bedroom and the tire iron.

"It was one of the bloodiest crime scenes I'd ever been at," Carrillo later said.

They walked outside, hoping there was a flowerbox under

the window, but there wasn't, though the window screen was lying on the patio.

The killer had never used a tire iron before; there were no Avia shoeprints, nor a gun or knife or handcuffs. However, because of the brutality, they suspected it was him. Carrillo called the office and requested criminalists Gisele La Vigne, Debbie Green, and Ron George. They had each worked Valley Intruder crime scenes, and all were familiar with the evidence and factors that linked them. They figured the killer had come in by way of the window. Salerno thought they should interview Whitney right away, and he and Carrillo drove over to Arcadia Methodist, after telling Officer Skinner not to let anyone into the crime scene.

They found Whitney being treated in the emergency room; she was still unconscious. Her hair had been shaved off, and they could see the terrible beating she had received. The doctor said she would live, but she'd been struck more than twenty times. There were open blood-red welts crisscrossing her entire head in a waffle-iron pattern. She would need 478 stitches—equivalent to four feet in length—to piece her scalp together. It was, the doctor said, amazing she hadn't been killed.

They found Steve and Anna Bennett in the waiting room. When they first introduced themselves as homicide detectives, Steve panicked, thinking Whitney had died. They assured him that that hadn't happened and told him the attending physician had said she would survive the attack.

Steve Bennett told the detectives how they'd had company earlier, watched the fireworks, and retired before Whitney had gotten home, and how they'd found her in the hall. "All bloody and beaten and moaning," Steve said. "Gave me the biggest shock I've ever had in my life; it looked like she'd been in some kind of terrible car accident."

Yes, he had noticed the tire iron, but no, it was absolutely not his.

Satisfied for now that they couldn't learn anything more at the hospital, the two detectives returned to the house to run the crime scene.

The criminalists arrived and Salerno had Ron George dust for prints and take photos. Gisele La Vigne and Debra Green searched for evidence. The tire iron, the phone, the blue sash, and the brown tie were bagged for evidence. It was easy to see by the blood smeared on the walls and windowsill that the assailant had been wearing cloth gloves.

Whitney was, they thought, his second living victim, and they were anxious to interview her, hoping she'd give them a description, a lead, some direction.

Carrillo and Salerno were standing in the living room, discussing the possibility that the killer had come in through the front door, when Gisele La Vigne approached them. "Hey, boys," she said, "come look at this." Gisele was 5′4″, thirty-six years old, with dark, curly hair cut short. She was one of the best criminalists the sheriff's office had.

Inside the bedroom, Gisele, wearing thin plastic gloves, carefully unfolded a corner piece of Whitney's pink comforter, and there, clearly discernible, was the distinct waffle print—in blood—of the entire Avia Aerobic shoe.

"That's it, it's him," Carrillo said.

"It's him all right," Gisele said.

Carrillo would later say of that moment, "When I saw the print, I got goosebumps all over, chills, and a tight feeling in my gut. It was him—no doubt."

Salerno reminded everyone there how important the smallest clues were—and to triple-check everything. He called the office and requested more detectives. They stayed until 4 that afternoon, dusting for prints, scrutinizing, taking pictures, and gathering clues. Then they shut down the crime scene and agreed to meet back at the office after catching a few hours' sleep. Neither Frank nor Gil had slept in twenty-four hours.

Salerno had never before heard of so varied and vicious a killer, and this crime affected him more than the others. Carrillo was also profoundly disturbed by the assault on Whitney. He had two teenage daughters. He told Pearl about the Valley Intruder and they discussed her and the kids sleeping at her parents' house. Gil was out working the case every night, and she and the kids were home alone. Pearl was frightened, and Carrillo took it as a personal affront.

Back at the office later that day, there was another meeting with Capt. Grimm. Salerno and Carrillo told him about the Bennett assault—the shoeprint in blood, and how vicious the attack had been. Salerno asked the captain about the car that

LAPD officer Stavros had pulled over; Grimm said he was still making calls.

"If that was him—and we think it was—his prints could be in that car, Captain," Salerno said.

"I'll scream, I'll yell, we'll get it."

They didn't get it that day.

The next morning, after a few uneasy hours of sleep, Salerno and Carrillo returned to Arcadia Methodist Hospital where Whitney, in a private room on the second floor, was being guarded by a sheriff's deputy. Her face was wrapped in wide gauze bandages. Just her nose and eyes—black and swollen closed—were visible.

Salerno introduced himself and Gil, and asked whether she was up to talking. She said she was. Salerno explained how important it was that she tell them exactly what had happened. He spoke in a low, concerned voice, his eyes never leaving hers. She told them about her evening. When asked if she'd been followed home, she said no, that she'd looked for the police in her rearview mirror frequently, as she was late for curfew and was speeding. She was certain she'd not been tailed. When asked about her attacker, she truthfully told the two detectives she'd never even seen him.

Whitney, Salerno thought, was an exceptional sixteen-year-old. Even after what had happened, she was polite and eager to help, and she didn't complain. They didn't tell her they suspected her attacker of many other horrific crimes. They thanked her and left.

Salerno arranged for pictures of Whitney to be taken to be used in court when her attacker was apprehended. He was certain that as vicious and active as the killer had become, it was just a matter of time before they got him. The killer was like a shark that had gotten the scent of blood—and he wouldn't stop until he was either dead or incarcerated.

They turned their attention back to the police teletype reports and memos, hoping to find more of his crimes—and, hopefully, clues—which had been overlooked or not yet tied to him. They coordinated a list of all known sex offenders who had recently been released from prison. They were looking for a man who was approximately six feet tall, had bad teeth and shaggy black hair, was Hispanic, was into sodomy, handcuffs, and Satan, and wore a size 11 1/2 shoe. He was probably a Vietnam veteran.

Suspects were popping out of the woodwork all over Los Angeles County. Carrillo was constantly getting calls from police officers in different jurisdictions who were sure *they* had captured the Valley Intruder. The first question Carrillo asked was how big were his feet. If they were not size 11 1/2, he wasn't interested.

The fact that there were so many police jurisdictions involved made their task a monumental, exceptionally difficult one.

While reading the teletypes, Salerno and Carrillo came across the name of Carol Kyle. Gil called up the Burbank Police and asked them to send over a full report on the case.

When the two detectives read the Burbank report, they realized they'd found another of his victims. The phone disabling, his bad odor, the handcuffs, the ransacking, the rear-burglary-type entry, and the sodomy were all his traits.

Salerno sent detectives out to Burbank to interview Carol. She, without emotion and in cold detail, told the detectives about the man who'd invaded her home and body on May 30.

She said he wore all black, was extremely vicious, and smelled like "wet leather." She described him as a good-looking light-skinned Mexican with some kind of accent, which she couldn't put her finger on. She also said she was not at all happy with the composite drawing the Burbank police artist had done. Sheriff's department artist Malon Coleman was contacted and went out to visit Carol. Working with him, she did a second composite of her attacker.

This time the composite looked, Carol said, much more like him, and when Salerno and Carrillo compared it to Maria Hernandez's, they were very similar.

ELEVEN

On July 7, the temperature was in the low 90s, cool compared to much of the hellish weather of that dreadful summer.

In another stolen car, the killer cruised Glendale, Rosemead, and Arcadia and finally ended up back in Monterey Park at a little after 9 P.M. He knew people in Monterey Park were uptight because of the Doi and Yu assaults, but that didn't stop him. He was protected and guided by Satan himself. How could he ever get caught, with such an ally?

He cut the engine and lights on East Andrix Street, coasted to a noiseless stop, and let his senses read the night.

Herald Examiner deliverywoman Launie Dempster came driving down East Arlight. She immediately noticed him and realized he was the same guy she'd seen the night Bill Doi had been murdered. As she passed him, he said, "Hey, what the fuck you looking at, bitch?" but she didn't hear him. She thought about stopping and calling the police, but didn't.

The killer decided this was a good place for what he had in mind, got out of the car, and leisurely walked to the front of a house off Andrix on East Arlight, the home of sixty-one-year-old Joyce Lucille Nelson. The house, pale yellow, was a hundred feet wide and forty feet deep. The entrance was on the left; a large oak tree on the sidewalk blocked any light from street lamps, creating a wide shadow. He decided this was the place, and he walked straight to the front door, only fifteen steps from the sidewalk. Dressed all in black, he was impossible to see. He tried the front door; it was locked. He went to the left window, stepping on the soil, leaving clear, well-defined shoeprints. The window was unlocked. He removed the screen and slid the window up easily. Before he went in, he carried the screen to the backyard and left it there, lest it cause undue suspicion. He tried the back door—locked—and returned to the open window.

Joyce Lucille Nelson, residing there since May of 1949, was a divorcée who had lived alone for the last twenty-one years. She worked in the production line at the Coast Envelope Company in Commerce for thirty-three years. She would be retiring soon and planned to spend much of her free time on the golf course. She had two sons, Dale and Don, and five grandchildren. Joyce was very young at heart, often getting down on the floor to play board games with her grandchildren and was still able to do somersaults.

She knew about the killer; she'd read about the attacks. Her son Don had even suggested she put bars on her windows, but she'd refused, saying, "I'll not be a prisoner in my own home."

Now the killer stepped into the front window of Joyce Nelson's home and found her asleep on the couch, in front of the television. He made sure no one else was in the house, then put the .22 automatic to her head and woke her up.

Startled, her eyes bulging, she said, "Oh, God! Who are you? What do you want?"

"Don't look at me, bitch! Just do as I say, and you'll be all right!"

He grabbed her hair and pulled her toward the bedroom, but Joyce Nelson resisted him and demanded he leave immediately. Her defiance infuriated him, and he knocked her to the ground with his fist, bent over, and beat her with rapid, piston-like blows, knocking her out.

He dragged her to the bedroom by the hair and beat her to death, kicking her in the face so hard that she spun around the floor one complete time. He left a clear imprint of the Avia shoe embedded in her face.

He ransacked the house, taking what he wanted: a VCR, jewelry, watches, a radio—and walked out the front door as though he'd been living there for years.

Sex and murder were all he could think about, and again he continued to hunt, driving to Alhambra, then Rosemead, but he couldn't find a situation he was comfortable with.

At 3 A.M. he returned to Monterey Park and again cruised the quiet, sleepy community—correctly figuring Joyce had not yet been found.

He parked on Hollywood Oak Drive, got out of the car, and walked along the sidewalk, carrying a set of handcuffs and a nickel-plated .22 automatic in his belt. There was not a soul out.

He stopped in front of the home of Sophie Dickman, a sixty-three-year-old psychiatric nurse. It was a well-kept yellow one-story house with a little driveway leading to the garage, which was on the left. Its single front window faced the street. There was a cypress tree on one side and a tall pine on the other, no gates on the windows, and a lot of shadow.

Satisfied that this was the right place, he walked to the front window, getting the screen off in seconds, but the window was securely locked, and he couldn't get it open. He wasn't ready to give up. The needs that drove and propelled him made that impossible. He walked to the left side of the house and found a doggie door, reached in to unlock the door, and entered the house.

As always, he stayed low, letting his eyes get used to the darkness.

With a penlight in one hand and the .22 in the other, he moved toward Sophie Dickman's bedroom, found her, and made sure she was alone. He put on the lights and charged her bed.

She woke up with him running at her from the doorway. He slammed his hand across her mouth, saying: "Don't look at me! Don't make a fucking sound, or I'll kill you!" He put the gun to her head. "Undermotherfuckingstand?"

She nodded that she understood. She knew instantly who he was, that somehow, the Valley Intruder in the papers had made his way to her home and was now leering down at her with ink-black eyes filled with a hatred that seemed inhuman, it was so intense. He took out the handcuffs and put them on her wrists. She stayed quiet and as calm as she could, sensing his terrible combustible temperament, knowing instinctively she must not incite him in any way. He put a pillowcase over her head so she couldn't see him. Taking her to the smaller of the two bathrooms in the house, he made her sit on the floor. He disconnected the phones and began to ransack the house furiously, coming back to her within two minutes.

"Where's the diamonds, and where's the money?" he demanded.

"I don't have any," she said.

He punched her hard. "Liar—where's the jewelry, or you are fucking dead!"

"In the other bathroom," she told him.

He dragged her into the second bathroom and she showed him her secret hiding place: in a cup in the medicine cabinet. Quickly he looked through the cup's contents, knowing instantly the difference between zirconia and real diamonds, pocketing it all. While he was engrossed in the cup, she slipped the diamond ring from her finger and threw it behind the sink, but as soon as he turned his attention back to her, he noticed she'd taken off the ring and demanded to know where it was. She nodded in the direction of the sink. He punched her in the face, found the ring, and dragged her back to the bedroom, where he ripped off her underpants and told her to spread her legs; she complied. He tried to sodomize her, but couldn't get an erection. She stayed as calm as she could, trying to avoid doing anything that might incite him further. It was obvious how much he had to be in charge, to dominate, and she was careful about doing anything to make him feel he wasn't in control; that could be deadly. Sophie had worked with psychiatric patients for thirty-eight years and knew the ways of the psychopath.

He undid the cuffs, handcuffed her to the bed, and unsuccessfully tried to rape her again. He demanded to know where other jewelry was hidden. She swore to him he had gotten it all, that she was not a wealthy woman. He made her swear on Satan, which she did, all the while asking him not to hurt her in a calm, even voice. He ransacked her entire house some more, put everything he wanted in a pillowcase, and left her cuffed to the bed after warning her not to scream, or he'd come back and kill her.

"Remember, I know where you live!" he threatened, and departed, leaving yet another witness alive who could identify him.

He went to his fence to turn the Dickman and Nelson booty into cash. The fence had a loupe, and he looked at the stones through it, to decide how much he'd pay. They settled on a price and it was agreed the man-in-black would come back later for the cash.

He dumped the stolen car in Hollywood and took a bus back to downtown Los Angeles. The sun was coming up and the sky was alive with blood reds, hot oranges, pastel yellows and pinks; the air was still and very warm.

Sophie Dickman was nearsighted and hadn't had her glasses on, but she had seen the intruder up close and she had heard his voice; she'd never forget that voice—"demanding, demeaning, and threatening all at once," she would tell police.

When she was sure he had gone, she tried to get her hands free. The cuffs were not of a good quality and could be found in variety stores all over Los Angeles, but they held. Sophie knew a woman who was in law enforcement lived across the street. She got up, and using every ounce of strength she had, pulled the bed over to the window. With her feet she opened the shutters and window, bent over, and began shouting: "Mrs. Arthur! Oh, Mrs. Arthur, would you help me, please? I'm just across the street, Mrs. Arthur . . ."

Deputy Linda Arthur, from the sheriff's office, lived opposite Sophie Dickman. She was a little over five feet tall, very attractive. Coincidentally, she had worked the Doi crime scene and was familiar with the havoc the Valley Intruder had been causing.

In June of that year, Linda's own husband had been murdered while on duty. He, too, was with the sheriff's department. Carrillo often met her at murder scenes, and they had become good friends.

Linda was sleeping soundly, but Sophie Dickman's pleas woke her. At first, she thought she'd been dreaming, and she lay there perplexed as Sophie again called out, "Mrs. Arthur, please help me!" Linda sat up. Suddenly, she realized a woman was calling for assistance. She put on a robe, went outside, and walked straight to Sophie's front window, which faced the street. The two women had never met and Sophie apologized and told Linda what had happened. Wide-eyed, thinking it might be the Valley Intruder, Linda ran back to her house and dialed 911.

Pearl Carrillo refused to be alone anymore, and she and the kids had gone to stay at her parents'. When Gil arrived home that night to an empty house, he cursed the killer. All he could do was lie alone in bed, wide-eyed, unable to sleep, thinking about the killer, consumed with him. He wondered where he was—if he was stalking, raping, murdering, or laying up somewhere, waiting. Carrillo wondered if the killer knew he was looking for him. His quarry was clever and capable of just about anything—even killing a cop and his family. Maybe he had gone to Rodriguez's house purposely to kill a deputy sheriff. Anything was possible with this guy. Carrillo got out of bed, took his gun from its holster, and laid it on the nightstand within arm's reach, a .38 with a two-inch barrel. He had told Pearl earlier, "I'm sleeping with a gun next to the bed, so make sure you call before you come home; don't just come home."

A little after 3 A.M. he started to doze off, but he woke up with a start at exactly 3:20—the time Sophie Dickman was being attacked in Monterey Park, he would later realize. He was covered with sweat from having a nightmare about the Intruder.

He heard a noise inside the house, and in his mind, he believed the killer had somehow found out where he lived and had gotten into the house. Carrillo grabbed his gun, got down low, and crept toward the living room, holding his weapon in combat position. He kept the lights off so he wouldn't be a good target. The detective went from room to room and searched closets, under beds, the tubs—even the backyard, looking for the familiar Avia print, but he didn't find it.

There was no way he could go back to sleep. He realized the Valley Intruder had gotten to him and he sat in the living room and vowed to keep his emotions and imagination in check. He turned on the television.

When the phone rang, Carrillo jumped a foot in the air. The office told him Linda Arthur had phoned and wanted him to call her immediately: "There's been another attack in Monterey Park."

Linda Arthur picked up on the first ring. She explained what had happened to Sophie Dickman and suggested it was their man. At first, Carrillo doubted it, because thumb cuffs had not been used and Sophie Dickman had lived, but he told her he'd get dressed and come right over.

Somewhat reluctantly, he left his home and sped to Monterey Park. Arthur had been through an awful lot with the loss of her husband and the horrific crime scenes she'd been working lately. Maybe it had gotten to her, Carrillo thought. He had no jurisdiction in Monterey Park and knew he would not be welcome there, but Linda had called him and asked him for help, and nothing was going to stop him from going.

Linda Arthur was standing grim-faced in front of her house. She explained exactly what had happened as she'd heard Sophie Dickman—who was now at the hospital—tell it.

"Let's take a look," he said, and they went over to Sophie Dickman's place. A detective sergeant with the Monterey Park Police was standing at the front door, and when he saw Carrillo, his eyes widened and he looked shocked. "What are you doing here?" he asked. Carrillo explained that Linda Arthur was his "personal friend" and had called him.

Politely, he asked if he could view the crime scene. The sergeant said he could, "When *we're* finished." Somewhat awkwardly Carrillo stood there until a Monterey Park captain arrived and was nice enough to invite Carrillo into the house.

He noted the ransacking, the disabled phone, the source of entry, and the handcuffs on the bed. It had taken fifty minutes for the Monterey Park police and fire department to get the cuffs off Sophie.

Gil was thinking it *could* be his man, but he wasn't sure. Had the Avia print been present, he would have known immediately. Although ransacking and phone disabling were the Intruder's stamps, many thieves disabled phones and ransacked.

He thanked the Monterey Park police and went back to Linda Arthur's house. She made him cinnamon coffee and they sat down in the early-morning silence of her kitchen and discussed the case.

Linda knew if this was the Intruder, he could have checked out her house, too. She had all the windows locked, but both she and Gil knew the Intruder was good at what he did and mere locked windows weren't about to stop him. Linda vowed to sleep with a gun near the bed.

At 6 A.M. they went back outside; it was light now and they wanted to see if there were any Avia tracks around Linda's house. They found no prints but did see what appeared to be drops of dried blood leading to her backyard. These later turned out to be sap from a tree she had recently chopped down because she didn't want anyone to be able to hide behind the tree. The Intruder had made her, as well as just about everyone else in L.A. County, very security conscious.

With nothing more he could do in Monterey Park, Gil called Pearl at her parents' house. He missed her and his kids terribly and wanted to see them. It was a little before 7 A.M., and he suggested he'd pick them up to take them all out for Sunday breakfast.

He hugged and kissed Linda on the cheek, told her to beep him anytime she needed him, and left for his in-laws' home. He hadn't slept the whole night and figured there was enough time to have breakfast with his family and catch forty winks at Pearl's parents' before he had to meet Salerno at the office come noon.

Gil Carrillo hated his wife sleeping at her parents' house; it implied he couldn't protect her and his family. He was withdrawn at the breakfast and didn't say much. When they got back to his in-laws' house, Pearl told him he'd better take it easy and get some proper rest, that the case was getting to him. This was the last thing Gil wanted to hear. He told Pearl she should put a lid on it. "Please wake me up in one hour, at 11 A.M."

He went into a spare bedroom, his bones and muscles aching. He'd barely put his head on the pillow before his beeper went off. The office wanted him to go back to Monterey Park, as one Joyce Lucille Nelson had been brutally murdered.

When Carrillo heard the Avia shoeprint had been found there, he was suddenly no longer tired; the adrenaline kicked in and he was up and moving.

TWELVE

Gil arrived at the Nelson residence before Salerno. The press was already there in full force.

For the first time, the press *knew* there was a serial murderer entering homes at random all over Los Angeles County, killing people and raping women. They had been hearing and reporting rumors, though no one in law enforcement had publicly acknowledged there was a bona fide, very active serial murderer in their midst. All the crimes had been reported, but no one in the news had genuinely tied them together yet.

Now, the Monterey Park detectives on the scene were acknowledging a serial killer.

Quickly, word of the incredible brutality, missing eyes, pentagrams, torture, sodomy, and brutal rapes spread among the newspeople like blood on white satin. There were camera crews from every network, as well as print reporters with photographers from all of the newspapers, Spanish and Japanese included.

No one in the Monterey Park Police Department asked Gil what he was doing there this time; they knew he'd been saying "serial killer" all along and had sent out a flier on the Avia print, with his and Salerno's names on it.

Monterey Park detective Sgt. O'Connor showed Carrillo the prints in the flowerbed and on the front and rear red-painted patios. He took Gil inside and showed him Joyce, left between the bed and the closet, beaten beyond recognition.

Gil couldn't believe it, but the distinct waffle print of the Avia sole was clearly visible on Joyce's face. Salerno arrived and both he and Gil walked the crime scene, inside and out, as Gil told Frank about Sophie Dickman.

The Nelson murder had happened in Monterey Park, and it was the Monterey Park police's case; however, the two sheriff's detectives had a right to be there because this murder was now clearly one in a series the sheriff's office was investigating.

As police and tech people came and went, the camera crews recorded their every move, which would be plastered all over the four, five, six, eleven, and one o'clock news shows.

It looked, Salerno thought, like Joyce had been handcuffed, because both her hands were behind her back, frozen in rigor mortis, but there were no bruises or hematomas to indicate she'd been cuffed, and he thought that strange.

Certain it was their man—unless two killers had the same footwear—Salerno and Carrillo went back to the sheriff's office and reported the details of the Dickman and Nelson attacks to Capt. Grimm, and a meeting of the detectives working the task force was called. Criminalist Jerry Burke was just back from Portland and had very interesting news to report on the Avia Aerobic Shoe: only 1354 pairs had been made, and only six of those had found their way to the West Coast and been sold in L.A. Of those six pairs, only one was an 11 1/2. It was the only such shoe in L.A., and somehow the killer had found it.

That meant there were no two killers wearing the same shoe; it was one guy, and now, finally, that was an absolute certainty. All they had to do was find the guy wearing a size 11 1/2 Avia Aerobic shoe and they'd have their man. Pictures taken of the Avia shoe were sent to all sixty-three police jurisdictions in Los Angeles County.

In the morning, Salerno and Carrillo went to visit Sophie Dickman in her home. In a calm, collected manner, she told them exactly what had happened: how she had been awakened with the light in her eyes, the gun, the ransacking, the rape; she described her assailant as being white, tall, and thin, with bad teeth. She said he was dressed in black and that he was "good looking."

They thought it an odd way to describe a rapist. She

worked with a police artist and helped create a likeness of her assailant.

When the public, just after the Dickman and Nelson assaults, fully comprehended who was walking freely among them, a collective terror was born the likes of which had never before been seen in Southern California. The sale of guns, guard dogs, window gates, and alarm systems soared. Locksmiths had never been so busy. In the gun stores, people were lining up three deep. A gun salesman in Northridge said, "I had wall-to-wall people up to the ceiling wanting guns for protection. Never saw anything like it."

Editorials screamed for the capture of the Valley Intruder. Mayor Tom Bradley, Sheriff Block, and Police Chief Darryl Gates all said his apprehension was imminent.

When the news media learned that *the* Frank Salerno, of Hillside Strangler fame, was running the task force for this new serial killer, which the press had now dubbed the Night Stalker, they wouldn't leave him alone. He, and soon Carrillo as well, were hounded by reporters as they came and went; they couldn't answer the phone anymore because so many reporters were calling from all over, as far away as England, Israel, and Brazil.

Carrillo thought it would be a good idea if he did a video about the crimes for all L.A. County police departments. It would help centralize the investigation and make clear the evidence tying the crimes together—the killer's M.O., his description, etc. Salerno thought that was a great idea, and Carrillo went over to the Sheriff's Media Resource Center and taped a twenty-minute piece laying out what they had. Copies were sent to all L.A. sheriff's stations.

The tape was done the day after the Nelson murder, and it shows how exhausted Carrillo was; his voice is hoarse and strained.

It was that day, finally, that the LAPD let the sheriff's office have the car Officer Stavros had pulled over. It had been in an outdoor police parking lot, and any prints left behind had been burned away by the scorching California sun.

Salerno and Carrillo learned, for the first time, about a dentist's appointment card in the wallet and the six phone numbers in a little black phone book. LAPD said they were subpoenaing the phone company to learn the identity and addresses of the people whose numbers were found.

This, Salerno knew, was the first and biggest break they'd had. All LAPD had to do was find out who belonged to those numbers, put them under surveillance, and wait; it was just a matter of time.

The dentist appointment was in the name of Richard Mena, which proved to be an alias. The two homicide detectives went to visit the dentist, Dr. Peter Leung, a no-nonsense Asian who ran a dental clinic that opened at 7 A.M. and closed at 9 P.M., seven days a week.

He said Richard Mena had abscesses and was in pain and should be back. He had come in for treatment on July 3, which was weeks after he'd gotten away from Stavros.

Carrillo and Salerno realized that had the dentist's office been staked out right away, as it should have been, they would have caught him on July 3.

They asked the doctor if it would be okay if the sheriff's office placed undercover detectives in the office until Richard Mena came back. Leung didn't like the idea, saying it was disruptive and a nuisance, but he finally acquiesced. They would have to be, he stipulated, of Asian ancestry, for most of his practice was Asian. They agreed, and two Asian detectives from the sheriff's office were planted in Dr. Leung's office. They were told many times over by both Salerno and Carrillo not to take any chances; that the guy they were looking for was a stone-cold killer who knew what he was doing and would move very fast, very decisively.

From when Dr. Leung opened his office to when he closed, detectives, guns at the ready and keyed up, waited for "Richard Mena" to show. If he grabbed for a weapon, he'd be dead before he hit the ground.

Salerno and Carrillo felt very positive about the success of the operation. Dr. Leung said Mena had a condition which absolutely needed attention and was very painful. They reasoned if he came back once after being stopped, he'd come back again. Carrillo showed Mena's X rays to a friend who was a dentist, and he confirmed what Dr. Leung had said: "This guy will need medical attention soon."

At that point, they had no way of being certain Mena was

the Intruder, though his description and M.O. matched abductions where the Avia prints had been found.

The sheriff's task force began to grow in size, ferocity, purpose, and focus; lines of communication were finally opened between all L.A. police jurisdictions. Tips and leads pouring into the sheriff's office had to be followed up on. Salerno assigned Bumcrot and Robinson to run down every Richard Mena in the criminal justice system, which turned out to be forty individuals.

"Our biggest clues were his teeth and feet, and that's where we focused our energy," Salerno would later say.

Indeed, when Bumcrot and Robinson were checking out the forty Richard Menas in their computers, they were so busy looking at their feet and shoes that Buncrot said if they'd really come across the Stalker he'd have gotten the drop on them for sure.

Smaller task forces were put together by the LAPD and the Monterey Park police. At stationhouses all over L.A. County, cops going out on patrol were shown the video Carrillo had made. Many of them taped composites of the killer to their dashboards. There would be promotion and adulation for the cop who caught him. He'd be an instant hero. They all knew that, and how terribly vicious he was, and finding the Night Stalker became the top priority in every cop's mind.

Carrillo continued to sleep alone, with his gun near the bed.

Salerno, too, took precautions; his face, name, and reputation had been shown all over newspapers and news broadcasts, and for all he knew, the Stalker might decide to come looking for him—or his family. Salerno would not underestimate him.

He had two well-trained hunting Labrador retrievers who barked when strangers came around. To make certain his dogs didn't miss *anything*, he tied garbage cans to the two doors to the left and right of the house that led to the yard and rear bedrooms.

Salerno also took to sleeping with his gun near the bed. Frank Jr., who was working as a deputy sheriff at the time, was still living in the house, and he also slept with a gun near the bed. If the Stalker came to the Salerno house, he'd leave in a body bag.

* * *

On July 13, Sophie Dickman went to a town meeting called by the Monterey Park Police, held at the city council chambers. The police were shocked by how many people showed up, nearly 2000, and this was without any formal notice. They had expected just block captains to come, but once word got around, people couldn't be kept away. Lt. Joe Santoro was first to address the frightened citizenry.

He told them about the crimes the killer had committed outside Monterey Park. There were, he conceded, more attacks in Monterey Park than in any other community. He said plainclothes detectives were now cruising the streets at all hours. If he came back to their city, they'd have him. He told the audience that the Stalker enjoyed hurting his victims—that mutilation and very vicious sexual assaults had occurred. "He works at night. If you hear or see anything suspicious, don't hesitate, call us. Because he comes at night, practice dialing 911 in the dark. Know where your phone is, and keep it within arm's reach. And keep your curtains closed."

When Sophie Dickman heard Lt. Santoro talk about the realities of her assailant's viciousness, she realized how fortunate she had been. She had been trained to deal with psychopaths, but she realized she'd still been *very* lucky.

She wanted to get up and tell everyone there what had happened to her—how he was suddenly standing over her, leering down at her, snarling, raping her, but she remained seated and listened to Lt. Santoro.

"There are," he said, "hundreds of detectives looking for him. We'll get him soon. In the meantime, you can't be too cautious!"

On July 17, Mabel Bell died of the wounds she had suffered at the killer's hands on May 29. Dr. Sara Reddy did the autopsy. In her report, she noted the cause of death as massive brain trauma. Dets. Robinson and Bumcrot never had a chance to question her.

Nettie remained in a comatose state and was being fed intravenously.

THIRTEEN

The Stalker read, with great interest, the news accounts of his assaults. When he first saw them, as he casually passed a downtown newsstand, he stopped still and was in shock, his stomach turning and his heart racing. He'd had no idea they had connected all his crimes. He bought the newspapers, and as he listened to heavy metal music, read them in a roach-infested hotel room with windows too dirty to be seen through. The stories said nothing of the Avia footprints or the ballistics match-ups; he knew, though, that he'd have to be much more careful from now on, that it was getting hot for him.

Yet he stayed in L.A. and planned new, more horrific crimes.

It was now, after the Nelson and Dickman attacks, that he made up his mind to take what he was doing to a new level, one that would shock and horrify the world in a way never known before. He wanted everyone everywhere to know of his power.

On July 20, as detectives waited for him in Dr. Leung's office, as cops all over Southern California looked for him, he casually went into a downtown knife store, Ross Cutlery, and bought an industrial machete. He was going to remove the heads of his next victims and leave them on the front lawn for the police to find; that, he figured, would show them who they were *really* dealing with. With his pass key, he easily stole another Toyota and got on the freeway system, headed north this time, to Glendale, a large community with a population of 170,000, ringed by the Verdugo mountains and Angelo Buono's hometown. Glendale was the third-largest city in Los

Angeles County, founded in 1880, and a quick six miles north of Los Angeles. The people in the Chamber of Commerce like to say it is a great place to work and invest.

After getting off the freeway, he slowly cruised Glendale's streets, lined with darkened lawns and palm, eucalyptus, cyprus, and acacia trees. He parked at Stanley Avenue and Zerr Court, shut off the engine and lights, and listened to the silence carefully. Here, in Glendale, he sensed he'd have what he coveted and craved.

He tied his shoelaces tightly and tucked his pants in his socks so they wouldn't get caught on anything, got out of the car, and walked to the home of Maxon and Lela Kneiding, one block from the freeway. He stood still and let his hyper-keen senses feel the night. A fog had rolled in and hung two feet above the sidewalk. He was fascinated by fog: it reminded him of Jack the Ripper. He decided this was the place and walked to the front windows. They were locked, as was the front door. He went around to the back of the house, which was beige stucco with a slanted terra cotta tiled roof. Two large orange trees filled with fruit grew in the front yard. In the rear of the house, all the windows were locked. The Kneidings had been following his crimes in the news, and they were not keeping their windows open. The horrible assaults of Mabel Bell and Nettie Lang had upset them deeply.

He cut the screen on a French door, reached in a large, gloved hand, and easily opened the lock.

But he didn't enter the house. Instead, he went back to the car for the machete, walking quickly, all his senses sharper and more defined. He retrieved the large blade and returned to the yard, keeping his hand down, the machete hidden in the fog, which swirled around his legs as he moved. Before he entered the house, he knelt on the ground and prayed to Satan: *By all that is evil, I, your humble servant, invoke Satan to be here and accept this offering.*

Staying low, he entered the Kneiding residence, remained statue-still, then moved straight to the Kneidings' bedroom.

Max Kneiding was sixty-eight. He and Lela, sixty-six, had been married forty-seven years. They were high-school sweethearts and had been married shortly after graduating. They had three children and thirteen grandchildren. Max owned a service station. Lela worked for the security force at Robinson's Department Store. They made a nice living and were comfortable. She was an avid Dodgers and Lakers fan and would often listen to the games on her radio while doing chores so she could enjoy the games. Max was a hardworking man who was a deacon at the Glendale Seventh Day Adventist Church. They had known one another for fifty years and were as much in love today as they'd been when they'd first met.

As always, the Stalker found out who was in the house. When he realized it was just Max and Lela, he entered their bedroom, turned on the lights, walked straight to their bed, kicked it, and said, "Rise and shine, motherfuckers!"

Max bolted up, not believing his eyes, shocked, startled— seeing death as clearly as an oncoming train in this soldier of Satan's face. Lela screamed. The killer swung the machete, its blade hissing in the air like a poisonous snake, and struck Max in the neck, giving him a deep gash. The Stalker had thought the head would come off, but it didn't. Max went down, pleading for him to stop. Instead, he swung at Lela and missed. The machete wasn't sharp enough to kill them quickly, he realized, and he pulled out the .22, put it right to Max's head and pulled the trigger, but the gun jammed. As they pitifully begged not to be killed, he cleared it and again put the gun to Max's head and fired, ending Max's life instantly. Lela screamed hysterically. He put the gun to her face and pulled the trigger three times, killing her.

They were both still.

He proceeded to cut and jab them with the machete, then ransacked the house.

He had the scanner with him and over it he heard a report of "shots fired" go out. Quickly, he put what he wanted in a pillowcase and walked back to the car, carrying the bloody machete in one hand and the Kneidings' possessions in the other, the fog surrounding him. He got in the stolen Toyota and pulled away as a police car began slowly to cruise the block.

In thirty seconds he was back on the freeway, and in minutes was at the fence's house, getting rid of the Kneiding valuables: a radio, a camera, a VCR, watches, rings, and other jewelry. The fence saw the blood on him, but said nothing of his being the killer in the paper. If he really was the killer, he was dangerous beyond words, the fence knew, and so he kept quiet and woodenly went about doing business with him.

Soon, however, he would stop dealing with him. There was just too much blood on everything he brought him, and if he *was* the killer, there would be a big reward if he called the police; and that's what he thought about now as he took the Kneiding loot.

Still not satisfied, the Stalker again drove north, a quarter moon low in a mostly clear night sky. He got off the Sun Valley exit of the freeway and began to cruise the pristine community of 60,000. The town had been known as Roscoe until 1948, when a public referendum overwhelmingly voted to change the name to Sun Valley.

At 4:15 A.M. on this night, the city of Sun Valley was soundly sleeping. Everyone there knew about the murderous assaults in people's homes, but there had never been one in Sun Valley, which was much farther north than any of the other attacks. The people of Sun Valley felt removed from the danger of the Stalker.

He found his way to Charbonne Street, shut off the lights and engine, and coasted to a noiseless stop. He decided this would be a good place, got out of the car, and walked up Charbonne, leaving the machete in the car. There was no fog in Sun Valley. He stopped when he reached the home of Chainarong and Somkid Khovananth, a modest, L-shaped house with a garage and a curved driveway.

Chainarong Khovananth was an immigrant from Thailand who had come to California ten years earlier. He worked long hours as a parking attendant. He was a handsome man with thick black hair who dearly loved his wife and his children, an eight-year-old boy and a two-year-old girl. His hobby was gardening, and he spent many hours in the back yard of the house. Somkid, too, had been born in Thailand, and like her husband, she'd immigrated to Los Angeles ten years earlier, in May of 1975. Her first year in L.A. she had met and married Chainarong. Petite and very pretty, Somkid had large, round, dark eyes and short, thick black hair.

The Stalker walked to the front of the Khovananth residence and tried the windows and doors. They were all locked.

He went to the back of the house and saw the beautiful garden Chainarong had created with love and patience, got down low, and made sure the vibrations were right. When he was satisfied all was clear, he tried the sliding-glass doors. They were open, and he silently slipped into the den.

There was a nightlight on. Somkid had been sleeping on the couch in the den. She was a very light sleeper, and his presence, his sudden movement, woke her. He ran to her and put his hand over her mouth. Trembling, she stared at him with huge, frightened, liquid-black eyes. He put the gun, a .25 auto, to her head.

"Don't make a fucking sound, bitch, or I'll kill you! Understand?" he hissed.

Crying, she nodded.

He left her, found the two sleeping children in different rooms, then went to Chainarong, who was snoring loudly as he slept. There was a fan on a dresser facing the bed, and it slowly moved back and forth, offering little relief from the heavy, cloying heat.

The Stalker walked straight to the bed, put the barrel of the gun one inch from Chainarong's left ear, and pulled the trigger. There was a muffled pop, and the .25 slug zigzagged through Chainarong's brain, killing him instantly. As blood poured from the wound, the Stalker covered him with a blanket and went back to Somkid, anxious to terrorize and rape her. She had taken off her diamond wedding ring and hidden it in the couch. He immediately noticed her ring was missing, took off his glove, and slapped her hard, putting the glove right back on.

"Don't play no fucking games, bitch! Where's the ring?"

She told him it was inside the couch. He found it and put it in his pocket, then viciously ripped off her flimsy nightgown, grabbed her arm, and dragged her to the bathroom, where he picked up a hair dryer.

"What are you going to do with that?" she cried.

"I need a knife."

"A knife? Why?" she asked, all wide-eyed, fear bulging her eyes.

"To cut this cord."

Together they went to the kitchen, where he found a butcher knife and severed the cord from the dryer. He took her back to the bathroom and tied her hands behind her back with the wire. He took her to the bedroom where her dead husband lay and raped her. She was terrified and her fear turned him on and excited him, and probably saved her life. If she had resisted, if she had put up a fight—defied him—he would have killed her.

An alarm clock in the eight-year-old's room went off. He tied her legs and ran into the boy's room, bound and tied him, and put a sock in his mouth.

He left the boy's room and began his frenetic ransacking. Soon, he came back to her and made her sit in a chair and fellate him, then he sodomized her, climaxed—and demanded jewelry and money. She told him where her jewelry box was, but there was nothing except costume pieces in it, which infuriated him.

He dragged her by the hair around the house, cursing her, threatening her, slapping her, kicking her.

"Where's the good stuff, and where's the cash?" he demanded.

She told him where her purse was and he found eighty dollars and pocketed it.

"I killed your husband, okay, and I'll kill you and your kids. Now, where are the fucking valuable things, bitch?" he said.

"If I give you everything will you go?"

"Yeah, I'll go."

She told him she had hidden her valuable pieces in the kitchen; he dragged her there. Somkid showed him her secret hiding place, an envelope hidden behind a drawer. In it were rubies, diamonds, a diamond bracelet, and a ring. Somkid's brother was a jeweler, and she had some unique, very valuable pieces.

He took them all.

"And where's the money?"

"No money, no money! I swear, I swear to God!" she said.

"No! Swear to Satan!"

"I swear to Satan, no money! I swear to Satan! I swear to Satan!" she pleaded.

He dragged her, still naked and bound, back to the bedroom and raped her again.

There was a time when he had discovered a fortune in gold Krugerrand coins in the trunk of a stolen car, and now, after the third rape, he wanted to go outside so he could look in the trunk of their car for cash. In order to open the garage door from inside the house, a button on the wall in the bathroom had to be pushed. Somkid showed it to him, but he wouldn't push it because he thought it was some kind of police panic alarm. He put the gun to her head and told her he'd kill her and her kids if she tricked him. She repeatedly swore on Satan that she wasn't trying to trick him. He pushed the button. The garage door automatically opened and they went outside after he put a robe on her. All he found in the car was fifteen dollars in Chainarong's wallet under the driver's seat.

Back inside, he slapped her and demanded more valuables. She told him about a piece of jewelry she'd hidden in her son's blue jacket in the hall closet. He went and retrieved it, a gold brooch with diamonds. He made her swear on Satan there was nothing more, which she did; he laughed, laid her down, and tied her ankles together with a belt. Finished, finally, he put his booty into a large suitcase of theirs and silently exited, leaving Somkid tied on the bedroom floor.

When she was sure he was gone, she freed herself, ran to her son, and made certain he was okay. She then went to the bedroom, lifted the blanket, and saw the bullet hole in Chainarong's head, and knew it was true—that he really had murdered her beloved husband. She began to shake and sob, but she knew she had to keep her composure for the sake of her children. Quickly, she gathered them up and ran from the house, crossed the street, and frantically rang the bell of a neighbor.

The first Homicide people to arrive at the Khovananth home were Carlos Brizzolara and his partner, Al Michelorena, from the LAPD Foothill Station. By the time they got there, Somkid had been taken to the hospital.

Initially, this assault was not tied to the Stalker. He'd never come so far north, and Michelorena and Brizzolara weren't thinking Stalker, though that would change soon enough. The two LAPD detectives worked the crime scene and directed fingerprint people, clue gathering, picture taking. They found a Martinelli Apple Juice bottle the assailant had drunk from, but there were no prints on it, nor were there on the butcher knife or the blow dryer. They found the Avia prints on the rear patio and in the hallway, but these were not immediately connected to the Stalker assaults. A representative from the coroner's office arrived, pronounced Chainarong dead, and he was removed to the county morgue, becoming the ninth person the Stalker had killed.

At 2 P.M., Somkid returned from the hospital with LAPD uniformed police. She had two black eyes, a huge swollen lip, two concussions, and thirty stitches inside her mouth to close a gash he had given her with one of his punches. She was heartbroken and distraught, crying, sobbing, yet she reenacted everything for detectives Brizzolara and Michelorena.

What kind of man, they asked one another, could rape a woman and have an orgasm just feet away from her dead husband?

Somkid described him as being "brown-skinned, bad teeth, thirty to thirty-five, 150 pounds, six foot one or so." She said he had black hair with soft curls and sweated an awful lot. The detectives sincerely promised her they would do all that was humanly possible to bring her husband's murderer to justice. She kept asking them why it all had happened, and they kept saying they didn't know.

At 5 P.M., Somkid and the detectives left the house. It was locked up by Det. Brizzolara. Yellow police tape surrounded it. Somkid went to join her two children, who were staying with family members.

Back at the Foothill Station, detectives Brizzolara and Michelorena wrote up their reports. The attack in Sun Valley still was not linked to the Stalker.

Judy Arnold called her mom and dad, Mr. and Mrs. Kneiding, at 7:40 that morning, without getting an answer. The family customarily met for Saturday breakfast before going to church together. Judy figured her mom and dad had left for the restaurant already, and she, her husband, and her children drove over to the Toasted Bun in Glendale to meet them. They weren't there. Thinking perhaps her parents had gone on to church, Judy drove there, but their car was not in the parking lot. They went to the house on Stanley Avenue and saw Lela and Max's cars in the driveway. Perplexed, Judy rang the front door bell—and got no answer. The door was locked. She went around back, noticed the ripped screen, and with some trepidation, entered the house, saw the ransacking, and then found her parents wrapped around one another in a large bloody knot in their bedroom. She screamed and ran outside.

Officer Tom Kuh from the Glendale police pulled up in front of the Kneiding home at 9:15. He was met by an hysterical Judy Arnold. Through sobs and tears, she told him how she'd found her parents. He went into the house alone, gun drawn, found the Kneidings, realized this was indeed a very bloody murder, and backed right out of the house, called it in, and sealed the perimeter. As he was putting up the tape, Glendale officer Fox arrived and helped him. From the sidelines, crying, brokenhearted, Judy Arnold watched.

Glendale detective Jon Perkins arrived and Officer Kuh took him through the crime scene. Perkins, unlike his Sun Valley colleagues, immediately thought it was the Night Stalker's work and he told his partner, Gary Montecollo so, but they did not contact the sheriff's office.

It was obvious the Kneidings had been brutally murdered, but until they were turned over by Fred Corral from the coroner's office, the detectives had no idea how truly brutal the attacks had been: both Max and Lela had multiple deep gashes across their throats, one of which was three inches deep and six inches long, and all over their upper bodies. They each had lost a lot of blood. Criminalists Lynne Harold and Sally Jimenez looked for prints and clues. They found pieces of a .22 slug under a dresser, which they bagged. There were also tufts of hair from Lela's head that had been torn from her scalp by the bullets and had stuck to the curtain and the wall above the curtains. There were blood splatters all over the walls and ceiling, going every which way, indicating blows delivered from many different angles. The Kneidings were taken to the morgue.

At 2 P.M. that afternoon, the killer woke up in the Cecil Hotel, went next door to Margarita's, and ate breakfast. He went into a porno shop and looked at magazines involving bondage.

It would be just a matter of time, he believed, before he had enough money to buy his torture house, and as he scanned the magazines depicting women bound and terrified, he became aroused.

He proceeded to the bus terminal and hung out with a few of his contemporaries, guys who stole for a living, showing off the stones and gold bars he'd stolen from the Khovananths, proud of his prowess. He copped a dime bag of pot and smoked a joint as he walked to the Cameo Theater and watched pornographic films—thinking about ways he could torture and kill women up on the screen.

He was still confident he'd not left any clues at any of the crime scenes, but he knew all the women he'd let live could identify him. He had made them look down and away, but still he realized they'd glimpsed his face, especially Somkid, and they had heard his voice—his threatening commands and snarling, clenched-fist threats. But he believed so long as the cops didn't have any of his fingerprints, they'd never catch him. He'd always worn gloves and would continue to do so. He knew as long as he stayed evil in his heart, Satan would protect him, watch over him, and keep him out of harm's way—which, in his case, would surely be the Green Room at San Quentin death row (the gas chamber).

If he was caught, he vowed there in the theater, he would not let them take him alive. He fervently believed when he did die, he'd go to hell and be a hero, be recognized and appreciated for his deeds, not prosecuted, scorned, and punished. Sitting there in the Cameo, masturbating, he remembered the rape of Somkid. She had been the most attractive woman he had taken like that, with a gun to her head, her hands trembling with fear.

He left the theater and went to the Ye Hi pool parlor and shot a few games of pool. No one there suspected him or pointed at him. If, as he walked down the streets, people had known who and what he really was, they would have run, terrified, pointing at him, he was sure.

However, no one knew his real identity, and he passed people on the sidewalks like everyone else. He had never told a soul the truth; that was his secret . . . the key to not being apprehended. Serial killers very rarely, if ever, let people into their confidence. Murder is their secret and they guard it carefully. This is one of several reasons police agencies have difficulty apprehending serial murderers: they keep their mouths shut about who they really are, and after the truth does come out everyone is always shocked.

After the pool hall, the Stalker went to the home of his fence and turned some of the loot from the Khovananth assault into cash.

Again, nothing was said about him being the Stalker, but as soon as the fence could figure out how to turn him in without himself getting into trouble, he would. He was afraid the police would make him an accessory after the fact. He was hoping he could get immunity if he cooperated, but it was something he had to think about long and hard. If he made a mistake in judgment, in his course of action, it would surely cost him his life.

Most of the loot he had bought from the Stalker was still in his possession. Stolen property had to be sold slowly, discreetly, lest it cause undue attention.

If the press had reported exactly what articles had been taken from the homes of the victims, others would have known that this man who always wore black and was known by different names was the Night Stalker.

When he left the fence's house, he bought the evening's papers and read, with relish, about his latest assaults.

Neither the Glendale police nor LAPD contacted the sheriff's office and told them about the Kneiding and Khovananth assaults.

Carrillo didn't get wind of them until July 21, from Scott Carrier at the Medical Examiner's Office. He immediately went to Salerno and told him about these new attacks. They were angry no one from either police jurisdiction had contacted them. Salerno phoned Glendale Homicide and made an appointment with Jon Perkins so they could view the Kneiding crime scene. During the Hillside Strangler case, Frank had had a lot of trouble with the Glendale police being uncooperative and not sharing information. Jon Perkins knew about it and assured Frank it would not happen again.

Salerno thanked him and they made plans to meet at the Kneiding residence. The two Homicide detectives drove out to Glendale together. The temperature was 101 degrees, hot enough to literally fry an egg on the hood of the car.

There were no Avia prints, but Frank and Gil knew it was their guy because of the viciousness of the assaults, the rear entry, and the ransacking.

LAPD detectives Brizzolara and Michelorena attended the autopsy of Chainarong Khovananth as Salerno and Carrillo studied the Kneiding crime scene. Frank, who had heard about the Sun Valley attacks from a contact at the morgue, told the LAPD detectives he and Gil wanted to take a look at the crime scene. The detectives agreed to meet at the Khovananth residence. When Frank and Gil heard he'd left another witness alive, their hopes soared. If they could get a true rendering of what the Stalker looked like, that could bring him down much quicker. Somewhere, someone knew this guy, and for the $80,000 reward being offered now, they were confident they'd have the Stalker's name soon.

They drove to Sun Valley and Brizzolara took his colleagues through what Somkid had told him. They found the Avia footprint in the back yard and in front of the eight-year-old's room. Gil wasn't surprised at the perverse, sadistic nature of the sexual assault. He contacted the sheriff's crime lab and asked Chuck Vander Wende and Jerry Burke to come out to Sun Valley and lift the shoeprints.

The sheriff's detectives were anxious to speak to Somkid and have her help with a composite. They felt this crime, more than any other, brought together all the elements involved in the Stalker assaults—burglary-type entry, Avia shoeprint, murder with a small-caliber gun, ransacking, phone disabling, robbery, rape, sodomy—and there was a living witness.

His leaving Somkid alive was evidence of his cockiness—and it would do him in soon, Salerno told Carrillo: "The fucker's just too active not to get caught."

In the morning, they told Capt. Grimm and the other detectives working the case the details of the Kneiding and Khovananth assaults. They discussed ways to improve communication between the different police agencies. If, Salerno pointed out, Scott Carrier from the M.E.'s office hadn't called them, they might never have heard about the crimes. Capt. Grimm said he'd talk to Sheriff Block.

Salerno and Carrillo interviewed Somkid at her brother's home. She was truly grief-stricken but agreed to speak to them; more than anything, she wanted the man who'd raped her and murdered her husband to be captured, tortured—killed. A beast like him, she told them, had no right walking free among human beings.

"He is dangerous beyond words," she said. "So brutal; so mean—so cruel. His eyes were like an animal's, wasn't human. Why . . . why did he have to kill him? He was such a good man."

There was no answer to her question.

Carrillo and Salerno were both tough men inside and out, but to see Somkid's pain and hurt moved them deeply. They assured her everything possible would be done to catch her husband's killer.

She worked with an LAPD artist and put together a composite that looked like the Stalker. He had large eyes, hollow cheeks, high cheekbones, and full lips. Salerno and Carrillo implored LAPD to release this composite, it was given to the press for publication and telecast, and every cop all over Los Angeles taped the composite on his dashboard.

Salerno and Carrillo knew the Stalker often hunted at night, and they felt confident it wouldn't be long before a black-and-white or a sheriff's deputy pulled him over. Word went out to all police personnel not to take *any* chances with the Stalker. They knew he realized he'd get the death sentence and had nothing to lose by killing a cop to get away.

After the Kneiding and Khovananth attacks, the Night Stalker became front-page news all over California. He was the lead story for all the local news shows, as well as on CNN. Journalists from many countries around the world descended on Los Angeles like vultures, hungry for the gory details of the Stalker's grisly deeds.

The population was in a panic; never before had a single killer had such a profound effect on a whole community. He was what people were talking about over breakfast and the last thing on their minds as they tried to sleep at night, tossing and turning in the oppressive summer heat because of him, deathly afraid he might come to their home.

Coincidentally, most of his attacks had been in beige and yellow houses, and people began painting their homes different colors, hoping that would make him pass their place.

The sale of defensive items reached record heights; gun shop owners found people in line when they opened their stores; locksmiths were so busy putting in new locks and bars that they were working almost twenty-four hours a day; there was such a run on guard and attack dogs that animals from other states had to be brought in to fill the demand.

He was a killer who entered your bedroom in the middle of the night; could there be anything more dreaded? He frightened people deeply, both consciously and subconsciously.

All over L.A., the police were getting reports of a suspicious man in black. Elderly women were terrified of being alone. Girls had to be home early from dates. Husbands sat up all night standing guard with bats and guns at the ready. Children insisted on sleeping in their parents' beds; many people couldn't sleep at all. Communities pooled their resources and set up patrols that walked the streets until dawn. Psychiatrists and psychologists all over Southern California heard stories from their patients about how frightened they were, that they couldn't sleep; that even their love-lives had been affected.

The pressure on the police to solve the case became enormous. The Stalker was thumbing his nose at all things good, and nothing was sacred so long as he was free. Hundreds of thousands of letters and phone calls poured into the mayor's office, begging and demanding he do something.

Finally, all the different police jurisdictions began cooperating "somewhat." The infighting and the concern for career opportunities and politics seemed to be put aside. There was a killing fiend in their midst, and if the police didn't cooperate with one another, he'd simply continue to hunt, rape, and kill.

Later in the afternoon of July 22, Salerno and Carrillo were in Grimm's office when the Firearms section of the sheriff's office called to say that the gun in the Kneiding attack had been the same one that had killed Veronica Yu and Dayle Okazaki. This, in Salerno and Carrillo's minds, confirmed an earlier theory that the killer had several guns. If he was captured alive with any of the guns still in his possession, they could use the ballistics and the Khovananth I.D. to send him straight to the death chamber.

After the meeting in Grimm's office, another meeting was called of the sheriff's task force, now over twenty-five detectives, a third of Homicide. Salerno presented the details of the Stalker's newest crimes and everyone else reported on the progress of their particular tasks. Salerno reminded the task force to treat every lead from every call like *the* one that could crack the case. It was just a matter of time before someone the Stalker knew gave him up.

Later, Salerno and Carrillo went to Flora's to brainstorm about the case over a drink. Other detectives from the task force joined them. They all had different theories but were agreed that the Stalker was an ex-con, had done hard time somewhere, and had probably been in the service. The investigation would concentrate in the direction of a recently released veteran-convict.

When Salerno got home that night he, like many others in the huge expanse of L.A. County, had trouble sleeping. There was a closet opposite his bed, which he normally left open at night, but now he got up and closed it lest the Stalker use it for cover. He slept with his gun within easy reach.

When Carrillo got home, he slept in an empty bed, his hand only inches from his service revolver.

The next morning, Frank Salerno called the FBI's Behavioral Science Unit (BSU) and asked them to come to Los Angeles and help with the Stalker investigation. They were the most informed law enforcement people in the world on the subject of serial killers and had, beginning in 1978, done extensive interviews with fifty-one incarcerated serial murderers. The information they'd gathered was ultimately used to help do profiles on active serial murderers.

Agent Bill Hagmeyer and program coordinator Terri Green arrived with two crime analysts from VICAP (The Violent Criminal Apprehension Program) on August 6. Hagmeyer was one of the originators of the BSU and had personally interviewed two dozen serial murderers. Salerno and Carrillo picked them up at the airport and began laying out all they had on the ride back to the sheriff's office. The agents asked few questions. At the sheriff's office, they were shown the shoeprints and the crime scene and autopsy photos. They didn't give much importance to the pentagram on Mabel Bell's thigh. They gave the agents copies of all the written reports on the Stalker crimes.

"Look, fellas, I don't want to mislead you, but all we have is based on what we've been told by killers. What you've described to us is unique. We'll still do a profile, but what you've got here is a first," Hagmeyer said.

Salerno had already known that, but to hear Hagmeyer say it was sobering. Salerno and Carrillo were let down; they'd been hoping the BSU people might see something they'd missed.

FOURTEEN

He stole still another Toyota from a hotel parking lot in Burbank, and drove north on the freeway. He knew it was hot in the areas where he'd already gone hunting, so tonight he figured he'd travel to a place where they'd least expect him.

He ended up in Northridge, twenty-five miles from downtown Los Angeles. Northridge, with a population of 78,000, was again one of those perfect communities that epitomized the American Dream. Its streets were immaculate, lined with maple, palm, oak, and walnut trees. Up until 1929, the town had been known as Zelzah, the Biblical name for an oasis, but it was then changed to Northridge. Surrounded by the beautiful Santa Susana Mountains, it was a fine place to live and to bring up children.

At 2 A.M., the Night Stalker pulled off the freeway and cruised Northridge. The night was clear, thousands of stars filled the sky.

He found his way to Acre Street, shut off the lights and engine, and coasted to a silent stop. His eyes moved from house to house, window to window, door to door, making certain he hadn't been seen. He unloaded his bullets, kissed them, put them back in the gun, tucked his pants into the tops of his socks, and got out the car, being very careful not to make a sound as he opened and closed the door.

He proceeded up Acre with an unhurried gait, his eyes moving from residence to residence. After half a block, he stopped in front of the home of Virginia and Chris Petersen and their five-year-old daughter. Chris was a strapping 6'1", a thirty-eight-year-old man in the prime of life. His wife, too, was a large woman, twenty-seven years old, blond, and blue-eyed. Chris had worked as a warehouse manager for the past eleven years. Virginia was a U.S. postal clerk. They were very much in love and had worked and saved hard to buy their house on Acre.

Like the Khovananth home, it was modest, though well kept. There were the ever-present orange trees growing in the front yard, which created webbed shadows. The house was just off the corner of Nestles and had three stone steps to the front door and three picture windows on the right.

As if he lived there, the Stalker walked straight to the front door and tried the knob; it was locked. He then tried the windows; they, too, were locked. He moved to the back of the house, all still and quiet. Off the yard, there were sliding glass doors, which led to the living room. They were open. He pulled out the .25 automatic, knelt down, and told Satan what he was about to do he was doing for him. Silently, he stepped inside, stayed low to the ground, and listened.

Chris Petersen had gone to sleep after his wife, who had retired at 9:30. He'd left the living room light on because their daughter was afraid of the dark. The Stalker stood and quickly moved through the den and along a foyer that led to Chris and Virginia's bedroom. Before he entered the room, he cocked the gun. Virginia was a light sleeper, and the cold metallic click woke her, just as he reached their room and turned straight toward her, holding the gun out with two hands, as if he was praying.

"Who the hell are you, what do you want?" Virginia said. "Get out!"

"Shut up, bitch," he told her. He moved closer to the bed and shot Virginia under the left eye, just to the left of her nose. She felt like she'd been hit by a bat and went down. Chris woke up. Virginia's face went all numb and she said, "I think he shot me with a stun-gun."

"Is this some kind of sick joke?" Chris said.

Virginia turned toward Chris. He saw the bullet wound in his wife's face and all the blood. "My God, your face is gone!" he exclaimed. The Stalker shot him in the right temple, knocking him back down. Laughing, he fired another shot at Virginia, missing. The Petersens' five-year-old woke up and began crying, screaming.

Chris knew he was all there was between his wife and young daughter and the laughing madman with a gun.

He must be the Night Stalker, he thought, and like an angry bear, stood and attacked the Stalker, who shot two more rounds at him, missing each time. The gun was now empty. The two men grappled. Chris tried to pull the Stalker to the ground, to rip his head off, but the Stalker tossed him over his back and ran for the sliding glass doors. Chris chased him to the doors, where he stopped and began yelling for help.

The Stalker was going to reload the gun at the car and go back to kill Chris, but he knew the police would be there in minutes and he took off, got on the freeway, and sped back toward downtown Los Angeles.

Miraculously, Virginia got out of bed, ran outside, and went to a neighbor's for help. They weren't home, and she came back to the house and dialed 911. Chris gathered up their daughter and went outside to wait for the police. Virginia joined them. By now she was bleeding profusely. He decided there wasn't time to wait for help and put his family in his pickup truck and drove over to Northridge Hospital, where he and Virginia were promptly treated.

It would later be revealed that the Stalker's ammunition was old and the gunpowder had lost much of its potency. The slugs that had hit Chris had not been able to penetrate his skull. The bullet Virginia had taken had gone through the roof of her mouth and down her throat and exited at the back of her neck, missing her brain entirely; she'd been very lucky.

LAPD homicide detective Lewis Bobbitt arrived at the Petersen home at 4 A.M. Black-uniformed LAPD were already there and had put up the now all-too-familiar yellow crime-scene tape. Bobbitt ran the show, directing fingerprinting and picture-taking. Criminalist David Weller found the four shell casings and bagged them in clear plastic coin-envelopes for evidence. He also found a bullet hole in the windowsill and dug out the slug, which proved too damaged for any exact ballistics work.

Quickly, the LAPD Stalker task force heard about the assault on the Petersens. Chris never got a clear look at the man, but Virginia had, and based on her description of him, the task force took the case from Det. Bobbitt.

At the Petersens' there was no ransacking, robbery, or phone disabling, and there were no Avia shoeprints, so no one in the LAPD task force was certain this attack was by the Stalker. However, he had called Virginia "bitch"—one of his favorite words. And he was wearing all black and was the right height.

That same morning, Salerno had called a meeting of all police jurisdictions in Los Angeles County. It was held at the LAPD police academy and detectives from Montebello, Monterey Park, West Covina, Monrovia, Arcadia, Glendale, Burbank and Sierra Madre were there—as well as representatives from the FBI. Fifty people in all.

Gil said the Stalker knew there were different police jurisdictions involved and was exploiting it. If they didn't share everything, Gil warned, the killing would continue.

During the meeting they received word about the Petersen attack. Salerno suggested Gil run over to Northridge with detectives Paul Tippin to check it out.

Carefully, Carrillo scrutinized the Petersens' home. At first glance he saw nothing to indicate it was their man. But in his gut Carrillo felt it was him.

Back at the meeting, he reported to the group, "There were no prints, no ransacking, but there was a silent rear entry and a .25 automatic used."

The meeting ended with everyone promising to share information and to cooperate.

After the press got word of the Petersen attack, they hounded Salerno and Carrillo for a quote, some kind of statement. It was the detectives' policy never to talk to the press, but they were surrounded by reporters when they left the office that night, and Salerno decided he would go public with his feelings to try to draw the Stalker into a dialogue.

He said, "In this attack, the Stalker showed his true colors," meaning the Stalker was a coward.

The following day, all the Los Angeles newspapers carried the story about the Petersen assault with the quote from Frank Salerno.

FIFTEEN

The Stalker read what Salerno had said about him, and it made him angry.

He believed it took courage to enter someone's home in the middle of the night; he never knew who or what he faced: a gun, a dog, a bat-wielding husband. He knew, too, that the police, given the chance, would kill him without a second thought, and none of that had stopped him.

He decided he wanted to be better able to defend himself against the police's shotguns and high-powered .9-mm sidearms. He bought an Uzi machine gun from a black-market gun dealer he'd met at the bus terminal. The weapon fired thirty rounds per second. He loaded up, kissing some of the bullets—three thirty-clip magazines—and taped two of them end-to-end so it would be a simple matter of ejecting an empty clip, turning it around, and slamming in the new clip. It could be done in seconds. He also carried a .38 pistol, a .25 automatic, and a pair of handcuffs.

On August 8, he again stole a car, jumped on the freeway, and began to hunt. This night he drove further east than he'd ever gone—to the community of Diamond Bar, nestled in the scenic hills of La Brea Canyon, thirty miles from central Los Angeles. A lovely city of 42,100 surrounded by soft, rolling hills, its streets had many twists and turns, endings and beginnings, ups and downs, and even with a compass and map, it was not easy to find a particular address. It was an upscale community with ten beautiful parks and streets shaded by oak, walnut, and pine trees. It was an idyllic community, sleeping soundly on a summer night.

He reasoned correctly that the people here would not be

so vigilant and he'd find less resistance. As with all serial killers, he traveled the path of least resistance.

The stolen car had a nice sound system, and while he negotiated the twisting, rising, and falling streets of Diamond Bar, he listened to the pounding, pulsating rhythm of heavy metal. He did not have the scanner tonight.

As he stalked the picturesque streets, he thought about murder and sex, sex and murder. Somewhere in the swirling recesses of his bubbling psychosis, they were one. He coasted to a stop on Pinehill Lane. When he was sure he wasn't seen, he got out of the stolen car and walked the quiet street, the handguns in his belt, the Uzi in a black knapsack on his back.

By Diamond Bar standards, it was a modest beige tract house with two large picture windows to either side of the entrance, over which a lantern—whose light was now out—hung from a shiny black chain. There was a garage on the right. Two large pine trees grew in the front yard and cast the house in shadow. This was the home of Sakina and Elyas Abowath. The Stalker walked straight to the back yard. The windows were locked, but he managed to open the rear sliding glass door.

Sakina Abowath was a twenty-seven-year-old Burmese immigrant. Elyas Abowath, thirty-one, had been born in Pakistan. He was a computer programmer; Sakina worked as a medical technician. She was a petite, attractive woman with thick, short black hair and large, round eyes. The Abowaths had two boys, one ten weeks old, the other three years.

The Stalker slid the glass door open and entered their living room, got down low, and listened. The light in the living room was on. After a few heartbeats, he was up and moving through the house with silent deadly intentions. The first room he came to was the bedroom of the three-year-old. He moved on to Sakina and Elyas's bedroom. The ten-week-old was sleeping in a crib near their bed. Sakina and her husband were both sleeping soundly. She had just fallen asleep after breast-feeding the infant at 2:30 A.M. There was a nightlight on in the small room. The Abowaths had a king-sized bed, and there was little space to move about the bed's perimeter.

He turned and went back out to the car. He wanted it closer for quick escape, and he brazenly parked it right in the Abowath driveway, where it would be less conspicuous.

He returned to the rear door, went in, quickly walked to the sleeping couple, sweating, his heart pumping like he'd run a great distance, seeing the killing even before it happened, consumed with the need to do it. He reached the bed and without hesitation put the .25 close to Elyas's head, just above the left ear, and pulled the trigger.

Elyas was killed instantly by the twisting, searing-hot .25-caliber slug.

The Stalker then jumped over Elyas's convulsing body and straddled Sakina, punching her in the face and stomach, making her nose bleed, then turned her over, handcuffed her, and said, "Don't scream, bitch, or I'll kill you and your kids here and now!"

Horrified beyond words, she stayed silent. He struck her again, went to the closet, and blindfolded her with a shirt by tying it tightly around her head. He forced part of the shirt so far down her throat that she began to gag and choke. She bit down on it to prevent him from sticking it further down and he slapped her hard, saying, "Don't bite it, bitch, or I'll kill you," and slapped her again. Her mouth began to bleed. He tied another blouse around her ankle and hit her four times more on the side of the head, making her ears ring and nearly knocking her unconscious. He stood over her and kicked her so hard she flew off the bed and landed on the floor.

He left the room, disabled the phone in the kitchen, and ripped the phone out of the wall in the bedroom. He began to look through the closet, throwing things to the floor, which landed on top of Sakina. He came back to her, took off the blindfold and pulled the gag out.

"Where's the jewelry, bitch?" he demanded. She tried to tell him, but she was bleeding from the mouth so heavily she couldn't talk. He hit her again.

"Where's the jewelry, bitch?"

She indicated the closet with her head.

"In a suitcase on the floor," she managed to say.

There were several suitcases and he couldn't find the right one, which infuriated him further. He beat her again and demanded the jewelry. "You said it was in the closet—"

"In the briefcase, on the floor on the left," she said. He

found the right one, but couldn't find the jewelry, and he kicked her.

"Where?"

"In the zipped compartment, in a zip-top plastic bag," she pleaded.

He found the sealed plastic bag containing bars of gold, gold bracelets, and rings, and he pocketed it all.

"Don't make a motherfuckin' sound, understand, bitch?"

"I swear to God I won't scream."

He hit her. "No! Swear to Satan!" he demanded.

"I swear to Satan I won't scream. Please don't kill me! Please don't hurt my children."

"So, then, where's the money—the cash?"

"There's some in my pocketbook and in my husband's wallet."

He grabbed her by the hair and dragged her across the floor to the empty bedroom.

When he was in a killing mode, his strength increased, and he carried her like she was a weightless rag doll. He ripped off her pajamas and nursing bra and forced her to fellate him, then he raped and sodomized her—ripping and tearing, deriving excitement from her obvious pain and discomfort.

All Sakina could think of was her children—giving this monster from hell what he wanted so he'd leave. She knew he would kill her if she resisted him in the slightest; that was very evident.

Her three-year-old son woke up and began crying for her.

"Shut that kid up!" he said.

"Please let me go to him; I'll keep him quiet; please don't hurt him."

"Swear on Satan you won't scream."

"I swear on Satan," she said. "I swear on Satan I won't scream."

He untied her feet and followed her, naked and handcuffed, torn and bleeding, to the child. She couldn't hold her son because her hands were bound behind her, but she nestled her head up against the three-year-old and tried to lull him back to sleep, soothing him, calming him, speaking softly in his ear as only a mother can.

Inside, she wanted to scream, to yell for help, but she

stayed with her son, comforting him with her mother's warmth. The child, thankfully, fell back asleep. The Stalker dragged her to the empty bedroom, and slapping, kicking, and punching her, turned on by his total domination, he proceeded to rape and sodomize her again, even drinking and swallowing milk from her swollen breasts.

His mind was on everything at once—her body, her sex, the gun, her husband, the car outside . . . the police, the children—

He sensed that something was wrong and suddenly pulled out the .38.

"Please don't shoot me! I do what you say!" pleaded Sakina.

"Shut up, bitch!"

The door burst open and the three-year-old walked in.

"Daddy's not waking up," the toddler told his mother.

The Night Stalker grabbed the child, put him on the bed, and tied him up, putting a pillow over his head to muffle his protestations. Sakina tried to intercede, to go to the child, but he punched her and told her to stay put. He resumed his conquest of her.

When he finished, he let her go to the child; he proceeded to the kitchen and came back eating a honeydew melon he'd found in the refrigerator, spitting seeds on the floor.

He took Sakina by the hair back to the bedroom where her dead husband lay motionless and demanded more jewelry and cash. She repeatedly swore on Satan that there was nothing more of value, that he had already taken it all. He took a gold band ring her brother had given her and a gold chain from her neck. "Where's your wedding ring, bitch? This isn't your wedding ring. Where's the one with the diamond?"

"In the bank—in the vault—"

He slapped her. "You're lying, where is it?"

"No, I'm not lying, I swear on Satan, it's in the bank."

He laid her down on the floor.

"You have any Scotch tape?"

"No . . . no tape."

He left and returned after a few minutes, saying, "I only knocked your husband out," then laughed.

"What, what did you do to him?"

"Nothing. I only knocked him out."

He blindfolded and gagged her.

He had a sense again that something was wrong. He went to the front window and peered through the blinds. A police cruiser was slowly prowling the street. He watched it go to the corner and turn around. He figured someone had heard the gunshot and called the police. As the cruiser slowly returned toward the Abowath house, he prepared for a shootout, putting the .38 near the rear door with an extra clip for the Uzi. He took out the Uzi and went back to the window, ready to shoot holes in the lone cop if he got out of the car. This was a war he was determined to win.

The cruiser soon left the block, but he remained at the window, peering out of it, soaked in sweat, his heart racing, until he was satisfied they weren't laying a trap for him. That, he figured, would be how he would go down—surrounded by the police when he was in someone's home, boxed in. After five minutes, he returned to Sakina and removed the gag. Again he demanded more money and valuables, and again she swore there was nothing more.

"I've given you everything—everything, I swear to Satan! *I swear!*" she said.

So obsessed was he for things of value, he made her go out to the garage with him so he could search the car trunk. There was nothing worth stealing, and he took her back inside, again raped her—in the room where Elyas had been killed. Afterward, she put her head against his stomach and turned it back and forth and implored him not to kill Elyas.

"Please don't kill him, he's such a good man," she said. "Please don't kill him!"

"He's all right," he said, "I just punched him and knocked him out."

For the first time, he felt a pang of guilt, but it was gone very quickly.

Sakina had no idea that the popping sound she'd heard was her husband being killed, and she believed the Stalker—her husband was still alive.

He finally left, carrying the booty in a pillowcase, after handcuffing her to the doorknob on the door to the empty bedroom. Sakina heard his car start up and pull away. She waited a few minutes, then tried to reach her son. She was able only to grab his feet, and holding him tightly with one hand, she pulled him toward her and undid his hands. He untied his own feet.

She told him to go to his father and wake him up. The boy obediently went to Elyas. Sakina heard him say, "Daddy, wake up. Daddy, Daddy, wake up."

She screamed, "Elyas, Elyas, Elyas, wake up! *Elyas!*"

The boy returned to his mother and said, "Mama, Daddy won't wake up; he won't wake up, Mama. Please don't scream; you are scaring me."

"Go again and take anything from his mouth, Aamar. Go, go!"

He obeyed, came back quickly, and said there was nothing in his mouth. Sakina had seen melon bits in the hall, and she thought the killer had pushed melon into Elyas's mouth and somehow taped it closed, but here was the child saying there was nothing.

"Elyas! Wake up! Elyas!" she called to her dead husband.

She thought about her neighbors, Roswitha and Bob Wilson, and she screamed their names, too, imploring them to come and help her.

Sakina tried to talk her small son into going next door to the Wilsons' and getting help, but he was reticent about venturing out into the dark by himself. Sakina told him, promised him, the neighbors would have popsicles and candy and they would give him some—all he wanted.

That got the boy's courage up and he dutifully, though with much trepidation and hesitation, went outside and over to Bob's and Roswitha's house, on a mission for popsicles.

At 3:43 A.M. the Wilsons' doorbell rang. Bob was a light sleeper and woke up immediately. He looked at a red digital clock on the nightstand. Wondering who the hell could be ringing the bell so late, he got out of bed, slipped on pants and a T-shirt, and went downstairs, with Roswitha just behind him. As they reached the front door, the bell rang again. Bob looked out of the peephole and there was no one there, yet the bell rang. Bob opened the door and saw little Aamar, who said, "You have ice cream?" He was in his pajamas, obviously frightened, and there was a robe-belt still tied to his left arm. Bob asked where his parents were. Aamar said, "Daddy won't wake up."

Bob removed the belt from his arm and walked toward the

Abowath house. He noticed the lights were on and thought it odd. As he got within ten feet of the house, he heard Sakina screaming for help. Slowly, he entered the house and quickly found Sakina. A very modest woman, she was terribly embarrassed by her nudity. She asked him for a robe, which he promptly gave her.

She said, "Please, Bob, go to Elyas. He's not answering; help him."

Bob found Elyas as the killer had left him. He felt his forehead; it was cold. Sakina shouted for Bob to make sure Elyas, who was epileptic, hadn't swallowed his tongue. She still had no idea her husband was dead.

Bob could see Elyas's tongue, swollen and purple, protruding from his mouth. He pulled it and tried to clear the breathing passageway, but that was not possible, for his tongue was too swollen. He tried to resuscitate Elyas, to no avail. The two men were friends as well as neighbors, and Bob began to cry, realizing that the Stalker had killed Elyas just feet from where he and his wife slept. He returned to Sakina. Bob told Roswitha to call the police. She ran back to their house, dialed 911, then summoned neighbors Emily and Ron Ledesma. Bob told Sakina that Elyas was dead. She burst into tears and became hysterical. Emily Ledesma entered the bedroom and tried to comfort her.

Sheriff's deputies John Knight and his partner, Kirk Smith, pulled up in front of the Abowath house at 4:07 A.M. Bob Wilson met them on the sidewalk, told them what he had observed. They followed him to Sakina, still handcuffed and crying. The moment she saw officer Knight, who was 6'6" and had broad shoulders, she begged him to help her husband. The deputies noted the handcuffs and the fact that Sakina had been severely beaten. Knight tried to get Sakina to tell him what had happened, but she kept insisting he help Elyas. The two deputies went to the master bedroom, and Officer Knight felt for a pulse in Elyas's neck, noting the small bullet hole just above Elyas's left ear. No pulse. He shined a flashlight in Elyas's eyes; they didn't react. The two deputies went back to Sakina and confirmed that her husband was indeed dead.

"Please," she implored the deputies, "get this off me, please, please!" indicating the handcuffs.

Deputy Knight knew his handcuff key wouldn't work on the cuffs. He tried to slip her hand out of the cuffs, but they were too tight. Normally the deputies would not have disturbed a crime scene in any way, but Sakina kept asking them to free her so she could go to her husband and children. Deputy Knight went to the other side of the door, and as his partner held it still, he kicked the doorknob off.

The cuffs still hanging from her left wrist, Sakina ran to the master bedroom, wailing "Elyas! Elyas! Elyas!" She shook him; he remained still. She looked in the crib to make sure her ten-week-old hadn't been hurt. He was still sleeping soundly. She picked him up and left the house with Emily Ledesma. Officer Knight followed her—anxious to get a description of her assailant on the radio—to the Ledesma house, where she sat down and cried uncontrollably. More police and a Medivac arrived, and Sakina was examined and treated, as she told about the man who had attacked her. She described him as being light-skinned, 6'1" or 6'2", with dirty blond hair, wearing boots. She said his teeth were stained and crooked, and that he was wearing all black.

She told how she'd been awakened by a popping sound and suddenly he was there, beating her, kicking her, demeaning her. "Many times he make me swear on Satan I wouldn't scream."

She described the nature of the sexual assault and the deputies became convinced her attacker had been the dreaded Night Stalker. Sgt. Paul Bear arrived with a pair of bolt cutters and cut the cuffs from Sakina's thin left wrist. Knight used his radio and called in the description Sakina had given him.

At Gil's urging, Pearl Carrillo had returned to the house that evening, but she refused to sleep with any of the windows open. She had wanted to be up when Gil returned home, but she had fallen asleep. He didn't get home until 3 A.M. and had slept very little when he got the call about the Abowath assault. Pearl asked him where he was going at 4:30 in the morning. He told her the Stalker had struck in Diamond Bar, which was only a five-minute drive from where they lived.

"You're kidding," she said, sitting up, suddenly wide awake.

He just looked at her, got dressed, and hugged and kissed her. She said, "Gilbert . . . get him; stop him. He scares me; he's scaring the children. He's scaring everybody—"

It bothered Gil deeply . . . the fear and terror the Stalker was causing on his beat, in his own home, and as he sped over to Diamond Bar, he silently cursed the killer and prayed for help.

Carrillo arrived at the Abowath house. It was a little after 5 A.M. and still dark, though a hot, fiery dawn was rapidly swelling in the east.

Dep. Knight brought Carrillo up to date on the facts. Sakina had been taken to the hospital. The detective decided to wait for Salerno before he entered the crime scene, though he looked in the back yard, hoping there were shoeprints. Using a flashlight, he very carefully walked to the rear of the Abowath residence. He didn't notice any prints outside, but he spotted one on the kitchen floor, just inside the sliding screen door. It wasn't the Avia, but it was as large as the Avia. He thought, *It's him!* He noted the screen door had been bent near the lock, then made his way to the front of the house. *He's gotten himself another pair of shoes,* he thought.

Homicide sheriff's deputies Mike Robinson and Mike Bumcrot were up for the next murder, and they arrived at 5:20. Carrillo told them what he'd seen and said to wait for the criminalists and Salerno before they entered the crime scene.

By 5:40, Giselle La Vigne, Jerry Burke, and Ralph Salazar were there, and as soon as Frank pulled up, they entered together. The press had gotten wind of the assault, and news trucks and reporters with cameras, lights, sound bites, and questions lined the crime perimeter.

The detectives noted the ransacking, the disabled phone, honeydew seeds on the floor, and the bullet hole in Elyas's head, exactly where Chainarong Khovananth had been shot. Burke found a spent .25 shell on the floor and bagged it. He and Salazar took pictures of the print, then lifted it.

As the criminalists worked, Salerno, Carrillo, Bumcrot, and Robinson scrutinized the crime scene, but they didn't find anything more that might be of help. Bob Wilson told them how three-year-old Aamar had rung his bell and asked for ice cream.

At 6:10, they got a call from the San Bernardino Police. They had a suspect who looked exactly like the Stalker. He'd been picked up as he was leaving a porno shop. Salerno and Carrillo decided to take a ride over to San Bernardino and take a look at their suspect, primarily because he was seen exiting a porno shop.

Porn, they felt, was something the Stalker would most definitely be into. They jumped into Salerno's car and drove to the San Bernardino County Jail.

The suspect looked exactly like the composite, but he was neat and clean, and had good teeth, the wrong size feet, and no Avias. When Carrillo and Salerno got back to Diamond Bar, police brass were there, as well as more news trucks with their long telescopic poles and satellite dishes. When the reporters saw Salerno and Carrillo, they hurried over, hoping for a quote, but both detectives remained tight-lipped.

Giselle walked over to them with a long face. The brass, she complained, were traipsing in and out of the house, seriously contaminating the crime scene, and she pointed to honeydew seeds which had been tracked onto the front lawn.

"If you want me to do my job, you're going to have to do yours," she said.

The two detectives went inside and insisted everyone but the criminalists leave, which caused some anger, hurt egos, and resentment from the higher-ups, but neither Salerno nor Carrillo cared what they thought, felt, or said.

Salerno said, "No one, and I mean *no one*, goes in there but our tech people."

A representative from the medical examiner's office arrived and removed the body to the morgue for autopsy. Charles Vander Wende dusted the screen door for prints but found only fabric marks, which indicated the attacker had worn gloves.

Salerno and Carrillo learned Sheriff Block was calling a press conference for 12 noon to officially announce there was a serial killer loose in Los Angeles County. The detectives were ordered not to talk to the press on their own.

When Gil arrived back at his place, Pearl and the girls were packing suitcases and paper bags. She said she and the kids were just too frightened to stay home alone anymore, that J. R. had taken to sleeping with a bat he was so scared. Gil said he understood; that in truth he too would feel better knowing she and the kids were at her parents' place.

Sadly, he helped put what Pearl had packed in the car, hugged and kissed her and his daughters Rene and Tiffany, told them he loved them, promised the Stalker would be caught soon and they'd be able to come back home.

As Gil watched his wife's car pull away, his children waving, he could feel a warm lump lodge in his throat and a hot simmering anger rise inside him. He hated the Stalker for driving his wife and children from their home.

At his press conference, Sheriff Block told the press a shaggy-haired man with bad teeth had been linked to fourteen attacks involving rape, murder, and robbery in Los Angeles County. He assured the public everything humanly possible and more was being done to catch the killer.

In the morning, all the newspapers' front-page headlines screamed the Stalker's most recent attack and reported the sheriff's news conference. As the public read the details of the Abowath assault, they were even more horrified and shocked: Diamond Bar was farther from Los Angeles than any of his other assaults had been.

Was there anywhere he wouldn't strike?

That morning, the task force was called together. This case now had top priority.

Salerno laid out the similarities between the Diamond Bar assault and the killer's previous crimes: phone disabling, ransacking, same size shoeprint, a small-caliber gun, rear entry, sodomy, and the killer's phrases—"Don't look at me, bitch," "Swear on Satan."

Hundreds of tips were pouring into the sheriff's office daily, and each had to be followed up on and indexed so that all the detectives had immediate access to the information. Salerno ordered the most recent composite of the killer's picture sent to 5000 dentists with a copy of his dental X ray. The killer's teeth needed attention and he knew he was too hot to return to Dr. Leung's office.

After the meeting, Salerno and Carrillo drove to the morgue and with detectives Robinson and Buncrot, attended Elyas's autopsy. It was done at 11:30 A.M. by senior deputy medical examiner Dr. Joseph Cogan, the coroner who had done the autopsy on Chainarong Khovananth.

Dr. Cogan noted that the cause of death was a bullet wound to the head. The gun, he said, was approximately an inch from the deceased when fired, as indicated by the stippling (gun powder burns) around the wound. The bullet, when removed, was handed over to Det. Bumcrot, who bagged it for evidence. Dr. Cogan noted it was steel jacketed and had bounced off the right side of Elyas's skull and back into the brain, flattened out somewhat, coming to a stop in the right posterior cerebral hemisphere. Death, he said, had to have come very rapidly.

Gil and Frank were sure someone somewhere knew the Stalker's identity and it would be just a matter of time before they had a name, an address, a direction. The rewards were in excess of $80,000, the most ever offered for a serial killer. The Stalker had an incredible run of luck. Knowing he was a Satan worshiper, they had each taken to silently praying for the forces of good to intercede and stop this bloodthirsty soldier of Satan.

Carrillo and Salerno visited Sakina at her brother's home. She was a modest, shy woman, and it was very difficult for her to tell the detectives what had been done to her. Gil and Frank were professionals, but listening to this little woman describe what had happened to her in her own home profoundly disturbed them; she could have been either one's daughter. Sakina became so upset that they had to cut the interview short. They thanked her for her cooperation, gave her their sincere condolences, and silently drove back to the office.

The *Los Angeles Times* decided to do a cover story on Frank. He was, they felt, a colorful, larger-than-life character who intimately knew the inside story. It had been widely reported that he'd headed the Hillside Strangler investigation. *Times* staff reporter Roxane Arnold contacted the sheriff's office and asked if he'd do an interview. Sheriff Block okayed the story, hoping it might assuage the public's fears. Salerno had reservations about doing it: he knew the Stalker would read it, and he didn't want to do anything that might compromise the investigation—or his own safety. On August 14, the piece appeared on the front page under the headline, "Homicide Cop is Perfect Man for the Job."

It described Salerno as a good cop who worked a case tirelessly. Salerno explained how all information was being cross-indexed and shared between different police jurisdictions. He also described how different this serial killer was. " 'This is a complex individual as far as trying to get a handle on [his] psychological profile. . . . Investigators are running out of shoe leather. There's a lot of good old-fashioned police work where people are going out knocking on doors and talking to people. We'll get him soon . . .' "

SIXTEEN

The Stalker read with great interest the *Times* article on Frank Salerno. He was pleased someone of Salerno's stature was after him; it made him feel important and fanned his warped ego. He soon, however, began thinking it was time to make himself scarce in Los Angeles County for a while.

He was still confident he walked with Satan, but the public outcry in Southern California had reached a fevered pitch; and he sensed it, felt it. People around the Greyhound Bus Terminal were looking at him too long and too hard, and asking too many questions. Like Jesse Perez.

Perez was a sixty-two-year-old small-time thief, hustler, convicted murderer (he'd killed a man with a knife in a bar fight in Texas), and gypsy cab driver, with bad teeth and eggplant-colored circles under baggy eyes.

He decided the man he knew as "Rick" was the Night Stalker. The description of him—clothes, hair, and especially the teeth—too closely resembled Rick for Perez not to contact the police and claim the reward. He decided he would ask his daughter, who worked for the Los Angeles marshall's office, to contact the sheriff's task force for him.

But the Stalker left Los Angeles and drove north in a stolen Mercedes Benz.

In San Francisco, the Stalker knew, it would be easier to get in and out of people's homes; they would not be so cautious and vigilant about security as everyone in L.A. had become. The thought of stopping never entered his mind. There were only two ways he would stop: he'd either die or be incarcerated.

In the late afternoon, he checked into room 315 of the Bristol Hotel on Mason Street. The Bristol was a four-story transient hotel in the heart of San Francisco's Tenderloin District, perfect for his purposes. There were porno shops, cheap hotels, seedy bars, and pool halls, and the streets were peopled with crackheads, junkies, alcoholics, and broken-down, toothless prostitutes with black eyes. It was the San Franciscan counterpart to the Los Angeles downtown area.

The Stalker left the hotel and entered a porno shop on Mason that showed XXX-rated movies in little booths at four minutes for a quarter, twenty-four hours a day. When he was finished there, he walked over to Mission Street to cop some pot, then smoked a joint, drove to Chinatown, parked, and shadowed a small Asian woman, sixty-five to seventy years old, for a block. When she entered a two-story building, he followed her into the vestibule. She was startled by his sudden appearance, but before she could even say a word, he knocked her to the ground, kicking and pummeling her until she was a bloody mess.

It was over in seconds.

He left her in the hall, not sure if she was alive or dead. No one had seen anything. As he walked away from what he'd just done, he felt powerful, whole, and in charge, complete; he knew his brutality would please Satan, and he was always eager to do that.

That night he broke into a house in the scenic Marina District. No one was home. He stole some jewelry, a VCR, and a jewelry box, and went back to the Bristol Hotel.

Peter Pan was sixty-six, his wife, Barbara, sixty-two. They lived on Eucalyptus, in the Lakeside District, near Lake Merced. Peter was a smiling, upbeat, gregarious man who'd worked as an accountant for the San Francisco General Hospital for sixteen years. Barbara Pan was a bank teller.

Peter had been born in Taiwan, had attended Wharton Business School in Philadelphia, had returned to Taiwan, and had worked for a railroad company. He'd opened a successful import-export business in Hong Kong in 1961.

The Pans had immigrated from Hong Kong to Northern California in 1969. They had two sons and three grandchildren. Mr. Pan was very proud to be an American citizen and often said how great it was in America, where the people had true freedom.

At 2 A.M. on August 18, fate brought the Stalker to the Pan home, a two-story yellow stucco house on a quiet street. He randomly parked the stolen Mercedes on the block, walked to the Pan residence, and stood there, making certain this was the right place; then, quickly, as silent as the coming of night, he walked to the side of the house, took the screen from an open window, and went in.

Upstairs, he found the Pans sleeping soundly. He walked up to Peter, put the .25 to his right temple, and pulled the trigger, killing him instantly. He then slapped and terrorized Barbara, sexually assaulting her, but she resisted him. He shot her in the head for not being compliant enough.

He ransacked the house, and feeling omnipotent, defiant, and daring, wrote in lipstick on the wall of the Pan bedroom, "Jack the Knife," and drew a pentagram.

He put Peter and Barbara's rings, a VCR, and Peter's watch and cufflinks in a pillowcase and left. Sexually keyed up by the violence, he drove to the Tenderloin and picked up a skinny prostitute on Mission with big, sad eyes and a broken nose. He took her back to his room at the Bristol, paid her ten dollars, and had sex with her feet. When he asked her if she liked it, she said she liked it fine as long as he paid her. After she left, he slept.

At 10:30 that morning, Peter and Barbara Pan's thirty-year-old son, David, went to his parents' home and found his father dead, his mother near death, and the house ransacked. With trembling hands, choking with grief, he called the police.

Carrillo and Salerno heard about the Pan assault in San Francisco from a Glendale detective who had learned of it over a CB channel as he'd driven to work that morning. Salerno called San Francisco and spoke to homicide detective

Carl Klotz. He told Frank about the burglary-type entry, the bullet to the head, a sexual assault, a .25-caliber automatic being used, the pentagram on the wall, and the words "Jack the Knife." Thinking it might be a copycat killer, Salerno asked, "Is there a red circle around the primer on the shell casing?"

The answer was yes.

They now knew their man was in San Francisco. Carrillo contacted Paul Tippin and Leroy Orozco at the LAPD task force and invited them to join them on a late-afternoon flight north. As the detectives were walking to their seats, Frank noticed crime reporter Laurel Erickson, who worked for KNBC news, taking a seat in the rear of the plane. She was with her cameraman; they both were busy eating hamburgers and she didn't notice the detectives. The plane took off and Gil, Frank, Leroy, and Paul discussed the ramifications of the Stalker's going to San Francisco. Salerno had always said they'd know immediately if he changed location because of the frequency and the vicious nature of his attacks.

The flight ended quickly, and as they disembarked, Laurel Erickson spotted them, and hurried over when she saw the lead investigators in the Stalker case. She believed it confirmed that the Stalker had traveled north. She begged for an interview, but Salerno said simply, "No comment." They went to police headquarters, where they were briefed by the San Francisco Homicide people, and plans were made for the L.A. detectives to see the crime scene early the next morning. They checked into a Holiday Inn and the four exhausted men were soon asleep.

In the morning the Pan crime scene was swarming with press. The detectives shouldered their way through a phalanx of pushy reporters, perhaps the most aggressive of whom was Laurel Erickson.

The L.A. homicide men studied the source of entry, the ransacking, and the pentagram on the wall. They found the Stalker's "Jack the Knife" very interesting. It seemed like a challenge to the police—as if the Stalker was thumbing his nose at them, daring them, laying down a Satanic gauntlet. Carrillo answered a loud knock on the door to find Erickson, insisting that Salerno come out and talk to her. Salerno refused politely and closed the door in her face.

Back at police headquarters, they sat down with the leaders of the San Francisco Stalker task force, Carl Klotz, and Frank Falzon, both excellent detectives. Opening with everything they had, the L.A. detectives laid out their case, comparing the similarities in the San Francisco assault with theirs.

Promises to share information were made and the four L.A. detectives returned home to resume the hunt.

Word of exactly what the L.A. authorities had on the Stalker quickly passed up the chain of command in San Francisco to Mayor Dianne Feinstein (now Senator Feinstein). She ordered a news conference at City Hall, boldly took the podium, and, tight-lipped and stern-faced, told the press about the evidence they had linking the Night Stalker to San Francisco, focusing on the Avia sneakers and ballistics. She assured the public that everything possible was being done to capture him and described the large task force which she had ordered put together. She added $10,000 to the reward money being offered, saying, "Somewhere in the Bay Area, someone is renting a room, an apartment, or a home to this vicious killer. If you know who he is or have seen him, if you know anything, please contact the task force. We'll have him, and we'll have him soon."

Salerno and Carrillo saw Feinstein's press conference on a television in a ground-floor office and became livid. By divulging the particulars of their evidence, the mayor was giving the Stalker the opportunity to get rid of the evidence—the shoes, the .25 automatic, and other guns. Dianne Feinstein was shooting holes in their case. They went upstairs to their desks speechless with anger. Leroy Orozco called and said they'd already complained about Feinstein to their captain, who'd gone to Police Chief Darryl Gates.

Capt. Grimm was at Flora's, and Carrillo and Salerno joined him, telling him about the mayor's comments and ordering drinks. The captain had missed the news conference and became as outraged as the detectives. He left to make phone calls, returning in thirty minutes to tell them the sheriff wanted to meet with them and hold a press conference.

At 8 o'clock Carrillo and Salerno were in the sheriff's office. Block was a balding, red-faced man, 5'11", with broad shoulders and a no-nonsense way about him. He had been a career deputy and in office three years. He loved his work and planned to stay in office for many more years, which would never happen if the Night Stalker wasn't caught soon. The sheriff listened to Salerno and Carrillo explain why they felt Mayor Feinstein's comments had undermined their case. The sheriff shared their outrage at what the San Francisco mayor had done. At the 9 o'clock press conference he slammed public officials for making their case public, saying, "This places our community in jeopardy . . . and it impedes our ability to go forward with the investigation."

Salerno and Carrillo appreciated Block's support and were somewhat placated by his public position; however, personally, they'd never forgive Feinstein for her press conference.

The population of San Francisco was suddenly just as frightened and in an uproar as the residents of Los Angeles. The monster had come there to satiate his bloodlust, his sadistic sexuality, and nothing could stop him. It proved he could go anywhere he wished. The sales of guns, guard dogs, and alarms soared, as they had in L.A.

The Stalker had also seen Feinstein's news conference. He hadn't realized he'd been leaving distinct shoeprints or that his .25 had been so quickly connected to the L.A. murders.

At 8 P.M. on the day of Feinstein's public revelations, as Sheriff Block prepared for his news conference, the Stalker walked onto the Golden Gate Bridge and casually made his way to its middle. The August sun was setting and laid a sheet of fiery oranges and hot reds over the beautiful, famous bay of San Francisco. At the middle of the bridge, he dropped the size 11 1/2 Avia sneakers into the water. The currents were swift and strong, he knew, and the sneakers were soon carried to obscurity.

In the days following the Pan attack, the Stalker slept late, constantly smoked pot, listened to heavy metal music, watched porno movies, and stayed away from Los Angeles. In the afternoons, he'd play outdoor dice with a bunch of guys who always had a game going on Mission Street, for the most part total strangers.

On the twenty-fifth he decided to go back to L.A. San Francisco, he thought, was too small, too hot, and he was thinking that people he knew had become suspicious of him. He jumped into the stolen Mercedes and boldly returned to Los Angeles.

SEVENTEEN

Back in L.A., the Stalker stayed away from the downtown area. With the rewards as high as they'd become and the uproar he'd caused, he knew he had to be very careful, even with Lucifer's protection.

He went to Chinatown and rented a room where he read all the L.A. newspaper accounts of his crimes. He was shocked, though pleased, by so much press; it made him feel strong and invincible. In Chinatown, the streets were crowded, and he moved about without being noticed.

He needed money, but he did not go back to the fence's house. He had to be very careful with him from now on, and he started thinking about killing the fence. He knew too much and was too great a liability for the Stalker to let him live.

As he moved about Chinatown, he fantasized about committing violence on the people he passed. He imagined them tied up and begging for mercy as he cut them and had sex with them. He thought more and more about buying a secluded house and carrying out his sadistic fantasies.

On Sunday night, he dumped the Mercedes and stole a 1976 orange Toyota station wagon parked in front of a Chinatown restaurant and hit the freeway, the lust for blood propelling him forward. The car belonged to Bill Gregory, a fifty-six-year-old carpenter who was a member of the Christian Vineyard Fellowship Church. There was a stack of pamphlets for the church on the back seat, as well as two Christian Bibles.

Mission Viejo, in Orange County, seventy-six miles south of Los Angeles, was the farthest away from the downtown area he had ever hunted. It was another fine Southern California city that seemed too good to be true, full of people who worked hard, raised families, and went to church every Sunday.

He reached Mission Viejo at 1 A.M. Earlier, he had pulled off the freeway and cruised Anaheim, Garden Grove, and Santa Ana, but he'd been unable to find a situation he felt comfortable with.

Everywhere people were more vigilant; he could see it clearly. There were bars and bright lights and suspicious eyes where before there had been none.

Fate now stepped in and dealt a crippling blow to the Stalker's incredible run of luck: a thirteen-year-old boy was fixing his motor scooter on a warm summer night when he looked up and saw the orange Toyota with its lights off slowly drive by. James Romero III had straight blond hair and looked like Dennis the Menace. There was something about the driver, the way he looked around—a malevolence—that alerted James to danger. He watched the car carefully but did not write down its license plate number, though he thought about it.

When the killer reached Chrisanta Drive, he parked and walked back along it. He had not seen the boy.

The Stalker moved up the street at a pace calculated not to draw attention to himself, keeping, as always, in the shadows. He had nothing with him tonight but a gun—the .25 automatic. Anything that could tie him to the Stalker assaults he'd left behind. Even if he went down fighting and was killed, he didn't want to be linked publicly to the crimes. Somewhere there were people who loved and cared for him deeply, and he didn't want them to know. His family was the only thing that made him sorry for what he'd become; but as long as they never found out, it wouldn't matter, and so tonight he had only the one gun; no handcuffs, no thumbcuffs, no knives, no police scanner. They were all hidden away—safe from Carrillo and Salerno. However, he had on the same shoes he'd worn during the Abowath and Petersen attacks.

Tonight, he chose the home of twenty-nine-year-old Bill Carns, who lived with his twenty-seven-year-old fiancée, Carole Smith. Bill was tall, thin, and muscular, and he wore a mustache. His fiancée had blond hair and was attractive, with blue eyes and an athletic figure.

Earlier that evening they had talked about the Stalker on the way home from the movies—and they'd discussed getting bars, and maybe even a gun.

Bill was a computer whiz who worked for the Burroughs Corporation. He had been transferred from their Dakota branch in 1983 and had settled in Mission Viejo, only a mile away from his job. He was very much in love with Carole.

Their house was beige with a wood-shingle slanted roof and two large bay windows. There were pine and maple trees growing in the front yard, which again created the shadows the Stalker embraced like a lover. There was a thirteen-foot black tar driveway to the garage on the right and a little lawn on the left, the front door was in the center of the house. He first tried the front door and windows; they were locked. He walked to the back of the house and managed to get into a rear window after removing the screen. As always, he got used to the house, the dark, then moved forward with a small penlight.

As he reached the master bedroom, he saw the sleeping figures of Bill Carns and his fiancée and he cocked the automatic. That sound entered Bill's sleep, perhaps because they had been talking about the Stalker earlier—

He opened his eyes, felt Carole next to him, saw the light of the flashlight, and as fast as he could move, started out of bed, knowing somewhere in his mind what that light meant. The Stalker pulled the trigger and shot Bill in the head, knocking him back down as if he'd been struck by a bat. He moved closer and shot Bill twice more, both times in the head. He saw movement under the blanket, pulled it back, and revealed Bill's terrified fiancée.

"You know who I am?" the Stalker asked, laughing.

"No, who are you?"

"I'm the Night Stalker!"

"Oh, God, nooo!" she wailed.

"Don't say 'God,' say 'Satan.' Say you love Satan!" he said, and slapped her so hard her ears rang.

"I love Satan!" she said.

He punched her in the face. "Louder!" he demanded.

"I love Satan!" she said, terrified, trembling, and beginning to cry. "Please don't kill me! Please, please!"

His answer was to pull her from the bed, throw her on the floor, and hog-tie her with ties he found in Bill's closet, while demanding jewelry and money—threatening her, slapping, and kicking her—as blood poured from the bullet wounds in Bill Carns's head.

She was scared, and that gave him the feeling of power over life that his psychosis so craved.

He ransacked the bedroom with quick, knowing moves. By now it seemed he knew instinctively where to look, and he pulled out drawers, dumped their contents on the floor, stuck his gloved hands anywhere there might be valuables. He found some jewelry and watches, which he took. He made her swear on Satan that he'd gotten all there was. She complied. He dragged her to another bedroom to rape and sodomize her.

When he was finished, he kissed her somewhat tenderly, shocking her further. He tied her up again and demanded cash. She told him there was some hidden in the bedroom. He went to find it. She heard him demand more jewelry from Bill, who was unconscious and bleeding, then laugh in a high-pitched cackle. He couldn't find the cash and angrily returned to the terrified woman.

"You're lying, bitch. I'm going to kill you—"

"I'm not, it's there! I'll show you!"

"Swear on Satan!"

"I swear on Satan!"

He untied her and she showed him where $400 in cash was hidden, which he promptly pocketed.

"There any more?"

"No, that's all; I swear on Satan."

"You know, this is all that saved you. This is all your life is worth. I would have killed you if it weren't for this money." He dragged her to the bathroom and hog-tied her hands and feet.

"Tell them the Night Stalker was here."

"I will."

"Say you love Satan!" he demanded.

"I love Satan," she said. He laughed and was gone. In the sudden silence she prayed.

He exited the house by the front door, calmly walked back to the stolen car, started the engine, and pulled away.

Romero looked up and saw the car again and "the weird-looking guy in black." This time he made sure he got the plate number. After he memorized only three of its digits, he went into the house he shared with his parents and wrote them down.

The Stalker got back on the freeway and sped toward downtown Los Angeles. Normally, while he drove, he kept his gloves on, but when he was halfway to L.A., he took them off. It was very hot, and his hands were sweating. He'd wipe the car down well before he left it. He got to the Wilshire area in mid–Los Angeles and parked the car in a small shopping center lot at Sixth Street and Alexandria Avenue.

Using the cloth gloves, he carefully cleaned the prints, making sure to get the steering wheel, the shift, and the rearview mirror, which he'd adjusted earlier.

But he missed one fingerprint on the outside of the rearview mirror. He did not notice the two Bibles on the back seat.

He took a bus back to Chinatown, rented a room, and went to sleep, totally unaware of James Romero III or the fingerprint.

When Carole Smith was sure he was gone, she untied herself and tried to bring Bill back to consciousness, but couldn't. The phone had been disabled, and she ran next door and asked a neighbor to summon help. Quickly, a Medivac team arrived and took Bill and Carole to the Mission Community Hospital. She was treated for bruises and given a rape examination, which proved positive. Bill went into surgery. Only two of the bullets could be extracted from his brain. The third was in too vital a place for it to be removed witout causing even more damage.

When word of the Carns attack reached James Romero, he immediately told his mom and dad about the strange-looking guy in the orange Toyota. They called the Orange County sheriff's office. When James described the man he saw and when he'd seen the car pass, the Orange County police were certain he'd seen the man who had attacked Bill Carns and

Carole Smith: the Stalker. Orange County homicide detective Jim Sidebothem called Salerno and Carrillo and they drove to Mission Viejo to view the crime scene. Everyone half-suspected it really had been the Stalker, for he'd identified himself to Carole Smith and the language had been the same. When Carrillo and Salerno saw the ransacking, phone disabling, and the shell casing of the .25 auto, and heard the nature of the sexual assault, they were dead certain their man had come back to L.A.

Jesse Perez's daughter contacted the sheriff's task force on August 27. Perez had waited a week before he'd told her, and she had first contacted a lawyer; she didn't want her father getting into any kind of trouble. She reached Homicide detective Louie Danoff and told him that her father knew who the Night Stalker was, and wanted to tell the authorities. She said her father was acquainted with him from the bus terminal, and that he had bad teeth, talked about Satan, and was a professional burglar. His name was Rick, and he was from Texas. Her father was certain he was the Night Stalker.

Perez's daughter explained further to Det. Danoff that her father was frightened and wanted protection. Danoff assured her the sheriff's office would guarantee her father's safety unequivocally and set up a meeting.

When this tip came in, the task force was in the middle of a meeting. Det. Danoff brought it to Salerno's attention, saying it was "hot." Salerno dispatched Det. Ike Aguilar and his partner, Mike Griggs, to meet with Jesse Perez's daughter in her East L.A. home. As they were interviewing her, Jesse came home. He was, at first, upset she had let the police come to the house, but Griggs and Aguilar calmed him down.

Sweating, his eyes moving about like nervous fish in a glass bowl, Perez told the sheriff's detectives—after he was repeatedly assured of his safety—about a guy named Rick. He didn't know his last name, but was sure he was the Stalker. He told them he had first met Rick through his brother and saw him a lot at the bus terminal. He had once bought a gun, a .22 automatic, from Rick.

Aguilar and Griggs became excited. They asked where the

gun was now, and Perez said he'd given it to a female friend, Esperanza Gonzales, in Tijuana for protection.

Rick, he said, was an obsessed burglar who had bad teeth like the guy in the paper. He came from somewhere in El Paso. He had told Perez he had killed an Asian couple in Monterey Park, and Perez had later read about it in the papers. Rick had been arrested the previous year for stealing a car, which he had crashed into the back of the bus terminal after being chased from the freeway by five LAPD squad cars with sirens blaring and red lights spinning. "You find that arrest, you'll find the guy," Perez guaranteed. The detectives agreed it was the lead that would give them Rick's full name. They pressed Perez about the date of the arrest, and he said it was sometime in early December of 1984. If Rick had an arrest record, they'd have their man in a flash.

They took Perez back to the sheriff's office and he repeated for Carrillo and Salerno what he'd told Aguilar and Griggs. After prompting, he added that Rick often hung out around the bus terminal.

"He's a loner and always talkin' 'bout how great Satan is," Perez said. "I don't believe in none of that shit, but he for sure and for real does. He likes that heavy metal music. Always has a Walkman." Gil showed Perez the Somkid Khovananth composite and he said it looked like Rick, " 'Cept his hair ain't so curly, you know."

Salerno asked Perez if he knew where all the things the Stalker had stolen were. Perez wanted to know, if he told them, would he get the reward. The detectives assured him sincerely that they'd make sure he got it.

With renewed vigor, Perez, his eyes always moving nervously, told them about a fence named Felipe Solano, who lived near Dodger Stadium and had a lot of stuff in a garage by his house. "He's got all kinds of shit in there—televisions, radios, VCRs, jewelry . . . a ton of shit, man, all the way up to the fucking ceiling . . . he's Rick's fence."

Salerno wanted the gun Perez said Rick had sold him. If it was one of the murder weapons, it would seal their case against this Rick. However, before he had Perez taken to Tijuana, he had him show them where Solano lived. It was in a two-story pink house with a garage on a quiet street lined with modest one-family houses.

Frank put Solano's house under surveillance, using an LASD crime impact team trained in surveillance and combat situations. He also had them stake out a bar in MacArthur Park, where Perez said Solano hung out. Carrillo reminded the LAPD people not to take any chances if Rick showed up, to shoot first, then ask questions. They also staked out the bus terminal.

The police arranged for a female snitch named Sandra Hotchkiss to try to set Solano up by having him buy stolen property, which would give the detectives probable cause to search his home.

Hotchkiss had a long list of burglary arrests, was a junkie, sometime prostitute. She approached Solano in a downtown pool hall, but he wasn't interested in buying the jewelry Hotchkiss was given to use as bait.

They decided to take Hotchkiss to Solano's house and have her try to sell him a gold rope chain. She didn't want to do that, because Solano knew she didn't know where he lived and he'd realize he was being set up, but the sheriff's detectives insisted. Sandra finally agreed. As she was making her way up the alley to his house, Solano pulled up, parked, and started toward his door. When he saw her, he was shocked, and said, "Are you a policewoman?" Before she could answer, the impact team ran up the alley, grabbed Solano, threw him to the floor and pummeled him.

He agreed to let the detectives into his house, where they discovered a bonanza of evidence—almost everything that had been taken in the Stalker robberies. Salerno ordered it brought to the sheriff's office. When they questioned Solano about Rick, he swore up and down he didn't know his last name, address, or phone number. He said Rick moved around a lot, stayed in different hotels, and would call him if he had something to sell.

Carrillo called LAPD again and asked them to find the December 1984 arrest form for a stolen car bust that had been made at the back of the bus terminal, in which a few LAPD black-and-whites had been involved. The suspect's name, he said, was Rick, or maybe Richard or Ricardo. LAPD finally called back and said they couldn't find any arrest like what Carrillo described. Salerno called them and asked them to look harder.

* * *

Every cop in Southern California was looking for the orange Toyota used in the Carns attack, knowing the car might very well crack the case.

A break came when a friend of the car's owner called Homicide and reported that the car they were looking for sounded like one stolen from Chinatown. He gave a deputy the full number of the plate, and it matched the partial number James Romero had written down. The sheriff's office decided to release the full number to the press, and on the morning of August 28, the car was located in a shopping center in the Wilshire District of L.A. County, exactly where the killer had left it. They staked it out all day and night, hoping the Stalker would return, but he didn't. It was taken on a flatbed truck to the LAPD Rampart Station and then to the Orange County sheriff's garage lab in Santa Ana, where technicians went over it. There seemed to be no discernible prints anywhere.

But when they were just about ready to give up, a female technician found a clear print on the outside of the rearview mirror and enhanced it with black powder. The print was removed with lifting tape.

Back in San Francisco, the Stalker task force made a very clever decisive move: they published pictures and descriptions of the jewelry stolen from the Pan residence. They figured someone somewhere was buying it, and with the high rewards being offered for the killer's identification, this might be the way to nail the Stalker.

Her name was Donna Meyers. She was 5'6", overweight, and unkempt, with shaggy, ill-cut, dirty brown hair.

Donna had a friend named Rick from El Paso, Texas. She knew he did burglaries for a living and had on several occasions asked her to hold jewelry for him. The last time had been just a couple of weeks ago. He had given her a few pieces, a gold bracelet and some rings. The gold bracelet was too small for her wrist, and she had given it to her daughter,

Deleen, who was married to Earl Gregg. Donna also gave one of the rings to her granddaughter, Deleen's kid, Ophelia. She gave another ring to her son, Lloyd Vorack, Jr. The Greggs were also acquainted with the man who'd given Donna Meyers the jewelry.

They had become suspicious of him soon after Peter Pan was killed. He was tall and lanky, like the Stalker, always wore black, had bad teeth, and was constantly talking about the many virtues of Lucifer.

Earl Gregg was the first to recognize the bracelet in the papers as the one his mother-in-law had given Deleen, and he found the driver's license number on it that was published in the papers. He showed the newspaper to Deleen and they decided to contact the authorities. Gregg called the task force and was put in touch with Det. Carl Klotz. He told Klotz about a satanic burglar friend named Rick who fit the Stalker's description. "And he looks like the drawing in the newspapers; just like him, 'cept his hair isn't as curly and his chin is different, you know," Gregg said.

Klotz treated the call from Gregg seriously; a satanic burglar sounded right. He and his partner, Frank Falzon, drove to Lompoc to interview the Greggs. Falzon was an outgoing, gregarious man, 5'9", dark-haired, heavy-set, with a robust laugh. Klotz had thinning gray hair, was nearly six feet tall, and wore gold-framed glasses. They were a good team.

Klotz and Falzon were greeted at the front door by Earl and Deleen. She had dirty blond hair, and looked like she needed sleep. Earl had a long, narrow face with sagging cheeks, lifeless eyes and buck teeth; they each looked like they could use a bath.

Earl told the two detectives that he met Rick—he didn't know his last name—through his mother-in-law, Donna Meyers, who had met him through a friend of hers named Rodriguez. Rick was from El Paso and was "always robbing places. He's a professional thief," Gregg said, "and he's real good." Gregg told the detectives Rick was always talking about Satan being the "supreme being." Rick was obsessed with heavy metal music and was constantly listening to it. The San Francisco detectives knew about the AC/DC cap left at the Okazaki/Hernandez residence. This Rick sounded better and better. They asked about Rick's teeth and Gregg told them they were stained and chipped. He said Rick had been a coke fiend and had needle marks on both arms, but he now just smoked a lot of pot and drank. When asked if he ever saw Rick with a gun, Gregg said he sure had—a silver .25 automatic which he'd tried to sell to Gregg for $150, "much more than it was worth." Gregg didn't know where Rick lived now. He said he moved around a lot, sometimes staying in cheap hotels in the Tenderloin District.

Klotz and Falzon drove to Donna Meyer's house. They showed their IDs and asked her to answer some questions about Rick. Donna was polite and invited the detectives in. They were direct and to the point, wanting to know where Donna had gotten the jewelry she had given her daughter.

She told the two San Francisco detectives about Rick, who was a friend of her friend Armando Rodriguez. She said she had lived with Rodriguez in 1979 in Richmond, California. They had traveled to El Paso together that year and she had met Rick for the first time. When they'd returned to Richmond, Rick had begun visiting Armando and started living at the house for days, then weeks at a time. When Donna moved to San Pablo, she didn't see that much of Rick. She knew he was a burglar, but she was quite surprised that he was suspected of being the Stalker. She had never seen him get violent. She had seen him with gardening gloves. Donna told the detectives Rick had come around on August 16 and asked her to hold an octagonal jewelry box which he'd retrieved on August 23, when he came over with Armando. He had given her the jewelry she had given her daughter then, as well as the jewelry box, which she now handed over to the detectives.

Once, she told them, he'd given her $500 for her to hold for him. If anything happened to him, she was to give the money to his sister, whose phone number he gave her. But that had never happened. He'd returned and retrieved the money. She said she hadn't kept the sister's number.

The detectives wanted Rick's last name. They had a place— El Paso; now, all they needed was a last name and they'd have broken the biggest murder case in California's history. Rick fit the profile of the killer, and his having the stolen jewelry, and having shown Gregg a .25 seemed to sew it together. They asked Donna to call Armando for Rick's last name, but Armando told her he didn't know it. The detectives told

Donna not to leave town. Using the phone number they'd gotten from Donna, they found Rodriguez's address and drove to his home.

Armando was tall and thin, with dark hair. He hated cops and refused to talk to Klotz and Falzon. They knew Armando was very likely the key to the case, so they cuffed him and took him to police headquarters, threatening to charge him as an accessory to murder. He was there, they pointed out, when Rick picked up the jewelry from Donna Meyers. That made him an accessory after the fact in the Pan killing. At first, Armando wouldn't talk at all. They put him in a cell and let him sweat. He soon decided to talk. He wanted nothing to do with the things the Night Stalker had done.

He admitted he knew Rick, but "not too well at all." His last name was Ramirez; that's all he knew.

The detectives put the names Rick, Richard, and Ricardo Ramirez into their computers, and there were thousands of them on file.

Task force detectives flooded the Tenderloin District, asking questions, showing the Los Angeles composite, questioning hotel managers, putting the squeeze on people. The manager of the Bristol Hotel, a burly Russian immigrant, told detectives there had been a guy staying in room 315 who'd looked like the composite and sounded like the fellow they were talking about. He didn't know his name; names were not needed at the Bristol. When asked by the detectives if the guy in 315 had caused any kind of disturbances or done anything out of the ordinary, he said, "No, nothing. He came; he paid and went. Sometimes he played music loud and I had to tell him to lower it. Other than that, you didn't even know he was here. Very quiet. Very to himself." The detectives went up to room 315 and found a pentagram on the bathroom door—just like the ones at Mabel Bell's and Peter Pan's. They removed the whole door for evidence and called in tech people to dust for prints.

Det. Carl Klotz called Orozco and Tippin in Los Angeles and told them about Earl Gregg, Deleen, Donna Meyers, the jewelry, Armando Rodriguez, Rick Ramirez, and the Bristol Hotel. Orozco called Salerno and told him. Salerno said they already had a suspect named Rick who sounded like the same guy. The two detectives promised to let the other know as soon as either of them learned anything more.

Salerno told Carrillo about the call and Rick Ramirez from El Paso.

They went to Grimm and told him they'd gotten a last name for Rick from San Francisco. The next step was to try to match the print they'd retrieved from the Toyota with all the Rick, Ricardo, and Richard Ramirezes on file.

The true account of what happened next has never been made public before. The *official* story the police released was that the Cal-ID, a new twenty-five-million-dollar Japanese computer the California Department of Justice had just bought, broke the case. Actually, the fingerprint Orange County found on the mirror in the orange Toyota was flown up to Sacramento, and with the computer's help, all the Ramirezes on file were searched. They found the name of a Richard Muñoz Ramirez—a tall, gangly El Paso drifter, thief, and sometime drug dealer with a record for small crimes, petty thefts, and stealing a car—which apparently was the December 1984 arrest Perez had told them about and the LAPD had never been able to find.

Could this two-bit criminal be the terrible, fear-inspiring Night Stalker?

His mug shot was shown to Jesse Perez, who verified that Richard Muñoz Ramirez was the fellow he'd been talking about.

When the information reached Sheriff Block, he excitedly conferred with LAPD Chief Darryl Gates, Orange County Sheriff Brad Gates, and San Francisco Police Chief Con Murphy.

They reluctantly agreed they *had* to release the picture to the press. If, in fact, the Stalker *was* Richard Ramirez, then going public with it would tip him off and give him the chance to disappear, Salerno pointed out. But if they held the information back, it left him free to kill or rape again before they picked him up. For the public's safety, Sheriff Block decided to release the name.

A press conference was hastily called despite Salerno's and Carrillo's being against releasing the name. Right now,

Richard Ramirez didn't know they were looking for him. With the information they'd gotten from Perez, they were confident they'd pick him up soon, within hours. However, they were overruled, and Sheriff Block held the news conference.

Word quickly spread among the news media that the police had a suspect in the Night Stalker assaults. Hundreds of reporters invaded the wood-paneled press room at the sheriff's office.

Sheriff Block, looking haggard and tired, flanked by the Gates and banging on a microphone-covered table for emphasis, told the assembled press they had a suspect in the Night Stalker slayings named Richard Muñoz Ramirez. He was "a twenty-five-year-old man from El Paso with a record of petty crimes." The reporters were ecstatic to learn there was now *finally* a face attached to the gruesome crimes. As if speaking to Ramirez, Sheriff Block said, "We know who you are now, and soon everyone else will. There will be no place you can hide."

Everyone everywhere was now looking for Richard Ramirez. Television broadcasts all across the country were interrupted for a news bulletin showing the most recent mug shot of Richard Ramirez and identifying him as the prime suspect in the Night Stalker crimes, linked to them through fingerprints.

Ramirez had an angular, high-cheekboned face and full, heart-shaped lips. His eyes were dark, large, penetrating; his hair was black, wavy, unkempt. He was looking at the police camera as if he wanted to kick it over and spit on it.

Salerno ordered thousands of copies of Ramirez's most recent mug shot—the arrest for the car theft downtown—and had every police department send someone to the sheriff's office for pictures to distribute among the whole rank-and-file of all of Los Angeles County law enforcement jurisdictions. He ordered detectives Ike Aguilar and Mike Griggs to take Jesse Perez to Tijuana and retrieve the .22 Perez said he'd gotten from Ramirez. If the gun had been used to kill people in L.A., it would be a very strong piece of evidence.

Salerno and Carrillo stayed at the office until 4:30 A.M. that

Friday night, overseeing the deployment of surveillance people all over the downtown areas, in the places Richard Ramirez supposedly frequented. They all knew it wouldn't be long, but no one celebrated or opened any champagne. "Until we had Ramirez in custody, alive or dead, there was nothing to celebrate," Salerno later said. "He was a very wily individual."

When Salerno got home, Jayne was sleeping; she had seen the news bulletin and knew the man her husband had been obsessed with catching had been identified. Salerno undressed and got into bed, but sleep was elusive. He couldn't keep his mind off Richard Ramirez.

Before Gil went home, he drove over to downtown Los Angeles and slowly cruised its sleepy streets, hoping he'd spot Ramirez, but no luck. After an hour, he went home for a few hours' sleep. His house was empty. Although the killer had been identified, his wife was still too afraid to come home.

In the morning, Richard Ramirez's picture was on the front page of every newspaper in California. His name was the first word spoken by every newscaster on every channel.

BOOK II

RICHIE

My brother never slept. He was always up and moving around at night.

Ruth Ramirez

EIGHTEEN

Richard Ramirez was the fifth and last child born to Julian Tapia Ramirez and his wife, Mercedes. They had had three boys, a girl, and finally Richard—or Richie, as the family affectionately calls him.

Richard's father was born in Camargo, Mexico, on February 16, 1927. He was a large, powerful, handsome man with jet-black hair and high, well-defined cheekbones, the second of eight children brought up on a dirt-poor farm. His mother, Roberta, died when he was twelve, and much of the burden of raising the large family fell on his shoulders. He was the oldest male.

His father, Jose Ramirez, was an extremely serious man who rarely smiled. He had a perpetually stern Mexican face with dark, piercing eyes and tight, firm lips—traits he had inherited from his father, Inacia, a large, brutal man with a bad temper who often beat his kids whether they misbehaved or not. Like the land around Camargo, he was mean and unforgiving. Jose Ramirez also believed in corporal punishment. If any of his four boys and four girls didn't do what was expected of them, he was quick to beat them. Like his father, he had a bad temper, and often his beatings went on longer than they should have. However, in Mexico, it was a normal thing for a father to beat his children. It was the way things were done. It was commonly felt it taught the child respect and discipline and to accept the consequences of their actions. Often, though, the line separating punishment and correction was crossed, and Julian Tapia was beaten too hard, too long, too often—by both his father and his grandfather. It was his grandfather, Inacia, who beat Julian the most. If Julian did a particularly bad thing—like sleep late when there was work—his grandfather would tie him to a tree and lay into him with rope. The beatings made Julian quiet and withdrawn, and his face often seemed to be in an unhappy shadow.

Because he was the oldest son, Julian received the most beatings. He took them stoically, not crying or begging for them to stop. He would just wait until his father's and grandfather's irrational rages were spent.

It was not an easy life for Jose Ramirez. He had lost his wife at an early age. He felt cheated; it angered him deep inside, and he often vented his anger on his eight children.

When Julian, who was big for his age, was fourteen, he stood up to his father, pulled the belt from his hand, and threw it on the ground. "You are not beating me anymore!" he proclaimed defiantly. This was a crime punishable by death in Camargo, Mexico, in 1944. A son did not defy his father. There were customs and regulations that had to be adhered to, but after that day, Jose Ramirez and his father did not beat Julian anymore.

In truth, the beatings were never really necessary, for Julian was a good son; he worked hard on the farm and did everything he could to help feed and support his seven siblings. He, as well as all the family, went to church every Sunday; he believed in the virtues preached by Jesus Christ and the powers of Christ's enemy, Satan. Julian never stole, smoked, or cursed, and he very rarely drank.

He had been taken out of school in the first grade; he was needed on the farm, and there was no time for the luxury of an education. He worked from sunrise to sunset and would turn a deep chestnut brown under the strong Mexican sun.

Camargo was a small, dusty town without railroad, electricity, or phone, and everyone there knew everyone else, either directly or indirectly. Julian first met Mercedes when they were both just fourteen.

Mercedes had been born in Rocky Ford, Colorado, one of seven children, four boys and three girls. There was much love in the Muñoz family, but little money. When World War II came to America, Mercedes's mother, Guadalupe, made the decision to leave the United States and move to Camargo. She did not want her sons being drafted. She was against the war—all wars—and would not allow her boys' blood to be spilled because of the whims of politicians. Governments were corrupt. Everyone knew that, and neither she nor anyone in her family would suffer because of their corruption.

Julian's sisters became friendly with Mercedes upon her arrival in Camargo, and through them he was first introduced to her. She had large, innocent doe-eyes and was tall and lanky, with a high, broad forehead. Her hands and fingers were long and finely tapered, beautiful enough to have modeled. However, it wasn't until they were nineteen that sparks began flying between Julian and Mercedes and they began dating, going to the only cinema in Camargo and for long walks around Camargo's only park.

There was very little work in Camargo then. One of Mercedes's brothers, Nacho, had moved to Juarez, Mexico, in 1946 and gotten work in the post office right away. Juarez was a border town next to El Paso, Texas. The war was over now and there was a lot of work in both towns. Born in the States, the Muñoz children were American citizens and it would be easy for them to go back and forth from Juarez to El Paso. Guadalupe decided to move. Mercedes would have to go, too. Any relationships she had would have to be put on hold, maybe ended. The family came first.

In August of 1947, the Muñoz family moved to Juarez. Quickly, everyone in the family old enough to work got a job. Mercedes secured employment in El Paso as a housekeeper. Like many border towns, Juarez was a wild and dangerous place. For a small price, anything could be gotten—sex with minors, drugs, stolen American cars and jewelry. Mercedes did not like it there; she was frightened and intimidated by the illicit activity.

She and Julian wrote to one another. Writing was very difficult for him, as he had only a first-grade education, but with his sister's help he struggled and learned how to write. His letters were short and to the point: he told Mercedes how much he missed her and how empty Camargo—and his heart—had been since she'd gone. She, too, wrote of feeling empty without him.

Julian was drafted into the army. He learned how to shoot and take care of all kinds of weapons, until he contracted scarlet fever and had to be discharged. When he returned to

Camargo, he was thin and sickly with fever, and his sister, Augustine, had to nurse him back to health.

Julian wanted to go to Juarez to be with Mercedes. His father and grandfather still tried to dominate him, and told him he was still needed on the farm. But Julian felt he had already done far more than any three sons put together. Although he loved his brothers and sisters very much, he loved Mercedes in a way that made living without her difficult. Julian wrote to Mercedes and proposed. She said yes.

Guadalupe was a strong, domineering woman with a shrewd mind. She forbade the marriage to take place. She felt that Julian, though good looking and a fine physical specimen, would never amount to much. He had no education, no skills, no money. He was not a suitable husband for her Mercedes. Julian's family felt the Muñozes were uppity and acted as if they were better than everyone else, and they didn't want Julian marrying her, either.

Mercedes rarely defied her mother, but she was going to marry Julian whether her mother and her family approved or not.

Julian arrived in Juarez with all his possessions contained in a single battered cardboard suitcase on August 3, 1948. He and Mercedes were married on August 9 at Juarez City Hall, in the Presidency Building, before a few friends and no family. They were both nineteen. They could not afford a honeymoon and they had nothing but their love for each other and a desire for a big family. All their lives they had managed with little, and they would see to it their children got all the things they hadn't had.

And in Julian Tapia Ramirez's house there would be no beatings, he vowed.

Soon after their marriage, Julian got a job as a laborer in a Juarez clothing factory. Mercedes continued working in El Paso as a domestic. The poverty and crime in Juarez in the 1940s was extreme and Mercedes was unhappy living there. Because she'd been born in the States, she could, if she chose, live in El Paso. Julian was not an American citizen and could not move to El Paso until he was approved by the U.S. government. He was content in Mexico, but Mercedes wanted out of Juarez and for her children to be born American citizens. She had heard many times over about the great

American Dream and she wanted some of it for her family. Julian finally acquiesced and the young couple took a small apartment in El Paso, one room and a bathroom, at Fourth and Canal. Between them they earned very little, but they managed to save the amount necessary for the first month's rent and security.

Guadalupe's feelings slowly started thawing toward Julian Ramirez. She saw that he was hardworking and ambitious and loved her daughter very much. The apartment in El Paso was not far from Guadalupe's house in Juarez, and Julian and Mercedes began going there for meals and visits.

Several months later Mercedes was pregnant. When Julian heard the news, he was all smiles. He felt certain that it was a son, and that made him very proud and very happy, for his boy would be something special . . . he would be a professional, and unlike his father, he would have a fine education.

During this time, the U.S. government was conducting nuclear bomb tests in nearby Los Alamos, New Mexico. Little was known about the detrimental effects of nuclear fallout in 1949. Juarez was about 200 miles from Los Alamos, and when the winds were right, fallout from the bombs was regularly carried to Juarez and El Paso, where it settled on the populace and the cattle and in the milk and water.

During the years when the testing was most frequent, 1950 to 1954, there was an unusually high rate of birth defects: babies born with too few limbs, half-formed hearts, and deformed heads—a host of physical as well as mental problems and abnormalities. In years to come, it would become common knowledge that nuclear fallout causes birth defects, but then there were only rumors about it. The A-bomb had won the war and the government did not want to publicize any complications the testing had caused.

Mercedes and Julian's firstborn was named Ruben. The pregnancy and birth were not particularly difficult, but the baby was born with a series of golfball-sized lumps all over the back of his neck and head and was very sick.

The doctor wasn't sure what was wrong with the infant, though he intimated that the condition could have been a result of the bomb tests in New Mexico.

Julian and the Muñozes knew nothing of this. Ruben was put into an incubator. His respiration was slow and labored, his blood pressure too low. A priest was called and gave the infant last rites. Julian and Mercedes turned to the only power who had any say in death and sickness and prayed fervently to Jesus Christ and the Virgin Mary that Ruben would get better, that the terrible lumps on his neck would go away. But Ruben's condition did not improve, and a priest had to administer last rites again.

A few days later, Ruben began to get better: his vital signs stabilized, and the lumps began to disappear. The whole family vehemently believed their prayers had been answered by divine intervention. Ruben was taken home and his health continued to improve. It seemed, for all intents and purposes, that he was healthy, despite his frequent crying.

Julian often held the boy in his arms, walked the unpaved roads of El Paso's Second Ward, smiling and telling Ruben secrets. Julian and Mercedes had never learned to speak English, but they agreed the boy would have to learn English well to prosper in the United States.

Mercedes was soon pregnant again—just two months after she'd given birth to Ruben. She would have liked a girl and to have had a little more time between births, but all that mattered was that the child be healthy. By now she had also heard the rumors of how atomic bombs were causing an invisible poison to come down from the sky and hurt unborn children still in their mothers' wombs. She did not understand why this had come about. She just wished it would go away.

Mercedes's second pregnancy was uneventful. She gave birth on time to another boy they named Jose, or Joseph, after Mercedes's favorite brother. This time when the obstetrician came to Julian, he said the child was healthy.

Julian Ramirez considered himself a lucky man—two sons in a row. He bought big cigars in Juarez and passed them out to everyone. He would hurry home from work every day so he could spend time with his boys. Guadalupe Muñoz clucked and cooed over both her grandsons. Two consecutive boys was a good omen, she said.

When Joseph was six months old, they began to notice that he cried too often, as if he was in pain. The clinic in El Paso examined him and pronounced him healthy, yet still he cried. Every day it was more, longer, and louder. Julian would hold the infant, walk him back and forth, and coo to him, but nothing helped. They took Joseph to the clinic a second time when he was nearly a year old. This time the doctor told them the boy's bones were not growing correctly; his kneecaps weren't developing as they should.

The doctor didn't know why, and said the child would need tests and a specialist. The Ramirezes were given the name of Dr. Perry Rogers, an orthopedist with a large practice in El Paso. Dr. Rogers himself had had polio and walked stiffly, with thigh-high braces. He examined Joseph, did some tests, and told the Ramirezes that their son had Collier's disease, which was causing the child's bones to curve as they grew.

The condition was believed to be a result of nuclear fallout and radioactivity from New Mexico.

Dr. Rogers told them there was no cure, but he could cut away the curved part of the bone—in Joseph's case, the os calosis, and add a metal heel, which he'd construct. With specially designed shoes, Joseph "should be able to walk all right." However, the boy's bones would always continue to grow at an angle, and there would have to be more operations in the future.

The news hit the young parents hard.

Julian wanted only good for his sons, but here, so early in life, his second-born was seriously handicapped. He thought long and hard about the atomic bomb tests and began asking questions around Juarez and El Paso. He soon learned there were many children, in both towns, who'd been born with strange deformities. He learned there was a camp in Arizona where these children were being kept in secret. The government knew the bombs were very dangerous to the unborn, yet they tried to keep it from the public.

Whatever surplus money the Ramirezes had went to Dr. Rogers. They were very proud and would not ask anyone in their families for help. They simply worked harder, longer hours. The operations began on Joseph when he was seventeen months old. The surgery helped for a while, but the bones continued to grow incorrectly. Joseph would often be in pain and crying again. Both Mercedes and Julian Tapia went to the Sacred Heart Church on Oregon Street often, knelt down next to one another and prayed for Joseph's bone disease to go away.

But Joseph's condition worsened.

Julian found employment in El Paso as a construction worker. He did not have the proper papers yet, but they needed money desperately, and the construction job paid considerably more than the factory in Juarez. He was an excellent worker, big, strong, muscular—and always eager to do well. The foreman was very pleased with Julian and wished all his workers could be as serious about a job well done.

NINETEEN

In 1952, three immigration border guards visited Julian's construction site. When he was asked for his papers, he sheepishly explained that they had not yet been granted. His wife, he said, through a fellow worker who acted as an interpreter, was an American citizen. Stone-faced, they told him that without the proper papers, he had no right to take wages away from some American citizen and would be deported immediately.

They drove him to his apartment so he could tell Mercedes. Once there, they told him his wife and children were to be deported, too. The immigration people were not interested in their being American citizens. They just wanted the Ramirezes and their meager belongings out of the apartment and over the border. Despite the protests of their landlord, who knew they were citizens, their belongings were loaded into the immigration workers' truck, and Mercedes, the two children, and Julian climbed into the back. It was 3 P.M. and it began to rain as they were taken to the Mexican side of the Santa Fe bridge, where their things were dumped on the corner.

Julian decided he would stay with their possessions while Mercedes and the children walked to her mother's house, a mile east of the Santa Fe bridge. Juarez was a very dangerous border town. On the average weekend there were twenty murders. Julian knew he might have to fight off thieves who saw his misfortune and would take advantage of it and steal all he had in the world. There were such men always near the bridges.

Julian and Mercedes hugged and she started towards her mother's house. The rain let up some, but now lightning began to split the low dark sky and thunder boomed like cannons.

Ruben walked, holding Mercedes's hand, while she carried the crying Joseph. As Julian watched his wife and small sons walk away, he prayed she would reach her mother's house without problem. In Juarez you never knew what could happen. Anyone who looked at Julian guarding their belongings that stormy day would have seen a dark-eyed man willing to fight to the death for what was rightfully his.

Mercedes reached her mother's house without mishap. Her brothers, Joseph and Manuel, borrowed a neighbor's truck and in two trips moved everything into Guadalupe Muñoz's back yard and house.

Julian needed work right away. He went to the Presidency Building, which housed the Juarez City Hall and police department, hoping he'd find something there. He met a childhood friend from Camargo who was working as a Juarez policeman. After shaking hands and embracing one another, Julian told his friend how desperately he needed employment.

"Well, no problem," said his friend. "I can help you. I will recommend you and you too can become a policeman."

"Me? A policeman, but I know nothing about being a policeman."

"That doesn't matter, you are big and you will learn. You've never been arrested—have you?"

"No. Never. Of course not."

"Good. Come with me."

Julian was introduced to the *commandante* of the Juarez Police. He immediately liked the way Julian looked and was pleased to hear he knew about the handling of guns from his time in the army.

He was sworn in right away, given a uniform and a gun, and told to report for duty the next morning.

Life was so unpredictable, Julian mused. He walked back to his mother-in-law's house with his new job, boots, gun and uniform. Now Guadalupe and the Muñoz clan would truly respect him.

However, Mercedes was not happy about his becoming a policeman. In Mexico, like in Colombia, South America, the Policemen were killed if they got in the way or did their jobs too well.

Julian's experience with guns led to his being put in charge of teaching the Juarez police how to shoot and maintain their firearms properly. Mercedes worried when he told her of arrests during which he'd been shot at. She wanted him to find other work, but he was happy with the respect and authority his job offered.

Mercedes gave birth to their third son, Robert, who seemed healthy. She continued to press for Julian to quit the police force, and to apply for American citizenship.

When Julian's citizenship papers were approved, for the good of his sons, for their education, and to give Mercedes what she wanted, he quit the Juarez police department.

The Ramirezes moved back to El Paso in the spring of 1954. They rented a small apartment in the Second Ward, at Seventh and Canal. El Paso was a much cleaner, safer place than Juarez, and Julian knew he'd made the right decision to leave Mexico.

Julian found a job with the Santa Fe railroad, laying track. The wages and benefits were good, but it meant he had to be away from his family, and it would be backbreaking work. Julian loved the outdoors and would make the best of the situation.

His sons would be raised in the Land of the Free.

Julian's new job took him out of town with work gangs for days at a time, laying track all over the southwest. He had always been an unusually strong man, but his lifting railroad ties and tracks and swinging a heavy sledgehammer all day made his muscles huge and as hard as steel.

Mercedes found work with Tony Lama—the famous Texas bootmaker. The wages were better than that of a housekeeper. She was able to find a Mexican woman to stay with her three boys while she was away at work. She didn't like leaving them alone, particularly Joseph, but in order to provide for them, she had to work.

Her job at the factory consisted of mixing the pigments and chemicals for the boots' brilliant colors and shines, then painting the boots and treating them with fixatives so the color would remain. The chemicals were very strong, and under certain circumstances they were toxic; ventilation and a mask were necessary when using them, but neither was provided to Mercedes. She stood up in the back of the factory seven hours a day, five days a week, without the benefit of a window, fan, or mask. She began to get dizzy spells and had to sit down often. It was 1955, and no one yet realized how toxic benzene, toluene, and xylene were.

She became pregnant with her fourth child after being employed at Tony Lama's for six months. When Julian heard the news, his heart soared—four pregnancies in five years! He was blessed with a fertile woman who loved him; life was good. He and Mercedes went to the Sacred Heart Church several nights a week and always on Sundays and prayed that their fourth child would be born healthy.

It was a girl they named Ruth. On examination she seemed healthy enough, and Julian and Mercedes were very pleased.

She would always, Julian thought, have three older brothers to protect her. Mercedes had wanted a girl very much. A daughter was necessary if a family was to be complete. Her daughter would be able to help her with the things that were expected of a Mexican housewife, and with three boys and Julian, Mercedes had been hard pressed.

Mercedes was not a strong woman. Her bones and limbs seemed too fragile, as if they could break easily if she were pushed or fell. It had taken her months to recover from each birth. She was an extremely sensitive woman, and the brutalities she had observed in life had given her a seriousness beyond her years. She put her faith in God and believed Satan was always there, tempting people with all things bad. One always had to be vigilant against the forces of evil.

Laying track for the Santa Fe railroad was hard work, but it suited Julian fine. One or two nights a week, and always on weekends, he would dress up and visit his police buddies in Juarez. Often he would take his sons along on these trips and talk to them in Spanish. He wanted them to have a shot at the American Dream, but he did not want them ever to lose their Mexican heritage.

* * *

Julian's sister, Victoria, moved to El Paso that year. Her son, Miguel, was Ruben's age. From the day the two boys first met, they struck a special bond, and in later years, for a time, they would be inseparable.

Mercedes's sister, Julie, who was also employed at Tony Lama, said she never felt well on weekends. Mercedes also noticed *she* felt anxious and irritable on Saturday and Sunday, until she went back to work on Monday. The two sisters began to suspect they were in some way addicted to the fumes they were exposed to at work and were experiencing a kind of "weekend withdrawal," but neither sought any medical attention or advice.

Before Julian knew it, it was time for Ruben to be enrolled in school. He was put in a special class that focused on teaching English. The school system in El Paso was geared to accommodate children of non-English-speaking parents.

Ruben soon knew many English words and could string them together in sentences. Julian would make him speak English with his friends and his grandmother in Juarez. The boy sensed how important it was to his father that he spoke English, and he worked hard at mastering the difficult words. He had a sharp mind and picked up whatever he was taught quickly. Julian and Mercedes had been warned that some damage could have been done to his brain by the fallout of Los Alamos, but the child seemed normal, and both his parents prayed and gave heartfelt thanks to the Lord, Jesus Christ.

When it was time for Joseph to go to school, he was wearing special shoes he had gotten in Juarez. They enabled him to walk, though awkwardly. His right leg was considerably longer than his left, and the artificial heel on his left foot needed frequent adjustment, but he did not complain. He did his best and walked to school with the other children. Julian knew how cruel children could be, and he prayed Joseph would be thick-skinned and strong.

It was a good thing, Julian thought, that Joseph had an older brother, who would be there to protect, help, and defend him. Julian would teach those traits to all his family.

Soon Robert joined his brothers at school. When Julian heard his boys first speaking English to one another, it made him very proud, though also sad, for he could not speak English with them. Learning a new language was a very difficult task, and he didn't really need to speak English. Nearly all the men he worked with were Mexicans and always spoke Spanish among themselves.

Joseph was a kind, good-natured, sensitive child, and he took his classmates' teasing and taunts to heart. He had apparently inherited Mercedes's sensitivity. But Ruben had inherited his father's fierce temperament and soon was chasing children who had harassed Joseph.

Julian did not lose his temper often, but when he did, it was very unpleasant. What was odd was how placid and easygoing he was normally—but if something set him off, he'd become like an angry bull teased by a red cape, and he'd break and throw things and beat the walls and doors with his hamhock-sized fists. Mercedes noticed early on that each of her boys seemed to have the violent, explosive temper of the Ramirez men. Even Ruth, provoked enough, would start hitting people and breaking and throwing things. "I'd just black out when I got mad," she'd say years later. "I couldn't control the anger. There would just, like, be an explosion inside of me, and I'd go off." Her older brothers gave her a wide berth when she "went off."

TWENTY

Mercedes's final pregnancy was by far the most difficult. She was still working at Tony Lama's, and the fumes from the chemicals were still causing her problems. Frequently now she was getting dizzy and had to sit down. She often was fatigued and nauseated. She had cramps in her joints and was always tired. The pregnancy with Richard caused her much discomfort, and Mercedes had to go to a specialist. It was later believed that the chemicals from work were causing her body to reject this last child. She had to get many injections to retain the fetus in her womb. She knew it was a boy by the way he kicked and moved.

Julian was caught off guard by this last pregnancy. It had been four years since Mercedes had last conceived, and they'd both thought four children were all they'd have. Guadalupe Muñoz was worried that the fifth child was sapping the life-force from her daughter, and she prayed for her and her unborn child.

The specialist told Mercedes that if she wanted to keep this baby she'd have to stop working at Tony Lama's—that the chemicals and all the standing would kill the child. Mercedes quit. She was already at the end of her fifth month.

Richard was born on February 29, 1960, at 2:07 A.M. Julian, Ruben, Joseph, Robert, and Ruth all went to the hospital. Ruth was tickled pink to have a younger brother. He would be like her doll, and she'd be able to play with him all she wanted. He'd be unlike her older brothers, who only wanted to roughhouse and boss her around.

Julian was overjoyed. He now had four sons to carry on the Ramirez name. Who knew? One of them might be famous someday.

They had decided to name him Ricardo. Ruth automatically made herself a surrogate mother to Ricardo, or Richie, as he became known within the family.

From the first day he came home from the hospital, Ruth was all over him. He was her little precious, dark-eyed, dark-haired doll come to life. Ruben, Joseph, and Robert didn't pay one-tenth the attention to Richie that Ruth did.

A month after she gave birth to Richard, Mercedes went back to Tony Lama's. Another woman who'd worked there had gotten sick and had sued the bootmaker, citing the chemicals as the source of her illness. Now ventilation and a mask were available to those who worked with the chemicals, and Mercedes no longer experienced the dizziness and nausea. She hired a babysitter to stay with Richie while she worked. When the other older children came home at 3 P.M., the sitter would leave. Mercedes would be home by 4:30 and begin to cook supper. During the summer months, when the children were not in school, the sitter would watch over them a few hours every week. Mercedes didn't like being away from the house so much, but the money she earned was necessary if they were ever to buy their own home. Buying their own home in America was a dream Mercedes had vowed would come true.

By now, Joseph had had fifteen operations. They were done in the summer so he would miss the least amount of school. In the afternoons Mercedes would visit him, and on Saturdays the whole family, including Richard, would go. Joseph had learned to deal with the pain and the months of hospitalization while he recuperated. He rarely complained. The specially designed shoes enabled him to walk to school a quarter mile away, but they weighed four pounds each and the walking was very difficult for the child. He had to rest every half block or so. Ruben, Robert, or Ruth would walk to and from school with Joseph.

Robert was big for his age. When he was seven, he was nearly the size of Ruben. He was the most easygoing of the three brothers; Ruben was the rebel, with a bit of a chip on his shoulder; Joseph went along with most everything and never made waves. Ruth had the best qualities of each of her three older brothers. She never had to be asked to do anything twice and was always willing to help Mercedes. Although well behaved, she had a rough-and-tumble side. Ruben and Ruth often fought, and he'd hit her if she didn't do what he wanted fast enough. If it hadn't been for Joseph, and later, Richard, she says, Ruben and Robert would have hit her a lot more often.

Ruben began to have problems in school. He didn't follow instructions well, he argued with other children, and he got into fights. At first, his father attributed his problems to the teachers and to other children, but it soon became evident that Ruben had a mind of his own and did what he wanted, not what his teachers told him to do. He was a "behavioral problem."

When Ruben began bringing home bad report cards, his father's response was to beat him with a water hose, intent upon teaching him that he must change his ways, or there would be punishment. But the beatings didn't help.

In 1963, the children witnessed their father's capacity for rage for the first time. Julian was working on his car out front and couldn't get a filter to fit into the engine the way it should. He started cursing, then got so mad he banged his head against the house until blood ran down his face in thick ribbons of red.

"I've never seen anyone ever get so mad," Joseph said later. "He would just lose it totally. To see him doing that, making himself bleed and all—it was scary. When that happened, all the kids ran. My mom would stay out of his way totally. The funny thing was, he got more mad at objects than people."

Because of Joseph's illness and his having to miss so much school, he truly appreciated being able to go to school. It was much better than being in a hospital bed with his bones freshly cut, fighting a losing battle with a disease he didn't understand. He did his best, but he was still a below-average student. Robert clearly had learning disabilities and was put in a special class. Ruben had also been put in a slow class. It was not because he couldn't master the work; his IQ was average—he just didn't care. No matter how much his father beat him, yelled, or threatened, it didn't matter.

Richard continued to be Ruth's personal doll. For hours she'd play house with him like he was her child, talking to him softly in both English and Spanish. Richard was a good baby, didn't cry much, and ate and slept well. He was particularly good looking, with a well-formed face and big, round, long-lashed eyes. As with his father and brothers, his hands and feet were large.

Richard loved music, his mother later said, even before he was a year old. When the radio was on and there was a song he liked, he'd start moving his head and feet in time to the music.

Now that the family had grown to seven, the Ramirezes needed a larger place to live. They started shopping for a house, after having saved and scraped for eleven years. They bought a house on Ledo Street, in Lincoln, also known as La Roca, "the rock," because of nearby Cordova Cemetery. The area was more residential than where they were now, with well-kept single-family houses lining the tree-lined, sun-baked streets. The one-story tract-stucco with three bedrooms, a large kitchen, and backyard was in the middle of the block. There was a driveway on the left and no garage.

Mercedes found a woman named Socorro to babysit Richard until Ruth and her brothers came home from school. Julian was frequently away for days at a time. He traveled on the railroad with a work crew of thirty-five to wherever the Santa Fe Railroad wanted tracks laid down. He didn't like being away from home so much, but he didn't complain. As he and his crew laid more track, they had to travel further and further away from El Paso, and he had to stay away from home for longer periods of time.

The first troubles began when Ruben started hanging out with "a bad group of boys," Mercedes would say later, who sniffed glue and burglarized houses outside the neighborhood.

Julian was on the road, Mercedes worked from 8:30 to 4:30, five days a week, and the Ramirez boys didn't have enough supervision. Socorro had little to say, and as long as no one talked, how were Mercedes or Julian to know what they did?

When Socorro was not in the house, Ruben would have his friends over and they would sniff glue. Ruth saw the glue sniffing and Ruben told her if she said anything he'd beat her, so she kept quiet, knowing her parents were away working too often for her to be spared Ruben's revenge if she did talk. Ruben's rebellious nature attracted the kind of trouble that put him in direct conflict with his father's heartfelt hopes, dreams, and prayers.

For the most part, Ledo Street was in a good, though tough, area of El Paso. Everyone who lived on the block was hardworking and family- and church-oriented. Most were Mexican-Americans, first- and second-generation.

When Richard was two, he was nearly killed by a dresser that fell on top of him. He was home alone with Socorro. She had the television on and was watching a soap opera. Richard asked her to put on the radio so he could listen to it and dance. After ten minutes of his asking her and her saying no, he decided to put it on himself. The radio was on a heavy, tall wooden dresser in his parents' room. He couldn't reach the top of the dresser, so he used the opened drawers as a ladder. When he got to the third drawer, his weight brought the dresser forward and on top of him, knocking him unconscious and giving him a deep gash on his forehead, which bled profusely. The scar is still evident today. Socorro panicked when she saw the dresser on top of the unconscious, bleeding two-year-old. She called Mercedes at work, got the dresser off Richard, and put a towel on his wound. They took the now conscious boy to the hospital. Thirty stitches were needed to close the wound. Socorro said Richard had been knocked unconscious for fifteen minutes. The doctors said he'd received a concussion and a sharp eye should be kept on him. If he had dizzy spells or trouble with his equilibrium, he was to be brought back to the hospital.

When Julian heard what had happened to Richard, he was angry. What the hell were they paying Socorro for, if not to keep an eye on Richard and make sure he didn't hurt himself? He was hyperactive, never sat still, and needed close attention. Julian insisted Mercedes find another woman to stay with his youngest son. Socorro was fired, and the incident was forgotten.

It seemed the backbreaking work of laying track was changing Julian's temperament; he'd never been easygoing to begin with, but now he was even more serious and severe, and he rarely smiled.

Often, when he came home, he would just want to sit in his chair and be left alone. It was as though something was troubling him deep inside, but he said nothing to Mercedes, and she didn't press him. He'd talk when he was ready.

When the phone call from the police came to the Ledo house, Julian Ramirez was home. Ruben and his cousin, Miguel, had been arrested in a stolen car with some of their glue-sniffing buddies. When Julian showed up at the police station to pick up Ruben, he was in a rage that knew no bounds; he felt let down and betrayed. Whether Ruben was guilty or not didn't matter—just the fact that he'd been arrested was enough to disgrace the Ramirez name, Julian felt. No one in his family had ever been arrested. They were all poor people, but they were *honest* poor people.

To have a police record in America was very bad. Julian slapped and cursed his son at the police station, and when he got home, he fully lost his temper and beat the boy mercilessly. All the other children ran and hid. Mercedes prayed that whatever was making Ruben do these bad things would stop. Richard, too, felt his father's rage, heard the blows, and heard his brother's pleading for the beating to stop. Richard trembled and cried.

Finally, it was over. Julian had vented his anger at his son, leaving Ruben black and blue all over his body, very much as his grandfather and father had done to him. Julian had vowed never to bring violence against his children, but he had never thought a son of his would be arrested and handcuffed for stealing! He made Ruben swear he'd stop hanging out with the boys he'd gotten in trouble with.

But while Julian was away laying track, Ruben did what he pleased. He was like a wild horse who didn't want to be tamed. What he wanted to do was get high and steal things.

His grades progressively worsened, which only further fueled his father's anger.

The second time Ruben was arrested, it was for breaking into someone's house.

Disgraced, Julian again went and got his firstborn out of the police station.

Breaking and entering was a serious crime, though it had been viewed by Ruben as more of a lark than anything criminal. Julian hit his son at the jail, and when they got back to Ledo, his rage took over and he again beat Ruben senseless; he didn't realize he was going too far with the beating, that it had crossed the line from discipline to abuse.

Shaking, six-year-old Richard again heard the blows breaking on his brother's body as he pleaded with his father to stop. Ruth went to Richard and held him. Robert and Joseph hid. Mercedes prayed.

She felt her husband was disciplining Ruben in a way that was necessary: breaking into someone's home was very serious. But she also felt that Julian's rage had taken over. She knew how incredibly strong her husband was and interceded to stop the beating by putting herself between her son and Julian.

It was too much; it had gone too far, she said.

Julian, still in a rage, left the house, went to a bar, and drank. He didn't drink often—he was diabetic and couldn't—but when he was particularly troubled he would sometimes look to the bottle for solace and solutions. He came home later that night and went to sleep.

Mercedes prayed to Jesus to intercede and make everything all right. She knew how badly Julian was hurt by Ruben's actions, and it was not a good thing for a man to be so angry at his son; it could only lead to something bad.

The next day, Mercedes went to church, lit candles, and prayed some more. Her prayers, however, were not heard, for Ruben continued to sniff glue and do even worse in school.

Then Robert, influenced, perhaps, by what he saw Ruben and his friends doing, began sniffing glue. Soon Joseph was sniffing glue, too. It took away the pain and made him forget the disease that was crippling him. But Joseph soon stopped; he knew it was something he shouldn't be doing and didn't want his father to find out. Joseph had never been beaten by Julian.

Ruben and Robert kept getting into trouble with the police, having arguments and fights with kids on the block and problems at school. Julian would lay into them with his volcanic rage and awesome strength. His anger was so bad it became a kind of unspoken dread that lurked about the house at all times; even when Julian was away laying track, the echo and presence of his anger hung thick over the house like a dark stormcloud alive with thunder and lightning.

The next time Julian got so mad he beat himself, was over a kitchen sink. It was a Saturday. He had been meaning to install the sink for weeks but had never found time. He was staying away from the house more and more, and his chores around the place piled up. Richard, Ruth, Joseph, and Robert were home. Ruben was playing stickball on Ledo. Julian was in the kitchen, working on the sink, and Joseph was helping him. Julian could not get the drain to fit into the wall connection. He started cursing the pipe for not fitting. Joseph saw what was coming and thought of taking off, but he didn't want to do anything to contribute to his father's anger. Julian began yelling about the sink. Ruth and Richard heard him and stayed away from the kitchen. Julian stood up, so infuriated he couldn't get the drainpipe to fit, he began to bang himself in the head with a hammer until blood ran down his face. Joseph took off. Ruth never forgot that day, nor the other ones like it.

"My father," she said, "would get so mad at things that he'd lose it totally. He'd get more angry at objects like the sink than at people. It was scary. Richard, all wide-eyed and frightened, was there, and he saw the blood as my father hit himself."

The children hid until their father's rage was spent; when it was over, they all acted as though it hadn't happened; the storm had passed and the sea was temporarily calm again.

TWENTY-ONE

With five high-spirited children so close in age all growing up in the same house, there was much practical joking—and a lot of water and egg fights. Often the three older brothers would conspire against Ruth, and they were always laughing at her expense. But Ruth was a good sport and was quick to laugh at herself—and come right back at her brothers with jokes and gags of her own. Richard didn't always think it was funny. He was very protective of his sister. There were times when Ruben or Robert hit Ruth for some infraction and Richard saw red and got between Ruth and the brother. He would not allow Ruth to be hit.

During the day, while his siblings were in school and Richard was home alone, he'd amuse himself for hours on end, playing cowboys-and-Indians in the yard. He was a tireless child who never sat still, and he would assume both roles, acting out each part with great drama. He would aim and fire at air, then run where he had fired his toy gun and make believe he had gotten shot, falling down histrionically. A neighbor who saw Richard playing in the yard, later went to Mercedes and told her Richard was doing "very strange things" in the yard.

Mercedes thanked the neighbor for her concern, but thought the woman was nuts for criticizing her Richard's game of cowboys-and-Indians. She thought it was wonderful he could play alone for so long and be content. A child, she felt, should have a good imagination. It was the sign of an active mind, and what harm could there be in that?

For the most part, the Ramirezes kept to themselves. On Ledo there were a lot of Mexican couples their age with children, but Mercedes and Julian were private people and didn't associate much with their neighbors.

When Richard was five, he went to a nearby park with Robert to find Ruth. When Richard saw her on a swing, he ran to her, and before she could stop her swing, it slammed into his head with terrific force, knocking him out and giving him a deep gash. Robert picked him up and carried him home. When Mercedes saw him, bloody and unconscious in Robert's arms, she screamed and started making the sign of the cross. They took him to the hospital, where his gash was stitched closed. The doctors said he'd be fine.

Richard's first day at school was not as a joyous time in the Ramirez household as the other children's had been. None was doing well in school. Joseph and Ruth got by and stayed out of trouble, but Ruben and Robert were always in trouble, getting failing marks and getting into fights.

This was a serious disappointment for Julian Tapia Ramirez. He'd had such high hopes for his boys. He was now regularly away from home for weeks at a time, and when he got back he was quiet, withdrawn, and distant. He felt the farther away he could get from the family, the less he'd be hurt.

The Ramirezes first realized Richard was epileptic when he had an attack in the fifth grade. Patricia Kassfy was there that day, and she would later relate: "I used to sit just behind Richard. He was always turning around and playing little jokes on me. We lived on the same block and he used to walk me home sometimes. The day I saw him have the first attack, we were taking a math test. He turned around and the teacher yelled at him. The next thing I knew, he started sinking down in his seat. He was always doing things like that, so I thought nothing of it, but then he fell down on the floor and started cursing, and his eyes rolled to the top of his head. Mrs. Woodard, our teacher, made all the kids get up and go to the window. She told me to go and get the nurse. I was real frightened. I'd never seen anyone have an epileptic fit before. I didn't even know what one was. Anyway, the gym teacher, Mr. Mares, came in with the nurse and took him, I mean, carried Richard back to the nurse's office.

"Mrs. Woodard explained to us something about what

epilepsy was, how the brain had a kind of seizure, and we just went on with class like nothing had happened. Richard did not come back to class that day."

The school principal called Mercedes at work. She rushed to the school and found Richard in the nurse's office, lying down, shaken up. He had no idea what had happened; he had no memory of falling on the floor, convulsing, cursing. The nurse told Mercedes he should be taken to a doctor, examined, and given medication.

Mercedes took Richard right home. She wanted him to get in bed and rest, but he wasn't interested. He felt fine and wanted to go out and play, watch television, listen to the radio, and dance—anything but stay in bed in the middle of a sunny day. Mercedes insisted, reminding him that he'd passed out and that she had had to leave work all worried to come and get him. Richard was a very stubborn child. If he didn't want to do something, he wouldn't do it. His father was the only person he wouldn't argue with. Richard was deathly afraid of Julian's temper and hands.

"More than him actually hitting me," Richard said later, "I was afraid of it in my mind. I'd seen him beat Ruben and Robert, and I'd seen him lose his temper over the television not working right when he wanted it to. They say it's worse to see someone you love getting tortured or hurt than being tortured or hurt yourself. I don't know if that's true or not, but I was real frightened of my father. When he lost it, I ran and hid, scared shit."

At school the next day, Richard had a second seizure. This time it was in the hall. Patricia saw that seizure, too.

"I was on my way to class. Richard went down in front of the lockers, cursing and shaking real hard this time. I knew what to do and I ran straight and got the nurse right away. Mr. Mares, the gym teacher, returned with the nurse. His office was near hers and he would frequently help out during emergencies."

"Richard was very sweet, quiet—in a way shy," Patricia remembered. "Because we lived on the same block, I saw him just about every day. He kind of watched over me. Made sure nobody bothered me. He was a good-looking boy. The girls liked him. He was nice."

Mercedes took Richard to the hospital. He was examined

perfunctorily and Mercedes was told he was an epileptic and was experiencing grand mal seizures. There was nothing to worry about—he'd "grow out of it." He was not given any medication, nor was Mercedes asked to bring him back.

At home, Ruth began noticing that her baby brother was having long staring spells in which he would just sit still and look at something—a wall, a table, the floor—for five, ten, fifteen minutes without speaking or moving. He was having petite mal seizures, but no one realized it then, and Richard wasn't diagnosed or treated.

Richard had one to two dozen of these petite mal attacks every month until he entered his early teens, when they, as well as the less frequent grand mal seizures, lessened and eventually stopped altogether.

According to Dr. Ronald Geshwind, a certain number of people who suffer from temporal lobe epilepsy have altered sexuality and hyper-religious feelings, are hypergraphic (have a compulsion to write), and are excessively aggressive. Van Gogh, Julius Caesar, Napoleon, Dostoevsky, and Lewis Carroll all suffered from temporal lobe epilepsy. Years later, after all the trouble, Richard would be diagnosed as having temporal lobe epilepsy.

Richard loved watching television. He was often the first child up and in front of the screen, wide-eyed, drinking Coca-Cola and eating sugar-covered cereal. His favorite shows were the scary ones; he would often have vivid dreams in which horrible monsters were after him. Sometimes he'd be looking out the window and see monsters actually running around the yard. These visions frightened him to the core of his seven-year-old existence. They were, experts now say, part of the petite mal episodes, but Richard didn't know any of that then, and when he told Ruth, his brothers, his mother, and even Julian, they all dismissed his claims of monsters as just a product of his wild imagination.

Other than the epilepsy, Richard had few problems during his first years of school. He liked to make people laugh, and that caused him to be disciplined sometimes, but he was a good student who paid attention in class and tried to do well,

work hard, and get along with others. He did not, like Ruben and Robert, fight with the other children.

In the second grade, his marks were five Bs, two Cs, and an A, in writing, and he had perfect attendance. His grades stayed that way until he reached the seventh grade, when he got four Cs and three Ds.

It seemed, that year—1973—Richard stopped paying attention.

Joseph was Richard's favorite brother, and he loved him dearly. Richard admired Joseph's courage and bravery. Even though Joseph's legs hurt tremendously and he was always in pain, he went to school whenever his health allowed. He'd put on his special large-heeled flat black shoes and hobble along to school as fast as he could, stopping every fifty feet or so to rest.

One time, Joseph later said, Richard asked him to walk more like he was normal because it was embarrassing to Richard to have his brother hobbling along all crooked. Nearly crying, Joseph said, "Don't you think I want to? I can't help it, Richie."

Richard apologized and never again asked Joseph to try to walk better.

Children often made fun of Joseph, until Ruben or Robert found out. They, like their father, had bad tempers, and inevitably some kid would end up getting a beating. Julian had taught his children to stay close to family through thick and thin.

"It is a terrible thing when a brother doesn't help a brother," he would often say.

Ruben, then Robert, had been put in the slow class at Bowie Junior High School for children with learning disabilities. The class was headed by a teacher named Frank McMan. He was a ruddy-faced, dark-haired man, seemingly a concerned teacher whose only interest was in helping the troubled children under his care do well and toe the line. In truth, McMan was an obsessed child molester who, over the years, sexually abused dozens of kids who'd passed through his classes. This was during a time when the extent to which child molesters had permeated society was unknown. None of the children in his classes ever told anyone about McMan's obsession.

He had a particular fondness for Ruben, then Robert. He even began going to the Ramirez home when Mercedes and Julian were working, and he abused Ruben and Robert there. Both brothers knew it was wrong, but it felt good, and it was a way to stay on Mr. McMan's good side.

"He would," Robert would later say, "come over to our house in the afternoon, do things, and take us back to his place. Like a couple of times a week, for a while. My mother and father knew, but we told them we were doing work for him at his house and that he was helping us with schoolwork. But he was sucking our cocks and getting us off."

When asked if McMan had gotten to Richard, Robert said:

"I don't know . . . Richie used to be there a lot, you know, but I never saw him do it. Maybe . . . I think so. He would even give us blow jobs in the bathroom at school. It felt good; what the fuck—so I never told anyone."

When Richard was recently asked if McMan had in fact sexually accosted him, he said he didn't remember. He would have been seven or eight and it was an event which, he quickly concedes, he may have blocked out.

He does, however, remember a degenerate pedophile who lived on Sapian Street, one block east of Ledo. He says he saw the man stick a candle in a boy's rectum as the boy screamed. Then he sodomized the boy very hard while he continued screaming. Richard says he left at that point and saw no more.

Ruben's problems with the law continued; he was arrested for breaking and entering and for stealing cars. Every time there was a new arrest, Julian would again beat Ruben, but it didn't help. As angry and hurt as Julian was over Ruben's troubles with the law, he would never abandon his son. He tried to talk to his son about his problems, but Ruben wasn't interested in talking.

Ruben needed lawyers, and little by little Julian was forced to sell property he had acquired in Juarez to pay for Ruben's and Robert's defenses. Within three years, Julian had sold all the property he had bought with money he'd earned laying track. What little he owned for security had been taken away from him.

Julian blamed his sons' problems on drugs—marijuana and pills—and the bad influences of certain boys in the Ledo area. He still felt his nephew, Miguel, was one of those bad influences. Miguel had grown into a very strong young man who beat to a pulp everyone he fought, regardless of their size, in no-holds-barred street fights. He was very quick to move and had no second thoughts about stomping an opponent into submission, then beating him some more. Miguel had also inherited the fierce Ramirez temper. Julian told his son to stay away from Miguel, but Ruben would not stop hanging out with his cousin. Until Miguel joined the Army in 1965 and went to Vietnam, he and Ruben remained tight.

Richard was not a gregarious child; he preferred to be alone. He was able to amuse himself for hours at a time, usually playing some game that involved shooting an enemy. At eight, he was tall for his age, with thick black hair and large dark eyes. He was quick to smile, though quite shy. He continued to do well in school, which made his father proud; he hoped and prayed his lastborn would make his dream of a college graduate for a son come true.

By the time Richard was nine, he and Ruth were the only children still living at home. Robert had dropped out of school in the tenth grade, Ruben in the eleventh. Ruben had first moved out, gotten an apartment with friends in El Paso, then moved on to Los Angeles. Robert and Joseph had rented a place together for a few months.

Joseph had graduated from high school, but did not want to go to school anymore. He had met Sofia, and he wanted to work and save so he could settle down with her. He, like his brothers, had had enough of living under Julian's tyrannical rule. Joseph lived with Robert until Robert secured a job in Morinze, Arizona, a four-hour drive from El Paso. Joseph then began living with Sofia, his childhood sweetheart.

With all his older brothers out of the house, Richard was suddenly alone. He no longer had three protectors. It was just Ruth, his mother, and Julian at the dinner table.

Julian was not a happy man. He'd been profoundly hurt by his sons' decisions to move out of the house. He didn't know where it had all gone wrong; he only knew it had.

People who used drugs were depraved, yet his sons, his

flesh and blood, were users of drugs. He often wondered if the atomic bomb tests had had something to do with the troubles his sons had had. It all made Julian a bitter man, and Richard could constantly sense it. As hard as Richard wanted to please his father and do the right thing by him, he could never live up to Julian's stringent expectations.

Ruth suggests Richard first changed when he was thrown off the football team at the Lincoln School for his epilepsy. He was the quarterback, and Julian attended the Saturday games whenever he wasn't away laying track. Richard was an excellent athlete and was very proud about being the quarterback. He was a fast runner and could think quickly on his feet. However, when Richard had had a grand mal seizure at the end of one game, the coach had unceremoniously and without apology thrown him off the team. There was medication Richard could have been given, but no one ever suggested it.

Richard was very disappointed; it wasn't his fault he had blackouts, and it was unfair for him to be thrown off the team. He protested to the coach, but the coach said, "If something happens to you while you're playing, it'll be all my fault. No, thank you."

TWENTY-TWO

Cousin Miguel or, "Mike" as he was often called, returned from Vietnam a war hero with two tours of duty under his belt and four medals on his thickly muscled chest. His Green Beret platoon of twenty men had been surrounded by the Vietcong at one point, and Mike and another soldier had been the only ones who'd made it out alive. Mike took to guerilla fighting like a champion boxer to the ring. It was a situation in which he could vent his anger and aggression—kill and not get into any kind of trouble. According to Richard, Mike had twenty-nine known kills.

Mike grew to actually enjoy war. When the American soldiers learned the Vietcong believed they wouldn't ascend to heaven if they lost a body part before dying, the soldiers began mutilating their bodies. It was not uncommon to see an American soldier with a necklace of human ears. The raping of the enemy's women was commonplace, too, and Mike had more than his share of Vietcong women.

When Mike returned from Vietnam, Richard began hanging out with him. He was twelve. To Richard, Mike was special—a bona fide, real live hero, a man who'd gone into battle and come back victorious, with medals and Polaroid photos to prove he had been there and done it.

In these pictures—which Mike showed Richard many times—there were Vietnamese women on their knees being forced to perform fellatio on Mike. In each he looked grimly at the camera and held a cocked .45 to the woman's head, genuine fear in the woman's eyes. Mike kept these black-and-white pictures, all bent by handling, in a shoebox at the top of a closet. He also kept eight shrunken heads he'd brought back from 'Nam in a battered suitcase under his bed. He told Richard he'd used the heads as pillows in Vietnam.

Mike was married to a shapely Mexican-American redhead named Jessie with a full figure and strong personality. He needed a strong woman as he was not an easy man to get along with. Jessie and Mike had two boys, Paul and Orado.

Mike hadn't received the kind of psychological counseling he'd needed when he'd returned from battle. In a war setting, he had no problem getting along. He'd been trained to kill with stealth and finality, and he realized he'd enjoyed it. "Having power over life and death was a high, an incredible rush. It was godlike. You controlled who'd live and who died—you were God," he told Richard.

To Richard, in a sense, Mike *was* a god. He listened to his older cousin's war stories of rape and killing wide-eyed, fascinated beyond normal curiosity. The photos had a profound effect on Richard. They aroused him sexually in a way far more intense than the girlie magazines his brothers had.

In some of the pictures Mike was holding the decapitated head of a woman. It was the same woman who had been forced to fellate him in another photograph. Richard didn't know why these pictures excited him so much; he knew it was wrong for him to be aroused by such brutality, but he would often masturbate thinking about those pictures.

The Church and Jesus, he knew, would frown deeply on such things, but he had no control over the whole process. He couldn't help becoming excited by Mike's photographs and stories.

Satan, he began to vehemently believe, would have approved of the thoughts and feelings he was having, and he started to think maybe Satan would be a more appropriate god, a power, for him to follow and worship.

Richard and Cousin Mike would cruise up and down Alameda Street in El Paso. They'd smoke pot and listen to the radio, and Mike would regale the boy with colorful, bloody, sexually sadistic war stories.

Richard had been smoking pot steadily from the time he was

ten. His siblings were always lighting up joints in the house, and Richard was quick to pick up the habit. It made him feel grown up. Pot was cheap in El Paso and easy to come by.

Richard's brother Robert had belonged to a Chicano movement called the Brown Berets. They would protest vocally and stage rallies about how unjustly Chicanos were being treated by the U.S. government. Ruth joined the group and talked of how inequitably Mexican-Americans were treated, a subject hotly discussed in the Ramirez house.

Richard became Mike's pupil. All his older brothers were away from the house, and Mike took it upon himself to show Richard the ways of the world—and the ways of war: how to fight to win, and how to protect himself. "It's us," he told Richard, "the poor and downtrodden, against them, the rich and influential."

He taught the boy the tricks and nuances of jungle warfare: showed him how to become invisible; how to kill with stealth and absolute certainty. Richard was a willing, particularly bright pupil.

During this time, Julian and Mike became close. He blamed Mike for much of Ruben's troubles, but Mike was his blood and was now a war hero. He was a man to be reckoned with, a fierce fighter with rock-hard muscles covering his body, which was heavily adorned with tattoos.

Julian knew Richard was spending too much time with Mike, but he couldn't put a stop to it, so he quit trying. Richard was stubborn like no one else in the family except Julian, and no matter how Julian beat, yelled, swore, and threatened Richard, Richard did what he wanted to do.

He was very quick, wiry, and resilient, and it became extremely hard for Julian to catch the boy if he didn't want to be caught. He'd run, "Fast like a rabbit," said Joseph, "before my father even moved in his direction."

Often Richard would sleep in the Cordova Cemetery to get away from his father's rage and bad temper. He'd grab his sleeping bag and run out of the house in a flash. The cemetery was on the other side of the newly constructed "Spaghetti Bowl" highway, three blocks away.

Richard thought the cemetery at night was peaceful and tranquil; on evenings of the full moon, there was something mystical and magical about it. Though he was frightened by horror movies and monsters, the cemetery never scared him. When he slept there under the huge expanse of the purple-black star-studded El Paso nights, he would sleep deeply and well. His father would be at work when he returned home in the morning.

Jessie was not happy with Mike or the lifestyle he'd chosen for himself. All he wanted to do was work out, drive around with Richie, smoke pot, and brag about the things he'd done in 'Nam. Jessie told him to get a job, stop hanging around with a kid—and and stop smoking pot. Mike was not the type to do anything but what he wanted to do.

Jessie complained to her mother, Larcerda, who was a tough, determined woman with a sharp tongue, and she, too, got on Mike to get a job.

Mike and Jessie and their two sons lived on Fruta Avenue in a small, one-story red brick building located in a residential complex called Truth Apartments. It was on a quiet, dusty street.

On May 4, 1973, Richard was in Mike's house, playing miniature pool. Thirsty, he went to get a Coke from the refrigerator. It was late afternoon and Jessie was out shopping. Inside the fridge, he saw Mike's gun, a .38-caliber with a two-inch barrel, on the top shelf.

"Hey," he called to Mike, "what's that doing in the refrigerator?"

"I may be using it, and I want it to be cool," Mike said.

Richard wasn't sure what the hell Mike meant and went back to the pool table. His long, nimble fingers and steady hand made him a naturally good pool player. As he was about to take a shot, Jessie came in carrying groceries. Immediately she started complaining about money and Mike's not working. Mike was not lazy; he just wasn't ready to take on the responsibility of a job yet. Why should he work unless a job that suited him came along?

He told Jessie to shut up—that he was sick and tired of her complaining, whining bullshit. She continued to nag him. He walked calmly, to the refrigerator, took out the .38, and faced Jessie. She wasn't frightened. She demanded to know what he was going to do with the gun. He told her he'd kill her if she didn't put a lid on it. She didn't believe him and she dared him to shoot her, spreading her legs defiantly, sticking her chin out. In one quick move, Mike raised the pistol and shot Jessie right in the face at point-blank range. The bullet entered just above her lip and exited the back of her head. Dead, she hit the ground hard, a finger of blood squirting from her wound as her body shook, trembled, and quaked in death's final embrace.

The report of the .38 sounded like a cannon in the small, cramped apartment, and Richard's ears were ringing. The room reeked of gunpowder and blood. Mike's two sons were crying. Mike told a wide-eyed Richard to leave and not tell anyone he was there when it happened. He didn't want Richard to be involved in any way.

"You don't *ever* say you saw this!" he said. "You understand?"

Numb, shocked, Richard left the house and began walking back to Ledo, along one of the many Santa Fe Railroad and Southern Pacific tracks crisscrossing much of El Paso. The day was gray, overcast and windy. Clouds of dust made it hard to see.

Richard was very upset, but he said nothing to Ruth, Mercedes, or his father when he arrived home. Just before dinner, the phone rang. It was Julian's sister, Victoria, telling Julian about the killing and asking him to come to the police station to help. Julian went to see what he could do. Mike's father had been gone for years, and it was Julian's place to help his sister's son.

Richard remained mute when he heard his father tell Mercedes of the shooting, the death, and the arrest of his cousin. Richard stayed home that night, sullen, quiet, and withdrawn. Everyone thought it was because Mike was in jail, charged with murder. Richard wanted to go see him, but he was too young.

Mike did well in jail. He became the boss of the section he was in while he awaited trial. El Paso jails are notoriously tough, but Mike had everything he wanted. In jail, as in war, "kill or be killed" was the order of the day—something Mike understood and had mastered quite well.

* * *

A few days after Mike killed Jessie, Richard returned to the Truth Apartments with his parents. Mike had called Julian from jail and asked him to go to the apartment and retrieve some pieces of jewelry. It was late afternoon, the sun shining brightly, the day very hot.

When Julian opened the front door and saw Jessie's blood in a large circle on the floor, he told Mercedes to wait in the car, but he let Richard come inside to help him find what Mike had asked for.

Now, for maybe the first time, Richard realized there was something very different about him. He recently said: "That day I went back to that apartment, it was like some kind of mystical experience. It was all quiet and still and hot in there. You could smell the dried blood. Particles of dust just seemed to hover in the air. I looked at the place where Jessie had fallen and died, and I got this kind of tingly feeling. It was the strangest thing. Then my father told me to look in her pocketbook for this jewelry my cousin wanted, and I dumped Jessie's pocketbook on the bed and looked through her things. It gave me the weirdest feeling—I mean, I knew her, and these were her things, and she was dead. Murdered. Gone. And I was touching her things. It made me feel . . . in contact with her."

Richard had never told anyone he'd seen Jessie murdered. Richard, a very impressionable twelve-year-old at the time of the shooting, should have gotten therapy, but that luxury was never made available to him.

Julian found the slug which had killed Jessie; it had gone clear through her head, hit the wall, and fallen to the floor. He'd figured out the trajectory and located the slug within two minutes. He showed it to Richard, both marveling over its destructive force, and Julian put it in his pocket. They retrieved what Mike wanted and left the still, hot silence of the place where there had been a murder.

Seven months after the incident, Mike went to trial for the killing. His defense was temporary insanity. His lawyer argued that Mike had been exposed to too much combat, had never gotten therapy, and was not legally sane. The prosecutor argued that war or not, Mike had killed his wife in cold blood and should be sent to jail, not to an asylum where he could be released when and if the doctors deemed him cured.

The jury, sympathetic toward Mike, a hero who had fought gallantly for his country against the dreaded Communists, found Mike innocent by reason of insanity, and he was committed to a Texas state mental hospital.

After Jessie's murder, Richard's life began to change radically. He had less and less interest in school and more and more interest in getting high, stealing, and getting high some more. He clashed with his father frequently, but there was nothing Julian could do to force his youngest back on the straight and narrow line he had walked up until Jessie's murder.

Joseph would later say, "My Dad would tell Richie, 'Just stay here at the house. You don't have to do anything. Just let me go to work in peace, with a clear mind that you are here and not in any kind of trouble. Please.'"

Richard grew his hair long and with Ruth smoked pot every day, all day and night.

That summer, Richard Ramirez left El Paso for the first time, and went to Los Angeles to visit his brother Ruben.

TWENTY-THREE

Ruben had started using heroin in El Paso, and he took his habit with him to Los Angeles. To support his addiction, he worked odd jobs, stole cars, and burglarized homes. Ruben was tall, thin, and lanky, and he had the fluid grace of the natural athlete. With stealth, rarely seen or heard, he got in and out of peoples' homes.

When Ruben was twenty, he and his wife, an El Paso woman named Suzanna, jumped on a Greyhound Bus and took the sixteen-hour ride to the Los Angeles Greyhound Bus Terminal. In 1972, as now, there was much crime and the selling of drugs and sex around the terminal. Julian and Suzanna wanted to get away from the downtown area, and they took an apartment in Watts, where it was even cheaper to live than downtown L.A.

Soon Suzanna was pregnant, and by the time Richard came to visit, he was uncle to a baby boy named Juan. After the birth, Ruben rarely used heroin, though he continued to smoke marijuana and drink. Ruben had never been a strung-out junkie; he'd always stop for a while, cold turkey, then begin all over again. It was a vicious cycle, numbed and made foggy by the reality of heroin.

Ruben teamed up with other Mexican-American burglars who hung out at the bus terminal. They were the black sheep who'd come to L.A. looking to rip off the system and get high. Every day, dozens of houses all over Los Angeles were robbed by them and the loot quickly sold to fences who lined the front of the terminal seven days a week, including Christmas and New Year's. To a professional burglar, L.A. was like a beacon in the night, summoning those who would steal from far and wide. The thieves knew L.A. was made up of ninety-six different communities, many of which had their own police forces, and if they moved around, they were a lot less likely to come to the attention of any given police department and thus elude capture.

Julian Ramirez had some trepidation about Richard's being in Ruben's company without any adult supervision. Had he known how bad it truly had been in L.A., he would have unequivocally forbidden Richard's going. Since Richard had seen Jessie killed, he'd become very quiet and morose, and Julian and Mercedes thought it would be a good idea if he left the bad influences of El Paso to spend the summer of 1972 in sunny Los Angeles.

The bus ride to L.A. was uncomfortable and arduous. Richard was not able to sleep. He was too excited at the prospect of being in the city of movie stars, beautiful women, palatial homes, and great wealth. Richard felt, even then, the only way he'd ever have any of that wealth was by stealing it. He viewed that as his destiny and didn't question it.

He had begun breaking into people's houses shortly before Mike had been arrested for killing Jessie. He loved the feeling of being in a stranger's house when they weren't there, alone, looking through their personal things, taking what he wanted, fantasizing about sexual scenarios involving bondage. It gave him a feeling of power. He had given his cousin much of what he stole of value. Mike had in turn sold it, then given the money to Richard, minus his share for acting as the middleman. Richard quickly warmed to the idea of getting money so easily. It certainly beat working.

He knew stealing was wrong—that it was against the teachings of the Church and the Ten Commandments—but he had seen his brothers and other boys do it regularly for years, and he was extremely adept at getting in and out of people's houses without being seen or leaving clues.

Richard was met at the terminal by Ruben. At nearly thirteen, he was 5'9" and weighed ninety pounds.

Richard looked up to Ruben because he had stood up to their tyrannical father and had always done what he'd wanted. He was his own man, and nothing, including all of Julian's beatings, could dissuade him from what he wanted to do. Ruben had promised his mother on the Sacred Heart of

Jesus that he'd watch over Richard and make sure he didn't get into trouble.

Richard had brought some marijuana up from El Paso, and the two brothers smoked a joint together as Ruben gave Richard a tour of the downtown area. He proudly introduced him to a few of the fences as his kid brother just in from El Paso. Richard couldn't get over all the tall buildings in the downtown area above Main. Ruben told him how enormous Los Angeles really was, and that the movie stars and beautiful homes were in Beverly Hills, Malibu, and Bel Air, far from where they were now.

That summer Richard saw the ocean for the first time. He thought the Pacific was one of the most beautiful things he'd ever seen, and his eyes nearly popped out of his head when he saw all the shapely, nearly naked beautiful women who filled Santa Monica. Bikinis were new to Richard, and he couldn't take his eyes off the women.

Richard was equally fascinated by all the L.A. prostitutes, who so openly, blatantly, and without shame offered themselves. He'd seen prostitutes before in Juarez on trips with his friends, but the Mexican prostitutes were not so bold as their Los Angeles counterparts. In L.A., they were half-naked, smiling, winking, gyrating their hips, and moving their tongues across their lips, covered with blood-red lipstick.

Richard saw all the movie-houses showing XXX-rated films, and he stared at the porno shops wide-eyed. He was too young to go into the shops legally, but he was tall and looked older than he was; he walked in and out of the shops with impunity. Seeing so much hard-core sexuality got him excited. For the first time he realized how sexual society truly was—that the intese thoughts and fantasies he'd been having for so long were normal, and by downtown Los Angeles standards, tame.

He saw men driving around in expensive cars and wearing expensive suits, trying to pick up hungry young boys. He was approached many times. Every day kids from all over the Southwest arrived at the bus terminal and the child molesters and perverts were there to meet them. Most of the kids were runaways, and being abused by strangers who paid them was often better than what had been done to them in their own homes. Sexual deviates, Richard Ramirez quickly learned, hid and were hypocritical about who they really were.

Richard accompanied Ruben on a few burglaries, and he learned from his older brother the ways of locks: how to open windows, the things to look out for—dogs, alarms, motion detectors.

When Richard returned to El Paso, his troubles began in earnest.

He had no use for school anymore; he had made up his mind that school wasn't for him. The things he wanted in life, he was sure, were not to be found or acquired in El Paso's Jefferson High.

Julian knew an education was the key to getting anywhere in the world, and he still secretly prayed Richard would change his ways and do well in school, excel in life, make something of himself. Richard could pass his classes if he wanted to; his teachers had said he had the aptitude, but not the desire.

Mrs. Trejo, the assistant principal of Jefferson High, remembers Richard as a tall boy who was always at the back of lines because of his height.

"He was not," she said, "a problem child. He was quiet and shy and behaved himself. He was a very good-looking boy."

Mr. Cesar Mendosa, a graying bull-dog of a man, was the principal of Jefferson. He also remembers Richard well. "He was not a bad boy, though he fell in with bad company. He played a lot of hookey. His grades were all failing. It was a shame because he was a smart young man. He just didn't seem to care; wouldn't apply himself. Richard seemed troubled."

Richard's school performance put him on a direct collision course with his father, who'd yell, threaten, and beat him—when he could catch him, but there was no altering Richard's behavior. He did not like school, he wanted nothing to do with it. In the ninth grade, he got failing marks in every subject except physical condition, in which he got an A.

Richard loved to hunt; his father had taught him how to shoot. With Mike's further tutelage, he had become an excellent marksman.

He would often go out hunting with a .22 rifle Julian had given him. Richard and Robert both enjoyed shooting, but Robert was away working the mines of Morenci and Mike was in jail, so Richard went alone. He stalked and hunted rabbits, coyotes, and birds in El Paso's wide-open deserts.

He soon became very adept at sneaking up on animals and taking them by surprise. He would then gut the animals he killed; he didn't know why and told no one, but he enjoyed sticking a sharp blade into the still warm animals and eviscerating them. He'd then feed their entrails to his dog, a brown mutt named Indio whom he loved very much. The Ramirezes had gotten Indio when Richard was three, and he had made the dog his own.

Richard loved scary movies and looked forward to going to the Capri Theater on Saturdays. There he'd watch a horror film triple-feature. At the frightening parts, everyone but Richard would scream. He'd take home what he saw on the screen and fantasize that he was the monster everyone was running from. He also liked martial arts films and took karate classes at a nearby karate school. He learned the basic moves, dropped out of the class, and practiced punching and kicking for hours on his own. He was very thin, though muscular and wiry; he, like all the Ramirezes, had large hands that made formidable weapons. He did not, like his cousin Mike, fight often, but when he did, he was vicious and fought to win. Mike had shown Richard how to take out an opponent quickly and where to kick and punch for the optimal effect. Mike had been trained to kill with his hands, and what he learned he passed on to Richard. However, Richard did not like to fight; if he could avoid a fight, he would.

Like his brothers, father, grandfather, and cousin Mike, Richard had a very bad temper.

Richard began going to Jehovah's Witnesses meetings on Sapian Street with his friend Eddie. At the meetings, he heard about the treacherous, terrible power of Satan—how if a man wasn't careful, he'd be in the grip of Satan before he knew it, destined to all kinds of pains in hell. Richard often had thoughts of violence fused with sex that were far from

Christian. He knew they were diametrically opposed to the teachings of the Church.

At first deeply confused, he'd ask himself why the images of blood and sadism affected him so. He didn't then attach the fleeting scenarios of women being tied up and raped, pleading for mercy, to the pictures his cousin Mike had shown him, or to his vivid stories of lustful sexual conquests.

Richard and his father clashed more and more, and the boy slept in the cemetery frequently; he tried to make its peace and tranquility his own. Even with the cemetery as a sanctuary, he found it harder and harder to live under Julian's roof, with his strict rules, his bad temper, and when he turned thirteen, he moved into Ruth's and her new husband's home.

Ruth had married Roberto Avala, a good-looking six-foot Mexican-American who, according to Ruth, was oversexed.

Ruth, like her brothers, couldn't live with Julian—he was too strict and too demanding, and too old-fashioned in all things. By getting married, Ruth was able to leave her father's house without incurring his overt wrath as her brothers had done. Julian didn't like her husband. He was a very good judge of character, and there was something about Avala that made him uncomfortable.

Roberto demanded sex from Ruth constantly whenever they were alone. He couldn't be satisfied. She wanted to be a good wife, but she wasn't as interested in sex as he was. She found it tiring. She did her best to keep him pleased, but it was never enough. She hoped his libido would diminish with time. She had grown into a beautiful, clear-skinned woman with big, dark round eyes, full lips, and the Ramirez high cheekbones. Her hair was a shiny, wavy chestnut brown.

The fights began between Ruth and Roberto when he started going out at night—just after they'd made love—to skulk about people's back yards, hoping to get a glimpse of a naked female neighbor or people having sex. Sometimes, he'd tell Ruth what he'd seen. At first she found it mildly amusing, but when she came to believe Roberto was an obsessed Peeping Tom who would rather watch strangers through windows than have sex with her, they began to fight.

Richard moved out of his father's house and into the Avala's, a place of romantic discontent and sexual incompatibility, in 1973, in the fifth month of his thirteenth year. Julian didn't want him to leave, and Mercedes was brokenhearted.

Richard began going out with Roberto on his nightly forays. Roberto had the neighborhood all staked out; he knew which windows to look in to and which yards to be in—and at what time. Richard enjoyed stealing about the El Paso dark, checking out windows: it was exciting and sexually stimulating.

When Ruth realized what they were up to, she demanded that Roberto stop, saying she'd leave if he continued. He apologized, but continued, leading to a separation after only two years of marriage. Richard continued to live with his sister and to spy on the neighborhood's unsuspecting women. Several times he had sneaked into houses while its occupants were sleeping. He had learned from Mike how to use the night as a cape to cloak himself with. It gave him a thrill, being able to sneak in and out of a place without being seen; to him, it was like a game—to see if he could really do it and get away with it.

"My brother never slept," Ruth would later relate. "He was up all night all the time. He was one of those people who functioned with only a few hours of sleep. He'd watch television or he'd go out somewhere. He just never slept."

Richard began to experiment with hallucinogens. LSD was still popular with America's youth, and he tripped many times on acid. He also took magic mushrooms and peyote, which were both plentiful and readily accessible in El Paso. High, he'd go out to the desert at night and hunt by the light of the moon, imagining he was in touch with Satan, that Satan was communicating with him.

The closer he drew toward Satan, the more estranged he became from society, as well as his parents. Richard began to conceive of Satan as a friend, an ally he could be himself with, share his inner thoughts with, and not be judged by. He remained close to Ruth and Joseph. He visited Joseph and his wife Sofia often. She was a short, reserved woman with a shy smile, almond-shaped doe eyes, and a very soft voice.

Sofia had fallen in love with Joseph from their first meeting. She understood the terrible cards life had dealt this up-beat, giving, quick-to-laugh man. She admired and respected him, and when he asked her to marry him, she said yes. He was nineteen, she eighteen, and they eloped.

Sofia was a perfect mate for Joseph. She loved him deeply and would gladly do anything for him. Joseph, as with all the Ramirez children, had been brought up a Catholic, and he truly believed in the Lord, Jesus Christ, above all things and did everything he could to be a good Christian.

Since he was twelve, Joseph had repeatedly tried to get Social Security and medical benefits and had been repeatedly turned down. The government's position was that he was able to stand and walk, and if he could do that, he could work. Through a federal work program, Joseph learned about an apprentice position for a butcher at Furr's. It was very difficult work for him, handling the large pieces of beef, but he did his best and complained little. After a few months he was promoted to meat cutter and was given a raise to eight dollars an hour, a good wage in 1975. Julian suggested Richie get a job there, too. If he didn't want to concentrate on school, then he should concentrate on work, mastering a trade. Joseph secured a part-time job for his younger brother, but Richard didn't like the work, and after he almost cut off his thumb, he quit.

Mike did not want his mother-in-law, Larcerda, near his two boys while he was in the mental hospital. He had never liked her, and he thought she was crazy. She felt the same way about him.

Larcerda was a bold, fierce Mexican woman who was not afraid of anything in this world. She believed fervently in spirits and in the power of Satan. She often went to a black *macobero* in Juarez to have spells cast. She took the murder of her only daughter very hard, and vowed to fight to her dying breath to have her grandchildren. She hated Mike and she hated his family with a passion bordering on insanity.

Julian did not want to tangle with her, but Mike had begged him not to let Larcerda have his two boys. As his uncle and the elder male in the family, it was Julian's duty to go to war with Larcerda over custody of the boys.

When Larcerda realized Julian was going to fight for her grandchildren, she ran to the *macobero* and begged him to cast a spell, the most potent one he was capable of. For a price, a curse was duly prepared and cast.

It was no secret to anyone, including Julian, that Larcerda used black magic, and it was something that concerned him. Perhaps because of Julian's deep-rooted belief in the power of Satan, of evil, of black magic, shortly after the problems with Larcerda began, he did become ill. At first, he was lethargic and listless, not wanting to do anything. Soon he lost his appetite and began wasting away.

Mercedes took Julian to the hospital, hoping it wasn't a spell. He underwent many different tests, which all said nothing was wrong with him. Specialists from Tucson and Albuquerque looked at him, and they couldn't find anything, either. He just lay in the hospital bed—not moving, not talking, not recognizing his children when they came to visit. Whatever problems Julian had had with his children were forgotten when he became sick. They rallied behind him unequivocally.

Ultimately, the doctors said they just couldn't find anything physically wrong with Julian. Mercedes decided to fight fire with fire. Priests were brought to the hospital, prayers were said, holy water was sprinkled, but Julian didn't improve.

Mercedes then went to a different, renowned *macobero* in Juarez.

"This man's power was legendary. People came from all over Mexico to see him; there would be lines many blocks long of people waiting," Joseph would say later. Mercedes told him the whole story, beginning with Mike's shooting of Jessie and ending with Julian's mysterious illness. He listened attentively, asked a few questions, then told Mercedes that a spell had been cast.

This *macobero* was a white witch, unlike the witch Larcerda had gone to, and he was always happy and willing to do battle with Satan's disciples.

"When," he said, "they show themselves for what they are, they must be beaten."

He agreed to go to Julian's hospital room.

He was a small man with intense eyes that seemed to see everything—the past, the present, the future—all at once.

As soon as he walked into Julian's room, he proclaimed that a spell had been cast, and he immediately began to battle it, summoning the appropriate spirits to chase away the evil forces, rubbing Julian's head and hands with different yellow-colored oils that smelled sweet. He finished after twenty-eight minutes, told Mercedes it was done, and left. She tried to give him money, but he wouldn't take it.

One hour after the *macobero* had left, Julian got up and acted normal. For three weeks, he hadn't moved or said a word. It was a miracle. He said he was hungry and wanted some food. Mercedes's joy overflowed, and she cried and held Julian tightly.

Julian was soon released from the hospital; he quickly regained the weight he'd lost and said he had little memory of the illness.

After that, Julian and Mercedes became even more religious. They had seen with their own eyes the power of good over evil and they were believers.

Julian wanted nothing to do with Larcerda anymore. She was given custody of the two boys. Neither of them, today, has any memory of their mother being killed.

Richard found a job at the Holiday Inn, keeping the place clean, carrying luggage, and doing light maintenance work. The money wasn't bad and there were lots of women for him to look at. He had become acutely aware of women and sex; he would masturbate frequently as he imagined different scenarios—most involving bondage—with the attractive women he saw around the hotel.

His first problems at the Holiday Inn occurred when he was in the hotel elevator with two girls in their teens. He smiled at one of them and told her he thought she was pretty. She said thank you and promptly told her parents Richard had made a pass. Her parents complained to the assistant manager, who told the manager, who promptly summoned Richard to the office.

Richard was told he was not to flirt with the guests' daughters and was warned that if another such incident happened he'd be fired. He promised it wouldn't. The manager made him apologize to the girls' parents and the incident was forgotten.

After being employed at the Holiday Inn for three months, Richard was given a master key to the hotel's rooms. He says he got it from his friend, who had worked at the hotel but had been fired for being late and not showing up.

By now Richard was 5'10" with taut, sinewy muscles. He was very well coordinated, the fastest runner in his class. He was still enrolled in Jefferson High, but for the most part he didn't attend classes.

From the very first, Richard had gone back to the hotel at night to look in the windows. The hotel had curtains of stiff fabric, and there was frequently an inch or two where someone could look in. The unsuspecting guests had no idea he was there, spying on them, fantasizing about them. He began testing himself, becoming bolder and entering the rooms with his pass key while the guests were sleeping. That's when the most valuables were there, he realized.

He'd first make sure the guests were asleep by listening at the window. When he was satisfied, he'd open the door, enter quickly, get down to the ground, and wait, making certain the guests weren't disturbed. Then he'd crawl across the floor, as Mike had taught him, and find the wallets, cash, and watches using a penlight to see.

The guests, management, and police were baffled by these thefts. Richard was not a suspect; he was discreet and didn't commit too many thefts at once. He'd wait weeks between them, and no one knew he had a pass key.

Frequently, he would see beautiful women undressing, toweling themselves after their showers. He was very turned on by the fact that they didn't know he was watching. But he wanted more.

He wanted, needed, to *have* one of the women he'd been looking at through the windows, and he devised a plan. At the right moment, he would go into the room of a lone female, overpower her, blindfold her, bind her, and then have her the way he fantasized about constantly.

The first one was in her late twenties. She was attractive, with black hair and large breasts. When he peeked into her room, it was 1 A.M. She was wearing a bra, panties, and an unbuttoned nightgown, preparing, he thought, for bed. He could see she was alone because he had a view into the bathroom of the single room.

When she went into the bathroom, he put the pass key in the lock, opened the door, and entered. Quickly, catlike, on the balls of his feet, he made his way across the room and hid in the open closet. The element of surprise was part of his plan. As she left the bathroom, he took her from behind so she couldn't see him. He first got his hand over her mouth, just as he'd planned. Then he got her to the floor and gagged her with a piece of her underwear, warning her not to scream and not to look at him.

She obeyed, knowing her husband would be back at any moment. He was a large, fierce, jealous Mexican, and she knew he'd be in a rage when he saw what was being done to her. He had just gone to get something to eat. What if he didn't have the key with him she wondered in a panic; or if this man tearing at her underwear had a gun? She prayed.

After Richard tied her up, he pulled off her undergarments and was attempting to have sex with her when the door opened and the woman's husband walked in.

He went berserk, attacking Richard with fists and feet. Richard tried to fight back, but he weighed only 120 pounds and the husband was thick and bull-like. He beat Richard to the floor, knocked him out, then beat and kicked him some more. He untied his wife and called the front desk which summoned the police. Richard remained unconscious and bleeding, his face swollen all out of proportion. He had two huge black eyes and was almost unrecognizable. He was handcuffed and arrested. Taken to the hospital before jail, he was treated for a concussion and given thirty stitches to close up a gash inside his mouth.

Julian was away laying track. When the call came from the El Paso police, a Spanish-speaking officer told Mercedes what happened. She couldn't believe her ears.

It wasn't possible that Richie, her baby, had attacked a woman in a hotel room. There had to be some mistake. Richard got on the phone and confirmed he'd been arrested, though his version of what had happened was entirely different. He could never admit to his mother what he'd done. It would hurt her beyond words.

Richard didn't know why he had these uncontrollable desires involving bondage and rape, but they were there, and he had no say over their comings and goings (as with his epileptic attacks). He knew they were wrong—were against the Church—but they, to him, were bigger than the Church, bigger than life itself, and not about to go away.

Mercedes, in a panic, called Ruth, who picked up her mother, and together they hurried to the hospital. Richard would always be the baby of the family; he was a good boy, not like his brothers; he was special.

Richard was lying handcuffed to a hospital gurney. His face was twice its size, both his eyes swollen closed. He looked more like he'd been hit by a truck than an irate husband.

Barely able to speak, Richard told Ruth and his mother that the woman had invited him in and came on to him. Then her husband had arrived and gone crazy. He was innocent; he was the victim.

Ruth and Mercedes believed him.

It was impossible their Richie had raped a woman. He was a gentle boy who wasn't capable of such a ghastly deed. Neither had any idea about the inner turmoil and conflict that lived inside Richard.

After he was treated at the hospital, he was detained overnight for observation. In the morning, he was booked and taken to court. The judge released him to Mercedes. He was fifteen and would be treated as a juvenile.

The couple at the hotel lived out of state. They wanted nothing more to do with the incident and wanted to forget the whole ugly affair. They refused to return to El Paso and testify against Richard, and the charges were dropped.

Richard received no probation, no therapy, no dialogue with anyone about the demons dancing in his head. Julian, like Mercedes, believed Richard's story and had arranged for a lawyer to represent him.

TWENTY-FOUR

Mike was released from the Texas State Mental Hospital in late 1977, four and a half years after killing Jessie. The doctors felt he had stabilized and was fit to be returned to society. The doctors reasoned that his not having gotten extensive therapy after the horrors of Vietnam was to blame. He deserved another chance.

Soon after Mike got out of the hospital, he and Richard began hanging out together again. Richard had changed: He was taller and had filled out some, though he was still lanky. His eyes were no longer wide and innocent. They'd taken on a certain hardness beyond his years. Richard was Mike's favorite cousin. He was loyal and knew how to keep his mouth shut, rare attributes in a man, let alone a boy. Mike resumed his training of Richard. He wanted him to be prepared for the world. Mike believed that only the strong survived, and he took it upon himself to make Richard strong.

Julian and Richard were now almost totally estranged. Ruben was still in Los Angeles. Joseph had a son, Jesse, and a daughter, Lupe, and had had his left leg amputated at the knee. Robert was in jail in Arizona for getting into a fight over a traffic incident. Mike became a surrogate older brother to Richard.

"Miguel [Mike] filled the vacuum," Joseph said later.

Mike explained the concepts of guerilla warfare to Richard and told him more about his sexual conquests in 'Nam. These stories hung inside Richard's head like obscene, perverse paintings.

Mike still had the pictures of his conquests, which he showed Richard, and these photographs gave dimension, life,

and sustenance to Mike's tales of sexual dominance and
sadism and Richard's subsequent fantasies.

Mike and Richard again drove up and down Alameda
Street, listening to music and smoking pot—just as they had
done when Richard was twelve. The good old days were back.
Cousin Mike was free as a bird, cracking jokes and making
Richard laugh. Richard marveled at Mike's strength and re-
silience. They never talked about the day Jessie had been
shot, but it was always there, always in the back of Richard's
mind: one minute she was there, talking, breathing, then she
was gone.

Richard, aside from hanging out with Mike, became a
loner. He didn't trust people or like them particularly. He
perceived society as unfair, vicious, and hostile.

In the early-morning hours, when all of El Paso slept,
Richard Ramirez dressed in black and burglarized people's
homes. He used what Mike had told him—"Watch out for
gravel, clotheslines, garbage cans, and dogs"—and became a
very proficient thief.

By the time he was sixteen, his nickname had become
"Dedos," or "Fingers." If it wasn't nailed down, he'd take it.
He often sold what he'd stolen: a radio, a leather jacket, a
television, stamps, coins. Julian knew nothing of Richard's
nightly forays.

Richard often thought of Los Angeles, of all the wealth
there—his just for the taking. Through his burglaries in El
Paso, Richard was growing more and more confident. Soon
he would be ready for the big city. If he ever expected to score
big, he knew it wouldn't be in El Paso.

Los Angeles, the City of Angels, was what he saw in his future. He used El Paso as a training ground. If he went to L.A.
before he was ready, he'd only end up in jail for a long time.
It was like a war and you had to be in fighting condition if you
wanted to win.

In Los Angeles, there were large, palatial homes, and the
people in them were rich. Richard knew Los Angeles was
made up of many communities, and if he stayed on the move
and didn't leave clues, they'd never catch him. "It's an easy
thing to steal, any jerk could do it, but to steal and not get

caught, ever, that's something else. That's something you have to train for. And to learn it properly takes years," Richard later said.

Richard returned to the desert to hunt, practicing what Mike had taught him: how to approach game with stealth, and when to pull the trigger. He'd see just the tips of a rabbit's ears as it hid among rocks, and he'd crawl up to it without being seen. It was a game he enjoyed, but he knew it was a game which could become real at any time.

"You never know," Mike had taught him, "when you'll have to provide for yourself, kill or be killed. You have to always be prepared. After all, life is like living in a jungle. It's a fuckin' dog-eat-dog world, and if you don't eat first, you get eaten. Period. It's that simple."

Richard would now often stay out in the desert after it had gotten dark. Mike had taught him how to read the stars, and he never got lost. When there was a full moon, the desert was very beautiful, Richard thought—a silent, surrealistic world of black and white through which he moved, hunting. Sometimes, the moon was so close it was as if he could reach up and touch it.

Richard was still taking hallucinogens. When he tripped, he saw monsters doing all kinds of horrible things to people. The monsters wanted and took sex.

Nancy Avila lived across the street and down the block from the Ramirez residence. She was a petite teenager with curly dirty blond hair and a quick smile. Nancy had had a crush on Richard since 1976, when she was twelve and had first noticed him at a birthday party for his niece. She thought he was very good looking and couldn't take her eyes off him as he walked up and down the block. Although he was living with Ruth, he was at the Ledo house frequently, visiting his mother. Nancy would smile and wave to Richard; he'd smile back and wave, but did nothing more; he was shy, and she was only twelve.

Some time later, when she was fifteen, Nancy became a little bolder and one day crossed the street so she could talk to him. She liked him even more after that and began thinking about him before she went to sleep at night in her room, alone in bed.

She soon made up her mind to have Richard. She didn't know what she'd do exactly when she did have him, but she wanted him. Her parents were very strict Mexicans, and if they'd known the kind of thoughts she was having about Richard, she'd have gotten a serious thrashing and been grounded. But Nancy's parents knew nothing of her fantasies.

According to Nancy, she instigated what happened next: she looked in the phone book, located the Ramirez number, and called. Richard was home and answered the phone. They talked a long time, about "nothing in particular," she'd later say. They had a few more extended phone conversations over the next month or so. He then asked her if she'd meet him so they could be alone together. She agreed and suggested they rendezvous at her school. By now, Richard had dropped out of school altogether. He and Julian barely spoke anymore.

One day Nancy's father, as always, drove her to school, kissed her, and told her to have a nice day. He was very strict, but he rarely had reason to admonish or punish Nancy. If he had known what Nancy and Richard had planned, he would no doubt have gone looking for Richard with a shotgun, as a Mexican girl's virtue is of great worth. Richard picked her up in a borrowed old, beat-up jalopy. He rented the room at the Flamingo Hotel on Alameda. It was a tense moment for Nancy. Never in her wildest fantasies did she think she'd really be in a hotel for the purpose of sex, but here she was, entering a room with Richard Ramirez, the boy of her fantasies. Finally, they were alone. They kissed gently and took off all their clothes.

"He was," she later said, "patient and kind. I was so nervous, but he wasn't pushy at all.

"But as it turned out, it couldn't happen. No matter how hard he tried, he couldn't, ah, do it. I wanted him to, but it just wasn't possible that day. He didn't get mad or anything like that; he was nice about it."

A week later Richard again picked up Nancy after her father had dropped her off at school. They went to the same hotel, and this time, perhaps because Nancy was more relaxed, Richard and she had sex. She hadn't known really what to expect, but it wasn't, she thought, all that it was cracked up to be. Over the next few months, Richard and Nancy saw each other surreptitiously. She was fifteen and he was seventeen, and if anyone found out they were having sex, there'd have been trouble. Both Richard and Nancy went to great lengths to protect their affair. They would meet blocks away from Ledo and go off together. He could not always borrow a car, nor did he always have money for a hotel. Whatever money he made quickly left his hands; he gave it to Ruth, to his mother; he bought things. He sometimes went over to Juarez and had sex with a prostitute.

One night, Richard suggested to Nancy that they go to the cemetery together. It was private and peaceful, and they'd be able to relax, he said. Without really thinking about it, she said okay. That evening there was a half moon low in the El Paso sky. Everything was quiet and still. Richard knew the cemetery well, and he took Nancy to the spot where he'd been sleeping for years to avoid his father's anger. He had a blanket hidden there and they lay on it and began kissing. Soon Nancy forgot where she was, and they made love.

"Richard was a good, very gentle, considerate lover," she would later say.

When asked by a journalist if he ever forced her to do anything, she answered, "Oh, no, never anything like that! I was willing and we just did it. I felt guilty sometimes, but I still did it. I was young and I really loved him and I thought he loved me. There was something very different about Richard; he had an aura about him that just drew me in. He was generous and he was fun."

Mercedes knew about Richard and Nancy and she warned him to be careful.

The cemetery was close to Ledo, and Nancy and Richard continued to go at night. It was peaceful and private in the cemetery and no one ever bothered them. When asked if she was afraid of ghosts or spirits in the cemetery, she laughed nervously and said no.

Nancy had heard rumors about Richard being a thief, but she dismissed them as jealous gossip. To her, Richard was soft, generous, and sincere.

Nancy knew nothing about his other side.

TWENTY-FIVE

By February of 1978, Richard had had it with El Paso. It was too small, and he couldn't live the way he wanted to there. Mike had remarried and was having problems with heroin and with his new wife. Richard's affair with Nancy had run its course; she wanted to spend more time with him and that wasn't possible, considering her age, so Richard stopped seeing her. What he wanted, the thing he craved, he couldn't get from Nancy. "She was a good girl," he'd say of her later.

Richard had a plan to make some quick money: he could buy pot in El Paso for next to nothing and sell it in Los Angeles for considerably more.

Without telling anyone, Richard left El Paso for good on a dirty, battered Greyhound bus. He'd just turned eighteen. Richard listened to heavy metal music over earphones and slept when possible.

He was drawn to musical groups whose rhythms were hard-driving and whose lyrics had something to do with his innermost thoughts on religion and sex. He no longer believed in the Catholic Church. The things in his head and heart now were far from Christian; he didn't know when exactly the change had occurred, though he had an idea.

Intense sadistic sexual images filled Richard's head, as much a part of him as his heart or legs. He had no idea how to make them go away, and there was no one he could talk to about his thoughts, not even Mike.

For such thoughts, Jesus Christ, he knew, would scorn him and make sure he went to hell and stayed there forever. Because Richard had so fervently believed in Jesus Christ, he now as fervently believed in Christ's counterpart—Satan. The two went hand in hand. It was really very simple: Jesus represented good, and Satan represented evil.

"But then, who's to say what is evil?

"A man's beliefs are his own business. Neither the Church nor anybody else has any right to tell you how to think and how to act; that's what real freedom is about: to be able to be who you really are, not what you are expected or supposed to be," he later said.

Richard arrived at the Greyhound terminal in downtown Los Angeles. If Satan hung out in L.A., that's where he would have been, for sure: the downtown area was alive with all that's wrong with human nature.

Richard was eager to get on with his "career." He'd be so successful he'd be able to retire young and live high on the hog, in a fancy house, with a pool and slaves. The idea of having slaves appealed to him; he would frequently have dreams of being the master of many women, sitting on a throne, as they groveled obediently at his feet.

He carried a large black knapsack and nothing more. He knew how to live on the go, and luxuries meant nothing to him. He was a soldier in a war, and war was tough.

Unlike Jesus, Satan, he felt, would not scorn him, but embrace him and give him solace, protection, and understanding. It was a very cruel world, and if a man didn't believe in some power higher than himself, he was hollow and empty inside, and the power Richard turned to was Lucifer in all his glory.

He walked west on Seventh to Main, a half-mile away. He passed broken-down hookers with no teeth and black eyes and tattooed junkies who were rail-thin and lost in a haze of heroin. He passed cokeheads whose eyes were bugging out of their faces, their movements erratic, their mouths working away aimlessly, foaming. There were bars that smelled like stale whisky and dirty bodies, laced with the sweet aroma of marijuana, filled with the distinct drone and hum of human misery and hustle. Richard walked through this jungle of degradation with a quick, easy step. If any place was ever a bad influence on a boy, it was downtown Los Angeles.

But to Richard then, this was home. This was a place he

could be comfortable in. Here he would not be scorned or looked down upon or judged. Here he could be who he wanted. Here, he felt, he was among his own kind: the people of the street, the people of the night, the black sheep of society.

On Main Street, Richard went into Dave's Adult Bookstore, next to the Cecil Hotel. He gave the guy behind the counter, a cantankerous balding man with a stump of a cigar protruding from his mouth, the dollar required to look at the magazines and books, which later would be applied toward any purchases. Richard perused the magazines. He was immediately drawn to the ones involving bondage. He bought one, rented a room in the Frontier Hotel, and retired for the night.

Over the next few weeks he sold the pot he had brought from El Paso. With the money he lived in different hotels, bought food, and played pool, sometimes for money. He loved being on his own with no one telling him what to do. Some nights he'd visit Ruben and Suzanna.

On one of the nights when Richard stayed at Ruben's place, three men tried to break into the apartment. It was 4 A.M. and Richard was sleeping on the couch. As the men tried to break open the door, Richard woke up. Their plan, apparently, was to rush inside, take what they wanted, and leave. But in a flash Richard was up and yelling for Ruben. As the door was opening, Richard swung and hit the first guy in the eye. Richard was now six feet tall, 150 pounds and he knew how to throw a punch. He'd die before he let these men into the apartment with his brother's wife and children. Quickly Ruben joined Richard at the door, and together they fought the three men. When Richard screamed for Suzanna to bring the gun, the intruders took off. There was no gun, really, but if there had been, Richard would have used it in a heartbeat, and the law would have said he was within his rights.

Richard told Ruben he was going to get some guns for protection, and Ruben thought it was a good idea. He was shaken up by the experience. It was the first time anything like that had ever happened. He knew if Richard hadn't been there, he and his family might very well have been killed, Suzanna and his daughter hog-tied and raped.

Richard was able to find pistols at the Greyhound terminal.

He bought a .22 revolver and gave it to his brother for protection. Ruben slept with the gun near his bed. He'd also put new locks on the door and reinforced the frame. If those guys came back again, Ruben was ready. He knew how to shoot well and would use the gun without hesitation. Everything in the world he loved was in that apartment, and he'd protect it with his life.

Problems between the two brothers began when Ruben accused Richard of coming on to Suzanna. Whether it was true or not was never made clear, but Richard stopped going to his brother's house.

That first year in L.A., Richard became addicted to cocaine. It was 1978, and coke was the "in" drug, selling for $100 per gram. This was prior to the Colombian cartels appling modern corporate techniques to the importation and distribution of cocaine in the States, which brought the price of a gram down to thirty-five dollars by the mid-eighties.

Richard became obsessed with the rush and the feeling of power cocaine gave him. When he was on it, he felt strong, cunning, and invincible. Richard had seen Ruben using a needle since he was twelve, and it was an easy transformation from snorting cocaine to injecting it intravenously.

Mainlining cocaine is far different from snorting it. The drug goes right into the bloodstream all at once, causing an immediate, thunderous rush with the intensity of a speeding train. Cocaine stimulates the right side of the brain, where much that is dark and abstract about human nature resides, and with the drug saturating Richard's brain, he was drawn further and further toward Satan and sadism. The drug became a key that unlocked a door behind which lurked nightmares in living color.

Richard knew there were a lot of people who were drawn to the devil and what he represented. One only had to look at the music scene. There were a dozen groups with songs espousing the virtues of evil—Black Sabbath, Ozzy Osborne, Billy Idol, Ronnie James Dio, Judas Priest, and AC/DC were some of Richard's favorites, and he knew the lyrics to all their songs.

To support his cocaine habit, Richard committed scores of

burglaries. Without difficulty, he was earning the money he needed for the cocaine—which was now between $1,200 and $1,500 a week. The fences at the bus terminal gladly bought whatever he had of worth, though they preferred televisions, stereos, jewelry, stamp collections, watches, any kind of gold, and diamonds.

The cocaine accelerated and fueled Richard's fantasies, his psychosis. When he wasn't stealing or getting high, he thought more and more about sadism as a means of getting off sexually. He was no longer interested in conventional sexual relationships. What turned him on was S&M, with him in the role of master. The porno films and books he saw in the downtown area further fueled the fire burning inside his tormented libido.

Within fifteen months of his arrival in L.A., Richard began sleeping and living out of stolen cars. He'd keep one a few days, abandon it, and take another. He'd either hot-wire the car or steal it from a gas station while the owner went in to pay for gas, both tricks that he'd picked up in El Paso. It was in these stolen cars that he began to traverse and learn the complicated Los Angeles freeway system. He studied maps and made up his mind to rob houses in every community. He couldn't get over the size—or the wealth—of Los Angeles County. He'd never seen such beautiful homes and estates. Why, he would ask himself, did these people have so much, when he and his family and so many others had so little? He was sure it wasn't fair, and through his stealing, he was balancing out the scales of this injustice. He viewed himself as a sort of Robin Hood, who kept his booty rather than doling it out to strangers.

Richard worked mostly at night. He'd sneak into people's houses while they were sleeping, take what he could, and leave without being seen or heard. He was stealing just as he had done at the Holiday Inn, only now he was using the proceeds of his ventures to feed an insatiable hunger for cocaine.

Soon Richard discovered P.C.P., or angel dust, a powerful narcotic that is smoked and has been blamed for many deaths and psychotic episodes. Emergency wards all over the country have had to deal with people who had done dust and gone off the deep end, who had to be restrained and sedated.

On a hot summer night in 1978, Richard met a pretty brunette who came downtown looking to cop some dust. She approached him on Spring Street and asked him if he knew where she could score. He copped for her, she took him back to her apartment, and they smoked the dust and got stoned. Richard put the moves on the brunette, but she turned him down cold, telling him she was a lesbian and not to waste his time. He couldn't accept that. He was going to have her whether she was willing or not.

At 3 A.M. they ran out of dust and she told him to leave. Instead of going down the stairs of the building, he went upstairs, to the roof, waited a while, then slinked down the fire escape to her window, which he had earlier unlocked. The lights were out and she'd gone to bed and was sleeping. He came through the window and surprised her, immediately covering her eyes, gagged her, and tied her up. She fought him, but she was no match for the forces driving Richard. When she was bound so she couldn't move, he ripped off her underwear and raped her several times . . . excited by his domination over her.

At dawn he left, alive with the power of having had a human being in his total control. It was the first time he'd actually overcome a woman and had sex with her, and he'd enjoyed it profoundly.

That same week Richard read *The Satanic Bible*, a book glorifying the virtues of Satan written by Anton LaVey, founder of the Church of Satan in San Francisco. LaVey, a former circus animal trainer with a shiny bald head, had also written a second book, *Church of Satan*.

LaVey's approach to Satanism was much like that of a ringmaster in a circus—unapologetic, loud, and boisterous. He openly endorsed Satan and was proud of this. In LaVey's organization there was no sin, no guilt, and one could do what one wanted—whatever it was—whenever one wanted to do it.

Richard stole a car and drove to San Francisco to meet LaVey. It was important for Richard to see and be among others who were followers of Satan. He believed in his heart that

LaVey was the real thing, that he had a personal rapport with Lucifer.

LaVey had opened a second church of Satan in Amsterdam's red-light district. Many of the prostitutes hustling sex from store windows became members, as did some sexual deviants who called Amsterdam home and some transient perverts.

Richard was deeply impressed when he met LaVey and treated him as though he was something holy.

"I thought Richard was very nice—very shy. I liked him," LaVey would say of Richard years later.

Richard said he attended a ceremony over which LaVey presided. Everyone was naked, and LaVey did a ritual above the unclothed body of a woman. During the ceremony, Richard felt the ice-cold hand of Satan touch him and he felt Satan's presence. It shook him to his core.

Afterward, he hurried from the ceremony and called his mother in El Paso, beseeching her to pray for him. When she asked why, he said, "I was touched by Satan tonight, Mama. He came to me."

She told him she'd pray for him and begged him to come home. He refused, saying he didn't want anything more to do with El Paso.

Mercedes hurried to church, got down on her knees, and prayed that her youngest would not fall victim to the Lord of Darkness, that he'd come home. To Mercedes, Satan was as real as anything in life—a car, a house, a thunderstorm. The fact that she'd never seen him didn't mean anything; she'd never seen Jesus and she was sure he was there.

Richard left San Francisco and returned to L.A. He read LaVey's second book and became a different person—much more serious—and drew further .nto himself. He was no longer Richard Ramirez, the El Paso burglar and sometime pot dealer; he was now Richard Ramirez, the unsmiling, mean-eyed Satanist.

Soon after, Richard was arrested for driving a stolen car. He spent several months in jail, where he met a long-haired blond man with tattoos and bleeding gums who was also an avowed Satanist, and who did not shut up about how great Satan was.

He said Satan would protect and help anyone who was true

to him. "You don't ever have to feel guilty about anything. The only law is that you are true to your inner self. If you want to kill somebody, that's okay. What's bad to them is good for us. Get it?"

Richard "got it" only too well, for when he was released from jail, he became what is known as a "lone practitioner." He did not make it a secret that he followed Satan; in fact, he drew perfectly shaped pentagrams on his hands and arms, but he stayed away from groups and cults. He was untrusting of them. He felt that they (including Anton LaVey) might have been compromised by police infiltration.

Richard continued doing burglaries, stealing cars, and shooting cocaine, and he withdrew further and further into himself. Days melted into weeks and weeks into months, and his life became a monotonous rollercoaster ride of cocaine, stealing, more cocaine, and more stealing—with an occasional prostitute. Personal hygiene didn't much matter to him anymore, and he walked with a tawny, leathery smell. He didn't pay much attention to his teeth and constantly ate sweets and fruit and drank Cokes, giving himself large, painful cavities that he reluctantly sought care for. He didn't like dentists, having to sit still with his mouth open as strange hands prodded and probed, hurting him.

As time went by, Richard became more and more estranged from his family. He rarely visited, and when he did, he'd stay in the Pink Flamingo on Alameda. Julian did not like the way Richard looked. He was too thin and didn't appear to be at all healthy, he said. He was sure Richard was using narcotics, and when he tried to talk to his youngest, they'd inevitably end up arguing and Richard would go back to L.A., to more burglaries, more cocaine, and more bizarre sexual fantasies. Ruth often tried to reach him through Ruben, but to no avail. Julian rarely saw him or even knew where he was.

At one point in mid-1983, Ruth traveled to Los Angeles to see Richard. The family had not heard from him for months. Julian said he wanted Richard back in El Paso with him, and Ruth was dispatched as an emissary of the Ramirez clan. Her mission was to bring her baby brother back home.

Ruben told Ruth he hadn't seen Richard for weeks. They went downtown together and tried to find him, but he was not at his usual haunts. Ruth slept in Ruben's car that night. She did not get along with Suzanna and blamed her for starting trouble between her two brothers. Watts was a dangerous place for a good-looking woman to sleep alone in a car. Ruth hid under her raincoat in the back seat until the sun came up. She'd barely slept the whole night. There were huge rats in Watts, and Ruth watched horrified as Ruben's black cat pounced on the rats and killed them right there on the sidewalk. The cat was so good at killing rats, Ruben would rent him out. On the third day of Ruth's search for Richard, she finally found him in front of the bus terminal. She hardly recognized her brother; he was thinner than she'd ever seen him, and he didn't look like Richie anymore. He was like somebody else. "He'd changed," she'd later say. "It was mostly in his eyes—they were hard and unfeeling."

There was still some bad blood between Richard and Ruben over Richard's supposed advances to Suzanna, and Ruben left Ruth and Richard at the bus terminal and went back to Watts.

Ruth was totally shocked by her brother's appearance and his erratic behavior. He took her back to a seedy room he had in a hotel on Main. She was mortified at the squalor of the place, the characters in the lobby and halls. He sat her down in a ripped chair and proceeded to shoot up cocaine in front of her. She began crying, beseeching him to stop what he was doing, and begged him on her knees to come back home. He didn't want any part of what Ruth was selling. He was up and moving about the little room like a caged jungle cat. He had a ghetto blaster and put on AC/DC's *Highway to Hell*.

"Please, Richie, I beg you to stop this; it will kill you. Papa wants you to come back home; he says everything will be different now; he'll do anything for you, Richie. He loves you so much. Please stop with this cocaine. It'll destroy you. Richie, open your eyes—"

"My eyes are open! Fuck El Paso . . . I'm not going back. There's nothing there for me—"

"Your family's there, Richie. Your roots are there. You don't belong here, in this kind of place with these people—you're better than this—"

"Ruth, I'm where I want to be and doing what I want to do! You know all we'll end up doing is fighting, and I've had it; I don't want to hear his shit anymore. 'Do this, do that.' I'm not going back, ever; El Paso's too small—I could never find what I want there . . . I belong here, where I am."

"Where you are? You're in hell, Richie."

"Then that's where I want to be."

"You are going to get hurt—"

"No, I won't—I know how to take care of myself."

"Richie, with this kind of lifestyle, it's just a matter of time before something real bad happens . . . really bad—"

"Nothing bad's going to happen because I'm protected, okay?"

"Protected by who?"

"By Satan," he said.

"Oh, god, please don't start with that—"

"Ruth, fuck that—don't start putting down what I'm into, okay? I don't want to hear it, all right?"

"Why Satan, Richie? Why? *Why?*"

"Because Satan represents what I feel. I'm not like other people; I'm different."

"You are not different, Richie. I know you better than anyone in the whole world, and you're good and pure inside—"

"I'm not. I've changed."

"Richie, I love you more than anything in life, more than my own child, and I beg you, please leave L.A. Papa will give you money for school and you can learn a trade, something in electronics—you like that—"

"I've got a trade. I'm a thief, Ruth . . . and a good one."

"How long can you go on with that before you end up in jail?"

"I'm not going to any jail, okay? I told you, I'm protected."

Ruth looked at Richard long and hard. She could see he really believed what he was saying, and she knew there was no changing his mind once he'd made it up. His eyes were filled with defiance and fire, and his hands fluttered about like angry, nervous birds.

"So you won't come home," she said in exasperation.

"No. No way. Stop fucking asking me, or I'm outta here."

The next day Ruth took the sixteen-hour bus ride back to El Paso. She didn't want to leave Richard. It was very difficult for her, but she had a job and responsibilities she had to get back to. On the bus, she prayed for Jesus to intercede and make her brother see the light. She prayed so hard she gave herself a throbbing, blinding headache.

Ruth was honest with her father and told him how Richard looked. Julian was a very hard man to lie to: he had dark, penetrating eyes that seemed to see right through you to the truth.

When he heard about Richard's condition, the drugs, the hotel, Satan, he was brokenhearted—but what could he do? Even if he went to Los Angeles, he couldn't make Richard come back. He was now old enough to be on his own legally.

"What was I to do, handcuff him and throw him in the trunk of my car?" he'd often ask later.

Julian and Mercedes went to church and prayed Richard would come home . . . that Richard would see the light.

But he never did.

BOOK III

CAPTURE

He's really nothing but a poor boy who was brought up to believe in Christ.

Julian Tapia Ramirez

TWENTY-SIX

On the morning of Friday, August 30, 1985, Richard Ramirez stepped onto a Greyhound bus to Tucson, Arizona. He wanted to visit his brother, Robert, who was now living in Tucson with his wife Samantha and their daughter, two-year-old Betty. Richard knew nothing of his being linked to the Night Stalker crimes. All the way to Tucson he listened to heavy metal music. He'd switch from a radio station to cassette tapes he carried in a black shoulder bag. When he arrived in Tucson he called Robert; there was no answer. He hung around the Greyhound station a while and tried his brother again. This time Samantha picked up the phone. She told Richard that Robert should be home soon. She did not invite Richard to the house, nor did he ask if he could come over. As with Suzanna, Ruben's wife, Richard had been accused by Robert of coming on to Samantha and saying inappropriate things to her. The two brothers fought and for a while they didn't speak, but that had been last year and was mostly forgotten, though Richard still didn't want to be alone with Samantha. He felt no good could come of it.

After an hour, Richard called again, Robert still hadn't gotten home. He told Samantha he'd call back. As he killed more time in the bus depot, he noticed plainclothes cops starting to enter the terminal. He had no idea that after getting word from the L.A. sheriff's office that Richard had a brother in Tucson, they were looking for him. He didn't like all the cops and decided to leave; he thought about continuing to El Paso, but he didn't have enough money for the fare, so he bought a ticket back to Los Angeles.

He was wearing black pants and a short-sleeved black shirt

with a white Jack Daniels logo on the chest. The Tucson detectives were watching vehicles that arrived from L.A., not those going to Los Angeles, and Richard went unnoticed as he headed for the departing bus. As he was getting on the bus, he dropped his Walkman, which broke open, and its two AA batteries rolled under the bus. Richard was about to retrieve them, but the driver said, "Hey, if ya' gettin' on, ya' better get on, buddy, 'cause we're leavin'."

Reluctantly, Richard paid his fare and found a window seat in the back. The bus was half full and scheduled to arrive in L.A. at 7:45 Saturday morning.

He tried to sleep but couldn't—he had an antsy kind of tingling in the back of his neck that something was wrong.

Sullen and angry that he couldn't listen to music, and not having access to the news on the radio, he looked out the window. No moon or stars were out, and he stared blankly at his own gaunt reflection in the glass. The bus picked up speed and was soon doing a steady seventy-five miles per hour. The land on either side of the road was flat and desertlike. As the bus sped north, it entered a lightning storm. Huge bolts of jagged lightning danced across the sky, casting the flat, bleak landscape into momentary daylight as thunder boomed and roared. He associated lightning with heaven. He closed his eyes and tried not to see the lightning, but that was impossible; it lit up the inside of his closed eyelids. They were in the storm for nearly an hour. When they finally got past it, Richard was thankful. He closed his eyes and soon a restless sleep enveloped him. The bus sped toward L.A.

When Richard woke, they were just entering Los Angeles proper, getting off the freeway. It was 7:25 A.M. The day was clear, ninety-five degrees, humid, without so much as a hint of a breeze. In just a few minutes they'd be at the terminal. Richard was hungry and thirsty, and his eyes were puffy from his restless sleep. When they pulled into the busport on the roof of the terminal, Richard got up and waited to exit the bus. There were fifteen SIS men stationed in and around the terminal. They had good reason to believe Richard Ramirez might try to leave L.A. via the terminal. They didn't know whether or not Ramirez was really the Stalker, but none of them was about to take any chances. In their minds, he was guilty until he proved himself innocent.

All the SIS men paid close attention to the outgoing buses; none of them thought for a moment Ramirez would be coming into L.A. Without being challenged, Richard walked casually through the terminal. It was air-conditioned and cool. He was not spotted by the police, but he saw plainclothes cops all over and quickly left the terminal, having no idea his picture was on the front page of every Los Angeles newspaper and on the minds of many of Southern California's citizenry. At that very moment, people in every community in L.A. were staring at his mug shot in the paper, trying to see some sign of the beast that lived behind those eyes.

Outside, the heat hit him in the face like a hot, wet towel; even before he'd gone ten steps his brow was beaded with sweat. He copped a nickel bag of pot and headed toward Mike's Liquor Store on South Town Avenue. There he bought some coffee and a sugar-coated pastry. As he was waiting for his change, he noticed a few elderly Mexican women in the back of the store pointing at him, looking at him with obvious fear on their faces. Richard heard one of them say, "El Matador," which, strictly translated means "the Killer," and has nothing to do with bulls.

Why, he wondered, perplexed, *would these old women be thinking he was* the killer? Then Richard's eyes dropped to the news rack and he saw his picture all over the newspapers. Suddenly he knew why they were pointing at him.

Unbelieving, shocked, he grabbed a copy of the Spanish newspaper *La Opinion* and hurried from the store.

Even before he'd gone a few feet, the store owner had called the police, and soon every cruiser in East L.A. was speeding toward South Town Avenue. Helicopters were also dispatched.

As he ran, Richard read *La Opinion*'s account of his identification and Sheriff Block's press conference the night before. He heard the police sirens and knew they were coming for him, looking for him—anxious to kill him.

He had to get away—no matter what, he had to escape. He ducked into a yard and effortlessly vaulted a six-foot fence. Running for all his life was worth, he headed toward the Santa Ana Freeway, leaving his black knapsack in the yard of a house that abutted the highway. He went over another fence and ran down a hill covered with thick foliage to the freeway. Cars zoomed by at seventy miles per hour. Breathing hard, his heart pumping blood furiously, his legs weak, so covered by sweat it looked as if he'd just stepped from a shower, Richard waited for the right moment and darted across the freeway, nearly getting run over. Once on the east side of the freeway, he made his way up another hill, vaulted yet another fence, and grabbed a bus going south, paid his fare, and sat down.

Right away people on the bus recognized him from the picture on the newspapers and television and started pointing. The bus stopped and he got off, realizing for the first time everyone everywhere knew his face. There was nowhere to hide.

He needed a car. With a car, he'd go south to Mexico; once there, he thought, he'd be able to blend in and not be noticed. He could change his appearance, grow a beard, bleach his hair, and wear glasses. As he hurried down the scorching, sun-drenched street, people on their porches and in their yards recognized him, and they, too, called the police. Three teenaged Mexican boys began to follow him, until he told them he had a gun, and to "get the fuck away from me." In the blue sky over East L.A., Richard saw police helicopters searching him out as if they were hungry birds of prey and he was food—and he heard police sirens coming from all directions.

A car: no matter what, he had to get wheels. He spotted a lone woman sitting in a running auto on the corner of Indiana and Whittier. Her name was Manuela Villanueva, and she was waiting for her boyfriend, Carmello Robles, who'd gone into a grocery store to buy tamales and coffee for a breakfast on the go. It was a little after eight. She saw Richard running toward her on the left side of the street, thinking he looked peculiar, worried, and very upset about something, and dangerous—she thought he was a *cholo* (tough guy), and as he got closer, she became even more frightened, for, she realized, he was looking at her; all his attention was focused on her. As he reached the car, he said, *"Mataron mi mama* [my mother has died], I need the car; get out!"

"No, I can't—I'm not giving you my car," she said.

He said he had a gun, grabbed her arm, and tried to pull

her out. She began screaming, *"Auxilio, auxilio* [Help]!" As Richard grappled with her, Carmello Robles, short and strong, with a rock-hard jaw and black mustache and eyes, rushed from the bakery. He was joined by Arthur Benavedes, who ran out from his small two-seat barber shop, having just put down the Saturday morning paper.

"Hey, get away from her!" Carmello yelled. Richard saw the two men hurrying toward him—the shock in Arthur's face as he recognized him—and he bolted off rabbitlike, running into an alley. Carmello chased him and was soon joined by Frank Moreno, who was exiting the building whose alley Richard had ducked into.

Richard went over another six-foot fence and across a woman's yard to Perry Street. Rather than chase him over the wall, Carmello and Frank jogged around the block to see if they could cut him off. Both men knew the neighborhood well. Richard reached Perry and walked into the front yard of a woman who, upon seeing him, began to scream and slammed the front door of her modest house. She, too, hurried to the phone and dialed the police. Richard heard the cacophony of police sirens as a deafening, maddening sound. It was so hot he felt like he was in a furnace, like he was being licked by the flames of hell.

Exhausted, stumbling as he moved along, his heart feeling like it was about to burst, his muscles burning, his lungs screaming for oxygen, Richard Ramirez headed toward Hubbard Street. He couldn't have picked a worse place. It was a block made up of hard-working people, for the most part Mexican-Americans, who toiled and battled with all the inequities of life every day; what they had, they'd gotten with sweat and aching muscles.

Everyone on Hubbard Street knew Richard Ramirez had been identified as the Night Stalker, that he was a Mexican—one of them—and the news of his identification had caused an uproar and spread like wildfire in the very substantial Mexican-American community of East L.A.

Richard hopped a fence and ended up in the rear garden of Luis Muñoz, who was cooking hamburgers and ribs on a barbecue, holding a long iron spatula. He demanded to know what Richard was doing. When Richard wasn't forthcoming with the right answer, Muñoz whacked him a couple of times with his cooking utensil. Richard vaulted another fence and landed in Faustino Piñon's back yard. Faustino, a burly laborer, had been working on the transmission of his daughter's red Mustang; the car was running, jacked up, and on boxes. At the sight of the unoccupied car with a running engine, Richard saw his chance to get away, the light at the end of a very dark tunnel. He did not see Faustino, who was coming out of the house with a tool. Richard jumped in the Mustang, put it in gear, and stepped on the pedal.

Faustino was not going to let him take his daughter's car; he had bought it for her with very hard-earned money, and he knew his daughter loved the red Mustang. Faustino would sooner die than let the car be stolen. He ran and grabbed Richard by the neck with one hand while he tried to take the car keys with the other. Faustino's hands were strong and like a vise around Richard's neck.

"Get away, I'm taking the car—I have a gun, I'll kill you," Richard said.

"You are not taking *this* car," Faustino said, grabbed the wheel, and turned it, steering the car into the chimney of the house. Faustino was thrown to the ground. The car stalled.

"You cannot take this car," Faustino repeated, reaching in and grabbing the car keys, which he dropped on the floor. Richard got out of the car and bolted toward his destiny. There was a five-foot fence across Piñon's driveway, and he went over it easily, "like it wasn't even there," Piñon would later tell the press.

He ran inside and called the police.

When Richard got to the sidewalk, he saw Angela De La Torre, in a bright red dress, getting in her car, which was parked in front of the house she shared with her husband, Manuel, and her daughter, Amber. It was Amber's fourth birthday, and Angela was going to the market on Whittier Street to get candies and sweets for a piñata at Amber's party, planned for 3 P.M. that day. Angela was twenty-eight, had dark hair, and was attractive, with a heart-shaped face and rounded, naturally pouty lips. She looked up and saw Richard rushing toward her, his eyes wild and frantic. She knew who he was at first glance, recognizing him from the news reports, and began to scream, *"El Matador! El Matador!"* He demanded her keys, threatening her. She bravely declined; he punched her in the stomach and took the keys out of her hand.

Already in the car was Angela's neighbor, Lourdes Estupinion, who leaped from the front seat and ran back toward the house, taking up Angela's cries of *"El Matador!"*

Across the street, Jose Burgoin was watering his lawn when he looked up and saw Richard, stiff-legged, shoulders hunched, approach Angela. The moment she began screaming for help, Jose dropped the hose and rushed to her aid, his two sons, Jamie and Ernesto, a few feet behind him. As he reached the car, his head cocked belligerently, he demanded to know what Richard, who by now had gotten behind the wheel, thought he was doing. "Get out, man, get out of the lady's car!" he demanded.

Richard ignored him and put the key into the ignition. Manuel, Angela's husband, came running from the back of the house. He had been in the yard when the fracas had started. Lourdes had come for him, yelling that someone was hurting Angela. Manuel loved his wife passionately and would defend her to the death. He, like most Mexican males, would sooner die than let his woman be harmed.

He heard Angela's screams of "El Matador" and he knew who she meant just by taking one quick look at his wife's panic-stricken, tear-streaked face. Anger filled Manuel's heart. He grabbed for a metal bar he used to close the front gate. It was two feet long, curved into an L at the end, as thick as a fat cigar.

Bar in hand, Manuel ran up to Richard, who was still trying to start the car. He opened the door and slammed Richard in the back of the head with the pipe and demanded he get the hell out of his wife's car. Without saying anything, Ramirez leaped from the De La Torres' car and began running up the middle of Hubbard Street, toward Indiana Avenue. Angela and Lourdes continued to scream as more people came out of their homes with bats and clubs.

Hot on Richard's heels, Manuel and Jose and his sons gave chase as cries of "El Matador!" began to echo up and down the block. As Richard ran, he turned around and began sticking his tongue out, hissing, serpentlike, at his pursuers.

At the sight of him doing that, the women made the sign of

the cross, looked down, and turned away; he looked, they thought, like a deranged madman—a demon.

Manuel swung the metal bar again and now it hissed through the air. He missed. They went a few more steps and Manuel swung again, hitting Richard on the top of the head. He went down. Manuel stood over him, raising the metal bar high above his head.

"Go ahead, go ahead, get up, man, and you're fucking dead!" he said. "Get my gun—go get my gun!" he called to Angela.

She was about to, but Lourdes talked her out of it.

"Only no good could come from that," she said.

Jose Burgoin's boys stood by menacingly. Blood ran down Richard's neck and fell in droplets on the hot black tarred street.

By now both LAPD and LASD police cruisers were on their way to Hubbard. The first to arrive was sheriff's deputy Andres Ramirez. A call had come to him reporting a "man with a gun." He had, as he came to a stop near where Richard sat bleeding, no idea what had happened, what was going on. He saw De La Torre, Piñon, Burgoin and his boys, and the metal bar in Manuel's hand. A large crowd was gathering. Dep. Ramirez got out of his cruiser and approached; he had been brought up on Downey Road, just four blocks away.

"It's him, it's him, we caught him," someone said to Dep. Ramirez.

Him who? he was saying to himself, when he looked down, saw Richard, and immediately recognized him. He had the mug shot of Ramirez taped to his visor. "What's your name?" Dep. Ramirez asked.

"Ricardo Ramirez," Richard said, still panting heavily and bleeding.

Jesus Christ. It's him! Dep. Ramirez thought.

"How badly are you hurt?"

Richard didn't answer, just looked down. Dep. Ramirez handcuffed him, made him get up, frisked him, sat him down, and called for an ambulance.

"What happened?" he asked Manuel, who calmly described the sequence of events as he knew them. More and more people gathered around them.

LAPD had been chasing Richard, who had initially been in

their jurisdiction, but Hubbard Street was on the sheriff's beat, and technically, Richard was the sheriff's prisoner. Overhead, helicopters that had been chasing Richard circled expectantly. As word of Richard's capture spread through the police community, every cruiser in the area headed toward Hubbard Street.

As Dep. Ramirez took down names and addresses, a Medivac team arrived. They cleaned two wounds on Richard's head and covered the wounds with gauze, wrapping it around his entire head.

LAPD officers Dave Strandgen and John Vidal were the next to arrive, their siren winding down, red lights spinning anxiously. They, like all of the LAPD that morning, had been briefed about Ramirez and had his mug shot with them. Officer Strandgen got out of the car with the picture in his hand, compared it to Richard, and saw the suspect was indeed Richard Muñoz Ramirez. He, too, placed Richard under arrest, frisked him, and found a black wallet, which he took. In it were papers with some phone numbers and a yellow baggage claim ticket for a piece of luggage at the bus terminal.

Just a few minutes earlier, he and his partner had been directed to a yard on Bestwick, where Richard had left his black knapsack. They had retrieved the knapsack, locked it in the trunk, and gone on to Hubbard Street.

"Are you Richard Ramirez?" Strandgen asked.

"Yeah, it's me, man," he said.

They sat him down on the curb and cordoned off the area as more and more police cruisers continued to arrive. The press was just behind the police, and in no time they had their cameras running as they hustled up and down the block, looking for witnesses, sound bites, scoops. It was big news. Not only had the Night Stalker been captured, but he had been taken by the people—not the police.

In no time a crowd of a few hundred had formed, and it grew, pulsating and swelling with anger, as people spit in Richard's direction and cursed him and his ancestry out loud. LAPD officers James Kaiser and Danny Rodriguez did not like the look of the crowd. Rodriguez made Richard get up and put him in his patrol car as the crowd jeered under the scorching August sun and waves of heat rose from the ground.

It was collectively decided by LAPD to take Ramirez to their Hollenbeck Station, even though he was in the sheriff's jurisdiction and had first been arrested by a sheriff's deputy.

"They ended up stealing our prisoner," an official in the sheriff's office would later say. "They had no right taking Ramirez; he was ours. They wanted the glory of the arrest for themselves."

Officers Kaiser and Rodriguez took Richard to the Hollenbeck Station. It made no sense to keep him on Hubbard Street any longer; the crowd was becoming more and more unruly. With Richard in the back seat, they drove through the crowd as reporters pushed and jostled for a picture. Ramirez kept his head down and remained silent, and neither Kaiser nor Rodriguez said a word. They didn't want to do anything that could later be misconstrued in court as being improper or coercive. However, they would later testify in court that as they'd left Hubbard Street and the crowd cheered, Richard had said: "Why don't you just shoot me? I deserve to die. Now they're going to send me to the electric chair. I was being chased all the way from Olympic, you know. All the killings are going to be blamed on me. You see, those people wanted to kill me."

Officer Rodriguez said, "Nobody's going to hurt you—don't worry. You are in our care, and nobody is going to harm you."

They all remained quiet. The ride to the Hollenbeck Station took eight minutes. Richard looked out the window, his head throbbing, knowing he'd probably never walk the streets a free man again: no matter what he said, no matter how much he protested his innocence, they'd never believe him.

He thought of his mother, and of Ruth and the family. What would they think? What were *they* going to say? He dreaded the thought of having to face his father.

He turned around and saw news trucks following them.

When they got to the station, reporters were already waiting for them, but Richard ducked down and they couldn't get any usable shots of him. He was taken out of the car and upstairs to the second floor. As he passed LAPD personnel, they stared at him solemnly, in awe, for if he truly was the Night Stalker, he was one of the most vicious serial murderers ever.

He was a bona fide homicide superstar. Richard kept his head down and didn't make eye contact with anyone.

On the second floor, in the detectives' squad room, Kaiser and Rodriguez sat Richard in a swivel-type chair. They handcuffed his hands to the chair, again behind his back. Richard asked for a drink of water. He was dehydrated and suddenly felt very thirsty, nauseated, and slightly dizzy. Officer Kaiser got him the water and held the glass while Richard drank.

Officer Rodriguez kept checking the handcuffs. He viewed his prisoner as the most dangerous man alive and was afraid he'd slip his hands out of the cuffs.

He decided to handcuff Richard's legs to the chair and used Officer Kaiser's cuffs to put one around Richard's ankle and the other on the base of the chair.

Richard, they would say, suddenly said, "The .32 automatic is in the Greyhound bus locker, and that is where I keep it. In my wallet is a ticket for the locker."

LAPD detective Sgt. George Thomas and his partner, Paul Joy, arrived. They had, with Leroy Orozco and Paul Tippin, been working marathon shifts on the Night Stalker task force. Their eyes first went to Richard's shoes; they were not Avia Aerobics, but they were large.

They thought it best if Richard was isolated from the commotion caused by his capture, and they moved him to an industrial green six-by-ten-foot windowless room with a wooden table and six wooden chairs and again handcuffed Richard's hands behind his back. Det. Joy stayed outside and briefed task force detectives and brass as they arrived.

Thomas said, "I'm going to be taking your shoes." He bent down and undid the laces of Richard's low-top black Stadia sneakers. He put them in a corner for the detectives who actually had the case, Carrillo, Salerno, Tippin, and Orozco, knowing there could be evidence, blood, hair, and soil on the shoes. He made it a point of not talking to Richard. His job was to observe him and write down what, if anything, he said, and that was it. Richard put his head on the table, facing away from Sgt. Thomas, and gently started to bang it, as he began to hum "The Night Prowler" by AC/DC.

How, Richard wondered, *could Satan let all this happen?* It was, he decided, because he'd done something to displease

Satan, who was, he knew, vengeful, demanded strict obedience, and had little tolerance for weaknesses.

"What day is it . . . Friday?" he asked.

"No, Saturday," Sgt. Thomas responded, as he took out a pad and pen.

Richard, Thomas would later testify, then said: "I want the electric chair. They should have shot me on the street. I did it, you know. You guys got me—the Night Stalker . . . hey, let me have a gun to play Russian roulette. I'd rather die than spend the rest of my life in prison. Can you imagine? The people caught me, not the police." He stopped, laughed, and continued, "You think I'm crazy, but you don't know Satan. Of course I did it, so what? Give me your gun, I'll take care of myself.

"You know I'm a killer, so shoot me. I deserve to die. You can see Satan on my arm." At this point Richard looked up and saw Thomas had been writing.

"Are you writing down what I say?"

"Yes," the sergeant said.

After that, Richard, Thomas would report, said nothing more.

At 6 A.M. that morning, Gil Carrillo had awakened from a restless sleep. The first thought he had when he opened his eyes was of Richard Ramirez, where he was, how long it would be before he was caught. He was up, showered, dressed, and out of the house by 6:30. He stopped for coffee and went on to the Industry Station. He had made plans with Salerno to meet him at the Temple Street office at 9:30.

While Carrillo was looking at a map of downtown Los Angeles and coordinating the armies of detectives who would soon be saturating it, he heard that Ramirez had been spotted near the bus terminal. He wasn't surprised. If Ramirez was in L.A., he knew, he'd be seen unless he crawled into a hole and stayed there. His picture was everywhere.

In the twenty minutes between when Ramirez had first been seen and his capture on Hubbard Street, Carrillo paced back and forth like an expectant father. When word reached him that a sheriff's deputy actually had Ramirez in custody, Gil's spirits soared and a huge smile broke open his face. Finally, he'd be able to face the man who had been his nemesis for what had seemed a lifetime. He ran from the station-house, jumped in his car, and sped toward the Sheriff's East L.A. Division. Once there, he was told Ramirez had been taken to LAPD's Hollenbeck Station, that he had been stolen from the sheriff's department and taken there. Carrillo wasn't annoyed or mad at this news. What was important was that Ramirez was in custody, not whose custody, and, he knew, he'd soon be in his and Salerno's hands. He hurried back to his car and sped to the Hollenbeck Station, very interested in talking with Richard Ramirez, looking into his eyes.

In a strange kind of way, Gil respected Ramirez: Gil knew Ramirez was very good at what he did and couldn't be dismissed as just another crazed killer. Gil made up his mind in the car that he would be tactful; he believed Ramirez might warm to that. He didn't seem like the type who could be browbeaten or influenced with heavy-handed tactics. Ramirez was from the street, and, Carrillo believed, he'd just clam up if anyone came on too strong.

And he'd play up the fact that he was Mexican—that he and Ramirez had a cultural link, a heritage.

By the time Gil reached the station, a very large, angry crowd had gathered. At the first sight of him, reporters hurried over. He told them he had nothing to say and made his way in the intense August heat through the crowd and upstairs.

Orozco and Tippin were already there. They told him Ramirez had been making incriminating statements and it seemed like he wanted to confess. They showed him the black knapsack and told him about the Greyhound luggage ticket. Gil's eyes lit up.

They told him Ramirez had said the guns were supposed to be in the bag. They had decided to wait for Frank, and all four of them would enter at once; it seemed like the democratic thing to do. Gil, though, had to see Ramirez and walked to the door, opened it a match-thin crack, and eyeballed him.

That's him, he said to himself. *That's the man who chased my wife and kids from my home.* He closed the door without a sound. LAPD brass arrived, as well as officials from the sheriff's office. There were congratulations, handshaking, and loud back-slapping. They had done it. They had caught him, the mad butcher who had been making them all look like inept fools for months on end.

It was over.

They had won.

Good had triumphed over evil.

Frank arrived ten minutes behind Gil, parking his car two blocks away from the Hollenbeck Station because the crowd had grown so large. Reporters circled Salerno. He told them he didn't know any more than they did and made his way upstairs. He was briefed by Carrillo on what they had. Before they went in and talked to Ramirez, Salerno ordered the bag at the terminal brought to the sheriff's office. It would not be opened until they had a proper warrant, which Mike Bumcrot was drawing up. Salerno borrowed a handheld tape recorder from LAPD and the four of them discussed strategy before the interview.

Word was sent to LAPD detective Dennis Lee to retrieve the bag at the Greyhound station. He and three other detectives had been stationed at the bus terminal since 7:30 A.M., with orders to be on the watch for Ramirez. Det. Lee and his colleagues had been there when Richard had arrived from Tucson and casually strolled through the terminal and out the front door.

They retrieved the two-foot high black leather bag with a shoulder strap and a zipper sealing it closed. They did not open it. The bag was put in an unmarked police car and taken to the sheriff's office on Temple.

At 10:10, Carrillo, Salerno, Orozco, and Tippin entered the room where Richard waited. Salerno held the tape player in his right hand. As he got near Richard, he pushed the record button. Thomas took off the cuffs per Salerno's orders.

"I'm Sergeant Salerno, with Sheriff's Homicide. This is Deputy Carrillo, with the sheriff's office. These are detectives Tippin and Leroy Orozco, with LAPD."

"I know who you are," Richard answered. "Yeah . . . you brought down Bianchi and Buono, right? You're the one they wrote about."

Salerno was caught off guard by this revelation. He'd known his picture had been in the paper, yet to hear Ramirez tell him he knew all about him had a chilling, sobering effect, "Like taking a cold shower," he'd later say.

The four detectives sat down. Frank asked Richard if he'd like to eat something or have a drink.

He declined the food but asked for a Coke. The detectives' tack was going to be one of diplomacy and congeniality. They were under the impression that Ramirez wanted to confess, and if he wanted to talk, they'd make it as easy for him as possible. Frank asked him how his head was, if he required a doctor. Richard said he didn't need a doctor. He was shy and respectful, mostly looking down.

Frank read Richard the Miranda warning. When he was finished, he asked, "Will you talk with us?"

"I want a lawyer," Richard said, surprising and disappointing the detectives.

"So, you didn't want to talk—?"

"I'd like a lawyer."

Salerno and the others stood up. "Well, I guess we've got nothing to talk about," he said.

They started to leave, but Richard said he'd talk to them, but not about any crimes.

They all sat back down, Carrillo opposite Salerno, Orozco opposite Tippin, Richard on the end. Frank began by asking Richard questions about his family and El Paso, which Richard freely answered. After forty minutes or so, Gil began to talk with Richard in Spanish. Richard was quick to respond and seemed more comfortable speaking Spanish. Gil had worked street gangs for years and he knew how to "talk street," and that's what he did now—gently, with humor and even respect.

Ramirez told him how he'd been chased and pummeled by "a bunch of punk nobodies." Gil commiserated with him, nodding understandingly. Richard sensed Carrillo's sincerity and he obviously warmed to him, for he began readily answering Carrillo's questions. Gil, at first still speaking Spanish, then slipping into English, took Richard back to El Paso and asked him about his family. He already knew from Richard's rap sheet that he had three brothers and a sister. He knew, too, that one of his brothers lived in Tucson and another in L.A., on Bannick Street, in Watts.

Richard, Carrillo would later say, told them his father beat him and his brothers and had a fierce temper.

Richard spoke calmly, in a weak, beaten voice; he seemed

like a man who had had the life force sucked out of him. Salerno was very pleased with the quick rapport Gil managed to create with Ramirez and had a newfound respect for Gil as a detective: it was easy to get mad at Ramirez and call him names, but that was not their job—their job was to relax him and get him to talk willingly, even after getting the Miranda read.

Gil steered the conversation toward Ruth. "Did your father abuse your sister, too? . . . Did he maybe abuse her sexually?" Richard's persona suddenly changed, Carrillo reported later. "He started to hyperventilate. Muscles in his jaw tightened, veins in his neck welled.

"It seemed like he was going to lift right out of his chair."

Richard began drawing a small circle on the table.

"Go ahead and fill it in," Gil prompted.

"What do you mean?" asked Ramirez. "Fill what in?"

"You want to draw a pentagram? Go ahead; it's okay."

Richard wiped over the spot as if he was erasing what he'd been doodling. Gil turned the conversation to the time Officer Stavros had stopped him—and asked if he'd drawn the pentagram on the hood of the car. Richard admitted he had been stopped, but he didn't know the officer's name, though it was LAPD.

Carrillo asked him about his belief in Satan and Richard readily admitted that he followed the ways of Satan, walked the left-hand path, and wholly believed in the existence of Satan and his omnipotence over all things in this world and the spirit world.

"It's he who really rules," said Richard.

Gil turned the conversation back to El Paso, where Richard said he'd been brought up a Catholic, and told Gil his mother took him to church all the time.

Salerno was very pleased with the progress Gil was making, and he kicked him under the table to encourage him to get Richard to talk more about his family. They, Salerno felt, could be used as a catalyst for Richard to talk about his crimes.

Gil misunderstood the message: he thought Frank was telling him to back off. This case was the only one they'd ever worked together, and they had not yet had a chance to perfect signals.

Richard became quiet and stared at his unusually long, thickly veined hands. There was a heavy silence, which Richard ended by saying again, "I want a lawyer."

Frank, then Gil, tried to get him to talk further, but he was reticent to speak any more, and at 10:40, the interview was ended and Richard was left alone. All the detectives felt if given a little time and the right kind of treatment, Ramirez might very well confess, which would make everyone's life much easier. None of the survivors would then have to come to court and relive their horrible ordeals.

Arrangements were made by Salerno to bring Ramirez to the county jail, where he would stay until his case was adjudicated.

The entire second floor was packed with task force members and police brass. Mayor Bradley showed up to shake everyone's hands and bask in the excitement of the moment. The mayor told the press: "California can breathe a sigh of relief. A very dangerous man is off the streets."

Gil fingerprinted Richard.

By now the crowd outside had swelled to over a thousand. They called threats to Ramirez and chanted: *Give him to us; give him to us!*

So there wouldn't be an incident when Richard was taken to the county jail, two dozen more uniformed officers were assigned to crowd control, carrying long wooden nightsticks.

When it was time for Richard to leave, the four detectives took him downstairs and put him in a caged bullpen as final arrangements were made for the transfer. They would use four cars, eight motorcycle cops, and a helicopter. They wanted to make sure nothing happened to Ramirez. They all knew how angry the citizenry had become and would not have been surprised if someone came looking for Ramirez with an automatic weapon in his hand and revenge in his heart. They knew the Night Stalker had frightened people in ways no serial murderer had ever done before. LAPD uniformed officers walked to where Richard was being detained. Officer John Stavros had a grimace on his face and gave Richard curious, angry looks. Salerno wanted none of that. He walked over to Stavros and told him to stay away from Ramirez, and not too politely.

When it was time for Ramirez to go, he was taken out of the

bullpen and led into the Hollenbeck Station's inner court-
yard. Huge and forbidding, Carrillo led the way. Salerno and
Paul Tippin were on Richard's left and right, respectively;
broad-shouldered and bull-like, Orozco brought up the rear.
They walked through a phalanx of tight-lipped uniforms to
the traveling car, a dark brown Plymouth with black-walled
tires. Word that Ramirez was being brought out quickly
spread through the crowd, and angry chants and epithets
sailed at Richard through the intense, fetid East L.A. August
heat.

Paul Tippin drove, Carrillo rode shotgun. Ramirez was
seated between Salerno and Orozco. With a roar, the motorcycles started up, and as they moved forward, the crowd
slowly opened up and the brown Plymouth followed the lead
cars and motorcycles through the throng of angry faces and
clenched fists and curses toward the L.A. County Jail. When
they were a block from the Hollenbeck Station, Carrillo spotted and pointed out to the others a full-figured woman on the
hood of her car. She had raised up her T-shirt, and with a big,
toothy smile on her face, was showing them her breasts. They
all laughed; Ramirez thought she was doing it for his benefit.
The detectives felt it was her way of saying thanks. In five minutes they arrived at the jail and Richard was taken to the hospital wing on the second floor.

Again the detectives asked if he'd like to make a statement.
He declined and again was booked—fingerprinted and photographed, given a shower and a baggy blue jumpsuit, then
put in a cell with a solid steel door and no window, with a slab
of metal attached to the wall for a bed, a small aluminum
sink, and a toilet bowl.

Pacing back and forth, Richard cursed the cell, heaven,
and hell—and all the people on Hubbard Street.

Salerno and Carrillo went straight to the Sheriff's Homicide office, eager to see what was in the leather bag found at
the terminal. They felt confident it would contain evidence
that would help secure a conviction against Ramirez.

It would be John Yarbrough's job to file and index all evidence as it came in, and he, as well as Jerry Burke and Chuck
Vander Wende, were there. Salerno, wearing tight plastic

gloves, opened the bag and gingerly removed a jar of Vaseline, a black pair of Stadia sneakers, a bottle of vitamins, a pair of brown gardening gloves, long-nosed pliers, locking pliers, two sets of keys, a .32-.20 revolver, a box of .32-.20 ammunition, four .25-caliber and five .22-caliber cartridges, a pair of sunglasses, a can of Weight On, and an AC adapter. Pictures were taken of all the items, which were then put in numbered plastic evidence bags. There were, Salerno noted, red circles around the primer of the .25s. The name on the bag ticket was Gregg Rodriguez, and the detectives learned later in the day that the Brannick Avenue address was Richard's brother Ruben's.

Frank had the lab match up shells and slugs found at crime scenes to those in the bag, and they were, according to LASD firearms, like those used in the crimes.

When Phil Halpin, who would be prosecuting the case, heard this, he was all smiles. It was, he said, the kind of evidence that would assure conviction, and ultimately make his job easier. Halpin was 6'1" and had a tight, muscular body, graying hair, and a well-trimmed salt-and-pepper beard. His eyes were dark and penetrating. Halpin had a well-deserved reputation of being a fierce fighter in the courtroom and was always extremely well prepared. He was unquestionably one of the finest trial lawyers in the Los Angeles district attorney's office. He had been co-counsel on the prosecution of Charles Manson and had secured convictions in the famous Onion Field murder case. Once, during a heated legal argument with a lawyer who was defending Charlie Manson, Halpin had challenged him to a fistfight outside.

Philip Halpin was indeed a two-fisted prosecutor who would, it seemed, gladly fight to the death for what he believed was right. And what Halpin felt was right in this case was to send Richard Muñoz Ramirez to the gas chamber at San Quentin.

In all the years he'd been a prosecutor, he'd never come across a more vicious killer. There was no way, he was certain, an insanity defense would be successful in the Ramirez case. He felt that Ramirez—if he truly was the Stalker—had shown far too much advance planning and cunning for his sanity to become a legal issue. Working with Salerno and Carrillo, coordinating and organizing assiduously, Halpin began weaving an airtight case against Richard.

The first order of business was to arraign Ramirez. It was scheduled for Tuesday, September 3.

Gil and Frank focused their attention on getting Halpin what he needed and coordinating a lineup at the county jail for the Night Stalker's victims to view. They decided to have all stolen items received from Solano laid out so they could be viewed by survivors and family members of those killed. The lineup was set for 12 P.M., September 5.

Salerno sent Dets. Uloth and Olson to talk to Richard's brother Ruben at his house. Jesse Perez had told the sheriff's task force that Richard had a 1976 green Pontiac, and Salerno wanted it.

Uloth and Olson later reported that Ruben readily agreed to show them where Richard's car was, and that he and Suzanna got in his own car and took the two detectives to Avenue 23 in Lincoln Heights, a lonely stretch of road littered with beer cans, condom wrappers, and cigarette butts. It ran parallel to the freeway. A green 1976 Pontiac with a flat tire and a damaged right front fender was there, exactly as Perez had described. Photographers and lab techs were summoned, and Chuck Vander Wende and Jerry Burke hustled out to Lincoln Heights. They could all readily see a pentagram drawn on the dashboard. The car would not be searched until a warrant was secured. It was towed to the sheriff's East L.A. Station and an addendum to the warrant for the bus station leather bag was drawn up.

When the warrant had been signed by a judge, the car was searched with a fine-toothed comb. The pentagram was cut out of the dashboard by Jerry Burke. They found a white coffee cup in the glove compartment and a pair of cheap handcuffs under the right front seat. Richard Ramirez's prints were on the cup as well as on the rearview mirror, seat belt buckle, and steering wheel.

TWENTY-SEVEN

The news that Richard had been identified as the Night Stalker hit El Paso like an atomic bomb.

At 11:15 Friday evening, Joseph and Sofia were home in bed, sleeping soundly, when the phone began to ring insistently. It was a very excited Robert. He said, "Have you heard, Joseph?"

"Heard what?" Joseph asked, annoyed that Robert had awakened him and Sofia so late; he had to work the next day.

"Richie has been identified as the Night Stalker—"

"The Night Stalker? What's a Night Stalker?"

"The guy killing all the people in Los Angeles."

"Are you crazy or what, Robert?"

"I'm not crazy; go put on the television—it's all over the television, on every channel; go see, go look, man!"

"I'll call you back," Joseph said. He turned to Sofia, said, "Robert said Richard was arrested," and told her to turn on the television.

Richard's December 1984 mug shot filled the small black-and-white TV screen. Joseph's eyes bulged. "It was like getting hit by an ugly stick," he'd later say. They heard the announcer report that Richard had been identified as the man responsible for a series of murders, rapes, and robberies all over Southern California. He'd become known as the Valley Intruder, the Walk-in Killer, and finally, the Night Stalker.

"We've got to get to my mother and father," Joseph said, knowing what this news would do to his parents. He didn't know if it was true or not, but he prayed this was all some kind of perverse mistake. He knew his father would be deeply distraught. As quickly as he could, he dressed, put the kids in the car, and drove to his parents' house.

When Ruth heard the news, she was sitting on the edge of her bed, combing her hair before retiring. There was a news bulletin on television and suddenly her baby brother's picture was there, all over the screen. She heard the announcer and her jaw fell open. It was like being struck by a speeding train. Robert's daughter was staying the weekend, and she and Ruth's daughter, Gloria, were sleeping.

Ruth rarely drank, but she felt if she didn't have a drink, she'd go mad. She slipped on jeans and a top, walked outside, numb and unbelieving, drove to the store, and bought a can of beer. She opened it on the ride back to Ledo, then pulled over, and with the windows up, screamed over and over with all her strength, like a woman possessed. Then she cried. She, like Joseph, had no idea if what she'd heard was true. How could her baby brother, her Richie, her play-doll, be a murderer? It was all wrong. They'd made some gross mistake. She collected herself as best she could, suddenly remembering her mother and father. Back home, she got her daughter and her niece up and hurried toward her parents' home, a two-minute drive away.

When Joseph pulled up in front of the house, all the lights were on. "They know," he said, and got out of the car. He could hear the television. As he and Sofia entered the kitchen, they met Julian and Mercedes, "both with looks of amazement, hurt and confusion on their faces all at once," Joseph later said. Ruth arrived. The children were put back to sleep in a spare bedroom.

Mercedes said she needed to get away from the house, that she had to cry. Carrying her Bible, she, with Ruth and Sofia, went to a nearby park, where Mercedes looked up to the large black star-studded expanse of the El Paso night and asked why.

She began to cry. It turned into a wail, as though from an animal that had had a hot spear thrust through its heart. Ruth joined her, then realized that she must calm her mother and with Sofia's help bring Mercedes back from such terrible despair. Ruth was afraid it would actually kill her mother.

"Listen," she said, "we don't know that Richie did the things they are saying. They make mistakes all the time. Let's wait and see if this is even really true; how could he—? Richie could never do the things they are saying, Mama."

Ruth was right, Mercedes realized. Mistakes were made all the time.

Slowly, arm in arm, they walked back to the car and returned home.

Julian rarely drank alcohol because of his diabetic condition, but he couldn't face the reality of what his youngest had been accused of. When the women returned, he and Joseph drove to a 7-Eleven and Julian bought a few bottles of wine and beer. In the car on the way to the house, Julian said, "Why? Why do these things happen to me; what did I do to deserve such a fate, such a thing? I always did my best, didn't I?"

"Dad, it's all probably a mistake. Don't go getting all so worked up, please."

When they returned to the house, they looked for the women and found them in the back yard, Mercedes with the Bible open. She said, "Come, we must all pray that this terrible thing is a mistake. If any of you cannot pray, I will pray for you. Let us all hold hands."

Under the velvet black Texas night, the Ramirez family held hands and prayed that what was said on the television was some perverted untruth, schemed up by the devil himself, for who else, Mercedes asked, could ever think up such a thing? When the prayers were over, they all felt a little better knowing Jesus and the Virgin Mary were now, thanks to Mercedes, aware of this grave injustice which had befallen the Ramirez clan.

Joseph and Julian went back inside to Julian's bedroom. There, as always, Mercedes had a white candle burning, causing bending, twisting shadows to dance on the wall. Julian cracked two cans of beer and gave one to Joseph, saying it would help calm their nerves. After Julian drank some beer, he poured a glass of wine and drank it, too, knowing the beer-wine combo would get him drunk sooner.

"Haven't I been a good father?" he asked Joseph. "I always worked; I always sacrificed; I did everything I could. What did I do to deserve such a thing?"

"It's a mistake, Richie didn't kill all those people. No way. He stole things, yeah, but he's no killer. No way. It's a mistake, Dad."

"I hope so . . . Marijuana. It's all because he smoked marijuana," Julian insisted, taking large drinks of both the beer and wine.

His resistance against alcohol weak, Julian became drunk and his mood turned foul. He began to curse, then went to the lower drawer in the dresser and took out a .38 revolver with a four-inch barrel. He'd had it since he was a Juarez policeman.

"What are you going to do with that?" demanded Joseph.

"I can't take the disgrace of Richie being arrested for killing people; I'm going to kill your mother, then kill myself." He headed toward the kitchen.

As fast as he could, Joseph jumped up, grabbed the gun, and said, "You ain't going to kill my mother," and the two men grappled with the gun, but Julian relented and gave it to his son, who promptly locked it in the trunk of his car. Julian cried himself to sleep.

Ruth gave Mercedes some sleeping pills, and thankfully, she, too, soon fell asleep. Reporters kept calling for interviews, and finally the family had to take the phone off the hook.

Ruth was so upset by the accusations against Richard that her hands trembled constantly. She, too, couldn't sleep until she took some sleeping pills. She prayed, until her mind went blank and the sleeping pills kicked in, that the police would not kill her baby brother—that all of this was just a big mistake.

For the last few years Richard had been mailing Ruth costume jewelry, which he'd told her he'd bought from some fence. Ruth kept it all in a box in the garage. Despite the accusations that her brother was a thief, it had never occurred to her that the jewelry might be stolen and she should hide it.

At 6:40 Saturday morning, as Richard was sleeping on the bus to L.A., Joseph had left his parents' house and gone to work. He'd asked Sofia to stay with his family until Robert, who was speeding in from Tucson, got there. Joseph prayed in the car on his way back to work. He tried to concentrate on his job, but he was so distracted, it proved very difficult. His boss noticed something was wrong and Joseph told his supervisor about Richard's being identified as the Night Stalker. The supervisor suggested he could go home. Sofia called to report that Richard had been apprehended in East L.A. by an angry crowd and that news trucks were lined up and down the block and reporters wouldn't leave them alone. Joseph left work and drove to his parents' home, praying and thanking the Lord that Richard hadn't been killed.

When he got to the house, his eyes nearly popped out of his head at the sight of all the news trucks and the incredible hurly-burly this had caused. He'd never seen anything like it. He parked and was questioned and hounded by press as he hobbled along the sidewalk and into the house, shaken.

Julian was up. Sofia, who had not slept the whole night, had fallen asleep, and Mercedes was still sleeping. The television was on low, and they kept showing film clips of Richard's capture, in the police car leaving Hubbard Street, and entering the Hollenbeck Station.

Robert arrived and the three of them watched the news reports, slack-jawed and shocked at the enormity and viciousness of the crimes Richard was being accused of.

Ruben called from L.A. and told Joseph he'd gotten to Hubbard Street just as Richard had been taken away, and that the crowd would have killed him if the cops hadn't shown up.

Ruth arrived and the family talked about getting Richard a lawyer and going up to L.A. Among all of them they didn't have much ready cash, but whatever they could scrape together they would.

Julian did not want to go to L.A., nor did Robert, and Joseph couldn't go because of his medical condition. It was decided Ruth would leave that night and see what help she could give Richard.

Reporters coming to the door kept being turned away by Joseph. When Mercedes woke up and heard that Richard had been captured relatively unharmed, she insisted on going to church.

As soon as they left the house, the reporters wanted Richard's mother, but Robert's size and his dark, angry eyes kept them at bay until he had a chance to put her in the car and drive away. The reporters turned their attention back to the Ramirezes' neighbors.

Richard's old girlfriend, Nancy Avila, was devastated by the accusations against Richard. She was sure it was all a big mistake. The sweet, gentle boy she knew could not have done the things they were saying. She went to the Ramirezes' and asked if there was anything she could do to help. She readily agreed to go with Ruth on the night bus to Los Angeles so they could be there in the morning and see Richard.

Spanish-speaking reporter David Hancock, from the *El Paso Times*, politely asked Julian if he'd agree to an interview. Julian wanted people to know the truth, his feelings about certain things. In a weak, strained voice, looking down, he explained how his eldest son, Ruben, from Los Angeles, had called and told them the news, and then he'd put on the television and seen for himself. He described Richard as "stubborn," a boy who would do what he wanted. "When he was eighteen, he first decided to move to Los Angeles, and he picked up and went. I tried to stop him but couldn't. I believe all the marijuana he's been smoking put him out of control. There was a break between us. He didn't want to do what I told him."

The reporter asked Julian what he thought about the murder charges. "In my heart I cannot believe he would have arrived at that! But if the authorities have proof, what can we do?"

"Will you get him a lawyer?" the reporter queried.

"No . . . I don't have that kind of money. In a case this heavy, it would be very difficult."

When Carrillo and Salerno again tried to see Richard, he refused to talk to them.

A representative from the public defender's office assigned to Richard's case went to see him Sunday evening. Alan Adashek was a tall, thin man with a long face, black hair, and thick wire-rimmed glasses. This case would be the biggest one he had ever tried, and he didn't want to make any mistakes, knowing everything he did would be scrutinized and reported in the press. Adashek was a careful man who liked to be in control. This would put him on an inevitable collision course with Ramirez.

When Adashek first spoke to Richard at the jail, Richard was despondent, humble, and shy. He said he didn't think he'd ever get a fair trial, that everyone already felt he was guilty, and he wanted to plead guilty to get it all over as fast as he could. Adashek advised him not to plead guilty and to fight the case. Richard said he'd think about it and was then taken back to his cell.

He didn't like Adashek. He felt he was part of the system that would take his freedom—and, ultimately, his life.

Ruth and Nancy took the crowded 8 P.M. bus to Los Angeles. When they reached the Greyhound terminal it was 9 A.M. They walked through the terminal as Richard had done the day before and caught a cab to the county jail. Ruth told the guard who she was visiting and showed them her and Nancy's identification, and they were let into a benched waiting area that was thick with people.

Ruth and Nancy had to wait half an hour. Then the name "Richard Ramirez" was called over the loudspeaker, booming and echoing over the din of the crowded room.

At the sound of that name, everyone became quiet, even the children. Slowly, hesitantly, Ruth stood and walked through the thick silence toward the visiting booth where her brother had been seated. Every pair of eyes was on her. Nancy didn't stand, and Ruth walked alone. She found her brother sitting on the other side of a thick, smudged glass partition set into a cement wall. She could talk to him only over a phone.

When Richard saw his sister, he started to cry. Quickly she picked up the phone and said, *"No enseñes el cobre,"* a phrase her father had always used, which meant, "Don't show your inner feelings." Richard understood and pushed away the weakness, which quickly turned to anger.

When Ruth asked what had happened, he told her it wasn't him, that he wasn't this Night Stalker guy, but with all the publicity he was getting—which already had him guilty—he was sure he'd never be able to get any kind of fair trial, and therefore he wanted to plead guilty.

Ruth told him to fight the charges if they weren't true. "Don't give up so easy; you must not give up, Richie! They'll kill you."

He insisted that as a poor Mexican, a nobody, he'd never be able to get any kind of justice. He told his sister about Adashek, how he didn't like or trust him. Public defenders, he said, worked with the prosecution and the courts. They were part of the establishment. Ruth said she would find another lawyer for him. When he asked her with what money, she didn't know what to say.

"No," he said, "I want to plead guilty and get it over quickly."

She reminded him of California's death sentence.

He said he didn't care, he was going to plead guilty to everything but the abduction-molestation charges they were trying to hang on him. She noticed the missing hair at the back of his head and asked after his injuries. He said it was nothing, that some rats on Hubbard Street had hit him with a metal bar. "My own people—can you believe it? Mexicans gave me up."

"I wish you came back to El Paso when—"

"Well, I didn't, and let's not start with all that now; how's Mama and Papa?"

Ruth told the truth, how devastated their parents were, about all the reporters, cameras, questions, and hostile stares. Richard saw Nancy and called her over with the wave of a hand. She hadn't seen him for three years. She got up and walked toward him as everyone watched her.

He'd changed much, she thought, as their eyes met and locked. He didn't look like the same person anymore. She took the phone from Ruth.

Richard told Nancy that he wasn't the Night Stalker, that they had to arrest someone and they had chosen him; he was a scapegoat. He thanked her for coming. She said she felt terrible and would do whatever she could to help. He put his hand to the glass and Nancy raised her hand and they touched palms.

He asked her about school and her family. She wanted to tell him how her heart had broken when she'd seen his gaunt face on television, how horrified she had been when she'd heard about the atrocities he was being accused of, how she had locked herself in her room and cried. But she said none of this. He asked her to write and she said she would, regularly.

Ruth took the phone back and told Richard he should fight to the end if he was innocent; this talk of pleading guilty was all wrong. He was giving up too easily. She would find a good lawyer who would help them and advise them correctly and properly. "If you are innocent, then it will come out," she said.

"You don't understand. They've already convicted me. Read the papers. I'll never get any kind of fair trial."

"You will. The whole world is watching this, Richie. They'll *have* to give you a fair trial."

"No way, not here. This Night Stalker dude is hated beyond words, and everyone in Los Angeles is already convinced I'm him. Yesterday, Mayor Bradley said the people of Boyle Heights did the right thing by getting a dangerous criminal off the streets."

A sheriff's deputy approached and told them their time was up. Ruth said goodbye. Richard thanked her for coming and told her he loved her. He again thanked Nancy. Ruth said she'd come back to L.A. as soon as possible. He threw his sister, then Nancy, a kiss, and was taken back to the cell.

TWENTY-EIGHT

Tuesday morning, September 3, Richard Ramirez was shackled and taken downstairs by a half dozen sheriff's deputies. He was put in a sheriff's van with barred windows, and with a caravan of deputies' cars and motorcycles and a helicopter overhead, he was taken to the Los Angeles courthouse, just a few blocks from the jail. The court was a fifteen-story building, a square modern structure. From this building justice was meted out to all of Los Angeles County's ninety-six communities, rich and poor, obscure and famous. As the van entered the carport for vehicles with prisoners, Richard saw, for the first time, how interested the press was in him, and it shocked him. There was a virtual mob of reporters and newsmen who had come to get a glimpse of the fear-inspiring Night Stalker. Richard ducked down so the cameras couldn't get a shot of him.

He was taken from the van to the thirteenth floor and put in a holding pen outside Judge Elva Soper's courtroom. As he passed other prisoners, threats and curses were hurled at him, which he ignored; he just kept his eyes down, walking awkwardly with rattling chains keeping his feet close together.

Judge Soper's courtroom was packed with reporters, police, and the public. Oddly enough, a varied assortment of women who found Ramirez "extremely attractive" had come to court. They'd seen his picture and wanted to see him in person. He was to them, because of his perceived danger, a turn-on.

Alan Adashek told Richard how crowded the courtroom was and what to expect. Richard again in no uncertain terms told Adashek that he wanted to plead guilty and get it all over with. He did not want to go through a long drawn-out court battle only to be found guilty, which in the end he was sure would happen. Adashek tried to explain that there were many legal options and avenues open to him and at this early juncture it was premature to seriously entertain pleading guilty. Adashek told Richard about producers who had called to indicate interest in acquiring the rights to his story.

As Richard entered the courtroom, he kept his head down low. When he was seated in the prisoner box, he put his head between his legs; he did not want to be photographed. All the newsmen were surprised at how shy he was.

Phil Halpin stood up, his suit well tailored, his beard well trimmed, and told the court that the State of California was charging Richard Ramirez with the murder of Bill Doi, the robbery of his home, the rape of Lillian Doi, and the robbery of Clara Hadsall's home, eight counts in all. There were, Halpin added, many more charges being drawn up, which would be lodged against Ramirez soon. He asked for no bail, because of the gravity and the enormity of the crimes. Judge Soper, a hawk-eyed woman, was in agreement with Halpin about no bail.

Halpin further informed the court that the sheriff's office was coordinating a lineup for Thursday, September 5, and asked for a second court date shortly thereafter at which more charges could be filed. Judge Soper set September 9 as the next day Richard was to be in court, and it was all suddenly over.

Hiding his face, acting like a spooked deer, Ramirez was led out of the courtroom. The reporters hurried to get a shot of him leaving the building.

Again, when Ramirez was taken from the courthouse, he saw the sea of curious faces as the newspeople looked at him through the van's thick, somewhat tinted bulletproof glass, trying to see the scaled, fanged monster they were all so certain lived inside Richard Muñoz Ramirez. After the van pulled away with sheriff's vehicles in front and behind it, the reporters hurried off to write and file their stories. All of California had an insatiable curiosity about Ramirez; he had suddenly become a very hot news item.

When Richard got back to the jail, he found a stack of letters from women who had seen him on television. In the letters, they wrote how sure they were that he was innocent and how they would do anything to help him. He also found letters from Satanists in Los Angeles and around the country who told him how "cool" they thought he was.

Richard, for the first time, realized that to people like him, people of the night, he was a hero; he was somebody. He liked that. For his whole life he'd been a tall, lanky nobody, just another angry-eyed hungry face in a hungry crowd, but now people stopped—people paid attention, stared, and pointed.

He vowed next time he was in court he'd show a different side to the world. He figured no matter what he did they were going to convict him and kill him, so he decided to take control.

An award ceremony honoring the Hubbard Street citizens who'd helped capture Ramirez was given by the Los Angeles County supervisors. Deputy Andres Ramirez was there, too. Supervisor Ed Edelman gave them all plaques, proclaiming their good deeds and citizenship. Carmello Robles, Manuel and Angela De La Torre, Jose Burgoin, Frank Moreno, Faustino Piñon, and his son, Julio, attended.

A few hours later, there was a second ceremony at City Hall, hosted by Mayor Bradley, honoring the people who'd helped capture Richard. In front of a wall of cameras and reporters, Mayor Bradley said they were brave heroes and society owed them a debt of gratitude.

Twenty-five-year-old Doreen L. of Burbank watched the awards ceremony with disdain. She thought it was unfair that awards were being given out for Richard's capture before he was convicted. Doreen was 5'2", with dark brown hair and eyes and a full figure. She worked as an editor for various entertainment magazines and lived with her grandmother. When Doreen had first seen Richard's mug shot on the Friday news, she had fallen in love with his face; she'd later say there was something in his eyes that made her want to reach out and hold him, and when she'd seen his bandaged head the morning he was captured, she thought the people on

Hubbard Street should have been arrested. "They weren't heroes. They were a mob of criminals."

Doreen was a college graduate with a B.A. in English from Cal State at Northridge. She didn't smoke or drink or curse and had been brought up Catholic in a strict household with her twin sister and one brother.

Doreen made up her mind she was going to protect Richard from how unfairly society had been treating him.

When public defender Alan Adashek heard about all the awards and the mayor's comments, he was outraged. How could Ramirez ever get a fair trial with these award ceremonies polluting the prospective juror pool?

To air his protest and hopefully counteract some of the overwhelming bad press, Adashek agreed to an interview with the *L.A. Times.*

At 11 A.M. the following morning, as people all over L.A. read about the awards and looked at the "heroes'" pictures on the front page of the newspapers, eight detectives in three cars pulled up in front of Ruth Ramirez's house. The day was cloudy, humid, and windy, with a promise of rain hovering over El Paso. Two of the detectives were Sheriff's Homicide men, the other six El Paso detectives. The L.A. detectives had flown down to El Paso that morning with warrants to search Ruth's and Julian's homes. The items specified in the warrants were serrated knives, bloody clothes, binoculars, guns, bullets, handcuffs, shoes, VCRs, photographs and/or videos of murders, satanic paraphernalia, and a pair of brown human eyes.

Perez had told the task force that Richard had mailed "a lot of stuff" to his family, and at that point they weren't ruling out any possibilities.

Ruth heard their car doors slamming out front and saw the procession of grim-faced lawmen, all wearing ties and suits, approaching her house. They told her that her house was going to be searched. She signed a form giving them permission, saying she had nothing to hide. The detectives looked for items that might have been stolen by Richard. They took,

Ruth would later complain loudly, pieces of jewelry in her bedroom and a jewelry box that belonged to her. Unless, she was told, she had receipts for any given item, they were taking it. They also took several kitchen knives.

They soon found the wooden box in the garage where Ruth had kept the pieces Richard had given her. When they asked her where this jewelry had come from, she was honest and told them Richard had given her it. It was, she quickly pointed out, all cheap costume jewelry. The detectives weren't concerned about their worth; they were concerned about their origins and their validity as evidence. When they told her they were looking for a pair of brown human eyes and asked if Richard had sent them to her, Ruth was horrified and stood there dumbfounded, her mouth agape. "Eyes? What do you mean, eyes?" she asked. They told her.

"No, of course not, absolutely and unequivocally not!" she said, and asked what kind of people did they think they were dealing with, cannibals or something? To which she got icy stares and no reply.

When the detectives finished at Ruth's, they went to Julian and Mercedes's house. Ruth tried to call her father to tell him what to expect, but she couldn't get through. The Ramirezes had taken the phone off the hook for relief from the constant calls from the media. Ruth decided to go to her parents' home to help them deal with the shock of what she knew they'd soon be hearing.

As she got in her car, the detectives arrived at her parents' home and were showing their badges to Julian. A Spanish-speaking El Paso detective told Julian they were there to search for certain stolen items, which had been laid out in a warrant. Julian respected the law. He'd never been in trouble once in his life; disgraced, he stood aside and invited the detectives in. He explained that Mercedes had not been feeling well and was sleeping. They asked him to wake her so they could search the bedroom, but he refused. His wife was ill, and he was not going to have her disturbed. The detectives began to search the rest of the house.

When Julian was asked if he'd ever been sent any jewelry by his lastborn, he said no; when they asked him if Richard had left any kind of weapon or handcuffs, Julian said no. When they asked if Richard had ever sent a pair of brown human eyes to him, Julian, like Ruth, did not know what they meant. After having been asked three times, he finally understood what they wanted to know—he felt as if he'd been hit in the face, and his stomach turned over.

"No," he said, never had such a thing been sent to him by his son.

Ruth arrived. She took one look at her father and knew they'd asked him about the eyes.

TWENTY-NINE

Richard didn't want to stand in a lineup. He knew his face had been plastered all over the newspapers and television and that the people coming to view the lineup—the victims—had seen the news broadcasts.

There was also the matter of the wound on the back of his head. It had been widely reported that he'd been hit by Manuel De La Torre on the head by a metal bar. The newspapers had used photographs of him leaving Hubbard Street, with gauze wrapped around his head. There was a shaved area at the back of his head about the size of a silver dollar, where the wound had been treated. There wasn't any way a person could not help noticing it.

Alan Adashek, Richard would say later, told him he had to stand in the lineup, that he didn't have a choice. According to experts, because of the distinct wound at the back of his head, Richard didn't have to stand in any lineup until the wound had healed and hair had covered it. All of the surviving victims of the Night Stalker—except a comatose Nettie Lang and a sick Clara Hadsall—went to the central jail Thursday morning, September 5.

Some, like Virginia and Chris Petersen, still had bandages, walked slowly, and had attending nurses with them. The lineup was held in an auditorium on the second floor. Half of its fifty seats were filled, and a palpable nervous tension hung in the air. The seats faced a stage two feet off the ground. The far wall of the stage was painted black, with white horizontal lines and measurements to indicate heights.

Gil Carrillo and Frank Salerno stood at the back of the auditorium.

Ramirez and five other men of similar height, weight, and general coloring walked out onto the stage. Ramirez was number 2. All six men squinted in the bright overhead lights as they tried to see who was in the auditorium, but the witnesses sat in the dark and weren't visible.

At the sight of Ramirez, people in the audience gasped and began to cry, their hearts racing, hands shaking. The sheriff's deputy in charge of the lineup told each of the men in turn to come forward, face left, face right, and say the words, "Don't look at me, bitch, or I'll kill you." When Ramirez's turn came, he walked forward and spoke. Carrillo and Salerno could see the witnesses squirm in their seats uncomfortably, and as Ramirez walked back to the wall, the witnesses saw the bald spot on his head. There were so many witnesses that a second lineup was held to accommodate everyone. After each lineup, paper and pencils were given to the witnesses for them to write down the number of the person they had chosen. Nearly all of them wrote down number 2, Richard's number.

After the lineup, the witnesses, along with relatives of those killed, were led down the hall to a large industrial green room where three twenty-five-foot tables had been set up. On them were all the items that had been removed from Felipe Solano's house, over two thousand pieces, mostly jewelry—earrings, rings, watches, cufflinks—but also VCRs, televisions, tape players, and answering machines. Somkid Khovananth, Sakina Abowath, Carol Kyle, Sophie Dickman, Linda Doi (the Dois' daughter), and the children of the other victims slowly entered the room and walked the length of the long tables, crying and whimpering softly. They all identified items that, they said, had been stolen from them or their relatives. Carol found a necklace she said was hers; David Nipp found the tape player he'd given Ma Bell. The pieces were identified, given numbers, and categorized so Halpin could use them as evidence when and if the case actually proceeded to trial.

When Alan Adashek, in a holding cell where inmates could talk with their lawyers, told Ramirez about the identification of both him and the jewelry, he wasn't surprised and said it was because his picture had been plastered all over; coupled with the comments of the officials, he didn't have a chance. Adashek couldn't argue with that reasoning; he felt Ramirez was right.

In the interview Adashek did with the *L.A. Times* later that day, he publicly agreed with Richard's sentiments and said, "The publicity is so intense . . . so intense and constant, over so many days, it's really a problem. A major problem . . .

"The effect of all this massive publicity can be very negative in terms of a fair trial."

In El Paso, they took the news of the identification, which they received from Adashek, very hard. No one in the family thought Richard had any kind of fair chance with all the publicity against him. He had already been found guilty before having a fair day in court.

Ruth made plans to visit Richard that weekend and Robert agreed to accompany her. The bus, as usual, was crowded and noisy. Robert's 6'4" frame was hard pressed to fit in the seat, but he didn't complain; he viewed it as a mission to protect his kid sister, and he just sat stoically and said very little. Ruth, exhausted and beaten by all the turmoil of the last few days, secure with Robert beside her, fell asleep and didn't wake up until they reached Los Angeles.

Richard was despondent; he told his siblings that he was being framed—that he was a scapegoat. He felt he'd been identified because all the witnesses had seen him in the news. Robert and Ruth believed Richard. It was a very hard thing to accept that someone they loved dearly was a sadistic homicide junkie.

Again Richard told his sister how he wanted to plead guilty and get it all over quickly. Again she reminded him he'd get the death sentence. He said he didn't care, that he'd been convicted already in the public's eyes.

"I have a chance like a snowball in hell has a chance," he said.

He went on about how he didn't trust Adashek and how Adashek was part of the system, out to get him and certainly not to be trusted. "I should never have been put in that lineup with this on my head," he said, showing Ruth the injured bald spot.

"Tell Mama and Papa that's why they picked me out. They all saw me in the news and they all knew I'd been hit in the head; and that creep rat Solano got all that shit from some other dude, not me," Richard very convincingly told his sister, the person he'd been the most close to all his life. Ruth beseeched him to have hope and promised to do all she could to find Spanish-speaking lawyers he could trust and who would defend him properly.

Robert, who'd been following the conversation by listening to Ruth, took the phone from her. "Hey, Richie, if you aren't this Night Stalker guy, you gotta fight them. Don't give up so easy—you're a Ramirez, remember!"

Richard told Robert that it was all stacked against him, that he didn't have any kind of chance.

"Mama's praying for you all the time. You don't give up and everything will be okay; you'll see, you'll see, man."

When Ruth and Robert left the jail, they met Ruben in a downtown coffee shop. They all agreed Richard was in more trouble than any of them had ever heard of. Ruben, like Richard, was tall and gangly, with long hands and fingers and needle marks on his arms. He was very depressed about Richard's being arrested, blaming himself for everything that had happened. If it weren't for him, Richard would not have come to L.A. in the first place and been subjected to all the negative influences. Ruben knew he'd not been a good role model for his younger brother as he was growing up. Ruth saw how despondent Ruben was and tried to bring him out of it.

They needed to find a lawyer for Richard. They had heard about producers calling up with movie offers and talk of a book deal. Ruth suggested that could be a way to get the money for a lawyer and "a proper defense." Ruben didn't think it was legal, but it was worth looking into.

He told Robert and Ruth about the awards being given to the people on Hubbard Street, and about Mayor Bradley's comments. They would have to find one hell of a good lawyer, with negative publicity like that. He said, "It's like he's already guilty in the people's eyes."

He told them he'd heard about Richard's capture on the radio and had hurried down to Hubbard Street in time to see Richard being driven away. "The crowd was wild; it was like they really would have killed him," he said.

"He can't get over that it was the people and not the police who caught him," Ruth said.

Robert and Ruth stayed in an inexpensive downtown hotel.

The following morning Ruben went to the jail with Ruth. Richard was in a foul mood. He said he'd been receiving threats and that the guards were putting something in his food that was giving him bad headaches. He repeated his dissatisfaction with Adashek and how he wanted to plead guilty and get it all over with fast. Ruben told him about the mayor's comments and the continued bad press. He explained how the cops had tricked him into telling them where the green Pontiac was. Richard said he understood through tight lips. There wasn't, he pointed out, anything in the car that amounted to a hill of beans. Ruben told him the police were very interested in the pentagram on the dashboard.

"Fuck, man, there are pentagrams all over the place! That doesn't mean anything."

"They're saying there were pentagrams at some of the crime scenes."

"Well, I don't know anything about those pentagrams," Richard said, watching Ruth's intense brown eyes bore into him, searching for the truth.

Richard knew he could never let Ruth know what was truly in his heart. Instead, he complained about the headaches he was having. They were so severe, he said, it felt like hot drills were boring into his head. He was convinced the guards were putting drugs in his food. He'd told Adashek, but he'd acted like Richard was crazy. That was another reason he wanted to get rid of Adashek. Ruth assured him the new lawyer would make sure he wasn't drugged and that he received proper medication for his migraines.

El Paso lawyer Emmanuel Barraza read about Richard in the *El Paso Times*. Barraza was married to Joe Manna's sister, who had been the Ramirezes' neighbor on Ledo Street for many years. Through his wife, Barraza learned that the Ramirezes were godfearing, hardworking people and didn't deserve all the public scorn and ridicule they were getting. The worst, she said, that could be said about Julian and Mercedes was that they were strict. Barraza called the Ramirezes and offered his help. The quotes he read from Julian in the paper had touched him, he said.

To the Ramirezes, his offer was a beacon of light in a dark

hostile place filled with nosy reporters and their barbed questions. Barraza invited Julian Ramirez to his office, and Ruth and Mercedes went with him.

Manny Barraza was 5'5", considerably overweight, with a round cherubic face above a double chin. He wore aviator-style silver-framed glasses. His hair was a tight knot of black curls, so thick it looked like he was wearing a hat. Barraza had graduated from the School of Law at the University of Texas at Austin in 1979. Though young and relatively inexperienced—he hadn't ever handled a capital case—he had dark, intelligent eyes whose wisdom was beyond his years. He seemed, to the Ramirezes, sincere in his desire to help.

Ruth told him about the press in L.A. and Richard's feelings toward Adashek. Barraza offered to fly to L.A. to confer with Richard and see what help he could offer. Julian thanked him profusely but was quick to point out that the family had little money. Barraza said he would do it pro bono, knowing he'd get plenty of publicity if he had anything to do with the Ramirez defense team.

From now on, he said, he'd handle the press for the Ramirezes and they should refer all reporters to him.

The Ramirezes left the meeting feeling Manuel Barraza was a godsend. He was one of them, the son of Mexican immigrants, from El Paso, and he would advise them properly.

Monday, September 9, Richard was again taken from his cell, where he had suffered from migraines all weekend, back to Judge Soper's courtroom, which was again packed with press.

This time he acted like a different person; he was no longer shy and trying to hide his face. He stared defiantly and angrily at the press and snarled at Phil Halpin, moving from foot to foot as a boxer might, his nostrils flaring. His hands, chained to a waist belt, opened and closed, his knuckles bulging.

Alan Adashek told the court that he had not had enough time to read all the police reports, and that Ramirez was not yet ready to make any kind of plea and asked for an adjournment. Halpin had expected this and had no objection. September 13 was set. Adashek asked the court to put a gag order on irresponsible statements being made by public officials about his client's guilt. Judge Soper said she'd take his suggestion under advisement. She was aware of the coverage and knew that finding an unpolluted jury would be very difficult.

Adashek didn't want Richard talking to any type of reporter and asked the judge to forbid visitors to Ramirez unless his attorney approved. With no objection from Halpin, Judge Soper ordered it.

Wearing a light-colored suit, Halpin stood and addressed the court in a strong, bellowing voice.

He was very concerned, he said, about the defendant's teeth. They'd been described by many of the surviving victims and he was planning to use them in the People's case. He wanted Judge Soper to sign a court order giving the state the right to plaster-cast his teeth, as well as take pictures of their present condition. He said the defendant's tooth structure might change due to jailhouse fights or naturally losing more teeth. The judge saw the request as reasonable and said she'd allow it over Adashek's objection.

Back in El Paso, Emmanuel Barraza was busy. The Ramirezes were giving the reporters his number, telling them that he was going to be representing Richie. Suddenly Barraza was an important man, giving phone interviews to AP, the *El Paso Times,* the *Daily News,* the *Los Angeles Times,* and anyone else who called.

He told Dave Holley and Bob Stewart of the *L.A. Times* he was flying up to see Richard. Defending Ramirez was going to be, "like a *Mission Impossible* assignment. It's going to be tough . . . but I haven't seen anything that concretely connects him to the murders." He said the case was so large and complex, he might have to move to California. When queried about his fee he readily admitted he was working pro bono.

The press quoted Barraza as saying all the publicity had polluted the Los Angeles jury pool. "The first step would be to get it [the trial] out of Los Angeles. We'll definitely explore the possibility of going out of state . . . there's just been too much adverse pretrial publicity. It's almost like in the eyes of the public he is guilty."

When deputy district attorney Sterling E. Norris, head of the prosecutor's special trials unit, heard about Barraza's comments, he said there was no legal authority under California law to move the trial out of state. "The only transfer possible," said he, "was to another county in California."

Barraza flew to L.A. to see Richard. His way into the jail, however, was barred by Judge Soper's order for Ramirez not to have any visitors. Displeased, Barraza called Adashek and convinced the public defender to let him visit Richard on behalf of the Ramirez family. Adashek didn't like the idea of another lawyer being brought into the case. He told Barraza that once private counsel was involved, the public defender's office had to drop the case. Whatever happened, Adashek didn't want to leave this case.

When Barraza finally did get to see Richard, he was struck by how polite and intelligent Richard was, and how lucid his arguments about his innocence were.

Ramirez was very angry that Adashek had gotten the order forbidding him to have visitors. He had, he said, no use for Adashek. "All he's interested in is the press. I want to plead guilty. I've told him that. I don't care what they do to me. I don't want to go through a whole trial. I'll be found guilty no matter what. I'll plead guilty to the murders, but not to any molestation charges." Barraza noticed Richard looked directly at him while speaking and seemed to be a man completely in charge of his faculties. If Richard was the Night Stalker, then he had to be insane: one just had to look at the things the Night Stalker had done.

But the man who was sitting in front of him was not insane. Therefore, he couldn't be the Stalker. He had to be innocent.

Richard liked Barraza; he warmed up immediately to the fact that he was of Mexican ancestry and from his hometown. Barraza explained to him that he did not have a license to practice law in California, but he could oversee Richard's defense and interests and help with any book or movie deals. Richard liked that idea and Barraza became Richard's counsel.

The first order of business, they both agreed, was to get rid of Alan Adashek. Barraza said that he would explain Richard's feelings in no uncertain terms to the public defender.

Richard told Barraza about his terrible headaches and his theory that he was being poisoned by his keepers. Barraza had heard of much worse happening to men in jail and believed Richard; he said he would see what he could do. Richard also heatedly complained about not having proper access to the phone. All the other prisoners did, but not him. Barraza again said he'd do what he could.

Barraza contacted Adashek to tell him he was taking over Richard's defense. Adashek told him that *he* was Richard's lawyer until such time that the court said he wasn't, and hung up. The battle lines were now drawn between Manny Barraza and Alan Adashek.

When Adashek went to see Richard the following day, Ramirez again told him he didn't want someone from the public defender's office representing him and that Barraza was taking over. Adashek pointed out Barraza's weaknesses and Richard accused him of only wanting the publicity. He wanted to plead guilty, and if he received the death sentence, dying didn't scare him. He'd end up in a place of honor in hell with Satan.

That reasoning, Adashek knew, was impossible to argue with, and he didn't try.

Manny Barraza began making phone calls, looking for, preferably, Latino criminal lawyers who were licensed to practice law in California and would work on the Ramirez case for no money up front. He said he could assign book and movie rights for payment, which would eventually amount to something quite substantial.

He consistently ran into brick walls. It seemed no one was interested in representing Ramirez, even if there was cash available now. Barraza conferred with Ruth and the family, and she suggested Melvin Belli, the former San Francisco lawyer, whose specialty was matrimonial litigation.

Barraza knew it was a wild shot, but to his surprise, Belli said he'd go talk to Richard in L.A. and let him know if he was interested in taking on the case. He made plans for the following week, on September 19.

In the meantime, just in case things didn't work out with Belli, Ruth thought about calling Daniel Hernandez. She'd met him at the University of El Paso, while he was studying law, and, had heard he was practicing criminal law in San Jose.

* * *

During his first week in jail, Richard says he suffered terrible hot-knives-through-the-head migraine headaches because of the food. He tried not eating at all and that helped; the headaches seemed to diminish; but then he got hungry, ate, and the headaches returned with a vengeance.

On Friday, September 7, Dr. Gerald Vale, the chief forensic dentist, arrived at the county jail to take photographs, X rays, and plaster casts of Richard's teeth. The examination was done at the jail for security reasons. Dr. Vale was assisted by Dr. Betty Hoffme and dental lab technician Kay Gong. Richard was cooperative and his eyes were often on the women. Dr. Vale's complete forensic examination of Richard's teeth took nearly three hours. Richard was returned to his cell, his mouth filled with the taste of dental plaster.

When he didn't have headaches, Richard read letters from Satanists who held him in esteem, and from women around the country who found him attractive, with his high cheekbones and full lips. He began answering the letters, being careful about what he said, afraid the police might be trying to trick him.

Ruth and Ruben went to Los Angeles again on Friday and were turned away at the jail because of Adashek's order. Ruth was told by his associate, Henrey Hall, that Richard had been in a dentist's chair nearly all day and perhaps it would be better if they came back the next day.

Ruth was livid with anger, but she could do nothing.

The following day she and Ruben went back to the jail, and this time she had no problem getting in. Richard was brought from his cell and put in a booth after the other prisoners were cleared away. When his name was announced over the loudspeaker, all eyes were on Ruth and Ruben as they approached where Richard sat.

When he heard they'd been turned away Friday, he began cursing Adashek and Hall, the veins in his neck bulging. As far as he was concerned, this was the straw that broke the camel's back. He wanted another lawyer. Ruth told him Melvin Belli was coming to talk with him on Wednesday or Thursday. Richard would not believe Belli was coming until he saw him in the flesh. He wasn't about to get his hopes up.

Ruth told him she'd spoken with attorney, Daniel Hernandez, and he was very interested. He and a colleague, Arturo Hernandez, could take the case, she said.

Richard repeated his intentions to plead guilty the next time he was in court on September 27, no matter what Adashek said. Ruth begged him to hold out on pleading guilty until Belli had talked with him. Richard said he wasn't about to go through any lengthy trial where he was going to be scorned and accused of all kinds of atrocities. He didn't want to put his mother and father through that. "It will be much simpler—and easier on them—if I just plead guilty, and that's what I'm doing.

"I'm not going to let them parade me out there like I was some kind of curious freak so they can pat themselves on the back and sell newspapers. I'm not giving them the satisfaction. And dying is better than jail for the rest of my life—"

Ruth and Ruben returned to the jail on Sunday and again tried unsuccessfully to change Richard's mind about his pleading guilty. Ruth knew he was as stubborn as a rock, and she began to cry. She could not, she told him, deal with the idea of losing her baby brother to the executioner's hand.

Even Ruth's tears had no effect on Richard's plan to plead guilty on September 27.

On September 17, *Daily News* reporter Arnie Friedman called Ruth in El Paso. She agreed to do an interview, wanting to vent her anger about Adashek and her not being able to see Richard. She felt he had arbitrarily and unfairly taken over, and she wanted the world to know it.

Ruth said, "My brother is being held like a prisoner in Communist China, where you don't have any rights. He should, like all the other prisoners, be able to see his close family."

When asked about the jewelry taken from her home by the police, she admitted she'd gotten some of it from Richard as a gift, but much of it was her own, including her wedding bands and her communion ring. She told Friedman adamantly that Richard did not want Adashek representing him. She protested further that her brother was being kept in constant solitary confinement, and she wanted to know why.

When asked about the Night Stalker's task force's suspicion that Richard had sent her a pair of human eyes, she got angry and said, "I don't think . . . any civilized person could receive parts of a human body and not be overwhelmed by it to the point of going crazy."

Friedman contacted Hall at the public defender's office and he told her the only reason Richard was in solitary confinement was for his own protection. Numerous threats had been hurled at him by the other inmates. Asked why Ruth had been kept out of the jail, Hall said it was a mix-up. Ramirez had just gotten out of the dentist's chair when Ruth and Ruben had come for a visit.

Melvin Belli arrived at the jail on September 19. He met Adashek and Ruth, who had traveled on the bus all night to be there, and they went into the jail together.

Belli knew he didn't have the time to represent Ramirez if his case proceeded to trial, but he thought it was a very important, interesting case, and he viewed Richard as a unique phenomenon, if all they were saying about him was true. He only knew what he'd read in the papers, and it was enough to pique his professional interest.

When Richard met Belli he was shy, very polite, and respectful, far from the bloodthirsty monster he had been portrayed as. Richard repeated for Belli his list of complaints, ending with his displeasure with Adashek, who was sitting right there. He told Belli that he wanted to plead guilty and get it all over with quickly. Belli asked if he had thought of an insanity plea. Richard said he wasn't crazy and had too much pride to say he was.

"It could save your life," Belli said.

"I don't want to plead insanity."

Belli told Richard if all he was interested in was a guilty plea, he *might* be able to come aboard. He didn't have the time to try the case, but he might be able to bang out a plea bargain for him. Richard said he would be very grateful for any help.

Belli came away with the impression that Richard was very complex. He told reporters, "It might sound strange, but I like the guy, and he has something to say. I hope the whole story will come out, for people will learn an awful lot from this case."

Belli told Ruth he'd let her know and returned to San Francisco.

The following day, Melvin Belli told Ruth he couldn't, in any capacity, work on the case, citing money and time as the main obstacles.

"If," he told the *L.A. Daily News,* "I were to represent him, I'd want a thorough, thorough mental examination of him before I would consider going into the case; that would cost lots of money, and the family just can't afford it."

Richard was not surprised by Belli's position.

Oxnard attorney Joseph Gallegos had heard that Ramirez was looking for new counsel. Gallegos had recently represented on murder charges a Mexican gang member who had been convicted and sentenced to twenty-seven years.

At fifty-six, Joseph Gallegos had a thick head of well-coiffed silver hair. He'd been practicing criminal law for twenty-two years, primarily cases dealing with possession, burglary, or simple assault.

He called the public defender's office and spoke to Henrey Hall to offer his services. Hall passed on his name to Adashek.

After Melvin Belli turned down Ramirez, Alan Adashek went to the jail. He'd accepted the fact that Richard did not want him and told him about Gallegos's offer. Richard liked the idea of a Mexican criminal attorney; with a Mexican, he felt, he'd get a fair shake, and that's all he said he was looking for. He again complained about his headaches and told Adashek that no matter what, he was pleading guilty on the twenty-seventh, and he didn't want to be paraded into court every day like some circus freak in a nonsensical trial in which he had no chance. Adashek tried to convince him to wait at least until his new attorney was on board, and he explained to him why Belli could not represent him.

THIRTY

To be able to be in court with Richard on Friday the twenty-seventh, Ruth had to travel by bus by herself Thursday evening. Robert was unable to leave his job, Joseph was having problems with his legs, Mercedes wasn't prepared for the arduous travel or the task of facing the press, and Julian Tapia could not overcome his sense of shame. Even if his son was innocent, just for him to be arrested for such terrible crimes was enough.

Gil Carrillo and Frank Salerno had been busy with the detailed business of putting together an airtight case against Richard. They oversaw and directed the preparation of all the evidence for each of the sixty new charges which were to be lodged against Richard.

They didn't work now, though, with the pressure of not being able to stop the violence, and both slept well. Pearl and the kids were back home, and Carrillo's domestic life had returned to normal. The two detectives each felt confident they'd convict Ramirez. With all the identifications and the extensive evidence, it seemed a sure thing.

On the morning of the twenty-seventh, the district attorney's office held a press conference to announce the new charges before they were presented in court. The press had an insatiable appetite, and it had to be fed.

District attorney Ira Reiner stepped up to the podium, as Phil Halpin, Salerno, Carrillo, Orozco, and Tippin looked on. It seemed as if every reporter in California was there, as well as from places as far away as England, Israel, Spain, and Brazil. Because Richard was of Latino origin, the Spanish-speaking press was there in full force. His picture and story had been front-page news all over South America and in Spain.

Reiner announced fourteen new murder charges and forty-five other felony counts, including rape, sodomy, unnatural acts on a minor, abduction, assault, and robbery. He would not take questions from reporters about the particulars of the murders or the assaults and robberies. He said the papers would be filed soon and all the information would be in them.

After the news conference, as Richard was being taken from the jail, Ruth squeezed into a seat in Judge Soper's courtroom, alone, wearing large, round sunglasses.

Richard was in a foul mood that morning. He had a headache and knew what he was facing would only make it worse. The knives in his head would be a little hotter, go in a little deeper. In the holding pen outside the courtroom, Adashek told him about the news conference and the new charges being leveled at him. It didn't surprise him. He said he was going to walk into court and plead guilty, no matter who said what.

"I want it all over. Don't you fucking understand, man?"

Adashek went to Judge Soper's law clerk and requested a closed conference in the judge's chambers. Phil Halpin was informed, and he joined Adashek and Henrey Hall in the judge's chambers. Judge Soper listened to Adashek's argument that Richard be kept out of court altogether.

He was, Adashek said, not in his right mind and wanted to plead guilty against his advice. Halpin said he was going to charge Richard with sixty new felonies, and if the judge saw fit to keep Ramirez out of court, he had no objection.

In light of defense counsel's request, the judge agreed to keep Richard in a holding pen where he could hear the proceedings but not be part of them. Adashek thanked the judge, and everyone took his place. When Richard learned he was not going before the judge, he began cursing and yelling out that he wanted to plead guilty—that he wanted Melvin Belli to represent him.

Stunned, the reporters strained to hear what he was saying. Ruth wasn't stunned at all. She knew Richard's intentions to plead guilty and wasn't surprised to hear him yelling. With so many older siblings to contend with, Richard had learned early on to yell for what he wanted.

Phil Halpin stood and announced the new charges, contained in an eighty-four-page complaint, as the reporters rapidly jotted down the details. Adashek asked for and got a three-week adjournment to October 9 before entering a plea. Halpin was eager to get on with the proceeding, to get Ramirez convicted and off to San Quentin's death row.

Halpin had been involved with the case very early on and knew all the details of all the crimes. In his opinion, the world would be a better place without Richard Ramirez. Nevertheless, he could hurry the case along only so much. When Adashek went back to see Richard in the holding pen, Ramirez was pale with anger, told Adashek that he was history and that he would represent himself before he let Adashek represent him.

"What I am doing, I'm doing for your best interests," Adashek insisted.

Richard asked, "How could it be for my best interests if you aren't doing what I'm asking—if you are keeping me from where I want to go and what I want to do? Listen, man, I'm going to start calling reporters and telling them what the fuck you are doing—" He demanded Adashek call Joseph Gallegos and tell him to come see him.

Back at his office, knowing he could now never be Richard's lawyer, Adashek phoned Gallegos and asked him to visit Richard at the jail. To keep Richard from calling the press, Adashek phoned Judge Soper and asked her if she'd bar Richard from having access to the phone and telling reporters that he was guilty. Such a story would virtually destroy Richard's chances at trial if his new counsel decided to litigate the case. Judge Soper took his request under advisement.

After court on Friday, Ruth went to the jail to see Richard and waited with the others for her turn. She had barely slept all night and had had nothing to eat. She was, in fact, losing weight, and all the stress was clearly showing on her face. She was beginning to recognize women who were there to see their brothers, husbands, fathers, sons, and boyfriends, and she said hello to a few of them, with only her eyes and a silent nod.

Ruth found her youngest brother even angrier than he had been at the court.

She asked him why he hadn't come out into the courtroom. He told her about Adashek's decision to keep him away from the judge, and that he wanted all the glory, to be in charge of everything.

He told her about Joseph Gallegos. What he liked about him especially was he had represented someone in a gang. To Richard's street-oriented mind, this meant Gallegos could be trusted. Ruth told him Daniel Hernandez had called to say he and Arturo were very interested in representing him. "Manny Barraza even spoke to them and he likes them—he says they are for you," she said.

In Richard's mind the Hernandezes didn't have enough experience. Between them they had been practicing law for only five years. Joseph Gallegos had been practicing for twenty-two years. Richard agreed to meet with the Hernandezes.

Their visit came to an abrupt end. Ruth ate a small meal and took a bus to Ruben's. Wanting to visit Richard Saturday, she asked Ruben if she could sleep in his car. Ruben felt bad, having to make Ruth sleep out in the car, but if he brought her into the house, there would be a war. Suzanna, like Ruth, had a fierce temper, and it was much better keeping them apart. Ruben kept watch out the window, making certain nobody bothered Ruth. He knew if anything happened to her, no one in the family would ever talk to him again.

With all the new charges finally filed, the sheriff's Night Stalker task force decided to throw a party for themselves. Each of the twenty-four men and women who had worked so hard chipped in. Carrillo collected the money and arranged for a place and food and drink for what was sure to be a very thirsty crowd. The sheriff's office invited all the other police jurisdictions that had worked the case, LAPD, Glendale, Montebello, Arcadia, Orange County, etc. The celebration was to be for cops only; no family or dates were allowed.

Carrillo's sisters pitched in to help with the food, decorating, and serving. The owner of Walt's Liquor in Pico Rivera heard about the party and volunteered the liquor. He called the Budweiser people, and they donated all the beer the "heroes" could drink.

Gil spoke with the people who owned the Pico Rivera sports arena, which was constructed in the shape of a miniature bull ring, with an open-air roof where riding contests, small rodeos, and an occasional bullfight were held. They were only too happy to make the space available for the sheriff's department and they covered the dirt area with Astroturf.

September 28 was an ideal night for an outdoor party. The suffocating, strangling heat wave of August had passed and it was a pleasant 65 degrees, the sky clear and filled with stars.

Approximately 200 people, who had been personally touched as a result of working on the manhunt for the Stalker, attended. Salerno knew that the investigation had changed some of his detectives. They'd become quiet and morose, when before they were full of jokes and smiles. They all had felt helpless, as the crimes continued, progressively escalating in frequency, ferocity, and perversity.

As they ate, drank, danced, and joked, they shared the satisfaction of having caught a killer like no other.

Frank Salerno ended up leaving the party early. He was tired and wanted to be home with Jayne; he had been away from her, from his family, for what seemed like years. He knew his colleagues wouldn't let him go without a struggle, so he just quietly slipped away. Salerno, like Carrillo, had taken the Night Stalker attacks very personally. They'd been happening on his beat, near his own mother, yet he'd been able to do nothing but wait and hope the Stalker made a mistake. Now, with Ramirez off the streets, he had a peace of mind which had not been his since his getting the Patty Higgins and Mary Cannon murders.

Ron Salisbury owned six restaurants in the Los Angeles area called "El Cholo." He knew Jayne Salerno and told her he'd like to throw a party for Frank and the other detectives for the great job they had done in the Stalker case. All of the Sheriff's people who worked on the case, including technicians and criminalists, had a second huge celebration in Ron's West Avenue restaurant. Again they ate and drank, laughed and joked—and tried to put the horror of the Stalker's grisly deeds behind them. "It was a hell of a nice gesture," Frank would later say of Ron's generosity.

The weekend of September 28, Manny Barraza came up to Los Angeles with an agreement by which Richard would assign all the rights of his story to his sister Ruth. The district attorney's office repeatedly said it would not allow Ramirez to use funds from any sales of his story; such money, they said, would go to the victims. Nevertheless, Richard signed the agreement.

Again Ruth told Richard that the Hernandezes wanted to handle the case. They would, she assured him, do a good job. Manny wholeheartedly agreed. He said what they didn't have in experience they had in enthusiasm.

Richard said Gallegos was coming Monday, and after he'd spoken to him and the Hernandezes, he'd make up his mind.

On Monday morning Joseph Gallegos arrived at the jail. He was well dressed, sure of himself, and polished, Richard thought, and he liked him. They spoke Spanish and Richard felt Gallegos, with his Latin origin, would treat him more fairly than an Anglo public defender with a career agenda.

Richard told Gallegos he was intent upon pleading guilty to all of the crimes except the abduction-molestation charges. He knew, he said, he'd probably get the death sentence, but that didn't matter. He didn't want to go through with any long, drawn-out trial that he'd lose in the end because of all the negative publicity against him. He didn't want his father to suffer the disgrace of all the details that would surely come out during a protracted trial.

Gallegos's approach to criminal law, he told Richard, was like that of a fox toward potential prey—he moved slowly and cautiously, sniffed the air, and looked in all directions.

If, he said, Richard wanted to plead guilty, so be it. However, he pointed out to Richard that an insanity plea *might* be the way to go. Richard didn't like that idea and shot it right down; he was not, he said, insane. He was different, and he followed the dictates of his own mind and desires, rather than a hypocritically dogmatic society's, he said.

"If that's what you want, fine," Gallegos said.

Richard sneezed. Gallegos said, "God bless you."

"No," Richard corrected him, "Satan blesses me."

"Okay," Gallegos said, smiling nervously. "Satan blesses you."

Richard said he'd already assigned the rights of his story to Ruth, but he would sign them over to Gallegos in payment. That was agreeable to the lawyer; he knew the huge media attention would inevitably spark book and movie interest, and he agreed to accept the yet-to-be-made deals as payment.

The first thing they had to do was to get Judge Soper to take Adashek off the case and appoint him. He would call the judge and go to court on Richard's behalf at the next appearance, on October 9. They shook hands and Joseph Gallegos was Richard's new lawyer.

Gallegos told Richard he'd been arrested in 1975 for shooting a hooker over a blow job payment, and the press might bring it up. Richard said that didn't matter, that it was bullshit.

Shortly after Gallegos left the jail, Ruth arrived with Arturo and Daniel Hernandez. They knew Richard had been talking to Gallegos and were intent upon not letting Gallegos represent him. They had decided that they and they alone would be his lawyers. They viewed handling the case as the turning point in their professional lives. They would be famous, legal celebrities whose opinion would be eagerly sought. They both knew the case would take up a lot of their time, but in the end it would be well worth it.

Both Arturo, forty-two, and Daniel, thirty-one, had thick heads of black hair, dark eyes, and heavy brows. They looked like they could be related but weren't. Arturo wore a beard. Daniel wore a well-trimmed Pancho Villa mustache and had thick lips and a sarcastic wit. Based on the standards set by the state bar for attorneys in capital crime cases, the Hernandezes were woefully inexperienced. Neither of them had ever tried a murder case, let alone one of this complexity.

Richard wasn't particularly impressed by Arturo and Daniel.

They weren't as seasoned, sharp, and well tailored as Gallegos, and they had had very little courtroom time. Richard told them, after repeating his rationale about why he was pleading guilty, that he had hired Gallegos.

They pointed out that Joseph Gallegos had a police record and had even done time.

"You can't have a criminal speaking for you, Richie," Ruth said.

Richard told them he knew about the incident, but it really didn't matter. "That was ten years ago."

Word that Joseph Gallegos might be defending Night Stalker suspect Richard Ramirez quickly reached the reporters covering the case. By October 9, when he was first to appear in court on Richard's behalf, not everything about his background was known by the media. He was just another unknown lawyer.

During a closed conference in Judge Soper's chambers attended by Adashek, Hall, Gallegos, Alan Yochelson, and Phil Halpin, Ramirez told Judge Soper he did not, under any circumstances, want Alan Adashek representing him. He wanted Joseph Gallegos. Halpin had no objection to the change of attorneys. His only concern was getting a plea from Ramirez and moving forward. He did not want to make this case his whole career. Judge Soper granted Richard's request and appointed Gallegos as his attorney.

Sitting in the courtroom amid the reporters and a small group of women who thought Richard was attractive and misunderstood were Ruth, the Hernandezes, and Manny Barraza. The Hernandezes tried to speak to Judge Soper about the case, but she refused to hear them. Gallegos requested an adjournment so he could familiarize himself with the case before entering any pleas. Richard stood behind him, on the other side of a chest-high wire mesh and glass partition, his huge hands handcuffed to a chain belt around his waist. He made eye contact with Ruth and with his steely black eyes and a nod, noted some of the women who'd come to catch sight of him. It was like seeing a dangerous animal in an exotic zoo. Richard glared at Phil Halpin, the reporters, and the judge. He was no longer shy about showing his face; now he stood erect, shoulders back, defiant, arrogant—like a star matador. He was very good copy; no one was interested in a meek, apologetic killer.

After Richard was removed from the courtroom, Arturo Hernandez again tried to address the court, but Judge Soper said he had no standing in her court and wouldn't listen to him.

Both the Hernandezes and Ruth spoke to the press afterward. Arturo said he, Daniel, Ruth, and Manny Barraza were going to the jail to speak to Richard again, and that they ultimately would defend him. "The defense never rests," he said. "Isn't it a shame when you have to fight to defend your client? . . . We were retained by the family."

Ruth said, "We have confidence in Daniel and Arturo because of their track record."

Gallegos, too, gave interviews after court. "I'm representing Ramirez," he said.

From the court, Gallegos went to the jail and discussed strategy with Richard. Because he was with Richard, Ruth, Barraza, and the Hernandezes couldn't get into the jail that day.

It didn't take long for the press to learn about Gallegos's prior problem with the law. Both the *Times* and the *News* did detailed front-page pieces on his arrest and trial for assault with intent to commit murder and the subsequent reduction in charges by the judge which led to the guilty verdict being put aside.

Ruth stayed in Los Angeles that evening, and, armed with articles in the *Times* and *News,* she went back to the jail Thursday morning with Arturo, Daniel, and Barraza, showed Richard the articles, and read him the details. He realized that Gallegos's credibility had disappeared with the publication of his run-in with the prostitute.

"No judge will respect this guy," Ruth said, and the Hernandezes agreed.

Like Gallegos, they said, they would work on the case with no money up front in exchange for the book and movie rights sales for payment. They insisted Richard fight the case and go to trial. "I haven't seen anything substantially connecting you to the crimes," Daniel said. Arturo agreed. "It's all circumstantial. We can win this case!"

"I agree with them," Barraza added.

"You really think you can win?" Richard asked.

"We *will* win," Daniel told him.

"I believe in them," Ruth said.

"But the thing is, I don't want my mother and father having to go through a whole long trial and everything like that where all their lies will come out."

Ruth said, "Don't worry about that, Richie! If you are innocent, you've got to fight them, otherwise they'll kill you."

"You think if I plead guilty, they'll give me the death sentence?"

"I'd be surprised if they didn't, with all the press this has gotten. It's political. But we can try to work out a deal," Arturo said. "If that's what you want."

There was a long pause. Richard had a lot to think about.

"And you have the time and everything to go to trial?" he asked.

"Yes, we'll make the time. This case will have our top priority," Daniel said.

"You can't ask for better than that," Barraza put in.

"Okay," Richard said, "I want you guys to represent me. You've got a deal."

Ruth smiled. They all shook hands. Ruth truly felt the Hernandezes would do the right thing by her brother.

As they left the jail, they were again stopped by reporters. Ruth said Richard had changed his mind about Gallegos, now that he knew everything regarding his background. "There's no way he wants a lawyer with a felony arrest representing him," she said.

When Joseph Gallegos was contacted and asked if he was still representing Ramirez, he said, "When I left him Wednesday morning he was in very high spirits. He was very happy I had been allowed in."

Asked if he had told Richard about his criminal record, he said, "Yes, certainly. Everything. And he said none of that mattered. Monday I'm putting in a motion to get copies of all police investigative records in the case."

THIRTY-ONE

The Ramirez family decided to show a united front for Richard and their support for Arturo and Daniel. Mercedes, Robert, and Ruth flew to Los Angeles on Sunday, October 21. Mercedes wore all black, as if she were in mourning, with large dark sunglasses on her face and a black veil on her head. Since August 31, she seemed to have aged twenty years. The lines on her face were deeper and more pronounced; she walked slowly, with obvious strain. It seemed the weight of what had happened—a world of tragedy—had come to rest on her thin shoulders, bending her over and pushing her down.

When she saw Richard, her heart rolled over at the sight of her lastborn in jail, charged with the most terrible crimes she had ever heard of. No matter what, Mercedes knew they were wrong. Her son, her Richie, who used to love to dance to the radio, could never have done the things they were saying. She felt that drugs and Satan had caused it all and were at the heart of this nightmare. People looked at her, stared, pointed, and whispered.

Richard told his mother, over the black jail phone, looking at her through thick, dirty glass, that he did not do the things he was charged with. He'd been framed. "They needed someone, and they chose me."

No matter what, Mercedes told her son, she believed in him and supported him. She also told him he must fight the charges—that the Hernandezes would fight hard for him and he should not give up. She would pray for him. "You cannot just roll over and give up and let them take your life."

* * *

The next order of business for the Hernandezes was to get Judge Soper to appoint them as Richard's counsel. When they appeared in court on Monday, the press was there in full force, as were Mercedes, Ruth, Robert, and Ruben. Mercedes kept her face covered by the black veil and sunglasses. At a sidebar Judge Soper explained patiently and slowly why she didn't want to allow the Hernandezes to represent Richard Ramirez, citing contempt charges from previous cases, which both Hernandezes protested, saying the contempts weren't their fault; they were unwarranted and unfair. The judge's real objection was their very obvious lack of experience in capital crime cases. There were grave consequences at stake, she said.

No matter what, Richard insisted, he wanted the Hernandezes.

Halpin also felt the Hernandezes weren't qualified to handle such a complex, heavy case.

Judge Soper pointed out that the state could not pay the Hernandezes because they didn't meet the state's minimum criteria for a capital crimes case. The Bar Association recommended that such lawyers have ten years' experience as attorney of record in fifty trials, forty of them involving felony charges, and thirty of the forty felony cases had to have been completed before a jury. The Hernandezes countered by saying it was California law to allow a defendant the counsel of his choice. They were licensed to practice law in California, were members of the bar in good standing, and were going to represent Richard Ramirez.

She asked the Hernandezes how they expected to be paid, in that Richard was indigent. They said they'd drawn up an agreement in which Richard would give them the rights to any film or book deal. She said she would have to review it and would appoint private lawyer Victor E. Chavez to read it and see if it was legal or went against the laws preventing criminals from benefiting from their crimes. The Hernandezes said the agreement had been drawn up in El Paso, where there were no laws preventing assigning book and movie rights to lawyers for payment.

Gallegos said he had no problem withdrawing from the case.

The Hernandezes would cause Phil Halpin problems. He knew their representing Ramirez would slow the legal process down to a painful crawl and make an already exceedingly difficult case even more difficult; their lack of experience would inevitably be a burden on his shoulders.

"I want these lawyers," Richard growled, very annoyed, opening and closing his hands as if they were claws, making the guards weary.

Ultimately, Judge Soper decided to put it all on the record and moved the arguments to open court.

As Richard was brought to the bar, he seemed like a man possessed. He moved from his left foot to his right and glared at Halpin with fire in his eyes. Mercedes prayed that he would calm down, but he didn't.

Judge Soper began by saying the defendant wanted to change attorneys again, after she had just allowed a change of counsel not two weeks before. She went immediately to the heart of the problem, saying the Hernandezes didn't have enough experience and that they'd been held in contempt of court in Santa Clara County. Arturo Hernandez jumped up and objected, saying the judge had no right making public these "alleged contempt charges."

Richard, staring at the judge, shouted, "I want these lawyers!" startling everyone in court.

Phil Halpin stood and suggested Ramirez confer some more with Gallegos.

"I don't want to confer with him," Richard said to Halpin venomously. "I want *these* attorneys!"

Arturo Hernandez continued to register his dismay at the judge's making public the Santa Clara contempt charges. Halpin interrupted him and said that he, in fact, had no right to speak to the judge on the record because they had not yet been appointed and had no standing.

"They do to me!" Richard called out.

Mercedes prayed that he would calm down, but she knew he wouldn't. Like his father and all his brothers, like his cousin Mike, he had a wicked temper; it was a family trait she had never really given much thought to. She'd just accepted it—like the color of their eyes or hair. She knew there were television cameras on him now, and she wished to heaven he would just sit down and not present such an angry face to the world. He was, God knew, already in enough trouble.

Instead of being calmed by his family's presence, Ramirez seemed to be spurred on to be more defiant and angry. The reporters looked on wide-eyed, shocked and pleased by Richard's fury. He was the personification of defiance, obviously very dangerous, and didn't care, apparently, who knew it. Richard glared at the reporters as Judge Soper and Arturo Hernandez argued about the contempt charges.

The judge ended by saying she was appointing a private lawyer to review the assignment agreement between Richard and the Hernandezes, and she would render her decision on changing counsel on Thursday, the twenty-fourth. As Mercedes would not talk with them, the reporters took off to file their stories.

The Ramirez family went to the jail after court. When their turn came and Richard's name was announced over the loudspeaker, all eyes followed Mercedes, trying to see some sign of how she could have spawned a child such as Richard Ramirez. With dignity and poise she ignored the stares, the silence, the pointing.

Why, she asked Richard, did he have to act like that when the whole world was watching? What were people to think? Richard said he didn't care what people thought, that Judge Soper had no right not appointing the Hernandezes as his lawyers. It was supposed to be a free country and he had the absolute right to have the lawyer he wanted. Mercedes said she understood, but he mustn't act so aggressive, so hostile. Ruth agreed with her mother, telling Richard that scaring people only made everyone think he really was a killer.

"They already think I'm a killer no matter what I do—so fuck them," he replied.

Ruth couldn't calm Richard down, and when the sheriff's deputies took him back to his cell, he was still cursing Halpin and Judge Soper.

Outside, as Mercedes and Ruth left the jail, they saw a group of young women, all wearing black, milling about the entrance. One of them carried a sign that read, "I love Richard." Mercedes looked at them incredulously, wondering what the world had come to.

To malevolent occultists all over Los Angeles, Richard was a hero: someone who openly stood up and embraced the dictates of Satan and didn't care who knew it.

Zeena LaVey, Anton's daughter, went to the jail to visit Richard. She wore a long, skin-tight black dress over her intense hourglass figure and had bright blood-red lipstick on her full lips and long fingernails. She was with her then-boyfriend, a tall blond named Nicholas Shreck, who had cut off his left ear as a token of his devotion to Satan. Nicholas also wore all black and sported an ankle-length black leather coat. Zeena told Richard that her father and the Church sent their blessings and were praying to Satan for him; they were making him an honorary member of the Church. That made Richard's spirits soar. He held LaVey in high esteem, and Zeena's visit made him feel the forces of darkness were being marshalled behind him.

Thursday morning, October 24, 8 A.M., Richard was shackled, taken out of his cell, and driven in a sheriff's van to the courthouse, where the press were lined up hoping to get some kind of outburst from him. Quietly, he hobbled out of the van to a holding pen behind Judge Soper's courtroom.

Mercedes was too weak and distressed to go to court, and only Ruth, Robert, and Ruben took up seats at the back of the courtroom, not talking, sitting up straight, as if they'd been called to the principal's office. In the holding pen, the guards noticed Richard was laughing to himself, walking back and forth, hyperkinetic, his chains rattling. His jailers wondered if he was trying to lay the groundwork for an insanity defense. They knew he was smart and wily ... otherwise, he'd have gotten caught much sooner.

At the defense table sat the Hernandezes and Joseph Gallegos. At the prosecutor's table was Phil Halpin, with the very visible presence of Carrillo and Salerno sitting in the first row behind him. The bailiff silenced the packed courtroom. About a dozen women, who had become known as Richard's groupies—disgusting but not surprising Salerno and Carrillo—waited anxiously for Richard, the object of their dreams and sexual fantasies. The bailiff carefully watched all these women. After all, this was the same courthouse where Charlie Manson's women created an uproar. The bailiffs knew, only too well, the terrible things such women were capable of doing at the bequest of such a charismatic manipulator.

Richard's eyes searched the spectators, quickly identifying

his supporters, detractors, and family. He smiled at his siblings, then scowled and sneered at the press, and still he laughed to himself. He stood to the right of the Hernandezes, facing Phil Halpin.

Judge Soper, her eyes on Richard and his attorneys, told the packed courtroom that she'd given a lot of thought to letting the Hernandezes become Richard's counsel. She was concerned that a contract assigning book and movie rights to the Hernandezes in lieu of payment would violate Richard's rights, for a story that ended in acquittal would be less valuable than one that ended with a guilty verdict. But the defendant, she pointed out, had refused to see lawyer Victor Chavez, whom she had sent to the jail to explain to Richard his rights after he'd reviewed the contract.

Nevertheless, she said, the assignment was legal under California law, and the defendant, according to the Constitution, could choose his own counsel. Judge Soper had decided to reverse herself and allow the Hernandezes to represent Richard. The Hernandezes smiled at one another and shook hands. Halpin shook his head in utter disbelief and disgust.

Richard decided to play a card he'd had up his sleeve all morning, and he raised his large hand high, his face filled with defiance and malicious intent. He showed the spectators the perfect pentagram he had inked on his palm. Under it was the number 666, the Book of Revelation's number of "the beast," i.e., Satan.

No, Richie, no, Ruth thought, looking at Robert and Ruben, as the press and spectators were suddenly in an uproar. Judge Soper banged the gavel and demanded silence. She hadn't seen the pentagram and couldn't imagine what the court was reacting to. When she saw it, she understood.

To see Ramirez, the dreaded Night Stalker, standing there insolently with a "blasphemous mark" on his hand was very sobering; it took a few minutes for the court to calm down. Richard smiled at his family, proud of himself.

The Hernandezes asked to be allowed to read the charges before Richard entered a plea. The judge called for a short adjournment to give Daniel and Arturo the opportunity to go over the particulars of the complaint. As Richard was led back to the holding pen, he shouted, "Hail, Satan," again throwing the court into a tizzy.

The Hernandezes said they hadn't heard it, but the court stenographer heard him clearly and she put it in the record—"Hail, Satan."

If anyone had had any doubts about Ramirez's guilt, they didn't now. It had been widely reported that pentagrams were found on Mabel Bell's inner thigh, on Nettie Lang's bedroom wall, and on the bathroom door at the Pan residence in San Francisco, and now one was inside Richard's hand with diabolic defiance on his face.

As the Hernandezes read the complaint, Richard paced in the holding cage, laughing. Cameras had been on him when he'd held up the pentagram and the image had been beamed to televisions all over the country, making people move uncomfortably in their seats, and in their sleep that night.

The Hernandezes conferred with Richard after reading the complaint and told him they could win the case. The lineup had been unfair, as had all the suggestive statements. They felt confident they could get the contents of the luggage at the bus terminal thrown out, because the luggage had been gotten illegally. Richard had told the Hernandezes that he had never told any cops about the luggage in any "voluntary statement." They had found the ticket in his wallet and had just taken it. The Hernandezes convinced him they really could win, and he decided to plead not guilty.

They begged Richard not to make any more outbursts and not to show the press the pentagram; that kind of behavior could only hurt him in the end. Laughing, he said he would behave. The Hernandezes told the bailiffs they were ready, and court reconvened.

As Richard was led back to the dock, all eyes were on him. He was smirking, but he kept his left hand to his side and winked at some of his followers. "I don't know what he's got to laugh about," Carrillo told Salerno.

Judge Soper took her place at the bench and asked the Hernandezes if the defendant was ready to enter a plea. They said he was. Richard was ordered to stand and tell the court how he pled, which he did, saying in a loud voice, "Not guilty."

Again the courtroom erupted, and Judge Soper had to bang her gavel and demand order.

Ruth's heart soared. For weeks she'd been fighting Richard

not to plead guilty; she had worried herself into a thin, nervous wreck—but finally her work and effort had paid off. She was so happy she cried. She knew if her brother pled guilty, the state of California would surely kill him. Phil Halpin had said publicly he'd seek the death penalty. The thought of her baby brother being put to death totally unsettled Ruth; she knew him as kind, gentle, giving, and caring, not the monster the Los Angeles press, the mayor, and everyone else said he was.

Judge Soper set Friday, December 13, for the preliminary hearing to determine if there was enough evidence for the case to proceed to trial in front of Judge James Nelson.

She warned everyone involved in the case not to make statements to the press; the gag order was still in place—and this admonishment, she emphasized, was also directed to the Ramirez family. The judge had read Ruth and Ruben's comments in the press and was distressed by their loose tongues.

Phil Halpin did not like the idea of the two inexperienced attorneys being his adversaries. He knew they were in way over their heads, which would inevitably slow down the whole process, but he remained resolute in convicting Ramirez and packing him off to San Quentin.

Richard felt that he had changed the judge's mind with the help of Satan. He believed Satan was as real as the American flag in the courtroom and that in the end, Satan would protect him from all his enemies.

When it was reported in El Paso that Richard would be represented by Arturo and Daniel Hernandez, Julian felt his son would now at least have a fair chance, and that was all he could hope for. As always, Julian had arranged for one of his sons to have a lawyer—but never before for the kind of trouble his lastborn had brought to the Ramirezes' doorstep.

The change in Julian was readily apparent. He seemed to grow older and shorter under the stress of Richard's arrest. He was appalled and horrified at the things the newspapers were saying his son had done.

Julian continued to go to work every day. Staying home and sitting around only made things worse. When he worked, he was distracted. He was still laying track and was as strong as a cape buffalo.

At the Santa Fe railroad, everyone knew one another, and Julian could feel their eyes on him. He knew for as long as he lived people would point at him and say, "There goes the father of the Night Stalker," and little by little, it began to kill him, sap the life force from him.

He seemed to begin to actually shrink.

Doreen was sick and tired of how unfairly Richard had been treated. She wrote a letter, the first of many, to the *L.A. Daily News* in mid-October, which they published, outlining her grievances:

What heroes?

A *Daily News* story on Oct. 6 reported that the captors of Night Stalker suspect Richard Ramirez, Manuel and Angela De La Torre, are "tired of the fuss." That makes three of us. The feigned modesty of the so-called heroes of Hubbard Street is equally tiresome. Heroes, indeed. According to one "hero," Jamie Burgoin, the "heroic" Manuel De La Torre exclaimed upon Richard's capture, "Get my gun! Get my gun! I'll waste him right here!"

What makes De La Torre's brand of violence "heroic" while Ramirez's alleged violence is considered "Satanic?" If the man they chased and beat brutally had been an ordinary intruder, and not the Night Stalker suspect, the so-called heroes of Hubbard Street might just as easily have been hauled away for assault and battery.

The De La Torres have been lavished with praise, awards from the mayor, and scholarships to study English. While they and their neighbors dive for reward money, it must be remembered that Ramirez has yet to be convicted of any crimes.

While the minor players in this game may have had something to gain, Ramirez has lost something: his right to justice and a fair trial.

Doreen Lloyd
Burbank

She decided not to use her real last name.

THIRTY-TWO

By the time the preliminary hearing finally took place, it was Monday, March 3, 1986.

There was a great deal of friction between Halpin and the Hernandezes.

A preliminary hearing is held to determine if there is enough evidence to proceed to trial. Halpin was planning to put 140 witnesses on the stand. He would not put his whole case on display, just enough for Judge James M. Nelson to hold Ramirez over for trial. Halpin felt he had enough evidence to convince any jury that Richard Ramirez was the Night Stalker.

The Hernandezes felt confident they could get thrown out all the evidence the police had gotten as a result of statements Richard had made during and after his arrest, which would severely hamper the prosecutor's case.

They believed the lineup was overly suggestive to the point of being illegal for three reasons: the bald spot on Ramirez's head, after it had been widely reported he had sustained a head injury when captured; the witnesses had been allowed to sit next to one another and conversed; and a sheriff's deputy at the lineup had silently held up two fingers—Richard's number—while he was in front of all the witnesses in the viewing room. In a video of the lineup, the detective holding up two fingers, as in a "V for victory" gesture, could clearly be seen.

The Hernandezes complained bitterly to the judge that the prosecutor was very slow in handing over important discovery items—such as fingerprints and police and lab reports—hamstringing their ability to cross-examine.

Richard Muñoz Ramirez at age three on his first bike. He was a good child and able to amuse himself for hours on end. (*Author's collection*)

Ramirez at six in an El Paso playground where he was knocked out for several hours by a swing. (*Author's collection*)

Ramirez's father, Julian Tapia Ramirez, when he was a policeman in Juarez, Mexico in 1951.
(*Author's collection*)

Modest El Paso home where Ramirez was born.
(*Author's collection*)

Ramirez at age eleven,
shortly before epilepsy
forced him to leave
the football team.
(*Author's collection*)

The Truth Apartments on Fruta Avenue in El Paso where
Ramirez witnessed a murder when he was twelve years old.
(*Author's collection*)

Ramirez at age fifteen, shortly before quitting school for good. (*Author's collection*)

Robert Ramirez, Richard's brother, at forty-two. (*Author's collection*)

Richard Ramirez when he was arrested for car theft in downtown Los Angeles in December 1984.
(*Author's collection*)

BK 786740 121284
LOS ANGELES POLICE — JAIL-F

The Los Angeles Greyhound Bus Terminal where Ramirez bought drugs and sold stolen property to different fences.
(*Author's collection*)

TERMINAL ENTRANCE
ENTRADA A TERMINAL

Gil Carrillo (left) and Frank Salerno (right), who ran the
Los Angeles Sheriff's Night Stalker Task Force.
(*Author's collection*)

AC/DC cap found in the Hernandez/Okazaki garage
in Rosemead.   (*Author's collection*)

Avia footprint in
Zazzara backyard,
size 11½.
(*Author's collection*)

The Avia sole presented
as evidence during the
trial tied many of
the crimes together.
(*Author's collection*)

Thumbcuffs used to restrain Lillian Doi at her Monterey Park residence. *(Author's collection)*

Doi residence after being ransacked by the Night Stalker. *(Author's collection)*

Mabel Bell's bedroom, where Stalker drew pentagram on wall: the first indication that Satan worship played into the crimes. (*Author's collection*)

Close-up of pentagram drawn on Mabel Bell's wall. (*Author's collection*)

The plundered Kyle residence. (*Author's collection*)

Handcuffs used to restrain Carol Kyle in her Burbank home. (*Author's collection*)

Mary Cannon's office after a visit from the Night Stalker.
(*Author's collection*)

Avia footprints on new rug of rear bedroom at Cannon
murder scene.   (*Author's collection*)

Joyce Nelson's home after being looted by the Night Stalker.
(*Author's collection*)

Partially-eaten melon left by Night Stalker at the Abowath
residence in Diamond Bar.   (*Author's collection*)

PEDRO'S BACK, AND THE BALL'S GOING, GOING, GONE/D-1

Saturday
August 10, 1985 -

Final news
25 cents

LOS ANGELES HERALD
EXAMINER

BIRNBAUM: WATTS NEEDS INVESTMENT FROM WITHIN A-3

7 HEADED TO SPRINGSTEEN CONCERT DIE IN BUS CRASH A-6

WRESTLING IS REAL (WELL, AT LEAST THE THRILLS ARE) B-1

L.A. bolts its doors, windows

Residents brace for new attack by Night Stalker

Violent end to a place of peace

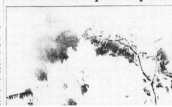

What makes this killer different

Serial murder experts piece together puzzle

By Annette Haddad
Herald staff writer

Some of the nation's top serial murder experts — including those who were involved in the notorious Hillside Strangler and Atlanta Child Murders cases — agree that the killer terrorizing much of Los Angeles...

By Mark S. Warnick
Herald staff writer

Frantic residents throughout Los Angeles County purchased guns and home-security alarms, called for neighborhood meetings and deluged authorities with questions and tips as the search continued yesterday for a vicious serial killer authorities fear will strike again.

The suspect, who enters darkened homes at night through unlocked doors or windows, has been linked to at least 14 recent attacks, including seven murders. He might be responsible for as many as 20 such incidents, authorities said.

The wave of attacks has prompted the largest local law-enforcement investigation since the grisly Hillside Strangler killings in 1977 and 1978, when at least 10...

Raiders fans get sobering news about acting rowdy

NAME GAME: IT CAN SPELL BIG BUCKS FOR A WINNER/A-9

Monday
August 12, 1985

Morning final -
25 cents

LOS ANGELES HERALD
EXAMINER

IN STYLE:
'TRADER JOE' TELLS WHAT'S IN STORE
C-1

IN SPORTS:
IT'S NO PUZZLE HOW DODGERS WON AGAIN
D-1

THE HERALD POLL
Are the Rams unfair to Eric Dickerson?
YES (213) 744-1405
NO (213) 744-1443

Night Stalker strikes again

L.A.'S MORNING BRIEFING

Frank Capra, 88, tested for stroke

Oscar-winning director-producer Frank Capra was admitted to Eisenhower Medical Center in Rancho Mirage last night to undergo tests for a possible stroke, the hospital said.

Capra, 88, was brought by ambulance to the emergency room suffering symptoms that could be the result of a mild stroke or a transient episode resulting in temporary changes at the level of consciousness, nursing supervisor Gini Chaney said.

Chaney said she had talked to Capra and he was alert.

Capra won Academy Awards for best Picture in 1934 for "It Happened One Night" and in...

WATTS — 20 YEARS LATER

The Watts business district, once called "Channel View," has been rebuilt in the Martin Luther King Jr. Shopping Center.

San Gabriel woman raped by intruder

By John Crust
Herald staff writer

A masked man who police believe might be the notorious killer of the nighttime "Night Stalker" at least seven people slipped through an unlocked window of a San Gabriel home early yesterday and raped and beat an 81-year-old widow.

A police task force — the largest since the Hillside Strangler killings of the late 1980s terrorized the county — is trying to catch the so-called Night Stalker, who is being linked to at least 14 recent attacks, including seven slayings. Detectives believe the man could be responsible for as many as 20 such attacks since February.

There are strong indications this could be the same person. Sheriff's Deputy Sam Jones. There are conflicting...

Union Carbide leak sends 125 to hospitals

INSTITUTE, W.Va. (AP) — A cloud of chemical fumes from a Union Carbide plant leaked yesterday, sending 125 people to hospitals, authorities said. Some of the people were complaining of nausea and eye irritation.

Officials at the plant feverishly, a few thousand more were sent to the hospital, and the chemical cloud drifted, prompting evacuation of some residents until several hours later.

Although many, the leak materialized in the pesticide trunk, broke from the plant's 700-unit chemical unit before it is when a valve failed, said Union Carbide spokesman David Henderson, a company statement...

Los Angeles Herald front pages of August 10 and 12, 1985 reporting the Night Stalker's savage attacks.
(Author's collection)

Survivor Carol Kyle helped authorities create the first
composite drawing of Stalker.　(*Author's collection*)

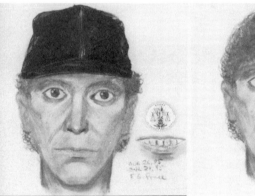

Police composite victim Sakina Abowath helped police
artist create.　(*Author's collection*)

The spot on East Los Angeles's Hubbard Street where Ramirez was captured by irate citizens. (*Author's collection*)

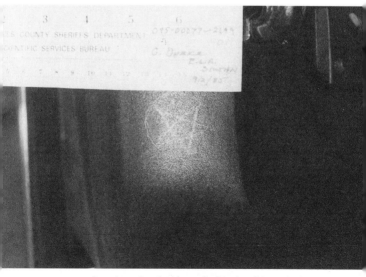

Pentagram found on the dashboard of Richard Ramirez's Pontiac. (*Author's collection*)

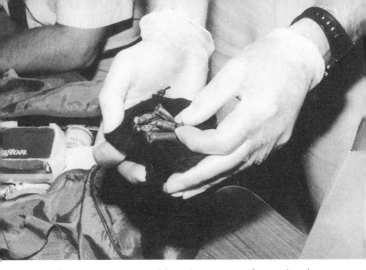

Ammunition removed from luggage confiscated at the
Greyhound Bus Terminal on August 31, 1985.
(*Author's collection*)

Jewelry show-up of valuables at the Los Angeles County Jail
on September 5, 1985.   (*Author's collection*)

Ramirez clenches his fists and pulls on his restraints at appearance in Los Angeles Municipal Court. *(AP/WIDE WORLD PHOTOS)*

A defiant Ramirez holds up pentagram at court appearance in 1985. Defense attorney Daniel Hernandez on right.
(AP/WIDE WORLD PHOTOS)

Asked by reporters what he thought of verdict convicting him as the Night Stalker, Ramirez responded, "Evil," and flashed a devil-worship sign. *(AP/WIDE WORLD PHOTOS)*

Ramirez looked around Los Angeles courtroom just before his attorney, Daniel Hernandez (right), launched his opening statement to the jury. *(AP/WIDE WORLD PHOTOS)*

Richard Ramirez (center) with San Francisco attorneys Randall Martin (right) and Daro Inouye (left). *(AP/WIDE WORLD PHOTOS)*

Juror Cynthia Haden, who fell in love with Ramirez during the trial, has become a private investigator so she can help Ramirez with his appeal.
(Author's collection)

Doreen, staunch Ramirez supporter and confidant, with her collection of Ramirez keepsakes.
(Courtesy of Doreen)

Laura Kendall, a New York admirer of Ramirez, says, "From the first time I saw him, I was drawn to him."
(*Author's collection*)

Recent shot taken by
Doreen of Ramirez
inside San Quentin.
(*Courtesy of Doreen*)

Ramirez in prison yard,
March, 1995.
(*Author's collection*)

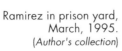

Doreen and Richard in the weeks leading up to their marriage. (*Courtesy of Doreen Ramirez*)

Mr. and Mrs. Richard Ramirez minutes after their prison marriage. *(Courtesy of Doreen Ramirez)*

In preparing their case, the Hernandezes had come to respect Richard. He had a keen mind, they felt, as evidenced by the caliber of the insights he offered into his defense.

Richard hated the idea of all the crimes he was being accused of—particularly the abduction charges—being made public.

Then, as now, he adamantly claimed that he never sexually abused any young people and that the police and the prosecutor had conspired to hang abduction and sexual abuse charges on him so they could pollute the L.A. jury pool further—hopefully, beyond repair. The Hernandezes planned to ask for a change of venue, to Oakland, perhaps.

As usual, the courtroom was packed. Richard's groupies took a dozen or so seats in the first row so they could be near him.

Ruth had come up from El Paso and sat with Ruben in the last row.

Richard was brought out chained and wearing baggy, jail-issue light blue pants and a short-sleeved shirt. On the starchy jailhouse diet and with no activity, he'd gained a good twenty pounds. His face was fuller and he seemed to have aged in the months he'd been incarcerated.

For Richard, jail was *very* difficult. He was a hyperactive person who had always moved around on the outside. Now he was locked in a six-by-eight-foot cell twenty-four hours a day and he hated every second of it.

Richard's eyes sought out his girls. As he spotted them he'd nod, giving them obvious thrills. His eyes then moved to the reporters and newsmen. He snarled at them and curled his lips, not shy about showing his disdain for them. *"Trematodes* [worms]," he mumbled, and sat down at the defense table, long and lanky and very annoyed at being there. Carrillo and Salerno sat in their usual seats just behind Halpin.

The Hernandezes made a motion to move the trial, which was summarily denied. They then told Judge Nelson they were objecting to an audiotape of Richard making incriminating statements to Carrillo and Salerno at the first and only interview at the Hollenbeck jail. Judge Nelson said he'd listen to the tape in a closed session in his chambers. Both sides moved to chambers, annoying the press and spectators.

Judge Nelson, a large, scholarly man who wore thick glasses

and parted his hair on the left, listened to the tape. There were clearly incriminating statements in it, but the judge said he would reserve decision until such time as Halpin tried to put it into evidence, and the proceedings were moved back to the courtroom. The Hernandezes asked that any evidence found in Richard's Pontiac and the bag at the bus depot be thrown out. Those things, Daniel told the court, were seized illegally because Richard had said he wanted a lawyer, yet still he was questioned. "His constitutional rights were seriously violated," he summed up. Judge Nelson reserved decision on that motion, too.

The hearing continued with Halpin calling witness after witness, including survivors of the Night Stalker crimes and criminalists. The case against Richard seemed airtight.

On all the important decisions, Judge Nelson ruled against the defense: he allowed in the evidence recovered from the bus station and from Richard's car and his sister Ruth's house.

While the hearing was still under way, Richard was taken under heavy guard to Orange County, where he signed a speedy trial waiver. He wouldn't be adjudicated on the Carns attack until the Los Angeles charges were disposed of. When Ramirez was driven back to the L.A. jail, he found scented letters from female admirers and a copy of *Justine*, by the Marquis de Sade, sent to him by Tamara Cruz, a Santa Ana Satanist who had been writing him.

Reading had become the only way Richard could escape the reality of his predicament. He had always liked to read but had never found the time to get intimate with a good writer. Now he had all the time in the world and nothing else to do. With books he could leave his cell and go wherever the story went.

In the Marquis de Sade, Richard had found an ally, someone who, he believed, was not hypocritical about sexuality and what he wanted. Society as a whole, Richard was sure, hid the truth—but de Sade told it and didn't care who knew it.

Halpin did not want Ruth or Ruben in the courtroom and he demanded they leave. He said they were going to be witnesses and had no right sitting in on the proceedings. The judge told them to leave.

Ruth was very angry about being ejected from the proceedings, as if she had done something wrong. She was sure Halpin was keeping them from appearing in court because he didn't want Richard to have any show of support so people would think the family didn't care, indicating he was guilty. She wanted to go to the press and complain, but she was afraid they'd arrest her.

Ruth went back to El Paso and followed the progress of the preliminary hearing in the papers. Her brother was the most infamous person ever to come out of El Paso, and his story was extensively reported. Julian kept reading the Spanish newspapers, and through them he learned the details of what they were accusing his son of doing. So far, he felt, the government hadn't shown anything that truly linked Richard to the crimes.

Wednesday, April 16, was a turning point in the preliminary hearing for many. Reporters who'd been thinking about writing a book on the case decided it was too upsetting a story to be that intensely involved with for months on end.

The Hernandezes and Phil Halpin argued over every issue. At one point, the judge moved their bickering into his chambers. The Hernandezes complained that Halpin was not presenting the case in the order of the crimes, and was, therefore, making it impossible for them to be properly prepared for cross-examination. Halpin said he was not required by law to present the crimes in the order in which they'd occurred. There were over 150 witnesses scattered all over the country, making it virtually impossible to present all the crimes in their actual chronology. Halpin called Arturo a clown and Judge Nelson took the case back into open court and on record.

Arturo Hernandez demanded Halpin apologize for calling him a clown. Halpin refused. The Hernandezes then asked Judge Nelson to hold Halpin in contempt of court for leaving the hearing Tuesday to check on whether or not Ruth and Ruben were talking to the press. The judge refused and warned: "Unless you are all very anxious to share the same cell, I would suggest you stop using the court record to cast aspersions on each other."

The court was called to order and twenty-three-year veteran sheriff's deputy Russ Uloth took the stand and testified about the day he was called to the home of Vincent and Maxine Zazzara.

He told the court how he and his partner had found Vincent Zazzara dead, on his couch, with a bullet hole in the left side of the head. He then described finding forty-four-year-old Maxine. "There was her eyes. There was a lot of blood and disfiguration, and the coroner examined that area, and the eyes were missing—"

Richard began to laugh, letting out a high-pitched hyena-like cackle.

The bailiffs closed in around him. Uloth stopped testifying and glared at Richard. If looks could kill, Richard would have fallen over dead. Richard continued to grin. The bailiffs' dislike for him was evident.

What kind of monster was he? The silent question hung over the courtroom.

Angry-eyed, hard-jawed, Uloth continued at Halpin's urging. "There appeared to be numerous scratch marks around her eyes. Her purple pajama top was pulled up and there were deep cuts, like an inverted cross, under her left breast. There were stab wounds in the chest, stomach, and pubic area. Her pajama bottoms had been pulled down."

People in the courtroom moved and squirmed in their seats uneasily. None of those details had ever been made public. Richard began to study photographs of Maxine Zazzara that had been given to the defense by Halpin as part of discovery, a slight grin still about his face. Could he, legal experts and members of the press wondered, be trying to lay the foundations for an insanity defense? He would have to be crazy to laugh in open court after such brutal descriptions and obviously risk further polluting the Los Angeles jury pool.

Russ Uloth described distinct shoeprints found in the flowerbeds under two windows and on the joint compound can under the small rear window the killer had used for access to the house. He further described the ransacking and the phone disabling that were trademarks of the Night Stalker's work.

Under cross-examination by Daniel Hernandez, Uloth admitted that Vincent Zazzara's son, Peter, had told him he thought his father had been killed because of Mafia ties and drug dealing.

Phil Halpin objected, saying the Zazzara killings were not a Mafia hit. Judge Nelson ruled against Halpin, allowing further cross-examination about Vincent Zazzara's alleged underworld ties, which didn't, Uloth summed up, amount to anything but "unfounded rumors."

Under cross-examination Sheriff's Homicide deputy Paul Archambault also admitted hearing rumors about Vincent Zazzara. He said, "He [Peter Zazzara] related to me at that time that his father was involved in Mafia operations . . . that it could possibly come from a drug sale."

Under redirect by Halpin, Archambault testified that the sheriff's office had thoroughly checked out what Peter Zazzara had said, which, in his opinion, was not true. As the Hernandezes protested, Halpin used this to get Judge Nelson to reverse his ruling regarding Vincent Zazzara's mob ties and have it stricken from the record.

The next fight between Halpin and the Hernandezes erupted toward the end of the day, when Daniel complained bitterly to Judge Nelson that the sheriff's office, the LAPD, and the prosecutor had not yet given them copies of fingerprint and footprint evidence they had in their possession, which the defense was entitled to by law. Judge Nelson ruled that all fingerprint and footprint evidence be brought to court on Monday, the twenty-fourth. Halpin complained to Judge Nelson that moving all the fingerprint evidence to the crowded court building could jeopardize and damage it. Judge Nelson was not interested. He said, "If we have to, I'll order every jar and bottle and have them put on the table here in court."

Halpin was very angered by this ruling. He wasn't going to put any of the fingerprint evidence up until the end of the case for the sake of expediency. He wanted the case to move along as quickly as possible, and with over 600 exhibits and 150 witnesses, that was not an easy task. There was another reason for hurrying to bring the case to trial: a few of the witnesses were close to death as a result of being attacked, and others could very well die of natural causes soon.

In the hall after court that day, he complained to the press about Judge Nelson's rulings, saying "Key evidence would be jeopardized in moving the fingerprints to the Traffic Court's building in downtown Los Angeles."

Judge Nelson reversed his ruling on the material being brought to court the next day but assigned a special master to make sure the defense received the items they were entitled to. The hearing went forward and Halpin put witness after witness on the stand, who pointed angry, often trembling, fingers at Ramirez.

Florence Lang was still in a comatose state and couldn't testify. But Maria Hernandez, Carol Kyle, Whitney Bennett, Sophie Dickman, Somkid Khovananth, Sakina Abowath, Virginia Petersen, Jesse Perez, and Felipe Solano all did testify—as did scores of technical experts, who all inexorably linked Richard Ramirez to the crimes, Halpin said.

It was heart-wrenching to watch Somkid Khovananth testify as she cried and sobbed, her shoulders shaking. "He just called me 'bitch' and every [bad] word. He dragged me by the hair; everywhere he go, he took me. He beat me up and put a gun to my head. He did *everything* bad to me." When Sakina Abowath's turn came, she was so distraught at the prospect of being in the same room with Richard, her legs were weak and she nearly had to be carried to the stand by bailiffs.

"Are you enjoying this?" Carol Kyle testified he had asked her while he was raping her. Unlike Sakina and Somkid, Carol was composed and matter-of-fact as she testified.

When Daniel Hernandez asked Carol why she had engaged the Night Stalker in a "twenty-minute conversation," she said she thought if she could make him care about her and her family, they might be allowed to live. She said the last thing she had said to him was, "You must have had a very bad life to do this to me." She said he laughed. Hernandez asked her if she had described her attacker as "very good-looking, painfully thin, with dark curly hair, who smelled 'very leathery.' " She said yes.

"I was afraid to make him angry," Sophie Dickman testified, and explained how she was eager to turn everything over to him. She described him as "tense, but in control of himself and the entire situation."

* * *

The animosity between Richard and his jailers grew daily to a palpable intensity. The bailiffs heard every witness's testimony, and the terrible details upset them and stayed with them.

To then see Ramirez smile and laugh, scoff and swagger, and show no respect to the system, the victims, or them personally, and to see all the women coming to smile at him, stick their chests out, and sit with short skirts and legs slightly ajar for him, made their dislike for Richard a very real tangible thing. It all came to a head at the end of April.

The woman in Tijuana to whom Jesse Perez had given the gun was called to testify. As she entered the courtroom and approached the stand, Richard turned around and glared at her. His eyes then moved to Amy Rio, and he smiled. Often during the preliminary, Richard would mouth words to the groupies and try to communicate with them, which was not allowed, and the bailiffs had to warn him a few times every day about communicating with spectators. Twenty-eight-year-old bailiff Stephen De Prima moved closer to Richard and told him to look forward. Richard ignored him and kept smiling at Bernadette and his fans. Apparently De Prima thought Richard was trying to intimidate the witness, and he grabbed Richard by the head and forced him to look forward. Richard stood up and yelled, "Get your fuckin' hands off me!" He grabbed De Prima. Two other bailiffs rushed in. De Prima put Richard in a neck lock, the two other bailiffs grabbed him, and as a shocked courtroom and judge looked on, they dragged Richard from the court and into the holding area.

Arturo Hernandez looked into a peephole in the door and saw the bailiffs pummeling an unresisting Ramirez.

"Hey," Arturo yelled, "you don't *have* to hit him anymore, he's not resisting!"

"Why don't you go in there and stop them?" Halpin said.

The animosity that had been building up between them spilled over, and Arturo took off his jacket and said to Halpin, "Come on, me and you. You think you're so tough? Come on, let's go outside." Carrillo and Salerno had to get between Arturo and Halpin. The judge banged his gavel, calling court to order.

Some minutes later, when Richard was brought back into the courtroom, he was smiling like a school kid who had gotten into a fight with the schoolyard bully. There was a pronounced red welt on his neck.

In chambers after court that day, Hernandez complained to Judge Nelson about bailiff De Prima's "excessive aggression." The judge agreed with the Hernandezes, saying, "There was no reason for the bailiffs to act that way," and removed De Prima from working the rest of the hearing.

In the hall afterward, Daniel told reporters their client was behaving properly and accused the bailiffs of overreacting. He said, "They don't think they are doing their job if they don't rough somebody up."

Richard would later say that De Prima had been angry because Bernadette had given him the cold shoulder.

Sheriff's dep. Jim Ellis was called to testify. Ellis had been guarding Ramirez on and off at the county jail, Halpin said, when Richard had made certain "spontaneous statements" to him. He asked Judge Nelson to let Dep. Ellis testify in the judge's chambers because he didn't know if Judge Nelson would ultimately allow the statements in. If Dep. Ellis testified in open court and the judge ruled against allowing the statements in, it could become an appeal issue. Halpin had vowed early on that he would give Richard very little he could use for a possible appeal.

Judge Nelson moved the proceedings to chambers. Dep. Ellis was sworn in, and as Richard gave him the evil eye, he stated that when he was guarding Ramirez on the evening of October 10, Ramirez had started talking to him. Ellis testified that he did not encourage or take part in any conversation with Ramirez.

Ramirez was angry about the food at the jail. He said it was always cold and filled with drugs that were giving him headaches. Ellis testified Ramirez proceeded to dump the food in the toilet bowl. "He stated that he killed twenty people in California, that he was a supercriminal, that no one could catch him until he fucked up. He said he left one fingerprint behind, and that's how he got caught.

"He made the statement that he went to San Francisco and killed Peter Pan. He stated he waited outside by their house by the garage, waited until it was dark . . . he said he went upstairs, saw two people living there, and the statement he made was, 'Boom, boom, I did them in.' "

Then, according to Ellis, Ramirez said he could have killed at least ten police officers and sheriff's deputies and that the next time no one would get away. " 'I would shoot them in the head and then they would wriggle and squirm all over the place and then just stop, or I'd cut them with a knife and watch their face turn real white. I love all that blood. I told one lady one time to give me all her money. She said no. I cut her and pulled her eyes out . . .

" 'I would do someone in and then take a camera and set the timer so I could sit them next to me and take our picture together.' "

Judge Nelson ruled that these statements by Ramirez were admissable because they were voluntary and had been made after Richard had been read his rights and spent many hours with attorneys.

However, statements Richard supposedly made to LAPD on the way to the Hollenbeck Station were not allowed because he had then not yet been given any Miranda warning.

When, later on, Richard was asked about the episode with Deputy Ellis, he said, "That's bullshit. What happened was I was pissed because of the shit they were putting in my food, and I threw it away and yelled and cursed at him. I told him I'd fuck him up."

Halpin questioned a second sheriff's deputy, Bob Anderson, in Judge Nelson's chambers, and he said that Richard had recently given him a postcard to mail, which was addressed to his former friend, Earl Gregg in Lompoc. On it Ramirez had drawn a scorpion and a pentagram, and he had written a threatening poem to Gregg, which, Halpin said, he wanted the judge to be aware of.

"Crybaby," Richard said.

When the proceedings were brought back to open court, Halpin told Judge Nelson he had no more witnesses and had presented the people's case.

The Hernandez strategy was not to offer any defense at the preliminary hearing. "We'll wait for the trial, where guilt has to be proven beyond a reasonable doubt, whereas with the hearing, the prosecutor only had to show a strong suspicion of guilt. There's no reason to use up all our ammunition at this time," Arturo said.

Halpin asked that eighteen of the charges be dropped. These included three abduction-molestation cases and the robbery of Clara Hadsall's home because of her recent demise. The families of all three victims in the abduction cases didn't want them to be retraumatized.

Richard would say later that that was the best news he'd heard since he'd been arrested. He hated the idea of being labeled a molester and said, "It wasn't true. The cops just made it up to get somebody to give me up."

Judge Nelson announced he'd found enough incriminating evidence to hold Ramirez over for trial. Because of the multiple murder counts Ramirez could face the death penalty. The judge read into the record all the counts: fourteen murders, five attempted murders, fifteen burglaries, five robberies, four rapes, three acts of oral copulation, and four acts of sodomy. The attacks were on sixteen different L.A. households, between June 27, 1984 (Vincow) and August 8, 1985 (the Abowaths). While the judge read the counts in a factual, dispassionate way, Richard sat low in his seat and looked forward as all eyes in the courtroom focused on the back of his head.

It was all over and the stage was set for one of the biggest murder trials in American jurisprudence.

Judge Nelson set May 21 as the date Richard had to enter a plea on the fifty new felony charges. There were now fifty-eight, including the initial charges leveled in September 1985. Richard was taken out of the courtroom, chains rattling, feeling triumphant, feeling that Satan's hand had helped in getting the eighteen charges dropped.

In the hall, reporters hungry for good quotes gathered around Halpin, Salerno, and Carrillo. Halpin said, "It's gone smoothly because there was a lot of preparation. There were a number of investigators who worked on the case for a long period of time, and we were very prepared. I'm satisfied. I felt confident we had enough evidence to hold him over for trial."

Frank Salerno, who hadn't said a word to the press throughout the whole preliminary, talked now. When asked how he felt about the long hearing being over, he said, "It's just a big relief to get it in the system and get it going. To move on to the next step, which is the one that really counts."

Halpin was hopeful the trial would start in the summer, and he would push for it.

The Hernandezes were also surrounded by the press. When asked how Richard felt about the day's proceeding, Arturo said, "He advised me to tell the media he thought there were a lot of politics involved with the position of the judge. He feels we won and there was a tremendous breakthrough in the case. At this early stage of the proceedings, I think that if you knock off thirty percent of the charges, you are talking about a significant breakthrough. The molestation charges in particular were bogus."

He said they had a slew of pretrial motions to file, the most important of which was to move the trial out of L.A. County. They would, Arturo said, take any ruling against a change of venue to a higher court.

In El Paso the news of Richard being charged with so many more crimes hit like a thunderclap.

Led by Mercedes, they had all been regularly praying, going to church every day, lighting candles, beseeching Jesus, Mary and the saints to help Richie.

Mercedes felt that Satan was the root cause of all these problems, and that ultimately the Lord Jesus would prevail. She constantly reminded everyone with an indomitable strength that seemed far beyond her capacity, to have faith and to continue to pray.

"Satan, in the end," she predicted, "will lose."

After the preliminary hearing, Richard often thought about suicide. If he hadn't been on suicide watch, he would have tried to kill himself. He believed they'd convict him; they were bloodthirsty and hell-bent on killing him.

To him, death was preferable to a life behind bars, in a small steel cubicle, being told what to do, and when and how to do it.

But the sheriff's deputies were always sitting there, looking in on him every fifteen minutes, staring at him like he was a caged human oddity in a zoo, then writing down what they'd observed.

Every day Richard received dozens of letters. He chose to answer very few. Some of the letters offered spiritual guidance; others, sexual fantasies; others, condemnation and scorn; still others, high praise and congratulations.

One of the women who wrote him the most often and seemed the most interesting was Eva O. She said she admired him for his courage and would love to have sex with him over "the bloody bodies of his victims." She told him that she, too, was a Satanist and thought of evil as a virtue: evil is, she pointed out, live backward. She said she slept in a coffin and did not go out during daylight hours unless she had to.

Little by little, Eva, Richard would later relate, pulled him out of his shell. Even before he'd been arrested, Richard had been a loner who'd very rarely confided in people or shared intimacies. He felt what was in his heart was his own business, and he had never revealed it to anyone. But Eva O, if she was sincere and not just looking for some of the heat from his notoriety, might be someone he could share intimacies, and perhaps secrets, with. He began writing back to her. She wanted to visit him. In order for her to be able to, the Hernandezes would have to get a court order, the requirement for anyone but immediate family. However, Richard wanted to first make sure Eva was the real thing, not a psycho Satanist or a police plant or a nut.

He received letters from born-again Christians, Protestants, and Catholics, all trying to convert him and turn him away from the clutches of Satan. And there were letters from women who wanted to mother him and show him the difference between right and wrong. One nurse who'd lost her son felt that Richard, because he didn't have *her* love, had gone astray and understandably vented his anger with guns, knives, and fists. There was also Tamara, a full-figured redhead who had made an altar with Richard's picture on it and a black candle always burning. She'd later say, "I used to go to a cemetery in Santa Ana and sit on a tombstone and write Richard poems and letters. I think he's gorgeous."

But Richard wrote only to Eva and to his family.

"If it weren't for the books and the letters, I would have done myself in," he later confided.

It was not only letters people sent him, but also books. It was during the weeks and months before, during, and after the preliminary hearing that he became "a book junkie." He read all day and all night. Frequently he couldn't sleep at all and would read for several days straight, stopping only to eat. He read Carlos Castaneda, Sigmund Freud, Gabriel Garcia Márquez, Arthur Conan Doyle, Norman Mailer, Truman Capote, and as much true crime as he could get his hands on. His favorite books were about serial killers.

Through the books, Richard acquired insights into human nature and the world he'd never known existed. The more he read, the more certain he became that society was hypocritical and malicious and would cut you up and spit you out like so much cow cud if you let it happen.

The Hernandezes' strategy was to delay the proceeding as long as possible. In a multiple murder case, the best friend a defense lawyer has is time: witnesses die (as evidenced by Clara Hadsall), move away, forget, confuse details, and change their minds about testifying at all—not wanting to air in public and relive what amounted to the worst experience they'd ever had.

"Any time a trial is delayed, you have the potential for the unavailability of witnesses. When we talk about justice delayed, it benefits only the defendant and his attorney," District Attorney Gil Garcetti would later say.

Defense attorneys say that overly swift justice is an abuse of the defendant's rights. "A criminal defense lawyer has to have time to prepare himself and plan strategy and counterattack, which in a case as large as Richard Ramirez's was very time-consuming," a noted criminal attorney practicing in L.A. said.

On May 21, Ramirez was back in court. Ruth and Ruben wanted to be there but couldn't. The courtroom was once again packed. Ramirez had become big business; it seemed people loved to hate him.

The groupies as well as press from all over the world were there. None of the reporters knew what to expect. Ramirez was an enigma who was capable of anything. He'd turned down all requests for interviews. He hated reporters and felt they'd been very unfair to him and made him guilty before he'd ever gotten to court.

Eva O was in the courtroom, wearing all black, as pale as white marble. She had dark hair parted in the middle, the part colored blood-red. Her heart skipped a beat as Richard was brought into the courtroom. He smiled faintly at her and scowled at the reporters. When asked how he pled to the charges, he said, "Not guilty."

Halpin was half expecting the Hernandezes to offer an insanity defense. "He had to be crazy to do those things," was a much-repeated statement in L.A. An insanity plea might work, particularly in light of the Zazzara eye removal and the pentagrams.

Ramirez pled not guilty, indicating to Halpin he was ready to do battle. Halpin believed Richard belonged on San Quentin's death row, not in some state hospital. In Halpin, Richard Ramirez had found a very worthy adversary: prepared, tough, experienced, and very smart.

Judge Nelson sent the case for trial to Superior Court Judge Dion Morrow. Halpin wasn't happy about it, but he had no choice. The problem, as Halpin stated in court, was Judge Morrow's busy calendar.

Sure enough month after month dragged by as Morrow kept giving the Hernandezes postponement after postponement until Halpin was red-faced and fit to be tied. He kept getting ready for trial, lining up all the witnesses, law enforcement people, and experts—over 160 individuals now—then having to cancel them all and reschedule everyone again.

By the end of November, Halpin had had enough. He made a motion to have the case moved to another judge, citing all the delays Morrow had allowed in the case. Morrow granted Halpin's motion, and the case was moved to Supreme Court Judge Michael Tynan, who would preside over the case to its resolution.

Tynan was a no-nonsense jurist who liked to move his cases along expeditiously. He had a gentle demeanor and was always polite. Halpin made the judge aware of the Hernandezes' delaying tactics and Tynan promised not to let the proceeding be held up unduly.

Judge Tynan wore thick wire-framed glasses, which often moved down the bridge of his nose. In 1981 he was appointed by Governor Jerry Brown to the Los Angeles Municipal Court, where he had been supervising judge of Traffic Court. In 1984, he was appointed to the Superior Court. On May 28, 1987, Judge Michael Tynan set September 30 for the trial, warning the Hernandezes to be ready.

On September 11, the Hernandezes again requested a delay of a few months, citing the prosecution's failure to turn over items the defense needed to plot strategy and plan defense. Tynan refused to give them six months and set trial for February 1, 1988, only to grant another delay before then because the Hernandezes appealed to the district court of appeals to get certain evidence the prosecution was refusing to give the defense—namely, crime-scene photographs.

On January 19, Tynan announced that the state court had granted a last-minute request by the Hernandezes for the state to turn over the evidence the defense wanted. On the twenty-fifth, he set March 22 for the trial date because of the uncertainty surrounding the appellate ruling.

On March 16, the defense asked for yet another delay to review the new material they'd gotten as a result of the appellate decision, which Tynan granted, making April 29 the date for trial.

Again, on the twenty-ninth, the defense asked for a delay, citing the huge amount of work as reason they weren't ready. Tynan then scheduled June 30 for trial, but on June 21, the defense filed a motion to exclude Tynan, citing him as being racially biased against the defense, a tactic expected to buy more time.

On July 8, Orange County Superior Court presiding judge Philip E. Cox ruled that Tynan was not biased.

Finally, on July 21, 1988, jury selection began, and the battle began in earnest.

Richard had gone through a metamorphosis during the long months of delays, hearings, and more delays. He had gained weight and was thicker around the middle. His face was fuller and not as boyish. His hair was to his shoulders now, black and unruly, like a lion's mane. He had not been allowed out of his cell for exercise, only to shower twice a week and for visits and court appearances. He mingled with no other prisoners.

All the reading had as notable an effect on him as the starchy food at the jail, for he'd become quiet and introspective—and he seemed much more sure about who he was and what he stood for, what he cared and didn't care about.

The visits from Eva and other female admirers had given him a newfound confidence and fueled his ego to new heights.

Richard had asked the Hernandezes to have Eva approved for visits a year after she'd first written him. Through her letters and poetry, he felt she was truly evil in her heart, and as such, someone he wanted to get to know. When she first went to the jail, everyone who saw her did a double take, stood still, and stared. It takes a lot to turn heads at the L.A. County Jail, where all sorts of characters regularly show up, but Eva did it, wearing all black with the blood-red strip down the middle of her head.

Eva told Richard that he was blessed with the power of Satan, that he was special and the most desirable man alive. She told him, too, about the macabre fantasies she had involving sex and cutting and killing people. She was obsessed with death; she'd even once had sex with a body, she told him. Richard listened to her wide-eyed—like a school kid hearing about sex for the first time from an older kid.

Soon, Richard asked the Hernandezes to have other female admirers of his approved by the court, which they promptly did. What Richard wanted, Richard got.

There were quite a few women now writing him every day, wanting to see him. When it reached the point of his having three different women on his visiting list, the jail stopped asking for a court order and relaxed visiting policies for Richard, and soon there were lines of women showing up at the jail to visit him.

Nothing like this had ever been seen before. It was a bizarre phenomenon that none of the guards at the jail could get over. It was almost as if Ramirez was a movie star rather than a man accused of entering people's homes while they slept and tearing their lives and bodies apart.

All the women who went to see him had different reasons,

but they each found him, they said, "Attractive and cute—so dangerous he's a turn-on."

"The forbidden fruit," added another. "I think he's the most attractive man I've ever seen."

"He didn't do the things they are saying, no way," said Dian Harrela, a Mexican-American woman who believed Richard had been sent from God to avenge all the wrongs society had perpetuated on her.

"There's something in his eyes—like a little boy who needs help. I just wanted to reach out and embrace him. He's so sexy," said Doreen, when asked why she was attracted to Richard.

Amy Rio began wearing a sticker over her heart that said "I love your smile." "He's vulnerable and so sexy," she said of Richard. "Just look at his eyes. They are like an animal's." The *Daily News* printed a large photograph of Amy on March 19, as she was sitting on the floor outside the courtroom. Amy was usually the first one there, with her heart-shaped face, big lips, and huge dark eyes, sitting on the floor, waiting to see a shackled Richard led to his chair, hobbling as he moved, chains rattling.

"He loves me," Patty, another of the girls, said. "He told me so. He's so nice. Gentle like a lamb. He talks so sweet. And he's very funny. He signs his letters, 'Yours Cruelly.' "

Some days as many as a dozen women would show up to see him. He was allowed only one visit a day. The rest would leave disappointed but would be back the following day and stand in line for hours hoping for a visit.

"It used to turn me on so much when he did that because he was so dangerous and so near, but he couldn't really hurt me," another Ramirez groupie admitted.

Doreen didn't get to meet Richard until shortly before jury selection had begun. "I was shy and I didn't want to be just another one of his groupies, so I waited." But Doreen continued to defend Richard mightily in the press with scathing letters condemning anyone she perceived as having done something unfair to him.

She finally sent him a birthday card in February with copies of all the letters she had written defending him. He was truly shocked that someone he didn't even know would so strongly take up his cause. He wrote right back and invited her to come to the jail. She was surprised when she got his letter, though quite pleased, and wrote him and invited him to call collect, which he promptly did.

"When I first spoke to him, my heart was going a mile a minute; I couldn't believe that it was him—that I was finally talking to him. He was so nice and so sweet, like a little boy."

Richard thanked her for taking on his cause. She told him she was in love with him, had been since she'd first seen his picture.

Here, Richard thought, was someone he could really trust—and he told her to come and visit.

The first time Doreen went to see him was at the end of June of 1988. She bought a new dress and fussed with her makeup and hair like it was her wedding day. When she was seated in a visiting booth at the jail and the sheriff's deputies brought him down, Doreen nearly fainted at the sight of him so close she could touch him, if not for the glass. "Right then and there I told him how much I loved him. He told me he loved me, too—that no one had ever protected him and cared for him like me."

Ruth Ramirez came up when she could. Money was tight, but every few weeks she'd show up at the jail and have to compete with Richard's groupies. Ruben, too, visited Richard in jail. Julian would call him and remind him to go to the jail so Richard knew his family was there, behind him, concerned, always praying for him.

From reports the Hernandezes gave Julian, there was a good chance they could win the case and prove his son had not committed the horrible crimes he was being accused of.

Julian prayed for that every day, morning and night. In the two years since Richard's arrest, Julian looked like he'd aged fifteen years; his shoulders had rounded, his face had thinned, his walk had slowed, and deep lines had formed on his face.

BOOK IV

THE TRIAL

These murders are in the first degree,
were premeditated, and occurred
during burglaries and other crimes. We
are asking for the death penalty.

> Prosecutor Phil Halpin, in his
> opening statement to the jury

THIRTY-THREE

By the time of the jury selection, the State of California had spent $1,301,836 on Richard Ramirez, and the case hadn't even gone to trial. There were editorials and news commentaries condemning a system that would let a murder case take so long to come to the bar and cost so much.

"It was an outrage" was the sentiment of many of L.A.'s citizens. Richard Ramirez had affected them in a very real, tangible way, and they wanted justice swiftly, not years after the fact.

Jury selection finally began on July 21, 1988, from a pool of 1600 citizens. The Hernandezes were looking for Hispanics and certain minorities; they felt that with a jury of all whites and Asians, Richard wouldn't have a chance. They believed Hispanics and blacks would have a more open mind.

Richard now wore a shirt and tie and a black leather jacket Doreen had bought him. She, with the rest of the groupies, was in court every day, her heart and libido doing a flip every time he looked her way. Doreen felt that she and she alone was good for Richard; all the other girls were nothing but a bad influence on him and were "a bunch of street sluts." Her love, she felt, was greater and more pure than any of theirs could ever be, and she would make sure Richard knew it.

"I loved him so intensely it hurt; all I would think about was him, day and night, night and day. I never thought of other men. I was a virgin and Richard knew it, and that's why I was different; that's why he loved me," she later confided.

On the first day of jury selection, fifty jurors were called. Thirty-nine were summarily excused, and the rest were questioned and grilled further. The Hernandezes knew that they had an uphill battle finding an impartial jury in L.A. County. They constantly complained to the press how biased everyone in L.A. was and repeatedly made reference to a study they had done proving it.

Richard felt the whole trial was a farce. If he hadn't been forced out of his cell, he would never have come to court. However, it gave him a chance to see his admirers and to stretch his legs.

The juror selection was a slow, tedious process. It bored Richard, and he soon began falling asleep. He'd stay up late at night reading and would be tired for court. Judge Tynan didn't like his sleeping and warned him to stay awake. Richard took to wearing large black Porsche-type sunglasses, also bought by Doreen, so he could close his eyes behind them.

Toward the end of July, Richard reportedly told a sheriff's deputy that he was going to have one of his girls sneak a gun into the courtroom and he was going to shoot Halpin to death, then people in the audience, then himself. Security was already tight, but the bailiffs took Ramirez's alleged threat seriously, set up metal detectors, and searched everyone coming into the courtroom.

On August 2, Halpin entered court in a huff, angry that he had been searched in front of eighty prospective jurors. "I was forced to remove most of my clothing while standing in the hall, surrounded by jurors. It seems a strange approach to search the district attorney, but not prospective jurors, Your Honor." Judge Tynan apologized for Halpin's embarrassment.

Daniel Hernandez told Judge Tynan that Richard didn't want to attend the jury selection; Tynan said that he had to, whether he wanted to or not.

Midway through the jury selection, juror expert Jo 'Ellan Dimitrius was brought in to help the defense. She had a long, thin face, intense dark eyes, and bouffant platinum hair. Richard often conferred with her.

Jury selection took six months, longer than most had anticipated. On January 10, 1989, a jury and twelve alternates were sworn in, comprised of six Hispanics and six blacks, seven females and five males. The Hernandezes felt it was a victory for the defense.

For most of the jury selection, Arturo Hernandez had stopped coming to court. Daniel had hired a paralegal named Richard Salinas, who had wavy black hair, a pointed hatchet face, and dark eyes. Daniel would often confer with Salinas on important issues. Arturo had apparently become disillusioned with defending Richard. There was no big movie or book deal, and the case was costing him money. A television movie about the Night Stalker was in the works, but the Hernandezes hadn't gotten a dime. As long as Richard refused to talk about his alleged crimes, nobody was willing to put up money. Daniel did his best, but the arduous task of being in court every day, staying in hotels away from his family in San Jose, and working without the benefit of co-counsel was taking its toll. He was tired, yet couldn't sleep at night; he'd toss and turn and worry about the case, his two little girls, and his wife. He began eating excessively, and by the time the jury was finally sworn in, he'd gained twenty-five pounds.

On the morning of the first day of the trial, the courtroom was packed. Photographers lined the top row of the jury box and reporters lined the benches tightly. The few seats in the courtroom not taken by press and lawyers held Richard's groupies, who had arrived early in the morning while it was still dark and waited in line, for the most part not talking to one another. Another of Richard's admirers, Diane Harrela, had said to reporters earlier that day, "The whole story hasn't come out. Richard is innocent. He's been framed, no matter what the prosecutor says. I know he's innocent . . ."

There was electricity in the air. When Richard was brought into court, everyone fell silent. He was dressed in a charcoal gray suit Doreen had gotten for him. The only sound was his leg irons as he hobbled to the defense table, wearing Porsche sunglasses. Ruben was outside in the hall, pacing back and forth and blaming heavy metal music for his brother's problems. "Maybe he'll save some souls if people learn the truth about that kind of music," he said.

Judge Tynan welcomed the jury and alternates to the trial. He warned them that it would be a long and arduous affair and suggested that if anyone on the jury was thinking of learning a new language or playing an instrument, now was the time. He also suggested exercise as a way to take their minds off the case while they were not in court.

He read every charge to the jury, then turned the proceedings over to Phil Halpin, who introduced Alan Yochelson, William Murk, Frank Salerno, Paul Tippin, Leroy Orozco, and Gil Carrillo.

Halpin made his opening statement in a matter-of-fact, dispassionate way, never raising his voice, never resorting to histrionics. With the help of enlarged maps and huge color-coded charts, he explained to the jury the series of crimes in chronological order, what connected them, and how he planned to prove it.

He told the jury he would link Richard to the crimes with surviving witnesses, gloveprints, fingerprints, and shoeprints at locations where he, Ramirez, had shot, stabbed, and beaten his victims to death while committing robberies in every case but Veronica Yu's. He made reference to the pentagram found at the Bell residence, on the thigh of one of the victims. As Halpin systematically described the crimes, Richard made notes on a yellow legal pad. Whenever he moved his feet, you could hear the chains rattle.

The attacks, Halpin said, stretched from Northridge to Sierra Madre in Orange County and were always near freeways for quick escape. Halpin told the jury about Felipe Solano, how he had much of the stolen property and would testify how he'd gotten it from Richard Ramirez, whom he knew as David Mena; that stolen property, mostly costume jewelry, had been recovered from the defendant's sister's home in El Paso, Texas. He spoke about the similar language used in different crimes and described Carol Kyle's attack, how she'd suddenly felt a gloved hand over her mouth and a gun to her head and heard, "Where's the money? Don't look at me, bitch." He told the jury that Ramirez had left a hand-cuff key on the mantel so Carol Kyle could free herself. "That key is identical to the key that was discovered in the home of Ma Bell and Florence Lang."

Of Mrs. Lang, Halpin said, "She cannot speak and she is fed through a tube, but she is still alive. Therefore, the defendant is only charged with attempting to murder her."

As Phil Halpin continued to describe the specifics of all fif-

teen attacks—for the first time made known to the public—
there were audible gasps among the spectators as well as the
press and Richard's groupies. There were public defenders
and ADAs in the courtroom who worked in the building, and
even they, who dealt every day with the incredible savagery
people perpetrated against one another, moved uneasily in
their seats.

Halpin told the jury about the luggage in the Greyhound
Bus Terminal, saying items found in it—a nail clipper and a
can of Weight Gain had the defendant's fingerprints on
them, and that there were .25-caliber cartridges with distinctive red marking in the primer. "The experts looked at those
cartridges . . . and . . . by examining [the] still live rounds, ascertained that they had been operated through the same .25-
caliber auto that had been determined to have been used in
the Abowath murder and the Petersens' attempted murder."

He said they'd be meeting Jerry Stubblefield, who had designed the Avia shoe with the distinct waffle pattern that
showed up at seven of the crime scenes: the Zazzara, Doi,
Bell, Cannon, Bennett, Nelson, and Khovananth residences.
With that, the prosecutor wrapped up his opening statement
and told the jury they'd first be meeting Jack Vincow, son of
Mrs. Jennie Vincow.

Jack now lived in Brooklyn, N.Y., where he'd been born
and raised. Since the 1984 murder of his mother, he'd been
turned off to Los Angeles. He had taken the loss of his
mother very hard; the pain and feelings of loss he felt hurt as
readily as if he had broken bones. He had turned to medita-
tion. "I chose for myself two simple words to meditate on:
calm and relaxed." Jack was now writing a book on medita-
tion.

Jack walked into the courtroom with a slow, shuffling step,
a big man with a very sad face. All eyes followed him as
Richard's chains rattled in the silence of the courtroom.

Jack described for the jury the afternoon of June 27, 1984,
how he entered his mother's apartment that hot June day,
finding things thrown all over.

He described how he found her, how he ran out of the
apartment in a panic, yelling for help, and the police arriving, taking his mother's lifeless body away in a black plastic
body bag.

Halpin finished his direct and turned Vincow over to Daniel Hernandez. Questioning a witness at a preliminary hearing without a jury present was one thing, but questioning a witness like Jack Vincow with anything but respect was inviting the jury to dislike you. Hernandez's strategy was that the first crime on Halpin's list was a third-party defense, i.e., someone other than Richard was the killer, and he was going to suggest Jack's brother, Manny, was that someone. The problem with this strategy was that Judge Tynan had already ruled the defense could not pursue that line of reasoning. (Halpin had investigated Manny and learned he'd been in Brooklyn with witnesses to prove it.)

Daniel's plan to pursue this defense before the jury put him on a direct collision course with Halpin and Judge Tynan.

He asked Vincow, "Did you ever see, yourself, any type of behavior on your brother's part that appeared to be aggressive or violent toward your mother?"

"Verbally abusive, but I corrected him. Nothing beyond verbally abusive that I saw personally. Never anything beyond verbally abusive," Vincow answered.

"But rumors you heard were beyond verbally abusive?"

Halpin's anger erupted. Standing, he said, "Excuse me, Mr. Vincow! Let me object on two grounds: both hearsay and irrelevant."

"Sustained."

Annoyed, Daniel asked for a sidebar, at which he described to the judge his third-party defense. Halpin told Judge Tynan about his certainty of Manny Vincow's whereabouts the night of the crime. Richard turned around and with a deadpan, sunglassed face, disdainfully looked at the press, snarling slightly, as his supporters admired his profile and pined for his attention.

When court resumed, Daniel took Jack through the day he had found his mother again. Most defense lawyers would have wanted Vincow quickly off the stand. It looked like he might cry at any second. Hernandez asked, "How long were you in the—in your mother's bedroom when you found the body? How long were you there before you ran out?'

"Very brief. Seemed like seconds."

"And what are the injuries you saw?" Hernandez wanted to

know, opening the door for details which could only work against the defense.

Vincow testified, "The major injury that there was a neck gash that looked like someone had attempted to remove her head and almost succeeded. Very serious neck injury—"

Hernandez interrupted. "Nonresponsive. I object and request that the latter portion be stricken."

"Overruled, denied," Judge Tynan said.

Hernandez then tried to suggest that Vincow had killed his mother because he had had a mental breakdown twenty years earlier. Halpin objected. Hernandez called for another sidebar, at which the judge slammed Daniel, telling him he was being cruel, that there was no evidence indicating either Jack or his brother had had anything to do with Jennie Vincow's murder, and that he was to stop implying they had. Daniel argued he should be allowed to impeach Vincow. The judge didn't agree and ordered his cross to continue. Daniel countered that Vincow had refused to take a lie detector test; Tynan said that that was irrelevant. Daniel continued to try to tie Jack Vincow and/or his brother Manny to the murder. His effort proved futile and made the jury restless and uncomfortable. He hammered away at Jack, trying unsuccessfully to shed suspicion on him, over Halpin's constant objections, right up to the end of court that day.

In the morning Jack Vincow was recalled and again Daniel Hernandez tried to link him to the murder and drilled Jack, clearly traumatized and suffering, on all the details of June 28, now implying he had killed his mother for money, as Halpin objected on grounds of relevance and was sustained. The jury began wondering what was going on.

"I felt so bad for that poor man, and here was Daniel Hernandez, showing no respect at all," one juror would later say of Hernandez's cross of Jack Vincow.

When Daniel asked Jack if it was he who'd handled his mother's financial affairs, Halpin strenuously objected and another sidebar on the record was asked for by Hernandez. Judge Tynan refused to let Hernandez ask questions concerning Jennie Vincow's money matters, stating it wasn't relevant. The sidebar ended and Hernandez repeatedly asked Vincow why he was frightened about talking to the police and taking a polygraph test.

"Mr. Vincow," Hernandez said, "do you remember telling me that there was something frightening about the interview with the police?"

"It was a poor choice of words," Vincow said. "I should have, well, said 'concerned.' That was just a poor choice of words at the moment. I meant 'concerned' and said 'frightened.' " With Halpin objecting, Hernandez persisted until the judge ruled the questioning irrelevant.

Daniel then tried to get Jack to admit he was relieved when he saw the time of death on the death certificate. Halpin again objected and the objection sustained.

Hernandez moved to a statement allegedly made by Wanda Doss, the owner of the building. Halpin objected, Tynan sustained, suggesting Hernandez make an offer of proof at the bench at another sidebar.

"What is the statement Wanda Doss was supposed to have made?" Tynan asked.

"That she saw someone like him having breakfast, or someone saw somebody like him having breakfast, and that would have made him—that made him develop some type of fear, fright, reluctance to cooperate . . . that goes to his credibility," Hernandez said.

Tynan said, "I'm going to sustain the objection. It is hearsay."

Back in front of the jury, Hernandez again asked about Wanda Doss. Halpin objected; the court sustained it. This would become a mantra—objection, sustained—through the whole length of the trial.

Halpin next put on the stand Jessie Castillo, the LAPD detective who had caught the Vincow homicide, and he told the jury how he'd arrived with his partner, Mike Wynn, secured the crime scene, and run the evidence-gathering.

Using photographs, Halpin helped bring Castillo and the jury back to that June day in 1984, five years earlier, and Castillo described the crime scene.

Halpin asked, "Can you describe the trauma [of Jennie Vincow] that you discovered during your investigation?"

"Sir, she had received many stab wounds to the upper chest area and some wounds to the hands."

Halpin handed him a photograph. "And finally, let me

show people's exhibit 1-H and ask you to tell the jury what is depicted there."

"Sir, that is the lower part of her body, the end of her dress, and depicting some of the panty girdle that she was wearing at the time."

"All right. And specifically with respect to that area of the body, did you notice any trauma?"

"Some to the legs and to—the inside was torn out, the inside of the panty girdle, the inner crotch area was torn."

Richard moved; his chains rattled. Spectators shifted uneasily in their seats, wondering why.

Halpin finished and Hernandez stood and began his cross, taking Castillo through every step of what he did that day, which took much longer than Halpin's direct.

Det. Castillo had, in fact, had some difficulty with Jack Vincow. "How would you describe his, Jack Vincow's, demeanor in terms of his cooperation with you?" Hernandez asked.

"Sir, he was difficult to interview."

"Can you tell me—can you describe his demeanor, what made it difficult?"

"Well, it would depend on what day you are talking about. Sometimes he was very cooperative, and then he would turn hostile and be very uncooperative."

Halpin didn't like that answer, but he could do nothing about it.

Daniel proceeded to ask Castillo if his investigation of Vincow had moved out of state. Halpin objected on grounds of relevance.

Judge Tynan thought that it was a good note to recess for lunch, reminding the jurors and alternates not to talk about the case among themselves or with the media, reserving decision on Halpin's objection.

Gil and Frank hurried back to the office and grabbed some sandwiches. Frank was still running team 3, and there was a lot of work on his desk. He did what he could, and he and Gil hustled back to court.

After lunch, and without the jury present, Judge Tynan took up Halpin's objections regarding Det. Castillo's going to

New York State. When asked for a show of proof for that line of questioning, Hernandez withdrew the question.

Halpin moved on to another matter: Hernandez's objections to his direct as being leading and his having been admonished in front of the jury. He complained to the judge that they gave the jury the impression he was doing something wrong, when in fact he wasn't, and said he didn't want the record to reflect any kind of improper questioning on his part. Tynan said he understood his concern and promised not to admonish him about how he did his direct. He then ordered the jury brought in.

Halpin was saving his ace for last; he was sure once Reynaldo Clara, the fingerprint expert, took the stand, he'd get a conviction on count 1. Clara told the court he'd had ten years' experience and had conducted 4,000 crime-scene investigations, including work on homicides and bank robberies. He described for the jury, at Halpin's patient, methodical prodding, how he'd dusted the window screen with magnetic powder and discovered five fingerprints, which he'd lifted with lifting tape and placed on a print card. There were, he stated, four prints on the screen and one on the window. Halpin took the print cards out of a sealed bag and showed them to Clara, and he identified them as the ones removed from the Vincow crime scene. He said he'd also found two more prints on the screen which were not identifiable at all. When Halpin asked if he had compared the latent prints with ones on file, he said he hadn't, that a colleague, George Herrera, at the coordination desk, had done that.

Halpin turned Clara over to Hernandez, who wanted to know if Clara had dusted anywhere else in the Vincow house for prints. He said he dusted the whole house, "Anything that is printable by powder I tried. The bathroom walls weren't porous enough for dusting, and the detectives decided to use ninhydrin in the morning," Clara said.

Hernandez's questioning of Clara also took far longer than Halpin's direct. After nearly an hour, he finished and Halpin asked a few questions on redirect about the exact place the four discernible prints had been found, whether they were on the inside or the outside of the screen, to which Clara said he couldn't tell.

Almost as an afterthought, Hernandez reminded Clara

that at the preliminary hearing he'd said that nobody could tell how long the prints had been there, a week or a few months or even a year. With that, Hernandez could later argue to the jury, his client's prints could have been put there long before Jennie Vincow's murder.

Richard felt that introducing the prints Clara had found was a travesty of justice; he'd later say, "These fingerprints should not have been allowed in at all. They had only three discernible loops, and for a print to be admissible in court, it's supposed to have seven loops."

Halpin then called John Herrera from the coroner's office and he told the jury how he'd been called to the Chapman residence and was directed to a bedroom where he saw the deceased. He said he took her body temperature at 4:50 P.M. There was rigor mortis about the body and lividity on the back and neck area.

There was the possibility that she had been sexually assaulted because "Her girdle was pulled down and her dress was partially lifted," Herrera testified. People in the courtroom cleared their throats and moved in their seats. As Richard crossed his feet, the chains rattled and all eyes moved in perfect unison like a school of small nervous fish in his direction.

Halpin had Herrera tell the jury what rigor mortis, lividity, and body temperature all meant. He knew there was going to be a lot of testimony about bodies, and the more the jury understood, the more they'd be able to evaluate and appreciate the evidence.

He finished quickly with Herrera and handed him over to Hernandez, who again had Herrera tell the jury the rudiments of rigor mortis and lividity and how they each had manifested on Jennie Vincow's body. It seemed he was trying to prove the time of death was closer to 9 A.M. or earlier, which he felt would tie Jack Vincow to the murder. Halpin repeatedly objected and Tynan sustained it.

In frustration, feeling the judge was conspiring to undermine his case, Hernandez finished with Herrera and court was recessed for the day.

Richard stood up and, tall and lanky, walked loudly toward the door leading from court. He never took off the sunglasses, and no one could tell where his eyes were. Doreen hoped they were on her; every woman there hoped his eyes were on her. As he looked in the direction of the press, his lips twisted into a silent snarl filled with genuine disdain.

Halpin's next witness, Dr. Joseph Cogan, from the morgue, was unable to be there that day. The prosecutor moved on to the next case and called Maria Hernandez, now married and pregnant with her first child. Halpin had her describe what had happened the evening she'd been shot and her room-mate killed. He showed her pictures of the garage and Dayle's car, marked exhibit 3C, and asked her if she recognized the AC/DC baseball cap in the foreground of the photo; Maria said she didn't. Halpin knew he had witnesses who would put that hat on Richard Ramirez's head. He had her tell the jury step-by-step how she parked in the garage and heard a noise as she was entering her apartment. Her eyes were big and filled with the pain of the memory, and they never moved in Richard's direction. When Halpin asked what she saw after she turned around, she said, "I saw a man pointing a gun."

She described being shot and told the hushed courtroom the details of how her assailant went into the condominium, and her then hearing a shot as she tried to flee.

For a moment, she told the jury, she thought he was be-hind her and had shot at her again, but there was no one there. She ran around front and saw the same man walking away from her condo. He saw her and pointed the gun at her, then ran.

Maria, testifying in a calm voice, told the jury how she found Dayle dead on the floor. Dayle's sister and other rela-tives were in the courtroom, and they began to cry.

"Now, Ms. Hernandez," Halpin asked, "do you see in the courtroom the man that shot you that night?"

"Yes."

"And will you point him out to the jury, please?"

She raised the hand that she'd been shot in, pointed at Richard, and said, "The man on the end," as all eyes moved to Ramirez.

"The defendant, Richard Ramirez, for the record," Judge Tynan said.

Maria was now Daniel Hernandez's witness. He complained that she was out of sequence and he needed until 1:30 to "review and prepare, perhaps move things along faster than to start right away and not be as prepared as I should be for the specific witness."

Halpin objected. "Counsel knew she was going to be here for a couple years now. The same thing happened at the preliminary hearing. We were out of sequence frequently, so we both had to be prepared."

Judge Tynan told Hernandez to do the best he could, but Daniel repeated that he wasn't ready, saying the district attorney was switching witnesses and trying to confuse the defense. At a sidebar, Halpin told Judge Tynan to stop Hernandez from insulting him in front of the jury. Tynan agreed and told Daniel that as a trial lawyer, he should be prepared. He ordered him to continue.

Hernandez took Maria through every aspect of her assault, without regard for the trauma she had gone through on the night of March 17, often asking what appeared to some to be impertinent or nonsensical questions. He seemed, however, to make some headway when he asked her to describe her assailant. She said, "From what I can remember at this point, it is very fuzzy. I can tell you he was five ten, something like that, at least as far as—as far as I know. I didn't have a tape measure with me. Dark clothes. Dark hair. That's all I really can remember." It had happened four years before and much of that whole evening was blocked and hazy. She answered, "I don't remember" to many of Hernandez's subsequent questions.

"Do you recall seeing any details of the person's face, the person's physical qualities or anything?" Hernandez asked.

"I remember testifying that I did, but my memory now, I don't have a clear picture."

"Today, here today, you can't tell me that you remember seeing your attacker's face?"

"No."

"So when you pointed out Mr. Ramirez today, you were relying on some other time, in terms of what you said then?"

"I was relying on my testimony then."

"So in your memory today, you can't really point at Mr. Ramirez and say that is the person?"

Everyone in the courtroom, it seemed all at once, leaned

forward to hear her answer, for she spoke softly now. "Not truthfully—not definitely," she said.

A hushed exclamation of surprise rose and fell. As much as Gil, Frank, and Halpin didn't like that answer, Hernandez liked it fine. If that didn't lay the groundwork for reasonable doubt, nothing did.

Daniel wanted to weaken the case even more, but his tactics caused Maria to seem more traumatized and vulnerable.

At noon Tynan broke for lunch and a shaken Maria Hernandez stepped down from the stand. Richard didn't take his eyes off her as he grinned broadly. He felt that Satan had interceded and forced her to tell the truth, "That she really couldn't recognize me. She saw me in the news and in the papers, that's why she ID'd me at the lineup. Her description to the police didn't look anything like me."

Maria hated being near Ramirez while she was pregnant; she believed in her heart that he was evil from his shoes to the top of his head and not someone to be around when you were pregnant.

At 1:30, Hernandez resumed the cross-examination, confident he could further show the jury that Maria Hernandez wasn't sure Richard was her assailant. He tried to get her to concede that she'd used her purse to protect herself and in so doing had never even seen who'd shot her, but Maria was firm and sure when she told him the purse had not blocked her view.

Halpin stood ramrod straight, absolutely determined to repair his case on direct. He had her detail the injury to her right hand, wanting to dispel any notion that her pocketbook had shielded her view. He then had Maria describe for the jury exactly what had happened at the lineup. "On September fifth of 1985, when you identified the defendant as the person who shot you, were you positive of your identification?"

"Yes," she said.

Daniel Hernandez objected, calling it hearsay, and Tynan ruled against him.

Maria didn't remember if she had identified Ramirez at the preliminary hearing, but at an April 9 motion in front of

Judge Tynan, she had recognized him as the man in black who'd shot her. Halpin conferred with Yochelson, then asked the court to let her read her testimony at the preliminary, to which Hernandez objected vehemently. There was now a question about her identification, Tynan said, and the people had the right to set the record straight. Maria silently read her testimony.

"And do you recall now if you identified the defendant as the man that shot you?" the prosecutor asked.

"Yes, I did."

Halpin questioned Maria on her recollection of how clear her memory was at her previous appearances in court and at the lineup, and she was confident that her memory of her attacker's appearance was fresh in her mind at those times.

It appeared Halpin had repaired the damage of Maria's memory lapse. Daniel Hernandez, though, was determined to take back the advantage. He questioned her again about her identification, but Maria held fast and he couldn't dissuade her in the slightest. He suggested Gil Carrillo had told her Richard was number 2 in the lineup, which she denied. He went over the same thing again and again, getting the same answer and losing the attention of the jury.

When Daniel finally sat down, a collective sigh of relief went throughout the courtroom. Halpin said he had no more questions; he wanted Maria to be able to get off the stand; he felt terrible that she'd been subjected to Daniel Hernandez's cross, but he couldn't do anything about it, and he apologized to her with his eyes. Judge Tynan told her she was excused and was subject to recall.

He recessed court until 3:15. At the defense table, Daniel felt triumphant. He was sure he had invalidated Maria's testimony by showing the jury she really didn't remember anything about the events of May 17. Richard wasn't so sure.

Joseph Cogan, the pathologist who'd done the autopsies on both Jennie Vincow and Dayle Okazaki, was called. He testified that Vincow's stab wounds were arbitrarily numbered from head to toe. Four occurred in the trunk, six in the neck area. He described in detail the injury each knife wound had caused.

"Any one of the wounds would be fatal," he summed up.

It was clear to everyone in the court that Jennie's killer had known exactly what he was doing.

Dr. Cogan testified that the neck wounds were peculiar because they were stab wounds incorporated with slash wounds and went from ear to ear. "And these stab wounds were—were driven in. One of them hit the spine and produced a small fracture in the spine, and then across the two stab wounds on either side of the neck was this—the slash wound, and the slash wound severed the trachea almost entirely, the trachea being the air tube which supplies air to the body and lungs, and [it] severed one of the deeper veins in the neck.

"There was evidence of blood aspiration into the lungs, indicating that the slash wound to the neck occurred while she was alive and that she had breathed blood into the lungs."

The eerie silence in the courtroom was tangible as the reality of the Stalker's work invaded people's minds. A few of the press members subconsciously reached for their own throats. One of Richard's groupies later admitted she became sexually excited by the description of all the blood.

Halpin asked the doctor if he'd found any hilt marks. Cogan said yes and explained that if a knife is driven into the body with force, black and blue marks form around the wound. He estimated that Jennie Vincow might have been alive for a few minutes after the wounds were inflicted.

Judge Tynan interrupted, saying it was close to 4 P.M. and they should call it a day. The reporters hurried into the hall to try for quotes from the key players for the evening news. Doreen and a few of Richard's other admirers hurried over to the jail so they could visit with him.

Halpin wanted to start with the neck wounds and show the jury close-up color shots of the slash across Jennie's throat taken during the autopsy. Hernandez objected heatedly, saying the photographs were inflammatory and the jury should not see them. Halpin countered that the wounds were "virtually identical" to injuries at other murder scenes and evidence in themselves. Judge Tynan was very reluctant about showing these photographs to the jury. They were horrible and would inevitably cause emotional turmoil and nightmares. He told Halpin that if he could show him that the wounds were identical he'd consider it; otherwise, only diagrams and drawings, which Hernandez had suggested, would be allowed. Halpin said he would need some time to go through all of the photos.

Halpin said he had photographs with the same slash wounds from incident number 4 (Maxine Zazzara), incident number 8 (Mary Cannon) and incident number 12 (Max and Lela Kneiding). Alan Yochelson was sent to get them. Tynan would delay his ruling on the admissibility of the photographs until he had seen them all. In the meantime, Halpin would resume his direct examination of Cogan. James Wegner had done the actual autopsy on Dayle Okazaki, but he'd left the medical examiner's office and wasn't available. Halpin intended to use Cogan to establish the facts. Hernandez objected on grounds of hearsay, but Tynan allowed it after much arguing, based on its being an "official business record."

Allowed to read Dr. Wegner's report, Cogan told the jury the exact cause of Dayle's death, a gunshot wound to the middle right forehead, had caused massive hemorrhaging and hemorrhagic brain damage. He testified there was a second injury—blunt force trauma that had probably been sustained when Dayle went down after being shot. Cogan said there was stippling (gunpowder marks) on Dayle's forehead, indicating she'd been shot at relatively close range. "The distance from the front of the barrel is about eighteen inches . . . It varies from firearm to firearm depending on various factors; the type of weapon, ammunition, et cetera."

Halpin handed the doctor a bullet envelope from the medical examiner's office containing the small, slightly dented .22-caliber projectile, which, according to the report, was the actual slug Wegner had removed from Dayle's head. Halpin had the doctor explain how an autopsy was done and how such a projectile would actually be removed. Then they broke for lunch.

When court resumed, Hernandez's first question was, "Doctor, as far as the wounds that you described to the body [of Jennie Vincow], can you tell me which of these wounds would be immediately fatal?"

"None are such that they would be immediately lethal. The

wounds to the neck I would say would be more immediately lethal than the wounds to the abdomen."

For nearly an hour and a half, Daniel asked questions about the wounds and how long a person would actually live after receiving such injuries. Richard fell asleep behind his sunglasses. It became a meandering, repetitive cross that went around in circles; one court observer likened it to a dog chasing its own tail.

Halpin asked a few questions regarding Jennie's time of death; he did not want the jury confused on that fact. The doctor reiterated that based on the liver temperature, she died somewhere between 1200 and 1600 hours (noon and 4 P.M.) on June 28.

Daniel's recross questions concerned rigor mortis and time of death. He was obsessed, it seemed, with getting Dr. Cogan to concede facts he was intent on not conceding, and this went on for another full hour as Richard slept, jurors moved about in their seats, and the journalists wished his testimony would come to an end.

When he was finally finished, the prosecutor had no further redirect and Judge Tynan dismissed him. He stepped down from the stand glad to be away from Daniel Hernandez and his questions.

After a brief recess, Gil Carrillo was called as the next witness. His huge presence a regular part of court proceedings since the start of the trial, he mounted the witness stand and told the jury about the Sunday night he'd received the call at home directing him to the Hernandez/Okazaki residence in the city of Rosemead, only a ten-minute drive from where he lived.

Using photographs Halpin showed him, Gil told the jury where he walked and what he did upon his arrival. Halpin had him describe everything he'd seen at the crime scene, and how he'd gone to the Beverly Hospital the next day to interview Maria. Halpin moved to Gil's relationship with Maria Hernandez's family and had him explain to the jury how her mom had been good friends with his sister on the block where he'd grown up. Halpin had him recount for the jury the incident in which Maria's mother had come to the house that night to collect some personal things for her daughter. Gil testified he'd attended Dayle's autopsy and had watched the .22-caliber slug being removed from her brain, as her sister in the audience let out a small, plaintive wail. He identified the slug for Halpin.

Halpin moved to the September 5 lineup; he didn't want any confusion about Gil's influence over Maria regarding her picking Richard out of the lineup. Gil testified he'd never shown Maria Hernandez any pictures of Richard Ramirez.

Halpin asked if Gil had communicated at any other time with Maria. Gil told the jury he'd met her at the house after she'd been released from the hospital and had her take him through every step of what had happened that night.

Halpin tried to establish for the jury that Maria had had ample light to see her attacker clearly. The bulb, Gil testified, was part of the door closer and was in the center of the garage, hanging from the ceiling.

Judge Tynan suggested they resume Monday morning at 10:30. Gil was just warming up and wanted to continue, wanted to get it over with, but he had no say in the matter.

THIRTY-FOUR

Richard hated weekends in the Los Angeles County Jail. On the outside, Saturdays and Sundays were always favorite days of his, and when weekends rolled around, the loss of his freedom seemed compounded.

Richard had always been the kind of person who was always on the move; ever since he was able to walk he'd never been able to sit still. That was one of the reasons he was so uncomfortable in school—sitting still for hours on end had been very difficult for him.

"My brother," Ruth said, "never stayed one place too long; I mean, it was like he had jumping beans inside him. He was always active, going somewhere or coming back from somewhere."

Now he could go nowhere; he lived in a six-by-eight-foot steel cubicle and probably would for the remainder of his life.

Richard, however, continued to escape from the jail with books, and whatever he read picked him up and transported him to where the story took place.

"No matter what they do to me, my mind is free and it can go where it wants to go and they can't do anything about it," he'd later say. An admirer of Richard's had sent him a story about Jack the Ripper and his grisly deeds, and that weekend Richard was, through the book, transported to Whitechapel in London, where he walked the cobblestone byways as fog swirled around his feet.

Letters were also a way for him to find relief from the flat steel walls and guards' hostile, curious stares. He would later relate that whenever a new sheriff's deputy hit high power, he inevitably come and take a look at Richard, at the fear-inspiring Night Stalker; to the guards—all convinced he was indeed the killer—Richard was the personification of the bad guy, the epitome of evil, as dangerous as a man-eating shark. Most of them wouldn't say anything; they'd just look at him with curiosity and apprehension. Richard didn't like people coming around and bothering him, staring at him. For the most part, he had very little contact with other inmates; even when he received visits, the guards wouldn't bring him to the visiting area when other inmates were still there.

Richard took to putting crime-scene photographs on the walls of his cell, using soap and toothpaste as glue. He'd gotten the photographs, which were part of the discovery, from Daniel Hernandez. Sometimes, an inmate mopping the floor or pushing a tray of books would pass by Richard's cell and call him names, curse him out. Richard would point to the photographs and say, "There's blood behind the Stalker," and the inmate would inevitably look once and go away pale.

One of the photographs was of Maxine Zazzara. The guards saw the photograph, but Richard was legally allowed to have it as part of his defense and the guards could do nothing.

Doreen, as well as a few of Richard's other admirers, came to see him that weekend. She wanted to be sure she wouldn't be shut out of a visit because other women had gotten there before she did and she was there at five in the morning, standing in the dark, leaning against the gray concrete wall of the jail.

She had become as obsessed with Richard as a holy man is with his Lord; he was her sunrise and her sunset, the moon and the stars. She thought of nothing but Richard; she was sure she could help him with the purity and sincerity of her love. Doreen wanted to marry him, to have his children and serve him breakfast in bed in the morning. She fervently hoped he'd win the trial and be freed so they could escape somewhere together, but with everyone lying about her true love and with all the unfair press, she knew his chances for acquittal were not good.

Whatever Richard wanted, Doreen secured for him. He was the boss in their relationship. She made sure Richard had money in his commissary account at the jail and sent him books and magazines, writing paper and stamps.

She wrote him religiously every day and often sent him funny cards. Richard was like no one she'd ever known. She'd come from a quiet, conservative background, had never been in any trouble, and was always more interested in studying for school and in romance novels than in men. With Richard, everything changed. He was the ultimate rebel. Combined with his dangerous Latin good looks, he turned Doreen on in a way no other man ever could, she says.

Doreen planned to give her virginity to Richard. She knew, however, that might never happen. She would sacrifice everything for Richard. "That's what real love is about—giving," says Doreen. "Isn't it?"

When she did finally see him, after waiting several hours, she could have only twenty minutes with him and they talked about how well Daniel had done with getting Maria Hernandez to admit she couldn't identify Richard in the courtroom.

Richard wanted to write a letter to Ted Bundy, on Florida's death row, and he asked Doreen to get Bundy's prison number and address. He had, he said, some things he wanted to ask Ted about.

Doreen was very good at locating information, having done it for her job at magazines. If Richard asked for something, neither storm, nor rain, nor sleet, nor flood would stop her from getting it. If he wanted Bundy's address, she'd find it. "I'd cut off my right arm for him," she'd later say.

Monday morning Gil was back on the stand. Phil Halpin, fresh from the weekend and anxious to get into it, asked Gil if Maria had described her assailant when he and his partner had gone to visit her at Mercy Hospital. Gil testified she had said, "A light-skinned Caucasian or Mexican, five-nine to six-one, nineteen to twenty-five years of age . . . with dark hair, wearing a black Members Only–type jacket, and also [with] a thin build." Halpin ended his direct examination.

Hernandez began with the AC/DC baseball cap, wanting to know if Maria had said her assailant had had a hat on. Gil said Maria hadn't said anything about a hat until he'd asked her if the AC/DC baseball cap was hers or Dayle's. Gil assumed that it had belonged to the assailant.

Daniel asked questions for an hour without eliciting anything that could help the defense and he sat down, seeming tired and sluggish.

"I have nothing further," Halpin said, in a hurry to put another witness on the stand and move the trial along. He made another motion to start showing the jury exhibits, particularly the photographs. Tynan asked for the prosecutor's argument to be made when they came back from lunch at 1:30.

Court then resumed with the introduction into evidence of photographs that depicted Dayle Okazaki lying on the kitchen floor in a pool of blood, her face obscenely swollen. Hernandez objected on the grounds that the photographs were excessively inflammatory and should not be shown to the jury, under statute 352. Judge Tynan said, "I think under 352 I will permit the photographs into evidence. It is not a pleasant picture, but it is not unduly gruesome and does depict the wound causing death and the appearance of the victim in the case, so the objection will be noted for the record." Daniel voiced more objections about the evidence.

Halpin moved to introduce photographs of the AC/DC cap found in the garage, but Hernandez again objected, saying the hat was on a brown-colored mannequin, connoting a Latino, which, Hernandez reasoned, was "unduly suggestive." Halpin said, "I don't understand the objection to the mannequin being Latin. I didn't notice any particular ethnicity of the mannequin." Judge Tynan said, "All I see is from the middle of the nose down. I don't think that that is a Latin face."

Hernandez said, "I'm not referring to a Latin face, Your Honor, and I realize that sometimes certain symbols are not adhered to or in any way given value, but some portions of the population [do] . . . It may have some type of suggestion to the jury."

Tynan did not agree and allowed the photo of the brown mannequin into evidence. Halpin moved to introduce the actual AC/DC cap into evidence, but Hernandez objected, saying the pictures were enough and there was no chain of evidence which proved that this hat was the hat Gil had seen on the floor. Tynan let it in.

Hernandez made a motion to exclude the next two witnesses, Jorge Gallegos and Joseph Duenas from testifying, citing statutes 402 and 352. Tynan said the matter had been litigated at the preliminary and he was going to allow their testimony.

Daniel wanted the charts Halpin had put up outlining the

crimes to be taken down, as they were "overly suggestive." Halpin had no objection. They were removed and the photographs were put on a pinboard on wheels that faced the jury.

June Wang, Veronica Yu's best friend, was called next. She was very nervous, as fragile and beautiful as a china doll, as she sat in the witness stand. Wang was deathly afraid of Richard Ramirez: she felt he was in league with Satan and hated being in a room with him, breathing the same air. She answered Halpin's questions about Veronica Yu's last day of life and told the jury, always conscious of Richard's eyes on her, how they'd been together Saturday and Sunday.

Halpin asked, "And did she, sometime that night, leave your home to go to her home?"

"Around eleven o'clock."

"And did you ever see her again?"

"No," June testified, and tears that had been brimming in her eyes spilled over and ran down her face. Halpin finished quickly.

Hernandez conferred with Salinas. June Wang was a sympathetic witness and most defense attorneys would have left her alone; she'd only been put on the stand to establish that Veronica was alive and well when she'd left June's house that March night, four years earlier. Hernandez stood up and moved to the podium. He asked her to tell the jury everything she and Veronica had done that Saturday and Sunday. Hernandez wanted the jury to suspect Veronica Yu's boyfriend as the vicious killer. Halpin objected on grounds of relevance and Judge Tynan sustained the objection.

Hernandez, flustered and angered by the block to his theory demanded a sidebar. Reluctantly Tynan agreed. To Daniel's defense of relevance, Tynan said, "This woman is simply testifying the last time anyone saw her alive. That is all. This other thing [Veronica's boyfriend] is totally irrelevant to any issue that I can even take a wild guess at. Sustained!"

Hernandez finished up with a few simple questions.

Halpin called Jorge Gallegos, who had been sitting in his uncle's truck with his girlfriend, Edith Alcaaz, on North Alhambra the evening Veronica was gunned down. Interpreter Cynthia Parker would translate. Gallegos looked in Richard's direction as he took the stand, openingly glaring at him as if to tell him and the world that he was not afraid.

Gallegos told the jury how he was able to see the incident in the mirror of the truck and described seeing a man trying to pull Veronica from her yellow Chevy. As the man took off, he saw his profile clearly. When Halpin asked Gallegos if he saw in the courtroom the man who was trying to pull Veronica from the car, he looked at Richard, pointed, and said, "He's over there; his hair is just a little longer."

Halpin now had Gallegos tell of his meeting with Monterey Park detective Anthony Romero and his identification of a car the police had as the one used in the attack.

The strain of the trial was showing on Daniel: there were dark circles under his eyes, his face appeared puffy, and he moved slowly, as if he hadn't slept enough. Arturo hadn't been in court since the selection of the jury, and the workload was far too much for Daniel.

"What was the description you gave Detective Romero?" he asked on cross.

"I told him that it was a man more or less my height, five-six or five-eight, wavy hair. He seemed to be Oriental in appearance."

The description didn't match Richard, and it seemed Hernandez had scored a point; he conferred with Salinas and Richard.

Hernandez asked if the man at the preliminary hearing looked different from the man he'd seen that night.

"Yes."

"The hair, the dress?"

"Yes, the hair, the clothing, the glasses."

"So he doesn't look the same as he looked that night?"

"No. He does not look the same," Gallegos said, peering hard at Richard. "Can he stand?" he asked Judge Tynan.

"Would you like him to stand?" the judge said.

"Yes, I would like to see his profile without glasses, and also from behind."

Richard turned to Hernandez and said, "Fuck him, man. I'm not standing up."

Hernandez addressed the judge, said, "Your Honor, he has already made an ID. I think this is just—"

The judge interrupted with, "Mr. Hernandez, are you making an issue of it? Mr. Ramirez, would you rise, please, take your glasses off, and face the clerk?"

"No!" Richard yelled, all puffed up with defiance, obviously ready to fight. The bailiffs moved in.

"Very well. Thank you," Tynan said to avoid trouble. He had no doubt Richard would resist rather than stand and accommodate Gallegos. He noted for the record that Richard had refused to stand and decided to end court for the day. As Gallegos stepped down, Richard snarled at him and cursed him under his breath, calling him "punk" and "rat." The bailiff removed Ramirez from the court.

That night on the television news it was heavily reported how Richard had defied the court and yelled "No" to Judge Tynan's request, and the next day this latest defiance made all the newspapers. As people read about it over breakfast, they shuddered—never had there been an accused serial killer showing so little remorse.

The next morning, Hernandez resumed his cross-examination. He tried to get Gallegos to admit that he had not really gotten a good look at the killer but had little luck.

Gil noticed that one of the alternate female jurors kept staring hungrily at Richard. She had big, round eyes, a pug nose, very white skin, dark-red shoulder-length hair, and bangs. He pointed her out to Frank, who said he'd already noticed. They both hoped if an alternate had to be called, it would not be this one. All it took for a mistrial was one holdout.

Hernandez's cross went on and on. Judge Tynan was getting annoyed and the jury was antsy. The judge admonished Daniel, and told him to move on.

Hernandez respectfully told Judge Tynan that he didn't appreciate being admonished in front of the jury. Tynan said he'd take his protest under advisement and court was recessed.

Phil Halpin very rarely ate lunch; it seemed the case never gave him the time. It was all he thought about from morning till night. He viewed his work as a life-and-death struggle between good and evil, and he was determined to win.

Both Frank and Gil saw how consumed Halpin was and

they were worried. They knew if he didn't get at least a little respite from it, his health would eventually suffer, but no matter how many times they asked him to join them for a drink, he was too busy. "Phil Halpin was the consummate professional. He was the most prepared, thorough prosecutor I ever worked with," Frank would later say.

During the trial, Richard had his lunch in a holding pen behind the court. Always by himself, still segregated from other prisoners, he had a bologna sandwich on stale white bread and heavily sugared tea. He hated bologna and he hated sugared tea, but there was only one item on the courthouse lunch menu.

After lunch, Halpin wanted to put crime-scene photos of the Yu incident on the board. One was a picture of Veronica with a tube forced into her mouth. Hernandez objected, saying it was unduly unpleasant and not necessary. Halpin said it was the clearest picture he had of her and that it was not, in any way, particularly prejudicial. He complained to Judge Tynan that Hernandez objected to *everything* whether it was objectionable or not. Tynan allowed the photos to be pinned to the board facing the jury.

Hernandez then tried to bar the next witness, Joseph Duenas, and requested a 402 hearing, based on Duenas's not being able to identify Richard at the preliminary hearing. Tynan denied the motion.

Joseph Duenas had heard Veronica Yu screaming for help and had called the police.

Halpin took him through the incident. Duenas said he could not positively identify the man he'd seen that night. He had described the man to the police as "About five-seven to five-eight, about 145, 150 pounds, light-complexioned, kind of long, shaggy hair, but I couldn't tell if his eyes were quite slanted or if they weren't."

People in the courtroom tried to see Richard's eyes, but he was wearing his sunglasses and wasn't about to take them off. Halpin finished with Duenas, itching to keep the case moving.

Hernandez stood and everyone dreaded another long cross-examination. He set out to show the jury that Gallegos and Duenas were liars, only out for the reward money, the limelight, some false sense of justice. Daniel had Duenas describe every minute aspect of everything he did, said, and saw. When Hernandez asked him if he'd heard any gunshots, he said no. Everyone knew Veronica had been shot twice before she'd gotten out of the car. Duenas testified he was put in a police car by himself when he said he'd seen the incident. At the police station, he'd told the detectives he could identify the killer if he saw him. Yet in court today, he couldn't positively identify Richard. Daniel wisely ended his cross on that note and court was recessed until 3:15.

Monterey Park officer Ron Endo was the next witness. He told how he'd been sent to Alhambra Street, what he'd found, and what he'd done. Hernandez had Officer Endo describe everything he saw and did again, questioning him as if he were part of some large conspiracy. The jury appeared to lose interest, yawning and fidgeting. One of them even fell asleep.

The following morning, juror number 4, Alfred Carrillo, couldn't make it to court because Route 5 was closed. Judge Tynan was forced to cancel the proceedings for the day and excused the jury with his usual admonishments about their not discussing the case.

Phil Halpin told the judge that he would like to introduce to the jury all the photographs from incidents already presented. He suggested they be put on the board and the jury allowed to look at them. He did not want the photographs in the jury room because they could cause dialogue and comments among the jurors. The judge suggested letting the jury pass the photographs among themselves, in groups relevant to each crime, for ten or fifteen minutes, and then let them have them when their deliberations began. Halpin and Hernandez agreed, and court was adjourned.

Halpin next put Dr. Richard Tenn on the stand; he'd been working in the emergency room of Garfield Hospital on the morning of the Yu shooting. He testified that Veronica had been brought in by a Medivac unit, and that he'd checked her vital signs, pronounced her dead, and filled out a coroner's report, noting two gunshot wounds as the cause of death.

As with previous witnesses, Hernandez had the doctor describe in detail the condition of the victim.

Halpin summoned Dr. Susan Selser and she testified she'd done an autopsy on Veronica at 10:30 A.M. on March 19, in the presence of Monterey Park detective Anthony Romero. The cause of death was two gunshot wounds, and she briefly noted the injuries each had caused.

Daniel Hernandez began his cross by asking, "Can you tell me which nerves were damaged or severed completely?" The question required Dr. Selser to describe the damage to Veronica in greater detail. He implied Veronica might have been bruised prior to being shot because there were some bruises on her legs, but the doctor said they'd probably happened during the time of the shooting. He asked if Veronica had any defensive wounds, to which the doctor said no. Daniel wanted the jury to believe Veronica had been killed by an estranged boyfriend in an argument that might have started earlier.

Before he moved to the next incident, Halpin wanted the jury to see the crime-scene pictures. With Frank and Gil's help the photographs were distributed to the jurors.

The jury comprised ordinary people leading everyday lives, and it was a very difficult thing for them to look at the bodies and not be disturbed. "They'd been changed forever," a juror would say later. But they all knew the worst was yet to come.

After lunch, Halpin told the court he wanted to show the jury crime-scene pictures of the Zazzara incident. Hernandez protested, saying the enlargements were enhanced by artificial lighting, were "excessively brutal," and would only inflame the jury—particularly the women.

Halpin disagreed. The male had been shot in the head which was consistent with other crimes yet to be presented, and the stab wounds Maxine had suffered were like others sustained in Stalker attacks.

Judge Tynan ruled, "Under 352, after careful weighing of all relevant factors, the court will permit these to be shown to the jury during testimony, and they—I assume—will be attempted to be admitted by the people after a foundation has been laid." The door was now open for all the pictures of the bodies to reach the jury.

Bruno Francisco Polo, Vincent Zazzara's employee, who had discovered the crime, was next on the stand. He was nervous and cowed by the enormity of the proceedings.

Patiently and professionally, Halpin had Polo tell the jury about how he'd discovered the tragedy on March 28. He described finding the bodies, the police, the fire department, and a Medivac arriving—then Peter Zazzara with his wife and small baby arriving.

Halpin asked for permission to approach the bench and told Tynan he was finished with Polo, but before he turned him over to Hernandez, he wanted it made crystal clear that he would not tolerate defense counsel asking about time Vincent Zazzara had done in prison, his having guns in his house, nor "his alleged underworld ties." Daniel said he had the right to ask such questions, but Tynan ruled that he didn't.

With the Zazzara murders, Daniel was hoping to show the jury that Vincent's own son had said his father had mob ties and that he and Maxine had likely been killed in a Mafia hit. Though he knew it was out of the scope of his cross-examination—unless Halpin brought it up first—he was still intent upon getting Peter Zazzara's statement to Russ Uloth out for the jury's consumption.

After a short recess, court resumed and Hernandez began asking Polo questions about his relationship with Peter Zazzara. Halpin objected to this line of questioning as "irrelevant and immaterial," and Judge Tynan sustained the objection. Daniel had Polo take the jury again through a detailed account of the events leading up to his discovering of the Zazzara murders.

Halpin eventually objected, as the questions seemed to become increasingly more irrelevant. The lawyers approached the bench and Tynan instructed Hernandez to find a more relevant line of questioning.

Daniel went back to the defense table and conferred with Salinas, then grilled Polo on how many bags of money he had left at the Zazzaras', trying to taint the pizza parlor receipts with some sinister underworld connection.

After only a few minutes, the judge interrupted Daniel's cross so Chris Olsen, the court reporter, who felt ill, could go home. He reminded everyone not to discuss the case and that the weekend would be for three days because court was dark on Monday. The next time they'd see each other again would be February 14, Valentine's Day.

THIRTY-FIVE

For the most part Doreen was the only one of Richard's dozen or so regular admirers who was still there every day, all day. Doreen's job at the magazine allowed her to set her own hours. The other girls, as well as many of the journalists, were now there just for the morning sessions, but Doreen was there for both mornings and afternoons, always hoping Richard would turn around and acknowledge her. She felt Richard had come to trust her; he knew she was out there protecting his rights, writing letters to newspapers denouncing his unfair treatment.

Samantha wrote him letters detailing how she would love to have sex with him in a cemetery at night, on a cold overturned tombstone, covered with the blood of one of the Night Stalker's victims.

"Eva O" told him when she came to visit him how she wanted to have sex with him in her coffin, which she slept in every night. It, the coffin, would be their love nest, the place from which, she guaranteed him, she'd fulfill his every fantasy, in the name of Satan; in the name of evil . . .

Laura Kendall, a former fashion model turned professional dominatrix in New York, wrote to Ramirez that she fantasized about having sex with him in his prison cell. "With Richard," she said, "I'd want to be submissive. You can't dominate a man like him."

Of all the women who claimed they were in love with him, Richard felt Doreen was the most grounded. She was a college graduate who didn't smoke, drink or curse. Doreen's idea of profanity was "gosh, golly, and oh my Lord." She was still a virgin, and was certain that appealed to Richard most of all. He felt she was his. All the other women he knew had had sex already. Many of them had sexual fantasies involving Richard, blood, knives, whips, and all kinds of sadistic abnormalities.

All the attention from so many women changed Richard. On the outside, in the real world, he never had intimate sexual relationships with women other than prostitutes. The last woman he had had any emotional intimacy was with Nancy, fourteen years before. He had never thought of himself as particularly desirable to women. He felt he was too skinny, and he was self-conscious about his teeth. He was shy to the point that he had become more comfortable with the demons and evil entities that dominated the spirit world than with people. He'd never cared how he dressed, never combed his hair, and living as he did, on the move, personal hygiene wasn't one of his primary concerns.

Yet now that his full-lipped, high-cheekboned face and his alleged deeds were one of the hottest news items in the country, Richard had become much sought after by females. That weekend he received scores of Valentine cards from women as far away as Israel, London, Germany, and Spain. All this adulation by so many females pumped up Richard's ego and aroused his sexuality. Some of the women who visited him would, upon his demand, when no one was looking, raise their dresses and discreetly show him their privates.

Of all the cards and love letters he had gotten that weekend, none was, Doreen felt, as important to Richard as her own.

"I was," she'd later relate, "the only one who truly cared. All the others were a bunch of freaks and weirdos who wanted to use Richard for their own aggrandizement and kicks. But I didn't want anything for myself. It was only what I could do for him, how I could help him." When asked about the crimes Richard was accused of and the dire consequences if he was convicted, she said, with patient finality, "None of that matters. I love him for who he is. You have to take the good with the bad when you're in love."

Doreen waited for hours to see him that Saturday and Sunday. She wanted to look extra nice because of Valentine's Day, and she put bows in her long black hair and wore a flowered dress she knew Richard liked. When she saw him she told him how much she loved him and how much she wished she could have a conjugal visit with him on Valentine's Day. They both knew that was not about to happen, so they did the next best thing.

Tuesday, February 14, court reconvened at 10:40 A.M. Judge Tynan announced that he had to go to a funeral the following day and court would be dark for the afternoon.

Sheriff's homicide detective Russ Uloth then mounted the witness stand to tell the court he and his partner, J. D. Smith, had gotten to the Zazzara home about noon, and after finding the footprints in the flower garden at the rear of the house, called for photographers and criminologists.

Using a series of photographs, Halpin had Uloth take the jury through the Zazzara crime scene. Uloth identified the close-up of Mrs. Zazzara with her pajama top pulled up to expose her breasts and wounds.

Halpin asked the detective to describe the wounds he and John Lorca, from the morgue, had discovered. "We noted that her eyes had been removed, that she had sustained a left gunshot wound to her temple. There were three large stab wounds to the left side of her neck and one on her cheek." He described the knife wounds in detail.

This testimony had a visible effect on the jury; they were very attentive, leaning forward and listening, horrified at the viciousness of the assault. As sad and troubling as hearing about the Okazaki/Yu incidents were, those attacks had happened with a gun. Killing was simply an impersonal matter of pointing and pulling a trigger. But here a knife had been used in unspeakable, nightmare-causing ways. Richard crossed his legs; the chains rattled. Doreen looked at the back of his head and wished she could hold him, stroke his hair, take him away from all this.

The following morning, before Judge Tynan broke for lunch, Uloth told about the autopsies.

Uloth, J. D. Smith, Frank, and Gil ate in a Chinese fast-food restaurant and discussed the effect Russ's testimony was having on the jury: hearing details like he'd described about the Zazzara incident was a very sobering experience and would, they all agreed, bring home to the jurors the true depth of the Night Stalker's horrible reality.

After lunch, Uloth described the ransacking, the three bags of pizza receipts at the front door, and the pillow with the missing pillowcase and identified the slugs removed at the autopsies.

Hernandez questioned Uloth about the pry marks the killer had left on the entrance window. Daniel implied that the marks had been put there when the Zazzara house had been robbed previously and that this had been an "inside job."

Daniel moved on to the Avia footprints. Uloth said they'd found the prints on the side of the house, under Maxine's bedroom window and on the container used to get into the house. Daniel wanted to know if Uloth had ever seen a pair of the Avia shoes like the ones that had made those prints. He said he had, "In a Foot Locker store at the Downey Mall."

"And during your investigation, did you ever find any similar shoes other than at the shoe store?"

"I didn't." Hernandez pointed out for the jury that no such Avia shoes had ever been found on Richard Ramirez.

Judge Tynan interrupted so the court stenographer could have a break.

During the break, some of the female jurors gave Valentine candies to the judge and to the defense and prosecution lawyers. Alternate juror Cynthia Haden had baked a few cupcakes that said "I love you" and asked a bailiff to give one to Richard. When the court reconvened, Ramirez found it on the defense table, and when he was told one of the alternate jurors had asked it be given to him, he picked it up and promptly ate it. Richard loved sweets, and this was a very welcome treat.

Judge Tynan said, "People versus Richard Ramirez, A771272. He is present with counsel. The people are represented. The witness is on the stand. The jury and alternates are in the box. The record will reflect that the court and staff, and I believe counsel, have received Valentines from the jury. I want to thank you very much. They are not to be construed as bribes or in any other way affecting the integrity of the people in this case."

Daniel took Uloth back to the crime scene and questioned him about what he'd seen and what he'd done, but none of these questions helped Daniel's quest for reasonable doubt.

Los Angeles County sheriff's criminalist Steve Renteria, who had worked the Zazzara crime scene, was sworn in. His job had been to make plaster casts of the Avia shoeprints. He told the jury how first photographs were taken of the prints, then the plaster was poured onto the prints. Halpin handed Renteria a sealed brown paper bag. Inside were the actual casts he'd made that March day. The killer it seemed had large feet as the casts seemed enormous. The jurors' eyes automatically moved down to look at Richard's chained feet.

When Phil Halpin finished with Renteria, it was 4 P.M. Daniel didn't look well; he was pale and sitting low in his seat. "Your Honor, I was hoping to start fresh with this witness tomorrow," he said.

"Give it a shot, Mr. Hernandez. Are you able to at all?"

"I'm somewhat exhausted. It has been really warm in here today."

"Well, I will expect you to move with alacrity, then, tomorrow afternoon, Mr. Hernandez," the judge said, and court was adjourned.

As the jury and the alternates stood to leave, Richard took off his sunglasses and locked eyes with Cynthia Haden. It seemed like electricity was passing between them. She wasn't a juror yet, but he figured with Satan's help he could get her on the jury. He knew what he saw in her eyes and he figured she would never convict him and send him to San Quentin to die if she became a juror. She had felt his eyes on her all day. She'd later say of them, "They have an animal quality that makes you feel he's looking right through you."

Gil, Frank, and Halpin had heard about the Valentine cupcake Cynthia had sent over to Richard. They also saw the way she and Richard had looked at one another as court ended. They only hoped she would never get picked if any alternates were needed. The chances were slim. There were eleven other alternates, and the present jury seemed healthy, well adjusted and running smoothly.

When Doreen saw the Valentine cupcake, she immediately knew Cindy had been the one to send it over. All along she'd been watching how Cindy had been "ogling and staring at"

Richard, and she didn't like it one bit. Cindy Haden was not some weirdo Satanist or sexually deviant street trash. She was well dressed and obviously intelligent, with good taste, looks, and breeding.

Later that day, when Richard and Doreen shared their first Valentine together, she told him that Cindy was in love with him and looked like she wanted to have sex with him right there in the courtroom with everyone watching. He laughed and said things like that only happened on television. "You mark my words," Doreen said, "when this trial is over she's going to come looking for you."

Richard let out a big laugh.

As Doreen left the jail that day, a dark-eyed, dark-haired female college student, was hanging around outside. She was carrying a sign that read, "I love Richard." Richard refused to see her. She knew who Doreen was and was resentful of her and gave her dirty looks. "If looks could kill I would have keeled over right there at the jail, dead," Doreen would later say.

At ten o'clock the following morning, Daniel Hernandez cross-examined criminalist Steve Renteria about the plaster casts he'd taken. Although Daniel could not change the facts, he seemed to feel if he asked the same questions long enough, the testimony would become beneficial to Richard. However, all it seemed to do was bore the jury.

The jury knew there were two sets of prints: one the killer's, the other Vincent's; and no matter what Daniel did or said, he couldn't change that fact. Finally, Halpin had enough and objected. The judge sustained the objection and Daniel finished with Renteria.

Halpin was ready to play one of his trump cards. He told the court the coroner in the Doi assaults was not presently available, so he was going to move on to a burglary case in Monrovia that he was certain tied the Avia shoeprint to Richard Ramirez. He called Monrovia officer Tom Wright, who testified he'd responded on May 9, 1985, to a robbery call on Olive Street at the home of Clara Hadsall, now deceased, and had found evidence of a break-in. A patio chair had been propped up against the back of the house, and someone had removed a lower window and, going into the house, had stepped into a kitchen sink and left a footprint there. When the intruder stepped down to the floor, he'd put his palm on the sink and left a latent impression, which Officer Wright had lifted with a fingerprint kit he kept in the trunk of his police car. As well as lifting the palm and fingerprints he found around the sink, he'd lifted the footprint right out of the sink using extra-long lifting tape and cards. He gave the lifts to Sgt. Christiansen of the sheriff's department.

Officer Wright stated he also found footprints in dirt on the north side of the house and made plaster casts of those prints, too. Halpin handed him a sealed brown paper bag containing the plaster casts of the Avia prints, the same size as the ones found at the Zazzara residence.

Hernandez knew he had to discredit this witness. The last thing he wanted was Richard's palm prints linked to the Avia prints.

However, Daniel's cross-examination was unable to weaken Wright's testimony. He was able to establish that Wright had not had any prior experience casting footprints at crime scenes.

During Daniel's questioning, Wright mentioned that he had found a pillowcase on the floor of the den. It was not lost on the jury that a pillowcase had been taken from the Zazzara residence and that Halpin had said missing pillowcases were a common theme throughout the Stalker crimes. It was not a point Daniel had intended to make.

Halpin's next witness was Monterey officer Mike Gorajewski. He told the jury how he'd been dispatched to the Doi residence a little after 5 A.M. on May 14 and had found Lillian and a bloody Bill Doi on the floor, being treated by paramedics. He described the ransacking and the sad emotional state of Lillian.

Halpin, as he would consistently throughout the long trial, kept his direct examinations short and to the point. Very little of what Gorajewski had to say was in dispute, and Daniel quickly ended his cross of this witness. Judge Tynan said he had to go to a judge's luncheon in Pasadena and told everyone to take an extra long lunch break and return at 2 P.M.

Richard was taken back to the court's holding pen, where he had the same sandwich and tea, lay down, and fell asleep, dreaming he was on a planet in outer space where he was a king on a throne with everyone bowing and scraping around him. There were alien creatures in the dream, tall monsters who called him master, with big muscles and pointed teeth, lurking in shadows. There were shrunken heads atop pointed spears around the throne.

He was rudely awakened for court.

Halpin continued with his presentation of the Doi incident and put on the stand Monterey Park policeman Bill Reynolds, who had also responded to a call for help at the Doi residence. It was Officer Reynolds who had removed the bloody thumb cuffs from Lillian's hand. He identified a picture of Lillian Doi—at the hospital, with the cuffs still hanging from her hand—and then the cuffs themselves. They were still covered with blood. Some journalists and court observers wondered where the Stalker had gotten the idea to use thumb cuffs. Gil remembered how he had thought the Stalker was a Vietnam veteran, for the U.S. Army had used thumb cuffs on captured Vietcong. Richard hadn't served a day in the service, and Gil would not learn about Richard's cousin Mike until after the trial.

Daniel's cross-examination of Reynolds did not gain any ground in planting reasonable doubt in the jury's mind.

Halpin called Monterey detective Paul Torres. He said the inside of the house "looked like a hurricane had gone through it," that there was a lot of blood on Bill Doi's bed and in the hall and den, where he had crawled to call for help. Richard had his head in his hand, daydreaming about being back in El Paso, hunting out in the desert. How, he wondered, did I get from that happy, carefree place to this courtroom, where everyone is so intent on killing me?

Often he thought of getting up and just making for the exit, forcing the guards to shoot him. A bullet in the head, he figured, had to be better than what life had in store for him. He hated jail, he hated being told what to do; he hated the idea of the system he despised so much dictating when he would die. With Satan's help, *he* would pick the time and place he died, not them, he mused, as he watched Paul Torres and listened to the sadistic havoc the Night Stalker had brought to the home of Bill and Lillian Doi. He turned around. All the journalists' eyes moved to him. They hoped he'd cause some excitement. As soon as he turned, his girls sat at attention, smiled and winked, and blew him quick, secretive kisses. Doreen nodded at him knowingly, as if she and he had secrets no one knew about. Because of his sunglasses she could never tell if he was looking at her or at one of the other girls, who stuck out their chests and pouted their brightly colored lips suggestively. Even if he was looking at one of them, it didn't amount to anything. She was the only one who mattered; she was the only one he trusted; she was the only one he confided in. Sometimes he'd be able to make phone calls to her and she'd tell him all the things she'd do for him to make him happy. She'd even play some of his favorite music in the background. Doreen was very optimistic about the trial, and she often talked about how they would go somewhere private after it was all over and live happily ever after.

After Torres's direct, Halpin moved to put the Doi crime-scene photographs into evidence, as well as the footprint casts, the thumb cuffs, and the bullets removed from Bill Doi. Daniel objected to everything and was overruled.

Judge Tynan also allowed two photographs of Maxine Zazzara in bed that Halpin felt were necessary to establish the eye gouging and the viciousness of the stab wounds.

Tynan then addressed the jury, warning them beforehand that they were going to see unpleasant pictures. He instructed them that seeing the horrible wounds was not to influence them against the defendant. He said, "You must not assume guilt simply because the photographs depict somebody who has been severely injured. Do you understand that? That is your rule as jurors. You are to be as neutral and objective as you possibly can be."

Given the intensity and the intimacy of the attack, that was a very hard thing to do, and Richard knew it. He didn't like the jury seeing those pictures. He was restless in his chair and moving around, rattling the chains. As the jury was given the pictures of the brutalized Maxine, Halpin moved to enter the palm prints, the fingerprints, and the footprints collected at Clara Hadsall's house in Monrovia. Hernandez objected strenuously. Judge Tynan offered a sidebar to hear the nature of the objection, which was that the crime at the Hadsall home was uncharged and as such, its evidence should not be allowed in. Also, it was irrelevant—no Avia shoe had ever been tied to his client. Halpin reminded the court that he had never mentioned any crime happening there. All it did was "put the Avia on his feet because the fingerprints and palm prints were his [Richard's]."

The judge allowed them to introduce the photographs, fingerprints, and shoeprints. Tynan told Daniel if he could cite cases which showed he would be wrong in allowing the Hadsall prints in, he'd be happy to reverse his ruling.

As the jurors studied at the pictures of Maxine, some winced, some paled, and a few prayed. They were given the plaster casts of the Doi footprints and the Zazzara shoeprints and asked to handle them carefully as they passed the foot-sized casts among themselves. They could clearly see the prints were identical.

After collecting all the exhibits, Judge Tynan called it a day and told the jury to enjoy another three-day weekend. Noticeably shaken and taking curious, angry looks at Richard, the jurors and alternates stood and left. Cynthia Haden stared long and hard at Richard.

When he turned around, Doreen was the only one still sitting there.

It wasn't lost on the bailiffs that Doreen was present every day, and they kept a close eye on her. Though she looked innocent and had no police record, they were leery of any woman who was that obsessed with a man who was accused of cutting out a pair of human eyes for the fun of it.

THIRTY-SIX

When court resumed on February 21, Judge Tynan announced that Daniel Hernandez was ill. He said he had spoken to him on the phone and that he was suffering from "nervous exhaustion," was under a doctor's care, and should be all right in a few days. Therefore, he had decided to postpone the proceedings until Monday, February 27, allowing a week for Daniel to recuperate.

Salerno and Carrillo welcomed the break; they would use it to catch up on lost time with their families and other cases piling up on their desks. Halpin said he knew something like this would happen and was concerned about Hernandez having recurrent relapses; he saw this move as a stall tactic Daniel would try to parlay into a mistrial.

The jurors welcomed the seven-day hiatus from court. It was an arduous, difficult task, sitting still all day, listening to horrible stories, and viewing photos of murdered people.

At 9 A.M. on February 27, an obviously annoyed Judge Tynan took the bench. Paralegal Richard Salinas sat at the defense table with Richard. "Is Mr. Hernandez coming into court this morning?" the judge asked Salinas. Salinas said no. Tynan told Halpin to approach the bench and explained that he'd received a letter from Dr. Pace, the San Jose physician who was treating Hernandez for nervous exhaustion and elevated blood sugar and blood lipids. The judge said Dr. Pace had told him he was putting Daniel on a weight loss program and that he was seeing to it that Daniel received "stress management counseling." Daniel was not fit for the arduous task of representing Richard Ramirez and would need one to four weeks of recovery. Salinas said Daniel's secretary had called Alan Yochelson the week before to inform him of Daniel's condition. Halpin was unconvinced. He had heard that Daniel had used this tactic during trials before. He thought about all the time, three and a half years, and hard work that had gone into this trial: the difficult tasks of finding the jury and setting up all the witnesses. Now he'd have to call the witnesses and reschedule everyone all over again.

The judge was not going to accept at face value Daniel Hernandez's medical disability. He ruled that not only Daniel was to be in court for a hearing on his condition on Wednesday, March 1, but Arturo as well. Arturo was still on record as representing Richard, and the judge wanted him in court. Halpin suggested he could draw up a subpoena and bring in Daniel's doctor as well. He said, "I have been through this before with one of our local attorneys and it turned out that he misunderstood his doctor and in fact was healthy enough to go forward with the case."

Tynan agreed and said he'd supply Halpin with the doctor's address for the subpoena. Tynan told a bailiff to tell the jury to come back to court on Monday, March 6, giving them another extended break.

All the jurors were anxious to get the trial over with, to be finished with this nightmare of civic duty and get back to the comfort and regular duties of their lives. Tynan decided to bring the jury in so he could explain Daniel's illness and apologize for the delay. He was only too aware of the jurors' discomfort; he told them to remember to keep their oath and stay away from the media.

It was widely reported in the press that Hernandez was holding up the trial, feigning illness, hoping to cause a mistrial.

Ever since the Avia shoeprint had been tied to Richard's fingerprints, it became evident that Daniel would have a very tough time winning this case. Reporters began digging into his past with a diligence that soon revealed facts that had not been known up until now. It was reported in the papers, for instance, how Daniel Hernandez had been fined twice for not showing up in Santa Clara County courts. It was also reported that Daniel had been given a hard time by the state of California in getting his license to practice law after he had passed the bar. Daniel attributed this to the FBI. having taken a dim view of his involvement with farm workers, his protesting the Vietnam war as an undergraduate at San Jose State, and staying in Havana for a few months as a guest of the Castro regime.

On March 1, as ordered by Judge Tynan, both Daniel and Arturo were sitting at the defense table with Richard. Richard was angry because Daniel was slowing up the trial process. He, perhaps more than anyone in the courtroom, wanted to get the thing over with, even though he knew it would lead to the death penalty.

In death, Richard still believed, he would have a place of honor in the court of Satan, and death neither scared nor unsettled him.

Judge Tynan read a letter from Daniel's physician, detailing the symptoms he'd been suffering, the tests he'd undergone, and an estimate of four to six weeks for recovery.

The judge told Daniel sincerely that he was concerned about his health, but after having a lengthy discussion with Daniel's physician, he did not find just cause to allow Daniel to miss any more court.

Daniel made a long speech about how tired he had been since jury selection, how he was the only attorney working the case, and how it was all just too much for one person. He requested a few weeks' recuperation time and asked Judge Tynan to assign another lawyer to the case to assist him. Arturo declined comment.

Halpin complained bitterly about having to keep rescheduling witnesses, some of whom had been terribly traumatized by vicious sexual assaults—and all these delays were further traumatizing and upsetting them. "These people are getting disgusted," he boomed.

Judge Tynan told Daniel that he knew death penalty cases were very stressful. "Some of us have chest pains, some of us have bellyaches . . . but the point is, we all suffer stress in these cases, even the court. And it is part and parcel of a death penalty case, and we have to deal with them as best we can."

The judge went on to say that he saw no good reason to delay the proceedings further and ordered both Hernandezes in court on March 6, ready to proceed with the trial.

Halpin remembered clearly how hard Arturo and Daniel had fought for the right to defend Richard. He'd known, when Judge Soper had ruled that Richard had the right to choose his own counsel, that it would come to haunt the proceedings, and quite possibly even cause a mistrial—meaning they'd have to do everything all over again. That possibility loomed over the court like a dark stormcloud sent by Satan himself to help Richard.

Halpin had vowed not to try this case again; it was too much for any man to go through twice. He already had an ulcer and high blood pressure. Both Arturo and Daniel said they would obey the court's ruling. They knew Tynan would hold them in contempt and throw them in jail if they didn't comply.

Monday morning, March 6, Daniel showed up in court with a new strategy. He was now certain he could not handle Richard's defense properly, even with Arturo's help, and he turned to seasoned trial lawyer Ray Clark, a light-skinned black man with salt-and-pepper hair and mustache. Daniel had been talking to him about coming aboard the defense team since January, and Ray had joined the defense team after Judge Tynan had agreed to see he was paid the standard rate for a capital crime case (one hundred dollars per hour) by the state. Tynan knew it would cost the taxpayers a lot more if Ramirez had to be tried all over again.

Before court, Tynan met Ray Clark for the first time in a closed meeting with Daniel and Arturo. The judge had researched Ray's background and knew he was a capable professional who had had experience with capital crime cases. He even had special training enabling him to be a member of the group of California attorneys who met the standards required for death penalty cases.

To Tynan, Ray Clark was a ray of hope. His arrival meant that this trial would actually move on to completion.

"No matter what," Clark told Tynan, "I'm in for the duration."

Ray Clark had been in private practice, handling criminal cases almost exclusively, since he'd passed the bar exam in December of 1973, the year he'd graduated from Southwestern School of Law. He was partners with his daughter, Dawn Blaylock, and Efrem Clark (no relation). They would be handling the firm's cases while he was committed to the Ramirez trial. Judge Tynan shook his hand and welcomed him aboard.

Back in open court, without the jury present, the judge announced for the record and for Phil Halpin's benefit that he had appointed Ray Clark to the defense team. Halpin knew Clark and his reputation and was very happy to see him sitting at the defense table. Now, he believed, the case would move along quickly.

Richard had no say in the matter. He knew Daniel was in way over his head, and he welcomed someone who brought as much experience to the defense table as Clark. Richard knew Clark didn't know anything about the case, though.

Clark's appointment raised grave appeal issues. There was a landmark 1976 case in which a conviction against Charles Manson follower Leslie Van Houten was overturned by the California appellate court when a new attorney was substituted in mid-trial, after Van Houten's attorney had disappeared. The court held that even if the new lawyer pored over the transcripts of trial testimony, he had missed the opportunity to view each witness's demeanor as he'd testified.

"It is elementary that the right to counsel means the right to effective representation," the appellate court had said in the Van Houten case. "In our opinion, an accused is denied effective representation if her trial attorney is unable to effectively argue the case."

Not only had Ray Clark failed to see any of the witnesses testify he still had not read the transcript. Tynan was in no mood, however, for more delays and didn't give Clark so much as an hour to read up on the case. He said, "It is my understanding, Mr. Clark, that you will be co-counsel and there will be no delays in the case for you to get up to speed, that you will do the best you can on your own time to prepare yourself, and that this case will continue apace, is that correct?"

Ray Clark answered, "That's correct, Your Honor."

"Very well, sir. You are appointed and welcome."

Tynan set up a hearing for March 24 to resolve a dispute the Special Master was having regarding the prosecution handing material over to the defense team scientist. The twenty-fourth was a Friday and the hearing wouldn't waste any jury time, Judge Tynan said. Daniel complained about the district attorney's office not trusting the defense and making things difficult. Tynan wanted to know why these issues hadn't been already resolved. Daniel, with new found vigor from his rest, new diet, and stress management counseling, and boosted by the presence of Clark and Arturo, said he'd tried to resolve them but the prosecution wasn't cooperating.

The defense table now looked like a formidable force, with Salinas, Clark, Daniel, and Arturo all sitting there, looking attentive.

Halpin countered by saying he'd been waiting to be contacted, and accusations went back and forth until the judge put a stop to them and ruled the issues would be resolved at the hearing on the twenty-fourth. The jury was brought in.

Halpin had pathologist Cogan tell the jury the details of Maxine Zazzara's murder. He described three gunshot wounds, eight stab wounds, ligature marks around her neck, and the way the upper lids of both eyes had been cut away to facilitate removal of the eyes. He described the stab-slash wounds in detail as the jury squirmed and moved uneasily in their hard wooden chairs, trying to see past Richard Ramirez's sunglassed facade of indifference as he rested his cheek on the palm of his huge right hand.

At this point Judge Tynan broke for lunch.

At 1:30 sharp, Dr. Cogan was back on the stand. Halpin showed him the bullets removed from Vincent and Maxine and had the doctor explain what damage each round had done and from where each had been extracted.

Halpin turned Dr. Cogan over to Ray Clark. Although he had not yet read the trial transcript, Clark asked questions that were precise and to the point. He knew what he was doing, and that soon became obvious.

There was little Clark could do to help the defense with Dr. Cogan, who had been put on the stand only to authenticate the autopsies for the court.

Halpin put Linda Doi Flick on the stand. She told the jury

she was an intern in family, marriage, and child counseling. Halpin asked her to describe her mother's condition. She said, "Cognitive-level thinking ability to process information is [at] about a two-year-old child level. In the last few years she's shown signs of senility. Certain things she is very sharp about and other things she can't respond to as well."

She testified that she lived four blocks from where her parents had lived. She had visited them early in the evening before the morning of the incident. Her dad was healthy and watching television, and her mom was "walking around the home." She'd received a phone call from the police at 5:20 A.M., directing her to Monterey Park Hospital, where her mother had been taken. She said her mother's face was swollen and black and blue, and she was disoriented.

Linda told the jury that she had been trained at Casa Colina Hospital in Pomona to work with the cerebrally impaired and with stroke victims. With this background, she had developed a way of speaking with her mother. Halpin showed her photographs of Mrs. Doi in the hospital, which Linda described for the jury's benefit.

Halpin moved to September 5, when Linda went to the jail with her mother to view the property lineup seized at Felipe Solano's house and other places.

"And did you on this occurrence see some items there that you recognized as property of your parents?"

"Numerous items," she said.

She had identified an inexpensive coin purse, a VCR, a Sernell Betacord, a coin purse of her mother's, a makeup bag, Lillian Doi's wallet, an Olympic pin her father had bought her mother, her grandfather's pocketwatch, and the Omega Constellation watch her father never took off. "In fact," she testified, "the jeweler used to complain to him about it because he kept saying that if he took the watch off when he went to bed, there wouldn't be so much lint in it and he wouldn't have to keep repairing it." When Halpin asked what was taken that wasn't there, she said a one-karat diamond wedding band set in gold, which had belonged to her father.

The prosecutor kept Linda on the stand for an hour and fifteen minutes.

Daniel Hernandez stood up to cross-examine Linda, asking her questions about the items recovered, as though he didn't believe what she was saying. He asked her about a crime report she had helped her mother fill out which contained a description that clearly did not sound like Richard. Halpin objected and asked for a bench conference, at which he said Daniel's questions were irrelevent, unless he was trying to impeach the witness, which he was not. He said he was not putting Lillian Doi on the stand, so it didn't matter what she said about her attacker.

Daniel said he might call Mrs. Doi because Linda had seemed to be able to communicate with her mother, despite her stroke, when they'd filled out the forms on the night of the attack. Tynan said he'd allow *one* question of Linda about her mother's description.

Halpin still objected but was overruled.

Daniel retrieved a police questionnaire from the defense table and asked for permission to show it to Linda, which Tynan gave. She said she remembered that detective Paul Torres had come to the house two weeks after the incident and helped her fill it out. "Did you assist your mother's putting together a composite for the police?" Daniel asked.

She said she had, at the hospital and at the house two weeks later.

Daniel conferred with Clark. The jury was getting restless. Doreen knew the truth about the discrepancy between Mrs. Doi's description and Richard's appearance, and she couldn't understand why Halpin was so afraid of the jury finding out. She started thinking about writing to some newspapers to point this out. Daniel announced he had no more questions.

Linda Doi slowly stepped down from the stand. Richard did not look at her. Judge Tynan called a recess.

Cynthia Haden sat with her eyes cast down. Gil Carrillo watched Cynthia closely to see if she communicated with Richard in any way. If she did, he'd have her ass thrown off the jury. The Valentine incident did not sit well with Sheriff's Homicide.

"You may call your next witness," Judge Tynan told Halpin after their break.

"We're starting into another incident, the matter of Mrs.

Bell and Lang that occurred between May 29 and June 1, 1985," Halpin said, and received permission to approach the bench. Because of the unexpected hiatus, he was going to have to present witnesses out of order and wouldn't be ready with his first witness until tomorrow morning. Tynan said he understood.

THIRTY-SEVEN

Phil Halpin opened by reading into the record the list of fifty-one photographs he'd be using in the Bell/Lang matter.

Ray Clark asked if he could have a bench conference without the court reporter. Judge Tynan said the reporter had to be present.

Clark asked for a copy of the list of photographs going into evidence because he couldn't write them all down fast enough. Halpin said he'd be happy to give the defense a copy, as long as there was no complaint about the order of the items listed.

"You may have a different situation with Mr. Clark," Judge Tynan said.

The prosecutor introduced Mike Bumcrot from Sheriff's Homicide, who would be sitting at the prosecution's table during the Bell/Lang presentation. Sitting behind Mike were Carrillo and Salerno in their usual places, as well as half a dozen of the homicide detectives from different cities in L.A. County. Family members of Mrs. Lang and Bell were sitting in court, on the side with the police, and seemed terrified by Richard's devotees.

Halpin called Carlos Valenzuela, the elderly gardener who had found the two sisters. Carlos needed an interpreter. He was a shy man who did not like talking about that day, but he knew it was his duty as a citizen and as a man. He, like most of the civilians who took the stand, did not look at Richard, or even in his direction. Carlos was a deeply religious man and he had heard about the pentagrams. He knew the hand of Satan had a prominent place in all this.

Carlos described how he had seen the newspapers and mail piling up at the front door at the residence of Nettie Lang and Mabel Bell and decided something might be amiss. He opened the door, calling their names to no avail. He found Nettie first, then Mabel, with the table the Stalker had left on her chest still there. He removed it, and saw the horrendous beating she had gotten and the pentagram on the bed, and hurried to neighbors to call the police. Clark stood for the cross-examination, asking Carlos how many papers were on the porch there. Carlos said four. Clark asked who he'd discovered first. Carlos said Nettie. Clark said he had no more questions of this witness.

James Olds, the first Monrovia policeman on the scene, was called next. He testified he had cordoned off the house and taken pictures of the wounds and the general areas where each woman had been found. He made certain to get clear shots of the pentagrams and of the hammer, still speckled with dry blood. When both sisters were removed to the hospital, Officer Olds went along so he could take more photographs of the injuries after they'd been cleaned, he stated.

He treated the assault like a murder because the wounds were so severe, he knew death was probable, and he wanted all the evidence needed to convict. As he described the horrible injuries for the jury, the people in the courtroom began to move uneasily in their seats. Several of the female jurors began to cry, and their sniffling filled the silence between Officer Olds's terrible words.

Halpin finished with Officer Olds and Judge Tynan called a lunch recess, knowing the jurors would need a break after listening to the wanton brutality upon two defenseless old women.

The jury and alternates stood and left. Richard sat there silently, alone with his thoughts; it was as though he was still a boy in school having an epileptic attack—he would just zone out and not be there at all.

Halpin's next witnesses would be out of order. He called Dr. Claire Paul Neiby, a general surgeon, who had worked on Nettie Lang in Methodist Hospital in Arcadia, then Dr. Michael Agron, who had worked on Mabel Bell. Claire told the court she had done an examination on Mrs. Lang's genitalia and found two stretch marks. Appropriate smears and washings had been taken and no usable secretions (i.e., seminal fluid) had been found at that time. "[The] injuries were very likely caused by sudden and violent stretching of tissues in that area," she testified, but she could not now say how such injuries had occurred. Halpin had her read her preliminary testimony, then asked if she now concurred with what she had said then.

"Reading my testimony from that date, it was my opinion that some attempt had been made at entry to the vaginal orifice."

That's what Halpin wanted the jury to hear: that eighty-four-year-old Nettie Lang, probably bound and already beaten, had been raped. The thick silence in the courtroom was broken only when Richard moved and the chains rattled.

Halpin had no more questions. Ray Clark stood to pick at what he perceived as the weakness in her testimony. "Could you assign a probability of likelihood to [the rape], Doctor? When you say 'very likely,' does that mean more likely than not?"

"I believe," she answered, "that the source of my speculation would lie in the instruments that might have been used to do this—make such wounds."

Clark got her to concede that she had no idea what had caused the vaginal tears.

Halpin summoned Sheriff's Homicide detective Bumcrot to the stand, and he told the jury how he and his partner, Mike Robinson, had received the call and described what he'd observed at the Lang house. He had also attended the autopsy of Mabel Bell in the middle of July, after she'd finally succumbed to her wounds. Halpin asked the detective if he had interviewed Nettie Lang. He said, "No, sir. . . . When she would wake up and see me or my partner, she would pull away from us, become extremely fearful, and begin to cry."

The best Ray Clark was able to do in cross to distance Richard from this crime scene was to ask if the soda cans had prints on them, to which Bumcrot replied, "One of the cans had some portions of a fingerprint, but it wasn't enough to make an identification."

Satisfied, Clark ended his cross.

Next, Charles Vander Wende testified he had found a "fabric print" on the Mountain Dew can, which meant whoever had held the can had been wearing gloves. Halpin planned to prove gloveprints were found at most of the Night Stalker attacks.

Clark wanted to show the jury that the print wasn't necessarily a cloth glove, that it might have been a leather glove, but Vander Wende testified that they could tell the difference between the texture of the surfaces: for instance, he said, the little pimples in pig leather would be picked up by the lifting tape after fingerprint powders were applied. Clark then had Vander Wende tell the jury exactly how the fingerprints were taken; they'd already been given that information early on but Clark wasn't aware of that.

When Vander Wende finished, Clark suggested the prosecutor show the crime-scene pictures now.

Judge Tynan addressed the jury. "Again, ladies and gentlemen, some of the photographs that you will be looking at this afternoon are not pretty. Remember, you are acting as judges here. You are not to be inflamed or emotionally involved in the photographs. They are evidence. You are to view them as evidence. They, in and of themselves, do not indicate that anybody is guilty of anything in this case. It is just evidence. You must view them as neutrally and objectively as you possibly can."

He warned them not to talk among themselves about the prints. Halpin read the numbers of them into the record and they were passed to the jury by Alan Yochelson. Stone-faced, each juror thumbed through the eight-by-ten black-and-white prints. They were passed to the alternates and finally collected by Yochelson.

Judge Tynan told the jury they were finished for the day.

THIRTY-EIGHT

Judge Tynan apologized to the jury for the air conditioning system not working well. The temperature in the windowless courtroom was in the high 80s or low 90s, and it made this difficult task even more difficult. He told court deputy Martinez to make sure someone from maintenance fixed the air conditioner.

Halpin called to the stand Dr. Sara Reddy, the medical examiner who had performed the autopsy on Mabel Bell on July 19. Dr. Reddy told the jury that Mrs. Bell had died of cranium cerebral trauma and that there were wounds to her chest, abdomen, back, and buttocks. At Halpin's urging, she said the wounds were those of thermal burns—i.e., electricity.

Halpin showed morgue photographs of Mabel Bell with tubes protruding from her neck and mouth. The head wound was so severe the surgeon couldn't repair it, and brain matter was still visible. Halpin asked what effect such head wounds would have on the cardiovascular system, and Dr. Reddy said, "These severe and fatal head wounds caused the brain tissue to swell and become soft and soggy and compressed the breathing center and also the heart-beating center, and that causes the stoppage of breathing and heartbeat."

She told Halpin similar head wounds she'd seen previously had been caused by hammer blows. After conferring with Daniel, Ray Clark said he had no questions.

Michelle Le Piesto testified next, telling the jury how it was she who'd picked up the alarm clock with the Avia print on it, and wrapped up the section of wall with the pentagram on it that Monrovia firemen had cut out for her. Ray Clark asked her questions about sketches she'd made and whether or not she'd found any hairs. There were, Daniel Hernandez had told Clark, human hairs mentioned at the preliminary that hadn't belonged to Richard or to either of the victims. She said she had found some hair under Mrs. Bell's bed but did not know if these were human hairs. Clark focused on these hairs, but all he could get from Le Piesto was, "I don't remember."

Clark felt the hairs proved that someone else did it. This was his basic defense strategy, as he really did not see any other viable defense except an insanity plea, which Richard was unequivocally against. Criminalist Le Piesto was excused.

Halpin said they were going to move on to incident 7, that of Carol Kyle. He read into the record the twenty-nine exhibits he'd be using in his presentation of the Kyle matter, then they broke for lunch.

Carol Kyle walked into the courtroom like a woman with a mission. Her head was back, her shoulders square, her step sure and confident, and when she sat down, she looked directly at Richard. She was clearly not cowed by or frightened of him. He let out a laugh. Halpin had her tell the jury about the night she had been awakened with a gun in her face and a light in her eyes. She testified that she had double-locked the front and back doors and windows, and that she was always careful about making sure the house was secure before retiring.

She had had a Lhasa Apso dog back then and had installed in the rear kitchen door a doggie door, which her attacker had apparently used to unlock a lock and gain entry. She said the doggie door could be locked, but she only locked it when away on vacation.

"What was the first thing you recall that person saying?" Halpin asked.

"I believe it was, 'Get up and don't make any noise,' " she said, and went on to describe her and her son's ordeal in detail.

Carol's words seemed to hover and quiver in the air as she spoke, evoking vivid images all too clear to the jury and court.

She tried to reason with the stalker, telling him that her son's father had been killed. " 'He has been through a lot in his life,' " she testified she'd said. " 'His dad died when he was six, and he's had a lot of trauma. Please don't hurt him.' And he told me shut up and took me into my bedroom."

She described how in the bedroom he looked for valuables, as he made her stare away from him. "He called me cunt and bitch." She told the jury how he kept asking her for valuables, that he was obsessed with gold, diamonds, and cash, and how she went to a drawer and reached in to give him a jewelry box. She said, "At that point he put the gun to my temple and said, 'Don't ever move fast like that or I'll kill you.' "

Carol testified that he then bound her hands behind her back with her pantyhose, left the room, ransacking as he went, came back and punched her a few times. He then told her to lie down on the bed. She knew what was coming and tried to dissuade him. "I told him just that I was having my period, that I had an infection, whatever, you know, to get him to stop. . . . He told me to shut up, and that if I made another noise, he'd kill me. He put the gun right to my head again." She said he got on top of her and began kissing her.

"Once he was on top of you and kissing you, what did he do?" Halpin asked.

Kyle gave a detailed description of the sexual assault. She said she knew he'd kill her if she didn't comply with his demands.

Women in the audience, and in the jury, moved uneasily in their seats. Carrillo looked at Cindy Haden and watched her stare intently at Richard, a blank, curious expression on her face.

"And for what period of time," Halpin asked.

"Three minutes."

"And then what?"

"Then he seemed satisfied and he got up off of me and I rolled over. As he was standing at the edge of the bed, he zipped up his pants. He was smiling at me and kind of chuckling and said I wasn't bad for my age."

Carol said he wanted more valuables and ransacked her home yet again, putting things in a pillowcase. She said he then disabled the phone, gave her a robe, and brought her son into the bedroom and handcuffed them together, leaving the key on the mantelpiece, where Carol's daughter could find it when she came home. He seemed, she thought, solicitous and oddly courteous.

At the end of her testimony, she identified Ramirez as her attacker.

Clark had decided to treat Carol like a woman who had made a mistake, not a victim. He was not particularly polite as he stood up and began his cross, first trying to underscore her identification at the lineup, which proved very difficult to do: Carol was positive about her identification of Richard, and no matter how many questions he asked, he could not make her waver. He tried to imply that there hadn't been enough light in the bedroom for her to see her attacker well, and that when she'd first awakened, the light had been in her eyes and she could not make out particular details. However, she did not agree with his hypothesis, saying she had had enough light to see him in the bedroom and that he'd been standing a foot and a half away when she'd looked right at him.

Clark then asked her if she had seen photographs of Richard before she had gone to the September 5th lineup. She said she and her son had seen a picture of him on television Friday night, and when she had seen that picture, she'd known he was the man who'd attacked her. Mark, too, she testified, had said Ramirez was the man. Clark asked Carol if she'd called the police and told them so. She said, "He, the next day, as I recall, the same person on the news flash, was apprehended."

She explained she'd gone to a class reunion. Her son was home with a friend and they had inadvertently activated the alarm system, which she had had installed after the incident.

"The police came to the house that night and Mark told them at that time that the person that we saw on the TV the night before was the one that was in our house."

Ray Clark waited a few seconds, trying to give the jury time to comprehend and appreciate the fact that she hadn't called the police as soon as she'd seen the picture of the man she was claiming was her attacker.

He asked her how many times "Richard" had struck her, and were the blows hard. She said she thought they were given one at a time, the first one the hardest, delivered to her right shoulder blade.

"Did he deface your home in any fashion, other than strewing these items about in an apparent search for valuable items?" Clark asked.

"Not that I'm aware of."

Trying to distance Richard from the Lang/Bell incident, he asked, "He didn't mark upon your walls or draw pentagrams or anything on your walls?"

"No."

"And other than obviously being an intruder in your home at that time of night, he didn't threaten your son. Is that a fair statement?" he asked.

"No."

Clark asked her about the type of guns she saw in the attacker's hands, but she didn't know the difference between an automatic and a revolver. He took her back to the lineup and asked her how many words she had heard Richard speak.

She said, "Whatever it was that he said, and I don't even remember what it was at this time, I just remember this horrible chill going through me, and thinking, 'That's his voice.' "

Clark moved to the composite Carol had helped put together, and she testified she had never been happy with the first one, that the second one was more like the image she had of her attacker.

THIRTY-NINE

The following morning, Tynan announced that Arturo Hernandez had called and would not be able to be in court because of another "pressing matter."

Halpin moved to incident number 8, the murder of Mary Cannon. He introduced photographs of the crime scene and morgue pictures of Mrs. Cannon, showing her gaping neck wounds. At this crime scene, a butcher knife and knife sharpener had been found on the bed next to Mrs. Cannon.

Mr. and Mrs. Frank Starich, the couple who lived next to Mary, testified first.

Frank told the jury about noticing that Mary's front window screen was down, entering Mary's home to find the ransacking, and calling the police.

Clark had a few questions about the distance the Stariches' house was from Mary's house, and he quickly got Starich to agree he had no idea how the screen he'd found on the lawn had gotten there. Christine Starich repeated with more detail what her husband had said.

Halpin wanted to show the jury pictures of Mary's body, but Clark objected on the grounds that they were gross and gory and likely to inflame the jury. Halpin countered that the force and viciousness of the cuts were important to the case and were very much like Jennie Vincow's injuries, which he contended the jury must see. Clark objected strenuously to exhibit 20G, a close-up of the neck wound. Halpin said he would be showing only 20I and 20H to the next witness, Lt. Ed Winter; one to identify the victim and one to indicate the wound. Judge Tynan agreed, saying, "The body has been cleaned up and the great masses of blood have been eliminated, and they are not pretty, either one of them, but I think they are necessary for the purposes of this trial."

Winter described the photos to the jury and testified about the ransacking, the disabled phones, and the arrival of Frank Salerno.

Clark understood that the tissue with the Avia print on it tied the Cannon crime to other crimes, and he wanted to get Winter to say that it might have been the shoeprint of a cop. Using a photograph of all the police and criminalists who'd been present, Clark asked Winter if he'd looked at the soles of the shoes of all ten. He testified that he had. In great detail, Clark had Winter describe the soles of the shoes he was wearing that day. Clark was unable to weaken Winter's testimony.

The prosecutor put Dr. John Shipley on the stand, and he testified he had performed the autopsy of Mary Cannon. "The cause of death was multiple trauma injuries as a result of blunt force trauma and an encircled wound to the neck to aid strangulation," he said. He described in minute detail the injuries Cannon had suffered, stating that there were at least ten blows with a heavy metal object. Halpin asked about the stab wounds to the neck.

Dr. Shipley answered, "What we're dealing with are four wounds, one of which is a large combined wound. That is, it has the features of both a stab wound and an incised wound, and then, in addition, there are three small stab wounds to the side of the neck . . . [the] single combined wound on the side of the neck is an extremely lethal enlarged wound. The knife penetrates from the side of the neck, and it is responsible for transecting the left carotid artery, and then it immediately cuts across the larynx so that it transects the epiglottis, which is the upper portion of the larynx, or voicebox, from the lower part and actually goes into the side of the mouth and back."

This testimony was crucial, Halpin felt, because the distinctive stab-slash wound was present in many of the Night Stalker attacks. He asked how long it would take for someone who had sustained such an injury to die. The doctor said a matter of seconds.

* * *

Halpin's first witness on March 13 was David Bruce Nipp, Mabel Bell's grandson. Walking slowly and not looking in Richard's direction, he took the stand, was sworn in, and identified morgue photographs of Mrs. Bell and Mrs. Lang and photographs of a cassette player he had bought his grandmother for her eighty-seventh birthday on April 6, 1985.

Clark tried to suggest the cassette player might have been stolen before the May 29 attack, but without success.

The prosecutor called Mark Krainbrink, David's brother, and he testified he had last seen Ma Bell and Nettie Lang two months before the attack, and that they were healthy and well on that occasion. He had gone to see them after the attack of June 1 in the Arcadia Methodist Hospital. They were both in a comatose state and could not communicate or acknowledge him. Halpin asked about the last time he'd seen his aunt, Nettie Lang. He said he had visited her at the Sophia London Hospital, the day before and that "She—she just lays in her bed, and she is unable to speak. She can move her head to look at you, but you can't be positive that she knows you are there or knows what you are saying."

"How is she fed?"

"She is fed through a tube."

Halpin moved back to the Cannon incident, and called criminalist Lloyd Mahanay, who testified he had responded to a summons by the sheriff's office. He was greeted by Frank Salerno, who directed him to two footprints on the bedroom rug of Mrs. Cannon's home. He cut them out with a carpet knife and they were rushed to the sheriff's crime lab, where they could be photographed under optimal conditions. Halpin showed the actual pieces of carpet, which over time had lost the impressions, and photographs of the rug with the prints still in them. They were very difficult to see.

Clark went at Mahanay with a vengeance. He felt trying to introduce evidence that had once existed but had since disappeared was bogus, and he asked dozens of questions about how he'd cut the rug patch out, what exactly he'd done with it, and was it the right or left foot. The criminalist said he didn't know, that he wasn't a footprint specialist.

Clark was unable to undermine Mahanay's testimony. In fact, his cross brought out something harmful to the defense.

The criminalist described for the jury how he had removed with a tweezer pieces of the glass lamp she'd been struck with, glass that had remained imbedded in Mrs. Cannon's face.

On redirect, Halpin clarified that the prints in the rug had been found in a second bedroom where there had been ransacking, not in the one where Mary had been attacked.

Judge Tynan soon recessed court until 1:30, at which point Halpin was going to present the next case.

Carrillo and Salerno ate together just about every day they were in court. If it was sunny, they'd leave the court building and take a leisurely stroll over to the mall, where they would sit outside and eat. It was relaxing to them both. Among the throng of people who worked in the downtown area and were at the mall, no one knew who they were and they could relax and not think of Richard or the trial. They ate silently and watched people walk by and didn't talk about much.

When court started up, Halpin announced they would be jumping forward to the residential burglary and attempted murder in the Bennett assault. He moved into evidence all the exhibits—photographs, the tire iron, and the comforter with the Avia print on it—then called Sierra Madre police officer Jerry Skinner, the first policeman to arrive at the Bennett house at 5:06 A.M. on the morning of the assault. He told the jury how he was greeted by Mr. Bennett at the door and appraised the situation, and he said a Medivac team had arrived thirty seconds later to take a very badly beaten Whitney to the hospital. He described how he had discovered a bloody tire iron on the floor of Whitney's bedroom, "Laying on the carpet, in the middle of a large pool of blood." Frank Salerno had arrived and taken over the crime scene.

Clark cross-examined Officer Skinner, having him repeat much of what he had already said, in greater detail: the jury learned nothing new and became fidgety.

Halpin told Judge Tynan the victim in this case had to be brought in from out of town and would not be available today.

The judge said he understood, congratulated Ray Clark on

moving the case along so quicky, and dismissed the jury until 10:30 the following morning.

Halpin moved to introduce, again, the coroner's pictures of Jennie Vincow's neck injuries. Ray Clark objected strenuously, particularly to the fact that they were close-up shots, which made them "twice as gruesome as they should be."

Tynan didn't agree. He said they were morgue shots of the injuries and should, because the prosecutor was trying to show a similar M.O. in the knife killings, be allowed in.

FORTY

Since the July 1985 attack on Whitney Bennett, Frank Salerno had grown close to the Bennett family, becoming personal friends with Whitney's father, Steve.

Frank thought the world of Whitney: she had been through a nightmarish ordeal yet rarely complained and often smiled when she should have been crying. Since her attack, she had had four operations to repair and remove the damage caused by the Stalker.

Steve Bennett came to the courthouse with Whitney; Frank and Gil stayed with them in the district attorney's office until it was time to take the stand. Whitney was nervous about testifying; she knew millions of people would be paying close attention to what she said, and she didn't like having to be in the same room as Richard Muñoz Ramirez. She thought of him as the embodiment of evil—a human being possessed of demonic force straight from the deep recesses of hell.

Frank had come to consider Whitney as almost a surrogate daughter. He was very protective of her, staying close and reassuring her that it would soon be over.

Frank's youngest son, Mike, took off work to be in the courtroom when his father would be testifying. Mike was six feet tall, muscular, and well built, with dark hair and large, dark eyes. He was a handsome man who had inherited his father's confidence. Mike was very proud of his dad and wanted to watch him testify. He knew his father had been particularly touched by Whitney and her ordeal.

"The people call Whitney Bennett," Halpin resumed.

Whitney entered the courtroom, took the stand. She was no longer a teenager, but a beautiful young woman with honey brown hair and large blue eyes. She saw Frank Salerno. He smiled reassuringly.

Halpin had her describe for the jury the July 4 night she had been assaulted. She testified about the party she'd been to, coming home very late, and going to bed. The next thing she remembered was waking up on her stomach in a pool of blood, and much pain about her head and hands. She did not remember being assaulted at all. She testified that she got up and made it to the hallway, where she collapsed and screamed for her father. She said she vaguely remembered him coming to her aid and the paramedics taking her to the hospital, where she stayed for eight days.

"And did you continue to receive medical treatment after that?"

"Yes."

"For how long?"

"Approximately for two and a half years."

"What about now? Do you still have some medical problems?"

"Occasionally I go and have my eyes checked, and cosmetic surgery. I'm still seeing a plastic surgeon." (The bone surrounding her left eye socket was smashed and had to be reconstructed.)

"What type of surgery did you have?"

"I has surgery on my hand and my face and my head."

Halpin had Whitney re-create the attack for the jury using crime-scene photographs of the bloody pink comforter with the Avia print on it; her bedroom dresser, where she testified she had put the jewelry she'd been wearing, which was stolen that morning; and the can of Coke she'd taken into her bedroom.

Halpin finished and turned her over to Clark, who asked Whitney if she had noticed anything unusual as she had driven home from the party, implying her attacker had trailed her home, rather than indiscriminately going in the window, as the prosecution was contending. She repeated that she had not been followed. She'd been speeding because she was late and had kept a close eye on the rearview mirror.

Clark seemed intent upon proving Whitney had been followed and asked her if her window was facing the street and had it been open, implying someone might have seen her through it, despite the fact that the window was above the surrounding landscape. He asked if she normally kept her window open with the curtain pulled back. She said she had earlier opened the window to tell her dad that he had a phone call and had never closed it.

Clark's questions did not undermine Whitney's testimony, and he finished without weakening Halpin's case. The Avia print on the comforter, he knew, tied this crime to others, and he could not change that fact.

Judge Tynan thanked Whitney and she left the stand and headed for the exit. As she moved through the courtroom, Frank's son Mike stared at her intensely, admiring her courage and feeling a tremendous sympathy for her. He thought Whitney had an inner beauty and a gentleness that was rare.

Halpin called Steve Bennett to the stand. Steve was a tall man with clean, well-defined features. As he sat on the stand, he looked at Richard, who stared at a yellow pad on the desk in front of him.

Bennett told the jury he and his friends had sat outside that night and watched the fireworks display over the San Gabriel Valley. He wasn't sure whether or not he'd locked the front door. He described how he'd gone to bed and awakened to Whitney's screams, finding her beaten beyond recognition. The tire iron was on the floor of his daughter's room when he went to get a pillow to place under her head. . . .

Halpin told the court he would be moving to the next count because there were no more witnesses in the Bennett matter; then, looking at Frank Salerno, he changed his mind and said he'd put Frank up next.

Clark stood and said that he was not ready to proceed because the Special Master was still having difficulties getting samples of evidence from the prosecutor's office. He asked for a hearing, based on papers the defense had presented to the court and the district attorney's office the day before. Judge Tynan had set the twenty-fourth to hear that motion and Halpin said he wouldn't be ready to argue until then. Tynan told him he would dismiss the jury until 1:30 so he could study the motion now.

When court resumed, Tynan announced he had gotten a note from juror number 11, Maria Santos, which said that

Steve Bennett was an employee of Southern California Gas Company, where she, too, was employed. Judge Tynan called Halpin, the defense team, and juror Santos to the bench.

She said she had seen Bennett in the company cafeteria, but did not know him personally, nor had she ever spoken to him. At Judge Tynan's questioning, she said this would not, in any way, affect her judgment or decisions. Tynan saw no problem, and neither Clark nor Halpin had any objection. Carrillo and Salerno worried that Maria Santos would be disqualified and that alternate juror Cynthia Haden would take her place. They did not want her on the jury. They had often caught her staring at Ramirez with an intensity that made them uneasy. Aware of issues pertinent to appeals, Judge Tynan agreed that Richard should be told about this development.

Halpin didn't want to be close to Ramirez at a sidebar and said so.

"Well, go back to your seats," the judge offered.

Halpin knew Richard hated him. For all he knew, Richard was capable of jumping on him and trying to bite his throat out. He did not trust Ramirez in any way. To Halpin, Ramirez was as dangerous and unpredictable as a rattlesnake.

Richard was brought in shackles from the holding pen to sit at the defense table. Clark leaned over and told him about Santos's working at the same company as Bennett. Richard's brows knitted together. He asked Clark and Hernandez what they thought, and they both said they had no problem with her still serving. Clark thought he would go along with their advice, but Richard didn't see it the way his defense team did. He said had he known she worked in a company where Steve Bennett was an executive, he would have said he didn't want her "right from the get-go. No matter what she says, she's fucking affected by him, if not consciously, then subconsciously. That's her boss, man."

Richard's point was not lost on Clark. If Richard didn't want her, she had to go.

"I want her off the panel," he said with finality. Clark turned to Judge Tynan and said, "Mr. Ramirez, in light of this fact, does not wish her to serve . . . he feels that it is—that there is something to it, the relationship, even though it is not apparently a one-on-one relationship, but it is something that had he known at the time, he would have urged defense counsel to exercise a challenge."

Halpin had no objections. "It seems to me appropriate, if that is what the defendant wishes, and he is correct, we really don't know what—what may exist. . . . We don't know at this point whether the witness might be somewhere in the chain of the juror's command. We didn't get into that, but I think the position of the defendant's table is well taken."

Halpin knew that if Santos stayed on the jury after Ramirez requested her removal, there would more than likely be an automatic reversal if there was a conviction. Halpin wanted to avoid giving Ramirez more ammunition than he already had because of the Hernandezes' lack of experience in capital crime cases. He still felt that Judge Soper had erred severely when she'd okayed the Hernandezes as defense counsel.

Judge Tynan turned to the defendant and said, "That is your request, is it, Mr. Ramirez, that juror Santos be excused for cause because of the relationship with the witness?"

"Yes," Richard said in a strong voice, and that was the end of juror Maria Santos. The judge asked her to be brought out and patiently told her of the court's decision, apologizing for having to dismiss her. She said, "Thank you," and left. Judge Tynan ordered the jury to be brought in and told them Santos had worked where Mr. Bennett was employed and for that reason had to be discharged. He asked his assistant, Josephine, to draw an alternate name from the round drum. Cynthia Haden sat upright, leaning forward, hoping to hear her name. She locked eyes with Richard.

Josephine read the name "Donald G. McGee," and Gil, Frank, and Phil Halpin all sighed in relief. Mr. McGee left the alternates and took place number 11 in the jury box. Cynthia Haden was clearly disappointed.

Salerno was recalled to the stand. All the newspeople were anxious to know what he had to say. They knew he had spearheaded the two largest serial killer cases in California's history.

Frank told the jury he had arrived at the Bennett residence a few minutes after 9 A.M., and Carrillo had gotten there five minutes later. He said he saw a bloody print on the windowsill, the tire iron, and the pink comforter.

"As of that morning, had you seen similar shoeprints?" Halpin asked.

"I had seen similar impressions at the Cannon residence and I was aware of a similar shoeprint that was found at the Zazzara location after reviewing the photographs of that crime scene with detectives Uloth and Smith and my partner."

Halpin then had Frank describe the visit to Methodist Hospital with Carrillo to see Whitney Bennett before she'd been bandaged. Frank identified the photograph he'd taken that showed a very badly beaten, unrecognizable teenaged girl.

Clark was very aware of Salerno's reputation as a thorough, tenacious pursuer and investigator who did his homework and came prepared. Clark focused his attention on the phone, knowing severed phone lines had been found at most of the Night Stalker crimes. He wanted to show the jury the Bennett's phone line had not been severed, but a photograph of the cut line made that impossible.

After the lunch break the prosecutor said they would move on to the tenth incident, the murder of Joyce Nelson. Halpin knew the Avia print had actually been left on Mrs. Nelson's face, and it was now fresh in the jurors' minds.

Court resumed. Halpin moved exhibits 12M to 12O into evidence, which related to the Bell incident. The jury was brought out and he read into the record all of the exhibits pertaining to the Joyce Nelson attack, then put Joyce's neighbor, Bob Blanco, on the stand. He told the jury how he'd become suspicious when he'd gone out to get the paper at 6 A.M. and noticed that a gate linking their two yards was open, and that the rear door to the Nelson house was also open. When the door was still open at 9 A.M., he had approached the rear patio, called Joyce's name, and noticed a screen had been moved. Receiving no response at the front door, he'd pushed it open. He saw that a dresser drawer was ajar, "like someone was going through them." He called another neighbor, Clifford Sharp, and the police were summoned.

On cross-examination, Clark had Mr. Blanco testify to what had happened that morning again and again until the end of the proceedings that day.

FORTY-ONE

Court resumed with Halpin introducing all the photographs relevant to the Sophie Dickman attack. That done, a heated argument between the prosecutor and the defense team erupted over the material the Special Master was supposed to have gotten from the district attorney's office. Halpin complained that the defense team had just given him a long list of numbers, without any description of the materials. He said the defense had been dragging their tails for years and suddenly they wanted everything all at once. He was clearly angry and frustrated.

Halpin was afraid the court would give the defense team a long period of time to review all the material they were now demanding. Tynan said he had no such plans and added he thought an agreement had been hammered out. He'd signed a rider that was prepared by the prosecution and everyone had been in agreement as to the manner in which it was handled.

Halpin felt he was being spoken down to by Judge Tynan in open court and requested a hearing. Judge Tynan tried to work out the complicated business of the DA's office sharing all the evidence with the defense forensic experts. He told both sides to have their experts in court on the twenty-fourth, that he would order the Special Master there, too. Until then, he wanted the trial to proceed as smoothly as possible.

The jury was brought out and Frank Salerno returned to the stand to testify that he'd arrived at Mary Cannon's house at 10:35 A.M. on the morning of the second. He saw the broken pane of glass in the window the killer had used to gain entry and the footprints on the rug. He got down on his hands and knees with a flashlight, scrutinized the prints, had them photographed, cut them out of the rug, tacked it to plywood and rushed it to the sheriff's lab.

He described finding a tissue on the floor with the distinct footprint of the Avia in blood. Halpin showed Salerno a close-up photograph of the victim as she was discovered.

"Her left arm is bent at the elbow and back behind her, with the palm of her hand facing up," he said, describing her pose for the jury. "There is a broken lamp, a milk-glass type lamp, that is on the bed directly next to her left elbow, and on the bed here, on the left side, I found a knife that was approximately ten inches in overall length that was blood-soaked."

"And up in the area of the shoulder and face, did you find other material?"

"I found what would appear to be pieces of the broken lamp about the bed, near her face. I found pieces of the broken lamp actually in her head and hair, and the pillow to the right of the victim is—had what appeared to me to be blood soaked into it."

Halpin had Frank now tell the jury how he had found that same shoeprint in the planter area in the front yard and on the rear patio porch of Joyce Nelson's residence in Monterey Park on July 7.

Salerno testified to assigning two detectives to learn everything they could about that particular shoe—the Avia Aerobic. Frank was about to tell the jury what he'd been told about the shoes when Clark objected, calling it hearsay. Halpin said it wasn't hearsay, that he was not asking "for the truth of the matter," just an opinion. Judge Tynan reserved his ruling until after lunch.

During lunch, Doreen grabbed a hamburger in a nearby fast-food place. She wished she could bring Richard a nice lunch they could eat together in his little cell. As Doreen ate, she wrote Richard one of the several love letters she sent him each day.

In them she made observations about what was going on in court; she didn't miss much and often had astute insights. Richard had grown to trust and care for Doreen very much.

She was, he'd come to believe, totally dedicated to him; she was probably the first woman he'd ever trusted.

When court reconvened, Judge Tynan told the jury that Frank's observations of the shoeprints were noted merely to indicate the avenues he had taken in his investigation, not that the shoe was any particular brand.

Halpin asked Frank to explain to the jury the great lengths the police department had gone to in analyzing and identifying the shoeprint. He stated they'd even sent criminalist Burke to Portland, Oregon, to interview the developer of the Avia Aerobic, a Mr. Jerry Stubblefield.

Halpin showed Frank crime-scene photographs of Joyce Nelson as he had discovered her that day, and Frank said he noted the imprint of a shoe on the left side of her face, though he could not "discern any particular pattern."

Clark knew the Avia print connected the crimes. Although the district attorney had no proof they were ever on Richard's feet, he would do what he could to undermine Frank's testimony. On cross he asked Salerno if the shoeprints had a serial number that distinguished them from all other shoes. Frank said, "Not that I'm aware of." Clark asked a few more questions about the samples Burke had brought back from Oregon and whether or not Avia had a copyright on the sole, which it did. Clark was soon finished. Surprisingly, he did not ask Frank if such shoes were ever found in Richard's possession.

Halpin now moved to the Sophie Dickman attack: residential burglary, rape, and sodomy. His first witness, Dr. Gerald Bross, had examined Ms. Dickman when she'd been brought to the emergency ward the morning of the incident. He stated he had given her a complete physical examination, finding rips and tears in the genital area and damage to Ms. Dickman's anus, where there were also tears and some bleeding. Clark had no questions and Bross was dismissed.

Sophie Dickman told the jury that she had a master's degree in psychiatric nursing supervision and had worked as a psychiatric nurse for thirty-eight years.

Halpin wanted her to identify Richard, but she had not worn her glasses and now had trouble distinguishing him from Daniel Hernandez. Halpin had to refer to Daniel's beard for clarification.

Ms. Dickman described how she was awakened at 3:20 A.M., as the light in her bedroom suddenly came on. "There was a man standing in the doorway, very tall, very thin, dressed in black, with black gloves on. He had a gun in his hand. He came around the table that the lamp was on, put the gun to my head [and] his hand over my mouth, [and] said, 'If you make a sound, I'll kill you.' "

She took a deep breath and described the gun as a silver metal automatic. Halpin asked her if she knew the difference between an automatic and a revolver. She said she did. "I was on the rifle and revolver team of Los Angeles County."

She stated she was ordered to stand up, turn around, and put her hands behind her back. Embarrassed by her nudity, she told her attacker that the shutters were open. He pushed them closed and put handcuffs on her. He had ransacked her home, noticing immediately she had slipped off her sapphire and diamond ring to hide it. He made her lie on the bed, pulled off her underwear, and put one of his gloves in her mouth, telling her to "bite down on this so you don't scream." She said the glove was leathery and had vertical and horizontal ridges, which she felt with her tongue. She told how he put a pillowcase over her head, threw himself on her, and proceeded to rape her. He asked her if she was enjoying it.

Several jury members stared at Richard in wonder.

Ms. Dickman said the sexual attack lasted two minutes. "I realized that he didn't have an erection. He was just thrusting and pounding, and that was it. He turned me over after two minutes . . . [and] tried sodomy."

"You say, 'Tried.' What was it he did?"

"He was thrusting and pounding against the rectal area, except it was more like my tailbone."

"Your hands still cuffed behind you?"

"Yes."

"And could you feel the defendant's genital area there against your rectal area?"

"It was against my tailbone. It felt like I was being torn in two."

How, alternate juror Cynthia Haden wondered, did it feel like she was being torn in two if he didn't have an erection, and how did she get those tears Dr. Bross had told the jury about?

Halpin seemed to come to the same conclusion. "Could you," he said, "determine at any time [if] the defendant actually penetrated your genital area?"

"I don't think so. He didn't have an erection," she said.

Carrillo looked at Salerno with a curious expression on his face. They both knew semen had been removed from Sophie Dickman by Dr. Bross at the emergency room of the hospital.

At this point, Judge Tynan recessed for the day. He asked Ms. Dickman to come back at 10:30, and she and the jury were excused. Tynan asked Halpin and Clark to come up to the bench. He wanted to know why Ms. Dickman had said she wasn't raped and if the charge of rape should be amended to "attempted rape." Halpin explained that Dr. Bross said she was confused about what exactly had happened to her. He wanted to leave the charges as they were because "the attempt is included in the act itself."

"I just asked," the judge said.

In the morning, Sophie took the witness stand again, facing a sunglassed, angry-faced Richard Ramirez. She saw Richard as a mentally ill person who had no right being free in society; she believed the forces that drove him were totally out of his control. Because she understood the ways of the psychopath, she harbored no wish for revenge. She just wanted him locked away—forever.

On the second day of her testimony, she seemed more composed and she was wearing her glasses. Halpin, like everyone else, noticed, and asked her about them. She said she was nearsighted and could only see well for four or five feet.

Halpin showed her the pictures of the crime scene, her home, and the pieces of jewelry that had been stolen, before directing her attention back to Richard. He asked if he looked different today than he had then. She said his hair was different and that he was wearing a suit and tie.

Daniel Hernandez stood for the cross-examination. He asked her if she was married or divorced.

"Divorced."

"And did you see your husband at all that evening?" he asked.

"I hadn't seen him since 1965," she said, derailing his intent to imply that she had had sexual relations with someone *other* than his client earlier that evening.

Daniel proceeded to have her again take the jury through what the man dressed in black had done to her, getting her to agree that she had told him at the preliminary that her assailant's shoes were "dark canvas topped with a white line around the sole," and not the now infamous Avia Aerobics. Daniel tried to create a scenario in which she'd never truly seen her attacker because he had ordered her from the beginning not to look at him. This, combined with her bad eyesight, the poor light, and her having a towel placed over her head for much of the time, would prevent her from ever getting a good look at her attacker. He suggested she had chosen Richard because she had seen his picture in the news when he'd been arrested and heard comments by public officials promoting his guilt.

She denied she'd told the police her assailant had been dressed like a camper and was five foot eight.

"No, I did not!" she countered.

Daniel asked if she had told the police her assailant was *not* Latino, and she said yes, she'd said he wasn't a Latino, Oriental, or black.

Judge Tynan interrupted, saying he had to go to a meeting. As the courtroom cleared, Cindy Haden and Richard stared at one another, to Doreen's displeasure.

When court resumed, Daniel had a police report from Det. Corrigan, the officer Sophie Dickman had spoken to at the Monterey Park Station the morning of the assault.

"Do you remember telling the person that you spoke to at the police department after the incident that the person looked like a hiker, or mountain climber?"

"Never!" she said.

Daniel smiled faintly. "You don't remember that?"

"I know I didn't say it." Her brows knit together and her lips tightened against her teeth.

Daniel asked permission to show her the report. He seemed calmer and more in control of himself than at the beginning of the trial. Having Ray Clark lead the defense team had taken a very draining strain off Daniel's shoulders. He handed the report to Sophie and pointed to the third paragraph down.

She read carefully. "The first sentence I did say, 'He smelled leathery,' but the rest of the sentence, no." (The report read that she had stated her attacker was dressed as a "hiker or mountain climber.") Daniel again asked her if that didn't refresh her memory, and Halpin interrupted, saying, "Excuse me, Ms. Dickman has already indicated that she did not tell him that!"

"I will allow the question, overruled. You didn't say that, did you?" the judge asked her.

"No, I didn't," she repeated.

"Then the report is incorrect."

"That line is."

Daniel again asked her if she had told Det. Corrigan her attacker was not Latino.

"I don't know if I said it that way."

Daniel directed her attention to the second sentence of the second paragraph. "Does that refresh your memory as to having told the officer—whether or not you told the officer that the person was not Latino at that time?"

"Well, I don't remember if I said it, if I said it at the time—but I did say he was not black, Oriental, or Latino."

"Okay," Daniel said, and he had what he wanted. Salerno, Carrillo, and Halpin all knew Dickman had very bad eyesight and wanted her off the stand as soon as possible; she was not a good witness for the prosecution.

Daniel moved on to the cans of soda she had found out of the refrigerator and on the floor of the rear patio. He knew there weren't any prints on them and asked her if they'd been there before the incident.

"No," she said.

He then asked her about the community meeting she'd attended in Monterey Park, if she had spoken there, to which she again said no. He wanted to know if the composite sketch she helped prepare was passed around at the meeting. She said it was. Daniel smiled. "And the description that was on it, was that also your description?"

"I don't remember," she told him.

Doreen squirmed uneasily in her chair. "Clearly Dickman had described someone other than Richard, but wouldn't admit it," Doreen would later say.

Daniel reminded Sophie that at the preliminary she had

told him the leaflet passed out at the Monterey Park meeting had the description she had given on it.

"Well," she said, "I don't remember telling you that, but if I did, I did."

With her testimony damaged on several points, Daniel soon finished and turned Mrs. Dickman back over to Halpin, who was eager to repair the damage. He moved back to the lineup and she said she had no confusion that Richard Ramirez was the man who had raped her and stolen her jewelry and dignity.

"How close did you get to him at that time [during the lineup]?"

"I got up on the stage and walked past him and back again. Only eighteen inches from him."

"Do you have any idea how this description of a mountain climber got into somebody's mind?"

"I cannot imagine," she said, with a light touch of indignation. He showed her another flyer of the Night Stalker suspect, which she said she'd had nothing to do with. Halpin put it down where the jury could see it. Daniel objected to the jury being exposed to this other composite without it being admitted as evidence. The judge agreed with him, and Halpin put the flyer in his folder.

Halpin asked why she hadn't called the police when she first saw Richard's picture on the tube.

"First it was eleven o'clock at night news. Secondly, I just figured they knew what they were doing. That is their job. They didn't need any hints from me."

Daniel asked her more questions about how many times she had actually seen Richard's picture before the lineup.

Richard hated Halpin. He viewed him as the embodiment of all that was wrong with the legal system. He often dreamt about Halpin, saw him in his dreams with horns protruding from the top of his head, devil-like.

Alternate juror Cynthia Haden was becoming nervous about getting on the jury; there were only five more cases which had to be presented and the trial would be over. Still, she knew deep inside it was her destiny to be called. She just wished it would happen soon.

When she and the other alternates and jurors entered the courtroom on Monday, Richard was already sitting at the defense table. He looked at her long and hard with his black eyes, deadpan. His stare made tingles slide up and down the skin on her back.

Doreen, ever vigilant, noticed him looking at her, then she saw Haden smile at Richard. It made her angry; ever since the Valentine incident, Doreen had perceived Cynthia as a rival for Richard's attentions and affection. She only hoped Haden wasn't picked if another juror had to leave the trial.

Newspaper deliveryperson Launie Dempster was called. However, before she could begin, the defense handed the court a motion to exclude her testimony because, as made clear at the preliminary, she was not certain of the days on which she said she'd seen Richard. The judge read the motion and offered the defense the opportunity to state their claim. Tynan ruled her testimony would go to the weight, rather than the admissability, of what she stated, and was going to allow it in.

Halpin moved into evidence a large Thomas Guide map and color photographs of the Pontiac.

Launie Dempster told the court about the three occasions she had seen a man in black near the Doi and Nelson residences, and on San Patricio in Monterey Park. She identified Richard as the man she'd seen. On cross, Clark tried mightily to undermine Dempster's testimony, but she was strong and unwavering and wasn't about to let any defense lawyer get the better of her.

FORTY-TWO

The following day Halpin told the court he would, because of conflicting schedules, have to move on to the next case, the murders of Max and Lela Kneiding, incident number 12.

Glendale officer Jon Perkins joined Halpin at the prosecutor's table. Halpin first introduced all the exhibits, then called a friend of the Kneidings', Roy Tesle Murley, who testified he had seen both Max and Lela alive and well at the Seventh Day Adventist Church on the evening of July 19, 1985. The defense had no cross, Mr. Murley was dismissed, and the Kneidings' daughter, Judith Arnold, took the stand.

As she was sworn in, she looked in Richard's direction. Like her parents, she was devoutly religious and viewed Richard as an actual extension of Satan—the embodiment of evil.

Without drama or tears, she told the jury how she'd gone to the restaurant that morning, then to the house, seeing her parents' car in the driveway, and entering the house through the rear door, which was ajar and had a broken window. "I walked down the hallway and found them in the bedroom." She took a long, deep breath and fought to hold back the tears the bloody sight of her parents brought on.

She said, her husband had called the police. Halpin did not question her about the condition her parents were in when she'd found them. He had the photographs, the most brutal and bloody of the trial, to show the jury, and he knew the pictures would speak for themselves.

Clark had no questions for Mrs. Arnold.

Next was Ella Francis, another daughter of Lela and Max Kneiding's. Halpin, using photographs, had her tell the jury about the individual items she recognized as her parents' at the property viewing room. When he showed her a photo of her mother's wedding ring, she began to cry. She identified a few other pieces of jewelry and was dismissed.

Halpin wanted to give the Kneiding crime-scene photographs to the jury, but Clark said the morgue shots were brutal and would inflame the jury, citing a blow-up of the stab-slash wound on Mrs. Kneiding, which Halpin felt was important for the jury to see. They argued and Tynan finally agreed to exclude some of the pictures.

Halpin next called Det. Jon Perkins. The prosecutor had Perkins describe in detail the specifics of the horrendous wounds the Kneidings had sustained.

The jurors and alternates looked at Richard. As usual, he sat slumped in his chair, his chained ankles crossed, his jaw resting on the palm of his right hand.

Halpin asked Perkins to identify the bullets taken from the bodies of the Kneidings. He described in graphic detail all the wounds, both knife and gunshot, that he'd observed at the autopsy.

When the afternoon session started, Halpin said he was not able to get the doctor who had done the autopsies on the Kneidings to court until the following week, so he was going to present the thirteenth case, the murder of Chainarong Khovananth and the beating and rape of Somkid Khovananth. The prosecutor put all the evidence he'd be using on the record, then called Somkid to the stand.

Doreen was not in court. No one had been available to babysit for Somkid's five-year-old daughter, and Doreen had volunteered. Somkid thought she was, in some way, attached to the court. Doreen watched the child in the hall as Somkid testified.

Somkid told the court she'd been born in Thailand and English was not her first language. She spoke so softly that Halpin suggested she bring the microphone forward.

She told the jury how her husband had come home that night and hadn't gone right to bed. It was very hot and she'd gone to sleep on the couch in the living room. The patio glass door was open, but the screen door was closed, though not locked. She was awakened by the sound of the screen door sliding open. Somkid had a Thai accent and spoke without syntax.

"What did you see?" Halpin prompted.

"I see a tall skinny man with a gun."

"Did he say anything to you?"

"Yes. He say 'shut up bitch. Do what I tell you, if not I'm going to kill you.' "

And she went on to describe how the stalker went into the bedroom where her husband was sleeping. She heard a gunshot.

"And after you heard the gunshot, did the man come back to where you were?"

"Yeah, the man come back, say, 'I killed your husband already.' "

"What else did he say?"

" 'Do what I tell you. If not, I'm going to kill both of your kids.' "

She told him she would give him anything he wanted if he did not hurt her children. He ripped her nightgown off, took her to the bedroom, said, "This is your husband. He's already dead." He then slapped her to the floor, put the gun to her head, raped her. Shaking, trembling, crying she continued her testimony, describing how he bound her hands with electrical wire he cut from a hair dryer in the bathroom and beat her.

Somkid testified that he then orally raped and sodomized her. The alarm in her son's room had gone off, and her tormentor had gone to the boy's room, tied him up, then returned to her and bound her legs with a belt. He then proceeded to the kitchen, returned drinking apple juice and demanded valuables and jewelry. He took her to the kitchen and she showed him where she had stashed her expensive pieces, taped under a kitchen drawer. He put the things he wanted in a pillowcase and soon left. She then untied herself and ran to her son.

Sobbing heavily now, she described returning to the bedroom with a neighbor, anxious to see if the intruder had truly killed her husband, said, as the jurors looked on spellbound, several of the women and two of the men crying—even hardened, seasoned reporters cried.

"I just open the cover and I see him is gunshot on the side of the head. I know he's dead and the police and the neighbors pulled me out. I don't want to go out."

Halpin offered her water and tissues to dry the tears. He then proceeded to show her the crime-scene photographs, and they further fueled Somkid's terrible, suffocating grief.

"Seeing her testify was one of the saddest things I've ever been exposed to in a courtroom," Gil Carrillo would later say. "Just about brought tears to my eyes."

Finally, Halpin asked, "Do you see the man in the courtroom today?"

Without hesitation she raised her right hand and pointed at Richard. He grimaced at her, then laughed. She began to cry harder.

Halpin showed her a photograph of Chainarong Khovananth as he lay dead.

"Is that the way you found him that morning?"

She said it was, and totally broke down.

Clark, during the cross, brought out the fact that the light in her home had been poor when the stalker had entered, but she said she had gotten a good look at him, particularly when he had put on the bathroom light. Clark tried to undermine the description she had given the police by suggesting she had described her attacker as a "white man."

She denied it, saying she had told the police he had brown skin, "like a Mexican," and curly black hair.

Clark asked her if she had seen Richard's picture on television and in the newspaper, intimating that was why she had picked him out at the September 5 lineup. She answered with resolution, "But I know it is him because I never forget his face, even today," and no matter how hard he tried, Clark could not dissuade her.

Diane Fitchner, the first police officer to reach the Khovananth residence that morning, was called next. Reading from her report, she stated that Somkid had "said that he was a male, possibly Hispanic, about six foot, thin build, about thirty to thirty-five years of age, and . . . he had wavy brown hair, soft waves, light curls, and he was wearing brown pants and a blue multicolored-type shirt."

"Did you then broadcast that description?"

She said she had.

Clark asked several questions about Somkid's description, before court was recessed for the evening.

The next witness was Carlos Brizzolara, who testified he and his partner, Al Michelorena, arrived at the Khovananth residence at 9:08 A.M. the morning of the twentieth. Halpin had Brizzolara re-create the crime scene for the jury. The prosecutor showed him photos of the ransacking and phone disabling, which were the Stalker's signature. Halpin made sure the jury saw a close-up of Chainarong's gunshot wound, which was identical to Vincent Zazzara's and Elyas Abowath's gunshot wounds. He also showed Brizzolara photographs of size 11 1/2 shoeprints that had been discovered about the house.

On cross, Ray Clark was unable to put distance between his client and the Sun Valley crimes. Brizzolara was dismissed and Halpin told the court he would again have to put a witness on the stand out of order because of conflicting schedules. He would present incident number 14, the attack on the Petersens, the next-to-last count. Judge Tynan said fine. Clark told the judge that Richard was not "feeling chipper," and wanted to waive his right to be in court the following day for a hearing. Tynan agreed and the paperwork was completed and signed by Richard.

Richard was convinced the guards at the jail were still putting something in his food to poison him. He was always listless and without energy, all his joints ached, and he felt sick in the morning. His dreams were becoming more and more bizarre, which he blamed on the poison. He didn't want to eat, but there was no other source of food.

"They had me locked up twenty-four hours a day, no exercise, no fresh air, no nothing. They were trying to kill me slowly, and they were succeeding. I felt like I was dying," he would later relate.

He complained to Doreen about his food being poisoned. She wrote articulate letters to the jail's warden, but nothing changed.

* * *

Assistant district attorney Yochelson read the exhibits in the Petersen matter into the record, and called Virginia Petersen to the stand.

Virginia was a large woman with wide, square shoulders and a strong, powerful gait. She gave Richard a dirty look on reaching the stand. She was sworn in and told the jury about the morning she was awakened by a footstep and saw a man pivot into her bedroom from the living room, where the light had been left on by her husband. "He was," she said, "ten feet away."

"Can you describe him as you saw him then?"

"He was over six feet tall, he was wearing dark clothing, and he had shaggy dark hair."

"What was his build?" Halpin asked. He wanted the jury to know Virginia had gotten a good look at the man.

"He was lean, muscularly built, not lean as in skinny. He was holding a gun in standard combat position," she said.

"Did that image put you in mind of something? Is there some way that you can describe it as it appeared to you at that time?" Halpin asked.

"Someone was sneaking into the house; someone was intruding."

"Did you say anything?"

"I sat up in bed and I said, 'Who are you? What do you want? Get out of here.' "

"And was there any reply from the man?"

" 'Shut up, bitch. Where is it?' " she stated the intruder had said.

She described being shot, falling back into bed, and feeling numb; the intruder's laughter; her husband waking up and his being shot, though he still jumped out of bed and ran at the intruder, who fired a third round at her husband, then a fourth shot. Her husband had gone down, but he'd come back up and the two men had grappled; her daughter had been screaming, and she, choking on her own blood, had retrieved her child and called 911.

Halpin showed her photographs of her house for her to describe to the jury, then asked if she saw her attacker in the courtroom. She pointed at Richard. Richard's eyes were covered by sunglasses. He laughed, making her skin crawl.

Halpin asked, "At the time you saw the defendant enter

your room with his hands up in front of him, could you see his hands?"

"Yes," she said.

"Could you describe their appearance?"

"They stood out from the rest of him in that they were much lighter in color and I was struck by how long and how large they were."

All eyes in the room, even Judge Tynan's, moved to Richard's hands. They, like his father, Julian's, were huge, and now they rested on the defense table defiantly.

The prosecutor asked her if she could tell if he'd been wearing gloves.

"It could have been gloves," she said.

Clark began his cross of Virginia after the lunch recess. Virginia was a difficult witness: she was sure of herself and had all her facts straight. She did not cry or become overwhelmed by emotion, and the hatred she harbored for Richard was real and tangible—easy for the jurors to perceive.

He began by clarifying the amount of light she had to see her attacker. She conceded it was a hundred-watt bulb under a shade, three feet off the ground, in a lamp against a wall in the living room. He used a diagram of her home and had her draw an "X" where the lamp would have been, which she said was about seventeen feet away. He asked her if the intruder was only "backlighted." She agreed, but added, "At times the light shone directly on his face by the way he was standing."

Clark asked her how many times she'd seen Richard's face on television and in the newspapers before she'd viewed the September fifth lineup. The question could only help Richard. There was no way, Clark knew, Virginia Petersen hadn't seen Richard's face multiple times before September 5. She testified she'd seen his picture on TV six or seven times.

On redirect Halpin returned to the intruder's hands, making sure the jury would not miss the resemblance between Richard's and the hands Virginia described.

Halpin moved all the photographs of the Kneiding and Khovananth incidents into evidence. Judge Tynan then addressed the jury, complimenting them on their behavior through the long weeks.

After his remarks, the Kneiding and Khovananth photographs were distributed among the jurors and alternates. Halpin wanted the images to stay with the jurors on the upcoming long Easter weekend. Tynan explained to Richard that he would not have to attend the hearing in the morning involving the differences between the Special Master for both the defense and the prosecution if he didn't want to. Richard did not want to be present and signed a 977 waiver.

The following morning, without the defendant or the jury present, Halpin argued his position on why the defense was not being given all the pieces of evidence they were asking for. He felt what the defense wanted was unrealistic, that their requests for material were lacking specificity, and that they failed to refer to the number system which appeared in reports throughout the case. He was also concerned about the length of time the defense was seeking to do their tests, which in truth should have already been done. Halpin accused the defense of purposely trying to "sabotage the trial."

Clark's answer was to put Brian Wraxall, the defense Special Master, on the stand. He was questioned by Clark, then grilled by Halpin, as Judge Tynan listened and made copious notes. He wanted this decision to be the right one. He did not want to be responsible for Richard getting a reversal, if he was found guilty. Tynan thought this likely, as too many eyewitnesses put Richard Ramirez into the Night Stalker's large shoes. He listened to arguments until the court reporter requested a break. Then Judge Tynan finally ruled on exactly how all the items would be shared by the prosecution and the defense, and he recessed court for the weekend.

FORTY-THREE

That weekend Ruth traveled to Los Angeles to visit Richard. It was a long, difficult trip. Early Saturday morning, she stood in line with the others who were waiting to see the 6,000 individuals housed at the L.A. County Jail. Ruth nodded hello to a few familiar faces but stood alone; she was the sister of the Night Stalker and no one wanted to get too close. When Richard was brought down he was in a foul mood because of the poison he was certain they were putting in his food. He complained and Ruth listened with a patient ear and looked at him with sympathy and much love.

All week, every moment of every waking minute, Richard wore a stone-cold face, but when he was with his older sister, it was different. He showed her his true feelings and looked to her for support and understanding, which he received. "He was like a little boy all over again," Ruth later related. "No matter what, Richie was still my brother, and no matter what, I love him and will be there for him to the end. Whatever it is."

Richard told Ruth he didn't have a chance; they would surely convict him and send him to San Quentin to die. Ruth hated hearing him talk like that, but she knew it could very well happen, and deep inside she prepared herself for that dreaded eventuality.

She tried to give him a pep talk; she was afraid he might go mad and kill himself after all was said and done. She told him how much Julian and Mercedes missed him and loved him and that Ray Clark was doing a fine job and he should keep up his spirits and not lose heart. "You are a Ramirez," she reminded him. "Remember that."

When Ruth left the jail, she met Ruben for lunch. Ruth

would still not go inside Ruben's house because of the running feud with Suzanna. That night she again slept in the back of her brother's car, hidden under her raincoat, afraid of the rats, of the police, and of men who got their kicks from hurting women. Ruth knew it was a cruel world filled with people who were capable of terrible things.

Richard didn't like her sleeping in the car and he warned her over and over to be careful. He told Ruben to keep an eye on her, that if something happened to her, their father would go bananas.

Early Sunday morning Ruth went to church, prayed for Richard, prayed for her parents, and prayed that her younger brother would turn away from Satan and embrace Christ. If he was to find salvation, he must stop looking to Satan for redemption.

Ruth visited Richard on Sunday, and their half-hour together was spent very much as it had been the day before. Richard complained. Ruth listened attentively, with love and understanding. She wanted to go to the trial, to show the world she believed in Richard's innocence, but because she was a potential witness, she still was not allowed in court.

That weekend Ruth met Doreen. She was at first leery of Doreen, but when she realized how much Doreen truly cared for Richard, she embraced Doreen as a friend.

When court resumed on Monday, all but one juror looked fresh and more relaxed. Juror Phyllis Singletary looked worried and distracted; Some of her fellow jurors noticed a little swelling around her left eye. They did not ask what had happened, and she didn't offer any explanation. Cindy Haden knew Phyllis was involved in some kind of abusive relationship, but she was not aware of how truly abusive it was.

Cindy wondered if it would be this week that she was finally picked as a regular juror. There wasn't much time left, she realized, though she still felt confident she'd be chosen.

Halpin told the jury they would be moving back to the Khovananth attack and put criminalist Charlie Vander Wende on the stand.

Vander Wende stated that he and criminalist Gerald Burke had photographed and lifted footprints from several different areas at the Khovananth home. The prints were the same as what he'd seen in Joyce Nelson's home and on the clock at Mabel Bell's. Halpin handed him three footprint lifts. The jury could see they were the now familiar Avia Aerobic shoe.

Because of witnesses' schedules, they would now have to jump forward to the autopsies of Chainarong Khovananth and Elyas Abowath. Yochelson read into the record all the exhibits in the last case, number 15, which included residential burglary, murder, rape, oral copulation and sodomy.

Dr. Joseph Cogan was called, and he told the jury he performed an autopsy at 10:30 A.M. on July 21 on Chainarong Khovananth. Halpin showed him photographs of the wound, which was just above the left ear. There was gunpowder residue around the bullet hole, indicating the gun had been very close when fired. Cogan estimated "an inch or less."

Dr. Cogan autopsied Elyas Abowath on the morning of August 9. The cause of death was also a gunshot wound to the head, also from "about an inch" away. This projectile was copper-jacketed, while the one removed from Chainarong Khovananth was solid lead. Clark had no questions.

Halpin had planned to put Sakina Abowath on next, but she was ill and would not be available until the following day. The prosecutor said he couldn't proceed any further. Court was recessed.

Sakina Abowath dreaded being in the same room with Richard Muñoz Ramirez. In her heart, she was sure he was the man who had robbed her husband's life and her dignity—who'd made her grovel and beg and swear on Satan.

Halpin called her name, she timidly entered the courtroom and slowly made her way to the stand, pale and trembling. She had been home in bed with the flu and a sore throat. Sakina was five feet tall, had pearl black hair, cut short, large black eyes. Halpin hated putting her on the stand, but he had no choice in the matter.

In a small voice thick with a Burmese accent, Sakina first told the jury she had awakened that morning at 2:30 to nurse her ten-week-old son. Their other child, a three-year-old boy, was asleep in his room. After she breastfed the child, she turned off the air conditioner, went to the restroom, took a glass of water in the kitchen and went back to sleep.

Halpin knew Clark would question the available light, so he had Sakina testify that the nightlight in the bedroom had been on as well as a lamp in the living room.

Sakina said she then heard a popping.

"And all of a sudden someone hit me on the head real hard and turned me on my stomach and he put handcuffs on me from the back."

"And what else was done?" Halpin asked.

"Then he started banging me in the ears a couple of times real hard and then beat me up like this," she said, indicating with open hands over her ears.

Crying and sobbing, she went on to describe how her assailant had jumped on the bed and kicked her in the head so hard she landed on the floor, where he'd beaten her still more. He then went to the closet and grabbed a shirt of hers and with it he bound her feet together.

It was extremely difficult for Sakina to talk; she looked at the ceiling as if searching for strength.

"He said, 'You bitch, you motherfucker, you don't scream, otherwise, I'm going to kill you. I'm going to kill your kid in the crib, and I'm going to kill your son.' " Then he stuffed a sock in her mouth.

"All right. Now, up until that point, had you said anything?" Halpin queried.

"No. I said, 'I swear I won't, I swear I won't scream. I swear I won't go out,' and he slap me one more time, and he said, 'Swear upon Satan.'

"And I said, 'Yes, I swear on Satan I won't scream.' "

Crying now, she said he gagged and blindfolded her, ransacked the house, came back, beat her some more, and demanded valuables.

Sakina's hurt and pain reached out and touched everyone in the courtroom. Even Judge Tynan, normally stoic and stone-faced, had tears brimming in his eyes.

Halpin asked her, "Do you see that man in the courtroom today?"

"Him," she said, pointing. "I can identify him in a hundred people, if you like. He is not even big change, except his hair is longer." She stood up, saying, "You son of a bitch! Why did you kill him? I give you everything! You bastard!"

"All right," Halpin said.

"Ma'am, I know this is tough for you," Tynan said.

"I give him everything," she wailed.

"I understand. Just try and stay calm. Just answer the questions, ma'am. If you need time off, we'll give you a few minutes. Just try and relax," Judge Tynan said.

"We have to do this," Halpin said. "There are five men sitting at the end of the defense table."

"Him," she said, indicating. "The one in the red tie."

"All right. The defendant, Richard Ramirez, for the record. Thank you," Judge Tynan said.

She sobbed, cried into her hands, and sat down, exasperated and beaten.

Clark and Daniel knew Sakina was very bad for the defense. The two defense lawyers conferred. They wanted to get her off the stand as quickly as possible. Daniel stood up and said, "Your Honor, may we suggest a brief recess?"

"No, you may not," the judge said.

Sakina, through tears and gasps for breath, went on to describe being beaten still more as her tormenter demanded cash and her diamond wedding ring.

Then, she said, he'd left and come back after a few seconds.

"He tear off my clothes."

"And were you still handcuffed behind your back?"

She said she was and went on to describe being dragged by the hair to the spare bedroom.

"And then he sit on the bed and he take out his penis and he grab me from the hair and he pull my mouth on his penis and I don't want to do it and he pulls me, he pulls me—" she cried out, broke down again, sobbed into her hands, cupped against her tear-soaked face.

Halpin, in as gentle a way as possible, led her through the details of the rape. She then told the jury about her son waking up, her going to him handcuffed, soothing him, lulling him to sleep, then back to the bedroom where she was raped again. She said that he tried to sodomize her but wasn't able to consummate the act, though he did vaginally rape her.

While he was engaged in this, her son had come walking

down the hall. The Stalker had grabbed the boy, bound him, and covered him with pillows.

"You bitch, you don't scream. Tell your son not to scream, otherwise I will kill him."

"I said, 'I swear I won't,' and he said, 'Swear upon Satan.' I said I swear upon Satan I won't scream and I won't let him scream either."

With that, she stated he closed the door and left her and her son tied up, and when he came back he was carrying the couch pillows, which he put on top of the boy to muffle his pleas, and the boy called out, "Mama, please, I can't breathe."

Sakina had begged him not to hurt her husband. In response to her plea, the killer laughed, undid her handcuffs, and cuffed her to a doorknob. He asked if someone would be coming in the morning so she could be released. She said yes, and he was gone.

She said she first untied her son and sent him to wake up her husband, but Elyas wouldn't get up.

"I get so panic. I thought that maybe he cut this cantaloup and stuff it into my husband's mouth and he wants the Scotch tape so he could tape it on [Elyas's mouth]. That's why he couldn't scream or nothing. I figure it out that way."

She went on the describe her making the boy go back to his father, telling him to remove anything from his mouth, that she heard her son trying to wake his father up, repeatedly called to him as she screamed Elyas, Elyas wake up!

"You could hear him saying Daddy, Daddy?" Halpin asked.

"Yes, and he was doing something and he came back to me and he said, 'Momma, there is nothing in his mouth and he's not waking up.'

". . . And I told him, 'Aamar, go back again and wake him and shake him so he can wake up.' And at the same time I was screaming Elyas, Elyas," she wailed, her pain and turmoil filling the courtroom. Women on the jury and among the alternates took out handkerchiefs and tissues and wiped at the tears streaking their faces; even the male jurors were wiping back tears.

Then, she said, she began the difficult task of getting the boy—still very traumatized and frightened by the Stalker—to go out into the night to the neighbors' for help.

Sakina now told the jury that her neighbors did come, that

Bob Wilson went and looked at Elyas and came back crying. He didn't tell her Elyas was dead, though she knew from Bob's reaction. When the police arrived several minutes later and she was freed, she ran to Elyas to see for herself.

Phil Halpin wanted to get Sakina off the stand as soon as he could so he moved to the September 5 lineup. She testified she identified number two and wrote it on the card they gave her. She said she also found jewelry that belonged to her at the property show up—two gold chains from Pakistan, a set of earrings and an engagement ring her mother-in-law had given her, among other things—including a television and a VCR.

Halpin proceeded to show her dozens of photographs of the inside and the outside of the house, which she described for the jury . . .

Then he came to photograph number 40-E, an autopsy photo of her husband's head. She took it in her hand, looked and her eyes swelled and her face winced in sudden agony. "You never showed me that before," she told Halpin, as if she'd been burnt.

"Please, just tell the jury who that is," Halpin said.

"My husband. This is my husband. Did he beat him up on the head, too? I didn't know that," she said, and again broke down.

She turned to the judge.

"What did he get out of killing him? He's such a nice man."

"Ma'am, I can't answer that, I'm very sorry. I'm concerned about you now. Do you want to take a little recess?"

"I want to go straight through," she said, anxious to get it over with.

"I have no further questions," Halpin said.

"You may cross-examine," Tynan said to the defense. Clark knew he had to be careful with Sakina. She was a very sympathetic witness. Before he could get up, Halpin stood and asked her, "Did you see anything on his hands?"

"Yeah," she said. "He was wearing gloves."

That was the answer Halpin was looking for. "Did you ever see a picture of the defendant after this happened?"

"No. It is our religion that after the husband died to give him respect. We didn't watch TV. We don't go out of the house, we don't do anything. Just for two months. We give him respect. We just stay in the house and pray and pray for him, and that is what I was doing."

"What about newspapers? Did you read any newspapers?" Halpin asked.

"You cannot do anything. You pray a lot for him."

"Thank you," Halpin said, and sat down.

Clark asked Sakina if the September 5 lineup was the first time she'd been out of her house since her husband's murder and she said yes. He proceeded to show her the police composite drawing she'd helped to create, and he asked her if she'd ever seen it. She said she had worked with a policeman on it, but "I wanted something better than this. It doesn't come out—"

Clark stopped her and asked her if she'd helped create it. "Yes. Yes," she said.

"Did you tell the artist he had light brown or dishwater blond hair?"

"I told him he got a light face, light-colored hairs."

"That means light in color?" he asked.

"Yeah. I told him that because the—the bathroom light, the restroom light was falling on his head. That is why I said light hair."

Clark grilled her about the available light she had seen her attacker in and how many times she'd seen him. She did not weaken or become distressed by Clark's thoroughness. She seemed to reach inside herself and get stronger with each question. He focused on whether she had noted her attacker's shoes.

"I can't because he's so huge and I'm so tiny, even if you kick me with the tennis shoes, I can't figure it out because it was hurting on my head so badly. I know that he was hitting me on the head [kicking her] with the shoes."

Clark said he had no more and sat down.

"We are very sorry for your loss, and God bless you," Judge Tynan said to Sakina.

"I hope you do good judgment," Sakina responded, and slowly stepped down from the witness stand. She looked at Richard and it seemed she was going to fall down; two court bailiffs rushed to her aid, took her by the arms gently, and led her from the courtroom as she sobbed.

* * *

Halpin called deputy sheriff John Knight, and he told the jury about finding Sakina handcuffed to the door, locating Elyas, and kicking the doorknob holding Sakina off the door. "Did she give you a sort of description?" Halpin asked.

"Yes, sir. She described the person who was responsible as a light-skinned male Mexican or a dark Caucasian. She described him as being tall, and I stood up in front of her and told her that I was approximately six foot six and asked her where he would come up to on me, and she said, 'You know somewhere, you know, down by your mouth,' and I said, six three, six four, and she nodded yes."

Judge Tynan ordered a break for the court reporter, and when court resumed, Halpin put Gil Carrillo on the stand. The prosecutor handed him the remnants of the handcuffs used to restrain Sakina to identify. There was no cross. As Carrillo passed the defense table, Richard smiled and said hello in Spanish. Gil returned the salutation and resumed his place at the prosecutor's table.

Judge Tynan told the jury the case would be getting somewhat technical now and suggested they resist the temptation to rest their eyes. If they needed more fresh air or longer breaks, they should let him know. Court was recessed.

FORTY-FOUR

When Richard returned to his cell, he lay down on his bed and read letters from Doreen and a few of his groupies. He wrote a few letters and fell asleep, dreaming he was in hell with a Satan who had a face like Phil Halpin. He woke in the middle of the night with a start and in a sweat and couldn't go back to sleep. He read Carlos Castaneda for a few hours, dozed off, and was awakened by the guard to get ready for court. He didn't want to go. He viewed the trial as a "total farce," and he hated being there, but he had no choice. He sat up cursing, in a particularly foul mood.

Halpin opened by showing a videotape of the lineup to the jurors. He wanted to clear up once and for all any ambiguities and accusations that anything untoward had been done at the lineup. The lights were dimmed, and the thirty-five-minute tape was watched in silence. The jurors saw Richard step out from the other five men, walk to the edge of the stage, say a few words, and return to the line. When the tape was over, court broke for lunch.

The first witness after the break was Richard's former friend Donna Meyers, flown in from San Francisco with Earl and De De Gregg for their court appearances. Of all the people in the world, Richard did not want to see Donna Meyers in court. She was the first person he actually knew on the outside to take the stand, and as she was sworn in, he glowered at her.

Halpin showed her a picture, which she identified as Armando Rodriguez. Halpin then asked her if she knew anyone at the defense table.

"Richard [Ramirez] Whitney," she said.

Judge Tynan asked what count Donna's testimony was relative to and Halpin said, "This will probably go to all of them."

Donna described first meeting Richard when she went to El Paso for a visit with Armando in 1979. She saw him again when he went to visit them when they lived in Richmond, California, from 1979 to 1981. Richard had stayed with them when he'd visited. She had moved to San Pablo, and Richard often visited her there, sometimes with Armando, sometimes alone.

She stated the last time he'd come to her house was in August of 1985, "the fifteenth or sixteenth." He came alone, she testified, then with Armando. He gave her an octagonal jewelry box, asking her to hold it for him. When he came back to retrieve it, he gave her a bracelet and three rings, which she then gave to her daughter, De De, and her son, Lloyd Vorack, who left San Francisco with one of the rings and returned to Utah, where he lived and worked.

On August 30, Donna said she was contacted by San Francisco policemen Frank Falzon and Carl Klotz. She'd told them where she'd gotten the jewelry, but said she did not know how to find Rick, that he stayed in different hotels and moved around a lot.

"Can you tell us how the defendant customarily dressed when you saw him?" Halpin quizzed.

"Dark pants and shirt and dark shoes."

"Did he ever tell you why he dressed that way?"

"So he couldn't be seen so well at night."

"Did he ever tell you what he was doing at night?"

"Yes. He said he was ripping off people."

"Did you ever see the defendant wearing gloves?"

"He wore brown cloth garden gloves," she said.

And went on to state Richard had often brought jewelry to her house and sometimes sent it to his sister. Once he'd given her $500 for her to hold, with instructions to give it to his sister if anything happened to him. He had not given her an address, just a phone number and the name "Ruth."

Halpin asked her if she had ever seen any tattoos on the defendant.

"No. He had a picture drawn of a pentagram on his arm, but it wasn't a tattoo. It was just drawn with ink."

"Did the defendant ever speak to you about Satan?"

"Yes. He said he was the 'supreme being.' "

She testified that Richard truly did believe in Satan, and that made him all the more menacing as he sat there with his sunglasses on, staring at Donna Meyers like he wanted to take a bite out of her.

She said she had seen Richard looking at a handgun Armando had for sale. Richard had said he wanted to buy an Uzi. When Halpin asked her if she knew what Richard was doing with the things he stole, she testified he had a fence in L.A.. Richard had also shown her master car keys he had for Datsuns and Toyotas.

"Was there anything about the defendant's teeth that to you were remarkable?" Halpin asked.

"They were decayed, and one of them was chipped, and they were discolored."

She said there was a second time, he had left money with her, seventy-five dollars. She ended up wiring it to him in L.A., under the name of Rick Moreno. She stated she saw Richard in possession of Japanese coins in coin pouches in the summer of 1985.

Halpin asked about Richard's weight and his build.

"He was complaining—he was always complaining he was too thin. He used to drink a lot of this stuff called 'Weight On.' "

"To gain weight?"

"To gain weight."

The prosecutor was pleased. He felt Donna had put everything in perspective and pointed the finger of guilt directly at Richard. Ray Clark knew how much Donna had hurt Richard, and he stood to do serious battle with her.

. . . "Now, you told Mr. Ramirez that he didn't have the guts to kill anybody?" he asked.

"Yeah, we were talking about it."

"The reason you told him that was [that] you knew his reputation for peace and quiet, didn't you? You knew his reputation was that of a nonviolent person, didn't you?" he demanded.

"He had never been violent around me," she said.

"That's right," Clark quickly agreed, seizing the opportunity to make Donna Meyer a positive character witness for Richard. "And he'd been in your home many, many times, right?"

She agreed he had been, and that seemed a plus for Richard. Clark returned to his client's passive nature. "Okay, and had he in fact been around any relatives of yours?"

She said he had. Clark asked which relatives.

"My daughter Deleen—most of my relatives. I have a lot of children living in the area. Most of them knew him."

The defense lawyer asked questions about Armando Rodriguez, implying maybe *he* was in some way involved with the crimes Richard was charged with. Clark asked her if Richard had bought the gun Armando had for sale, and she said no. He grilled her on the exact conditions of Richard's teeth when she had last seen him.

On redirect, Halpin asked Meyers to describe Armando Rodriguez. "He's about five-nine, five-ten. He has dark brown hair. He has a mustache, and his hair is kind of medium length."

"Would you say he and the defendant were the same size?"

"No, the defendant is taller and thinner. Armando is a little heavier."

The next witness was Earl Gregg, the fellow who had first gone to the San Francisco police and made them aware of Rick Ramirez. Gregg was tall, thin, and unkempt, and he looked like he wasn't eating or washing enough. He was very nervous, and he stole furtive glances at Richard as he took the stand.

Halpin had him tell the jury he'd known Richard Ramirez for ten years and had met him through his mother-in-law. He had seen Richard at Donna Meyers's home shortly after Easter of 1985. Richard had tried to sell him a .25 automatic and showed him a small-caliber black revolver. Halpin gave him the gun retrieved from Tijuana, and Gregg said it looked like the pistol Richard had shown him. Richard had wanted too much for the guns, $125 to $150 each. "It was high. That's why I didn't buy them," he said. "He also had a couple of rifles for sale," he added.

Clark stood to do the cross on Gregg, who was, according to Richard, "White trash, a drug user, and a two-bit burglar."

Clark asked a few questions about the bags Richard had the guns in and if he had seen them in a pillowcase at any point. Gregg said they were in a brown gym bag with white handles, and he had never seen Richard with any pillowcases. He testified the same gun Richard offered him for $150 he'd bought new in a store for $53.

Halpin now said he had a few "fill-in witnesses": people who weren't available in the correct chronological order because of previous commitments. He called Dr. Irvin Golden, the medical examiner who had performed autopsies on Max and Lela Kneiding. He told the jury in gory, heart-wrenching detail about the wounds suffered by the Kneidings. Clark had no questions for Dr. Golden.

The prosecutor announced he was almost ready to move on to the arrest phase, but he had a few witnesses coming from out of state on Monday and asked if the court could be darkened until then. Clark said he had no objections and Judge Tynan recessed the proceedings until Monday, April 3.

Jesse Perez was the first witness called. He took the stand tentatively and was sworn in. Richard hated Perez. He viewed him as a rat, a snitch, the lowest form of life there was in the world Richard had traversed.

Perez wore a rumpled jacket, tie, and shirt. He looked like he hadn't slept in a week.

He told the jury he was a little hard of hearing, sometimes wore a hearing aid, but wasn't today. He testified he had murdered a man in a barroom fight in Texas and had been arrested for burglary for stealing beer from a bar.

Doreen made a face of distaste in Perez's direction, as if he had a bad odor. Richard kept moving. Being near Perez was making him very animated, and each time he moved, the chains jingled, rattling Perez, whose eyes constantly darted about.

Perez identified Richard Ramirez as someone he had met through his neighbor, Ruben Ramirez, three years before. He drove people around L.A., to Tijuana and back, for a living; he had met Richard at the Greyhound Bus Terminal and started driving him places. He took him to Tijuana a few times and drove him to meet Felipe Solano at a barber shop on Alvarado and Third.

Richard had told him that Solano owed him money, and he had waited in the car while Richard had spoken to Solano.

Perez had a girlfriend in Tijuana who needed a gun for

protection, and he had asked Richard if he knew where he could get one. Richard sold him a .22 for fifty dollars on credit. Perez in turn gave the gun to his friend.

Halpin showed him a picture of Richard's green Pontiac and Perez said he had seen the defendant driving around in it.

Halpin moved back to the gun, intent on putting it in Richard's hands. The prosecutor had Perez tell the jury about his two trips down to Tijuana to get the .22 from his friend. Perez said he learned of Richard's arrest over the radio just as he and Sheriff's Homicide men were crossing the border into Mexico. He testified he got the gun, gave it to the homicide detectives, and returned to L.A. with them.

Daniel Hernandez's first question to Perez was to ask if the gun he received from Richard was loaded.

"That's right," Perez said.

Daniel didn't elicit anything that could help Richard, until he asked Perez when he'd bought the .22 from Richard. Perez said he didn't know, that he had nothing to hide—that it was he who had told the cops about the gun. Daniel asked him if he'd said at the preliminary that he had gotten the gun from Richard nine months prior to his being arrested, which was clearly well before all of the assaults except Vincow. Perez said he didn't remember. Daniel showed him a page of the hearing transcript and asked him to read it. That done, Perez said, "I don't recall saying this. I couldn't say this was definite. I am—"

"That's okay. I will ask you some questions."

"I'm senile. I cannot remember that, okay? I don't know," he said contritely. Halpin was not happy with that answer. Daniel asked Perez if he had known about the reward money. Perez said he knew there was a substantial reward but had thought the amount was half a million dollars, not $80,000 split up among a few dozen people.

Perez was contrary and uncooperative with Daniel; he often acted as though he didn't understand Daniel's questions or had not heard, forcing Daniel to repeat himself. Daniel tried unsuccessfully to get Perez to admit he'd scouted locations for different thieves to rob.

Daniel said, "Mr. Perez, when you were convicted in Texas of murder, what kind of weapon was used?"

"No weapon, no weapon."

"What was the method?"

"Knife. Knife fight. Knife."

"Okay, so you killed the person with a knife."

"We had a fight in a bar."

"My question was, did you use a knife to kill a person?"

"Did I use a knife?"

"Yes."

"Well, how else . . . can I do it? I cut him, and that's all. I was drunk."

On redirect, Halpin asked, "Did you ever have a conversation with the defendant concerning yellow houses?" Daniel objected. Judge Tynan allowed the question.

"He liked to burglarize them. That's all," Perez said.

"Did he say why?"

"Burglarize."

"Burglarize them. Why? Why did he like to burglarize them?"

"Jewelry."

"All right, did he say why he picked Orientals?"

"Because they were easy, easy to do and no retaliation," Perez testified.

"Thank you," Halpin said. "I have no more questions."

Daniel stood and pointed out that Perez had said nothing about yellow houses at the preliminary hearing. "That's because nobody asked me," the witness said. Judge Tynan soon dismissed Jesse Perez.

The trial moved to the capture of Richard. The first witness called by Yochelson was Manuela Villanueva. Visibly nervous about being close to Richard Ramirez, she told the court how a man tried to steal her car as she sat in it at Indiana and Whittier Boulevards, but was chased off when friends came to rescue her. Yochelson called Frank Moreno, Faustino Piñon, Angela De La Torre, her husband, Manuel, and sheriff's deputy Andres Ramirez. They all told about their role that scalding August morning of Richard's last day on the street. Clark did what he could on cross-examination, but they each told the facts the way they knew them, and nothing he or any other defense attorney did could alter it to benefit Richard.

FORTY-FIVE

In the morning Halpin moved into evidence the items found in a black backpack Richard was believed to have ditched in the chase from the Greyhound terminal. In it were a pair of binoculars, gloves, a white plastic flashlight, and a black leather jacket. Halpin put LAPD officer Bob Rysdon on the stand, who, with his partner, was directed to the black knapsack in a back yard on Bestwick Street. Rysdon identified the items found in the backpack.

On cross-examination, Clark asked if the officer had found any kind of gun, knives, or cartridges, to which he said no. Surely, Clark reasoned, if Richard was the Stalker, his backpack would have been full of weapons. He felt confident the jury would see it that way.

LAPD officer Kaiser told the jury Richard had made a "voluntary statement" on the way to the stationhouse. Referring to his notes, he read Richard's alleged statement to the jury: " 'Why don't you just shoot me. I want to die. Now they are going to send me to the electric chair. I was being chased all the way from Olympic. I know all the killings are going to be blamed on me.' "

He stated that when Richard saw his mug shot on the sun visor of the car, he said, " 'That's my picture.' "

Officer Kaiser testified that when they arrived at the station, Richard was given the drink of water he asked for. Richard had then said, "The .32 automatic is in the Greyhound bus locker, and that is where I keep it. In my wallet is a ticket for the locker."

"That," Doreen would later say, "didn't have the ring of truth. It seemed too pat." Kaiser told the jury that his partner,

Andres Ramirez, had since had a stroke and retired. Richard let out a laugh and moved around in his seat. He felt sooner or later Satan would exact revenge for him.

Ray Clark was anxious to question Officer Kaiser. Richard had told Clark very adamantly that he'd never made any statement about the luggage ticket or the gun. However, Kaiser proved to be a difficult witness; he was sincere and testified in a straightforward manner, and Clark was able to do little to help Richard, who wanted to stand up and scream at Halpin and Judge Tynan, telling them the trial was a fucking farce, but he stayed in his seat and said nothing.

Halpin moved into evidence all the items found in Richard's Pontiac Grand Prix, which included a coffee cup with Richard's prints on them, a set of handcuffs under the passenger seat, a handcuff key, a pair of gloves, and blown-up photographs of a pentagram drawn on the dashboard. He also moved into evidence photos of the items found at the bus terminal: a four-pound can of "Maximum Weight," Duracell batteries, fingernail clippers, channel pliers, a blue bag containing a revolver, bullets of various sizes, a Remington ammunition box, a pair of Stadia sneakers (no Avia Aerobics), and other items.

Halpin called LAPD sergeant George Thomas, and he told the jury that he had been part of the LAPD Stalker task force. When he arrived at the Hollenbeck Station, he had put Richard in a small interview room, searched him, taken his shoes, and handcuffed him to a chair in the room.

He testified he did not give Richard a Miranda and had not talked to him at all, other than to ask his name. However, he stated that Richard had said to him, "What's today, sir, Friday?"

"I replied, 'No, it is Saturday,' " Thomas testified. "There was a short pause and then he began with the following. He stated, 'I want the electric chair. They should have shot me on the street. I did it, you know. You guys got me, the Stalker. Hey, I want a gun to play Russian roulette. I'd rather die than spend the rest of my life in prison . . . Can you imagine? The people caught me, not the police,' at which time he began laughing.

"There was a short pause and he went on to state: 'You

think I'm crazy, but you don't know Satan.' And he began laughing, at which time he began humming a song."

"Did you recognize the song?" Halpin asked.

"It was 'The Night Prowler,' by AC/DC."

Thomas went on to testify how he and his partner, Det. Joy, had purchased AC/DC albums and reviewed the covers and songs, hoping to find some clue that might help the investigation. Thomas said he had to listen to "The Night Prowler" eighty to a hundred times to get the lyrics straight.

"After you heard him humming 'The Night Prowler,' what did he say?"

"He stated, 'Of course, I did it. You know that I'm a killer. So what? Give me your gun, I'll take care of myself. You know I'm a killer. So shoot me. I deserve to die. You can see Satan on my arm.'

"And then he stated, 'Are you writing down everything I say?'

"It was at that point he stopped talking," Thomas said.

Daniel stood up to do the cross, and the jurors moved about uneasily. Daniel had Det. Thomas describe the function of the task force and the role he played in it. "And would you say that your primary assignment on that task force had been to go and find some records and listen to the lyrics?"

"That was one of my many, many jobs on the task force, yes."

Daniel tried to wedge some doubt into Thomas's credibility, but Thomas believed what he said and was very specific on details and times. He had taken copious notes.

On redirect, Halpin asked Thomas to tell the jury when the defendant had laughed.

"Referring to my report, after making the statement, 'Can you imagine? The people caught me, not the police,' he began laughing.

"After making the statement, 'You think I'm crazy, but you don't know Satan,' he began laughing.

"And after humming a short portion of 'The Night Prowler,' he began laughing. And after those three times were the only three times he laughed."

"Did he cry at all?" the prosecutor asked.

"No."

After a ten-minute comfort break, Halpin put Frank Salerno

back on the stand, and he told the jury that he first became aware of Richard Ramirez on Friday afternoon, August 30, and thousands of copies of his picture were distributed to every police agency in Southern California. Frank explained how the bag confiscated from the terminal was kept in the sheriff's evidence locker until Det. Buncrot had a search warrant signed by a judge. When they learned about the Grand Prix, which Ruben had told them about, Frank had Buncrot add an addendum to the warrant which would give sheriff's detectives the legal right to search the car as well as the bag. Frank described in detail every item recovered from both the car and the bag. He said he'd found red circles around the primer of the .25 auto ammunition in the bag. Similar cartridges were found at several crime scenes. The prosecutor showed Frank a pair of aviator-type sunglasses that Frank testified he'd found in the Greyhound bag. Richard had been wearing the same style glasses since the beginning of the trial.

Although Cindy Haden was not on the jury yet, she was feeling the stress of the trial as much as any juror. As an alternate, she'd listened to all the testimony and scrutinized the crime-scene photographs. The sights and sounds of Somkid and Sakina's grief and pain would never leave her mind.

Often, in the middle of the night, Cindy would wake up and make sure the windows and doors were locked. Having learned how open windows, front doors, and screen doors had caused so many innocent people to suffer, she'd never sleep with an open window again.

Judge Tynan had told the alternates early on that capital cases were extremely draining and distressing and that the jurors should take some form of exercise to help cope.

As Cindy walked through the halls to the elevator, she could feel people staring at her. She was not allowed to talk to the reporters, and they left her alone. In the elevator, she stood next to a Ramirez groupie she had often seen in the court. She had blond hair and a very shapely figure, and in a low voice she said to Cindy, "He's really very nice, you know, really."

Cindy didn't know what to say and remained mute. She

didn't want to do anything that could get her thrown off the trial. She viewed serving on the jury as her destiny, and this blonde wasn't going to put that in jeopardy. Cindy turned away from the woman, left the court building, and walked to the Nautilus gym on Ninth Street. She changed into sweats and spent two hours lifting weights. She'd been going to the gym almost every night and had never been in better shape in her life. As she worked out, she tried to block out the blood and the suffering and got lost in the mindless repetition of her sets.

FORTY-SIX

When Felipe Solano entered the courtroom, Richard's lips tightened. He despised Solano. As Solano was sworn in, Richard cursed him under his breath. Daniel told him to be cool. Halpin was ready to show where all the items taken from the Night Stalker crime scenes had gone.

Richard had a notepad he brought to court every day. He had taped a piece of reflective foil on the back. He began reflecting the ceiling light in Judge Tynan's eyes.

Solano did not speak English well and a translator was provided for him. He was sworn in and avoided looking in Richard's direction. Richard began reflecting the light into the translator's eyes, too.

Halpin wanted it known for the record that Solano had immunity from prosecution for the handling of stolen property, and that he had testified at the preliminary.

Solano told the jurors in Spanish that in 1984 and 1985 he had lived on Lavetta Terrace in Echo Park with his wife and two children. He identified Richard in court, "The man with the red tie and vest," as someone he had known during that period. He had first met Richard in the Greyhound terminal, when Ramirez had approached him and asked if he'd like a car to Tijuana. Solano said he did, and Richard had brought him to Jesse Perez, who drove Solano and five other passengers to Tijuana. Solano told Perez that he took cars to Tijuana because his own large car was a gas guzzler and this way was cheaper. Richard said he could get a smaller car for him at a good price. Solano gave Richard his number, and he called, "maybe five or six days later." He gave Richard his address, and within two hours he was there with a Toyota. He didn't have the title, and Solano didn't buy it. He said Richard asked him if he needed something else. Solano said a television, and one week later, Richard was back with a color TV, for which Solano said he paid $200 or $225. Solano said Richard had said his name was Ricardo Moreno, then later said his name was David. Solano didn't know his real name until he saw his picture on the news bulletin of Sheriff Block's news conference.

Solano told the jury Richard was back some three weeks later with some jewelry to sell, but he didn't buy any. Richard made a gift of a few pieces of costume jewelry.

"When did you see him next?" Halpin asked.

"I'm not sure when it was—because I went to Mexico, and when I came back, I think he was in jail, and when he came out of jail, he came to see me."

It was in 1985, but Solano said he didn't remember when, exactly. On this occasion, he said Richard brought some rings and earrings with him, which Solano readily admitted buying. He stated further that Richard had come back eight or ten times more and that he had bought jewels, gold, a VCR, a television, radios, and cameras. Solano sold some of the items he bought to Jorge Castro, a man he met in a pool hall. After the police came to his house, Solano had gone back to the pool hall and brought back the items from Castro to turn them over to sheriff's task force detective Sgt. Carlos Avila.

"What did you plan to do with the jewelry?" Halpin asked.

"Wait to get enough together so that they would be worth something."

"And then do what?"

"Maybe buy something for my family or to leave something for my children."

Richard continued to reflect the light at the judge and interpreter. Tynan waved for him to stop, but he continued.

Halpin asked Solano about the prices the defendant charged him.

"They were ridiculous."

"In what way?"

"Cheap!"

Halpin asked the witness if he thought the things the defendant sold him were stolen. "At first, no, but afterward I convinced myself because of the cheap prices."

Halpin asked Solano if Richard was the only person he bought stolen property from, and Solano said yes. Richard's face bunched into a snarl and he yelled in a bellowing voice, "Liar!"

The bailiffs closed in on Richard. He didn't get up, and the bailiffs stood at the ready. Even though Richard's legs were cuffed, they believed his hands were lethal weapons, and they watched him very carefully.

It was the kind of incident the reporters hoped for, and they wrote down the details of the moment.

Solano, obviously shaken by Richard's outburst, told the jury he had wired money to Richard in San Francisco on two occasions, in the name of Ricardo Moreno.

Halpin wanted to know how the defendant dressed.

"Dark colors."

"Do you recall if he ever wore a hat or cap?"

"Yes, on many occasions."

"Can you describe the cap he wore?"

"I think it was a baseball cap."

"Do you recall if there was any writing on the cap?"

"Yes. It said 'DC' or 'CD,' something like that or both of those things."

Early on the jurors had been told about the baseball cap with an AC/DC logo that had been dropped in the Okazaki/Hernandez garage.

The witness stated he'd seen Richard with a star of David in a circle drawn on the palm of his hand. The last time he'd seen Richard, he said, was when he'd come to his house on Wednesday of that last week, looking for money, saying he was hot and wanted to leave town. Solano testified he'd moved his family from the house when he'd seen the orange Toyota the police were looking for on the news. "Monday of that week I saw on the television a station wagon, orange, that he had used in a crime, and he had—he showed it to me on Saturday night."

Solano conceded he couldn't be sure it was *the* car, "but it sure looked like it."

Judge Tynan was becoming annoyed at Richard's shenanigans with the aluminum foil. He again waved for him to stop, but Richard continued.

The witness told the jury that he gave his son a bag of jewelry to hold and brought some of it to work. He said the police arrived at his house at 7:38 A.M. on the morning after Richard was arrested. He described how the detectives confiscated all the stolen property, after he'd given them permission to search. He stated he was then taken to the sheriff's office, where he spoke to Det. Avila in Spanish and agreed to recover all the things he said he'd gotten from Richard, which he quickly did, in a hurry to distance himself from Richard and to ingratiate himself with the police. He hoped if he cooperated he would not be arrested as an accessory or for receiving stolen goods, which did happen.

At the end of Halpin's direct, he showed Solano a photo of the green Grand Prix, which Solano said he'd seen Richard driving on several occasions. Halpin announced he was done and Judge Tynan recessed court until Monday, April 10, telling Solano to return then.

As soon as the jury and alternates left, Tynan turned his attention to the defense table and complained about Richard having a mirror in court, that he was shining it in his and the interpreter's eyes, and maybe even in the witnesses' eyes. He instructed the bailiffs to remove the mirror.

"I don't know what he's doing with the mirror, but certainly it should not be brought to court," he said.

Richard's "mirror" was confiscated, and he was taken back to the jail. In the hall, Clark told reporters that any reflections were accidental, and that Richard used it to comb his hair. The incident was reported in the papers the next day and picked up by the wire services.

That weekend an earthquake rocked Los Angeles. Richard was reading when the jail started shaking and trembling. He watched the ceiling, thinking it was going to fall down and kill him, and he welcomed death, for then he'd be in a place of honor, at the table of Lucifer and out of the hated six-by-eight-foot cell he'd been in since September of 1985. The quake passed. The ceiling didn't fall down. He went back to his reading.

Solano again took the stand on Monday. Daniel asked him if he had initially told the police he had not bought any jewelry from Richard. Halpin, objecting on grounds of ambiguity, asked for a sidebar.

At the bench, the prosecutor argued that Solano did tell the police he didn't at first buy jewelry Ramirez had, which was exactly what Solano had testified to. Judge Tynan suggested Daniel make his questions more concise and clear.

He said, "You are always trying to trap somebody. And we get into these discussions all the time. I know it is your style, and it really isn't very effective."

"You'd be surprised," countered Daniel.

Daniel grilled Solano on what he'd said and when he'd said it. The witness remained sure in what he said and it seemed the longer he stayed on the stand, the worse it got for Richard. Solano said Richard was the only person he had ever bought stolen property from. According to Richard, Solano had bought items from other thieves in the pool hall, one called Jorge, and another called Cameron. Solano denied ever buying anything from them.

After the lunch break, the judge wanted to know where Arturo was. Daniel said he didn't know, that he had beeped him over the weekend, but Arturo hadn't responded. Tynan said he was issuing a "body attachment" notice for Arturo, but would hold it until Wednesday.

Daniel asked Solano if he had spoken at the House of Billiards on Seventh to a woman who'd offered him jewelry for sale, a few days before Richard's arrest. Solano said he saw this woman the day after Richard's arrest, but he did not know her name, nor had he ever seen her before. Daniel asked him about the conversation he'd had with her. He said she'd been given his name as someone who bought things. He told her he wasn't interested, but the woman was insistent. He ended up telling her he was maybe interested in some gold chains, but she didn't show him anything that day. He told the court the woman then came to his house the next day. He had not given her the address and he was angry. When she left, he tried to follow her, but she lost him. The police showed up half an hour after she'd gone.

Daniel brought up a woman named Eva who knew both Richard and Solano. Solano was evasive and said Eva would sometimes help his wife with cleaning and babysitting, and he had once seen her talking to Richard at the pool hall, though he didn't know what their relationship had been.

Daniel asked him questions for an hour more. After some redirect and recross, Solano stepped down from the stand.

Sheriff's deputy Durazo took the stand next and stated he had learned that Solano had bought stolen property from Richard Ramirez, but they didn't have enough information to get a warrant, so the police had decided to try and sell Solano some stolen property. They had recruited the help of a woman whose name he didn't know. She "lived in the area and was known to use drugs and deal in stolen property."

They outfitted the woman with a wire, and five detectives had waited outside the pool hall as she unsuccessfully tried to sell Solano merchandise.

The following day, they had brought her to the Solanos' house, but he wasn't interested in what she had to sell. Solano then readily let the police in his house and gave them permission to look around, after he had signed a consent-to-search form. They didn't remove anything until Sgt. Yarbrough and Dep. Ghan, who were in charge of marshalling and inventorying all recovered property in the Stalker case, showed up.

Clark asked a lot of questions about the woman the police had sent into the pool hall and Solano's home.

Halpin told Judge Tynan he would be putting some witnesses on out of order because they'd come from out of town and had been waiting for days. Halpin suggested it might be a good idea to take the jury by bus to all the crime scenes. He knew they'd seen the pictures, but nothing was better to get a feel of things than actually seeing the place. Tynan said he would contemplate it and recessed court for the day.

Doreen visited Richard at the jail that day after court. A few of his groupies were there, but she ignored them. When Doreen's turn came, she excitedly waited for Richard to be brought down from his cell. She knew he was upset about Solano's betrayal and how Solano had lied to hurt him. When Richard sat on the other side of the glass and picked up the phone, he was fuming. He said Solano had bought hot things from a lot of people, not just him, that all Solano was after was the reward money, that he was a no-good dirty rat, that he'd burn in hell for his treachery. Doreen sympathized and listened to Richard with understanding eyes. He told her Eva, a professional thief, had sold Solano many things, which he, in turn, took to Tijuana and resold. He said his lawyers were trying to find her so they could show the jury what a lying creep Solano was.

He said in the end none of it would matter because he'd be convicted and sentenced to die. Doreen begged him not to talk that way, to have hope. Just the thought of Richard being executed made her faint.

FORTY-SEVEN

Halpin told the court the following morning they would have to move from the recovered property phase to the Avia shoeprint due to witnesses' schedules.

"You may proceed," Tynan said, and the prosecutor read into the record all the items relevant to the Avia shoeprint. These included business and sales records of the Avia company, photographs of the Avia Aerobic prints found at the Zazzara, Doi, Bell/Lang, Cannon, Bennett, Nelson, Khovananth, and Abowath residences, and plaster casts of Richard's upper and lower teeth.

The prosecutor put the data processing manager for Avia, Jeff Brewster, on the stand, and he told the jury how he fed into a computer, by style and number designation, how many pairs of shoes and what sizes were sold in any given region. He testified that the records for the period January to July 1985 indicated twenty-four pairs were sold in Southern California, and only one pair size 11 1/2. Halpin asked how many Avia Aerobics, model number 445B shoes, were sold in the San Francisco Bay area. Brewster said forty-one pairs, two of which were size 11 1/2.

That testimony, Halpin felt, proved there were very few people walking around L.A. or San Francisco with the 445B in size 11 1/2 who also burglarized homes and killed people for the fun of it.

Clark made a gallant effort and asked a lot of intelligent questions but didn't elicit anything from Brewster that helped the defense. There were two 11 1/2 Aerobics pairs sold in Southern California, and nothing Clark said could alter that fact.

Halpin called Jerry Stubblefield, the owner of Avia and the designer of the Aerobic shoe. He described in great detail the sole pattern of the Aerobic and how different it was from other models they manufactured. On cross, Clark had Stubblefield concede that their Coach model was very similar to the 445B, and that with wear and tear, the impressions the Coach made were similar to those of the Aerobic.

Stubblefield told the jury he had been shown the crime-scene impressions by the sheriff's department, and that he had identified the impressions as those of the Aerobic shoe.

Dr. Kenneth Moore, a medical doctor who worked in Pomona Valley Community Hospital's emergency ward, took the stand next. Yochelson had Dr. Moore describe Somkid Khovananth's injuries to her wrists, face, and legs, as well as the tears which were consistent with a forced entry, "sexual attack."

The prosecution then moved to Richard's teeth. Dr. Jerry Vale was called and he testified he'd gone to the jail on September 13, 1985, and taken a series of pictures of Richard's teeth as they'd appeared that day. As Yochelson showed him the photographs, Dr. Vale described them for the jury: the teeth were jagged and decayed, and teeth were missing in both the lower and upper gums. He stated further he'd done a gelatin cast of the lower and upper teeth that were used to make plaster casts. Yochelson had Dr. Vale hold the casts and describe in detail each of the irregularities in Richard's teeth. On cross, Clark asked a few questions about some crowns and fillings in Richard's mouth.

Dr. Vale was followed by another dentist, Dr. Alfred Otero, who told the jury he had been the senior dentist for the Los Angeles Sheriff's Department for the past nineteen years and had seen Richard for the first time on September 3. Richard had nine decayed teeth. Over a period of nine months, the doctor had repaired nearly all the decay to Richard's teeth, filling them with a compound substance.

Halpin and Yochelson, with the help of Carrillo and Salerno, moved into position displays of the Avia shoeprints which had been secured at the Zazzara, Doi, Bell/Lang, Cannon, and Bennett crime scenes. Halpin moved the displays and the plaster casts of the Avia prints into evidence. He called to the stand Gerald Burke, the criminalist from the sheriff's crime lab who had been in charge of analyzing and categorizing all shoeprints relevant to the Stalker crimes. He told the jury how difficult it had been to identify the shoe.

On cross-examination, Clark unsuccessfully tried to muddy the waters, but the facts were clear and worked against his client.

Halpin moved into evidence in chronological order the fingerprints that tied Richard to the case, including photographs of all the items found in the Pontiac and in the Greyhound bag that had Richard's prints on them and photographs of latent palm prints found on the kitchen sink of Clara Hadsall's home.

He called sheriff's fingerprint expert Hannah Wood to the stand and she testified she'd been a deputy twenty-three years, fifteen of which she'd spent in the Scientific Service Bureau. She had compared in excess of a million fingerprints, resulting in positive identifications of "thousands of subjects," and had testified in over 500 court cases.

Halpin had her identify Richard as the person whose prints she had taken at the county jail on September 9, 1985. Richard smiled at her; she frowned. Halpin showed her every print she had lifted from the confiscated items and she testified they all belonged to Richard. She was the last witness of the day.

In the morning, Halpin introduced into evidence the items removed from Ruth's residence in El Paso, the warrant to search the premises, and photographs of drawings of "666" and the pentagrams found in Richard's car and Mabel Bell's home.

Gil Carrillo was called and he stated he had fingerprinted Richard the morning he'd been arrested at the Hollenbeck Station. There was no cross. Halpin put Sheriff's Homicide detective Carlos Avila on the stand, and he told the jury how he met Felipe Solano on several occasions and was given items Solano claimed he'd bought from Ramirez. He'd also told him a gun they'd found in Solano's Chevy truck had been left there by Richard. At that Richard moved in his seat and laughed.

"I never left any motherfuckin' gun in Solano's van," Richard would later say.

Next up was deputy homicide detective Bob Perry. He stated he had made plans to fly down to El Paso on August 31 to gather information on Richard. Before he'd left, however, Richard had been apprehended, so his task had focused on recovering stolen property, especially Maxine Zazzara's eyes.

Using the phone number he had been given by Sgt. Yarbrough, Perry secured the address of Ruth's home. The phone number, however, was registered to the Ramirez home in Hacienda Heights. Daniel objected to Halpin's putting the address into the record, saying that the parents were elderly and ill. At a sidebar Daniel told Tynan that nothing had ever been recovered from the parents' home and they had already suffered much because of Richard's arrest. Halpin agreed.

Back in open court, Perry testified he went to El Paso District Attorney Bill Moody's office for warrants. With three El Paso detectives and his partner, he'd searched Ruth's home and confiscated a wooden box filled with costume jewelry she said she received from Richard. They confiscated it as well as numerous other pieces which, Ruth would later complain, belonged to her. They went to the parents' home but didn't search it.

"Why not?" Halpin queried.

"Primarily the medical condition of Mr. Ramirez and more so his wife, who was bedridden [and] under a doctor's orders not to be disturbed in that residence . . . I felt from the totality of the information I had that there probably wasn't anything there for us to rescue or retrieve."

"So did Mr. Ramirez ask you not to search his home?"

"He did," Perry said.

As Richard sat there, he wished he'd never gotten Ruth or any of his family involved in his lifestyle. Again, he wanted to tell everyone in the court to fuck off and get up and leave; he had to fight hard to resist the temptation. He knew the guards were hoping he'd do something like that so they would have a reason to lay into him.

The prosecutor moved into evidence a chart of the recovered property and called sheriff's detective Yarbrough. He told the jury how he had gathered all the items in Solano's home and put them in a locked room, next to the Sheriff's

Homicide office. On September 3, he and twelve other detectives numbered, photographed, and categorized all the items taken from Solano and brought them to the county jail for the property viewing on September 5.

On cross, Clark got Yarbrough to testify that fewer than twenty-five percent of the items in the September 5 lineup (1500 in all) were identified. That, Clark believed, clearly implied Felipe Solano had other sources.

Det. Michael Griggs next took the stand and told the jury he had been there when the .22 was recovered in Tijuana. It was loaded with five rounds of live ammunition. There was no cross.

Halpin introduced photographs of a jail cell Richard had stayed in, where he'd drawn pentagrams and "666" in his blood on the floor. Deputy sheriff Neulhad had been on suicide watch for Richard when he was first booked into the county jail's hospital wing, on the day of his arrest. He stated he saw Richard sitting on the toilet bowl with some blood in his hand, and that he noted the 666 and the pentagram on the ground. "I watched him with his left hand take blood from his right palm and write the numbers and that five-pointed star directly on the floor in front of him."

He testified he then advised his supervisor of this, and photographs were taken of Richard's artistic statements. There was no cross.

Salerno was brought back to the stand to testify he was present at Richard's arraignment on October 24, 1985, in front of Judge Elva Soper, when Richard had raised his hand to the court and yelled, "Hail, Satan," as he held up his right palm, on which there was a pentagram.

Daniel stood up for the cross and asked Frank if he'd ever seen a pentagram and 666 together at a crime scene, other than at the Stalker crimes.

"No. Never in my life," Frank said.

Dep. Daniel Laws, the last witness for the prosecution, replaced Frank on the stand, stated he'd been on P.M. watch at the jail's hospital wing and had guarded Richard for about a year and a half altogether. He stated that on October 30,

Richard had beckoned him to his cell, saying, " 'Laws, come here.' "

"What did you do?" Halpin asked the deputy.

"I went over."

"What did the defendant do?"

"He showed me two pictures of a homicide victim."

"Can you describe them?"

"The first picture was of a woman [Maxine Zazzara]. The photograph showed from the face down. She was nude.

"And then the second photograph had the same woman lying on the bed with her head turned away from the camera."

"Did he—did the defendant say anything at that time?"

"Not at that time."

"Did you ask him why he was showing you the pictures?"

"Yes. I did."

"What did he say?"

"He said, 'People come up here and call me a punk and I show them the photographs and tell them there is blood behind the Night Stalker and they go away all pale.' "

Halpin handed the deputy two photographs of Mrs. Zazzara and he identified them as the ones Richard had shown him.

Halpin now moved into evidence a four-page list, then announced, "The state rests."

Judge Tynan ordered a fifteen-minute break. As the jury and alternates got up to leave, Gil watched Cindy Haden stare at Richard and was thankful she had never been put on the jury.

When court resumed, Judge Tynan asked Ray Clark if they would be putting on a defense. Clark said he needed time to prepare, at least two weeks, as there were items that had still not been received by their experts.

Tynan gave the defense two weeks to prepare their case and set a firm court date of May 1 to begin.

FORTY-EIGHT

Richard didn't want to put on any defense at all. He had continually told his lawyers the trial was a circus and a farce. He refused to take it seriously or give it the dignity of putting on a defense. Clark strongly urged him to plead insanity and try to show the court through expert medical witnesses that he was crazy, but Richard told him he would never plead insanity. He had his pride, his dignity.

Clark and Daniel spoke to Ruth and implored her to try and change her brother's mind. She came up from El Paso to visit Richard that weekend, but even she couldn't alter his resolve not to put on a defense.

"If they convict you, the judge will sentence you to die," she said, her big brown eyes brimming with tears.

"I'd rather die than spend my life in jail."

"Any life is better than no life; if they execute you, Richie, it will kill Papa and Mama."

Richard stayed silent. Ruth began to cry in earnest. She knew when her baby brother made up his mind about something, neither flood nor fire could change it.

Against Richard's wishes, Daniel and Ray Clark went ahead and put together as good a defense as they could muster without their client's cooperation, support, or input. They hired private detectives to dig up more information on Solano, and they had found several other thieves who'd dealt with him. They had also located a burglar who used to do burglaries with Richard, Sandra Hotchkiss, who was also the woman the police tried to entrap Solano with.

On May 1, the courtroom was filled with press, spectators, and Richard's groupies. Doreen took her usual place. Phil

Halpin stood and told the court that a prosecution witness had lied and he wanted to make the court aware of it and asked to reopen his case to straighten the matter out. It would take no more than ten minutes, he said, though he was not quite ready to proceed and asked for a little time to prepare. Tynan ordered the proceeding to resume at 10:30 the following morning. He asked to see defense counsel without Halpin present.

The reporters gathered around the prosecutor in the hall. A witness lying in the Night Stalker case was big news, and they beseeched Halpin to tell them who it was. He refused to give any names but said the lies were not earth-shattering. The witness had lied "to protect a woman. There's nothing so unusual about that," he was quoted in all the Los Angeles newspapers as saying.

In the morning, after Clark and Daniel Hernandez had had a chance to discuss the matter, Clark told Judge Tynan he thought that, because the people had clear, accurate information that Solano had dealt with other thieves and knew he was lying on the stand, his testimony should be stricken altogether.

Clark told the court a woman named Sandra Hotchkiss had a wire on when she went to Solano's house and he talked on tape about buying items from people other than Richard Ramirez.

Hernandez said the people having information that Solano was lying could be seen as "subornation of perjury." He had spoken to Ms. Hotchkiss and she'd claimed Solano was wrestled to the ground by task force detectives and dragged into the house, where he was beaten and coerced into signing a form giving the police the right to search his home.

These were grave charges, and Judge Tynan was suddenly interested in what Daniel was saying. If it could be proved all the materials confiscated at Solano's should not have been allowed in as evidence, the prosecution's case would be weakened considerably. This could ignite a mistrial, or a reversal, if the jury convicted. When Daniel finished, the judge asked for Halpin's response.

"Certainly this is a good example of the incompetence

demonstrated by Mr. Hernandez. I am going to object. I'm getting *tired* of his ridiculous accusations."

Judge Tynan tried to calm him. "Mr. Halpin, why don't we just—"

"The man is an incompetent! He has accused me of being a felon."

"Rise above it," Tynan suggested.

There was, between Daniel Hernandez and Phil Halpin, a genuine intense hatred, and they argued back and forth heatedly.

Daniel said the only reason Halpin was reopening his case was because he found out the defense had witnesses lined up to testify and prove that Solano was a liar. The police and the prosecutor knew about it, yet they let him get on the stand and perpetrate a perjury. Tynan told Daniel to make his objection on the prosecutor reopening the case and he would rule on it. Daniel said he wanted a full 402 hearing to determine if the district attorney knew about Solano's other transactions and through the hearing determine if there was indeed subordination to perjury.

Judge Tynan ruled there would be no hearing, that the defense had the right to cross-examine Solano when the people reopened the case. He said, "As I've indicated before, I've had my skin abraded by Mr. Halpin, but I have never known him to be dishonest and I see nothing at this juncture that would lead me to believe that he has been."

The jury was brought in. Tynan told them he was allowing the prosecution to reopen its case for the purpose of calling back a witness, Felipe Solano. Richard glowered at Solano as he took the stand. Solano was not happy about being recalled. In the few weeks since he'd testified, he seemed to have aged ten years.

Halpin went right to the point and said, "Were there some things you testified to that weren't true?"

Solano said there were. He had known Eva Castillo, also known as Rosa Solis, since August 1983, and he had bought stolen property from her on three occasions. "But she had *given* things to my family as a gift a few times." Halpin asked Solano if he'd received any of the property identified at the September 5 lineup from Eva Castillo, and with certainty he said no, that he'd received that property from Richard

Ramirez. Richard moved about in his seat nervously and his leg irons rattled.

When Halpin asked why Solano had lied about receiving stolen property from Eva, he said, "Just because I wanted to protect her. She's a mother." He said he had also bought things from a thief named Monje, and from another who went by the name "Cuba."

Halpin showed photographs of confiscated items Solano identified as some he'd gotten from Eva, Cuba, and Monje, and the prosecutor said he had nothing further.

At 2:50, Daniel Hernandez rose to do the cross on Solano. He tried mightily to rake Solano over the coals, but Solano had already admitted lying to protect Eva, and no matter how hard Daniel worked, he couldn't undermine Solano's character or truthfulness any further. Solano had never been a credible witness—he was a fence who worked the denizens of downtown L.A., and his credibility was inherently limited. When Daniel asked him if he'd voluntarily let the police into his home, he said he had. After an hour on the stand, when Daniel's cross began to go in circles, Halpin starting objecting. Court was recessed at 3 P.M. Cindy Haden made wide, syrupy eyes at Richard.

Ray Clark and Daniel went to talk with Richard in the court's holding cell, and Richard repeated that he didn't want to put on a defense. Clark tried hard to change his mind, but Richard said no, got angry, and showed the fierce Ramirez temper, cursing and yelling and demanding, "No fucking defense, man! This trial's a fucking joke!" The guards had to intercede and stop the shouting.

After the break, Daniel asked Solano if he'd known, when he was lying on the stand, that Richard Ramirez was facing the death penalty. Solano said at the beginning he'd thought there was no death penalty, but he had since learned otherwise.

"But still you lied to protect a woman?" Daniel asked incredulously.

Solano repeated that he lied only to shield Eva. It was a point well made, and it was not lost on the jury. When Daniel finished, there was some redirect and again Halpin announced, "The people rest."

Ray Clark asked to approach the bench and told Tynan they were still undecided about whether there would be a defense. He asked for a little more time to decide and Judge Tynan gave them until the following morning. Daniel said they would need more time than that. Clark said if they did put on a defense, they would be doing it against Richard's wishes. He recounted to the judge the heated shouting match with his client, and that Richard was adamant about not putting on any defense. Daniel said he would need to talk to Richard's family and couldn't do everything in just one day. Judge Tynan relented and gave the defense lawyers until Monday.

FORTY-NINE

According to Julian Ramirez, his youngest son was in El Paso for the communion party of Ruth's daughter Gloria during the time he was supposed to have attacked Mrs. Bell, Nettie Lang, and Carol Kyle.

Julian told Daniel over the phone he would be willing to come up to Los Angeles, take the stand, and swear on a stack of Bibles it was true. Julian insisted he had a picture with Richard, himself, Mercedes, and his granddaughter in her communion dress standing in the front yard of the Hacienda Heights house.

When Daniel and Ray Clark went to the jail to tell Richard of his father's willingness to help, and about the photographs, Richard threw a fit, saying he didn't want to put his father through that. He yelled and screamed in a temper tantrum.

Ruth came up to Los Angeles with Joseph and they tried to convince Richard to put up a fight, but Richard yelled and screamed at them, too. Ruth begged him, but he stayed adamant and unmoving. "There will be no defense!" he said.

Monday morning Ray Clark, with large circles from stress under his eyes, asked Judge Tynan for an ex parte meeting in the judge's chambers with defense counsel and the defendant. Halpin objected, saying at this juncture the prosecution had the right to be privy to all proceedings. Tynan disagreed and moved the proceedings to his chambers, minus the prosecutor.

Richard was in a foul mood. When Tynan asked him if he wanted a defense, he yelled "No!" and cursed the judge, calling him a motherfucker. He told him that he thought the whole trial was "a scheme, a joke," and that he wouldn't take part in it. He said that he would put up a fight *not* to come to court. "They'll have to bind me and fucking drag me in the courtroom. I won't go."

Tynan said that could be arranged. He quickly saw the futility of trying to reason with Richard and ordered the proceedings back into court, after Daniel and Ray asked for a little time to talk with their client.

In open court, a motion to drop the sodomy charges in the Sophie Dickman matter got under way. Clark argued that according to Ms. Dickman, Richard was humping her tailbone, "and tailbone does not equal anus, which does not equal sodomy."

Halpin said, "In fact, as the court knows, penetration is not located in the definition of either rape or sodomy in the penal code of this state."

Clark and Halpin argued as Judge Tynan listened and then ruled the charges would remain. Court was recessed until 1:30, when Daniel and Ray Clark had to let the court know if there was going to be any defense or not.

As Richard was being led from the courtroom, he turned and faced the press, an angry snarl on his face. He said, "Media: sensation-seeking parasites," and was led from the court. The press was taken aback for a few beats, then hurried to phone in this latest defiance of Richard Ramirez.

Ray and Daniel returned to the holding pen and worked hard to convince Richard to change his mind. They both knew if no defense was put in, he would surely be convicted and given the death sentence. They didn't want that to happen; neither of them wanted Richard's execution on their hands.

Clark said it was stupid not to put his father on the stand. Daniel told Richard he had spoken to his mother and she had cried and begged him to convince her youngest-born to put up a defense.

That seemed to strike a chord somewhere deep inside of Richard. He said he would like to talk with Dr. Jo 'Ellan Dimitrius and ask how the jury might react if he didn't put up a defense, didn't take the stand and deny the charges.

* * *

When court resumed, Clark told the judge Richard had changed his mind and was now thinking about putting on a "limited defense," but he wanted to speak with Dr. Dimitrius. Reluctantly, Tynan agreed to give the defense until morning to decide what direction they were going to take.

Halpin moved into evidence all the documents he had relative to Eva Castillo's arrest and incarceration. Daniel didn't want them in and objected strenuously, but Tynan allowed the documents in and the jury would see them.

That evening Jo 'Ellan Dimitrius went to the county jail to visit with Richard. He trusted her judgment, thought she was very observant and knew human nature. Dr. Dimitrius advised him to tell his counsel to put on what defense it could and that it would be a good idea for him to allow his father to testify. Richard told her he did not want to take the stand and asked her if that would hurt him in the eyes of the jury. She said it would not, that frequently defendants in capital crime cases do not take the stand and that during the charge, the judge was obligated to tell the jury not taking the stand was not to be held against him.

The next day Richard showed up in court wearing all black. Daniel announced they would be going forward with a defense and told the court he was ready to make the opening statement.

Halpin had no objection. Judge Tynan gave Daniel the go-ahead to make his remarks. Arturo was now at the defense table again.

Daniel faced the jurors and, using a large chart of the evidence as the defense saw it, began systematically to go over all the counts, pointing out weaknesses and discrepancies. He said, often using his hands for emphasis, there was only one fingerprint, of "questionable origin," connecting Ramirez to Vincow, and that Maria Hernandez could identify Richard only tentatively. Daniel referred to the different guns that were used, but his remarks weren't completely clear, and a few of the jurors looked at him with some bewilderment. No one looked more bewildered than alternate Cindy Haden.

Daniel had difficulty explaining away the eyewitnesses. He spent a long time breaking down the credibility of Felipe Solano and Jesse Perez, describing Solano as "a downtown fence, a liar, a man who couldn't be believed about the correct time." He said Solano had recruited Richard and others to sell stolen items he'd bought at very cheap prices in the downtown area. He returned to Maria Hernandez, saying she had never had time to see her assailant because the lights had gone out. Richard took off his sunglasses, turned in the direction of his admirers, and smiled.

The judge interrupted him and suggested a lunch recess. Halpin asked for a sidebar, complaining that Daniel's statements of facts were off base and that he wasn't just making an opening statement, but was arguing his case. The judge agreed and warned Daniel to move along.

Daniel brought up a September 4, 1985, *Daily News* article by Arnie Friedman which clearly implied that Richard Ramirez was the Night Stalker and said that he would be in a lineup at the jail on the fifth. It had accompanying photographs of Gil Carrillo, Frank Salerno, Phil Halpin, and Ira Reiner. Halpin objected. There was no offer of proof that Maria or, for that matter, *any* of the witnesses, had seen the Friedman piece. Tynan agreed.

Unless Daniel had "eyeball witnesses" (i.e., people who had identified Richard) testify they'd been contaminated by the press, his argument was moot.

Tynan ruled Daniel could not make reference to newspaper articles in his opening statement unless he made an offer of proof that witnesses had, in fact, seen a particular article. Daniel continued with his opening. He said no expert witness for the prosecution had come forth to testify that the AC/DC cap left in the Okazaki/Hernandez garage definitely belonged to Richard. DNA tests on the sweatband could reveal that Richard never wore that hat. He claimed the defense had had such tests done and would put witnesses on the stand to say that the DNA in the sweat was not Richard's.

He moved to the Yu matter and said Duenas had admitted on the stand he could not honestly identify Richard as the person who'd shot Veronica Yu. Daniel continued that Jorge Gallegos could not have perceived Richard as the assailant, as the headlights were shining directly in the rearview window and in Gallegos's eyes during the entire incident. Daniel pointed out Gallegos had told the police officers on the scene that he could not identify who'd shot Veronica. Daniel added that the Catholic medallion found near Veronica Yu's hand, lying on the street, could very well have belonged to her assailant. It was no secret to anyone on the jury that Richard was a Satanist, and the last thing he'd be walking around with was a Catholic medallion. Daniel stated that there was evidence Veronica Yu was sitting in the car when she was shot, which clearly implied she had known her killer.

Concerning the Zazzara incident, there a fingerprint was found on the screen at the point of entry and that fingerprint did not belong to Richard or to either of the Zazzaras. Daniel mentioned the Avia prints found under the window but didn't offer a viable reason for their presence. He moved to the Mary Cannon murder and said she'd been struck by a milk-glass lamp, "and that weapon used against Ms. Cannon didn't fit any pattern."

Again, he mentioned the Avia print had been there without addressing how it had gotten there. "But more importantly, there was a light brown hair found in the bed that was not Richard's, as well as an unidentified fingerprint located on a green metal file in Mary's home."

Daniel made reference to blood other than Richard's, and at Ms. Cannon's, the police had found blood on the knife left on the bed and the lamp. He said, "And that when a lamp is struck against someone's head and broken, that the person holding that lamp could very well get cut and lose some blood onto that glass, onto that weapon."

Halpin moved about in his chair anxiously, having difficulty with Daniel's view of the facts.

The defense lawyer moved to the Bennett assault, skirted over the shoeprint and made reference to a beer bottle found in the home with a print on it that didn't belong to the Bennett family, or to Richard. More important, he said, were bloodstains the police had found on a blue sash on Whitney's bed, which was neither Whitney's blood nor Richard's. He said fingerprints found on the air conditioner near the point of entry also were "not Richard Ramirez's."

Daniel told the jury there had been testimony about gloveprints being found at crime scenes. But no gloveprints like those had ever been linked to Richard. He moved to the Bell matter and the open can of soda seen by Carlos Valenzuela, who thought it was odd for the sisters to just leave it lying around. "The criminalists," Daniel stated, "had collected that can and inspected it and tested it for fingerprints . . . and there were no fingerprints found."

About the Kneidings, he said both victims had been killed and there were no witnesses. He again offered no explanation for the presence of Avia prints. Instead, he told the jury about a T-shirt found at a construction site next door to the Kneidings' home, which had been photographed and tested by the police. It contained light brown hair similar to hair found on a nightstand in the victims' bedroom, which didn't match Richard's.

Daniel was sweating profusely now. He consulted his notes, took a few deep breaths, and told the jury that there had been Avia prints found at the Joyce Nelson murder scene, but he skirted over them, too, making reference to some brown hairs and fingerprints found in Joyce's home which did not belong to her or to Richard.

Finally, Daniel addressed the Avia prints at all the crime scenes. No such shoe had ever been found on Richard, even though all his things had been confiscated. Nor had a receipt for any Avia shoes been found, nor any witness who could say Richard wore Avia Aerobic shoes.

He said of all the gloveprints found at so many crime scenes: "No such glove had been located in Richard's belongings."

Daniel seemed winded, obviously needing a break, and suggested to the judge they take a recess, which Tynan agreed to.

Richard, Ray Clark, and Richard Salinas congratulated Daniel on the fine job he was doing. Halpin thought Hernandez was going in circles and grabbing at straws. Whatever might be said about Daniel's opening statement, he was impassioned and seemed to really believe Richard wasn't the Stalker.

When court resumed, Daniel brought up the murder of twenty-six-year-old Patty Higgins in her Arcadia apartment, wanting to tell the jury about her. This was one of the murder counts against Richard which had been dropped by the state. Daniel said there was a similar M.O. in this murder—the slashed throat. Serological tests done on Ms. Higgins showed that there was another party there "other than Ms. Higgins or the defendant." Judge Tynan asked Halpin his thoughts on that, and he objected on grounds of relevance. Tynan sustained it, saying he'd instruct the jury to disregard anything Daniel said about Patty Elaine Higgins.

The defense lawyer again reviewed all the inconsistencies he perceived with the people's case, then moved on to the Abowath assault, pointing out more brown hairs and fingerprints found on the premises which didn't belong to the Abowaths or to Richard. He said Mrs. Abowath had told police her attacker had light brown hair. He mentioned a private security officer who had heard the first police call go out and was speeding to the Abowath residence to assist when he ran into a man in a Datsun pickup truck who seemed to be fleeing the direction of the attacks. Daniel promised the jury this fellow would be testifying.

He attacked Jesse Perez, pointing out there would be testimony that Perez had received the recovered gun in Tijuana, "many months before Richard Ramirez's arrest, up to a year before," and he ripped into the credibility of Perez and his testimony.

He moved to Sophie Dickman and her statements that her assailant had brown hair and "was *not* Latino." He reminded the jury she had admitted on the stand having seen many news shows and read many papers about Richard's capture. "The evidence is going to show . . . that she was identifying the person she saw on television, rather than the person she saw the evening that she was assaulted."

He described how terrible the light had been when Virginia Petersen had seen her attacker. "There was no way that person could be seen." He pointed out that Chris Petersen, who was closer to the attacker, was not able to identify Richard as his assailant.

Daniel now tore into the lineup, saying there had been a lot of media waiting for witnesses, that there was an air of celebration, that "Ramirez was on stage." He said the witnesses waited in the halls of the jail together and spoke to one another, and that there was some communication from the people running the lineup about which person to focus on. He said Richard clearly had a shaved spot on his head, and it was reported widely he had sustained a head injury as a result of the chase on Hubbard Street. He would be putting Alan Adashek on the stand to tell the jury how concerned Adashek had been about this obvious head injury on the day of the lineup. Daniel talked about James Romero III, and said he was flown by helicopter from Orange County to the lineup and had been given rewards and plaques and even a motorcycle. The press had virtually crowded the streets and stopped traffic around the jail during the lineup. Daniel said of Romero's identification, "And this gentleman will testify that he felt obligated, after the awards and after all the congratulations, he felt obligated to identify Mr. Ramirez."

Daniel again reviewed his salient points, sincerely thanked the jury for listening to him, and ended his day-long opening.

Judge Tynan wrapped up the proceedings and the jurors stood to leave, weary and anxious to be out of the courtroom. The press didn't move, hoping Richard would show some new defiance, but only his chains rattled as the bailiffs led him from court.

The first witness for the defense was Dave Frank, a private detective with thirteen years' experience. A small, unassuming man, he testified he went to the Petersens' former home in Northridge and the present owner had let him in to take pictures, which Daniel now showed to the jury. According to Frank, it would have been nearly impossible for Virginia Petersen to have had enough light to make out the features of her attacker. Using the window as his focal point, he'd taken photographs from where he surmised the Petersens' bed had been on the morning of the assault.

On cross, Halpin tried to undermine the private detective's testimony and his pictures, but the angles were clear and it appeared it really would have been difficult for Virginia to be able to see the man who had shot her and her husband.

Clark told Judge Tynan he wanted to call either Salerno or Carrillo. The prosecutor said it was Salerno's day off and he was out of town. Carrillo was attending a function, but would be available the next day.

Monterey Park policeman Dan Romero was called by the defense, and Clark, using Romero's report, got him to quickly concede that Jorge Gallegos had said he could not identify the man who'd shot Veronica Yu.

"Did Mr. Gallegos tell you he never heard or saw a fight between the suspect and the victim?" Clark asked.

"That's correct."

"And did he also tell you that he did not hear any shots being fired?"

"That's correct."

"And did he also tell you that he would not be able to identify the suspect?"

"That's correct," Officer Romero said.

Halpin wasn't happy, for that destroyed any credibility Gallegos had. Clearly he had lied on the stand: he had testified he'd seen the shooter, heard the gunshots, heard arguing. Clark had Officer Romero tell the jury that Alhambra was a dark street with a lot of trees on it.

Phil Halpin stood to try and repair the damage, but this time the facts worked against the people. Officer Romero repeated under Halpin's questions that both Joseph Duenas and Gallegos had said they could not identify the shooter. On redirect, Clark asked if either of the witnesses appeared retarded, and Romero said no.

Next, the defense put Monterey Park officer Anthony Romero on the stand, and he stated he spoke Spanish and had asked Gallegos on the night of the crime if he would like to add anything to the statement he'd made to Officer Dan Romero, and Gallegos had said no. Halpin had no cross and the officer stepped down. He did not seem happy about his testimony helping Richard Ramirez.

Ray Clark asked for a sidebar. They had run out of witnesses and wanted a postponement for the day. Judge Tynan pointed out that Det. Carrillo was now here. Daniel said they weren't prepared to examine him.

Judge Tynan criticized Daniel for not being prepared. "I'm going to let it slide this time, Mr. Hernandez. I really don't want this to happen again, please." Daniel apologized.

In the morning Gil Carrillo took the stand. Daniel began with the AC/DC cap Gil had seen in the Okazaki/Hernandez garage and Halpin objected.

At a heated sidebar Tynan ruled that Daniel could question Gil about the cap if he did his questioning in a professional manner. "If you begin the usual meandering that I put up with for the last two, three years, I will probably change my mind about allowing you to or taking you at your word that you are simply laying a foundation."

Daniel didn't like the judge saying his examinations were "meandering" and complained, but Tynan was adamant. "Let's go," the judge demanded, losing what patience he had left.

Daniel asked Gil when he had first observed the baseball cap, and Gil again took the jury through what he had done the Sunday night he was called to the Rosemead condo. He testified he didn't recall whether he or his partner had first picked up the cap, but the criminalist had placed it into an evidence bag to be removed for testing after it had been photographed.

Daniel asked Gil what other crimes he had investigated that he believed were connected to the Okazaki killing. Halpin objected strenuously, asking for a sidebar. He felt Daniel's question could cause a mistrial because Gil would have to say there were molestation crimes, which the court had ruled could not be admitted.

Daniel said he had meant crimes Richard was being charged with and that his question was misinterpreted by Halpin. Judge Tynan warned Daniel he was not going to allow him to recross-examine Gil or any other witness, unless his questions were focused and to the point. Tynan said he'd been very generous with what he'd allowed in Hernandez's cross-examinations.

Ray Clark told the judge that another witness of theirs, who would be testifying against Solano, was afraid of retaliation. He asked if the witness could take the stand under an assumed name and not have his photograph taken. Judge Tynan said he had no problem allowing the witness to testify under an alias.

Carrillo returned to the stand. Daniel asked him questions about the photo lineup Maria Hernandez and Sophie Dickman had reviewed. Carrillo explained the surveillance that was placed on Paul Samuels, the man Maria had said most looked like her attacker. Samuels was arrested and his house was searched, but he was let go because the sheriff's office came to the conclusion that he was not their man.

Daniel next tried to get Gil to admit that something untoward had been done at the lineup. He asked if investigating officers at the lineup had discussed whether Richard's picture in the paper tainted the lineup and made it unfair. On grounds of relevance, Halpin objected—there was a sidebar; annoyed, the prosecution said the issue of the lineup had been litigated a half dozen times and to do it again was "ridiculous." Clark argued that if the police had had such a conversation, it was not irrelevant.

The prosecutor got into a heated argument with Judge Tynan and was asked to calm down. They broke for lunch.

After lunch, the prosecutor opened up volume 21 of the trial transcript, for February 25, and read the judge's previous ruling: Carrillo's state of mind and what he thought of the lineup and Richard's picture being in the paper were all irrelevant. Clark argued that what the investigators knew about the lineup's fairness was relevant. Halpin pointed out that other officers, not Carrillo, had been in charge of it. The judge agreed and again ruled Daniel could not ask Gil about what he thought of the lineup. Halpin seemed satisfied.

Ray Clark asked the court if they could recall Gil. They had other witnesses they had to examine because of pressing time restraints. Tynan said that would be all right.

"The defense will call Julian Tapia Ramirez," Clark announced. Richard's father entered the courtroom, looking confused. Tynan swore Julian in and an interpreter was provided. Richard did not look in his father's direction. He kept his head bent, busying himself with some papers. Clark asked Julian his relationship to the defendant.

"He is my son," Julian said. There was a heavy silence in the courtroom. "He seemed as much a victim as anyone else," Juror Choclate Harris would later say.

Clark moved to May 24 and 25, 1985, asking Julian if he knew where Richard was on those days. Julian testified he was in El Paso, that he remembered this distinctly and clearly because it had been the time of his granddaughter's first communion and there was a party. Richard had been there, he was sure. Clark showed him a communion certificate, which he identified as belonging to his granddaughter.

"And do you have any doubt in your mind that Richard was in Texas during the time that you just testified to?"

"No; I'm telling the truth," Julian said, with sincere finality.

Clark thanked him. He had nothing further. The prosecutor asked to approach the bench.

At a sidebar, Halpin said that according to the penal code, he had a right to look into the alibi and he requested Julian be held over until Monday, at which time he would do his cross-examination. Daniel said Halpin had known all along that Richard had been in El Paso then as it had been noted in police reports. The prosecutor said he had never heard of Richard being in El Paso in May of 1985. Clark asked for a recess so he could look for the reports, which Tynan granted.

When court resumed, out of the presence of the jury, the judge said he wasn't himself quite clear on when Julian was saying Richard had been in El Paso. Julian said he'd arrived May 23, a Thursday, more or less, and stayed eight days, which indicated Richard was out of L.A. during the Bell/Lang and Kyle assaults. The judge ruled that the people had a right to "a reasonable continuance to ascertain the correctness of the information testified to" and said Mr. Ramirez should stay in Los Angeles for the weekend so he could be in court Monday morning. He stated further that the court would pay for a hotel and give Mr. Ramirez a hundred dollars a day to cover his costs. Ray Clark told the court Mr. Ramirez was "taking care of children" and would like to return to El Paso for the weekend. He asked if the court would cover the round trip airfare, which was $450. The judge agreed.

The jury was brought in and Tynan told them Mr. Ramirez would be cross-examined on Monday and ordered him to return to court at 10:30. Julian said he understood and stepped down from the stand. Clark told the judge that two other witnesses the defense was going to put on, who were in the hall, were not going to be called, and Carrillo was asked to retake the stand.

Daniel asked if Gil had been aware "that Richard Ramirez had been portrayed on television and his picture [had been] in the newspapers," during the period between Richard's arrest and the lineup. Gil said he had been and Daniel tried again to find fault with the lineup. Gil told the events the way he knew them and Daniel was able to do little to assist the defense.

Julian Ramirez did not visit Richard at the jail after court that day. He flew back to El Paso to be with his grandchildren. They were the only source of pleasure he had left in life.

Monday morning, May 15, Ray Clark was given permission to put Rosa Solis's corrections counselor at Corcoran State Prison on the stand first. He told the court the testimony would be short.

The courtroom was packed with spectators and press. The senior Ramirez was news. He had sired the man who was being tried for the most brutal, frightening murder spree in California's history.

The correction officer Alex Lujan took the stand and testified he had gone to Felipe Solano's residence to verify that the address Solis had given was not bogus. There he had spoken to Solano's wife, learned from her Solis was not there, and issued a Prisoner-At-Large report. Clark was still trying to show Solano had lied, and that Halpin knew it and was trying to cover up the fact that Solis was one of the many thieves who had sold property to Solano. That was important for the jury to understand, Clark knew, if he was going to have a viable "someone else did it" defense.

Halpin's cross-examination of Lujan was interrupted because he didn't have all the pertinent files with him. Julian Ramirez was called back to the stand. Mercedes, who had returned with him, waited in the hall, sitting on a wooden bench and praying to Jesus that the jury would see the truth.

Julian mounted the stand; Richard stared down, avoiding looking in his father's direction. Tynan told Julian he was still under oath and Halpin asked Julian how many grandchildren he had, to which he replied six. Halpin asked the name of the grandchild who had received communion in May of 1985. Julian said it was Gloria.

When the prosecutor asked him to spell her last name, Julian Ramirez said "No," and looked at Halpin defiantly, his eyes hard and cold and unwavering. Julian did not want his grandchildren to suffer any more than they would already because of Richard's notoriety; they were young and they were innocent, and Julian wasn't about to spell Gloria's last name. Halpin sensed his resolve in this matter and understood, though he asked Julian when Gloria had been born, and Julian answered, "I don't remember." Halpin picked up the communion certificate and asked when Julian had first seen it. Julian said just a week ago. Using a calendar, the prosecutor asked him to put a red circle around the day his granddaughter had received her communion. He circled May 25 and stated that Richard had come to El Paso to attend the communion party they'd had for Gloria at his home. Richard started to move about in his chair.

"It was just the family," Julian said.

Clark interrupted, requesting a sidebar, at which he stated Richard was "going bananas" at the defense table. He didn't want any pictures taken of his father, which the court had agreed to, but Richard had seen the camera facing his father, and that had set him off.

The cameraman was warned not to photograph Julian and the proceeding continued with Halpin asking what date Richard had left. The father said May 31.

Julian said Richard had come to El Paso a few times in 1985, but he didn't remember the dates. He said Richard had stayed in a hotel the first night he was there in May, that Mercedes had gone and picked him up and brought him to the Hacienda Heights house, where he'd stayed the full week.

The prosecutor moved on to when the L.A. detectives had come to El Paso and searched his home. Julian said they had searched Ruth's home, not his. Halpin ended his cross, requesting Julian Ramirez be subject to recall. The prosecutor believed Julian was lying. He was sure Richard had been in L.A. between May 22 and 31.

Judge Tynan thanked the senior Ramirez, who in turn thanked him and the jury. As he left the courtroom, he passed within inches of Richard. He wanted to hold his youngest-born close to him, tell him everything would work out, and to be strong, but he did none of those things.

After a five-minute recess, Alan Adashek was called by the defense, with Arturo doing the direct. Adashek testified he had been practicing law for nineteen years, was a public defender in September of 1985, and had represented Richard

Ramirez. He was now a traffic court supervisor for L.A. County. He stated he and five other public defenders and two investigators had gone to the lineup, that they had sat in the audience to observe what took place and make sure everything was done fairly. He stated how he had seen a few witnesses waiting in the hall together and that ultimately there were so many witnesses, the police had needed two separate lineups. He described how a witness sat in every other chair in a room about the size of the courtroom, which was thirty-six feet by forty-six. There had been a camera, eight rows from the front, set on a tripod by the sheriff's people to document the lineup's correctness. Arturo asked if Richard's hair had been shorter during the lineup. The witness said it was longer now. Arturo then addressed the heart of what the defense felt was wrong with the lineup: "Did he—did he have any injuries prior to—did he sustain any injuries?"

Adashek said Ramirez had and that there was a bald spot on the back of his head. Arturo had Adashek tell the jury all the details of the lineup, then showed him a series of photographs which depicted the people in the lineup. He directed his attention to a photograph which showed the lineup from the rear and asked Adashek if it depicted the bald spot as it appeared that day on the back of Richard's head, and Adashek said it did and added that the bald spot was visible in the photograph, as well as to the witnesses at the lineup that day.

The judge interrupted them for the lunch break.

All the jurors except Fernando Sendejas left. The judge's clerk told Tynan that juror Sendejas had a problem. Sendejas wanted the court to know that he had gone to school with Alan Adashek. Neither Tynan nor Halpin had a problem with that, but Clark said he would like to discuss it with Richard.

Cindy Haden went to lunch with Choclate Harris and Phyllis Singletary. As they waited for the elevator to take them downstairs, they saw Mercedes and Julian Ramirez also waiting for an elevator, with reporters surrounding them and asking questions, which got no answers. Cindy thought that they looked like nice, hardworking people and was sorry they had to publicly be a part of the trial. Cindy could see clearly that Julian's heart was broken, that his son's troubles sat on his shoulders like a two-ton weight.

The three women did not get into the elevator with the Ramirezes, but they did discuss how sad it was to watch Julian Ramirez walk past Richard and with neither one acknowledging the other. Cindy would very much have liked to have talked with Julian, to hear about his son's childhood and perhaps learn about some root causes for Richard's path in life. She hadn't yet made up her mind about whether Richard was the Stalker, but he'd obviously been living on the wrong side of the law.

As the women talked, Cindy thought Phyllis Singletary seemed troubled and distracted. She wondered if hearing Julian's testimony was the reason, and asked her. Phyllis said it certainly had saddened her, but added she was having "trouble at home"—that her boyfriend had a bad temper and he drank and became abusive.

Cindy realized how hard it must be for Phyllis to go home to an abusive relationship after she had been subjected to all the gruesome testimony and terrible pictures every day.

Ray Clark, Daniel, and Arturo asked Richard if he minded having Sendejas on the jury, Ramirez said he did because Sendejas knew Adashek and his impartiality would be affected. He said he wanted him off the jury.

Richard realized this would probably be the last chance for Haden to become a juror, and he had come to believe, through what she told him with her eyes and sympathizing little smiles, that she would never convict him. He demanded his attorneys tell Judge Tynan that Sendejas was history.

After lunch Clark explained to Tynan that Richard adamantly wanted Sendejas off the jury. The judge had no choice but to thank Sendejas and dismiss him. He ordered an alternate be drawn. The clerk reached into the drum, drew a name, and read it out loud: "Cynthia Haden."

"Ms. Haden, you are now juror number 1. You will sit in that seat henceforth," Judge Tynan ordered.

Cynthia Haden got up, walked to seat number 1, and sat down, with a huge smile on her face, extremely happy and apparently not caring who knew it.

Finally her turn had come. Richard saw the smile and her

attitude, and he leaned over and said to his defense team, "She looks like she won the fucking lottery."

"She certainly does," Clark said.

"She'll never convict you," Daniel added.

Salerno, Carrillo, Halpin, and Yochelson were not pleased: it took just one holdout to cause a hung jury. Halpin shivered at the prospect of trying this case over again. Coordinating all the witnesses and exhibits had been a Herculean task—and he didn't know if he wanted to, or could, go through it again.

Doreen didn't trust Cindy Haden and felt no good could come from her being on the jury.

Cindy Haden had been born in Portland, Oregon, the oldest of four children. She had one brother and two sisters. Her father, like Richard's father, worked for the railroad, and, like Richard's father, he had a very bad, excessively violent temper.

"He'd often hit my mother in front of us, and he often hit me; would beat the shit out of me. He liked it quiet at the dinner table, and one time I talked and he actually threw a knife at me, nearly knocked out my eye."

Much of the responsibility of raising Cindy's brother and sisters fell on Cindy's shoulders, and she had aged before her time. "It was like I was never a teenager. I went from being a little girl to being a mature woman."

Cindy married at twenty-one. Though her marriage was a good one, she was not happy; she wanted something more out of life than just a good marriage. She didn't want any children of her own, perhaps because she had been a mother to her siblings at an early age.

After seven years of marriage, Cindy left her husband and moved in with another man she'd become involved with. He told her he wanted to move to Los Angeles, and that, Cindy says, was the main reason she hooked up with him.

She'd later say, "I always felt that there was some kind of important destiny for me in L.A."

She stayed in the relationship a while longer, then split. He had begun to drink too much and was getting pushy and abusive.

Soon after, she got called for jury duty for the murder trial of Richard Ramirez, and she knew that was why she had come to Los Angeles: that the Richard Ramirez trial was her destiny.

Arturo went back to his examination of Alan Adashek as Cindy Haden looked on from seat 1 of the jury box, the smile still on her face.

Arturo showed Adashek the photograph of Capt. John Jones making the "V for victory" sign, showing two fingers, and asked him if that represented what had taken place that day. The former public defender said it did, and Arturo said he had nothing further, feeling confident the jury appreciated the significance of the gesture.

(Capt. John Jones had held up two fingers indicating Richard's place in the lineup to the witnesses).

Halpin asked Adashek if he remembered speaking with him at the lineup about whether or not Richard's injury was evident, and Adashek said he didn't remember. To nearly every question the prosecutor asked Adashek, he said he didn't remember. He couldn't even remember whether or not he had objected to the bald spot on Richard's head.

Solis's corrections counselor retook the stand for Halpin's cross but said he didn't have the files because his superiors wouldn't release them. Annoyed, Tynan ordered Halpin to draw up a subpoena for the files and told Lujan to return to court at 10:30 in the morning with the files.

Arturo called public defender Roy Wallen to the stand, and for the most part, he testified to the same facts that his former colleague had. He gave Halpin a list of concerns the public defender had had, namely that the participants of the lineup didn't smile, showing good teeth; that Richard's head wound was exposed; that the young people at the lineup would say something to their parents, which might be inadvertently overheard by other witnesses; and that all the participants didn't have angular faces.

On cross, Halpin first said he had never gotten any objection sheet from Wallen, then looked through his file and found the objection sheet. He handed it to Wallen, who read it out loud for the jurors, proving Halpin had been wrong. The prosecutor got Wallen to concede nothing overt had been done to draw attention to Richard's head wound. He stated he hadn't seen any police officials indicating the number 2 but that public defender Judy Crawford, who also had been at the lineup, had come to him later at the office and told him she had seen policemen indicating the number 2 with extended fingers toward the witnesses.

Alex Lujan retook the stand and testified that Rosa Solis's real name was Eva Castillo, that she was now a fugitive from justice, and that the address she had given prison officials was not Solano's address, which Halpin was intent upon showing the jury. Solano was a strong link in the prosecutor's case and he didn't want it weakened by the jury learning that Solano had dealt with many thieves. Lujan also stated that Eva Castillo was supposed to have been deported after her release from prison, but she had fallen through the cracks and gotten away. She was, according to the record, a junkie, an alcoholic, a thief, and a prostitute.

Richard was bent out of shape about his father's picture being shown on the news, and he complained bitterly to his lawyers. He told them he didn't want his father to suffer any more than he already had because of his troubles. He was very agitated and walked back and forth in the holding pen like a caged panther.

After lunch, Clark complained to Judge Tynan about Julian Ramirez being seen on the news when the defense had specifically asked he not be photographed. He would be putting on other witnesses who would not testify if their pictures were going to be broadcast. The judge apologized and said he would have the bailiffs speak to the camera people. From now on he would make sure no one would be photographed if they didn't want to be.

Halpin complained to Tynan about the defense subpoenaing civilian witnesses, saying there was no reason to put them back on the stand after they'd already been grilled during cross-examination.

Tynan agreed and reminded the defense to clear any subpoenas they had for civilians with him. Carlos Valenzuela (the gardener who had discovered Mabel Bell and Nettie Lang) was already there, waiting to testify. The judge reprimanded the defense for bringing in a civilian without asking permission. Daniel apologized. Their investigator had misunderstood his instruction and brought Valenzuela to court. Clark said they would forgo calling Carlos, if the people stipulated that he had seen an empty can of soda, which was out of place, on the dining table, when he'd initially entered the house. Halpin agreed to so stipulate and the next witness was summoned.

Judy Crawford, a public defender from 1982 to 1989, was one of the seven lawyers who had come from the public defender's office to the lineup on September 5. With certainty and sincerity, she told the jury how she had been standing in the left aisle to note any irregularities in the lineup and seen Dep. John Jones hold up two fingers in front of the audience at the first lineup. She stated she didn't think much of it until she realized Richard was number 2; then, she testified, she noted a second sheriff's deputy, Tom Hyeboeck, hold up two fingers as he addressed the second lineup, and say, "Does anyone have any questions?"

Arturo then showed a photograph made from the police video of the proceedings the defense had received with discovery, and in it one could clearly discern Dep. Hyeboeck holding up what she referred to as a "V for victory sign." She didn't say anything to anyone until later, she stated.

After a comfort recess, the prosecutor went at her with a vengeance, asking why she hadn't said anything of these "illegal" improprieties at the lineup.

"There was nothing I could do," she said.

"Well, now, what makes you say that?" Halpin asked.

She stated the lineups were in progress and it was "already after the fact." Those answers didn't sit well with the prosecutor, and he made sure the jury knew it. Knowing laws had been broken, how could she not do anything until so long after the fact? he asked. She said she had tried to tell Adashek, but he was very busy and there was a lot going on. She had told him when they were leaving the lineup, but she didn't know what he'd done with the information, and it hadn't been her case. Halpin asked if she kept notes and wanted to see them, but she refused, saying they were "work by-products."

Cynthia Haden found Crawford's testimony hard to believe, but she saw the photograph of Hyeboeck holding up two fingers, and Crawford's certainty and resolve were unwavering before Halpin's cutting questions.

Halpin turned to the preliminary hearing transcript and had Crawford read into the record what she had testified then—she had not told Adashek about the fingers at the lineup. On that note, Judge Tynan released the jury for the day.

At a sidebar, Carlos Valenzuela was discussed again. The defense wanted the people to stipulate the dates on the newspapers that had first drawn Carlos's suspicion. Halpin said there was no proof as to what those dates were. Tynan agreed with the defense, ruling Valenzuela could take the stand and testify about what he knew of the dates. Halpin changed his mind and agreed to stipulate that the dates on the papers were May 30 and 31.

FIFTY

Felipe Solano, Jr., took the stand at 10:50 the next morning to tell the jury that his father had given him a bag filled with jewelry to hold, then returned with the police for the bag, and that was the sum of his testimony.

Monterey Park policeman Dave Corrigan was next and he further undermined Jorge Gallegos's credibility. He testified Gallegos's description was "vague and imprecise," and that he hadn't been sure if the attacker was Latino or Oriental.

Photographer Dennis Lee testified, at Ray Clark's urging, that he had gone to Alhambra Street, the spot where Veronica Yu had been shot to death, and with Richard Salinas's help, had taken 35-mm photographs there, as well as at the spot where Launie Dempster had said she'd seen Richard near the Doi residence in Monterey Park. Clark showed the photographs to Lee and the jury, but not much could be seen in them. Halpin knew the photographs were not objective. Film ASA, shutter speed, and f-stop could all affect a photograph's clarity, and in cross he made that clear to the jury.

Criminalist Gisele La Vigne was recalled by Clark. She had found, on parts of the lamp that had been used to crush Mary Cannon's skull, blood which did not belong to either Mary or to Richard.

Sheriff's criminalist Gerald Burke testified after La Vigne about hairs found at the Abowath residence that didn't belong to the Abowaths or to the defendant.

At a sidebar, Clark requested more time to interview Sandra Hotchkiss, who was in jail and was a very important witness for the defense. The judge gave him an hour and a half instead of sixty minutes for lunch.

Without Richard's knowledge or authorization, the defense team went to the holding cell in the courthouse where Ms. Hotchkiss was being held. She was serving a fourteen-year sentence in the California Institute for Women for a violation of a parole she had gotten. As a result of help she'd given police in the Stalker investigation, as well as in three other cases, her sentence was commuted. Back in court, Hotchkiss was called as the next defense witness. When Richard heard her name, he looked up, startled and surprised. He had told his lawyers he didn't want her called and they had gone against his wishes. He was furious.

Sandra was forty, thin, with dirty-blond hair, and had a jailhouse pallor. Through Clark's direct the jurors learned she used to "caper" with Richard, but had stopped because he was "too messy and amateurish." She preferred not leaving a mess in any of the homes she robbed, unlike Richard, who threw things all over. She added that Richard was never violent, and she never saw him with any weapons. She described how she had been cooperating with Burbank police and setting up fences. She had been caught burglarizing a Burbank home and the police told her if she gave up some fences, they would write letters to the judge. She testified Det. Knight had said if she gave up three fences, he'd personally make sure she didn't do any time on the Burbank robbery. " 'Three for one,' " she said he had told her; and she successfully had two men arrested who'd operated out of jewelry stores in the downtown area.

This brought her to the attention of the sheriff's task force when they decided to send someone to Felipe Solano to sell him stolen property, thereby giving them an excuse to enter his home. She stated she had known Solano before the sheriff's deputies had taken her to a downtown pool hall to try and set him up. Solano was a known fence who dealt with many thieves and even carried a jeweler's loupe through which he could often be seen looking at a particular piece someone was trying to sell. Sandra said she knew another fellow, named Huero, who had also sold Solano stolen property. One time she had seen Huero go after someone who had ripped him off with a tire iron.

Sandra had first met Ramirez in the Ye Hi pool hall. She had seen him try to sell jewelry that he obviously didn't know the real value of. Always ready to take advantage of an opportunity, she'd approached Richard and bought the gold chain, turned around, and tripled her money.

After that, they'd started burglarizing together. Part of Richard's problem, she sincerely told the jurors, was that he didn't know the value of jewelry and would take junk and costume pieces. They only worked during daylight hours, while people were away working.

Clark had her tell how she had met with Carrillo, Salerno, Yarbrough, and Ghan, that they'd put a wire on her and sent her into the Ye Hi pool hall to trap Solano. She had asked a woman who worked behind the counter to call Felipe, and the woman had used a black phonebook to retrieve his number. He'd shown up in twenty minutes. She had tried to engage him in conversation to entrap him, but he'd been wily and on guard.

The sheriff's deputies secured a gold chain from Robbery and insisted she go straight to Solano's house and offer it to him. She had told the deputies Solano would be suspicious as he knew she didn't have his address. They said that didn't matter; they did not have enough on Solano to get a proper warrant, and an arrest for buying stolen property would let them search his house.

As Hotchkiss testified, the jury listened attentively. She was the first person, other than family, who said she'd known Richard and the inner workings of the world in which he'd lived.

She didn't even get through Solano's front door, she said. As she walked toward his place, he pulled up in his car and asked her "Are you a policewoman?" Before she could even answer, the deputies knocked Solano roughly to the ground and put him in a choke hold. She was led away and taken home. She didn't know any of this had to do with the Stalker crimes, until she saw Solano linked to the crimes in the newspapers. She had then complained to Det. Knight, saying she didn't want to have anything to do with a multiple murder case and would not testify against Richard. Knight told her they had the "swirls and loop" of Richard's fingerprints at crime scenes and she would never have to face him in court.

Halpin had Hotchkiss tell the jury that she had overdosed on Valium and Methadone and was unconscious from October 26 to 31 of 1985. He had her tell them how many times she'd been arrested and grilled her until lunch.

From the defense point of view, Hotchkiss had illustrated for the jury that Richard was not violent, didn't carry weapons, and was a messy amateur, which clearly contrasted with the Stalker's M.O.—great strength, weapons, cunning, and severe jungle viciousness.

When Halpin began asking questions about what crimes she had committed with Richard and when, she requested a lawyer. Tynan was inclined to provide counsel for her and Matt Cooper was sent over from the bar panel to talk with Hotchkiss about her rights.

So time wouldn't be wasted, Clark asked Judge Tynan if they could interrupt Halpin's cross of Hotchkiss to accommodate their next witness, Chainarong Khovananth's sister, who had two small children and had to get back to them. Halpin objected about being interrupted and objected to the defense putting the sister on the stand at all, but Tynan ruled she could testify.

Debbie Piyarataphipat stated that Somkid had told her the morning of the crime that the perpetrator had dark skin and was black, with curly black hair. She cried as she testified, still devastated over her brother's loss. There was no cross of this witness.

The defense called sheriff's criminalist Melvin Kong and had him tell the jury that "Negroid" pubic hair had been found at the Abowath crime scene the morning of the attack, which didn't match up with Richard's. They had not been able to get a sample of either Somkid's or Chainarong's pubic hair.

After a recess, Cooper told the judge that Hotchkiss was afraid to testify. Her protective custody status had been taken away, and he had advised her not to talk about any of the robberies she had done with Richard in which the statute of limitations wasn't up or about a murder case she had been involved with. Tynan said he'd reinstate her protective custody status and Halpin agreed not to go into those crimes. Criminalist Kong was put back on the stand. He stated that brown hairs found atop the Kneidings' pillows did not belong to them—they both had gray hair—nor did they belong to the defendant. There were hairs found at the Nelson crime scene which did not belong to Richard, either.

Sandra Hotchkiss retook the stand on May 24. Cooper was not available, and a Harvey Sanford Perless had been found to replace him. Halpin was angry his cross-examination had been interrupted for so long, but he went at it with renewed vigor.

Hotchkiss said there was an audiotape of her approaching Solano as a result of the wire the deputies had made her wear. On the tape the deputies could be heard rough-housing Solano and coercing him into letting them into his house. When Halpin and Det. Yarbrough had come to visit her, the prosecutor had warned her not to "screw up his case." She testified she had committed twenty to twenty-five burglaries with Richard, from January through July of 1985, in Alwater, Los Feliz, Glendale, Montrose, and Santa Monica. She would check mailboxes and look at fliers under doors to determine if people were away, and she would either use lock picks or a "Lloyds" (a stiff piece of bendable plastic) to gain entry. When Halpin asked why she'd stopped working with Richard, she said, "It just wasn't smooth, or I would get, like . . . I would get nervous and scared myself and just—end up starting to toss when it should have just went smooth." She said they got into arguments about time limits, noise, and his leaving with the car one time when he was supposed to stay put. Hotchkiss denied telling Yarbrough that she had seen Richard write on a window with lipstick.

"Do you know," Halpin asked, "if during any of those twenty-five robberies the defendant had a gun secreted on his person?"

"Not to my knowledge, I don't."

Halpin's cross lasted to the end of the day, when Clark began objecting that the prosecutor was becoming repetitious. Clark's redirect was postponed until court resumed on June 5, giving everyone a needed break.

During the court hiatus Richard was kept in his cell at the county jail; the only time he was let out was to shower twice a week and for visits. His visitors became a topic of discussion among Richard's jailors and the press. So many women were coming to see him, the jail had to put limits on the number of visitors he was allowed.

Doreen didn't like having to compete more and more for Richard's time and attention. She gave her would-be competitors dirty looks and refused even to talk to any of them. Their interest in Richard, she felt, was for all the wrong reasons, unlike hers, which was all for Richard—his welfare, comfort, and protection.

At this time actor Sean Penn had been sentenced to thirty-two days in the Los Angeles County Jail for punching out a photographer. Because of his celebrity status he had to be kept in protective custody and was lodged in the cell next to Ramirez. At the time he was still married to Madonna and when she came to visit Sean, she saw Ramirez as she stepped off the elevator. When Sean was brought to the visiting booth, the first thing she said to Sean was, "Who's that good-looking guy?"

Sitting down, smiling mischievously, Sean said, "That good-looking guy is the Night Stalker, . . . wanna meet him?"

"Gives me the goose bumps," Madonna said—"but yeah, I'd like to meet him," she joked.

"I don't think so," he said, laughing.

During the course of Sean's stay in the jail, Ramirez asked Penn for his autograph.

Sean wrote:

Dear Richard:
   It's impossible to be incarcerated and not feel a kinship with your fellow inmates. Well, Richard, I've done the impossible. I feel absolutely no kinship with you. Sean Penn

Richard wrote back:

Dear Sean:
   Stay in touch and hit 'em again. Richard Ramirez, 666.

Penn said Ramirez masturbated excessively. "He was like an animal in heat. He had pictures of his victims on his cell walls. He kept them up with toothpaste."

When court resumed on the fifth, Sandra Hotchkiss took the stand for the entire morning. She stated that neither she nor Richard ever used gloves on any of their heists, though they sometimes covered their fingertips with nail polish.

During the afternoon's redirect at Clark's urging, she testified she often saw guns being sold and traded at the Brunswick pool hall; however she had never seen Richard with any. She said because of her cooperation with the police she had been shot at twice: once outside the Brunswick pool hall, and once in front of downtown's Cameo Hotel. She was not hit either time.

On recross, Halpin asked, "While committing those burglaries [with Richard], you did not wear gloves?"

"No."

"Never wore gloves?" he pressed.

"No," she repeated, looking directly at the prosecutor.

"Did the defendant?"

"No."

"Ever?"

"No," she insisted, and explained that she had shown Richard how to hold things—by their side and on an angle—so as not to leave any prints. She mentioned her efforts to contact district attorney Ira Reiner to tell him how Solano had been roughed up, but her efforts had been fruitless.

When Hotchkiss left the stand, Gil, Frank, Halpin, and even Richard were glad to see her go. Richard still strongly believed she should have never been called, and he was still angry at Clark for putting her on the stand without his permission.

"I didn't even know the broad," he'd later say angrily.

In regard to the Veronica Yu murder, Dr. Susan Selser was resummoned to testify. Halpin objected to her being called, saying she had already been cross-examined extensively. Clark complained that he had not yet come on board when she'd been cross-examined. After an exchange of pointed remarks, Clark was allowed a few questions about trajectory.

Dr. Selser testified that Veronica had been shot twice, that there was gunpowder around one of the wounds, and that the bullet had gone from left to right, which contradicted what Jorge Gallegos had testified.

Halpin cross-examined her extensively, but no amount of questioning could change the trajectory of the bullet and the gunpowder around the wound. Clearly, unless Veronica was sitting in the car backward, she'd been shot from the passenger side of the car.

After Dr. Selser, LAPD criminalist Michelle Le Piesto was recalled. Before she could be asked any questions, Halpin objected on the grounds she, too, had already been lengthily cross-examined. Tynan agreed and told Clark to go to the record and stop recalling people just to ask the same questions.

After lunch, Clark told Tynan the defense wanted to call Le Piesto to ask her about hairs at the Lang/Bell scene, and would make an offer of proof to do so. They also wanted to recall Det. John Yarbrough to ask him about the description Sakina Abowath had given police the morning of the assault.

Halpin again complained, but Tynan decided to give the defense some latitude, warning the defense to be "speedy and not redundant."

The animosity between Halpin and Hernandez was becoming more apparent every day and stood between the defense and prosecution tables like a thick, impenetrable wall topped with razor-sharp barbed wire.

Judge Tynan called the jury out and Clark, distant and aloof from the acrimony between Daniel and Halpin, began his direct. From Le Piesto the jury learned that she had booked into evidence bloody pillows, electrical cord with human hairs stuck to it, bloody sheet and bed pad, and a long list of other items from the Bell/Lang crime scene. Clark had no more questions of Le Piesto and there was no cross. The defense knew if Richard's hair or blood had been on any of the items collected by Le Piesto, Halpin would have used it against Richard.

John Yarbrough was again summoned to the stand and Clark asked him how Sakina had described her tormentor. Reading from his notes, Yarbrough said, "Male, possibly Caucasian with Latin features, but not Negro, tall, thin, with receding chest, light brown or dishwater blond hair that had some curl to it, approximately twenty-five to thirty years old." All but the hair fit Richard. Yarbrough continued, "She recalled no accent, but said he was light complexioned, with a yellow tint to his skin color. She described his teeth as wide, but didn't recall any gaps in his teeth . . . The only odor she recalled was his shirt area, and it was stale sweat . . . When he walked it sounded heavy—like boots. She remembered after the rape, the suspect pulling on boots as opposed to lace shoes."

Knowing boots didn't fit in with the prosecutor's case, Clark said he had nothing further and sat down.

On cross, Halpin established that Yarbrough had first interviewed Sakina at the hospital where she was suffering from shock, then the next day, at her friend's home. Halpin established that Yarbrough had police artist Marlon Coleman with him and that Coleman had done a sketch based on Sakina's description, which did resemble Richard.

Halpin had little cross, and Clark again went at Yarbrough, asking him if Mabel Bell kept a diary. The detective said she had been making several entries a day until May 29.

On recross, Halpin asked Yarbrough when Mrs. Bell's electrical clock had stopped.

"5:29 A.M. on May 30," he said.

Which meant, if Julian was telling the truth, Richard was in Texas.

The trial resumed on July 9, with Judge Tynan announcing the proceedings would be canceled for Monday so that alternate juror Bonita Smith could attend a funeral; that meant a three-day weekend, and no one on the jury had any complaints.

Gisele La Vigne was recalled by Clark. He first apologized for not asking her all the questions he had the first time she'd testified, and proceeded to have her tell the jury all the items she had recovered from the Bennett crime scene. He then had her explain the facts known about blood in general, and state that Richard's blood type had not been present at the Bennett, Kneiding, or Cannon residences.

Steve Renteria was called and asked if a rape test had been done on Sakina Abowath; he said there had been one and the tests on the semen recovered proved to be "inconclusive." He did find a two-plus band (a genetic marker), which did not belong to Richard.

As Cindy Haden got up to leave at the end of the day's court session, Richard took off his sunglasses and stared at her. It seemed he was talking to her with his eyes, telling her to acquit him; telling her he'd give her what she most craved from a man.

"His eyes gave her goose bumps all over," she'd later relate.

As she went down in the elevator, she realized that Doreen and some of Richard's admirers were also in the elevator. She could understand why these women were attracted to Richard. "The guy was fiercely good-looking and dangerous. Since the beginning of time women have never been able to resist that combination."

The defense called Dr. Werner Spitz, who stated he had studied the morgue photographs of all fourteen murders in the case. In his opinion, Veronica Yu was shot inside her car, and going by body and ambient temperatures, Jennie Vincow had died two hours before she'd been found.

Not happy with this witness, Halpin demanded to know why the doctor was so sure Veronica had been shot from inside the car. Spitz replied that the wound was on the right side of the chest and the bullet's trajectory left-to-right. He then told the jury how he had calculated Vincow's time of death.

Thirteen had always been a very unfortunate number for Richard—he knew it and was very leery of the number. He was being tried in Department 113 on the thirteenth floor for thirteen murders. When court resumed, it was the thirteenth of July and he was sure something bad would happen. A little after the jury settled back into their seats, the rear door opened and Zeena LaVey with Nicholas Shreck and five others entered the courtroom. Walking in single file, all grim-faced and wearing black, they took seats on Richard's side of the courtroom. Zeena wore blood-red lipstick and smiled seductively at Richard when he turned in their direction. They wanted Richard and the world to know that they were his supporters, that he was not alone in the world. The jurors stared at the six Satanists with guarded, wary curiosity. They all knew the power "charismatic characters" had over people—Charles Manson, for example—and were concerned for their safety.

It was, a juror would say, a scary thing, sitting in judgment of Richard Ramirez with six Satanists all giving them the evil eye. "Who knew, they could've been casting spells . . . I mean, we are in Southern California here, and this guy has become the poster boy for the church of Satan."

Daniel Hernandez announced the defense wanted to call invalid Lillian Doi to the stand, but needed the court's permission. When asked why they wanted to call Mrs. Doi, Daniel said because of the description she had given to the police the morning of the attack.

Halpin was beside himself. He called this another example of Daniel's "inattention." The police had trouble communicating with Lillian and this issue had been gone over many times. He had spoken to Mrs. Doi himself and she could only barely make herself understood—though, he added, she had identified Ramirez at the September 5 lineup.

Tynan sided with the defense and said if they wanted Mrs. Doi on the stand, they should draw up a subpoena. He did not want to be reversed for unfairly hamstringing defense to create reasonable doubt.

There was a lunch recess and when court resumed, Clark said they wouldn't be calling Mrs. Doi. Clark said they had no more witnesses for the day.

In the morning, the defense called paralegal Richard Salinas, who explained he had taken the videotape of the lineup which they'd received as part of discovery to the Video Lab in Burbank and had the lab make photographs from the tape of the instance where Det. John Jones had held up two fingers. Clark now showed the photograph to the jury, who could clearly see the sheriff's detective with two extended upright fingers.

At a sidebar, Clark again said they were out of witnesses, that their next witness would probably be on for the whole day, and he asked the court to be recessed. Tynan was not happy; he wanted this case over with. Halpin asked the judge to quash a subpoena the defense had issued for James Romero, who had seen the orange Toyota in Mission Viejo.

The defense wanted Romero on the stand so the jury could see he had received rewards even before Richard was arraigned, let alone convicted. Halpin warned if they put Romero on the stand he would, under section 1101 of the evidence code, bring in the attack on Carns and the fingerprint in the orange Toyota. Judge Tynan warned that if Romero was called, the defense would be "opening up a can of worms" and he wouldn't be able to help them. Clark said they'd like to rethink their strategy.

The defense's witness, Dr. Linda Loftus, took the stand. She was a professor at the University of Washington who had written fifteen books on human memory and the processes eyewitnesses go through under stressful situations. She stated she often worked for the IRS, the Justice Department, and the U.S. Secret Service. Her credentials were quite impressive.

Under Clark's direct, she told the jury the human brain was not like a camera and did not retain exactly what had transpired. She said there were three stages to memory, the "acquisitive stage," in which events occur and register in the brain. The period after the event was over and some time had passed was referred to as the "retention stage." Then there was the "retrieval stage," in which an individual tries to recall information—tries to make identifications, tries to answer specific questions.

Clark wanted to know if stress affected memory. She said it did and that she had done many tests at the University of Washington in which a group of students were shown two different versions of the same film. In one version there was foul language and violence, and in the other no violence or foul language. "Overwhelmingly," she testified, the students remembered fewer details in the violent version. She said it was human nature to look away from ugly situations. Using an apparatus that attaches to the pupil of the eye, researchers had found that someone held at gunpoint looked much more at the gun than at the person who was holding it. A gun had been used in every nonfatal attack Richard was accused of.

She said of the gun: "It caused a reduced ability to remember some of those details."

Another factor that affected retention was passage of time, after which the mind begins to become vulnerable to "post-event information" which causes a "contamination or distortion" of what really took place. Additional factors that influenced post-event information were witnesses talking to one another or witnesses being asked leading questions.

She stated, "When witnesses are exposed to media coverage, newspapers, television . . . these are opportunities for new information to become available to a witness, that has the potential for distorting or changing the witness's recognition."

She then testified that when people of different races try to identify one another, an inordinate amount of mistakes are made.

When Clark asked if the media had an effect on memory, Halpin's objection that it was beyond her realm of expertise was sustained. Clark asked her if she had done any tests on media exposure and memory. She said, "They, witnesses, will adopt—what they've been exposed to in the media and claim that they experienced it themselves."

Halpin didn't like Dr. Loftus, feeling she was a hired gun who was helping a sadistic murderer, which he didn't try to hide from the jury. But she proved to be difficult to cross. She was sure of herself, had literally hundreds of experiments and volumes of research under her belt, and looked directly at the jurors when she spoke. When he asked her how much she was being paid for her testimony, Ray Clark objected. Tynan said he would consider the objection and ordered Halpin to continue. The prosecutor kept her on the stand right up to the lunch recess, grilled her, but did little to alter her opinion or testimony.

When they came back from lunch, Clark said they wouldn't be calling Romero, and Dr. Loftus returned to the stand. The judge ruled the people could ask the amount Loftus was being paid. Halpin, aggressive and unfriendly, proceeded to cross-examine Loftus the rest of the day; it seemed the more questions he asked her, the more bona fide and sure her position became. The jury was clearly becoming tired of Dr. Loftus, but Halpin kept banging away at her and the credibility of her work.

In the morning, Dr. Loftus again took the stand and the prosecutor asked one very salient question: he wanted to know if constantly telling someone not to look at you will cause that person to, in fact, look. "Like," he said, "telling someone not to think of an elephant, when of course they will."

The doctor agreed, saying that it would be human nature for the pupil to move in the direction of a person giving such an order.

On redirect, Clark asked her if the purpose of all the tests she had conducted was "to ascertain the truth." She said it was and soon stepped down from the stand.

After a short recess, Clark announced they had one more witness, and would then rest. The lawyers discussed schedules for their respective rebuttals and closing arguments and court was recessed.

FIFTY-ONE

The people's first rebuttal witness was Bob Knight, of the Burbank Police Department, the man responsible for Sandra Hotchkiss's becoming involved with the case. He testified he had heard the sheriff's department needed someone who had connections in the downtown area and had suggested Sandra. He told the jury that he had offered her the "three-for-one" deal and related how she'd delivered several fences and testified against them in court. He knew her to be, he said, a thief, a drug addict, and a prostitute.

On cross, however, he testified that Sandra was "honest and reliable" in all her dealings with him.

Halpin called Felix Estrada, another LAPD detective. He stated he had sent Sandra Hotchkiss into two jewelry shops with stolen property, wearing a wire, and that she had entrapped the store owners—known fences—whom he'd arrested. He had spoken to her about Richard Ramirez and she had said she hadn't known him—or Felipe Solano.

Most of the jurors found that hard to believe. From everything they'd already heard, they knew all three of them "hung out" in the downtown area and were involved in burglaries.

Estrada further stated that he had gone to visit her in jail in 1986, after she'd called him. She asked him for help with a case and for some money, but when he wasn't forthcoming with either, she said she'd go to the defense, "to see if they'd pay her."

He summarized that she had been "reliable" in bringing him information—but he had known her to lie.

John Yarbrough was called to the stand. He contradicted Estrada and said Hotchkiss had told him she'd known

Ramirez, that she had met him in front of the California Hotel and had shot cocaine with him, and that he was known as *"Flaco"* (Skinny) on the street. He stated Hotchkiss also said Ramirez lived with two lesbians, one named Baca. He then went on to confirm much of what Hotchkiss had said on the stand. When Halpin asked him if she had told him Solano had been jumped by sheriff's detectives, he said "Absolutely not!"

He testified she'd told him she was in a car with Richard in Aliso Village when he'd hit a drunken man and killed him. When he checked police records, he did in fact find a hit-and-run killing which corresponded with the date and time Hotchkiss had said it had occurred. When Yarbrough stepped down from the stand, court recessed for the day.

In the morning, rebuttal witness James Njavro from the medical examiner's office testified that coroner's photographer Steve Hansen had removed Veronica Yu's body from the crypt and photographed it, both with clothes on and nude. Halpin showed these pictures to Njavro and he identified them as the ones Hansen had taken. Halpin's objective was to prove that Veronica had not been shot inside the car and the photographs would remind the jury of the terrible, senseless brutality of this murder.

Richard turned to Daniel and said, "I bet you some of those goons at the morgue have sex with the bodies." Daniel laughed.

Halpin called Monterey Park police officer Ron Endo, and he told the jury, again, how he had been the first police official at Veronica's side and had given her CPR. He then identified photographs of how the body had been found, lying in the street rather than in the car, which is where, Halpin wanted the jury to believe, she should have been found if she'd been shot in the car.

On cross, Endo conceded he had never examined any of Veronica's wounds, which made his testimony moot, Clark felt.

Alan Yochelson called Steve Renteria, who testified there was no blood at all on the T-shirt found at the construction site next to the Kneiding residence. He was the last witness that day.

* * *

A little after 10 A.M. the next morning, the people called a few more rebuttal witnesses—the most important of whom was Dr. Peter Leung, the dentist who had worked on Richard's teeth in 1985. To show that Dr. Leung had worked on Richard, Halpin put Dr. Gerald Vale on the stand, who stated he had examined Richard at the county jail in September of 1985, had x-rayed his teeth, and had taken plaster casts of them, which were shown to the jury.

Dr. Leung was sworn in with the help of a Taiwanese interpreter and told the jury he had worked on Richard on March 8, March 17, May 21, May 23, and May 30. He described the kind of work he had done and the costs, saying that Richard, who had given the name Richard Mena, had paid cash.

Halpin was sure the jury would realize that if Richard was in a dentist's chair on May 30, it proved he was in L.A. and had the opportunity to assault Mabel Bell, Nettie Lang, and Carol Kyle.

Yochelson showed Dr. Leung the X rays Gerald Vale had taken at the jail and the doctor positively identified them as Richard's.

Sheriff's deputy John Jones was called by the people, and he stated he'd been at the lineup on September 5, that he'd brought Minnie Kelsey there. She was in a wheelchair as a result of an intruder breaking into her home and beating her. She had a crushed larynx and broken leg bones. Jones said she had not identified Ramirez. When asked if he had held up two fingers, as the public defenders had testified, he emphatically said no. After Jones's testimony, court was adjourned for the weekend.

Monday morning, Clark told Judge Tynan at a sidebar that the defense would like to call a rebuttal witness, but the witness was coming up from El Paso and would not be able to leave for a week. Tynan refused to halt the proceedings that long, saying the defense had had plenty of time to find witnesses. Reluctantly he gave them until noon the following day.

Finally, the people's last witness was called. Dave Hancock had worked as a reporter for the *El Paso Times*. He stated he had gone to the Ramirez Hacienda Heights home on August 31, 1985 and had found Julian Ramirez home. He stated further that he was fluent in Spanish and had asked Julian if he would agree to an interview. He was invited into the house for the interview and later wrote an article.

He stated that when he'd asked Julian when he'd last seen Richard, he'd told him, "Two or three years," which contrasted sharply with what Julian had said on the stand.

On cross, the reporter testified that the interview had happened on a Saturday at 4:30 P.M., and had lasted ten minutes, that Julian had been alone in the house, and that he had taken notes but had thrown them away. He had found his way to the Ramirez home by talking to old neighbors of the Ramirezes on Ledo Street, then calling his editor at the paper, who helped track Julian Ramirez to Hacienda Heights.

Clark asked him for a copy of the article, and Judge Tynan gave defense counsel fifteen minutes to read it.

Dave Hancock testified that he had taped his interview with Julian Ramirez and that Richard's father had been very distraught over what had happened. Clark also pointed out that Julian's remarks in the article were not in quotes.

The defense had an ex parte meeting with Judge Tynan in his chambers. Clark said the defense could prove, by way of two eyewitnesses, that Richard truly was in El Paso from May 22 to 31. Daniel would have to go to Texas to interview the witnesses during the court's July break. The judge was dismayed by the request, but he wanted to avoid a reversal at all costs, and reluctantly, after consulting his calendar, told Clark he would grant the request, give them until July 10. He added that all this should have been done already.

In open court, Tynan announced he was "reluctantly" going to allow the defense team to bring up witnesses from Texas to refute Dave Hancock's testimony and was going to give them until July 10 to do it.

Phil Halpin was livid at this news. He reminded the judge that Dr. Leung had identified Richard and even had X rays and dated charts to prove he was in his office.

The jury was told they were on vacation until July 10.

"Welcome back, ladies and gentlemen. I hope you had a nice little respite from our work," Judge Tynan told the jury the morning of July 10.

The defense called Raymondo Pantoja, a thick, powerful man with a tough, weatherbeaten face, for thirty years a friend of Julian Ramirez's. With the help of a Spanish interpreter, he stated that they'd worked together, and that he had loaned Julian a plumber snake to clean his kitchen drain on May 25, a Saturday.

When he went to the Ramirez home to lend the tool, Ruth's daughter was having her communion party; he had seen Richard there. Raymondo Pantoja had a lifetime of hard labor on his face, and he seemed quite sure of himself, "Like a man who was telling the absolute truth," a court observer would say.

Though Halpin stood and cross-examined him extensively, wanting to know everything about his visit to the Ramirez home, Pantoja said he didn't stay, didn't talk to Richard. He had gone there just to lend his friend a tool and had seen Richard.

"I just saw him, that's all!" he said with annoyance to the unbelieving prosecutor.

On redirect he stated that the trip to Los Angeles was the first time he'd ever been on a plane. The defense wanted the jury to know this was a simple, hardworking, honest man who didn't have a dishonest bone in his body. Clark tried to show a Polaroid of Richard at the party, posing with Gloria and his mother and father. Halpin's objection was sustained. The judge said there was no authentification as to when the picture had been taken. Halpin said the twenty-fifth had nothing to do with the thirtieth—that Julian Ramirez was lying when he stated Richard had been in El Paso on the thirtieth.

Clark in turn said it was the reporter who was lying, that he could've written anything he damn well pleased. "He kept no notes or recordings of his conversation with Julian Ramirez."

Judge Tynan ruled that unless the defense could prove the photograph had been taken in El Paso on that date there was no way that a photograph was getting before the jury.

The witness was excused. After lunch Clark said he wanted to introduce the photograph and was prepared to make an offer of proof. He had a witness who had actually seen the photograph come out of the camera. Maria Torres was called to the stand. She was the sister of Joseph's wife and would be the last witness to testify in the trial. Maria was sworn in and told the jury that she had been to Gloria's communion party and seen Richard there. When Clark asked her if she was sure of the date, May 25, she said she was absolutely positive because it was also her daughter's third birthday and she had had a party for her. Clark handed her the photograph and she stated she had actually been there when Ruth had taken the picture with Gloria in her communion dress.

She testified she had seen Richard in El Paso a second time, on May 29, at her sister's home. She was helping her sister clean when Richard entered, said hello to her, made a joke about some candy, and went to talk with Joseph, who was lying down, suffering from a migraine. Richard, she said, visited with Joseph for a few minutes and left. Ruth was waiting for him outside. She understood that Ruth was taking him either to the airport or the bus terminal. She was sure of the date because she had separated from her husband on April 29, and May 29 marked the end of the first month of her separation.

Halpin decided either she was lying or Richard had left that Saturday, flown to L.A., and attacked Mabel Bell and Nettie Lang. He'd be sure to point this out during his closing arguments.

Maria Torres stepped down from the stand and Ray Clark announced, "The defense rests."

They haggled about the times of their closing arguments and the judge's charge and Tynan excused the jury until the next day, when they'd enter a new phase of the proceeding and hear summations.

At 10 A.M., Judge Tynan told the defense the pistol the police had recovered in Tijuana had been "mislaid" and the people would give the jury a photograph of it to take into deliberations.

The judge thanked the jurors for their attention and asked them to try to concentrate on the attorneys' summations.

Phil Halpin began to outline all the strengths of the people's case and all the weaknesses of the defense. His summation was long and extremely detailed and went on for four full days. The air conditioner in the courtroom wasn't working well, and everyone was hot and uncomfortable as Halpin went through the case like an unstoppable tank, shooting holes in the defense's picture of Richard's innocence.

On the second day of the people's summation, Daniel didn't show up in court and Judge Tynan issued a warrant, which he quashed when Daniel came to court the next day, apologizing and saying he had told Clark he wouldn't be coming in, but co-counsel had "misunderstood me."

Tynan said his actions were "reprehensible and could be contrived by the bar as abdication of responsibility." He warned Daniel not to disappear again and ordered Arturo to attend the proceeding, though the next day, Daniel said he wasn't sure where Arturo was. Tynan told Daniel to get Arturo to court and ordered a subpoena sent to Arturo's office.

Halpin did not like his summation being interrupted because of the Hernandezes and complained to the judge about their lack of professionalism.

Tynan agreed and told the prosecutor to continue. At all costs Halpin wanted Richard to be convicted and sentenced to death. He was a methodical killing machine "who derived immense pleasure at the pain and hurt of others." He viewed Richard Ramirez as being in a class of his own in the world of serial murder.

Halpin finished his summation on July 21. The people had presented 139 witnesses and 537 pieces of evidence.

On Monday, the twenty-fourth, Ray Clark stood, thanked the jury for their kind attention, and began summarizing the weaknesses in the people's case and the strength of the defense's position. He pointed out the fallibility of eyewitnesses, how the descriptions of eyewitnesses were inconsistent and that the death penalty loomed imminently. His summation lasted for two days. He spent much time debunking Launie Dempster and spoke expansively of Sandra Hotchkiss's believability. He pointed out, toward the end of his summation, that Halpin had not proved that Richard had flown out of El Paso on the twenty-ninth. Richard always had taken buses and hung out at the bus terminal, he pointed out.

As is the law, Halpin was able to speak again after Clark, and he told the jury that Clark's take on the facts was all wrong and briefly reiterated the strengths of the people's case. He read into the record the testimony of Monrovia officer Tim Wright, who had found the Avia footprints, together with Richard Ramirez's palm- and fingerprints on West Olive in Monrovia.

He said, that put Richard in Avia Aerobics and placed him at all the crime scenes where footprints had been found. At the end of the day, Halpin said he was finished, satisfied he had done his best.

After the jury left, Clark asked Tynan if, during the jury's deliberations, Daniel would be able to leave town. Tynan asked Richard if that would be all right.

Richard said, "It's okay if he leaves," and court was convened.

The next day at precisely 10:13 Judge Tynan told the jury that it was now time for the final act in the trial process, his charge, and went on to explain the law and how to go about reaching verdicts on all the charges. It took Tynan two days, and when it was over, the jurors were itching to start deliberation and to get the trial behind them. They had been sitting for fourteen months. During that time they had become close, a family of sorts, and friendships that would last a lifetime had been born.

On July 26 the jury entered the jury room. They began their deliberations at 11:25 A.M.

FIFTY-TWO

The jury cooked up some popcorn, then sat at a long, rectangular wooden table with twelve chairs. As Judge Tynan had instructed, they began with the first charge, the murder of Jennie Vincow. The only thing that linked Richard to this crime was his fingerprint on the window, and the jury got into a long, heated debate about what legally constituted a fingerprint as evidence and ended up sending a note to Judge Tynan asking him the necessary elements for a fingerprint to be deemed "legal evidence."

The judge brought them back into court and again read to them what the law said about fingerprints. With that information they went back to their deliberations and took a vote. With his print present there—and the stab-slash knife wound, it didn't take them long to find Richard guilty of the Vincow killing.

They began to review all the elements that connected the crimes and soon focused on the Avia footprints. Using the prints as a guide, they discussed each of the crimes in which the print had been found. They went over the pros and cons of all the events, with Cindy Haden playing devil's advocate, saying things like "more than one person could have had such a shoe." They took votes on each of the crimes and Richard was convicted of all the assaults where Avia footprints existed.

They moved to the cases where there were no prints, talked over what other factors interlinked the crimes. They reviewed the ransacking, phone disabling, burglary-type entry, and similar language—"Shut up, bitch. Don't look at me. Where is it?"

Everything was moving very quickly, considering the volume of charges. There was little disharmony among the jurors; they got along well and were always courteous to one another.

The first problem they had was juror number 4, a black man named Lee, who kept falling asleep. They would be taking a vote around the table, and when they got to him he would be sleeping, his head bobbing about. The jury foreman finally wrote a note to Judge Tynan and complained.

The judge saw this as a serious problem and summoned the attorneys. Clark said he didn't necessarily want him removed—Halpin said he thought it best he be removed. Tynan ruled Lee had to go, that his sleeping could become an appellate issue. Lee was replaced by Vernon Sutton, another black man.

The jury continued its deliberations; some of the women brought in cookies and pies and everyone would munch away as the deliberations moved on.

On August 14, juror Phyllis Singletary didn't show up. Judge Tynan brought the jury into court and told the jury they couldn't continue without Ms. Singletary and court was recessed to the following day.

In fact the judge had learned that Ms. Singletary had been found murdered.

However the news media soon got wind of Singletary's death and swarmed over the story like bees on honey. The murder of a juror sitting on California's most famous serial murder trial was big news.

Cynthia Haden learned about the murder from juror Choclate Harris, who called her at her home that evening. Quickly, word of Singletary's death traveled to all the jurors and alternates; and that night few of them slept well. They were all haunted by the prospect of Richard Ramirez being responsible in some way. They had seen his groupies and the Satanists parading in and out of the courtroom daily for the last fourteen months. Charles Manson had, they all knew, sent people to kill Sharon Tate and her friends and Mr. and Mrs. LaBianca. After all, this was Southern California. Anything was possible.

In the morning, the jurors gathered in the deliberation chamber in numbed shock. The murder of Ms. Singletary hung over them like a dark stormcloud. Some of them wondered which of them would be next.

At 10:47, Tynan brought them into court. He apologized for not telling them about the murder the day before, saying he didn't have all the details. "Your friend and our juror here in court has been shot. I want to emphasize that it has, as far as we are able to determine, and I'm sure, nothing to do with this case. It is irrelevant to this case. Her death is tragic, and I think we all grieve for her. But what happened to her doesn't add or diminish anything to the evidence, as to whether or not Mr. Ramirez is guilty or innocent of these charges. And I beg you, I beg you, to remember that for deliberations . . . your grief must remain separate from your duties in this case . . . you are human beings . . . but we are also citizens with work to do."

Tynan now ordered his assistant, Josephine, to draw a name from the drum, and alternate juror Mary Helen Herrera was chosen.

Ms. Herrera burst into tears, her chest wracked with sobs. She was so upset, she couldn't stand and fill Phyllis Singletary's vacant seat. It had been learned at the voir dire that both of Ms. Herrera's brothers, who were in law enforcement, had been shot to death. Daniel was now sorry he hadn't dismissed her for cause.

Later that day it was revealed that James C. Melton, age fifty-one, had murdered Ms. Singletary. He was her live-in boyfriend, an abusive man with an explosive temper. Sheriff's detectives who learned about his whereabouts through a phone call he'd made raided a hotel where Melton was holed up. Melton saw them coming, and before the deputies could do anything, he put the gun he'd killed Phyllis with to his head and pulled the trigger, killing himself instantly. The deputies found a note in the hotel room in Melton's handwriting. In it, he admitted to killing Phyllis—saying he had shot her twice in the chest over "domestic disagreements."

The detectives later learned that Phyllis had told Melton that she felt sorry for Richard Ramirez because he hadn't gotten proper representation with the Hernandezes. Melton thought Ramirez was a mad dog that needed killing. An argument ensued, which grew into a senseless murderous rage.

When Clark and Daniel visited Richard in the county jail that day, he said he didn't want to go forward with the trial and his lawyers should demand a mistrial. There was no way, he insisted, the jurors could not be influenced by the murder of a fellow juror. He pointed out that the case was not about forgery, or a stock swindle; it was about murder, and he was being tried for murder.

"There's no fucking way they won't be affected against me!"

Clark, Daniel, and Salinas agreed wholeheartedly, and they promised Richard they'd prepare a motion for mistrial.

Amid a packed courtroom, Clark told the judge that the defense wanted the jury to have a period of at least a week to recuperate. If the judge wasn't inclined to give them a week, Clark asked that the jurors be polled to see if they could still be impartial. He had been in contact with two psychiatrists, Dr. Jo 'Ellan Dimitrius and Dr. Carlo Webber, and they had both unequivocally advised him it would be wrong and improper to let this jury sit in judgment of a murder defendant without their being polled. He reminded the judge that the jurors had become "as close as siblings, husbands and wives."

Halpin didn't agree. He didn't want any delay and polling the jurors would just serve "to stir up their emotions." Tynan decided to bring out the jury foreman and get his opinion about the capability of the jury to go on with an impartial deliberation.

Foreman Rodriguez was summoned and Tynan queried him about the jury's ability to move forward. Rodriguez, a mustachioed man with very black hair, said, "I feel it is somewhat tranquil, but it is—I feel that we can probably continue today."

"They all seem to be able to carry out their duties, then, as jurors?" asked the judge.

"Right. Everyone appears to have it behind them."

"I am delighted to hear that," Tynan proclaimed, an audible sigh of relief coming from him, and called for the jury to be brought out. He announced he was going to allow the trial to go forward. He looked at the defense table and said, "If there's any objection from the defense, I'll hear it now."

Richard leaned forward and said: "I have an objection. I think that is fucked up!"

The bailiff closed in. The press, not knowing what Richard would do next, leaned forward. Daniel calmed Richard and told Tynan the defense objected strenuously to the deliberations going on with this jury.

Tynan ruled they would continue with this jury, Richard scowled at the judge and moved about in his chair anxiously, chains rattling. The judge told the jury he was allowing their deliberations go on and read a prepared statement to them, imploring them to put Ms. Singletary's murder behind them. He reiterated her death had nothing to do with the trial and told them about James Melton, his suicide and the note.

At 10:45, the jury recommenced its deliberations.

On August 23, a motion the defense was making to poll the jury was to take place. Richard adamantly did not want to be there, Daniel told the court, adding he would not be able to control Richard if he was forced to come to court.

The judge didn't like this. He was not about to be bullied by Richard Ramirez at this late date. He told Daniel that Richard would have to attend.

Tynan said, "I don't want to play these games. I do appreciate the stellar job you have done in keeping him under control. If he wants to act like a jerk, we can deal with it at that time, restrain him."

Richard was ordered out of the holding cell. Surrounded by nervous bailiffs, he was brought out, openly scowling at Tynan, his lips silently mouthing curses.

"Hey, I don't want to be here, man. Don't you understand?" Ramirez said, as he sat down.

"I understand," the judge said.

"Then what is the problem?"

The judge ignored Ramirez and asked Daniel if he wanted his motion to poll the jury to be heard. Daniel said he did. Tynan ruled the people would be allowed ten days to prepare for the motion and offered the thirty-first as a date to hear arguments.

Richard said, "I won't come back in here again. You understand that? This trial is a joke—Fuckin' asshole . . . Piece of shit." As Richard shouted, the four bailiffs surrounded him, lifted him, and hurried him from court.

The jurors, spectators, and press looked at one another in amazement. Seeing Richard with the veins in his neck bulging, his face twisted into an angry, animal-like snarl, and his huge chained hands grabbing at the air futilely was a very sobering experience.

The judge cleared his throat. Halpin said he would be ready to respond to the defense's motion on the thirty-first. Daniel said that would be fine.

At a conference in the judge's chambers, Daniel reiterated that there would be trouble if Richard was forced to attend the hearing on the thirty-first—he was adamant about not being there. Daniel said he was upset about the trial going forward after one of the jurors had been shot. Richard would sign a waiver.

Tynan saw no reason not to grant this request. He knew Ramirez was very volatile and didn't want to deal with it. He agreed Ramirez didn't have to be present on the thirty-first and the proceeding returned to open court. Richard was brought out, more subdued now, politely saying yes when the judge asked if he waived his right to be in court for the hearing.

On the thirty-first, Richard listened, over a loudspeaker in the court holding cell he despised so much, as the hearing to poll the jury took place. Clark reiterated the defense's position. Yochelson stood for the people, saying Ms. Singletary's murder had happened two weeks earlier. It made no sense to rehash the tragedy and stir things up—after they apparently had been able to put it behind them.

Tynan said he thought letting the defense question the jury about Singletary's death would be a fatal mistake, and he denied the motion.

In his cell, pacing back and forth, Richard cursed the judge and told his jailers the trial was a joke; he spit and he cursed and he kicked the bars.

Daniel told the court, Richard refused also to attend a second motion to be heard on September 5. The judge said it would be all right, but he would have to sign another waiver.

Deputy Warden asked to speak to the judge at a sidebar and told Tynan that Richard was cursing and yelling and had stated he'd fight before he allowed deputies to bring him into court.

Tynan announced that for security reasons, the defendant would sign the waiver on September 5.

The jury's deliberations moved on.

On September 5, when Ramirez was led into court, he was subdued. Doreen was in her usual place, her eyes riveted to him. There was not an empty seat in the house. Ramirez signed the waiver form and was taken to the holding pen.

The defense had decided to seek a mistrial based on several points: one, the death of Singletary, the other, that the juror who had replaced her, Mary Herrera, had two brothers in law enforcement who'd been shot to death, which she had failed to mention on her initial questionnaire.

The judge refused to grant a new trial, court was recessed, and the jury continued its deliberations.

On September 14, court was convened because of Arturo Hernandez. He had been ordered to call the court daily but had failed to do so on the sixth through the fourteenth. Judge Tynan found him in contempt and issued a body attachment with $5000 bail.

On the eighteenth, Arturo showed up in court. Tynan bawled him out for not calling in as he had agreed to. He didn't want to hear any excuses, he just wanted to know how Arturo pled. The lawyer said he was guilty. Tynan fined him $2400 or twenty-four days in jail. He gave him until September 24 to come up with the money. The judge then had Arturo remanded to do a day in jail for a September 1 contempt charge.

FIFTY-THREE

At 10:50 on September 20, the jury announced they had reached a verdict—a unanimous decision. Daniel Hernandez and Ray Clark were summoned. Richard was brought from the jail. He refused to change into a suit and wore jail blues. The press packed the courtroom. All the networks interrupted broadcasts to announce that a verdict had been reached.

At 2:12, everyone was gathered in the packed courtroom. Carrillo and Salerno sat in their usual places. Clark told Judge Tynan that Richard did not want to be present for the verdict. Halpin said he wanted him there.

Tynan refused to have Richard chained up to hear the verdict. It wouldn't be good for the jury to see him that way before the penalty stage. He ruled Richard could hear the verdict from the court holding cell, citing "the *Ninth Circuit of California v. Spainer.*" He queried Richard on the record, asking him four times if he relinquished his right to be present during the verdicts, and each time Richard said yes. He signed a waiver and was taken back to the holding cell.

The jury was summoned. Solemn, and silent, heads cast down, they entered the courtroom. There was no sound but the soft shuffling of their feet.

"Good afternoon, folks," Judge Tynan said, and explained that the defendant had elected not to attend the verdict reading and that they weren't to infer anything from his not being present. He read each juror's name: Cynthia Haden, Martha Salcido, Verbe Sutton, Alfredo Carrillo, Arthur Johnson, Lillian Sagron, Felipe Rodriguez, Mary Herrera, Choclate Harris, Arlena Wallace, Don McGee, and Shirley Zelaya.

The judge then read the verdict sheets, announced they were in order, and gave them to Clerk Josephine Williams to be read out loud. Beginning with the Vincow charge, the jury voted guilty on every one of the forty-six counts.

No one in the audience was surprised. Doreen stood and, crying, hurried from the courtroom.

Judge Tynan, at the defense's request, polled the jury, and each one said he'd heard the verdicts read out loud and agreed with them.

It was over.

The judge thanked them and said they would now be moving to the penalty phase. He asked them to step into the jury room.

Judge Tynan asked the defense how long they would need to prepare for the penalty phase. Clark said three days. Daniel asked for at least two weeks, saying they were bringing people in from out of town.

Tynan told Daniel he should have already lined up any witnesses and gave the defense one week to prepare.

The jury was now brought out and told the penalty phase would take place on the twenty-ninth. The judge reminded them not to talk with anyone in the media. He offered them the use of the back elevator to avoid the waiting reporters and cameras.

As Cynthia Haden was leaving, Phil Halpin asked to speak with her up in his office for a minute. She followed him and Alan Yochelson up to the district attorney's floor. Halpin thanked her for the verdict and asked her not to talk with the defense if they approached her. She said she wouldn't and left, a bit bewildered about why they had apparently spoken only to her. When she got home, she called a few of the other jurors and they said they'd not been approached by the prosecutors.

That evening Richard Ramirez's conviction was the lead story on all the news shows. Commentators gave their opinion as to whether or not Richard would be given the death sentence.

In El Paso, Mercedes, Julian, and the rest of the Ramirez clan went to church and prayed Richard wouldn't be given the death sentence. In her prayers to Mary, Mercedes explained it was a big, Satan-inspired mistake, that her son could not have done the things they said he'd done, that Satan's hand was at work here. She implored Mary to speak to her son and tell him the truth.

As cameramen and reporters taped news pieces in front of their home, Mercedes Ramirez cried herself to sleep. Julian sat in his easy chair and stared at the floor, immobile, unspeaking. When Ruth and Joseph visited and tried to talk with him, he ignored them.

He had, Joseph thought, aged ten years in just a few hours.

When Richard's lawyers went to visit him at the county jail that evening, he said he wasn't surprised he'd been convicted. The trial was a farce and there was no way the jury would not convict him after Singletary's death.

He told his attorneys he didn't want to put on any kind of defense for the penalty phase. Clark warned him that would be foolish, a mistake. If he wanted the jury not to give him the death sentence, they needed mitigating circumstances, something they could hang their hats on not to vote for death. He suggested Richard's father, saying he was a good, hardworking man and he could very well stir up some sympathy among the jurors. Clark insisted if the defense didn't present something for the jury on Richard's behalf, they would surely sentence him to die: "You are as good as dead, Richard."

Richard said he didn't want to put his father through that—beg for his life, grovel in front of Tynan, Halpin, Salerno, Carrillo, and the rest of the detectives. He wouldn't stand for that. He insisted he didn't want anyone in his family put on the stand.

"They'll kill you," Clark repeated.

"Richie, they'll execute you, for sure," Daniel put in.

"Well, then let them. Fuck them. Dying doesn't scare me. I'll be in hell. With Satan. That's gotta be a better place than this. I'd rather die than live in a cage. Fuck that shit, man," he said, and laughed, then sat back, suddenly serious-faced.

"Please, Richard—" Clark began, but was cut off.

"We aren't begging. Period," Richard said, and that was that.

* * *

Daniel, against Richard's wishes, flew down to El Paso anyway and spoke to Richard's parents and siblings. He told them of Richard's decision not to put on any kind of defense for the penalty phase.

Hernandez beseeched Julian Tapia to overrule his son and come up to L.A., but the senior Ramirez said if Richie didn't want them to speak on his behalf, then by God, that's the way it would be.

No one asked Richard's cousin Mike to come to court and tell the jurors about the photographs, his war stories, or his having killed his wife Jessie in front of Richard.

Still, no one knew Richard had seen the murder.

On the day of sentencing, the defense announced they would not be putting any witnesses on the stand on the defendant's behalf, calling it "a tactical decision." Richard would not be taking the stand, either.

Tynan asked Richard if he was waiving his right to put on a defense and to speak on his behalf. Ramirez said yes.

The next issue was the jailhouse blues. Clark asked the judge if Richard would be able to wear them. He didn't want to change clothes. Tynan said that would be all right and ordered the jury brought in.

As they entered, Richard glowered at them. Cynthia Haden couldn't look him in the eyes. She felt guilty about having convicted him. She thought the Hernandezes were so woefully inadequate that Richard hadn't gotten a fair shake.

"He was sold down the river," she would later say, and would make correcting that "injustice" her life's work.

Court was recessed to 1:30 to give Judge Tynan time to read some amended charges the prosecutor had.

After the recess, a few issues involving the charges were ironed out between Halpin and Clark. The jury was brought out and told by the judge that the People would now present the reasons they felt Richard should be given the death penalty.

Halpin stood and, filled with anger and with fire in his eyes, told the jury that according to *Webster's*, the word "justice" meant "a reward or penalty as deserved; just deserts."

If the death penalty was ever warranted, it was in this case, he said.

He reminded them that they had each said, at the onset, that they could administer a death sentence if the evidence warranted it, and he went on to read the special circumstances the penal code outlined about extenuating circumstances, which precluded the death penalty. None applied to the crimes Richard had been convicted of.

He outlined each of the murders and why, in every case, Richard should be sentenced to death.

Of Jennie Vincow's murder, "Throat slit from ear to ear; very violent and very brutal—inexcusable . . . Not just a murder, not just a murder in the commission of a burglary, but an inexcusably violent act resulted in the death of that woman."

Of Dayle Okazaki's murder, "Very cold-blooded, deliberate act, and inexcusable."

Of Veronica Yu's murder, "Another terrible act, again with no time to mutilate [as with Dayle Okazaki] but someone obviously that—across whom the defendant just came at that particular time and place and took her life."

Of Vincent and Maxine Zazzara, "In their own home. Again, not only murdered, but Maxine Zazzara *horribly* mutilated. For what reason? Horribly mutilated, eyes cut from her head, why?"

Of the Doi incident, "Again, in the home where these old people had . . . some sanctuary, some place to get in at night so that they wouldn't be preyed upon. Another useless act."

Of Mabel Bell, "An elderly lady beaten, beaten terribly, and the cavalier drawing on the wall and that type of thing. But the—the unacceptable, just intolerable brutality at the scene of the crime."

Of Carol Kyle's ordeal, "The killing didn't end there. The killing went on. Some people he let live, and I submit to you that was for the simple gratification of this miserable human being."

Halpin stopped, letting his words sink in. There was not a sound in the courtroom. All eyes were on him. Spectators expected Ramirez to stand up, snarl, and curse at Halpin, but he stayed mute in his chair, looking at his hands—folded on the desk.

"Mary Louise Cannon," Halpin continued, "an elderly

woman, living alone in her home, beaten repeatedly beyond recognition, strangled . . . Her throat was slit from ear to ear! Little old lady that lived there alone. That wasn't necessary to steal whatever she had."

Whitney Bennett had lived despite Richard's repeated blows to her head with the tire iron. "Four-and-a-half linear feet of stitches on her head. No question the defendant tried to beat this sixteen-year-old child, lying in her bed, to death . . . He failed because of what—because of her constitution."

He said of Joyce Nelson, "Again, when we talk about this, a carbon copy of the Cannon murder, beaten senseless, multiple, *multiple* fractures to the skull and head."

Of the Sophie Dickman incident, "Somebody tells you that was an act in mitigation [not killing her], he could have killed her. Yeah, he could have, except that she was a psychiatric nurse and knew how to handle that type of situation."

Of Max and Lela Kneiding, "And why the mutilation again? Was it necessary to steal what these poor little old people had?"

Of the Khovananth attack, "A bullet deftly put in the head of Chainarong Khovananth, his wife terrorized and beaten and raped and sodomized, put through all sorts of things.

"August sixth of '85, Christopher and Virginia Petersen, both alive today, miracles. Both of them shot in the head. You recall what else? Remember the colloquy between Mrs. Petersen and the defendant. The usual language, and then he laughed. What was he laughing at?" Halpin demanded of the jury.

Of the Abowath incident, "Again, a bullet deftly placed in the brain of Elyas Abowath, and his wife brutalized, dragged down the hall by her hair, raped, sodomized, in the bedroom of her husband's dead body."

In summation, he said, "I submit to you that you *have* to look this case in the face . . . this man is the personification of evil, and if anyone ever deserved the death penalty, Richard Ramirez does . . . I urge you to vote for the death penalty. Thank you."

Ray Clark stood to try and save Richard's life. He knew it was an uphill battle, but he was going to give it his all.

He first spoke about mercy, Richard's father, the love of his parents.

He told the jury, by virtue of their verdict, Richard would die in prison, that he would live in a six-by-eight-foot cell for the rest of his natural life. "Life without the ability for parole means he will never see Disneyland again; he will never see Playa del Rey; he will never be free.

"This is severe punishment."

He pointed out that the Stalker had let people live, that he had asked Carol Kyle if someone would be coming so she would be freed, that he had left a handcuff key for her. He asked them to show Richard compassion and sympathy.

Then he tried to hang the blame on the devil. "And there is not a lot to be said here as to—as to he was a good boy, he did this, he went to this school, or that school. Obviously, you don't consider that. That wasn't presented, and I don't know what school he went to. You do know him between 1984 and 1985, principally in 1985. I think it is inescapable that something was wrong and that we don't know what it was. Even if we knew what it was, I'm not sure that that would change your task any. Let's say that we believed that he was possessed, if there is such a thing as being possessed. The extension of mercy goes to the devil, because I guess it is one thing to say he is considerably more in need of mercy than anyone else."

He went on about showing Richard Ramirez mercy, talking up a storm about why Richard should live, but the jury was as immobile as a rock, their countenances as fixed and still as the faces on Mount Rushmore.

In their eyes, one did not see the slightest glimmer of sympathy for the defendant, who had belligerently refused to take the stand or even deny the crimes he'd been convicted of.

Clark politely thanked the jury for their attention and wrapped up his arguments at 4 P.M. After a recess, Judge Tynan charged the jury as to the legal parameters of the death sentence and sent them home.

The jury began the deliberations of the penalty phase at 9:50 the next morning, September 28.

FIFTY-FOUR

After a few bowls of popcorn had been made, the jury got down to the business of deciding Richard's fate. They first took a vote to see if they could each recommend the death sentence if the law warranted it. All twelve jurors said they could. They began to discuss the particulars of each murder.

There was not, Cindy would later say, "Any mitigating circumstance which could have steered us away from the death sentence. It was criminal, absolutely criminal, that the defense had not put anyone on the stand on Richard's behalf."

Be that as it may, as difficult as it was—"It's very hard taking someone's life," Juror Santos would say—they voted that Richard should be executed on each of the first-degree murder charges.

They wrote their decisions on pieces of paper, which were then tallied. After they'd done Vincow and Dayle Okazaki, a few of the jurors began drawing little symbols—one drew a hangman's noose, one a gallows, one a tombstone with "RIP" on it. Cynthia Haden also drew a tombstone, though on hers she put a heart, which caused some raised eyebrows among the jurors.

In all, it took five days for them to cover all the counts. When they sent word to Judge Tynan that their task was done, it was 10:20 A.M. on October 3.

The lawyers were summoned. Richard was brought out and sat at the defense table, still wearing jail blues, cuffs and shackles. As the jury entered, he looked up; four of the women had tears coming down their faces and he knew they'd voted death. He'd always known they'd vote death.

Cynthia Haden was crying the hardest. She mouthed the words "I'm sorry" to him.

Tynan first called each juror's name, making sure they were all there. The clerk handed Judge Tynan the verdict sheets. He read the first one.

"We, the jury in the above-entitled action, having found the defendant, Richard Ramirez, guilty of the murder of Jennie Vincow in the first degree and having found it to be an intentional murder committed during the commission or attempted commission of the crime of burglary, within the meaning of section 190.2(A)(17)(VII) of the California penal code, as alleged on page two in count II of the information, fix the penalty therefore at death. Dated this 3rd day of October, 1989.

"Felipe G. Rodriguez, Foreman."

The judge read all the verdict forms into the record. As he spoke, his words hung over the crowded courtroom with a lethal finality.

When Judge Tynan finished, he queried each juror as to whether the verdict form reflected his decision. Each said yes. It was hard for a few of the female jurors to speak, they were crying so hard. The judge thanked them and set November 9 for sentencing.

Richard was remanded. He stood and hobbled from the court, head high, shackles dragging on the hard linoleum floor, as four sheriff's deputies walked in a circle around him.

Judge Tynan turned to the jury and asked them to come to his chambers. "For the record I would like to thank you on behalf of the people of the state of California, all the citizens perhaps of this country, for your work. You worked under extremely difficult situations and I'm very proud of you and I know you've had a tough time of it. And I think I speak for all the citizens of this state, we are very, very grateful for your service. We can't survive without you, but this was a highly unusual case, a very, very emotionally charged case, a difficult case for you for many reasons, and I do want to thank you and the public for your work. And God bless you and thank you."

The whole Ramirez family was gathered at the Hacienda Heights house when the verdict reached them.

Daniel called to tell them. Ruth picked up the phone. The lawyer said one word, *"Muerte"* (death). Ruth told him to hold on. With tears filling her big brown eyes, she turned to her father and repeated, *"Muerte."*

Julian Tapia got up and went to the bedroom to tell Mercedes. She was kneeling in front of her white candle. She took one look at her husband's face and knew the State of California would be killing her last-born.

"It should be Satan who is to die, not Richie," she said and began to cry. Julian held her, small and fragile, in his powerful arms and her tears ran down his chest, over his broken heart.

The day of sentencing, the judge told the press swelling the courtroom and hall outside the court that civilian witnesses, victims of the case, were absolutely forbidden to be photographed. He moved on to the sentence.

"The court finds that the evidence concerning the special circumstances pertaining to each of the counts enumerated above is overwhelming, and that the jury's assessment of evidence, that the aggravation outweighs the mitigation as to the selection of the proper penalties, that is, death, is supported overwhelmingly by the weight of the evidence."

He described each murder and crime in brief and said there were no mitigating circumstances in any of them that would forgo a death sentence.

He asked Mr. Clark if he wished to be heard.

"Counsel doesn't," Clark said. "However, Mr. Ramirez wishes to be heard."

"Very well," Judge Tynan said. "Mr. Ramirez, you may address the court."

All the reporters leaned forward, and the court camera zoomed in on Richard, who removed a piece of paper from his jacket, opened it up with his huge hands, and read, in a booming, angry voice.

"You don't understand me. You are not expected to. You are not capable. I am beyond your experience. I am beyond good and evil. I will be avenged. Lucifer dwells in all of us. I don't know why I'm even wasting my breath, but what the hell. For what is said of my life, there have been lies in the past and there will be lies in the future. I don't believe in the hypocritical, moralistic dogma of this so-called civilized society. I need not look beyond this courtroom to see all the liars, the haters, the killers, the crooks, the paranoid cowards. Truly the *Trematodes* of the earth.

"You maggots make me sick! Hypocrites one and all. We are all expendable for a cause. No one knows that better than those who kill for policy, clandestinely or openly, as do the governments of the world which kill in the name of God and country . . . I don't need to hear all of society's rationalizations. I've heard them all before . . . legions of the night, night breed, repeat not the errors of the night prowler and show no mercy."

Tynan cleared his throat and gave Richard the death sentence nineteen times—once for each of the murders and six for other crimes. He summed up each death sentence with these words: "This penalty is to be inflicted within the walls of the state prison of San Quentin, California, in the manner prescribed by law and at the time to be fixed by this court in the warrant for execution."

After disposing of all the murder charges, Judge Tynan sentenced Richard to six years for each of the other thirty-three charges in the indictment.

He then gave the victims and their family members a chance to speak before he signed the death warrants. The first was Virginia Petersen.

Virginia Petersen: "It has been over four years since the attempted murders of my husband and myself, an act which took only seconds, yet to this day reverberates with the original horror. Like a pebble cast into a pond that ripples outward, the effects of this crime touch not only us, but families and friends. When a crime of this magnitude is committed, it touches the heart of the community.

"These past years have been a constant strain on my family's emotional health. There have been many times for the two of us when walking away from each other would have been preferable, but we were determined not to let our marriage fail. Had we done this, we felt that he would have succeeded in killing us.

"We had to move from our home of nearly ten years, a home in which we planned our future and hoped to raise our daughter. It was [in] the neighborhood which my husband grew up in, close to our families, and we had wished to give our daughter the same childhood we had enjoyed.

"Over the last several months you have heard the facts of the night of our attack, but not of our daily struggles. Christopher lost his job of eleven years due to the injuries caused by the bullet. It rests at the base of his skull, very close to the spinal cord. The surgeons decided not to remove the bullet for fear of paralyzing him. He is in constant pain. At times the entire left side of his body will spasm, and he has lost a great deal of strength on that side as well.

"Last year I had to leave my employment due to the injuries that I sustained in the shooting. For the past four years I have had constant pain in either my arm, neck, or head. Without warning I have spasms in my head that can leave immediately, cause me to twitch for days, or cause me to lose control of my arms or legs.

"Nights are the worst. I suffer from a sleep disorder in which I wake up many times a night, sometimes with panic attacks. I scream in terror, not knowing why I'm frightened; it is beyond my control. I will then cling to Chris, who will comfort me until I calm down. Usually, then, I will stay awake until dawn. Medication does not help. In fact, it has a paradoxical effect. Here lies the greatest indignity. We had planned on having another child, but we dare not do so while I continually need medication for pain.

"My daughter was four years old in 1985, the joy of our lives, as any child is to her parents. I can still hear her screams of terror during the shooting, and her crying 'Mommy, please don't die, please don't die,' while I was bleeding uncontrollably in front of her. When we were released from the hospital, I reached for her, but she recoiled at my face, saying, "You are not my mommy, you are ugly." That wounded me worse than any gun could have. For days following the attack she would not speak but would wander aimlessly, uninterested in her toys or dolls.

"In kindergarten, she came to me one day to talk over something that was troubling her. She told me she could understand why people killed themselves because she hurt inside because of what the bad man had done. It is devastating when your child is severely troubled, but when the child is only five years old, it is unbearable.

"Despite what you have heard, I feel that I am the most fortunate of all women survivors. I have a husband I can turn to and a daughter whose only scars are emotional. Nevertheless, the future we face is not the one of our choosing, but one handed to us on the night of August 6, 1985.

"You, Your Honor, through your decision to impose the maximum penalty allowed, can help to secure a future for my family that we can face with dignity and peace."

The court: "Thank you, Mrs. Petersen. You have the profound sympathy of this court. Good luck."

Christopher Petersen took the podium. "Your Honor, I would like to add to my wife's statement.

"Now that Richard Ramirez has been found guilty for crimes committed against his fellow humans, it is time for him to become accountable for his actions. It is my belief that the death penalty be given without reservation. I'm sure he will now acquire a greater understanding for the value of human life than he had on the night we were shot. Thank you."

The court: "Thank you, Mr. Petersen. Good luck."

Joyce Nelson's son approached the podium.

Dale Nelson: "My mom—you know, she would have been retiring just about this time right now and kind of really starting to enjoy life—was brutally murdered by Richard Ramirez, and it is really the pits, I mean he has no, you know, emotion whatsoever about killing all these people, including my mother.

"And I just don't see why he should have any life left in him whatsoever. I mean, going to my mother's neighborhood, there are bars on windows, all through it.

"He terrorized the whole State of California, and you know, then there is the implementation of the death penalty after it is even given. It should be done, I think, rather quickly.

"And as far as it being a deterrent, I heard you mention that a little bit ago. It just isn't being used, so how could it be a deterrent? I mean, you have to start, I believe in the State of California, using the death penalty to make it effective, and as far as this even being other people, I understand there is two hundred and sixty people on death row, I mean, I don't know about there being a line, but this guy ought to be in the front.

"So that is what I have to say, sir."

The court: "Thank you, Mr. Nelson."

Don Nelson, also a son of Joyce Nelson spoke next.

Don Nelson: "Your Honor, Ray Clark, defense counsel, spoke of the quality of mercy demonstrated by my mother's murder, spoke of Richard Ramirez allowing several of his victims to live.

"I would like to talk about the other side of Richard Ramirez's mercy. Richard Ramirez murdered my mother three times. He beat my mother in the head with a heavy metal object. The same beating caused my mother to lose blood, blood that my brother and I cleaned up. People wonder when somebody dies who cleans up the mess. It is the family, the survivors.

"He then strangled my mother. My mother was found by the police the next day. She was in a fetal position with her arm locked behind her back. She weighed about one hundred and ten pounds, stands about five-two.

"Now, I just cannot imagine how anybody could get—could do this to a human being. This was the true nature of the mercy of Richard Ramirez.

"Thank you, sir."

The court: "Thank you."

Finally, a granddaughter of Joyce Nelson's addressed the court.

Colleen Nelson: "Basically, I'm just speaking for all my other cousins and my brothers and sisters because I don't think our lives will ever be the same.

"When I go outside, I'm scared of people because I just can't imagine how anyone can do this to people. For every person that he killed, he has put so many others through so much pain, a lifetime of pain that will always be there.

"My grandma didn't deserve to die. She was one of the best women I've ever known in my life and I just can't imagine that someone could do that to her and how scared she must have been.

"I think Richard Ramirez forfeited his right to live when he killed my grandma and all those other innocent people, and I think he should pay for what he did."

Tears in his eyes, Judge Tynan proceeded to sign the death warrants and ordered Richard to be taken to San Quentin for the execution of the sentence.

As the survivors wept openly, Richard Muñoz Ramirez stood and was taken from the courtroom, as his chains dragged behind him and his admirers looked at him forlornly.

EPILOGUE

FIFTY-FIVE

Frank Salerno and Gil Carrillo were anxious to speak with Richard. Early on, they say, he had told them when the case had been adjudicated he'd discuss the crimes he'd been charged with, as well as other murders and assaults the two detectives suspected he had done.

After the sentencing, they drove over to the county jail. They checked their side arms in lockers on the ground floor; made their way up to Ramirez's cell.

When they reached the cell, Ramirez was urinating. When he realized the two detectives were there, a smile broke on his face.

"Hi guys," he said. At this point the cell door was opened by a sheriff's deputy.

"You have a minute, Richard?" Frank asked.

"I've got a lot of minutes," he said, and they all laughed.

A prison cell is like a man's home, and the detectives wouldn't enter it without being invited.

"Come on in," Richard offered, and they stepped inside.

Richard told them he hadn't been referring to them in the speech he'd made in court. Frank reminded him he'd said he'd talk about his crimes after the case was over and asked if he'd be willing to talk now. Richard said he would not talk about any crime he wasn't convicted of, citing his family as the reason, but he'd be willing to discuss the crimes for which he had been convicted.

They moved to an interrogation room and began to talk.

NBC was airing a made-for-television movie based on the Stalker crimes. Richard said he was looking forward to seeing it. The two detectives said they'd be watching it, too.

Salerno suggested they could come back the following day to talk some more and discuss the movie. Richard agreed.

They discussed his sentence, his speech, the film, how packed the courtroom had been, and all the press the case had garnered. Salerno asked if it would be all right if they taped their conversation, and Richard said no. The detectives promised to come back in the morning.

"Could you use anything?" Salerno asked, knowing the only way to get anything out of Richard was to treat him "like a human being." Richard said he'd like some chocolate.

Later that day Richard was taken to the shower room and left alone. He saw a grated duct cover in the ceiling and decided to try and get it off. He couldn't move it with his hands, so he tried to kick it out of place. The sheriff's deputy on guard heard the kicks and caught Richard "vandalizing state property," he wrote in his report. As punishment, Richard wasn't allowed to watch *Manhunt*, the TV movie he had inspired.

Doreen hadn't been in court when Richard was sentenced. Daniel Hernandez had promised he'd call her at work and let her know what time to come to court, but he never did. She heard over the radio that Richard had been sentenced to death. She got pale and dizzy and nearly passed out, she later said. She was very angry at how the news people on the radio seemed happy Richard had been given the ultimate punishment.

She had to see him and console him and let him know she'd be there to the end, that nothing would stop her from helping him, that she'd do anything for him. She left work, went home, and cried her eyes dry.

With great effort she then pulled herself together, put on a yellow flowered dress, makeup on her face, combed her hair, set the VCR to tape the movie, and went to see Richard at the jail.

Visiting hours didn't begin until 5:30 P.M. She got there at 3:00 and took her place at a long line filled with hard-eyed women and unruly children. It was very difficult for Doreen, standing there, not to cry.

Two sheriff's deputies came out of the jail and asked her to come with them so they could look in her pocketbook. When the deputies were convinced she wasn't carrying any firearms or weapons, they let her get back into the line.

When her turn came, she took the elevator up to the second floor, where the sheriff's deputies again searched her pocketbook, and a female deputy searched her person thoroughly. She was told she'd have to wait for all the other inmates to have their visits, then they'd bring down Richard. She sat on a bench, "dazed, shocked, and stunned" for two hours, until the whole visiting area was cleared and Richard was brought out.

As usual, the visit was through dirty, smoked Plexiglas. He sat down as if the weight of San Quentin rested on his shoulders.

"Well, they did it," he said. "I told you."

"I'm so sorry, Richard."

"Me, too . . . but not for me. For my family, for my mother—for Ruth."

"You'll appeal it, and judging by how unfair the whole trial was, I'm sure you'll get a reversal."

"I don't know if I even want to appeal it. I don't want to go through another trial. Fuck that. Did you speak to my sister?"

"I tried calling, but the phone was busy and I couldn't get through."

"Call tonight. Tell them everything will be all right, that you saw me and I'm okay."

"I will. Daniel didn't call me—that's why I wasn't in the courtroom—I'm so sorry I wasn't there for you."

"Don't worry about it," he said, and looked down. Doreen had never seen him so sad and downhearted. Tears started rolling down her face. She told him that she loved him and in the end he'd win his appeal. He told her about the shower incident.

"So that's why they searched me and made me wait, you think?"

"That's why. Did you set the VCR?"

"Yes, of course, and I'll write you and tell you about all the highlights."

He thanked her and told her Carrillo and Salerno had come to visit.

"For what?" she asked.

"Just to talk. They are coming back to discuss the movie."

"Be careful."

"Careful . . . about what? It's all over."

"No, it's not. Don't give up. You can win an appeal."

"Fuck an appeal," he said, and the deputies came and announced time was up. Richard stood. He was taken back to his cell, angry he couldn't see the movie, hating what life had in store for him.

In El Paso, Texas, the news of Richard's sentence hit the Ramirez family hard. They were all gathered at Joseph's house. Reporter Tony Valdez from KTTV in Los Angeles was also there. He had been kind to Ruth when she was trying to get her brother a lawyer in the very beginning and had asked for permission to come to El Paso with a camera crew so he could capture the family's reaction to the sentence.

Right after Judge Tynan had finished the sentencing, a colleague of Valdez's had run to the phone and called El Paso from the courthouse. Ruth answered and gave Valdez the phone, as he ordered the camera put on the family.

The Ramirezes had turned down dozens of offers, some involving money, for interviews; only Tony Valdez was allowed near the family. He listened to his colleague say "nineteen death sentences," turned to Julian Ramirez, and said, *"Muerte, diecinueve veces."*

. A sudden sadness enveloped Julian. He looked down and appeared like a man whose heart had been cut in two. In Spanish, Valdez asked Julian what he thought. He looked up and said, "That jury may have sat in judgment of my son, but really there's only one who can judge him, and that is God."

The camera moved to Ruth. "I feel bad for the victims and their families, but we, too, have been victims."

Valdez signed off, saying the family were also victims.

The piece was shown on the four, five, six, and eleven o'clock Los Angeles news broadcasts and family members and survivors of the Night Stalker crimes called the station, complaining that Valdez had no right saying the Ramirez family were victims. They didn't want any sympathy extended to Richard's family.

When Mercedes Ramirez left Joseph's home, she and Ruth

went to church. Mercedes knelt in front of the Virgin Mary and prayed for her youngest boy's salvation. Ruth was crying too hard to be able to pray.

Julian went home and sat in his easy chair, his powerful shoulders bent by the weight of Richard's imminent execution. He told Joseph and Robert he wanted to be alone. The boys refused to leave him; they were afraid their father might commit suicide. Julian looked down and stared at the floor without blinking. Tears rolled from his unseeing eyes and fell on the backs of his huge, large-knuckled hands.

At 7 o'clock that evening the whole jury panel met at juror Shirley Jones's house. It was supposed to be a party, but there was a somber, sad cloud over everyone's head. It had been a very very difficult thing for some, not all, of the jurors to render a death sentence. "Regardless of how heinous the crimes were, Richard was still a human being, who was going to be put to death because of our decision," juror Martha Salcido said. Cindy, as well as Choclate Harris and a few of the other female jurors, felt Richard had been railroaded into the gas chamber. Cindy said she thought the Hernandezes should be prosecuted for incompetence—they had no right not putting some evidence forward when it came to the penalty phase.

Los Angeles Times photographer Mike Wu was there and he took pictures of the jurors, in which they wore serious stern countenances.

Later, when Cindy arrived home, she couldn't sleep. She felt haunted and deeply troubled by what she perceived as a "terrible injustice." Her heart ached at the thought of Richard being executed because of her: she felt that had she held out, she could have caused a hung jury. She was mad at herself for allowing the other jurors to convince her to vote for death; she was also mad at Daniel and Arturo and Ray Clark for not offering any mitigating circumstance that could have allowed her to vote differently about the death sentence. She was still crying at dawn, when she had to get ready to appear on *AM Los Angeles* along with two of the other jurors.

She was on the air at 8 A.M. At the host's urging, Cindy looked into the camera and told California that Richard deserved the death penalty. But, she added quickly, his lawyers had done a poor job representing him. She said she wondered what made Richard tick and hoped someday she'd be able to meet and talk to him.

Doreen made sure to catch Cindy's appearance on television. Of all the jurors, Doreen held only Cindy in disdain. She had seen the way Cindy had been looking at Richard during the trial "like she was hungry and he was food, or something."

She knew that Cindy had brought the valentine that said "I love you" for Richard's benefit.

Gil Carrillo and his whole family had gathered at his home to watch *Manhunt*. He was very proud of being portrayed on television. He knew there was much more to the story the film hadn't even touched on and hoped one day the "complete story" would be told the way it had really happened.

When the movie was over, the Carrillos had a celebration. It wasn't every day one of theirs was featured in a movie.

"It was a proud moment—one of the proudest moments in my career," Gil later said.

He had, he knew, helped root out, prosecute, and convict probably the most dangerous serial killer this century has ever known, for Richard Ramirez came when you were sleeping in your own bed.

Gil shivered at the thought of Ramirez stalking around people's darkened back yards, looking in windows, salivating at the very prospect of having a helpless woman in his control—it didn't matter what age—at his mercy.

He looked forward to talking to Richard some more, maybe getting some insight into what the hell made him tick, what he did to avoid apprehension.

"The fucker's a walking encyclopedia about murder and I'm going to find out what he knows," he said later.

Later that night, as they were preparing for bed, Pearl saw how sad Gil had become. She asked what was wrong. He sat down heavily on the bed and didn't answer. His lower lip began to tremble as if he might cry. "What's wrong, Gil?" she asked.

"I've been thinking about my dad. I wish . . . I wish he was here to share with me, with us, this triumph. I mean this is my shining moment as a detective; as a man. There'll never be another case like this, a killer as bad and cunning as Richard. I just wish . . . I wish he were here," and with that he did begin to cry in earnest, a thing Gil very rarely did. Pearl sat up and embraced his huge hulk.

"He is here, Gil. He is with you. I know it. I feel it," Pearl said.

Frank Salerno did not watch the movie. He didn't want to be reminded about all that had happened. Not yet. Jayne taped it for him.

When Carrillo and Salerno heard Richard hadn't been able to view the movie because of his antics in the bathroom, they decided it would be a good idea if they took a tape of the film to the jail so they could all watch it together.

The day after the movie had aired, they brought a bunch of chocolate bars, some popcorn, and some soda to the county jail. A VCR and a television had been set up in an interview room so they could watch the film with Richard.

Richard didn't think Greg Cruz, the actor portraying him, looked anything like him and said it appeared as if they'd put black wax over his teeth to make them look bad. Whenever a body was shown being taken from a house, Richard got excited. He thought A. Martinez, the actor playing Gil, was too small. They all got a laugh at that.

Richard asked if someday there would be a book about him, pointing out that there were a couple on Ted Bundy and half a dozen on the crimes of Jack the Ripper. Salerno said he didn't know of any book deals and explained to Richard that it would help the families of crimes they still suspected him of if he would now admit them. Richard said he wouldn't talk about anything but the convictions. Carrillo asked if it would be all right if they taped what he said. He said no.

They then began asking him about the crimes and how he did them. Richard gave them, the detectives later said—which Richard vehemently denies—the details of how he worked, lived, and avoided capture for so long. The detectives say he told them he capered in stolen cars, which he sometimes left in the parking lot of the Greyhound Bus Terminal. He always stashed any weapon he had in the terminal lockers until he realized the car might be staked out. At that point he began driving the cars around the block a few times before he retrieved his weapons.

According to the detectives, they began talking about the actual murders, beginning with Vincow. Richard told them what he knew. They weren't sure if he was bragging and making things up, but he seemed sincere, they thought.

For the next week, as Richard ate sweets, he told the two detectives the details of what he said had taken place. Both detectives enjoyed talking to him. "He had a likable side to him that was easy to warm to," Carrillo later said.

Their meetings were brought to a halt on November 16, when Richard was taken to San Quentin. The last time Salerno and Carrillo saw him, he asked them if they were going to come to his execution. Carrillo said he wasn't sure . . . didn't think so.

"You bet I'm coming," Salerno said, dead serious, looking Richard right in the eye.

San Quentin Prison was built in 1852. It is located on twenty acres of land at the foot of Mount Tam in Marin County, a thirty-minute scenic drive from San Francisco's Golden Gate Bridge.

Its south side runs parallel with the Bay of Skulls. The prison is painted a pale yellow with terra cotta roofs. It comprises five different buildings, or blocks, A through F. Death row is in E block.

Since 1893, 409 people have been executed at San Quentin, by hanging up to 1938, when the gas chamber was installed. Some of San Quentin's famous alumni are Caryl Chessman, the Red Light Bandit; James Watson, known as Bluebeard; and C. E. Bolton, or Black Bart. In gun towers in strategic positions around the prison are expert marksmen with automatic assault rifles with scopes. They man them twenty-four hours a day. It is a very scenic, lovely spot, with palm trees rustling in the gentle sea breezes and waves rhythmically lapping the coastline. An occasional shark's fin can be seen slicing the placid waters of the Bay of Skulls.

All men sentenced to die in California await their execution at San Quentin. Some of the serial killers presently housed in E block are Juan Corona, Randy Kraft, Lawrence Bittaker, Roy Lewis, David Carpenter, David Catlin, Douglas Clark, Mitchell Carton, and Bill Bonin (the Freeway Killer). These men would be Richard's neighbors.

Richard was taken to San Quentin ten days after he'd been sentenced. The authorities viewed him as a security risk: they knew he had many female admirers, and they knew about the Satanists who had regularly visited the trial, and there were always rumors that someone was going to try and break him out. For security reasons it was decided it would be better if he was flown to Quentin rather than driven.

The helicopter landed on the roof of the county jail in Los Angeles and picked up Richard, and with three guards watching his every move, he was flown up north. Richard had never been in a helicopter before. He was like a wide-eyed kid with a smile on his face, intensely looking out the window, though he began to get motion sickness. Still, he liked the idea of being flown to Quentin; it made him feel important and dangerous. He was shackled at the wrists and ankles and was wearing a blue Los Angeles County Jail jumpsuit.

At this point, he still had no plans to appeal his conviction; he viewed the system as corrupt and hell-bent on killing him. When the time came for him to die, he had decided to commit suicide. He didn't want a whole bunch of strangers watching him kick around in San Quentin's green room.

Death, as such, held no fear for Richard. More than ever he believed in his heart that he would go to Hell and sit at the right hand of Satan. He believed all the hardest criminals throughout history would be there and he'd get to know them. Jack the Ripper, Al Capone, John Dillinger, Ted Bundy, Adolf Hitler, and all the others sent to Hell for their deeds. Heaven and Hell were as real to Richard as the helicopter now taking him to San Quentin.

When the prison came into view, Richard sat up and stared at it; it looked, he thought, more like some vacation hotel, a Club Med or something.

In truth, Richard welcomed the change; he'd been locked

up in the Los Angeles County Jail for four years. Time was easier to do in a prison than in a jail: the visiting, food, and general conditions are much better.

Richard was handed over to heavily armed, grim-faced San Quentin officials. He was put in the A/C block, known as Reception. His prison number was E37101. All prisoners—except death row inmates—were kept in Reception while they were evaluated and it was decided where they would do their actual time.

Richard still had the Pan assault and murder charges against him, and until that case had been adjudicated, he would not be moved to E block after his obligatory three-month stay in Reception. He would, after evaluation, be transferred to the San Francisco County Jail, to be closer to court for hearings and motions on the Pan matter. Lawyers from the San Francisco public defender's office would be representing Richard in the Pan incident.

Richard was put in another six-by-eight-foot cell with an aluminum toilet, a sink, and a bunk bed. Prisoners in reception did not have access to phones, and their visits were for only two hours a week. In E block, the inmates were allowed twenty-four hours a week for visits, and Reception inmates were kept in the cell nearly twenty-four hours a day. Richard was assigned cell number 3AC8.

Cindy Haden was having a hard time keeping Richard Ramirez off her mind. He was all she could think of—his intense black eyes, his wavy black hair, his absolute and undeniable arrogance and danger. She dreamt of him nearly every night, often wondering if he had put some kind of spell on her. She would later say, "The truth of the matter is, I think I fell in love with him the first time I saw him. I know it's nuts and everything, but I couldn't help it; it was just one of those things."

A week after the sentencing, the Hernandezes asked to meet with her in the office of an attorney in downtown Los Angeles. After she'd waited for two hours, she called Ray Clark's office, hoping to locate the Hernandezes there. Clark didn't know they had requested a meeting with her.

Cindy took the opportunity to complain to Clark about the

defense, which she thought had been "woefully inadequate." It was "a sin" no evidence had been presented on Richard's behalf during the penalty phase. "Why didn't you do something during the penalty phase?" she demanded.

"Because he wouldn't let us," Clark said. "He's very stubborn."

When the Hernandezes arrived, they told her Richard wanted to talk with her. If she was interested, she could write him in care of San Quentin Prison and gave her his prison number and address.

Daniel then asked her what she thought of the defense they had mounted on Richard's behalf.

Cindy Haden laid into the Hernandezes, saying they had done a terrible job of defending Richard, that they hadn't had enough experience, that they'd missed the most crucial element to their client's benefit. When Daniel asked what that was, she told them it was Satan.

She believed Richard had been possessed by "some demonic force" when he'd committed the crimes and they'd not even mentioned it, let alone tried to highlight it as a viable defense. "It was something the jury should certainly have known about," she said.

When she got home, Cindy wrote Richard a long letter, saying how sorry she was about the death sentence, and tried to explain that she, and the jury as a whole, had had no legal alternative but to vote for death. She mailed the letter and anxiously waited for a response, which took only four days.

Richard wrote her back and said he understood, that she shouldn't feel bad about anything, not to beat herself up, and asked her to write him some more and maybe even come and visit.

Cindy was thrilled when she got his letter and immediately wrote him back.

The day after Richard left for San Quentin, Gil Carrillo left for Waikiki for vacation with Pearl, the kids, and four other couples. After ten days he went back to work. He couldn't help wondering when the next serial murder case would come his way.

During this time, Gil began thinking about running for

Sheriff. He had gotten a lot of publicity because of the Stalker case, and there were certain things in the sheriff's department that he would like to see changed. He talked it over with his wife, who said if that's what he wanted to do, she'd support him.

Something was wrong with Frank Salerno. The problems had begun at the end of 1989 and had escalated: he'd started experiencing dizzy spells, then vertigo so bad the room would seem like it was spinning and he'd have to sit down. He went to his family doctor, thinking there might be a problem with his inner ear, but the doctor couldn't find anything wrong. The dizziness and spinning not only continued but got worse, and he developed insomnia. He told Capt. Grimm, who sent Frank to see his own doctor, who did a complete physical.

When the results came back, the doctor had bad news for Frank which hit him very hard: Frank had high blood pressure and had developed a heart problem called arrhythmia. He told Frank he needed a lot of rest, little excitement, and to change his diet—no meat, no cheese, no fried food.

Frank was forced to take a leave of absence, which proved to be very hard for him at first. He was a homicide detective through and through; chasing and capturing killers was his passion in life, and now suddenly that was all taken away.

The first time Ruth Ramirez saw Richard after the sentencing, she had come up to Los Angeles by bus, then, with Doreen, flown to San Francisco. Ruth felt Doreen really loved her brother, and Richard had told Ruth he could trust Doreen. When Ruth saw the first editorial piece Doreen had written defending Richard, she really believed Doreen was in Richard's corner a hundred percent and accepted her as if she had been a childhood friend or a sister.

They drove to San Quentin and had to wait eleven hours to see Richard. There were always many prisoners in Reception, with a lot of visitors. The prison's facility for Reception visits was small, and ten- to fifteen-hour waits were the norm.

When Ruth finally did get to see her kid brother, she was

surprised at how well he had taken the death sentence. "It didn't seem to bother him," she'd later say.

Richard was, though, concerned about what his parents were going through. Ruth told him they were not taking it at all well. Mercedes often cried at night, and their father was quiet all the time, never smiled, and seemed to be "drifting away. He doesn't look well. His diabetes is getting worse," she said.

"Tell him I said this is a bunch of bullshit, that I didn't kill anyone—that this is all a big railroad job."

"I'll tell him," Ruth said. Richard thanked Doreen for helping his sister, for waiting so many hours for a visit. She told him she'd do anything for him, that she loved him.

Both Ruth and Doreen told Richard to appeal the conviction, that he could win an appeal on grounds of incompetent counsel. Richard said he'd think about it.

The following week Doreen flew to El Paso to meet with the family. She stayed with Ruth. After a dinner at Julian and Mercedes's house, Julian took her aside and thanked her for being so dedicated to Richard. He told her he would like to see her and Richard get married.

FIFTY-SIX

In February 1990, Ramirez was moved to the San Francisco County Jail, where he had access to a phone and a television and interacted with other inmates. Almost immediately, he got into a fight over the phones and beat up some guy who'd called him a punk. Richard knew he couldn't let anyone abuse him in any way, for the abuse would surely get worse and more than likely end up as an assault against him. He was quick to let everyone in the jail know if you bothered him, you'd better be ready to fight to the end. This resulted in his being left alone and he could do his time without being bothered.

Now that he had access to a phone, he called Cindy Haden collect and they talked for the first time. She felt like an errant schoolgirl getting involved with the bad kid in the neighborhood.

As a result of this first phone call, she thought he was sweet and shy and funny, nothing like the monster who had committed the murders and assaults she had heard about for so many months. Richard told Cindy he loved her. She was surprised and taken aback. "You don't even know what love is," she said.

"You are right," he said. "I don't. I had no one on the outside. Do you love me?"

There was a long pause. She laughed nervously, then said, "Yes, Richard, I do love you."

He invited her to come visit him in San Francisco, and that weekend she went to see him.

The visiting situation was much better at the county jail, and Cindy waited only an hour before they brought him out. They spoke to one another through Plexiglas and over the phone. Cindy later said she was so nervous her hands were shaking. Her heart was beating so hard she was afraid it would explode.

He told her he was very happy she had written him. He had wanted to talk with her since the very beginning.

Blushing, she said she had fallen in love with him the first time she'd laid eyes on him.

She cried and apologized for voting to sentence him to death. He told her to forget it—that he understood. She told him she wanted to hold him, to have him inside her. He told her maybe she could come with his lawyers when they came to visit. They'd then be able to have physical contact.

Their time was up.

When Cindy left Richard that day, she felt truly alive for the first time. As she flew back to Los Angeles, she thought about moving to San Francisco so she could be closer to Richard; for the first time she realized why she had left her husband and Portland, Oregon: she felt that being with Richard, as near to him as possible, "was my destiny."

As it turned out, it was very difficult for Frank Salerno to stay retired. After six months of recuperation, regularly swimming, hunting, and fishing, he told Jayne he was feeling much better and wanted to return to work. He wasn't experiencing the vertigo any longer, his heart condition had stabilized, and he had no trouble sleeping at night.

When he went back to work, though, the job wasn't the same. "Something had gone out of it," he'd later relate. He began to think he might have done it all when it came to homicide work and maybe it was time to quit.

A deputy sheriff was murdered and Frank, as an acting lieutenant, was put in charge of a task force of ten men to try and find the killer. Running this task force, however, was apparently too much for Frank, for he again started experiencing the dizziness and vertigo and shortness of breath.

Jayne didn't want him working homicides any longer and told him it was time to put police work behind him forever. He had to agree with her. He was still a relatively young man and could, he knew, have a long, wonderful life . . . if he got away from Sheriff's Homicide.

In August of 1993, Frank Salerno, the famous bulldog of Sheriff's Homicide, retired from police work for good. Jayne thought it would be fitting if he had a retirement party and, with Frank's approval, she and Jaquie Franco—a colleague of Frank's at Sheriff's Homicide—organized a huge affair at Steven's Steak House in Commerce. They invited all of Frank's friends and former colleagues and their wives, his and her families, and it turned out to be over 300 people. Among the guests was Whitney Bennett and her family.

Whitney had grown into a very beautiful young woman with honey-colored hair and large blue eyes. She had gone through a number of plastic surgery operations to correct the damage done to her by the tire iron, and one was hard pressed to see any scars.

At the party Jack Scully, Frank's ex-partner and master of ceremonies, introduced her to the audience, including Mike Salerno.

From the first time Mike had seen Whitney the day she had testified at Richard's trial, he thought there was something special about her. Later in the evening he asked her if it would be okay if he called her and she said yes and gave him her number. A few days after the party, Mike did in fact phone Whitney and they began dating; the two hit it off very well and soon were deeply in love.

It didn't take long for Michael to decide he wanted to be with Whitney forever and he asked her to marry him. She said yes without hesitation.

When Mike told his parents he and Whitney were getting married, Frank Salerno was a very happy man; he already cared for Whitney like she was his daughter and this news put a huge smile in his heart and on his face.

When Gil Carrillo heard Mike and Whitney were getting married, he too was overjoyed, saw it as maybe the only good thing that had come out of the Night Stalker case.

Cindy Haden continued visiting Richard every chance she got. She'd come mostly on weekends, when Doreen was visiting, too. The two women began seeing each other at the jail. Doreen felt Cindy was a "low-down, hypocritical bitch" who could have hung the jury. Whenever Doreen saw Cindy at the jail, she would narrow her eyes and regard her with utter disdain. When Doreen asked Richard why the hell he would allow that Benedict Arnold to visit, he said she was a juror and might be of help if he chose to appeal his conviction.

After a few months of Cindy driving all the way to San Francisco every weekend, she began thinking she would move north permanently so she could be close to Richard. She was in love with him and had pictures of him in frames on her night table and on the wall opposite her bed. Cindy had told her parents about her relationship with Richard and had actually brought her mom and dad to the jail so they could meet him. When Richard first sat across from them in the visiting booth, Cindy said, "Mom, Dad, this is Richard," as Richard smiled shyly. "I know you've heard some bad things about him, but he's got a lot of good points, too."

Richard sheepishly said hello, waved, and began talking to Cindy's father, who, like his father, had worked for a railroad. They had "something in common," as Cindy later put it.

Cindy agreed to do several national talk shows—"Donahue" once and "Geraldo" twice—and told the world, in a very passionate voice, that Richard Ramirez had had improper counsel and his convictions should be overturned.

Some of the groupies who had been visiting Richard in Los Angeles now began to go to San Francisco to see him. Doreen was unhappy with all the competition she had. She'd complain to him that they were taking visiting time away from her, but Richard enjoyed all the female attention.

Never before had he had so much female admiration—and he reveled in it, thrived upon it.

Cindy, unlike Doreen, didn't mind Richard's other visitors, as long as none of them bothered her.

But there was one woman Cindy and Doreen came to refer to as "the bimbo," who did, in fact, start getting aggressive with both Cindy and Doreen. The Bimbo, a heavy-set, well-built belligerent blonde with frizzy hair, and a big nose, began to challenge Cindy and Doreen when she ran into them at the jail. "He's mine. Stay away from him or I'll break your face," she'd say regularly.

Cindy stood up to her, telling her to fuck off, but Doreen

did not have Cindy's combative nature and would take the Bimbo's threats, taunts, and admonitions. The Bimbo began regularly to step on Doreen's toes and call her "Dogreen." It got to the point that Doreen began asking the jail guards to walk her to her car, she was so afraid of the Bimbo.

Doreen again complained to Richard, but he didn't stop the Bimbo from coming to the jail.

Several of the Ramirez women would bring phallic-shaped vegetables with them on their visits and would sexually excite themselves with the vegetables while Ramirez watched.

For many of these women Richard Ramirez was a turn-on.

"The fact that he was so dangerous and so close, yet couldn't hurt me, got me excited as soon as I sat down for a visit," one Ramirez groupie would later admit. "It was like the beauty and the beast kind of thing."

Cindy Haden wanted to be able to touch Richard, hold him, and be close to him, and she constantly thought of ways she could make that happen.

When her employer had a mass layoff and she was fired, she decided she would become a private detective. If she had a detective's license, she'd be able to work with Richard's new San Francisco attorneys and have a visit with Richard in a private room. She applied for a job with a San Francisco security firm, was hired, and moved to San Francisco. She took a quiet apartment in Richmond. The security firm sponsored her for a license, and she passed the required examination.

She went to one of the San Francisco public defenders representing Richard and talked him into taking her inside the county jail with him when he went to visit Richard. She and the attorney were shown into one of seven rooms allocated for lawyers who come to see inmates. It was ten by ten and had a wooden table and a few chairs. There were panels of glass in a wall so guards could look in. As Cindy waited for Richard to be brought down, her heart raced. She paced back and forth, her hands trembling. When Richard got there, the guard uncuffed him and he sat at the table. They were like two school kids, laughing and giggling.

Under the desk she raised her foot and put it on Richard's thigh; his eyes bulged. He couldn't believe he was actually sit-

THE NIGHT STALKER / 543

ting with one of the jurors who had handed him a ticket to the death room. After a few minutes, Cindy later related, the attorney went to look for a bathroom. When he left and Cindy was sure there were no guards about, she stood and quickly gave Richard a deep kiss as he groped her with his huge hands. She nearly passed out, she was so excited.

When later asked if she was afraid to be alone with Richard, she said, "No, absolutely not. He'd never hurt me."

When the lawyer returned, Cindy sat down, breathless, her heart pounding.

On subsequent visits to the jail, as she helped with Richard's legal problems, she says, she was able to have more contact visits and was actually alone with Richard.

Gil Carrillo decided to run for Sheriff; he felt there were grass-roots changes he could make which would vastly improve the efficiency of the sheriff's office. His platform would be that of a detective who had intimate working knowledge of the problems inherent in any huge police department.

He took a leave of absence in the spring of 1994 and began campaigning intensively. Pearl and his sisters pitched in and helped run his campaign office, made mailings and hung up posters.

His opponent, Sheriff Block, had become a giant in L.A. law enforcement. Gil's going up against him was akin to David taking on Goliath. Gil lost in the primary and dropped out of the race.

As a result of his involvement in the Stalker case, Gil is often asked to speak to police agencies around the country, including the FBI academy at Quantico, Virginia. And he always warns his colleagues to never discount any possibility when it comes to serial killers.

Gil Carrillo is presently working homicides out of the East L.A. Station. He is not at all bitter about losing the election. He always knew it was a longshot, but he had to give it a go. Today he is again trying to solve Los Angeles homicides, enjoying the work as much as ever.

FIFTY-SEVEN

Doreen continued to visit "her true love" on weekends and whenever she could get away. She wanted to move to San Francisco but couldn't because of her magazine job.

Whenever she saw Cindy, her stomach would turn. She'd later confide, "I knew she was up to no good and really wished she'd just get lost."

Doreen acted as Richard's confidante and secretary, took care of his correspondence, and passed messages to his lawyers and family. Often he received mail from all over the country, and Doreen helped him with his letters.

He'd call her collect from the San Francisco jail and she'd play heavy metal music for him over the phone. She put what money she made as an editor in his commissary account and did whatever she could to help him.

When asked if she ever thinks about the crimes Richard was convicted of, she says, "When you love someone, you only see the good in them. And that trial was a travesty of justice."

Doreen's family was quite displeased with her for getting involved with the likes of Richard Ramirez, but that didn't put a dent in her feelings for him; he was her sunset and sunrise, as she puts it, and she hopes one day to be Mrs. Ramirez.

Indeed, she says Richard has asked her to marry him and she's accepted.

Richard was becoming a problem for his San Francisco jailers—he was having just too many female visitors, some of whom argued and fought with one another at the jail. *A Current Affair* learned of Richard's admirers and did a story about all the fans coming to see him, which they appropriately called "Death Row Romeo." It was decided Richard should be moved back to San Quentin "for security reasons," the county jail told the press.

On September 21, 1993, Richard was returned to San Quentin. He didn't want to be there, for he'd be housed in the adjustment center, where visits were exceedingly limited, he had no access to the phone, and he was locked up almost twenty-four hours a day.

Doreen finally decided she had to be closer to Richard and she moved to the San Francisco area and got a job as a caretaker. Although she didn't have to drive the seven hours from Los Angeles anymore, in order to have a visit with him, she now had to go to San Quentin in the early morning hours to get a number. There were only three shifts of thirteen visitors each visiting day for inmates in Adjustment. Visitor's days were Thursday, Friday, Saturday, and Sunday.

Doreen was regularly waiting ten to twenty hours to get into the prison for a thirty-minute visit through glass, over the phone, though she didn't mind. She'd sit in her car eating sunflower seeds, and write him love letters as she watched the sun come up, glistening like fire on the Bay of Skulls. With a job and someone she had to account to, she managed to see Richard only on Sundays, her day off.

Likewise, Cindy Haden had to wait many hours for her Saturday visit. Richard tried to keep the two of them apart. They are, he laments, like oil and water.

Doreen kept pressing Richard to make Cindy and the other women stop coming, "especially the Bimbo," but her demands fell on deaf ears. At times Doreen would get so mad, she'd leave San Francisco and go back to L.A., but inevitably she returned to Marin County. She realized Richard wasn't the most rational person, and she fervently hoped he'd see how much she loved him and make her his bride.

She'd later say, "I'm not just another one of his numbskull girlfriends. I believed we were getting married. I mean, otherwise I'd have left."

When she pressed Richard for a specific date for them to take vows, he'd put her off. He'd tell her he loved her and that she was the only person he trusted outside his family—which was true.

No matter what, Richard knew Doreen would do anything for him.

When recently asked if she believes Richard is innocent, Doreen said, "I've always fervently believed in his innocence! I can't even conceive of his being guilty of the terrible things they say he did. He received an unfair trial with very inadequate legal representation. Someday the truth will be known."

Julian Tapia Ramirez took his youngest son's plight to heart.

After the conviction and sentencing, his diabetes progressively worsened; he lost weight every week. He had tomatoes and chilies growing in the back yard, but he stopped tending them and they died. His broad, powerful shoulders were shrinking and rounding. More and more lines formed on his high-cheekboned face. Nothing Mercedes did or said could bring Julian out of the deep depression that followed Richard's sentencing.

The only thing, that put a gleam in his eyes, that he looked forward to, was being with his grandchildren.

Like her husband, Mercedes had been devastated by the death sentence. She aged twenty years in the months following her son's sentencing. Deep, bitter lines, like cracks in fallow soil, completely mapped her face; she, too, lost weight. She went to church religiously every day and fervently prayed, eyes closed, hands clasped, for the salvation of the family.

Julian was diagnosed with bone cancer in the spring of 1991. The cancer spread quickly and he died of it on August 16 of that year.

Julian's death crushed Mercedes. Life without Julian wasn't worth living; and she surely would have died of a broken heart, but she had to be there for Richie and wasn't about to give up until she'd done all she could to help him and the rest of the family.

Joseph's children were stigmatized by being related to Richard. It was no secret the feared Night Stalker, now even more famous than John Wesley Harding, was their uncle. There were always taunts and rude remarks at school, though the children acted like they didn't notice the pointed barbs thrown at them or written on their lockers.

But they knew what was said and it hurt them deeply.

Troubled, they went to Joseph and complained to him. He'd tell them just to ignore those stupid people, though he remembered only too well the mean things that had been said to him as a child. He prayed his children would be thick-skinned.

Richard's oldest brother, Ruben, turned to heroin and found solace in its numbing embrace. He felt responsible to a degree about what had happened to his kid brother, and after the death of his father, he very rarely smiled.

Ruth never remarried. She lives with her mother and daughter in the Hacienda Heights house. Whenever she can, she goes to visit Richard. No matter what, Ruth will be there to the end for her baby brother.

"I love Richie to death. We were always the closest in the family," she would later relate. "If they kill him, I'll go crazy."

Joseph has a good job designating maintenance people at the Fort Bliss army base. He has many commendations, plaques, and awards. He works hard every day and goes to church several times a week. He still has much difficulty getting around, but he does his best and rarely complains. He, too, visits Richard when he can, twice a year or so, but it is a difficult trip for him, though he gladly makes it. Joseph loves Richard dearly. He gets a heavy heart and is brought to tears when he thinks of his brother's fate.

Joseph, like Richard, Robert, and Ruben, often gets migraine headaches that are so bad he must lie down in the dark. "You can't even talk to me when they come. It's like having hot needles in your brain."

Robert still lives in Morenci, Arizona, working in its mines. He is divorced now and sees his two daughters on weekends. When he can, he drives to El Paso to see his mother and his siblings. He has stopped using drugs and avoids trouble at all costs.

Cousin Mike, the person most people believe put Richard on the path he traveled, died of a massive heart attack in April of 1995. He was overweight and still haunted by the ghosts of things he'd done in Vietnam, regularly using heroin. The Army gave Mike a hero's burial with a twenty-one-gun salute.

* * *

For the first time since he'd been arrested, Richard has excellent, very competent legal council, in the form of five-foot-seven Michael Burt, with the San Francisco public defender's office.

Burt is a handsome, nattily dressed advocate who knows the law backward and forward and comes to court very well prepared. He was one of the lawyers who helped defend Lyle Menendez in his first trial, and he represented the very infamous Charles Ng, who, with Leonard Lake, tortured, sexually assaulted, and killed dozens of people in front of a video camera on a ranch in Wesleyville, California.

The San Francisco district attorney had been planning to try Richard for the Pan murder. Many in law enforcement say it was a waste of taxpayer money. However, when Burt had extensive psychological tests done on Richard (for the first time), and moved Richard's plea from not guilty to insanity, the San Francisco district attorney backed down. He said they would prosecute Richard only if he won an appeal in the L.A. convictions.

Gere Russell, out of San Diego, is Richard's appeals lawyer. She, like Burt, is an excellent attorney who leaves no stone unturned. She believes Richard has a very good chance at getting a reversal and is presently working hard on perfecting his appeal.

"There were many major mistakes, the least of which was incompetent counsel. The Hernandezes should have *never* been allowed to represent anyone in a capital case."

If, indeed, Richard wins the appeal, he will have to be brought back to the L.A. County Jail and tried all over again—a very daunting, unsettling prospect for the L.A. district attorney's office.

The appeal, Russell says, won't be ready until the end of the century—and by then it will be nearly twenty years after the crimes, which would put the prosecution at a huge disadvantage: witnesses die, move away, and forget details.

Today, Frank Salerno has adjusted to his retirement. He has no heart problems. The vertigo is all gone, and he sleeps well.

He doesn't miss being a homicide detective at all.

"I did it all and saw it all. There just wasn't anything left I'd not done. I got out just in time. It takes its toll on you. You think you are OK, but it breaks you down. Murder is not a healthy occupation."

Often, Frank is invited to speak at police seminars about the Stalker and the Hillside Strangler crimes around the country. He feels obligated to tell people in law enforcement what he learned about apprehending serial murderers as a result of all the experience in the two huge cases.

He recently said, "What makes serial murder cases so difficult to solve is the fact that the killer and the victim are strangers. You've got two ships passing in the night and for no good reason, one blows the other out of the water."

Today, Ramirez is still sitting in his cell in the adjustment center at San Quentin, waiting for his appeal to be argued, getting visits from Doreen, his family, and other supporters. He says he was railroaded and has hopes in the appeal.

He has changed much in the eleven years since August of 1985. He's gained thirty-five pounds and he's mellowed out. The seething anger he often expressed in court seems to be filed in a place he now has control over. But by no means has he adjusted to the reality of his existence. He does not like being in the adjustment center, saying it's cruel and unusual punishment, and he often paces his cell like a caged panther.

He recently said of his predicament: "I don't know how much longer I can hold out in here. This existence sucks big time. Boring as hell. No drugs, no pussy—might as well be fucking dead. Check this out—a little bit of philosophy—desire comes from the loins, emotions come from the heart, and knowledge comes from the head."

When not pacing, Richard writes letters and reads books— everything he can get his hands on about murder. He's become quite the expert on killers and killing.

Richard believes he will win the appeal, win at a new trial, and be set free.

He still has faith, as strong as ever, in Satan and believes he, Satan, will ultimately make him victorious and free.

In early 1995, when Richard was coming back to San

Quentin from court appearances on the Pan matter in San Francisco, the prison's metal detector went off. The guards searched him thoroughly and couldn't find any contraband, yet the metal detector still sounded when they passed him through it again. Officials put him in front of an X-ray machine and discovered he had a handcuff key and a hypodermic needle in a little vial hidden in his anal cavity, a very common practice in jails around the world known as "keistering."

Because of this incident, the San Quentin guards, these days, watch Richard Ramirez very carefully.

When Richard was asked recently how to avoid becoming the victim of a serial murderer, he said, "You can't. Once they are focused on you, have you where you are vulnerable, you're all theirs. Dahmer used to invite you home for a drink, and the next thing you knew, he's eating you. Same thing with John Gacy: he'd put on his clown face, do a couple of tricks, and suddenly he had you handcuffed and in his control. What people can do is not trust someone you don't know and to always be aware of what's going on around you. When you drop your guard—that's when a serial killer moves."

FIFTY-EIGHT

THE WEDDING

Thursday, June 27th of 1996, Richard Ramirez was moved out of the adjustment center to San Quentin's East block, "Death Row," where he would be allowed regular "contact visits" with his family and friends—the first since he'd been arrested. His attorney, Michael Burt, had been writing letters to the prison for many months, demanding that Richard be taken out of the adjustment center. His family had been praying for that, and Doreen wanted him to be moved more than anything in the world, for in "East block" Richard Ramirez would be allowed to wed.

Richard had taken the Bimbo off his visiting list and had told Doreen that if he was moved to East block he would marry her. Since the first time she'd seen Richard on TV being taken away from the angry mob on Hubbard Street, she had wanted to marry him, to fight his battles, to be known as Mrs. Richard Ramirez.

That day Doreen went to the prison for her regular Thursday visit, but was told that Richard had been moved. "Moved to where?" she asked the guard.

"Don't know yet," she was told curtly.

Doreen had always been afraid that something terrible would happen to Richard while he was at San Quentin. She knew it was a dangerous place. Men were being killed all the time in fights with other prisoners. In a panic she went back to her little apartment in San Rafael and sat by the phone, hoping, praying that Richard had been moved to East block.

She sat by the phone, not eating or sleeping the whole night. As each hour passed, her heart sank lower and the knots in her stomach grew tighter.

As dawn slowly broke in the east, she looked out the window. A low gray sky hung over San Quentin "like a funeral shroud," portending something ominous. At 8 A.M. the phone rang. She jumped at the sudden sound, nearly falling out of her chair. It was Richard calling from—East block. When he told her he'd been moved she cried with joy, almost unable to believe she would actually, now, be able to touch him . . . for the first time. He told her that his cell was smaller in East block and that he didn't know anyone there, and was very uncomfortable. There were, he said, some very infamous serial killers in the cells to either side of him—Randy Kraft, Juan Corona, Lawrence Bittaker, aka "the Pliers," because he ripped off the nipples of his victims with a pair of pliers.

Doreen was so excited she could barely hold the phone. She said, "Well, now that you are there, are we getting married?"

"I said," he said, "we would, and we will."

"Promise?"

"Promise."

"Oh Richard, I love you," she gushed, crying uncontrollably with joy now, gasping for breath. He told her to put away all the tears and come on over to the prison.

"I'm on my way, darling," she said and, in a whirlwind of activity, her heart pounding away as if she'd been running, she showered, did her hair, put on her makeup and a new special flowered dress she'd been saving for this occasion and ran out the door. She jumped into her car and sped over to the prison, went through security, and, with trembling legs and sweating hands, walked the 150 yards from the front gate to East block. Just above the entrance to the short, squat, red brick building streaked with water stains, stood a serious-faced prison guard, affectionately cradling a glistening blue-black assault rifle. He held it, she thought, as if it were a small child. She wanted to wave to him, to say hello, but she knew Richard wouldn't like that, and she walked up to East block's tall door. A guard opened it electronically from the inside. She gave him her driver's license and visiting pass and, with hesitation, walked slowly into the room where all death row inmates have their visits. It was 200 feet wide and 50 feet deep, the walls industrial-gray. A hundred hard orange plastic chairs were bolted to the gray cement floor in neat rows going left to right. On her right there was a bank of coin-operated machines that dispensed coffee, candy, hot soup and sandwiches—even foamy cappuccino.

Nearly all the chairs were filled with the condemned and their visitors. Wearing their Sunday-best, children of the convicts ran about. Doreen's eyes quickly scanned the room. Richard was not there yet. She recognized women she'd met over the years visiting with their men. One or two waved to her, small sedate movements. Doreen recognized notorious Los Angeles gang members and serial killers whose faces had been plastered all over the newspapers and television. She was so nervous her stomach felt as if there were huge butterflies fluttering about in it. Then, off to her right, on the far wall, a thick steel door opened and there, suddenly, was Richard Ramirez. She couldn't believe her eyes. She walked slowly toward him as if he were a mirage that might disappear any moment.

When people in the room realized who was abruptly among them, there was a hushed silence. Richard had not walked free among men, women and children, since the day of his arrest, one hundred and thirty-two months ago—"eleven years," she thought. He looked like a spooked deer caught in the headlights of a speeding car. He had to wear glasses now; they were silver, large and round, making his dark eyes appear huge, owl-like. He spotted Doreen and slowly moved toward her. As she got closer to him, Doreen felt as if she might faint. She reached out and embraced him. He flinched at her touch and led her to a corner of the room where there were two empty seats. Awkward, uncomfortable being around people, he sat. Doreen kept thinking he would disappear any moment. She couldn't stop crying, which annoyed Richard, and he kept telling her to "put away the tears."

"I can't . . . I'm sorry . . . I'm just so happy."

She reached out to caress his face. He recoiled. He was not, she'd later tell a journalist, accustomed to being touched affectionately. He again told her they would be married and they talked about getting his family up from El Paso. Marriages on death row occur every four months, and Richard promised her he would tell the prison to put him down for it. The next time they'd be able to wed, he said, was October 3rd.

Before she knew it, her time was up. They embraced goodbye and she said she'd be back the next day. Now that Richard was in E block he could have contact visits from 8 to 2 P.M., Thursday, Friday, Saturday, and Sunday. The thought of being able to spend so much "quality time" with Richard made her head swim. When she arrived home, feeling as if she were walking a foot above the ground, she called Richard's sister Ruth in El Paso and told her the wonderful news—that Richard had been moved, and that they were going to wed on the 3rd of October. Ruth, too, cried with joy, congratulating her soon-to-be sister-in-law. She, Ruth, knew how much Doreen wanted to marry her brother, and she was truly happy for her. She thought, also, that Doreen would be a positive influence on Richard, certainly a world better than the other women, the Satanists and freaks, that had congregated around Richard since his arrest. They made plans for Ruth to come up a few days before the wedding so they could spend some time together, and Ruth would be able to hold her baby brother. As if it were yesterday, Ruth remembered Richard as a little boy who used to love to dance to the radio. Thinking of him like that, with his wide-eyed innocence and easy smile, made her heart roll over in her chest. When Ruth hung up with Doreen, she told her family the good news. Her brother Joseph said he wanted to go to the wedding and he immediately arranged to take time off of work. His older daughter, now seventeen, wanted to come.

True to his word, Richard did ask prison officials for permission to marry Doreen on October 3rd. They gave him a form to fill out, which he promptly did, listing Doreen as his fiancée. According to the California Penal Code, prisoners have the legal right to marry.

The prison approved Richard's marriage, and his and Doreen's names were added to the list of ten inmates marrying that day, three from death row. It was quickly pointed out to a curious journalist by San Quentin's public relations department that prisoners on death row do not have the right to conjugal visits.

Doreen had to have an appropriate wedding dress, and went from store to store searching for one.

"I wanted something plain, not a gown with a veil, anything like that. I've seen women in bridal gowns at the prison and they . . . well, they looked silly. Mine, I decided, would be simple and plain. And, of course, white."

Doreen was, she would tell anyone who asked, a virgin and she would, she said, wear a white dress proudly. "Richard knew I'd never been with anyone else. I'm sure that's one of the reasons he asked me to marry him."

A suitable dress, though, was much harder to come by than she imagined. She finally found the right dress at Macy's. Tasteful and appropriate, it was satin and lace, knee-length with a wide neck and cost $145.00. Next she had to shop for the rings. She drove to San Francisco for them and picked out two simple wedding bands, hers gold and Richard's platinum. When later asked why Richard told Doreen not to buy a gold ring for him, he said, "Because Satanists don't wear gold."

The press got wind of the wedding on Saturday, September 22nd. The first reporter to contact Doreen was Marsha Ginsberg of the *San Francisco Examiner.* Doreen, for the most part, was very distrustful of reporters and what they thought of her impending marriage to Richard, but Marsha assured her that the piece would be respectful. Doreen agreed to an interview and the story ran on the front page of the *Examiner's* Sunday edition. The headline read: "Night Stalker Gets Virgin Bride: Death Row Wedding," and the article went on to describe Doreen as "a Catholic, who vowed to retain her virginity until marriage . . . says she loved the Satan-revering Ramirez from the first time she saw him in 1986, and doesn't believe he committed the crimes."

The *Examiner* story hit like a bomb in northern as well as southern California. It made all the wire services and overnight the Night Stalker wedding was the hottest story on the West Coast. Reporters descended on Doreen like "hungry vultures with no table manners," she would say.

They soon found out where she lived and staked out her house, but she saw them and took off, checking into a nearby hotel. Not able to get an interview with her, the reporters started interviewing her neighbors, told them Doreen was marrying the Night Stalker, and asked what they thought of that:

"An outrage."

"She needs a good doctor."

"How does that cold-blooded killer get married after killing people's husbands and wives?"

"What he should be is shot like a rabid dog, not getting married. Goes to show you—our society is going to pot."

"It's a travesty of justice."

"It's a dirty, rotten, sin," were some of the responses.

Even the *Los Angeles Times* did a story, a front-page piece, by Pam Warrick, with the picture of Doreen featured in this book. The *Times* headline read, "I saw something that captivated me." Jay Leno began doing skits on the upcoming wedding; he did four consecutive nights of jokes. On one show Leno said they had the actual wedding cake and a big cake was dramatically wheeled onto the stage and the groom on top of it had wild hair, holding a long knife over his head. The audience howled.

However, victims of Stalker attacks were outraged that the person who stole their loved ones' lives, their dignity, who beat, raped, and robbed them, was getting married, was having a "happy day." "A system," one said, "that allows such a perverted, disgraceful travesty to take place is truly wrong and should be changed, must be changed. It's an outrage!"

Indeed, victims, as well as a lot of police officials, including Attorney General Dan Lundgren, phoned the prison and demanded the wedding be cancelled, but they were all told it was Ramirez's right by law, and they couldn't intercede. Governor Pete Wilson said he would look into changing the laws right away. CNN picked up the story and ran it every half hour on "Headline News." It became the lead-off piece on every news show on every channel, day and night. Doreen Lioy had become very hot news and reporters searched high and low for her to no avail.

On the days before the wedding, she couldn't even leave her hotel room. Richard's sister flew up and stayed with her. They watched all the news shows and Doreen didn't like the things reporters were saying, but she knew she'd become a target, a big red bull's eye, when word of her imminent death row wedding went out.

Reporters soon found out she had a twin sister named Donna living in Burbank and news trucks lined the block where her sister resided. They relentlessly phoned her and knocked on her door. The *Burbank Leader* did a big cover story, with a 1973 photograph from Doreen's yearbook at Burbank High. Donna had always been afraid that the public would find out about her sister's relationship, and now it had become world news, the last thing she'd wanted. She wouldn't leave her house, she was so ashamed. But she did tell Therese Moreau at the *Burbank Leader* during a phone interview, "Our only connection is that we were born together, but other than that we have no ties."

She called her sister in San Rafael and told her she'd been disowned by the family. "From this day on you are not my sister—and you will not ever be allowed near my kids."

That, of all things, hurt Doreen the most: the loss of her niece and nephew. She loved children, yearned to have some of her own, but knew that was an impossibility and had made her sister's kids her own. "After all," she'd later say, "My sister worked and I used to watch them all the time. I love them so much."

But, for Doreen, to be known as Mrs. Richard Ramirez was worth any sacrifice. "Once I was married to Richard I would have a new family; his family would become mine," she proudly told a journalist covering the wedding.

The day before the wedding, which was scheduled for 8 A.M., the press descended on San Rafael, the home of San Quentin. CNN sent a crew, as did *Inside Edition, Hard Copy,* the Associated Press and all the local and Los Angeles news outlets.

Doreen was so nervous she could barely sit still. She paced back and forth, watching the news shows about her and her wedding, and critiquing every piece sharply.

It wasn't until 3 A.M. that she finally went to sleep, but was up at 6, primping herself, putting on makeup and doing her shoulder-length auburn hair in big fluffy curls.

The day was gray. Fog rolled in from the Bay of Skulls and hung a foot above the prison grounds.

Doreen, with Ruth, Joseph and his daughter left the hotel for the prison at 7:45 A.M. She knew there would be a lot of press outside the prison, but she wasn't prepared for the hundreds of reporters, all pushing and jostling to get at her, and the satellite news trucks all over the place. She turned her face and refused to answer questions tossed to her as she made her way through security at the front-gate entrance. The prison public relations man, Lt. Vernell Crittendon, a polite professional with a smooth, easy way about him, had let the press set up microphones near the post office just outside San Quentin grounds. He told the reporters he'd hold a press conference after the ceremony, and that he'd ask Doreen if she'd talk to them. The press were not allowed in the death-row visiting area. Ramirez's marriage was getting much larger coverage than such lead news stories as Mark Fuhrman's pleading guilty to perjury, even the Middle East Crisis that October week.

Doreen and the wedding party entered East block under the watchful eye of a prison guard cradling an assault rifle, wearing tortoise-shell mirrored sunglasses. When they entered the death-row visiting area, Richard was summoned from his cell. On this, his wedding day, he was wearing a baggy light blue long-sleeved shirt. He appeared thin and moved with the sure grace of a cat.

This was the first time since his arrest he'd be able to touch Joseph and Ruth. When he entered the room they rushed to him and he embraced them both. They cried; the guards did not intercede. They knew the family was innocent of anything and didn't want to intrude on this very special moment for the Ramirezes. On death row, at San Quentin, it's live and let live. If you behaved, the guards were polite and courteous.

Doreen, never letting go of Richard's hand, moved to a corner of the visiting area, along with the Ramirezes, and sat on the hard plastic chairs. Joseph could not stop crying. He wished their father could be there, to hold and embrace Richard, welcome him back to the family. Richard couldn't get over how big Joseph's daughter had gotten. The last time he'd seen her was when she was just a little girl. She smiled as she looked at her infamous uncle, more like he was some kind of rock star than her father's brother. After all, Richard was just about the most famous person from El Paso, and his celebrity had not been lost on her.

Soon, other death-row inmates were brought from their cells for their visits and the room filled up with convicted killers. Richard made his niece cover her legs. She was wearing a short skirt and he didn't want the other inmates looking at her bare legs.

The ceremony took place at 11 A.M. Mr. L. Weister, a civil servant would perform the ceremony. He was a tall robust man with a big, healthy red face and thick gray hair. Doreen was very nervous. Richard wanted to get the whole thing over with and get back to his cell. An author and one of Richard's attorneys joined the wedding party.

In front of an Alpine mural one of the inmates had painted, the ceremony took place. It was short and sweet—they did not say "until death do us part." They exchanged vows, wedding rings, and it was over in two minutes. Richard gave Doreen a peck on the lips.

Vernell Crittendon asked Doreen if she would talk to the press; he said they would probably not leave her alone until she spoke to them. Richard told her she'd better give a statement and she reluctantly agreed. Soon Richard went back to his cell and Doreen and an author walked out together. The family stayed behind, because none of them wanted to be on camera. When the press saw Doreen walking toward them in her white wedding dress, they hurried en masse toward the exit area, anxious to get footage of her for the news shows that evening. When she arrived at the gate, four huge prison guards gathered around Doreen and the author and walked them over to the makeshift podium as the reporters surrounded them. With resolve Doreen stood behind the podium and addressed the throng of reporters, cameras, questions. The sky had cleared and the bright October sun was in Doreen's eyes. Squinting, she told the press, "Thank you all for your patience. I just want to say I'm very happy to be married to Richard. I ask you please to let me go in peace and enjoy my day." She stepped down from the podium, got into a waiting car, and pulled away, speeding toward her destiny as Mrs .Richard Ramirez.

Special Update of the Tenth-Anniversary Edition

Often people ask me why I wrote *The Night Stalker,* "Why the hell would you want all that negative crap in your head?" This is a long, involved story, but to make it short: in 1992, I was intent on writing a novel about serial murder that truly would portray what goes on inside a serial killer's mind before, during, and after a murder. I planned to simply lay out in a compelling, suspenseful way the building blocks that make a serial murderer.

I am a staunch believer in doing research, getting out in the world and seeing for myself what's going on and talking personally to the players who know the truth. Toward that end, I began contacting convicted killers on different death rows around the country, intent upon shining light on this little-known, dark phenomenon—amongst whom were John Gacy and Ted Bundy. Some were interested in talking with me, others weren't; though, little by little, I began piecing together the hard-core realities, the building blocks, if you will, of what serial murder is about.

My friend and agent, Matt Bialer, suggested I contact Richard Ramirez—the notorious "Night Stalker," who, in 1985, held the entire state of California in a grip of fear unparalleled in the annals of crime history. I am a born-and-bred New Yorker and didn't live in Los Angeles when the Stalker was, at will, entering people's homes in the middle of the night, tearing, ripping, beating, and shooting them to death, but I did remember how incredibly brutal his crimes were, and that he was a Satanist, which I found particularly interesting and compelling. I wrote

Ramirez; he responded. We corresponded by mail for a few months. I invited him to call collect, which he did.

Quite to my surprise, I found him to be open and forthright, and, oddly enough, he possessed a keen sense of humor. He agreed to meet with me and I was soon on a plane to San Francisco and met Richard at the San Francisco County Jail, where he was being held because of crimes he was charged with in San Francisco—the rape of Barbara Pan and murder of her sixty-two-year-old husband, Peter Pan. I had press credentials and was able to meet with Richard, one-on-one, in a small conference room.

I arrived first. It took about twenty minutes for him to be brought down. When he got there, I was surprised at how big and fluid-moving he was, catlike, and his hands were enormous—the largest ones I'd ever seen. These were, I knew, hands that had done terrible, unspeakable things. They were like two malevolent vultures fluttering about before him as he spoke. I had seen crime scene photos of the Night Stalker's victims: heads had been nearly severed; eyes cut out; some victims were beaten so badly they were not recognizable as the people they once had been.

We talked for a few hours. Richard agreed to tell me the truth. I returned to New York and wrote a proposal for the book, sold it to Kensington Publishing, and I was soon back on a plane to California.

Richard, however, had been moved to San Quentin's death row and was only able to have visits through Plexiglas. Friends of mine in the NYPD Police Academy—where I had lectured numerous times—wrote a letter to the warden of the prison on my behalf and thus I was able to sit alone in a small room with Richard and pick his brain. Altogether, I spent three weeks with him, from 8 A.M. to 2 P.M., every day. I made it a point never to judge Richard or talk down to him. I treated him like just another guy and, like that, I was able to get inside his head with a flashlight and see what was going on. I found him to be surprisingly bright and well read; he clearly had a deep, reflective, introspective side, which, in my mind, made him all the more . . . interesting.

Here, now—for the first time—is part of my death row interview with Richard Munoz Ramirez, California's dreadful/infamous Night Stalker.

Carlo: Let's give it a couple seconds for the thing to start. Okay, it's February 8, about 9 A.M. I'm inside of San Quentin Prison's death row with Richard Ramirez. So, Richard, we'll be discussing some topics; you were just talking about death and what it means to society—would you continue?

Ramirez: Uh . . . now I'm freezing up! (laughter)

Carlo: So you find death funny?

Ramirez: No, I just think society is fascinated with death. Instead of giving it just a little part in this project you're doing . . . you should devote enough space to it because—

Carlo: What about *How We Die*—what's that about? That book *How We Die* you told me about. . . .

Ramirez: It talks about how people take death in . . . today, today's society. Long ago, it was taken as a spiritual thing because birth and death are two very major events, not only in the person being born and also dying, but in the people around them and the legacy that we leave behind. In today's society, it's more of the scientific and medical aspects that are most talked about in death. And in this book, it tells about how different people die and different ways of dying. . . .

Carlo: Different cultures?

Ramirez: Different cultures, I believe. I've read reviews on it; I haven't read the book myself. I've read reviews and it says there is such a thing as a death rattle; there is such a thing and it is a spasm of the voice box.

Carlo: You mean it's like the last breath?

Ramirez: Yes. (Tape shuts off.)

Carlo: About this death rattle—I've read about it a lot myself but I've never heard it. Have you heard it?

Ramirez: (Gets up and starts to walk out.)

Carlo: Hey, c'mon back!

Ramirez: No, I haven't heard it!

Carlo: Describe—

Ramirez: What I *think* it would sound like?

Carlo: Yeah man.

Ramirez: It's the last . . . breathing out. It's one last breath out, I don't think it's one last breath in. . . .

Carlo: The last breath out.

Ramirez: Right.

Carlo: And . . . what does it sound like?

Ramirez: I assume, I suppose, it—whoever is witnessing such a thing—it is sort of like the spirit leaving the body at the same moment this breath is given. But . . . uh . . . okay; some people actually fight, cling to life, some people even ask permission from their loved ones if . . . to die. See, because they don't want to leave their loved ones.

Carlo: What does the rattle sound like, and why? It's the last breath going out but does it affect the voice box?

Ramirez: It is a spasm of the voice box.

Carlo: It's a spasm of the voice box . . . I see.

Ramirez: Yes, I would assume it doesn't sound like any breath we take during our lifetimes. It is sort of like when a baby is born and he is slapped on the bottom, he takes a deep breath in. These things are to me mystical and spiritual, in that we don't experience them every day. When these things happen, we take notice. We have to. I don't think it's possible to not detect such things unless you're really stupid.

Carlo: Speaking of spirituality, let's talk about Satanism. There's been a lot in the press, Richard, about your devotion to and your affiliation with Satan. Can you tell a bit about what Satan means to you?

Ramirez: What Satan means to me . . . Satan is a stabilizing force in my life. It gives me a reason to be; it gives me . . . an excuse to rationalize. There is a part of me that believes he really does exist. I have my doubts, but we all do, about many things.

Carlo: When did you first turn away from Christianity— as I know you were brought up a Christian—and turn to Satanism?

Ramirez: From 1970—well, throughout my childhood and up to the time I was eighteen years old, I believed in God. Seventeen, eighteen years old. Then, for two or three years, I became sort of like an Atheist—I didn't believe in anything. When I reached the age of twenty, twenty-one thereabouts, I met a guy in jail and, uh ... he told me about Satan and I picked it up from there. (Richard had been arrested for stealing a car.) I read books and I studied and I examined who I was and what my feelings were. Also, my actions. Just like the Hezbollah and different terrorist religious organizations around the world—it is a driving force that motivates them to do things and they believe in it whole-heartedly. It had the same effect on my life.

Carlo: In other words, their spirituality was what was the driving force in their life, and Satan became, in a sense, your spirituality and the driving force behind you.

Ramirez: Yeah, exactly.

Carlo: Richard, do you believe that Satan helps people who ... (Tape shuts off.) Richard, do you believe that Satan helps people to be able to do things they wouldn't normally do? For instance, in Matamoras, Mexico, Adolfo Constanzo killed many people and he was committing human sacrifices to protect the Hernandez drug cartel down there from the police, and he fervently believed that Satan would protect him and so therefore made human sacrifices. Do you feel that kind of reasoning has any place—

Ramirez:—place in Satanism?

Carlo: Yeah.

Ramirez: I don't know the structure of Hell itself, or demons or demonology, but I do know when you tamper with witchcraft, when you tamper with Satanism, be it voodoo—

Carlo:—Santeria, Tayo Mayombe—

Ramirez: Yeah, any type of sacrifices or contacting the spirits, you're dealing with things that are very delicate— and dangerous. I myself am no warlock, I'm not a wizard. I'm not one of these types of individuals that knows his witchcraft from A to Z. But, I have heard and read of instances where people end up getting killed and ... uh ... arrested for tampering with the wrong demons and not using the right types of ... uh ... the right process of sacrifices and the right types of rituals. You have to know what you're doing. Everything from ropes to chalices—

Carlo: Everything has to be done right.

Ramirez: Exactly. From what I know, certain symbols—

like Pentagrams—are supposed to protect you from the demons themselves.

Carlo: Yeah. You were seen in court once with a Pentagram inside your hand and you held it up and showed it to the press and the audience. Why did you do that? Did you feel that it would protect you, or were you just making a statement that you were in alliance with the Devil?

Ramirez: Yes, it was a statement that I was in alliance with . . . the evil that is inherent in human nature. And . . . that was who I was.

Carlo: Richard, tell us about the Marquis de Sade. I know that since you've been incarcerated, which is about eight years, you've been reading an awful lot and one of the things you've read is the Marquis de Sade.

Ramirez: De Sade had a large . . . uh . . . a large . . . somewhat large following in his time. He had a philosophy, a way of thinking that was contrary to what people of his time thought and eventually he paid the price for it. They placed him in an insane asylum, where he died. His belief was that there was pleasure in painful sex. He wrote many stories, short stories; one of my favorites was *Justine*. He talked about the governments and how there were oppressors.

Carlo: Hypocritical?

Ramirez: Huh?

Carlo: And hypocritical?

Ramirez: Hypocritical. Takers away—they took away rights that belonged to individuals.

Carlo: Sexual rights, sexual freedoms?

Ramirez: Yes.

Carlo: But essentially de Sade was a sadist, right?

Ramirez: Yes, yes. He liked to inflict pain.

Carlo: He liked to *inflict* pain.

Ramirez: Inflict pain . . .

Carlo: Right. Do you feel he was ahead of his time in a sense? Do you feel he knew something about human nature—and explored it—that other people seemed to deny?

Ramirez: Well, I believe that—as time goes by, mankind will find new and different ways of living. Let's see . . . and . . .

uh . . . he may have been ahead of his time, or maybe he just came about at the right time with his ways of thinking.

Carlo: I believe they had the death penalty in the time period de Sade was alive.

Ramirez: I think it was the guillotine.

Carlo: The guillotine.

Ramirez: I think this . . . he . . . uh . . . all this took place in or about France.

Carlo: They did not give him a death sentence for his practices, but they indeed locked him up for the entirety of his natural life, but—

Ramirez: Because of the stories he wrote.

Carlo: Because of the stories he wrote?

Ramirez: I believe.

Carlo: They went against society. But what are your feelings about the death sentence, Richard? (Tape shuts off.) So, Richard, over the last ten years or so, there's been a lot in the press and there indeed have been a lot of people arrested all over the country for committing what amounts to a series of murders. These individuals are called serial killers because they kill in a series of crimes. Would you tell us why you think there's such a phenomenal number of serial killers being identified and captured these days?

Ramirez: You asked me why I think there's an abundance of serial killers . . . right?

Carlo: In society today.

Ramirez: Right, in society today. I believe that . . . uh . . . tension in the workplace, and also lack of jobs, and the way families are . . . are brought up, and child abuse, sure . . . it's like a recipe. Drugs, poverty, child abuse—all this creates angry individuals. And, then again, lust killers—people tend to lump all serial killers in the same category, but there are different types of serial killers, as you know.

Carlo: What are the different types of serial killers, Richard?

Ramirez: Some serial killers kill prostitutes, some serial killers kill young boys . . . uh . . . some serial killers kill homeless people. The only common denominator is that they kill people over a span of time. They keep on killing and . . . uh . . .

Carlo: The phenomenon of serial killers—is it a sexual thing, too, Richard? Is sex part of the crimes?

Ramirez: Sex? For some serial killers, sure. For some it is the very act of killing another human being that is . . . that . . . uh . . . that is sexual to them. It's a bloodlust, I guess you can say.

Carlo: Do you think a person who becomes like that is responsive to a bloodlust because of genetic propensity or because of environmental influences, or both?

Ramirez: Both. Very good. You oughta be—(Tape shuts off.)

Carlo: You think it's a combination of genetic and environmental influences.

Ramirez: Yes. Serial killers and most killers in general have a dead conscience.

Carlo: When you say a dead conscience that means they don't respond—

Ramirez: No morals, no scruples, no conscience. They are . . . uh . . . they sometimes . . . some of them don't even care if they live or die themselves and they are just the walking dead.

Carlo: The first really noted serial killer was Jack The Ripper.

Ramirez: Yeah.

Carlo: He killed seven prostitutes in London in the 1800s.

Ramirez: Yes.

Carlo: I think there were other serial killers loose and participating in those types of activities but they just never got the press that Jack got.

Ramirez: Jack The Ripper created an aura around himself, or maybe the media did.

Carlo: The press . . .

Ramirez: But it was one of mystique and . . . uh . . . a sinister character who was never identified. I remember in my childhood reading about him and I was intrigued by the way this . . . uh . . . killer, Jack The Ripper, was depicted. Wears a black cloak—

Carlo: Right—

Ramirez:—Fog—

Carlo:—Right—

Ramirez:—Nighttime—most of the time, the media tends to, if not glorify, but . . . paint him in a way that is very sinister and diabolical and to some of us, that is appealing. Certainly, it was to me. (Tape shuts off.)

Carlo: Why do you think it was particularly appealing to you? It seems appealing to everybody. . . .

Ramirez: Well, not everybody.

Carlo: People are interested, though.

Ramirez: Sure, I mean . . . they're interested, they're curious, but I don't think you could call it . . . I don't think they would call it appealing. I think people are . . . some people are fascinated by looking at how other people, such as killers, become who they are and how there are different types of people in the world. Certainly madmen in the world are something to look at because they are very . . . they are a minority in numbers.

Carlo: Do you think Jack The Ripper was a madman?

Ramirez: A madman?

Carlo: Yeah.

Ramirez: Some say—he was a doctor . . . I couldn't say. . . .

Carlo: Was he a psychopath?

Ramirez: A psychopath?

Carlo: Yes.

Ramirez: I could not tell you. I couldn't say. From what I've read about him, certainly he . . . if you came into his hands and . . . if you were a woman, certainly you would think this guy was mad. He would butcher you, he would cut your organs out and stuff and lay them right beside you in a very precise manner. Uh . . . madman . . . yes, there are certain types of mental illnesses, mental disorders that would characterize him as a madman.

Carlo: Richard, how would you suggest that people can become—can avoid becoming the victim of a serial killer?

Ramirez: There are ways. . . .

Carlo: How can society protect itself—

Ramirez: There is no protection against a mass murderer, if you will. A mass murderer will come onto the scene—whether it be a post office, supermarket, restaurant—and open fire. Unless the bullets miss you, you will become a statistic. A serial killer, if he's looking for certain type of women, certain type of victims, and you happen to match his preference ... it is possible that you could get away. You could even help in apprehending him, but it is said serial killers are very intelligent, otherwise they would not—

Carlo: They would not be able to commit crimes over a long period of time.

Ramirez: Exactly. What constitutes a serial killer right now is four murders or more, according to the FBI. Four murders is not that many but that's what categorizes a serial killer. I suppose to avoid being a victim is—

Carlo:—Being aware of the environment, being aware what's around you?

Ramirez:—Taking precautions, locking your doors, having your keys ready when you open doors ... being on guard.

Carlo: Your keys ready when?

Ramirez: When you open doors.

Carlo: Look over your shoulder?

Ramirez: Yes. Of course, one cannot live one's life like that in today's society, always aware. Especially if you haven't already been the victim of a crime. When you are the victim of a crime, a violent crime such as an assault or mugging, then throughout your life that will be at the back of your mind. Those types of people are more aware than those who have never been a victim of any type of crime. But, sure, a serial killer takes opportunities, in the victims being in the right place at the right time. He takes advantage of that.

Carlo: In other words, people are a victim of circumstance. But how can a woman be more insulated and more protected from a serial killer?

Ramirez: It's not possible because ... to detectives ... to apprehend a serial killer, they need to get inside the mind of the serial killer. Normal, ordinary people do not think like a serial killer. They have no conception of what is going on in a killer's mind, how he operates. They don't read, which is rightfully so ... if they have a life to live, they're not going to spend a lot of time reading up on killers if that's not in their interest. Certainly, serial killers and killers have the advantage in that they use the element of surprise ... uh ... darkness, and such things as this. . . .

Carlo: I see one of the conventional ways police manage to apprehend people who kill one another is usually the victim is known by their killer. But in serial murders, the victim is not known by their killer and therefore the conventional aspects that help homicide detectives— (Tape shuts off.) Do you think one of the reasons why serial killers are so successful in their crimes, and are able to go on for years and years, is because the police are not equipped to deal with this new phenomenon of serial murder, in that they don't have systems set up to help identify, categorize and apprehend?

Ramirez: Once they have a suspect, because of . . . the progress that has been made in forensics and all the new other evidence-gathering techniques, once they have a suspect there is a good chance they will catch the serial killer, because we all leave particles of ourselves wherever we are. So . . . yes, it is difficult for police. They are at a disadvantage because these are stranger-to-stranger crimes, and it will always be so. I don't think that can change.

Carlo: You mentioned that people always leave a bit of themselves behind and with today's technology, it makes it somewhat easier for them to identify serial killers. In an instance where a naked body is left out in a field and . . . uh . . . there are no clues left behind, it becomes virtually impossible, doesn't it?

Ramirez: Yes.

Carlo: Right. Can you suggest, Richard, to women out there—

Ramirez: Okay, there is no set rule, there is no proof positive, that once you come into contact with a serial killer that you will survive the encounter. There is no assurance of any of that because every individual is different and the same goes for every serial killer. Some serial killers will let you live if you talk to them, if you get to them, if they get to know you; some serial killers will take pity while others won't. This not only applies to serial killers but killers in general. Some killers are hell-bent on just killing regardless of circumstances or situation. They have made up their minds even before they encounter you and . . . uh . . . there is no way out of it. The victim is at a disadvantage because she or he does not know the mind of the killer or what he is thinking.

Carlo: You once told me that—(Tape shuts off.)—about what they call "the devil's dandruff"—cocaine, which is really prevalent in society today. What are your thoughts on cocaine, Richard?

Ramirez: I love it! (laughs) No, well . . . if you look at it in broad views, it's a supply-and-demand type of thing. I saw a show not too long ago where the CIA, I believe, actually had been working with this stuff to get arms to the Contras and stuff like that. That's on a big scale, but on a street level, I think cocaine is addictive and I think it's very harmful to the body.

Carlo: What about to the mind?

Ramirez: To the mind, sure. It depends on how you ingest it. If you mainline it, I've heard and read that it can cause brain clots that lead to strokes. Sure, it's harmful, but the sense of pleasure it gives is very profound!

Carlo: What could you compare that sense of pleasure to, Richard?

Ramirez: There is nothing . . . to me, anyway, that comes near it.

Carlo: You once described it to me as an intense euphoric heat, a rush, a light tingling that goes to the brain.

Ramirez: Exactly.

Carlo: Your feelings about capital punishment in this country are very profound.

Ramirez: You better take away that CIA shit—(Tape shuts off.)

Carlo: Your feelings, your opinions about the death penalty in this country are profound. Would you tell me your feelings about the death sentence?

Ramirez: As far as the death penalty is concerned, I think it is a power against the powerless. There are not many millionaires on death row. A lot of people choose to die, though; a lot of people, a lot of murder defendants actually get on the witness stand and tell the jury that they want the death penalty. They would rather die than spend the rest of their lives in prison. The death penalty is . . . to me . . . is not a very dignified way. They should have gladiator arenas like in the old Roman times because what I . . . it's just . . . you know, it doesn't seem right.

Carlo: Do you think that the government does not have the right to take a life, or do you feel that in certain crimes—

Ramirez: Well, they're doing it for the victims. If the relatives of the victims want the killer's blood . . . uh . . . I think one of the relatives should pull the plug, the switch. But they leave it up to the state and . . . uh . . . that is something to look at. I've given it a lot of thought and I've written some things down but I don't have—

Carlo: How do you feel about it only being in thirteen states, as opposed to it being in every state across the board?

Ramirez: Right. Well, the way crime is going nowadays, it'll probably end up being in a lot of states in the future. People in different parts of the country feel differently about it and it's ultimately up to the people in every state. They vote for it and some states vote yes and some vote no, they don't want it.

Carlo: Richard, do you think the death penalty is a deterrent?

Ramirez: No. No. Most criminals, the majority of criminals kill for . . . money, to get money for drugs. Some are not in their right minds, some are drunk . . . they kill for greed, lust, and things like this . . . and, uh . . . so, no, I don't think it acts as a deterrent because a criminal rarely thinks about his own death when committing a crime where such emotions as rage and hatred take hold of him. So, very little thought is given to his own demise when such feelings are raging inside of him at the time that he commits a murder or a crime. (Tape shuts off.) See, governments kill with impunity and sometimes they choose killers to go out and kill people for them. They justify it, they rationalize it, they pin medals on killers. Well, if you don't have a license to kill for the government, they won't pin a medal on you but they'll put you in the gas chamber.

Carlo: Do you think the gas chamber is cruel and unusual punishment? If a state has to have the death penalty, which way do you think is the best route to go? The electric chair, lethal injection, or the gas chamber?

Ramirez: That is up to the individual on which way he wants to go.

Carlo: Richard, as we sit here, you've got nineteen death sentences on your head.

Ramirez: Yeah.

Carlo: If . . . after your appeals are all exhausted and the day comes when you have to be executed by the State of California, which way would you choose?

Ramirez: Me myself, I don't really care because death is death and it is said that no man knows his own death. Sure, for a few minutes you might feel it—but then you're gone. I've really not given much thought to that. To me death is death and whichever way I choose to go out, I'll choose it when the time comes—if there is a choice open to me.

Carlo: Certain of the most notorious serial killers produced by society are Ted Bundy, Jeffrey Dahmer, Henry Lee Lucas . . . what do you think of a guy like Ted Bundy?

Ramirez: Say what?

Carlo: What do you think about Ted Bundy?

Ramirez: See, when serial killers come up in New York, Los Angeles, Chicago—these are media centers of the world. That's why more attention is paid to these guys, because of where they are located at. I've heard of serial killers in the Midwest who you've never even heard of but they've got twenty, thirty murders under their belts. As far as my views on Ted Bundy—was that your question? Ted Bundy was intelligent. He . . . he grew up and he found . . . in his mind . . . his own pleasures. These were his pleasures. A man's own pleasures are his own business, I think. He . . . he liked to do what he did, which was kidnap women, have sex with them, torture them, and kill them and whatever else. On the outside, to whomever he met on the street, he seemed like a very normal man, one you would never suspect of doing such things.

Carlo: It seems that many serial killers on the outside seem very innocuous, like the guy next door. For instance, Jeffrey Dahmer: of all the things he looks like, he does not look like a killer. What are your feelings about a fellow like Jeffrey Dahmer who on the outside seemed so normal but inside is far from normal?

Ramirez: I guess you could say like . . . the balances of the mind, the chemistry, the psyche of a killer—a wolf in sheep's clothing, and he has learned to perfect it. Uh . . . this is a guy you think it'd be okay to go to his house, have a drink, and smoke a joint, but it would be your last drink because you'd find yourself handcuffed and the next thing you know, this guy would be eating you. This is a very . . . uh . . . very interesting thing to look at in life. These types of individuals . . . because they're extra-ordinary. It's sort of like a strange car, a strange house. You ask yourself, "How was it built? How did it get here?" I've always been fascinated with killers, and crime, and murder, and death. I suppose I started when I was twelve years old (the murder of Jessie by Richard's cousin Mike). I started reading crime detective magazines and stuff like this and even the pages had a certain scent to them, a certain smell to them. It was very strange; it gave me a strange feeling.

Carlo: Can you explain the feeling?

Ramirez: Strange, because I had experienced the death of people I knew at an early age. I was four or five years old when I knew about a death of a friend of my father's. Then when I was nine I went to my grandfather's funeral. It's just . . . death had a very profound effect on me when I saw it. Death of my dog, death of a pet animal—just death.

Carlo: Do you feel that there's a life after death, that there really is a Heaven and Hell?

Ramirez: I couldn't say for sure what there is, you know? I can't sit here and tell you, "Yes, there's this or that," because I'm not sure. I can only speculate.

Carlo: Well, what do you speculate?

Ramirez: I think there is . . . uh . . . a divine force that is out there. I also believe there's a malevolent force that is out there. Then again, they could be one and the same. I also believe some in reincarnation. I mean, how do these child prodigies come about? A young child being able to play the piano very well at the age of three years old . . . everything is open. I have an open mind.

Carlo: Do you feel that evil can be reincarnated?

Ramirez: I hope so. [laughs]

Carlo: Like a killer like Jack The Ripper could come back in the form of Ted Bundy or Jeffrey Dahmer?

Ramirez: Yes, especially if . . . Satan grants that wish to the individual. If Lucifer gives his unworthy servant that opportunity, that chance. Satan would be saying to me right now, "Yes, you are unworthy." (Author's note: Because he was caught.)

Carlo: Richard, what are your feelings and opinions about women who are drawn to mass murderers and serial killers? It seems to be a phenomenon, somewhat prevalent in society today. . . .

Ramirez: A short comment on serial killers is that—is it a recipe that is created in their existence or is it a bad seed, chemistry, genetics?

Carlo: Is it environmental you're saying? What do you think?

Ramirez: That's a good question. Is there such a thing as a bad seed when a baby is born? Is he already a serial killer, already made, or is he created by his own deeds and feelings throughout his life and his environment?

Carlo: It's a new field of science but the connection between genetic propensity towards violence, as opposed to our environmental influences—indeed it's been proven and established that without certain chemical balances, people have much greater proclivity towards violence, sexual deviance, drug abuse, alcoholism. . . .

Ramirez: I've heard that a lot of serial killers—John Gacy, Ted Bundy, Jeffrey Dahmer—have had head trauma, head injuries when they were young. They were knocked out and so—like I told you the other day, I saw a show, *48 Hours*, where this doctor came out saying that there are pieces of brain, areas of the brain that are not functioning right, so that's always a possibility.

Carlo: Getting back to women who are drawn to serial killers and mass murderers, what are your feelings about that? Why do you think that happens?

Ramirez: Women . . . when I was on the street, I was a loner. I stayed to myself. I really had no contact with people. It's only been since I've been in prison that I have really developed relationships with people, and mostly women, though I now see that they have feelings, they have emotions . . . I mean, I always did but I suppose I locked it out most of the time. I didn't think about other people's feelings and needs.

Carlo: These women that you're making reference to, do you think they were drawn to you because of your notoriety?

Ramirez: Oh, they're drawn to me for all sorts of reasons.

Carlo: Such as what, Richard?

Ramirez: To get something out of me, to question me. Maybe they're intrigued by murder or murderers . . . some are religious, some are sympathetic—you know, they have sympathy for me. Some come just so they can tell their friends they came and talked to me. They've come to me from different walks of life, these women.

Carlo: Since your incarceration, which has been eight years, how many women would you say have come to visit you?

Ramirez: Nine years come this August. What was your question?

Carlo: How many women have come to visit you since you've been arrested?

Ramirez: It doesn't matter.

Carlo: Six hundred?

Ramirez: It doesn't matter.

Carlo: It doesn't matter. . . . (Tape shuts off.) Okay. (Tape shuts off.) Okay. Do you think that child abuse has anything to do with the development of serial killers?

Ramirez: Oh, it has *everything* to do with development of all malfunctions in the adult life. Child abuse, in its many forms, can . . . uh . . . produce many forms of . . . uh . . . life's miseries and griefs as an adult, you know? Mental disorders and such. Me myself, I've never experienced child abuse.

Carlo: You're laughing now. Why?

Ramirez: No, wait a minute! (Tape shuts off.) Not more so than anybody else, Phil.

Carlo: Well . . . so—(Tape shuts off.) You say a lot of people think serial killers should be studied.

Ramirez: Right.

Carlo: What do you mean?

Ramirez: Well, I've seen on TV a lot of people speak and say that serial killers should be studied. Me myself, I care about my life and already my life went downhill; it's already in the shit right now. I don't really give a fuck, you know what I'm saying? I don't concern myself with those types of decisions anymore because they have no effect on me; I'm on death row. So whatever society wants to do, they can do, you know? The legislators, the senators, all the lawmakers, they're the ones that make the decisions and the laws.

Carlo: What's it like living on death row, Richard?

Ramirez: Death row?

Carlo: Yeah.

Ramirez: It is monotonous, it is boring . . . because it is so boring it breeds tension. There's a lot of tension in here. Frustration . . . you never get used to it. I myself only tolerate it. I have acquaintances, no friends. Every day it's the same routine. The walls close in on you. It is like . . . uh . . . some people, though—every individual has his own program, has his own way of dealing with being incarcerated. Some can . . . it doesn't affect them at all—or so they say. Me myself, I try and not let the situation deteriorate my mind to a point where I will go crazy, where I will lose a sense of reality. I always try and keep a sense of reality with me. Uh . . . sometimes it feels very strange to wake up and be in that cage, in that cell and . . . uh . . . I don't think man was meant to be locked up in such a way. Maybe they had a thing going on in the Western days where they would just lynch the guy right off the bat, see what I'm saying, but they don't do it now like that.

Carlo: Do you think that's a better answer?

Ramirez: No, I'm not—I'm not—I'm not saying that. I'm saying that that is what they used to do back then. I'm sure the people they hung back then would have wanted to live in a cage, see what I'm saying, especially if they were innocent—but they were lynched anyway.

Carlo: How many hours a day are you actually in your cell?

Ramirez: Well, like I told you, the program they have me on now—which is maximum security—I got out sixteen hours a week. So . . .

Carlo: So, are you locked up twenty-four hours a day?

Ramirez: On some days, some days yeah. I go outside for about five hours on Tuesday, I got out five hours on Friday and I go out five hours on Sunday. The rest of the time I am on death row. Everybody has a single-man cell.

Carlo: How's the food on death row?

Ramirez: Edible.

Carlo: Are you able to eat with the prisoners on death row or do you—

Ramirez: They feed us in our cages.

Carlo: Richard, a lot's been said about you listening to heavy metal music with Satanic overtones. What influences, musically, inspired you?

Ramirez: Well, you might do some research on this, but I think it is believed that Satan was the one that made music in Heaven before he got thrown down into the pit. I'm not sure. A lot of religious people think that Satan— melodies—people believe Elvis and The Beatles with their gyrations and the beat of their music were conductive to a trance-like . . . uh . . . form of . . . uh . . . for people that they would become possessed with the music. Like I said, me myself, I'm not sure of it—but I have an opinion—but I don't think music drives anybody to do anything. People . . . uh . . . when they're feeling bad, they listen to a song and they feel better.

Carlo: When you were on the outside, Richard, before you got arrested, you listened to a lot of heavy metal music. Did it influence you?

Ramirez: Influence me? It gave me a good sense of being, but the being of what I was was already there before the music. The music just inspired me, it gave me inspiration. It reflected my feelings.

Carlo: What was some of the music that inspired you and reflected your feelings? Tell us.

Ramirez: Hmm . . . heavy beats—

Carlo: Like what groups? What album?

Ramirez: AC/DC . . . uh . . . *Back in Black* album, *Highway To Hell* album . . . uh . . . Pink Floyd, Led Zeppelin, Black Sabbath, Judas Priest—

Carlo: What about "Eyes Without a Face?"

Ramirez:—Iron Maiden.

Carlo: This is music you listened to a lot when you were on the outside?

Ramirez: Yes. I would have a walkman all the time and I would take cassettes with me to play in the cars. Uh . . . so, that was it.

Carlo: There was a song by AC/DC called "The Night Stalker"—

Ramirez: "Night Prowler."

Carlo: "The Night Prowler." Did you used to listen to that?

Ramirez: No, Phil, I didn't! (hysterical laughter) (Tape shuts off.)

Carlo: So, did you listen to . . . uh . . . "Night Prowler?"

Ramirez: No, I listened to Billy Idol—"Flesh For Fantasy." You know, lyrics that would reflect my feelings. He has a song called "Eyes Without A Face" that he says . . . uh . . . he's on a bus—which I was always on a bus most of the time—and he says that he's reading murder books to stay hip . . . uh . . . he's on a psychedelic trip . . . You know . . .

Carlo: So, basically, you . . . uh . . . listened to this kind of music—the heavy metal—for entertainment. Entertainment to clear your head and to—

Ramirez: Give me a sense of well-being.

Carlo: Give you a sense of well-being. Do you think young children, young teenagers, actually, should be kept away from music like that?

Ramirez: No, because I believe that a person that . . . a person that is destined or inclined to be evil will be evil with or without music. Music I don't believe has a part in anything.

Carlo: Even young, impressionable minds?

Ramirez: Yes, yes . . . because I believe that it is the environment that will determine who a child will grow up to be.

Carlo: Richard, when you were ten years old—

Ramirez: Or thereabouts.

Carlo: Or thereabouts. Your cousin Mike had just returned from Vietnam and he was stressed because of the war, from being in three tours of duty, and got into an argument one day with his wife and shot her and killed her.

You happened to be there that day. Could you tell us how that made you feel, to see that—and later on when you went back with your dad—

Ramirez: Well, yes it was—

Carlo: How old were you? Ten or eleven?

Ramirez: Thereabouts. I'm not sure, ten or eleven. I can't say for sure, I was probably eleven. It was a sunny day, I had been with Mike that day hanging out and . . . uh . . . he got to his house about 3 p.m.—I was with him. The incident happened . . . uh . . . he was arrested, taken to jail. His . . . Mike's mother called my father and my mother a week or two later asking them if they would go into the house and get some things for them. I remember me and my father and my mother going. We parked the truck. Me and my father went inside not knowing what we would find—(Tape shuts off.)

Ramirez: It was the strangest experience. I mean being there after Jessie had been killed. The . . . the aura of it was still kind of like hanging in the air. It was . . . kind of mystical. I could still smell her blood. Sunlight was streaming into the room and you could see particles of dust in the golden beams of sunlight.

Carlo: What kind of effect did this all have on you, you think?

Ramirez: Strange. I mean to see something like that—the line between life and death right there in front of me. Intense. When she went down I saw it all in slow motion.

Carlo: He shot her in front of you, Richard?

Ramirez: Yes, me and my two cousins, his two kids, boys three and six.

Carlo: How close?

Ramirez: A few feet away.

Carlo: Your cousin Mike also killed—raped and killed, women over in 'Nam, didn't he?

Ramirez: Yes.

Carlo: How do you know?

Ramirez: He told me all about it and I saw Polaroid photos he had.

Carlo: Please tell us about that, Richard.

Ramirez: He had a shoebox in his closet. It was filled

with these Polaroid photographs of women and girls he took into the jungle and did.

Carlo: Did?

Ramirez: Raped and killed them. Sisters, even a family, two daughters and the mother. He tore off their clothes and had them naked tied to a tree. In another one there they were dead. He cut off their heads.

Carlo: Did he rape them too?

Ramirez: Yeah, of course, while they were tied to the tree, all three of them, in front of each other.

Carlo: He told you this?

Ramirez: Yeah, told me all about it . . . exactly what he did. We used to go for joy rides all around El Paso, smoke pot, listen to the radio and he'd tell me what he did with the women.

Carlo: You know how many he raped and killed?

Ramirez: Over twenty for sure. He had photographs of them. Young girls mostly; but all ages. They were the enemy; they were, you know, V.C., no one gave a fuck.

Carlo: What kind . . . what kind of effect did this have on you?

Ramirez: Heavy. I used to think about them, I mean all that.

Carlo: Sexually, Richard?

Ramirez: Fuck yeah, of course, *sexually*. It was all about sex.

Carlo: They were a turn on? The photographs?

Ramirez: Yes, very much so.

Carlo: Do you think seeing those pictures helped you walk the road you eventually traveled?

Ramirez: It's hard to say. I'm not blaming my cousin for anything; I want that clear. This just happened.

Carlo: He also taught you about jungle warfare, guerilla fighting; how to kill people, correct?

Ramirez: Yes, he did. How to use a knife, where to shoot someone. How to be invisible at night . . . the whole enchilada.

Carlo: Invisible, how?

Ramirez: Wear all black, even shoes and socks, with a black hat with the brim pulled down to cover your face so no light can reflect off it. Avoiding the reflection of light, that's the key.

Carlo: Interesting.

Ramirez: For me it was all very interesting . . . I was already stealing, I mean getting into people's houses at night and stealing things and all that helped.

Carlo: Did he teach you how to shoot?

Ramirez: No. My dad did. But my cousin told me where to hit someone for the maximum effect.

Carlo: Where?

Ramirez: The head, of course.

Carlo: Any particular spot?

Ramirez: Above the ear.

Carlo: And the knife, I mean what is the best place to use it?

Ramirez: Across the throat. It's called a stab/slash wound. That is you drive the point into the side of the neck then pull it across the throat. That cuts both the windpipe and the arteries, always lethal.

Carlo: I see. (Tape shuts off.)

For me one of the more bizarre, compelling aspects of Richard Ramirez's mind-numbing, violent story was the individuals who were so drawn to him when he was arrested. In my research for the book, I did interview many of these women and wrote about them in *The Night Stalker*. One of Richard's many women back then—in 1993 through 1994—was Doreen Lioy. Doreen did eventually marry Richard in a death row wedding, which I attended.

The ceremony took place in the death row visiting room. As always, other inmates were having visits and they all became respectfully quiet when the ceremony began. Here were many other notorious serial killers, heavily tattooed gang-bangers, stone-faced, overly serious Arians— all becoming quiet and still for Richard's wedding. It took place in a cafeteria-type room, one hundred by one hundred feet, plastic chairs bolted to the floor. Vending machines lined the east wall. For me, it was kind of surreal to see all these stone-cold killers sitting there quiet, like they were in a church or some such place, because Richard was having a wedding. The pastor, I noticed, during the vows, didn't say the line "until death do you part." When I later asked him why, he said: "That would be bad form to say here, on death row."

Yes, of course.

Doreen Lioy had been one of many women who had been drawn to Richard after his arrest. They lined up at the Los Angeles County Jail during Richard's tumultuous fourteen-month trial, hoping to see Richard, have a visit with him. While free Richard had to pay for sex from lowly, downtown Los Angeles streetwalkers, now Richard suddenly was Rudolph Valentino, Mick Jagger, Brad Pitt, and the boogeyman all rolled into one. Richard, more than anyone else, was stunned and surprised so many females found him so totally, completely irresistible.

As per his instructions, some of them—indeed most of them—didn't wear underwear and would sneak him peeks at their excited charms as he masturbated himself—the old hand-in-the-pocket trick. They came in all shapes and sizes, colors and nationalities, tall and short and fat and skinny, teenage girls, women in their twenties and thirties, some of them exceedingly attractive, from all walks of society: secretaries, dental hygienists, teachers, college and high-school students, a few strippers, a bank employee, postal workers, hookers, and a Satanist or two. One of the latter was Zeena LaVey, the daughter of the once-infamous, now-deceased, Anton LaVey, the founder of the San Francisco–based Church of Satan.

Why—the question begs to be asked—were all these women so drawn to a cunning, remorseless, brutal serial killer . . . a man on trial for murdering seven women, nearly beating to death five others, raping old ladies, beating and kicking and sending them to the hospital barely alive. The crimes were committed across the wide expanse of Los Angeles County, as far south as Mission Viejo and as far north as Diamond Bar. Most of the Night Stalker's attacks—nineteen, in all, over a fifteen-month span—took place in lovely upscale communities. Yet, here were these girls and women wanting to have sex with him, do his bidding, fellate him, be sodomized by him, make themselves his willing, malleable sex toys.

Richard was being tried—it had been written about extensively—for not only vaginally raping female victims, but sodomizing them as well. These women all knew that, and yet it didn't matter. What Richard had done, sodomizing all his victims, apparently had given him some kind of unique, atavistic appeal. Indeed, to many of these women, it was a big turn-on—the sodomy was more giving, more painful, on their part. If that was what he wanted, demanded, they were collectively willing to pull down their drawers, bend over, and say "please" as they willingly spread themselves for him.

During the actual trial, females filled up whole rows in the courthouse, pressing close together, preening and strutting in front of him, his very own harem. They became known as the "Ramirez Groupies," so dubbed by the unbelieving, wide-eyed press. Doreen Lioy called all of these "ladies"—her competitors back then—"Pop Tarts," which, on face value, seemed uncannily accurate. As I mentioned, I did interview many of these women while researching the book, and I initially learned firsthand what was on these ladies' minds. One told me, "I'd get . . . you know, so wet when I went to see him. The fact that he was so dangerous, so close, yet couldn't harm me, caused me to have . . . to have spontaneous orgasms."

When *The Night Stalker* was released, however, I began hearing—via e-mail, phone calls, and letters sent to my publisher—from scores of women from all around the world. Because of my book, I wound up appearing in twenty hourlong documentaries on the Night Stalker case. These programs were and still are repeatedly aired all over the world, and thus Richard's infamy and unique appeal to women spread far and wide around the globe. Also, women who lived in Los Angeles during the Stalker's unprecedented reign of terror contacted me and admitted to me that they used to fantasize—and masturbate—that the Stalker would come in their windows and rape *them*.

Rape—for a whole host of reasons—is a fantasy "reality" that apparently many women secretly covet. Perhaps it is because all guilt is removed in forced sex; perhaps it is because of strange childhood traumas associated with sex;

perhaps it is some kind of built-in mechanism that some women use to protect themselves from ever becoming a victim: one cannot be the victim of a sex attack if, in fact, the attack is craved in some strange, unexplainable way. To some degree, in any society filled with stringent rules and regulations about sex—the repression of spontaneous, natural sexual desires and inclinations—rape can become a source of erotic stimuli, not a criminal act, as it indeed is.

I'm sure that many of these women didn't actually want to be raped by Ramirez. It was only a fantasy, a hidden sexual dynamic that played out in the secret recesses of their confused minds, whether they wanted it to or not. I received e-mails from Russia, England, Israel, Malta, Norway, Denmark, Finland, Italy, Germany, Japan, Paris, Holland, and from all over the United States . . . especially Los Angeles. Here were women begging for his address, asking how to visit him, wanting to know what he was *really like*. Even I, who had already interviewed many of these women, was taken aback and somewhat aghast by how many females found Richard so utterly irresistible. Truthfully, at first they were a bit annoying; here are a few queries, verbatim:

"Oh my God is he still alive—please tell me he is!"

"The devil is responsible, not Richard."

"Can you please-please tell me how to write Mr. Ramirez?"

"Thank you for scaring the pants off me. I can't sleep with the windows open anymore. Can you please please tell me how to contact Richard?"

"Hi, I'm a psych student doing a paper on The Night Stalker—can you tell me how to reach Richard." (I received over one hundred of these.)

"I'm a film maker. I want to do a film on Richard, all these groupies of his. Please sir, can you tell me how to visit him."

After a while I realized there was a little-known, little-understood phenomenon going on, and I determined to study it and find out what the hell was happening here. I began interviewing many of these females. Here is some of what I found out, a mere slice of this bizarre element in the mind-numbing, violent complexity of the Night Stalker case.

Julie: Julie is twenty-one years old, two years out of high school. She has thick black hair, large, dark, walnut-sized eyes. She lives in Paris, France. She is so taken by Richard, she changed her last name to Ramirez. She never has been in trouble with the law and is not overtly promiscuous. She is madly in love with Richard, however, and often fantasizes about having rough sex with him in a car. Julie was brought up by her grandmother. Her mother was a prostitute. As a child, Julie saw her mother turn tricks; as a child, Julie watched porn movies that her mother left around the house. This occurred before Julie went to live with her grandmama. When twelve, Julie was taken for a ride in a car by an older man, who orally raped her. He nearly made her choke when he orgasmed, forcing semen to come out of her nostrils.

This is what Julie told me: "I first heard about Richard on TV. I right away loved him. He is so beautiful. I bought your book and read about him and loved him even more. I began to write him. He wrote me back. He is so nice. So sweet. My fantasy about Richard is to make the love to him in a car, like he did with the prostitutes in your book. I want him to, you know, fuck me in the ass. He likes that, I know. I want to please him. For me this is more powerful, more intimate, then [*sic*] in the pussy. I love Richard so much; I would do anything for him; anything."

Carole: Carole actually lived in Monterey Park while the Night Stalker crimes were taking place. There were five Stalker attacks in Monterey Park. She was a single child in a loveless marriage of convenience. Carole is married now, not happily, with two children. She is thirty-four, and looks like the actress Jennifer Connelly (*A Beautiful Mind*). She works as a computer programmer.

She told me she was fourteen when the crimes were happening, that they were all over the news. She said, "Everyone was always talking about them. Many of them occurred just near where we lived. I mean blocks away. For the life of me, I don't know why, but I began fantasizing he . . . I mean the Stalker, would come in my room and rape me. Sick, I know. I'm . . . this is kind of hard for me to talk about, but it's the truth. I was, in fact, raped by my mother's boyfriend. I told my mother. She didn't believe me. I used to keep my window open and hoped he'd come in. Maybe . . . maybe I don't know I was trying to get back at my mother for, you know, allowing me to get raped, then not believing me. In any event, I used to think about that. Then when Richard was arrested, I really started having heavy sexual thoughts about him. He was—well, he was so cute and so bad at the same time. His badness drew me to him even more, you could say, you know. I was too young to go visit him then, but I did write him letters—love letters. Then, I . . . well, I grew out of it, you could say. Now I want to go see him. I know he's married, but this is between me and him."

Victoria: Victoria is Danish. As of this writing, she is twenty-two years old. She first became aware of Richard when she saw an HBO special about him and women who were drawn to him. She was sixteen then. She thought Richard very handsome, loved his big lips and high cheekbones. She then read my book and contacted me.

"Oh my God," she told me, "is Richard still alive? Please tell me he is! I'm madly in love with him. We all are. There is a chat room here in Denmark devoted to Richard and there are hundreds of girls on it and we all talk. I want to marry Richard. I know he married Doreen, but she is only a convenience. She looks like his mother. She is ugly. I think he sees her like his mother. What do you think? He doesn't really love her. I write him letters five or six times a week. My greatest dream is to go to America and see him. I will someday. If I could, I would like to make him breakfast and serve it to him in bed. Would they allow that? I'm saving myself for him. I know he likes virgins. He said I could come to see him. I'm going to go. That will drive all the others crazy with jealousy." Though I very much wanted to tell Victoria to get a life, I wished her luck. She'd need it.

Angelina: Angelina is Italian and lives in Milan. She is a tall, lanky runway model with never-ending legs and well-formed, chiseled, high cheekbones.

She told me, "Richard is the most beautiful man I ever saw. Those cheekbones and lips, my God, he is like a Latin god; like an Inca Prince, don't you think? I read your book after I saw the story on . . . I think it was the Court TV channel. I love the photographs of him as a child. My God, was he cute. I would love to make love to him. When I am with boyfriends, I close my eyes and make believe it is him—Richard inside me. I write him and send him photos of myself (naked). He loves them. It excites me so very much that he looks at them and masturbates. I sometimes send him a little money. Not so much, but he likes that. I send him books and magazines, too. Naked-women magazines. He told me he likes Asian women, so I sent him some of those. I want to go see him, but he tells me not to come because of Doreen. A man like him should not be married. No one woman could ever satisfy him. I'm waiting for permission from him to go see him. To hell with Doreen, you know."

Monique: Monique first contacted me when she was seventeen. She lives in Hyde Park, England. She was very troubled and seeking explanations and assurances she wasn't insane, none of which I could give her. She is Chinese, polite, and quite attractive, with long, silky black hair, a heart-shaped face, big kissy lips.

"I think," she said, "I need a psychiatrist—what do you think? I know everything Richard did. I've read your book many times over. I know whole pages by heart. It is the best book I ever read. I know he is very dangerous, like a wild animal, that he enjoyed raping and beating Asian women; yet I am so . . . drawn to him. Like a moth to a flame. It's like a sick obsession. I want him to tie me up and rape me. Sometimes I tie myself to my bed and fantasize he did it. I use different objects, all so big they hurt, like he would, and I have intercourse with myself, thinking it's him. I close my eyes and it is so real, so bloody real, I can smell him. He smells just like you wrote—wet leather, with an animallike odor. He is like an animal, a wild, dangerous animal. That's what I like, his danger—well, I can't honestly say I like it . . . I'm just uncontrollably drawn to it. To him. If my parents found out about any of this, they'd disown me, I know. I once told my sister I thought he was cute. She told me I'm sick. Do you think I am? I sometimes think I am. It all . . . it's like some kind of fever inside me, I can't get rid of it. I want to. I can't. Please, can you tell me if it's okay if I write him, or is it sick? I'm not one of his groupies at all, I'm . . . I just have this fever. If my parents knew, they'd lock me up. Do you think I should be locked up? Sometimes I think I should. Should I write him? That's sick, don't you think?"

"Do as your heart tells you," I told her. *Definitely see a shrink*, I thought.

Luda: Luda lives in Moscow. She has very white, creamlike skin, wears much makeup, is a bit overweight, but she's attractive in a dark, sultry way. She is a professional dominatrix. She abuses men for money. She likes her work a lot. She always wears erotic leather outfits that reveal her breasts and genitals. She has a golden ring through her clitoris. I have seen photographs of her naked. Like thousands of women, she has sent Richard nude photographs of herself. A while back, Richard wrote me and told me he had so many photographs of naked women he couldn't fit them all in his cell. He asked me if I'd "hold" a few for him. I said yes. He sent me a thick, big manila envelope brimming with photographs of women and girls; many of them were naked, quite a few "beaver shots." Luda's photo was among them.

Since the recent conviction of Scott Peterson, and the women who wrote to him subsequently, the media has newfound interest in this little-known, bizarre phenomenon: women drawn to killers, the infamous. Compared to Richard Ramirez, however, Peterson is like an innocent, wide-eyed altar boy lost in the woods. According to Venell Crittendon, the public relations liaison at San Quentin, no ten inmates put together ever got more mail from females than Richard. "He gets hundreds, boxes filled with mail, every week," he recently explained.

"It is my dream to have sex with Richard," Luda told me in heavily accented English. "He is gorgeous. He is the ultimate man. I would love for him to dominate me. I want to be his slave, his sex slave. I swear I'd do anything for him—anything. I mean it. I don't care for normal sex at all. It's boring. All these men come to me and pay me all this money to abuse them. They are a joke. Men are a joke. But Richard—he is my god!"

Tamara: Tamara is built like Jessica Rabbit. She lives in Sherman Oaks, Los Angeles. She is an avowed vampire. She sleeps in a coffin, has had her canines filed into points, is erotically aroused by the sight and taste and smell of blood. She works as a secretary for the city of Los Angeles. (She covers her canines with caps.) Tamara is in her midthirties today. When I first spoke to her, she was twenty-four. She has an altar in her bedroom devoted to Richard. It contains many photos of him, statues, burning candles, different crystals, quartz, and amethyst. One of the quartz crystals is in a penis shape. Tamara uses it to masturbate.

She explained, "My greatest fantasy is to have sex with Richard in a cemetery at night, on a black tombstone with only the light of the moon. I want him to fuck me with blood on his penis. I mean, I want our sex to be lubricated with the blood of one of his victims, and, you know what, I'm not ashamed of that at all. I know you think I'm nuts, but I'm not. I'm just honest. That's what I love about Richard. He never judges me, doesn't think I'm out of touch at all. He is one of the few people, perhaps the only person, who understands me, who can understand people like me. There are a lot more people—women—who would love to do what I just said—wild, crazy things. I know a woman who wants to be murdered by Richard as he fucks her. For her, that would be nirvana, the ultimate. . . .

"Who, tell me who, has the right to judge anyone about what they like sexually? No government, no church, nobody, has the right to police your passions. If it was wrong, against God or nature, I wouldn't feel it; I wouldn't think this way. Just the fact that I have these desires and needs makes them right. I mean, I don't want to force myself on anyone, force anyone to do something they don't want, involve children in any way. Consenting adults should be able to do whatever they please. Period. End of story. The church, isn't that a joke—*them* telling people what is right or wrong when it is filled with child rapists! Hypocrisy, talk about hypocrisy."

As of this writing, in 2005, Richard is still housed in San Quentin E block, death row. It is now sixteen years since he was sentenced to death nineteen times by Judge

Michael Tynan. The average stay on death row across the country is thirteen years. To some degree, Richard has become used to incarceration. He has books, a TV, and a radio in his six-by-eight cell. He gets hundreds of pieces of mail a week from all around the world, mostly from females. He has a lot of correspondence to keep him busy.

There has been much talk across the country about abolishing the death sentence, which very well could come to pass. If that does happen, Richard would be spared the lethal injection San Quentin now uses on the condemned. As of this writing, there are 667 men waiting to die at San Quentin's death row. Richard is one of the most infamous of all the condemned—a kind of homicide superstar . . . the Mick Jagger of murder.

Richard's attorneys are planning to appeal his conviction. His appeals attorney, Gere Russel, says there are numerous legal points she plans to perfect and argue, foremost of which is incompetent counsel. When recently asked when she will have the appeal ready to be argued, she said: "Well, truth is, it is a voluminous record and I won't have the appeal ready for quite some time."

The truth is, she told me off the record, there is no hurry to argue Richard's appeal; for the longer she takes, the longer Richard will live. He might very well live to a ripe old age and die in prison of natural causes. Then, again, San Quentin's death row is a very dangerous place and there is no telling when sudden violence can occur, and Richard could end up dead.

Meanwhile, Richard Ramirez, aka the Night Stalker, reads his fan mail, enjoys all the photographs of naked women sent to him, and dreams about being free so he can do all the grisly, ghastly things he did to get put on death row in the first place.

Philip Carlo
Montauk, New York
www.philipcarlo.com